Huntington Library Publications

CHARLES II

Engraved by Cornelis van Dalen,
after the painting by Pieter Nason, c. 1660

The

Restoration of

CHARLES II

1658-1660

by GODFREY DAVIES

SAN MARINO : HUNTINGTON LIBRARY

London: GEOFFREY CUMBERLEGE

OXFORD UNIVERSITY PRESS

1955

PRINTED IN U.S.A.
BY
ANDERSON, RITCHIE & SIMON : LOS ANGELES

TABLE OF CONTENTS

INTRODUCTION

A QUARTER OF A CENTURY has elapsed since Sir Charles Firth asked me to undertake the task of completing the history of England to 1660 which S. R. Gardiner had brought from 1603 to 1656 and he to Cromwell's death early in September, 1658. This work represents the fulfillment of a promise then made. It is, therefore, a continuation of the twenty volumes of those great historians. I have tried to make my narrative self-sufficient, and if I have been guilty of unnecessary repetition of what is to be found in Gardiner and, especially, Firth, I ask indulgence.

This book is essentially a history of England. The colonies have been deliberately omitted. The little space that might have been afforded them would have sufficed for no more than a summary of what is already known. Also, events in America or the Indies had no direct influence upon the Restoration, which is my theme. This is true to some extent of foreign relations, so I have confined them within narrower limits than my eminent predecessors. I have described how Englishmen regarded the situation abroad, what they hoped to achieve, and what means they used in pursuit of their ends, but have not attempted a survey either of Europe, or of the internal situation of any Continental power. The chapters on Scotland and Ireland necessitated some retrospection to make them intelligible. In both, but especially the latter, I found how scanty the materials are for the months immediately preceding the King's return. The discovery of a journal of the Irish Convention would be extremely opportune.

For the English Parliament I have found no diaries to continue Burton's, which stops in April, 1659. A diary kept by Sir John Gell, for a film of which I am indebted to Col. Philip V. W. Gell, a descendant of Gell's grandfather, covers part of the same ground as Burton but less thoroughly. The debates in the twice-restored Long Parliament remain unreported. Professor Caroline Robbins lent me a notebook of Sir Edward Dering for the Convention. Doreen Lady Brabourne kindly allowed me to quote it. I have been able to fill in part of the gap in the series of council records. The Marquis of Bath most generously permitted the register of Richard Cromwell's Privy Council to be filmed for the Huntington Library. The Bodleian Library was equally generous with regard to the register of the Council of State from May to August, 1659, and to a volume of miscellaneous papers of the same body which are styled Council Notes. It also allowed the filming of a number of documents selected for me by Professor Paul H. Hardacre of Vanderbilt

University from the Clarendon and Carte MSS. C. H. Wilkinson of Worcester College, Oxford, kindly had some volumes of Clarke papers photographed for my use. The Lansdowne MSS in the British Museum containing letters addressed to Henry Cromwell in Ireland have been available to me in a transcript made by the late W. A. Shaw. Mr. E. S. de Beer generously lent me his as yet unpublished edition of Evelyn's *Diary* and permitted me to quote from it. I have copied or had copied letters and other documents in the British Museum, Public Record Office, and Bodleian Library of too miscellaneous a nature to be described here.

In the main this book is based upon printed materials, many of them already well known. Its great novelty, apart from its scale, is that it incorporates the results of an examination of many hundreds of contemporary tracts and newsbooks. Relatively few have been cited, but the perusal of all the pamphlets I could find dealing with an event like the recall of the Long Parliament in May, 1659, has shown me which were the popular arguments in its favor and has guided my selection of the tracts to be mentioned or even quoted. One of the great difficulties of an historian is to see through contemporary eyes. For this purpose the day-by-day output of the press is invaluable.

As in all my historical work I owe a great debt of gratitude to the Trustees, Director, and Staff of the Huntington Library. Sir George Clark, during an all-too-brief visit, and F. P. Wilson during his fellowship at the Library, read my manuscript and made many valuable suggestions. Frederick B. Tolles, when a member of the Research Staff, and my wife cast critical eyes over many of my chapters. Mary Isabel Fry, Virginia Ruland, Margaret (Mrs. M. D.) Packer, Jane (Mrs. G. J.) Adams, and Isabel (Mrs. P. K.) Povlsen have in different ways given much assistance.

Though Sir Charles Firth had passed away before I wrote a sentence of this book, his inspiration has remained with me until its completion. Much of it has been written from books and pamphlets that were once his. The memory of many conversations with him has often guided me in my researches and composition. My debt to him is greater than I can find words to acknowledge.

G. D.

July 23, 1954

THE RESTORATION OF CHARLES II

CHAPTER I

The Accession of Richard

OLIVER, Lord Protector of England, Scotland, and Ireland, and the dominions thereunto belonging, died about three o'clock in the afternoon of Friday, September 3, 1658. A writer in the official newspaper, *Mercurius Politicus,* noted that "both himself and the day will be most renowned to posterity, it having been to him a day of triumphs and thanksgiving for the memorable victories of Dunbar and Worcester; a day which after so many strange revolutions of providence, high contradictions, and wicked conspiracies of unreasonable men, he lived once again to see, and then to die with great assurances and serenity of mind, peacefully in his bed."[1]

The latest constitution, the Humble Petition and Advice, had empowered the Protector to name his successor but had not prescribed the method.[2] Apparently Oliver had named a successor in a letter addressed to Thurloe, Secretary of State, but it had not been delivered and could not now be found.[3] By word of mouth he appointed Richard to succeed him as Protector on August 30, in the presence of Thurloe and Goodwin, and on September 2, when the two were again in attendance together with Fiennes, Whalley, and Goffe.[4]

According to the Humble Petition and Advice, the person nominated by Oliver was to succeed him immediately after his death.[5] The intention clearly was to follow royal precedent—*le roi est mort, vive le roi.*

[1]*Mercurius Politicus,* Sept. 2-9, 1658. Presumably the writer was Marchamont Nedham, editor from the beginning of the newspaper, June 13, 1650, until his dismissal on May 13, 1659 (*Commons Journals,* VII, 652). He was reappointed on August 15, but removed again April 9, 1660 (Bulstrode Whitelocke, *Memorials of the English Affaire* [Oxford, 1853], IV, 406). At the end of this number of *Mercurius Politicus* appears an advertisement of John Bunyan's *A Few Sighs from Hell or the Groans of a Damned Soul.* In this newspaper it does not come immediately after the announcement of Oliver's death, as it does, whether by accident or design, in *The Commonwealth Mercury.* See John Brown, *John Bunyan* (1928), p. 112n.

[2]The Humble Petition and Advice, passed May 25, 1657, and The Humble Additional and Explanatory Petition, passed June 26, 1657, defined the constitution. Both are reprinted in S. R. Gardiner, *The Constitutional Documents of the Puritan Revolution,* 3rd. ed. (Oxford, 1906), pp. 447-64.

[3]Probably the missing letter was the origin of the reports that Oliver had nominated Fleetwood as his successor. See *Reliquiae Baxterianae or Mr. Richard Baxter's Narrative of his Life and Times,* ed. Matthew Sylvester (1696), p. 101.

[4]The question is examined as minutely as the evidence permits in C. H. Firth, *The Last Years of the Protectorate* (1909), II, 302-307. Thomas Goodwin (1600-1680) was an independent divine, much trusted by Oliver; Nathaniel Fiennes (1608?-1669), an Independent (unlike his father, Viscount Saye and Sele, a Presbyterian), was a commissioner of the Great Seal, and a member of the Council; Edward Whalley (d. 1675?), regicide, colonel of horse, major general, and an active supporter of the Protectorate; William Goffe (d. 1679?), regicide, colonel of foot, major general, Whalley's son-in-law, and a stout Cromwellian.

[5]Clause I of the Bill of Recognition, introduced into Richard's Parliament but never passed, begins: "Whereas your Highness, immediately after the death of your renowned father, Oliver . . . became his lawful successor." *A Collection of the State Papers of John Thurloe,* ed. Thomas Birch (1742), VII, 603.

Nothing in this constitution provided for such a contingency as a defective nomination. Similarly, the Council was not authorized to examine the nomination and certify its existence. Nevertheless, inasmuch as Oliver had been capable only of a verbal choice, its verification seemed necessary. Oliver's Privy Council was the obvious body to act.[6] Eleven[7] of its members were available, and met the same day.

The Council Register[8] describes the proceedings. "Being fully enformed ... as well by writeing as by word of mouth, by certaine members of the Counsell, and others who were called in, That his late Highness did, in his life tyme, appoynt and declare the Lord Richard to succeed him," the Council resolved, *nemine contradicente*, that Richard had succeeded his father according to the Humble Petition and Advice. Other accounts add a few details. Fiennes and Thurloe described Oliver's verbal nomination of his successor, and Goodwin, Whalley, and Goffe were called in to attest the same on oath. After they had withdrawn, Disbrowe stood up and begged those present in the name of God to declare freely if they remained dissatisfied as, he said, he would have done had he felt any doubts.[9] No one expressed any opposition.

The Council then directed that the Lord Mayor of London should preserve the peace of the City with the help of the militia, and should discuss with three designated councillors where and when Richard should be proclaimed. It ordered a general embargo at all ports on shipping, English or foreign, and provided for the notification of all military and naval commanders of the Council's proceedings. Meanwhile Fiennes and Thurloe had been busy drafting a proclamation which, after some amendments,[10] was accepted and ordered to be printed. Another vote required Pickering, Jones, and Thurloe to consult the physicians about the em-

[6]The Instrument of Government, Clause XXXII, had empowered the Council to elect a successor to Oliver, and to issue a proclamation to announce its choice. Whether the Council in 1658 was influenced by this fact it is impossible to say. The Humble Petition and Advice did not suggest that any provision of the former constitution remained in force.

[7]Lord President Henry Lawrence, Lord Commissioner Fiennes, Lord Fleetwood, Lord Sydenham, Lord Mountagu, Lord Chamberlain Sir Gilbert Pickering, Lord Disbrowe, Lord Strickland, Lord Jones, Lord Skippon, and Mr. Secretary Thurloe. The absentees were Lord Lisle, Lord Wolseley, and Francis Rous. I have given the Cromwellian titles to show how many councillors were "Lords." Rous never attended Richard's Council. His life in the *Dictionary of National Biography* ignores the account of his elaborate funeral on Jan. 24, 1659, in *Mercurius Politicus*, p. 192.

[8]I am greatly indebted to the Marquis of Bath for his kindness in depositing the manuscript register in the Public Record Office where, thanks to the courtesy of R. L. Atkinson, it was filmed for the Huntington Library. Entries from the index to the Council records are printed in *Calendar of State Papers, Domestic Series, 1658-1659* (henceforth called *Calendar Domestic*), ed. M. A. E. Green (1885), pp. xvi-xvii. The "writeing" which confirmed Oliver's nomination of Richard is not known now to exist. It may have been a statement of Oliver's two verbal nominations signed by those present. A newsletter declared that the Council "opened the writing the Lord Protector had sealed up, which did declare that the Lord Richard should succeed as Protector." *The Clarke Papers*, ed. C. H. Firth, III (1899), 162. I believe this to be a mistake, because otherwise the deathbed nomination was unnecessary.

[9]Though I felt obliged to reject most of the narrative in Sir Richard Baker's *A Chronicle of the Kings of England* (6th ed., 1674) referred to in the next note but two, I have ventured to retain this episode, though I know of no other authority for it.

[10]The Council Register gives no clue as to the nature of the amendments.

4

bowelling and embalming of his late Highness' body. In their report the two physicians in ordinary and one other of their selection were directed to proceed with the embalming the following afternoon. The Council then decided to attend Richard to give him an account of their proceedings.

Not the least important of the many votes passed this day was the request to Fleetwood to send for as many officers of the army as was convenient in order that they should sign the original proclamation of Richard. It is of the highest significance for the history of the next eighteen months that the Council should have required the army's acquiescence.[11] In fact, the army was thus given what almost amounted to an official recognition as a kind of estate of the realm, if the phrase is permissible. Fleetwood proceeded to a council of officers then meeting at Whitehall. He urged that they should show how they honored the memory of Oliver by concurring unanimously in the proclamation of his nominee, Richard, as Protector, "to which there seemed a general consent."[12] Presumably Fleetwood was accompanied back to the Council chamber by the officers who signed the proclamation.

The first signatory was Richard Chiverton, Lord Mayor of London, then followed the thirteen councillors—the fourteenth, Rous, not signing. Others were the Protector's brother-in-law, Edward Whalley, and William Goffe. With the exception of Oliver Fleming, master of ceremonies, and Edmund Prideaux, attorney general, the remainder were army officers.[13] In the evening the members of the Council waited on Richard and informed him of their proceedings and of the proclamation they and others had drawn up and signed. To their condolences Richard made a "suitable return, in countenance and language."[14]

[11]The situation had a parallel at Rome where "the emperor was elected by the *authority of the senate and the consent of the soldiers.*" Edward Gibbon, *The History of the Decline and Fall of the Roman Empire*, ed. J. B. Bury (1900), I, 73.

[12]*Clarke Papers*, III, 162. This account differs materially from that to be found in Baker's *Chronicle*. The continuation is most valuable for the Restoration. According to Anthony Wood (*Athenae Oxonienses*, ed. Philip Bliss [Oxford, 1813-20], III, 148), those sections of the continuation which cover from 1649 to 1660 "were for the most part done by Sir Tho. Clarges . . . and put into the hands of the said Philips" (Edward Phillips, Milton's nephew, the editor or continuer). Clarges was Monck's brother-in-law and "agent for the armies and council[s] of Scotland and Ireland" (Baker, p. 654; confirmed by Thurloe, VII, 563). According to Baker (p. 653), those councillors who were best affected to the Protectorate met an hour after Oliver's death, heard from Thurloe of Richard's nomination and also of the letter referred to above, "wherein Fleetwood was declared successour." Two of the councillors were sent to Fleetwood and Disbrowe to learn whether they would accept Richard's nomination in spite of the lost letter and they solemnly declared that even if it were found, they would acquiesce in Richard's succession. I reject these statements for the simple reason that Thurloe (VII, 364) explicitly says that Oliver never revealed the name of the successor he had appointed in the letter.

[13]The proclamation is in the Council Register and bears 29 signatures. It is printed in *Mercurius Politicus*, p. 806. The proclamation bears the date Sept. 3, but Robert Steele (*Tudor and Stuart Proclamations* [Oxford, 1910], No. 3097) notes: "MS. date 4 September."

[14]*Mercurius Politicus*, pp. 802-805. This account may be regarded as official. It is reprinted in *The Parliamentary or Constitutional History of England* (henceforth referred to as the old *Parliamentary History*), XXI (1763), 223-31.

At an early meeting next morning the Council ordered the proclamation of Richard to be made at ten o'clock at Whitehall. Norroy King at Arms read it from a window in the presence of privy councillors, troops of horse and companies of foot, and a large crowd of citizens. It stated that Oliver had appointed Richard to succeed him, and that the Privy Council, together with the Lord Mayor, aldermen and citizens of London, the officers of the army, and numbers of other principal gentlemen, declared Richard the Lord Protector. The proclamation elicited loud cries of "God Save the Lord Protector" and great applause at Whitehall, Westminster, Temple Bar, Cheapside, and at the Royal Exchange in Cornhill.[15]

In the afternoon the Council met again and drafted a proclamation that all men in office at the time of Oliver's death should retain their positions until Richard's further direction. They then waited on the new Protector. They found the Lord Mayor and aldermen of the City and officers of the army in attendance. The Lord Mayor handed Richard and received back from him the sword of the City. After this little ceremony Goodwin prayed. Fiennes administered to Richard the oath prescribed by the Humble Additional and Explanatory Petition and Advice[16] to uphold "the true reformed protestant Christian religion," to maintain the safety and just rights and liberties of the people, and to govern according to the law. Returning to their chamber, the councillors subscribed to the oath required from them in the same document, to be faithful to the Protector, to keep secret all matters treated in the Council, and to perform faithfully their duties. After their departure the officers of the army made their personal addresses to the new Protector. The day closed with the firing of a hundred cannon at the Tower.[17]

Meanwhile the letters dispatched far and wide to tell of Oliver's death and to order Richard's proclamation were being received and acted upon. As a specimen of the ceremonial at Richard's proclamation, the case of Exeter may be cited. A correspondent wrote how on September 6 the magistrates and common council met at the Guildhall in their scarlet gowns and robes, together with the several liveries and companies. After hearing the letter from the Privy Council, they all agreed to proclaim Richard. When this had been done the crowds shouted, "Amen, Amen, God preserve my Lord Richard Lord Protector." The writer compared this proclamation with that of Charles I, which he remembered, and decided that he could not recall any event attended with so great a solem-

<hr>

[15]*Mercurius Politicus*, pp. 805-807. Whether the other heralds in turn read the proclamation at the other places after Whitehall is not stated.

[16]*Acts and Ordinances of the Interregnum, 1642-1660*, ed. C. H. Firth and R. S. Rait (1911), II, 1184-85.

[17]Council Register; *Mercurius Politicus*, p. 808.

nity in Exeter.[18] Similar ceremonies seem to have evoked equal enthusiasm throughout England. Sometimes wine and beer were distributed gratis to the populace; sometimes volleys of shots, the ringing of bells, bonfires, and "treatments"[19] were features of the celebrations. At Edinburgh the proclamation was made by order of His Highness' Council by direction of the English Privy Council. At the same time an order was issued to the sheriffs and provosts and baillies of the royal burghs to announce Richard's succession. The proclamation was made in Dublin and Dunkirk a few days later.[20]

The transition from Oliver to Richard took place in almost complete tranquillity. Well might Thurloe exclaim: "There is not a dog that wags his tongue, so great a calm are we in."[21] The only exceptions occurred at Oxford, where some undergraduates pelted Major Unton Croke, the sheriff, when he proclaimed the new Protector,[22] and at Waterford, when a recalcitrant ensign was cashiered.[23] The attacks of the Fifth Monarchy men and Anabaptists upon the Protectorate evoked no response.[24] For a few weeks the hopes of Royalists in exile ran high. The small group of exiles in attendance upon Charles II at Brussels waited eagerly for news of the consequences of their great enemy's death. Their optimism is proved by a rough draft of a declaration which Sir Edward Nicholas, Secretary of State since 1654, drew up for his royal master. It called upon all "lovers of the honour and peace of the 3 kingdoms and of the safety of their lives, liberties and estates and the ancient laws, religion and government" to take up arms immediately and end the usurpation.[25] But there is no reason to believe the declaration was ever issued: intelligence of Richard's peaceful accession demonstrated its futility.

[18]*Mercurius Politicus*, Sept. 9-16, pp. 817-18; Thurloe, VII, 377. Accounts of other celebrations are abridged in *A True Catalogue or an Account of the Several Places where Richard Cromwell was Proclaimed Lord Protector* ([1659], pp. 17-20) from the newspapers. Judging from a rather superfluous marginal note referring to Vavasor Powell as the author of *A Word for God*, the Welsh evangelist may have compiled this pamphlet, which reprints or summarizes newspaper accounts of Richard's proclamation and the subsequent addresses sent to him.

[19]This is an early use of the word. *Mercurius Politicus*, p. 826.

[20]The declaration at Edinburgh was dated Sept. 9 and signed by George Monck, Samuel Disbrowe, Edward Rodes, John Swinton, Nathaniel Whetham (*Mercurius Politicus*, Sept. 9-16, pp. 830-31); that at Dublin was dated Sept. 10 and is printed in Thurloe, VII, 383; the address from the army in Ireland was totally different from that of the army in England. It is undated but printed in *Mercurius Politicus*, pp. 875-76. The address from the Dunkirk garrison is printed in the same newspaper under October 3.

[21]*State Papers*, VII, 372.

[22]*The Life and Times of Anthony Wood*, ed. Andrew Clark (Oxford, 1891), I, 259. On Sept. 15 a blacksmith and two husbandmen were bound over to appear at the quarter sessions for uttering seditious words intending to draw persons from their due obedience to the Protector. "Justice's notebook of Captain John Pickering, 1656-60," ed. G. D. Lamb, in *Publications of the Thoresby Society*, XV (1909), 278-79.

[23]*A True Catalogue*, p. 23.

[24]Louise Fargo Brown, *The Political Activities of the Baptists and Fifth Monarchy Men* (Washington, 1912), pp. 171-72.

[25]*The Nicholas Papers. Correspondence of Sir Edward Nicholas*, ed. Sir George F. Warner, IV (1920), pp. 72-74.

Speaking of Oliver's death the Royalist historian wrote: "Contrary to all expectation both at home and abroad, this earthquake was attended with no signal alteration. . . . Never monarch . . . died with more silence. . . . His son inherits all his greatness and all his glory, without that public hate that visibly attended the other. . . . So the King's condition never appeared so hopeless, so desperate."[26]

The natural sequel to Richard's proclamation was the presentation of addresses to him. One of the first and the most important was from the "Armies in England, Scotland, and Ireland." According to Fauconberg, no friendly critic, "the close contrivers" were Fleetwood, Sydenham, Berry, and Hewson. Later Whalley and Goffe were called in, but all other officers remained ignorant of the address until offered for their signatures. On September 20, some two hundred and twenty commissioned officers then in London met at Whitehall and heard Fleetwood explain that they had come together to consider an address to His Highness. It was then read and signed, all present striving who should be first.[27] The presence of a few officers from Scotland and Ireland explains the title of the address. As Fleetwood told Monck and Henry Cromwell, the desire was to have all their armies united in one address, but not to have the army in England impose its will upon comrades elsewhere. To this end copies of the address were sent to Edinburgh and Dublin. Monck and the officers at headquarters in Scotland complied with Fleetwood's wishes, but Henry Cromwell disagreed, so the field officers in Ireland composed their own address to the Protector.[28]

Fleetwood, accompanied by the signatories, presented the address to Richard the following morning. It began by recalling how God had carried on his work in the three nations through several instruments, but most remarkably and eminently through his chosen instrument, Oliver, now deceased, who would be remembered by all good men for asserting the liberties of God's people, for restoring domestic peace, for loving civil rights, and endeavoring reformation. Now that their Moses was dead, they hoped Providence would enable his present Highness "to carry on that good old cause and interest of God and his people."

After this exalted language there followed more mundane passages: The army should be continued and kept under the command of honest

[26]Clarendon's *The History of the Rebellion and Civil Wars in England,* ed. W. Dunn Macray (Oxford, 1888), Book XVI, 1-2. The strictly contemporary Royalist view as seen in *The Calendar of the Clarendon State Papers* (henceforth called *Clarendon Calendar*), IV, ed. F. J. Routledge (Oxford, 1932), was the same as that expressed by Clarendon in his old age.

[27]Fauconberg to H. Cromwell, Sept. 21, Thurloe, VII, 406; G. Mabbott to H. Cromwell, Sept. 21, British Museum, Lansdowne MSS; *Clarke Papers,* III, 164. As the letters in Lansdowne MSS 821-23 have been rearranged in chronological order, the date only is supplied.

[28]Fleetwood to Henry Cromwell, Sept. 21, Thurloe, VII, 405-406; Monck to Thurloe, Sept. 25, ibid., pp. 411-12; Henry Cromwell to Thurloe, ibid., 399.

and godly officers, free to maintain the liberty of all righteous men, though these might differ among themselves, according to the true intent of the Humble Petition and Advice; the Privy Council should be filled up with men of known godliness and sober principles so that they, with His Highness and the army, might work to promote the interests of the godly; and suitable magistrates should continue "the work of reformation, tending to good life and manners." The ejection of "scandalous, ignorant, and insufficient" ministers, and their replacement by able preachers should continue, and any who should countenance profane persons in their attacks upon those ministers who denied the sacrament to loose-livers should be punished. In their conclusion the officers, after denying that they sought any private ends, declared that they would stand by His Highness against all who should oppose him or attempt to alter the present government by a single person and two houses of Parliament, as set forth in the Humble Petition and Advice.[29]

Fauconberg's comment on the address was that it was "pretty well featured, promises all good in show but in the end I fear will prove a serpent."[30] The impression it leaves today is that it represents a compromise, an attempt to please all by inserting the special interest of each faction. The eulogy of their late general would gratify most. The protestation of fidelity to Richard and the constitution met the wishes of the leaders and staunch Cromwellians (the court party), though the Commonwealthsmen must have viewed this paragraph with misgivings.[31] The requirements that the army should continue to be led by godly officers and that a generous toleration should be granted seem inspired by a fear lest the army might be remodeled and ecclesiastical discipline made stricter. The paragraph relating to membership of the Council, to the inclusion of the army, along with Protector and Council, as a constituent part of the state, and to the work of reformation was the most ominous. The control of the Council was soon to be disputed between Protector and army leaders. The implicit assertion that the army was a part of the government raised the issue whether it was, or was not, subject to constitutional control. The reference to the work of reformation was apparently an appeal for support to all groups of Puritans. While desire for a state church with selected ministers would

[29]*Mercurius Politicus*, Sept. 16-23, reprinted in the old *Parliamentary History*, XXI, 233-36. The compiler of this work, valuable for the documents it prints but unreliable in its comments on them, asserts that it was "highly probable" that the army's address was drawn up at court, and that Henry Cromwell contrived that all three armies should present the same address, and cites *A True Catalogue* and Thurloe, VII, as the respective authorities. Apart from the evidence already cited, the contents of the address disprove its alleged origin at court.

[30]To Henry Cromwell, Sept. 21, Thurloe, VII, 406.

[31]Of course, few junior officers, if any, were present. The reference to the "good old cause" may have helped to reconcile them.

alienate extreme sectaries, the protection of ministers who refused to administer the sacrament was a boon to Presbyterians, who required that communicants should first be certified after examination by elders.

Richard's private opinion of the address is unknown, but he warmly greeted the officers who presented it, and expressed his approbation of it. He mingled with the crowd and spoke heartily to old friends. Fleetwood said that "he hath hitherto much exceeded expectation," Whalley doubted not that it satisfied the Protector as his reception of it abundantly satisfied the officers, and *Mercurius Politicus* reported that all testified by their looks and words their elation.[32]

For the rest of the year and even longer, addresses poured in from outlying sections of the army, militia, garrisons, and separate regiments, from detached squadrons of the navy, from counties, cities, and boroughs throughout the three nations, and from groups of ministers and churches.

There are not many original sentiments in the addresses or in the speeches made at their presentation. Thomas Goodwin, on behalf of "above an hundred congregational churches from several parts of the nation," compared the liberty enjoyed under Oliver with the intolerance which had forced "almost a nation out of this nation" to seek refuge in the "howling desert" of America.[33] The gentry, ministers, and freeholders of Northamptonshire applauded Oliver's foreign policy for its zeal against the anti-Christian power in the world, its bounty and compassion to the saints suffering abroad, its efforts for Protestantism and for exalting the English name until it had become an honor and terror to the nations far and near. The citizens of Nottingham prayed Richard to keep the military sword in his own hands—the sole reference to a question which was to embroil the Protector and army. Scarborough urged the Protector to govern according to the laws of God. The Provost and Fellows of Durham College bewailed the death of their founder when they were still "an orphan scarce bound up in its swaddling clothes." The officers and soldiers of Ingoldsby's regiment vowed they were ready to expose their lives and fortunes to the greatest hazard on behalf of their lawful sovereign and general, and signed themselves as "Your Highness' most loyal and faithful subjects." The address from the navy, drawn up by Mountagu, was remarkable for its very emphatic promise to defend the Protector against all who should endeavor to alter

[32]Whalley to Cromwell, Sept. 18 [sic.?21], Lansdowne MSS. Fleetwood to the same, Sept. 21, Thurloe, VII, 405-406; *Clarke Papers*, III, 164. A protest against this address and others was sent to Fleetwood by an unknown officer at Plymouth, Oct. 23, 1658 (Thurloe, VII, 460-61); it gives the views of a Commonwealthsman.

[33]*A True Catalogue*, pp. 23-25. It is stated that most of the Baptist churches "by their great silence . . . did much connive at and own the last apostacy." Ibid., p. 60. A few separate churches only presented addresses, and the Fifth Monarchy men alone denounced Richard's accession.

the existing government by a single person and two Houses of Parliament or to replace it by a commonwealth.[34]

The author of *A True Catalogue*, in his "collection of the most material passages in the several blasphemous, lying, flattering addresses," listed ninety-four, relying, as he said, upon *Mercurius Politicus*, and admitted that more were presented than the newspaper printed. He claimed that similarities in substance and language begat the suspicion that they were hatched at court by Thurloe and "the old malignant pamphleteer, that lying railing Rabshekah, and defamer of the friends of the cause," Nedham.[35] A perusal of the addresses does not reveal greater uniformity than a common purpose would naturally dictate. All subscribers testified to their grief at the death of the late Protector and loyalty to his successor and—some added—to the constitution as established by the Humble Petition and Advice. It is not surprising that several addresses should make the same biblical allusions to Joshua's succeeding Moses, and Elisha's assuming the Mantle of Elijah, and to the lamentation, "Oh my father, my father! the chariots of Israel, and the horsemen thereof." If there was any conscious imitation of early addresses in later ones, the publication of the former in the newspapers may furnish the explanation.

The author of *A True Catalogue* mistook the intention of the government in promoting these addresses—if the gracious reception of individuals or delegations presenting them can be properly called "promoting." The wish was not to secure conformity to a pattern: it was to secure as many proofs as possible of fidelity. In spite of past experience when all kinds of oaths had been discarded, there was still a naive belief in the sanctity of political oaths. There was also the consideration that if officers should prove unfaithful, their signatures to addresses would record their perjury. Henry Cromwell told his brother Richard that he would send the address from the army in Ireland "as a witness against the treachery and falsehood of any officer of the army that may hereafter in the least manner warp from his due obedience."[36] But the primary desire of adherents of the Protectorate was to demonstrate the wide base on which it rested. Perhaps they hoped that the many signs of popular approval would deter opponents from interference.

Before the flood of loyal addresses ebbed, the condolences and congratulations of foreign powers began to stream in. The news of Oliver's death had been received abroad without regret even by friendly nations,

[34]Ibid., pp. 31, 44, 47, 48, 53, 24; *Calendar Domestic, 1658-1659*, pp. 133, 139, 154.

[35]Ibid., pp. 3, 53. In a very rare tract, *A Seasonable Word*, occurs the argument that, if the people had originated the addresses, they would have requested the summoning of a parliament.

[36]Sept. 18, Thurloe, VII, 400.

and with rejoicing by past and present enemies. Men breathed more freely now that the great champion of Puritanism was no more. France was an ally, engaged in a joint war against Spain, but her leading statesman, Cardinal Mazarin, no sooner heard of the Protector's death than he hastened to congratulate Queen Henrietta Maria. According to rumor he told her that his engagements to the "dead monster" would quickly expire and then something might be done for her son Charles II.[37] In Holland, George Downing, the English resident there, reported there was no need to recount the rejoicing, though the news of Richard's peaceful succession cooled the enthusiasm.[38] A Royalist at Amsterdam was less reticent. "They are mad with joy; . . . the young fry dance in the streets at noonday; the Devil is dead is the language at every turn."[39] The phrase expressed a general sentiment. An English sailor bound for Cadiz heard a Spaniard shout: "There is good news: Cromwell is dead. There is a great feast in Hell." It was good news for Spaniards, the Englishman thought, "for he made them cheap."[40]

Europeans clearly expected Oliver's death to be followed by the fall of the Protectorate, perhaps by the recall of the exiled king. They were amazed at Richard's peaceful and orderly accession, but soon adjusted themselves to the necessity of swallowing their true sentiments and of making overtures to the new Protector. Holland took the lead in recognizing him. John de Witt visited Downing on September 9 to express his pleasure that things had passed so happily and quickly in England to the disappointment of wicked men, enemies to the Dutch as well as the English. Nieuport, the Dutch ambassador in London, was instructed to offer condolences to Richard on the death of his father "of immortal memory" and congratulations on his protectoral dignity, and to assure him that the States-General was resolved to maintain "the ancient amity and the last alliance."[41]

As to France, within a day or two of his father's death Richard intimated to Bordeaux his wishes that the French court should go into mourning "as it is very necessary to his Highness that his Majesty should appear to regard him as highly as he has previously regarded the Kings of England and other sovereign princes, allies, and friends of France." At the same time a loan of £50,000 was requested for pressing expenses, because the situation of affairs made the summoning of Parlia-

[37]Jermyn to Charles II, Sept. 10/20, *State Papers Collected by Edward, Earl of Clarendon* (henceforth called *Clarendon State Papers*), III (Oxford, 1786), 415; *Calendar of State Papers, Venetian 1657-1659* (1931), (henceforth called *Calendar Venetian*), p. 245.

[38]Thurloe, VII, 379.

[39]*Clarendon State Papers*, III, 412.

[40]Edward Coxere, *Adventures by Sea*, ed. E. H. W. Meyerstein (Oxford, 1946), p. 113.

[41]Thurloe, VII, 379, 391; *Calendar Venetian*, p. 251.

ment inadvisable at the time.[42] Mazarin promptly informed William Lockhart, the English ambassador, that the French court had gone into mourning and that he had directed Bordeaux to compliment Richard on his accession and to take part in Oliver's funeral. Before knowing the course of events in England immediately following the late Protector's death, he had told Bordeaux to inform the family that they could count on the friendship of Louis XIV and himself in every eventuality. He added, however, that he regretted the impossibility of making a loan.[43] In reply to a letter from Richard he protested his devotion to the friendship his father had honored him with.[44] The refusal of the loan was felt to be more indicative of Mazarin's true feelings than the profession of friendship. Bordeaux reported that Fauconberg, whom he hoped to keep Francophile by a lavish present, had said that the government was "greatly offended" at the denial of so small a sum.[45] At the French ambassador's formal reception on October 18, however, all signs of resentment were suppressed, and assurances of good will were freely given.[46]

Two days after the French ambassador's reception Richard received a special envoy from Charles X of Sweden. Probably the Protector's remarks were in harmony with the advice of his Privy Council—that he could not immediately respond to requests for assistance, but desired to proceed with the treaty his father had begun with a view to entering upon "nearer terms of friendship and alliance."[47] Agents from other powers all presented their regrets at Oliver's death and their compliments to the new Protector. In fact, Europe, like England, appeared to acknowledge Richard as his father's lawful successor. With remarkably little dissent, the Protectorate had been transferred from father to son. All outward and visible signs looked propitious. What was not so clear was the dependence of the regime upon its head, upon personal loyalty. Oliver had prevailed, because he had been, not a symbol of the general will, but a very great leader in war and peace. The Protectorate, having no roots in the past and being clumsily grafted upon the old constitution, could continue only if upheld by another strong arm.

[42]Bordeaux to Mazarin, Sept. 5/15, Francois Pierre Guillaume Guizot, *History of Richard Cromwell and the Restoration of Charles II*, trans. Andrew R. Scoble (1856), I, 231-32.

[43]To Lockhart, Sept. 12/22, *Lettres du Cardinal Mazarin*, ed. G. D'Avenel, IX (Paris, 1906), 64.

[44]Ibid., p. 86.

[45]Guizot, I, 250-51.

[46]Ibid., pp. 245-46.

[47]Thurloe, VII, 440.

CHAPTER II

Richard and His Enemies

RICHARD, the third but oldest surviving son of Oliver Cromwell, was born on October 4, 1626. He was educated at Felsted school and entered at Lincoln's Inn in 1647, but whether he ever studied there is very doubtful. In or about September of that same year he was appointed captain of the lifeguard, but after its disbandment early in 1648 he held no commission for ten years. In 1649 he married Dorothy Major, the daughter of a wealthy Hampshire squire, and settled down to enjoy the life of a country gentleman. His later critics sarcastically described him as skilled in hawking, hunting, and horse racing.[1] Apparently immersed in these pursuits he neglected his affairs and ran into debt. His father, who had wished him to use his retirement for study, especially urging him to read Raleigh's *History of the World*, was vexed that his son should make pleasure the business of his life instead of fitting himself for the service of the state. Richard took the reproof to heart and, if he did not become more studious, grew more discreet in his amusements. Slander itself never assailed his morals. Even the righteous Mrs. Hutchinson allowed that he was "gentle and virtuous," though she thought that he "became not greatness" and was "a peasant in his nature."[2]

When his father became Protector, his oldest son, the Lord Richard as he was now styled, was inevitably thrust into prominence. He had a seat in the Parliaments that met in 1654 and 1656, and was a member of the Committee for Trade and Navigation, no doubt in order that he should learn what England's commercial interests were. After the Humble Petition and Advice had given Oliver the right to name his successor, dignities and offices were showered upon Richard. He succeeded his father as Chancellor of the University of Oxford (July 18, 1657), he was nominated a member of the new House of Lords, and of the Council of State (December 31, 1657), and given the command of Goffe's regiment of horse in January.[3] The official newspapers styled him "the most illustrious lord," and the local authorities received him with quasi-royal honors when he made a progress through the west in the summer of 1658. He was evidently regarded as his father's destined

---

[1] *A Second Narrative of the Late Parliament* (1658). There are at least two editions of this pamphlet, but the reprint in the *Harleian Miscellany* VI (1810) is incomplete.

[2] Lucy Hutchinson, *Memoirs of the Life of Colonel Hutchinson*, ed. C. H. Firth (1906), p. 298.

[3] After Oliver's death his two regiments of horse passed to Richard. Sir Charles Firth and Godfrey Davies, *The Regimental History of Cromwell's Army* (Oxford, 1940), I, 48, 73, 249, 286, 594, 674.

successor. Unluckily for him the highest position in the land devolved upon him before he was in any way fitted for it. With a longer preparation he might perhaps have made a constitutional head of the state. As it was, his experience in public affairs was too slight and limited to afford him either knowledge of men or insight into business. He himself complained of the heavy burden imposed by his position and confessed that he had thought to have lived as a country gentleman because his father "had not employed him in such a way as to prepare him for such employment" as was now thrust upon him.[4]

In the circumstances, inevitably the substance of power fell to the Privy Council. But that body was ill-fitted for a controlling influence upon affairs. As will be seen later, it was divided both by grave differences about public policies and by personal rivalries. Moreover, neither its composition nor its history under Oliver qualified it to direct affairs. Composed of mediocre men, its feebleness was bound to be exposed at the first major crisis. Like Richard, the Council lacked training in leadership. Oliver's imperious will had so dominated the Protectorate that his Council was reduced to a very subordinate position. Events were soon to demonstrate that the councillors could not grapple with the new responsibilities they had to assume. The sharp eyes of Bordeaux, the French ambassador, soon detected that Richard possessed only the shadow of authority, and he demanded more secret service money in order to bribe some members to reveal conciliar secrets.[5] A Royalist's view was that Oliver had made his own policy, running hazards his counsellors "trembled to think of," but that now they would make the decisions. Richard he thought more prudent and above all more docile, "ready to embrace and fit to execute the counsels of his father's old friends."[6]

Richard was in some respects admirably suited to be the figurehead of the state. As his task was to reconcile the victors and vanquished in the civil wars, his past detachment from politics was a positive advantage. The Presbyterian Richard Baxter noted that "many sober men that called his father no better than a traitorous hypocrite did begin to think that they owed him [Richard] subjection. . . . That this man having never had any hand in the war (but supposed to be for the King)[7] nor ever seeking for the government, and now seeking to own

[4]William Hooke to John Winthrop, Jr., Mar. 30, 1659, *Collections of the Massachusetts Historical Society,* Fourth Series, VII (Boston, 1865), 591. Hooke was an Oxonian who migrated to New England but returned in 1644. He became one of Oliver's chaplains and master of the Savoy.

[5]Bordeaux to Brienne, Nov. 22/Dec. 2, Guizot, I, 265.

[6]Broderick to ———— March 18, 1659, *Clarendon State Papers,* III, 440-441. John Barwick had written to the same effect not long after Oliver's death. Thurloe, VII, 415.

[7]A suspicion that may derive from his probable association with ex-Royalists in his recreations in Hampshire.

the sober party, was like to be used in the healing of the land &c. Such reasonings as these began to take with the minds of many, to subject themselves quietly to this man."[8] Pierrepont, traditionally known as "wise William," argued in Richard's favor with the Republican John Hutchinson on the ground that the nation could be restored to freedom "under this young man who was so flexible to good counsels."[9] The Royalist historian testified to the same effect: Richard inherited all the greatness and glory of his father "without that public hate that visibly attended the other."[10] In addition, unlike his younger brother Henry, he was not identified with any particular section of the Puritan party, so his elevation roused no jealousies among Cromwellians.

He possessed most of the external qualifications for his lofty position. Royalist satirists might depict him as a country clown, but in reality he was comely in appearance and gentlemanly in behavior. If his face showed none of the rugged strength of his father's, it displayed an attractive mildness and openness. A New Englander admired his "sweet countenance, vivacious & candid, as is the whole frame of his spirit, only, naturally, inclined to choler."[11] Many observers testify to his dignified and gracious bearing at public ceremonies. Some of his supporters, like Andrew Marvell, assumed that

A Cromwell in an hour a prince will grow.[12]

Others were agreeably surprised. Whitelocke, well-versed in the etiquette of courts, thought that at the French ambassador's reception Richard "did carry himself discreetly, and better than expected."[13] Another observer thought Richard's reception of multitudes of addresses proved, "among several other indications, more of ability in him than could ordinarily have been expected from him."[14] Embittered Republicans praised Richard's character in Parliament. "I never saw nor heard either fraud or guile in him," said Sir Arthur Hesilrige. "If you think of a single person," Scot avowed, "I would have him sooner than any man alive."[15] Moreover, both his public behavior and private life gave promise that he would uphold the best interests of Puritanism. After Richard's fall, Hugh Peters paid this tribute of praise: "His family,

[8] *Reliquiae Baxterianae*, p. 100.

[9] Lucy Hutchinson, in *Life of Colonel Hutchinson*, pp. 304-305, does not name Pierrepont, but there can be little doubt of the identification.

[10] Clarendon, *Rebellion*, Bk. XVI, 2.

[11] William Hooke, op. cit.

[12] A Poem upon the Death of his Late Highness the Lord Protector, l. 312.

[13] *Memorials*, IV, 337.

[14] William Hooke, op. cit.

[15] *Diary of Thomas Burton*, ed. John T. Rutt (1828), III, 104, 112.

himself, and lady, being truly godly; yea, such a family of godliness and sobriety not known in the Christian world."[16] These qualities compare favorably with those attributed to many English kings, and should have sufficed in normal times. Unfortunately for Richard, his lot was cast in a revolutionary era, and nothing in his character or record suggested that he would be able to face the sea of troubles before him. He might have exclaimed with Hamlet:

> The time is out of joint; O cursed spite
> That ever I was born to set it right!

The hour demanded a resolute leader, but Richard was self-effacing. Unlike his father, he seems never to have been conscious that he had a mission to perform, that he must be the militant champion of Puritanism or fall ignominiously. He failed to attract devoted adherents by personal magnetism or to convince men that he stood between them and a chaos out of which a restoration of the Stuarts would emerge. He had neither the will nor the wish to prevail when occasions arose that required stern measures. The father often hesitated until his mind was made up, but then he struck like lightning; the son continued to drift until upon the rocks. Difficulties similar to those that ruined the son— and more besides—had been overcome by the father. But the religious enthusiasm, fiery energy, and iron determination which had enabled Oliver to overcome every obstacle were all wanting in Richard. Well might his brother Henry ask: "Where is that person of wisdom, courage, conduct, and (which is equivalent to all) reputation at home and abroad, which we see necessary to preserve our peace?"[17] Anyone who peruses the authorities for the period of the Puritan Revolution will find that Oliver's life is largely the history of England, but that Richard's share in events from September, 1658, to the following May is small. The impression left is of a man of affable manners and gentle character in the web of extraordinary times from which he had not the ability and energy to disentangle himself.

The open and avowed enemies of the Protectorate were the same in September, 1658, as two years earlier, when Oliver had addressed his second Parliament. "Abroad," he had said, "your great enemy is the Spaniard. He is a natural enemy." He was also the ally of the Royalists on the Continent and at home. Though the Cavaliers might behave "most demurely," they would be ready to revolt whenever a fair opportunity offered. There were, according to Oliver, three groups of "dis-

---

[16]May 10, 1659, in *England's Confusion* (reprinted in *Collection of Scarce and Valuable Tracts . . . of the late Lord Somers*, ed. Sir Walter Scott [1809-15], VI, 525). Richard's wife is also praised by John Maidston, Cofferer of the Household, as "a prudent, godly, practical christian." Thurloe, I, 766.

[17]To Thurloe, Dublin, Sept. 8, 1658. Thurloe, VII, 376.

contented spirits" that played the game of the King of Scots, though some were not Cavaliers at heart. First came the Levellers who had prepared to join the Cavaliers in the insurrection in 1655 and tried to raise a mutiny in the army in Scotland. Secondly, there were the Republicans who liked to call themselves the Commonwealthsmen and, lastly, the Fifth Monarchy men.

Now all these opponents were even more hostile than before. Spaniards and Royalists, united by a treaty,[18] had fought against the French and a contingent of Cromwellian soldiers in Flanders. The enmity of Levellers, Commonwealthsmen, and Fifth Monarchy enthusiasts had been increased by the enactment of the Humble Petition and Advice, which approximated the Protectorate to a hereditary monarchy with a nominated House of Lords. These three dissentient groups were represented in the army. The Levellers had undoubtedly lost much ground since the mutinies they instigated in 1649 had been crushed. Many not then discharged seem to have regretted their disloyalty and to have served faithfully afterwards. But some retained their old political principles and grew more embittered after Oliver Cromwell became Lord Protector in 1653. However, the conversion of "freeborn" John Lilburne to Quakerism, and then his death, left them without effective leadership. Curiously enough, the lifeguards of Fairfax and of the two Cromwells contained a number of Levellers, perhaps because, as their pamphleteers claimed, they were men of superior intelligence.[19]

The Fifth Monarchy men or Millenarians (who were expecting that Christ would soon descend and establish the fifth universal monarchy) were now less numerous. Their leader in the army, Major General Thomas Harrison, had lost his commission for refusing to recognize Cromwell as Protector. Another of their supporters, Colonel Nathaniel Rich, was dismissed in 1654 for demanding that John Rogers, Christopher Feake, and other preachers be set at liberty. Five commissioned officers of his regiment were cashiered in Scotland in 1655, but Monck's army there, though not its general, continued to be regarded by Fifth Monarchy men as devoted to their cause. Their optimism was to prove excessive. They suffered another loss when Robert Overton, governor of Hull, was detected as sympathizing with, if not participating in, a plot and was strictly confined for the remainder of the Protectorate.

The Commonwealthsmen are often hard to differentiate from the Levellers, because both parties agreed in opposing the Protectorate and demanding a more democratic constitution. In 1654 the Petition of the

[18]By a slip of the pen Sir Charles Firth dated the signature and ratification of the treaty as 1657 instead of 1656, *Last Years*, I, 24; *Clarendon Calendar*, III, 109-10, 136.
[19]Firth and Davies, *Regimental History*, I, 48-50, 53-55.

Three Colonels (Matthew Alured, John Okey, and Thomas Sanders) attacked the Instrument of Government and demanded that the Agreement of the People be adopted. All three lost their commissions. After the enactment of the Humble Petition and Advice, Oliver found it necessary to purge Major William Packer and five captains from his own regiment of horse because they were unwilling to accept the new constitution, but insisted on the "old cause" though unable to define it.[20] There were, however, still some Republicans at heart among the field officers of the army—Colonels James Berry and Richard Ashfield being among the most prominent. But the Commonwealthsmen found their main strength among the junior officers, especially those of long service. They seem to have been most numerous in the regiments that had formed the New Model Army in 1645, and many of them had been promoted in 1647 for adhering to the army against Parliament.

The immediate danger to Richard came, however, not from any particular dissident group within the army but from its ambitious leaders. They were determined that the army should not resign its predominant position in the state. During Oliver's last days, meetings of officers filled supporters of the Protectorate with misgivings. At a general meeting on August 29 Fleetwood and Berry "prayed very notionally both, and in general, only begging of God to go on to own his people, and to keep up their hearts to do his work. Honest Ingoldsby and Fauconberg were the only persons not summoned to this meeting; by which you may guess at something."[21] Four days after Oliver's death Thurloe reported that there were secret murmurings in the army that Richard was not commander in chief as his father had been. At the same time Fleetwood was writing that the army was in a quiet condition.[22] Whether the Secretary was mistaken or the general willfully blind is hard to decide. A week later, Fauconberg reported that, although the army looked peaceful, something underhand was brewing. A secret cabal of "great ones" was resolved to rule, or to set all on fire.[23] Apparently the cabal was engaged upon an address to the new Protector.[24]

Some anxiety seems to have been felt in government circles as to the atttiude of the army in Scotland and of its commander, George Monck. Thomas Clarges was chosen to go immediately to Edinburgh in order to carry letters to the general and to ascertain his sentiments. Clarges

[20]*Regimental History*, I, 72-73.

[21]Fauconberg to Henry Cromwell, Aug. 30, Thurloe, VII, 365. Original in cipher (which accounts for the jerky style) but deciphered except certain letters which stood for individuals. "W." I have rendered Fleetwood, "B" is certainly Fauconberg, the writer.

[22]Thurloe, VII, 374, 375.

[23]Fauconberg to Henry Cromwell, Sept. 14, Thurloe, VII, 386.

[24]The same to the same, Sept. 21, ibid., p. 406.

found his brother-in-law "weary of the uncertain condition, wherein he found both himself and the nation inthralled by the overruling tyranny of the soldiers (who made themselves a divided interest from the rest of the people) so that they consulted of a paper to be drawn up to be presented to the new Protector."[25]

The policy which Monck proposed to the new Protector concerned religion, parliament, and the army. To establish himself more firmly he should endeavor to secure the adherence of those of power and interest among the people. The most considerable had a great regard for discipline in the church. Therefore, an assembly of godly divines should be summoned to agree upon "some way of union and accommodation," and put a stop to the progress of blasphemy and profanity which the existing toleration allowed. As a preliminary the Protector should countenance moderate Presbyterian divines like Reynolds, Calamy, Cooper, and Manton. The calling of a parliament would require much consideration. The position in the House of Lords could be strengthened by summoning the most prudent of the old lords[26] and some of the leading gentry in the several counties, such as Pierrepont of Nottinghamshire, Sir George Booth of Cheshire, Sir John Hobart ("Hubbart") of Norfolk, Hampden of Buckinghamshire, and Popham of Somerset.

The heavy debts owed by the government, he continued, made retrenchment imperative in the cost of the army and navy. In Ireland, the "loose" companies (not attached to any regiment) should be disbanded, especially as their officers were of doubtful loyalty, and replaced by a militia. Much expenditure on the three armies in England, Scotland, and Ireland could be saved by reducing two regiments into one. This economy had the further advantage of affording a plausible opportunity to get rid of "some insolent spirits." If the advice seemed bold, let His Highness rest assured that no officer in the army could induce two men to follow him in a revolt once he was cashiered, as a late example proved.[27] Every honest colonel should be allowed to nominate officers to fill vacancies in his regiment because he would choose men of his own principles, but others open to suspicion should be denied this favor. As for the navy, many who had fought bravely in the Dutch war were not now employed. A list of the names of eight captains well qualified to command the best ships followed, together with the warning that Whitehorn was a coward and that others were men of no estates and little interest. Finally, the Protector was urged, if he intended to carry out

[25]Baker's *Chronicle*, p. 654.

[26]I.e., those whose peerages antedated the Civil War.

[27]The reference is either to Lambert's dismissal in July, 1657, or more probably to that of Packer and the five captains in February, 1658.

the advice now given him, to consult Whitelocke, St. John, Broghil, Onslow ("Ansloe"), Pierrepont, and Thurloe.[28]

Clarges began his return journey about September 15 and probably arrived in London about five days later. He delivered the letter privately to Richard, who liked the advice it contained. The attempt to adopt its plan for remodeling the armies was, according to Baker's *Chronicle*,[29] "the main cause of all the divisions which happened in them, and the happy consequences thereof." Beyond these exaggerated words little is known of the reception of Monck's advice. That it was startling in its boldness admits of no doubt; less certain is its practicability. There were two main weaknesses. To rely more and more on Presbyterians to ensure the permanence of the Protectorate was decidedly risky, because their support could be purchased, if at all, only by sacrificing toleration, which all sections of the army fervently supported, and by establishing at least a modified form of Presbyterianism as the state religion—and the battle of Worcester appeared to have ruined forever any such plan. The second weakness was that there was no military leader in England of sufficient influence among the soldiery to be able to control the army while it was being remodeled, and it is significant that Monck named no officer among the councillors he recommended. Perhaps his plan might have been feasible if put into operation slowly but resolutely, beginning with the gradual substitution of reliable officers for the disaffected. But to change an army full of enthusiasts and extremists, the politically ambitious and the religiously fanatical, into a body of professional soldiers was a transformation that would require time—and time was to be denied Richard.

In the country at large Cromwellians formed a center party with Royalists on the right and Republicans on the left. In general, both opposition parties were irreconcilable, though some in each group were prepared to acquiesce in the Protectorate and a few to support it. Numerically the Royalists formed much the larger group, but its adherents were divided because, though many Presbyterians desired the King's return, by no means all wished his unconditional restoration. Even the Cavaliers who had adhered to the royal cause from the beginning found union difficult. Many of their old leaders were either dead or exiled. They were all impoverished by gifts to, or expenditures for, the King and by sequestration. They had been invariably defeated when they had risen, and traitors or spies had revealed their plans for other insurrections, so that they had grown weary of struggling. Not a few were satisfied to confine their loyalty to drinking toasts in secret. The

[28]Thurloe, VII, 387-88.   [29]P. 654.

King was a stranger to his supporters in England, and the reports of the evil life he led on the Continent—industriously circulated in the official newspapers—were not encouraging to men asked to risk life and estate on his behalf.

The Republicans formed a relatively small party which was formidable because it was compact under able leaders and because it was strong among the captains, lieutenants, and ensigns in the army. The left was composed, according to Baxter, of "democratical politicians that are busy about the change of government and would bring all into confusion under pretence of the people's liberty or power, and would have the major part of the subjects to be the sovereign of the rest."[30] Though thousands shared these democratic views, they had no effective political power. Some of the extreme sectaries and Levellers had asserted in 1656 their willingness to acknowledge Charles II as king, provided that he agreed to drastic changes in the constitution, to complete religious freedom without a state church, to the abolition of tithes, and to a comprehensive amnesty for all except those who continued to adhere to Oliver as Protector. This hatred of Oliver was the only real bond between them and the Royalists.[31] To have accepted their program would have lost the King all his other supporters.

The religious situation was similar to the political. The right was composed of Anglicans, Roman Catholics, and some Presbyterians. The first had lost their leaders by the abolition of episcopacy and cathedral chapters. About a quarter of the clergy had been deprived, but more than half[32] had accepted—no doubt with reluctance—the new ecclesiastical settlement, though some contrived to evade it either by using the forbidden Book of Common Prayer or by repeating parts of it from memory. The supineness of the hierarchy which remained in England was remarkable. Even the danger that the apostolic succession might be lost by the failure to consecrate new bishops was ignored. In striking contrast to the apathy at home was the energy abroad. The clergy in exile, over a hundred in number, published many learned and controversial works. The Laudians were the most zealous, and their fervor helped to form the alliance between high church divines and country gentlemen which was to influence politics so deeply.[33] Roman Catholicism was still proscribed, and a terrible penal code against its followers remained on the statute book, but there was very little persecution and

[30]A *Key for Catholicks* (1659), Epistle Dedicatory to Richard. Probably written late in 1658 judging from the references to addresses to the new Protector.

[31]See the interesting address quoted at length in Clarendon's *Rebellion*, XV, 105-30.

[32]Assuming about 9,000 clergy, 1,500 deaths, and 2,500 deprivations, about 5,000 would be left.

[33]Robert S. Bosher, *The Making of the Restoration Settlement* (New York, 1951), passim.

no martyrdom. Except for discriminatory taxation, they suffered as little during the Protectorate as at any period since the beginning of the century. It is noteworthy that Baxter, after mentioning the Spanish Armada, attempts to assassinate English rulers, the Gunpowder Plot, and the Irish Massacre, asked Richard to consider whether "you should be deposed or murdered as a heretic, and whether we should be tormented and burnt as heretics." Yet he concluded, "I speak not this to provoke you to deal bloodily with them."[34] The war against Spain actually benefited Catholics because French pressure on their behalf led to the release from prison of priests both in England and Ireland.[35] The frequent complaints by Royalists suggest that Catholics had become lukewarm in a cause they had at first supported so fervently.

The Presbyterians were divided. Some ministers and laymen openly supported the Protectorate, while more were willing to belong to the state church Cromwell had established. Nearly all deplored to a greater or lesser extent the toleration enjoyed by the religious parties to the left and advocated a tighter rein over them. No doubt a powerful reason why many adhered to, or did not oppose, the Protector was fear that his overthrow would place the extreme sectaries in power. When this happened in May, 1659, the Presbyterians became almost unanimous in their detestation of the restored Long Parliament.

The left included the more extreme Baptists or Fifth Monarchy men, Behmenists or mystics, visionaries and libertines, ranters, Socinians, Seekers and Quakers, and scores of small groups that gathered round some enthusiast or other. In general, all believed in toleration and denounced a state church supported by tithes. They wanted voluntary, self-supporting associations with or without ministers, according to the inclinations of the different groups.

Richard meant to uphold the ecclesiastical system he found in existence. Though the services of the Church of England had been proscribed and though bishops, deans, and cathedral clergy had been abolished and their lands sold for the use of the Commonwealth, the parishes had been retained as the local units. Two sets of commissioners had been established to supervise ministers. An ordinance of March 20, 1654, declared that henceforth any person before nomination to a benefice or as a "public settled" lecturer in England or Wales should be approved as a person with "the Grace of God in him," of "holy and unblameable conversation," and, because of his "knowledge and utterance, able and fit to

[34]The Epistle Dedicatory to Richard in *A Key for Catholicks*.

[35]Firth, *Last Years*, II, 221-22. It is noteworthy that on the eve of the Restoration a pamphleteer thought it necessary to refute the charge that Roman Catholics were enemies to the King. J. A., *A Vindication of the Roman Catholicks*, April 22, 1660.

preach the Gospel." No other standard was erected and no test of orthodoxy established. A mixed commission of laymen and ministers, but with the latter predominating, was named to sit in London and to enforce the ordinance.[36] They were often known as "the Triers."

The supplementary ordinance of August 28, 1654, provided for the ejection of "scandalous, ignorant, and insufficient ministers and schoolmasters." To execute it, commissioners were appointed in every county. They were nearly all civilians, with a sprinkling of soldiers, but when a case involved ignorance and insufficiency, the commissioners of any county were to be joined by five or more ministers named in the ordinance. The definition of scandal was very wide, and included, in addition to the sins to which flesh is heir, haunting taverns, frequent playing at cards or dice, profaning the Sabbath, use of the Book of Common Prayer since the previous January 1, countenancing wakes, morris dancing, or stage plays, and disaffection to the government. In fact, if rigidly construed, anyone not a strict Puritan and consistent supporter of the Protectorate might be ejected. Any minister already established in a benefice and approved by the first set of commissioners, or any substitute for an incumbent ejected by the second set was to receive the house, glebe, tithes, and other profits belonging to the benefice in question.[37] Another ordinance, of September 2, 1654, consolidating existing legislation, empowered the trustees of a fund for the better maintenance of ministers to augment the incomes of poor livings and to unite two or more parishes into one so that the combined revenues should yield a sufficient income.

From the point of view of those in authority the maintenance of a state church had the great advantage that the pulpits were subject to their control. At no time in English history has preaching been the organ for publicity to the extent that it was during the Puritan Revolution. Public opinion was molded by the thousands of sermons delivered every week.[38] Compared to these figures the circulation of political pamphlets was small; political meetings were still in their infancy, and

[36]Three of the civilians were Francis Rous, William Packer, and Robert Tichborne, of whom lives are in *DNB*. Among the ministers were many of the famous leaders and preachers of the time: Thomas Goodwin, John Owen, Philip Nye, Stephen Marshall, Hugh Peters, Peter Sterry, and Obadiah Sedgwick. The members seem fairly to represent the groups that supported the Protectorate.

[37]Sometimes ministers approved by the commissioners found great difficulty in securing possession of the church or parsonage or both. One, Edward Fletcher, in a petition to the Protector, left an interesting account of his misfortunes at Bagendon, Gloucestershire. His entry to the church was opposed by a cleric ejected from Rendcomb and the churchwarden. No magistrate would help him so he established himself, only to be stoned in the pulpit. When Oliver Cromwell died his opponents grew bolder and sued him at law, prevented his collecting his tithes and discouraged the villagers from working on his land, so that he was obliged to bring men from Gloucester to help with the harvest. *Calendar Domestic, 1658-1659*, p. 189.

[38]"As their ministers are, so for the most are people's minds." *The Case of Ministers Maintenance by Tithes* (1659), p. 34.

24

were liable to be dispersed if held. Of course, the majority of ministers was not composed of staunch Cromwellians. Indeed, the Anglicans, who had stifled their scruples and retained their benefices, and the Presbyterians, who had taken the places of the ejected, might be expected to refrain from denouncing from the pulpit the powers that be, but not to praise them. Yet, to suggest that favorable propaganda was a primary objective of Oliver Cromwell in his ecclesiastical policy would be a gross libel with no evidence to justify it. Although he benefited from a state church, he supported it for nonpolitical ends as the best way to ensure that every parish should have its minister. To maintain him Cromwell held tithes to be essential. Also, he may have felt, as others did, that if tithes were abolished, secularized church lands might be reclaimed. The ecclesiastical system under the Protectorate was assailed, therefore, on two main grounds—that a state church inevitably involved the use of force upon men's conscience and this in its turn would exclude the righteous but open wide the doors to "hirelings,"[39] and that tithes were contrary to Scripture and burdensome to the tillers of the soil. In general, Baptists, Fifth Monarchy men, and Quakers opposed tithes on religious grounds, and Levellers on economic.[40]

Richard wisely decided to tread in his father's footsteps, and he maintained the status quo. He was fortunate because, as Baxter remarked, "a spirit of peace and healing is lately risen in the hearts of many thousands in the land, and ministers that differed do lovingly associate."[41] One sign of this tendency toward unity was the continued though limited success of the voluntary associations of ministers which had begun in 1653 in order to secure a degree of uniformity in the ordination of ministers and admission to the sacraments. The Worcestershire association, first in order of time, was composed, according to its founder, of not more than four or five Episcopalians, no Presbyterians or Independents, and the rest "disengaged faithful men."[42]

Equally promising was a movement which started in the summer of 1658 toward an accommodation between Presbyterians and Congregationalists. It apparently began under official auspices and had Oliver Cromwell's blessing. A circular letter, signed by Henry Scobell, clerk

[39]Milton had already applied this term to clergymen in poetry and prose (see the index to the Columbia University Press edition of his *Works*). His tract, *Considerations Touching the Likeliest Means to Remove Hirelings* (1659), will be discussed *in loco*.

[40]For a very useful, short treatment see Margaret James, "The Political Importance of the Tithes Controversy, 1640-60," in *History*, XXVI (June, 1941).

[41]*Five disputations about church government*, Epistle Dedicatory to Richard. Thomason's date is March 2, 1659. Cf. M. Henry, *Life of Philip Henry* (1698), p. 60.

[42]For a succinct account of these associations see W. A. Shaw, *History of the English Church* (1900), II, 152-65; Frederick J. Powicke, *A Life of Richard Baxter* (1924), I, ch. 11.

of the Council, was sent to the Congregational churches announcing a meeting in London in June. Some two hundred representatives of one hundred and twenty churches met on September 29 and named six (Goodwin, Owen, Nye, Bridge, Caryl, and Greenhill) to draw up articles. The result was *A declaration of the faith and order owned and practiced in the Congregational churches in England: Agreed upon and consented unto by their elders and messengers in their meeting at the Savoy, Oct. 12, 1658.* A very interesting preface explained both the advantages and the need for a confession of faith. During the years when the churches had been gathering, there had been many seducing spirits at work "more perilous than the hottest seasons of persecution." A "great variety of spirits, doctrines, opinions, and occurrences" had tempted many, so that the "soundest professors" had been driven to a re-examination of essential truths. The principles followed throughout were that there should be, amongst all Christian churches, "a forbearance and mutual indulgence," and a desire for as great uniformity as possible with reformers and brethren in New England. Men should remember that the nation had not been accustomed to either Presbytery or Independency and that they were reaping with joy what the old Puritan nonconformists had sowed in tears, because they concurred in the substantial parts of church government. Now they lived in a time when their prince tolerated each persuasion, provided that the liberty to follow the dictates of conscience was not abused to the disturbance of civil peace. They should, therefore, do their utmost to support him and his government. Finally they should recognize that they differed from Presbyterians only as fellow servants, neither sect having the right to impose its opinions upon the other.[43]

This agreement on a national scale was followed by local attempts at accommodation by Congregational and Presbyterian ministers. At Manchester in July, 1659, the two groups of ministers agreed upon the qualifications necessary for admission to the Lord's Supper—a competent knowledge of religious principles, a life without scandal, and regular family prayers and Bible reading. Other propositions provided for the ordination of ministers, and the restriction of preaching to those duly appointed. These articles represented a genuine compromise, such as the likelihood that there would be one minister only in a parish rendered necessary. But it had hardly been reached when Booth's rising

[43]For preliminary correspondence see Francis Peck, *Desiderata Curiosa* (1779), II, 505-12; for a reprint of the *Declaration*, see Benjamin Hanbury, *Historical Memorials relating to the Independents* (1844), III, 517-48; for general accounts of this movement towards accommodation see Shaw, *History of the English Church*, II, 165-74, and Robert William Dale, *"History of English Congregationalism* (1907), pp. 383-90.

convinced the Congregationalists that they had been beguiled into a union with those whose ultimate purpose was a Stuart restoration.[44]

The attitude of Richard's government toward the insistence by ministers that the sacrament should be administered only to those fit to partake of it is shown by a curious case brought before the Council. At the assizes in July, 1658, at Derby and Lincoln, Wyndham, the judge, took a decided stand on the side of parishioners who complained that their ministers refused the sacrament to those they deemed unworthy. He is said to have declared that ministers who refused to administer it were guilty of a tyranny worse than prelatical, and to have advised parishioners not to pay tithes to such ministers. A report of "passages" between Wyndham and a minister of more than local reputation, Thomas Palmer, and a petition from Lincoln were referred to a committee of the Council, which advised that Wyndham's commission as judge should not be renewed. But another Council, eight months later, apparently took the opposite point of view—at least, it named Wyndham as one of the judges to ride the next circuit.[45]

A religious problem that Richard and his Council failed to solve was presented by the Quakers. In September a list of imprisoned Quakers contained a hundred and fifteen names and added that nine had died in gaol. In an accompanying address occurred the assertion that they had patiently borne the greatest sufferings of any people since the Marian persecution, having been "persecuted & despised, beaten, stoned, wounded, stocked, whipped, . . . & cast in dungeons & Noysome vaults." This treatment they had received at the hands of those who claimed to be the champions of liberty of conscience. They enumerated the offenses charged against them: that they were common disturbers of ministers, did not pay tithes, swear an oath or put off their hats, traveled up and down the country without a pass; they refused to pay fees to officials of a court of justice, to plead in the forms used there, or to give security for good behavior. Their answer was that they declined to obey all unequal and imperfect laws made by man and asserted they would bear the greatest suffering rather than sin against God. They had not been punished for breaking any just laws but chiefly for testifying against false prophets and hirelings.[46]

In response to this appeal the Council ordered its clerk to write to

[44]The Life of Adam Martindale, ed. Richard Parkinson (1845), pp. 128-33; The Autobiography of Henry Newcome, ed. Richard Parkinson (1852), I, 108; The Rev. Oliver Heywood, 1630-1702; His Autobiography, Diaries . . . , ed. J. Horsfall Turner (1882), I, 171-74.

[45]Register, Sept. 20; Oct. 5, 7, 1658; June 15, 1659; Calendar Domestic, 1658-1659, pp. 163, 194-96; Hist. MSS Comm. Fifth Report, p. 146a.

[46]Reprinted in full in Extracts from State Papers relating to Friends, ed. Norman Penney (1913), pp. 37-54.

the keepers of the various prisons in which Quakers were imprisoned to ascertain the cause of their commitment and detention. When the replies had been received, the President, Henry Lawrence, on behalf of the Protector and Council, addressed a circular letter to the justices of the peace. He urged that the prisoners had been moved by a spirit of error rather than a malicious opposition to authority, and recommended lenity and not severity in dealing with those who were led astray by defects in their understanding and not malice in their wills.[47] Whatever relief they obtained was temporary. The central government had little control over the local authorities who were hostile to Quakers. According to *A Declaration to the Parliament* delivered on April 6, 1659, the number of Quakers imprisoned had risen to one hundred and forty, and the number of deaths in gaol to twenty-one. One hundred and sixty-four offered to take the places of their brethren in confinement, but the exchange was not allowed.[48] Ten days later the *Declaration* was discussed by the Commons. Member after member denounced the Quakers. One moved they should be whipped home as vagrants. Others denounced them in opprobrious terms as a fanatical crew, disturbers of the peace, wolves in sheep's clothing, and so forth. A very occasional voice was raised on their behalf, but in vain. A resolution was carried that the House disliked the scandals cast upon magistracy and ministry, and the Quakers were ordered to resort forthwith to their respective habitations, apply themselves to their callings, and submit to the laws and the justices. Edward Byllynge and another were brought in to hear the Speaker deliver the judgment of the House. They were not permitted to speak but as they were led out one was heard to repeat, "The names of the righteous shall live; but the name of the wicked shall not."[49]

[47]Ibid., pp. 33-34, 55. The latter document is dated 1657, an error for 1658.
[48]Joseph Besse, *A Collection of the Sufferings of the People called Quakers* (1753), pp. iv-vi.
[49]*Diary of Thomas Burton*, IV, 440-446.

CHAPTER III

The Army's Unrest and Oliver's Funeral

WHILE addresses presented outward manifestations of loyalty to the new Protector, signs of underground intrigues in the army against his authority were not lacking. The first ostensible issue was command of the army, but this also involved control of the Privy Council. The Humble Petition and Advice had defined both the number of members and their powers. There were to be no more than twenty-one, seven of whom constituted a quorum. Each appointment was to be approved by the Council and afterwards by Parliament, whose consent was also necessary for any expulsion. Under Oliver's successors, the commander in chief and field officers, as well as the generals at sea, were to be nominated by the Protector "by consent of the Council and not otherwise."[1] Therefore, the question of who should be commander in chief under Richard, and which officers should be promoted to majorities and higher ranks, depended on the Council. At present the Cromwellians were in a majority, but whether they would maintain their superiority depended on the persons nominated to fill vacancies as well as on the attitudes of present members. Richard's inexperience might have been counterbalanced by a strong Privy Council. Its powers under the constitution were considerable. Its composition is, therefore, of great significance.

Oliver had been content with a Council of fifteen members. His son continued them in office, though his own elevation and the abstention of Rous left two additional vacancies. All the civilians, seven in number, may be considered supporters of the status quo; none was a member of the Council of State created by act of Parliament on May 19, 1659, after Richard's fall. They did not include any real statesmen; all were rather followers than leaders. The ablest of them was undoubtedly Thurloe, but though an excellent administrator, he was cautious to timidity and lacking in initiative. His ill-health during the first months of Richard's protectorate restricted his participation in public affairs. Of the rest, Lawrence was a Baptist and praised by Milton as the virtuous son of a virtuous father and, together with Mountagu, as "both men of the first capacity, and polished by liberal studies."[2] Fiennes, an original member of the Long Parliament but excluded from it by Pride's Purge, had found

[1] *Acts and Ordinances,* II, 1502.

[2] Sonnet xx; and *Defensio Secunda,* translated in *The Works of John Milton* (New York, 1931-1940), VIII, 235; cited henceforth as *Works.*

favor in Oliver Cromwell's sight and was called to his House of Lords in 1657. Wolseley, a Royalist's son, but the husband of Fiennes's sister, had been a councillor with whom Oliver Cromwell "would lay aside his greatness" and was equally trusted by Richard. Little is known of the parts played by John Lisle (a regicide, but otherwise undistinguished except as the husband of Alice Lisle whose trial and execution for sheltering a minister who had fought for Monmouth in 1685 are so graphically described by Macaulay); by Pickering, a brother-in-law of Mountagu and a member of the court which tried Charles I but not a signer of the death warrant; and by Strickland, an ambassador to Holland under the Commonwealth and an opponent of the Humble Petition and Advice, though a later convert to the proposal to make Oliver king. The two last named, never more than lukewarm in their loyalty, seem to have been the first to desert Richard. Certainly, neither the personal characters nor the past records of these councillors suggests that they would offer a rigorous opposition to their military colleagues or support strong measures to curb their ambitions.

Edward Mountagu was the only military (and naval) councillor likely to uphold the Protectorate through thick and thin. He had raised a regiment of foot in Cambridgeshire in 1643 when only eighteen years old, and served in the army of the Eastern Association. He was a colonel in the New Model Army, took part in the battle of Naseby and storming of Bristol, but then resigned his commission. He took no part in military or political affairs again until 1653, when he emerged from retirement to become a member of the Council of State, a position he retained. He was one of the two generals at sea in 1656, Blake being the other: he seems to have owed his position to Cromwell's friendship, because he had no naval experience at all. He had led those who wished to offer the crown to Cromwell a second time after the latter had refused it once, and had triumphed over the opposition in which Disbrowe was conspicuous,[3] though not over Cromwell's scruples. Probably the feud between Mountagu and the army leaders, especially Disbrowe, dates from the debates over kingship and explains the objections made by the military members of Oliver's Council to his appointment as a colonel of horse.[4] Of the other soldiers, Skippon was not a politician, and Jones's[5] military service had apparently been limited to garrison duty in Wales. Fleetwood, the Protector's brother-in-law and lieutenant general of horse, Disbrowe, the

[3]Another vehement opponent was Hewson. See Firth, *Last Years*, II, 167-68.

[4]Firth and Davies, *Regimental History*, I, 192.

[5]Among the index entries of proceedings in Council is: "Privy Seal for Lord Phil. Jones's regiment." *Calendar Domestic, 1658-1659*, p. 175. From a reference by Jones to his "lieutenant of the garrison at Beaumaris," I expect his regiment had not been completely disbanded in 1651-1652. *Regimental History*, I, xxiv-vi; Thurloe, VII, 539.

Protector's uncle by marriage and major general, and Sydenham, active in Dorset during the first Civil War and joint governor of the Isle of Wight with Fleetwood, had all opposed the plan to make Oliver king, the last two vehemently.

Richard's supporters won the first round in the fight to strengthen the military adherents of the government in the Council because Oliver's intention to make Mountagu a colonel of horse was soon carried out, and Theophilus Hart was approved as his major six weeks later.[6] But no progress was made after this initial success. "Matters certainly grow worse and worse every day," wrote Fauconberg. "Sudden clashing like to be in the council. None hereafter to be admitted members there or of the army that pronounce not Shibboleth," probably a new test, including approval on oath of the execution of Charles I. "The present aim conceived to be to exclude Fauconberg and Broghil from council. Henry Cromwell may imagine the sad consequence of this and that they will not rest here. I believe Henry will shortly be sent for over. . . . He is sure to be of the council when he comes over. Order is already in it."[7]

On some points Fauconberg proved a true prophet but on others he was in error. He and Broghil did not become councillors. That the military clique should object to the admission of Fauconberg, Broghil, and Henry Cromwell to the Council can be explained on several grounds. The former, an erstwhile Royalist, had married Oliver's daughter Mary the previous year, and the celebrations, including mixed dancing, had scandalized the stricter Puritans. He had been named colonel of horse to replace Lambert, who refused to accept the Humble Petition and Advice. Broghil, once an Irish Royalist, had been induced to change sides by Cromwell and to participate in his campaign in Ireland. Cromwell admired his political abilities as well as his generalship and had used him as an unofficial adviser during the Protectorate. By birth both were better fitted for a court than the army leaders. Probably jealousy of the favor they had enjoyed from Oliver and were enjoying from Richard actuated Fleetwood and Disbrowe, who saw in them enemies to the predominance of the army and of themselves in politics. Henry Cromwell was known not only to hold strong anti-militaristic views but to have put them into practice in Ireland. He had, as lord deputy, reversed the policy of Fleetwood, his predecessor, by governing in the interest of the settlers rather than the soldiery. Also, he had not favored the Anabaptists, whom Fleet-

[6]*Clarke Papers*, III, 164, 167; Lansdowne MSS 822, f. 225. On September 16 the Council received a message from the Protector that Mountagu should be given a regiment of horse and consented thereto. It passed a rule, however, that in the future its consent should not be given on the same day that the appointment was proposed and that on every such occasion the Council should be summoned. This procedure was followed in Hart's case. Register, Sept. 16, Oct. 28, Nov. 1.

[7]To Henry Cromwell, Sept. 21. Thurloe, VII, 406-407.

wood had countenanced. In the circumstances, therefore, it is surprising that Disbrowe rather than Fleetwood seems to have opposed Henry's coming to England and admission to the Council.[8]

Another question that is likely to have divided the Council was whether or not a parliament should be summoned. From the time that Oliver had dismissed his second Parliament on February 4, 1658, discussions within the Council as well as outside it had taken place about a possible new election. The need of money seemed to make a new parliament imperative. Disbrowe urged that taxes should be imposed and raised by force, and apparently was backed by Fleetwood, and by Lambert, who still retained much influence among the soldiery although he had lost all his civilian and military positions. This reckless proposal had been defeated in the Council but no agreement could be reached on the main questions—should Parliament be called together and, if so, what should be the government policy? The real crux of the matter was stated incisively by Henry Cromwell. "The calling of a Parliament signifies nothing until the army be sufficiently modelled; for that being full of its humors makes the honest party timorous, and the other insolent in their respective proposals . . . the well framing of the army would insensibly temper and keep steady the Parliament, which, no doubt, would provide well enough for a council." At present the civil and military parties were nearly equal at the board, and great changes required a decisive not a slender majority. Now was the time for action.[9]

Henry's words were as applicable to the situation after his father's death as they had been before it. The change was that a Richard had succeeded an Oliver. Parliamentary grants were even more urgently needed now, for expenses continued to exceed revenue. Inability to keep the pay of the army up to date created a most serious situation, because material grievances made the rank and file restless and ready to follow their leaders against a government that failed to pay them.[10] No account of any debates in the Privy Council about calling a parliament has survived, and the occasional references to the subject are not very enlightening. Thurloe informed Henry Cromwell that the question of calling a parliament would be debated in the Council on September 16. A Royalist asserted that the Protectorians dreaded the very name of a parliament because it might challenge Oliver's alleged nomination of Richard. An

[8]Francis Russell to Henry Cromwell, Oct. 5, Lansdowne MSS. Some of his friends wished him to remain in Ireland in order to maintain the army there in its obedience. There are many references in Thurloe and the Lansdowne MSS to the question whether Henry should cross over to England.

[9]This paragraph is based on Firth, *Last Years*, II, 270-272.

[10]Bordeaux, the French ambassador, reported on Sept. 19/29, that the pay of the cavalry had been increased by 4d. a day and of the infantry 2d. Guizot, I, 238. No other contemporary confirms this increase, and I believe it is an error.

anonymous writer thought that the Republicans were afraid that an election would give the Presbyterians a majority.[11] Fauconberg assured the French ambassador that, in spite of the great need for money, all other means of obtaining it would be tried before an appeal to the country.[12] On October 19, Fleetwood wrote that the old debate about summoning a parliament still continued. He clearly implied that financial needs rendered this the only, though hazardous, remedy.[13] How to regulate elections may have delayed a decision which was postponed for the time being. The threatening agitation in the army and the preparations for Oliver's funeral combined to make the holding of elections dangerous as well as inconvenient.[14] Another cause of dissension was provided by the renewal of the war between Sweden and Denmark. Differences are said to have arisen on personal as well as national grounds. That Fleetwood's brother was the Swedish agent in England sufficed to make some councillors averse to participation in the war, while others wished to avoid the risk of entangling England with Holland, which was pro-Danish.[15]

Viewed as a whole, these differences of opinion must have gone far to paralyze the government and to dishearten its supporters. It is not surprising to read the comment that some councillors, once very zealous for the Protector, were thinking of deserting him to avoid involvement in his fall.[16] Yet the hour required a firm and united stand by the constitutional authorities against military encroachments.

The movement in the army was not consistent, because no program commanded the single-hearted devotion of all its sections. It was united in its determination to be an estate of the realm,[17] and to uphold toleration, but there were wide differences of opinion as to the degree of interference in politics and of the latitude to be allowed to extreme sectaries and Quakers. There was no agreement as to the best form of government. From time to time various questions were brought to the front, now by the leaders, now by their subalterns, but most of them did not meet with unanimous approval. To use the contemporary phrase, there was a "divided interest" in the army. These considerations explain the devious course of discontent in the army, because its direction depended on which faction temporarily prevailed.

[11]Thurloe, VII, 386, 415, 496.

[12]Bordeaux, Sept. 23/Oct. 3, Guizot, I, 241.

[13]Thurloe, VII, 451.

[14]Bordeaux, Oct. 7/17, 14/24, Guizot, I, 244, 246; Calendar Venetian, p. 253.

[15]Bordeaux, Nov. 1/11, Guizot, I, 249. Anglo-Swedish relations will be dealt with at length in a later chapter.

[16]Bordeaux, Nov. 8/18, Guizot, I, 253.

[17]Lord Falkland in the debate on April 18 called the army the fourth estate, and Captain Baynes called it "a main ingredient in your government." Diary of Thomas Burton, ed. J. T. Rutt (1828), IV, 449-50.

The first stirrings in the army have already been noticed. Probably their renewal and intensification were caused by the nomination of Mountagu as a colonel of horse. "The cabal gets ground apace," Fauconberg wrote on September 28, and "will suddenly now pull off its vizard. They are demanding things which no magistrate in the world can grant without divesting himself of all but shadow. Officers have some dared already to move his Highness to give away his power of disposing all command in army to Fleetwood but this a great secret yet. . . . A false brother among them tells me all that they do even the closest debates." They will remonstrate if the next vacancy for a field officer is filled by his Highness. Unless he can draw strength to London immediately he is lost. "They are resolved to have the power of giving commissions in their own hands and will suffer no additions to the council because they cannot get the Protector's consent for such as they desire. In short the army is monstrous high."[18]

Some discontented officers prepared a petition, though none signed it, to present to the Protector, praying that Fleetwood should be appointed commander in chief of all the forces of the three nations, with power to give commissions to all but field officers, and that none should be cashiered except by court-martial.[19] At a general meeting of three hundred officers at St. James's on October 8,[20] Fleetwood told the group that he had given the petition to his Highness, who had refused to surrender his position as commander in chief or to yield his power to grant commissions, but would willingly consult him on matters concerning the army, and had assented to the rest of the petition. Then he and Disbrowe, Whalley, and Goffe deprecated any petitions at such a dangerous conjuncture and advised unity to carry on the good old cause, wherein his Highness resolved to live and die with them. Berry explained the good intentions of the petition, the meeting broke up, and all went their several ways very well satisfied.[21]

The under officers were setting too fast a pace for the leaders. The latter would be content if they were placed in control of the army and elevated to be the chief advisers of a nominal Protector. The former were still thinking of a government without an hereditary Protector or House of Lords—the good old cause, in fact. Fleetwood and his colleagues were

[18]To Henry Cromwell, Sept. 28, Thurloe, VII, 413-14.

[19]George Mabbott's newsletter, Oct. 9, *Clarke Papers*, III, 165. In this letter the petitioners are said to have asked that "none may be admitted or cashiered the army but by a court-martial." The first clause may be construed as a request that no field officer be named except by advice of the council of officers. The Dutch ambassador, Nieuport, stated, Sept. 8/18, that the under officers petitioned that Fleetwood should be general with authority to choose all officers. This appears more likely than the alternative explanation above.

[20]A Friday, the weekday on which meetings of this kind were usually held.

[21]Ibid.

simply deceiving themselves if they thought to reconcile the two very different principles of government. To assure the council of officers that Richard would live and die for the good old cause was either ambiguity or deception. Surely Fleetwood and Disbrowe cannot have forgotten that Major Packer and his fellow sufferers had refused to accept the Humble Petition and Advice because it was in contradiction to the "good old cause." Fleetwood might argue that Richard had granted what the petitioners wanted in substance though not in form, but the Republicans were not likely to be content for long with his platitudes. The army, he insisted, had a great desire that the "good old spirit may still be kept alive to carry on this work by, wherein his Highness hath declared himself very fully, which hath given very great satisfaction." He was conscious that his actions needed defense for he begged his brother-in-law Henry Cromwell not to condemn him unheard.[22]

Richard's complaisance toward the army caused misgivings in his own family circle. Fauconberg told Henry that if his Highness proceeded at this rate, the only service he could render his correspondent would be praying. "His Highness had a fine game to play a week since if he had had faithful counsel,[23] and I think there is yet some remedy. But alas! we want many of us either wit or courage. Fauconberg will be thrown out of the window if he stay, yet flees not upon that account, for if he had orders he has a regiment of honest fellows in town [that] would guard the best of them to the Tower. But I fear the master of that place is not right. I yet trust that God will in mercy look upon us, and deliver this nation from those that, I fear, under the notion of godliness are indeed serving lusts of their own."[24]

Henry Cromwell, the recipient of these gloomy reports, sympathized with rather than blamed his brother Richard. The only criticism he passed was that all officers should have been kept at their respective posts, and not allowed to settle in London in such large numbers. Now he thought the flood so strong that Richard must drift with it. "I thought those whom my father had raised from nothing would not so soon have forgot him, and endeavor to destroy his family, before he is in his grave. Why do I say, I thought, when I know ambition and affectation of empire never had any bounds? I cannot think these men will ever rest, till they are in the saddle; and we have of late years been too used to changes, that it will be but a 9 days wonder." As to calling Parliament, the trouble

[22]To Henry Cromwell, Oct. 12, Thurloe, VII, 436.

[23]"Councel" in cipher which may be either council or counsel.

[24]Oct. 12, Thurloe, VII, 437-38. The lieutenant of the Tower was John Barkstead, colonel of the Tower regiment of foot. As he lost both lieutenancy and colonelcy when the Protectorate ended he was probably "right" from Fauconberg's point of view. As Barkstead was rumored to be a harsh jailer, he may have been sacrificed mainly to gain popular approval.

would be to induce honest men to stand and to restrain the army from interfering in elections.[25]

On the same day Henry addressed a letter to Fleetwood, in which he asked some pointed questions. How came two or three hundred officers together? If they came without leave, how could they petition for a due observance of military discipline?[26] If they were summoned, were they not also told what to say and do—and was the summons issued with his Highness' foreknowledge? He then begged Fleetwood to remember how he had been honored by the late Protector, entrusted with the sword to preserve the succession. "Let the army be so governed that the world may never hear of them, unless there be occasion to fight. . . . God and man may require this duty at your hand, and lay all miscarriages in the army, in point of discipline, at your door."[27]

Whether Henry Cromwell was right in believing that the discontent in the army could not be resisted, or Fauconberg that it could be crushed by arresting the ringleaders, is uncertain. Oliver had found making a few examples sufficient on a number of occasions, but a more drastic purge involving scores of officers would probably have been essential now to remove all the would-be politicians from their commands. Even if Richard had determined to cast all on a single throw his gamble might have failed. The army might have acted as it had done in 1647 and instead of submitting to a purge, itself removed officers who supported Richard's attempted coup d'état. There is the further doubt whether Richard was sufficiently well informed of the personnel of the army, to which he was himself a stranger, to have expelled the dangerous. There is no sign, however, that so daring a move was seriously considered at this time. Instead, Richard continued to tread the path of conciliation.

At a meeting of officers on October 14 the old demands were repeated with illustrations of alleged victimization, including Lambert's. A great speech by Goffe dissuaded those present from further petitioning.[28] Four days later Richard himself took a hand. Summoning the officers then in London to his presence, he delivered a set speech prepared by Thurloe. He reminded them that the common enemy's main task was to create differences between them and him and among themselves. In their recent address they had defined the good cause his father and honest men had engaged in—liberty as men, toleration as Christians, keeping the army

[25]Oct. 20, Thurloe, VII, 453-54. Apparently letters took from five days to a week to reach Dublin from London. Henry had received the letters dated Oct. 12 but perhaps no later news.

[26]I presume the petition had used these words to paraphrase the demand that no officer be dismissed except by court-martial.

[27]Oct. 20, Thurloe, VII, 454-55.

[28]R. Temple to Sir R. Leveson, Oct. 18, Hist. MSS Comm. *Fifth Report*, p. 172.

in good hands, and a godly magistracy and ministry. He and they were at one on all these points. He realized his disadvantage in not being better known to them but time would remedy this and increase mutual confidence. He knew that there was some dissatisfaction, so he would speak plainly. Having been called to his place, he was resolved in conscience to exercise the trust committed to him. He meant to observe the Humble Petition and Advice which required him to appoint all officers, the higher ones by the advice of the Council, though as he had already informed some of their leaders, he would always consult them about the appointments. He had named his brother Fleetwood lieutenant general of all the army, so that he would be commander in chief under the Protector.[29] If any officer should neglect his duty, he should not be punished arbitrarily or at the Protector's sole discretion, but according to the discipline of the army. He concluded by deploring the arrears of pay and assuring them that he and the council gave this vital matter their constant attention.[30]

Apparently the officers were satisfied, at least temporarily, and parted from the Protector with kindness.[31] Thomas Clarges concurred in this view, and added that most of the unrest in the army was due to the lower officers, though influenced by some of their superiors. He drew the significant comparison with Scotland, where care was taken "that no officers and soldiers have any meetings to interpose in public affairs."[32] Fauconberg thought affairs had an outward appearance of quiet but were in reality farther from it than ever. His Highness had lost the fairest opportunities ever in a young prince's hands to settle the nation and himself. "Disbrowe, Berry, Cooper, and inferior officers, worse than themselves if possible, have daily meetings. I wish we had so too, but that is our weakness." He would resign his regiment but for his hopes to serve Henry with it.[33]

The storm died down but left an uneasy ground swell behind it. The officers continued to hold their meetings at St. James's on Fridays and still talked of the petition. A new demand was now added—that the officers deprived of their commissions by Oliver should be restored.[34] Ap-

[29]The Council Register contains no record of the appointment, but Clarges in a letter of October 19 asserts that the Council approved it. Thurloe, VII, 452.

[30]This speech is described as being written and corrected by Thurloe (VII, 447-49). It is undated and there is no certainty that it was delivered on this occasion. But there would be no point in the reference to Fleetwood's appointment if the speech were delivered at any other time, for the news was known on October 19 (Clarke Papers, III, 165). Richard Temple, in a letter of October 23, refers to a speech by Richard which seems to correspond with the above. Hist. MSS Comm., Fifth Report, p. 172.

[31]Newsletter, Oct. 19, Clarke Papers, III, 165.

[32]To Henry Cromwell, Oct. 19, Thurloe, VII, 452.

[33]To Henry Cromwell, Oct. 19, Thurloe, VII, 450-51.

[34]R. Temple to Sir R. Leveson, Oct. 23, Hist. MSS Comm., Fifth Report, p. 172. Downing to Thurloe, Nov. 15/25, Thurloe, VII, 507.

parently the friends of Lambert were active; whether he was responsible for their moves is uncertain.[35] A good sign was that no one complained when Fauconberg and Mountagu attended one of these meetings "to seek God." Against this must be set two disturbing factors. Fleetwood was dissatisfied with his commission as lieutenant general, and with the alleged failure of the government to live up to the promises he had made on its behalf in order to quash the petition.[36] Some army leaders were said to be holding daily conferences with the heads of the Republican party.[37] These rumors were exaggerated.[38] Whatever foundation they had may have been caused by a sort of coalition between the Commonwealthsmen and at least some of the army leaders—Berry, Hewson, and possibly even Disbrowe. Fauconberg refers to some such union when he wrote that the factious party, finding they were not strong enough to stand alone, were treating with the Commonwealthsmen, the Levellers, and that rabble.[39]

Time was on the side of those agitating because the material grievance of arrears of pay was becoming more acute. Already there had been a mutiny at Dunkirk, though it was suppressed easily. The pretense, wrote Lockhart, was that pay was not forthcoming, "but I am persuaded there is something else at bottom of it, and I hope to find it out."[40] The combination of resentment at lack of pay and political agitation was an ever-present danger.

To still the troubled waters was impossible so long as the Privy Council remained divided against itself. Fauconberg complained that it "did just nothing" either to win over or crush the malcontents, "whom only our negligence makes considerable."[41] By this time the army leaders

[35]Sir Charles Firth in his life of Lambert in the *DNB* stated that he "took no part in the military intrigues of October and November" and William Harbutt Dawson (*Cromwell's Understudy* [1938], p. 295) agreed. But Fauconberg asserts on or about November 25 that Lambert and Disbrowe were "the heads" of the factious party, and again on February 15, adding that Lambert appeared "only under covert." Thurloe, VII, 528, 612. The cipher "O" is not deciphered the first time, but it is the second as Lambert. He is said to have been stirring up trouble as early as October 15/25, *Calendar Venetian*, p. 255.

[36]Bordeaux, Nov. 1/11, Guizot, I, 251-52. The Frenchman noted that Fleetwood's mediocrity would make his dissatisfaction of little account if pay was not in arrears.

[37]Bordeaux, Nov. 8/18, Guizot, I, 253.

[38]Downing at The Hague noted a Royalist report that Sir Henry Vane "was to come into the council." If Richard's Council is meant, the rumor merely illustrates the credulity of exiles. To Thurloe, Nov. 15/25, Thurloe, VII, 507. Ludlow dates the reconciliation between the army leaders and the Republicans about the beginning of April, 1659. *The Memoirs of Edmund Ludlow*, ed. C. H. Firth (Oxford, 1894), II, 63-65.

[39]To Henry Cromwell, undated, but about Nov. 25, Thurloe, VII, 528 (I assume that the phrase "Our solemnity is well over" refers to Oliver's funeral on Nov. 23). The cipher is "I. men the D. and that rabble." I have not seen the letters I and D in any other letters and have had to infer for which parties they stood. I suppose the choices are Commonwealthsmen, Fifth Monarchy men, and Levellers. I have adopted the first and last but cannot be sure I am right.

[40]To Thurloe, Oct. 29/Nov. 8, Thurloe, VII, 466. Clarges to Henry Cromwell, Nov. 2, ibid., 492. Here the mutiny is described as very desperate and caused by want of pay.

[41]To Henry Cromwell, Oct. 26, Thurloe, VII, 462.

seem to have assumed the offensive and tried to remodel the Council. At a meeting of some of the principal officers and of the councillors, "to declare (as was said) the grounds of the dissatisfaction," the chief complaint was that his Highness relied exclusively on the advice of Jones and Thurloe. The latter, who knew that it was "industriously spread amongst the officers" that he was an evil councillor, offered to resign. He explained to Henry Cromwell that someone might do better who had not been "engaged in many particulars, as I have in your father's lifetime, which must be the true reason of these stirrings; for they were all set on foot before his now Highness had done or refused any one single thing, or had received any advice from any one person whatsoever."[42] The offer to resign was not accepted, but the effort to force a change in membership of the Council continued.[43]

These divisions did not escape notice abroad. The French and Venetian ambassadors' dispatches supplied their respective governments with all available particulars. From The Hague, Downing warned Thurloe that the Royalist exiles took the greatest interest in the domestic quarrels in England, hoping to profit therefrom.[44] According to his intelligence all but six of the councillors were to be removed, while the survivors would be Fleetwood, Disbrowe, Pickering, Strickland, and either Lawrence or Fiennes but not both. The sixth was not named, but Sydenham would surely have been retained. A well-informed, anonymous Royalist analyzed the factions at this time, and decided that Richard could count on Lawrence, Mountagu, Fiennes, Jones, Thurloe, and Wolseley in the Council and eight regiments.[45] The forces in Flanders and Ireland, and most of those in Scotland, together with the fleet, were all loyal.[46]

Richard made one more attempt to close up the ranks on November 19. Hearing that the officers were going to meet on that day at St. James's and fearing that the demands made a week before might be repeated, he summoned them to Whitehall and explained that he wanted them to come thither more often in order that he might enjoy seeing them. The whole palace was at their disposal. After this side glance at their private gatherings, he repeated the substance of his earlier speech, that he had taken an oath to rule according to the Humble Pe-

[42]Nov. 2, Thurloe, VII, 490-491; *Catalogue of the Collection of Autograph Letters Formed by Alfred Morrison*, VI (1892), 253.

[43]To Henry Cromwell, Nov. 16, Thurloe, VII, 510.

[44]Nov. 15/25, ibid., 507-508.

[45]Whalley's, Howard's, Fauconberg's, Hacker's, Ingoldsby's, Goffe's, late Pride's (Pride died in October, and was later succeeded by Richard Moss), and two more. The writer thus includes nine, not eight. In a newsletter of April 23, 1659, it is said the regiment late Lord Pride's marched into Whitehall, which suggests that it had not yet been given a new colonel.

[46]Intercepted letter from London, Nov. 5, 1658, Thurloe, VII, 495-96.

tition and Advice and meant to keep it. Because they had consented to his being Protector, he hoped they would assist him, "being young and not fitted for so great a work." All misunderstandings must be cast aside and they must work together in love and charity. They could be assured that he would protect the godly. Therefore let them not discourage him by their jealousies but judge him according to his actions. The majority present are said to have been much affected, but a few of the baser sort went away grumbling.[47] Except for a petition circulated for an increase of pay for the horse of three-pence a day, which was suppressed, the two troopers responsible for it being cashiered by court-martial,[48] no open manifestation of disloyalty was seen for several months.

The outcome of the agitation may seem a draw, because Richard had not parted with his supreme command of the army and had not permitted his Privy Council to be purged. He had made concessions—he had named Fleetwood commander in chief under him, agreed to consult the army leaders before issuing commissions, virtually consented not to cashier officers except by court-martial, and had tolerated the weekly meetings of officers. On the whole, he had lost ground—in fact, not to have won was really equivalent to a defeat, since time was on the side of his opponents.

While these dissensions, but half appeased and temporarily quieted, were threatening to wreck the life work of the late Protector, the day fixed for his funeral drew near. The government had decided that he should be buried among kings with regal solemnity. It determined, therefore, to take the ceremonies which had accompanied the interment of James I as a model.

On the night of September 20, 1658, Oliver's body, already embalmed and cased in lead,[49] was privately conveyed from Whitehall to Somerset House by the officials and servants of his household, headed by the Lord Chamberlain and Comptroller and escorted by the lifeguards and

[47]*Clarke Papers*, III, 168-70. The summary in *Mercurius Politicus*, Nov. 18/25, p. 24, differs from the above. According to this version he approved their meetings if restricted to praying. Jealousies are not mentioned, but Richard is said to have told the officers the more they knew him the more they would find he would encourage them in what was good. He praised the army as unparalleled for piety, obedience, and discipline. Bordeaux (Nov. 22/Dec. 2, Guizot, I, 264) represents Richard as warning the officers not to abuse the pretense of devotion in order to hold seditious meetings. "This language somewhat irritated them." A letter from Thurloe to Henry Cromwell, dated November 9, stated that Richard complained that his greatest trouble was the spreading of reports that he did not love godly men. The writer added that the officers wanted Fleetwood to be named their commander in chief so that Richard could not put another at the head of the army and that Richard had already assured the officers he had no such intention. *Catalogue of the Collection of Autograph Letters Formed by Alfred Morrison*, VI, 254.

[48]*Clarke Papers*, III, 170n.

[49]George Bate, *Elenchus Motuum Nuperorum in Anglia*, trans. Thomas Skinner (1685), p. 236. According to Bate, though his bowels were taken out, and his body filled with spices, wrapped in a fourfold cerecloth, and put first into a coffin of lead, and then into a wooden one, yet it "purged and wrought through all, so that there was a necessity of interring it before the solemnity of his funerals."

halberdiers. A month was spent in preparations before the doors were thrown open to those whom curiosity or respect moved to see the impressive spectacle. The visitors first passed through three rooms, formerly the presence, privy, and withdrawing chambers, all hung with black cloth and adorned with painted escutcheons. In the fourth, hung with black velvet, was the corpse of the Protector himself. Upon a bed of state, raised two steps above the rest of the room, lay the wax effigy of the Protector clad in a robe of purple velvet, with a cap of velvet and ermine on its head, a richly gilt sword at its side, and a scepter and orb in its hands. By the side of the bed was a rich suit of complete armor. Behind the head was a chair of state of cloth covered with gold and upon the cushion was "the imperial crown set with stones."[50] The effigy was enclosed with rails, at the four corners of which were pillars decorated with armorial bearings, banners, and trophies of military honors. Eight tapers of virgin wax in candlesticks five feet high shed their soft light upon the memorable scene.[51]

The date of the funeral had been fixed for November 9, but it was postponed until the twenty-third because the endless preparations could not be completed until then. But the actual corpse was removed on the tenth, conveyed through St. James's Park to Westminster Abbey, and buried in a vault in Henry VII's chapel.[52] Probably in consequence, the effigy was now placed upright, and a crown substituted for the cap.[53]

For the procession from Somerset House to Westminster Abbey the greatest care had been taken. All London had been scoured to find enough black cloth for all who held office, and many besides. Those holding the highest offices were assigned nine yards, the others six, or even four. The Latin secretaries, John Milton and Andrew Marvell, were first voted the nine yards, but then were reduced to six.[54] The infantry, lining the streets two deep outside the railings which had been erected, were given new red coats trimmed with black, but their captains and lower officers had to be content with a promise that they should

[50]In the Council Register the crown was ordered to be set on the head of the effigy, a scepter in one of its hands and an orb in the other. The profusion with which black cloth was used at Somerset House and Whitehall elicited the comment that because man could not mourn enough for His Highness the walls were taught to do it. Hist. MSS Comm., *Fifth Report*, p. 144a. The quotation describing the crown is from *Cromwelliana* (Westminster, 1810), p. 179. If the reproductions of engravings there can be trusted this crown resembled the crowns of the Stuarts rather than the crowns on coins issued during the Protectorate.

[51]*Mercurius Politicus*, Oct. 14-21. The relevant passages are reprinted in *Cromwelliana*, pp. 178-79; and with slight variants, in the old *Parliamentary History*, XXI, 238-41. The most minute particulars were set down in the Council Register for September 14.

[52]*Clarke Papers*, III, 168. Bordeaux, Nov. 17/27, recorded the rumor that the sole reason why the interment took place at 1 a.m. was fear lest the soldiery seize the corpse as security for arrears of pay. Guizot, I, 260.

[53]Illustrations of the effigy, recumbent and standing, are reproduced in *Cromwelliana*.

[54]*Calendar Domestic, 1658-1659*, p. 131.

be given an equivalent to the mourning they did not receive.[55] Those who were going to walk in the procession were warned to be at Somerset House by 8 a.m. The procession itself was late in starting, partly because of disputes about precedence among the representatives of foreign powers. The Swedish envoys wished to be treated as ambassadors, and the French ambassador declined to walk between the representatives of Portugal and Holland.[56] Another reason for the delay was the great number of mourners who took several hours to pass along the streets. Most of them preceded the hearse. Fleetwood followed it as Richard's representative, with Fauconberg walking at his side. Claypole, the third son-in-law, led the horse of honor. Evening was closing in before the Abbey was reached, where those with tickets were admitted. No candles had been provided to light[57] the mourners to the mortuary chapel where the effigy[58] was to be placed. There were no prayers, sermon, or funeral oration. Trumpets sounded for a brief time and then the pageant was over. The mourners returned to their homes in whatever order they could. The confusion was typical of the government.

The impression made by these long-drawn-out obsequies varied greatly. The French ambassador thought that its magnificence consisted in the number of mourners who followed the hearse, and the Venetian noted the huge crowds that watched the procession.[59] The poet Cowley, surprised at the curious multitude and the costly spectacle, commented: "Much noise, much tumult, much expense, much magnificence, much vain-glory; briefly, a great show, and yet after all this, but an ill sight."[60] Others were scandalized at the regal honors paid to the head of a republic. According to Ludlow, himself an unbending Republican, the folly and profusion so provoked the people that they threw dirt on the escutcheon placed over the great gate of Somerset House.[61] A Royalist

[55]*Clarke Papers*, III, 168.

[56]*The Protectorate of Oliver Cromwell* [letters from John Pell], ed. Robert Vaughan (1839), II, 341-42; Bordeaux, Nov. 29/Dec. 9, Guizot, I, 269; *Calendar Venetian*, p. 269.

[57]Probably the darkness made possible the snatching of the "majesty scutcheon" from the bier by a Westminster schoolboy. Margaret M. Verney, *Memoirs of the Verney Family* (1894), III, 424-25.

[58]I believe the description of the effigy in Harleian MS. 1438, fo. 79, refers to the effigy which was presumably left in Westminster Abbey until the Restoration. It begins "His effigies, curiously made to the life according to the best skill of the artist in that employed, viz., Mr. Symons, is thus habited: there being a body of wood carved by Mr. Phillips (being carver to the house and surveyor) a fine shirt of holland lace, a doublet and breeches of the Spanish fashion which was great skirts and close at the knees, being made of uncut velvet of a gray color, with silk stockings and shoestrings and garters, suitably laced with gold lace. . . ."

[59]Nov. 29/Dec. 9, Guizot, I, 268; Nov. 26/Dec. 6, *Calendar Venetian*, p. 266.

[60]"A Discourse by Way of Vision, concerning the Government of Oliver Cromwell" in *Abraham Cowley, Essays, Plays and Sundry Verses*, ed. Alfred Rayney Waller (Cambridge, 1906), p. 342. This comment was probably written after the Restoration.

[61]*Memoirs*, II, 48. Ludlow (p. 47) seems to be alone in stating that on November 1 Oliver's body was removed into the great hall and represented in effigy.

report that some Anabaptists tore off the nose and ear, and cut the hair of the effigy must be viewed askance, because attendants were present.[62] There is better authority for the distribution of printed papers in the streets of London, "inveighing no less against the vanity and expense of the funeral than against the validity of all the acts done in England" since the Long Parliament was turned out.[63]

The spirit of George Fox was grieved to hear "a great pudder [pother] made about the image or effigies of Oliver Cromwell lying in state; men standing and sounding with trumpets over his image after he was dead." So he wrote to those responsible a remonstrance: "Oh friends, what are ye doing? And what mean ye to sound before an image? Oh, how am I grieved with your abominations! . . . The sober people in the nations stand amazed at your doings, and are ashamed, as if ye would bring in Popery."[64] Another Quaker, Edward Burrough, found at Charing Cross a very great multitude of people and whole streets filled from one side to the other, with abundance gazing forth at every window and upon the balconies and housetops. When he learned that all had come together to see a lifeless image he was moved to reflect: "Oh abominable! Oh idolatry! O folly and vanity!" He wondered what Oliver would have said and felt his verdict would have been: "This will be a shame to my children, and a disgrace to my kindred, and a reproach to my officers and whole army, and all the nation will mock and be offended, and they may say: 'These are they that were once enemies to all images and dead idols, and pulled them down, and broke them down; and are these now making an image, and setting it up, and wandering after it from place to place?' "[65] Perhaps on this occasion the two Quakers spoke for more than their own followers.

Imagination would linger over the feelings of the two Latin secretaries on this November 23.[66] Marvell wrote "A Poem upon the Death of his late Highness." In it he described how he saw his leader dead, but it was the corpse he looked upon—"All withered, all discoloured, pale and wan"—not the bedecked effigy. Milton left no record of his feelings about the passing of the man he had hailed four years before as "Your country's deliverer, the founder of our liberty, and at the same time its

---

[62]Dr. Moore to Hyde, Nov. 26, *Clarendon Calendar*, IV, 113.

[63]Guizot, I, 270. Dr. Moore enclosed a copy of the paper to Hyde but it has not survived. *Clarendon Calendar*, IV, 117.

[64]*The Journal of George Fox*, ed. John L. Nickalls (Cambridge, 1952), p. 356.

[65]"A Testimony against a Great Idolatry," in Edward Burrough, *The Memorable Works* (1672), pp. 457-61.

[66]Curiously enough, biographers of Milton seem to have overlooked the assignment to him and his fellow French and Latin secretaries of a place in the funeral procession. Burton, II, 524.

protector," whose exploits had surpassed those of fabled heroes.[67] A conjecture is that both would have preferred a simple dignity to mark the passing of the head of the Commonwealth. They would have deemed ostentation a surrender to worldliness, a vanity of vanities, dishonoring to the great Puritan and to his cause.

Leaving the realm of speculation we find that the Secretary of State told Henry Cromwell that a great endeavor had been made to induce the soldiers to cause a disturbance, but all had ended orderly and quietly.[68] The soldiers do not appear to have been unduly impressed by the solemnity of the occasion. Evelyn, who was present, entered in his diary: "It was the joyfullest funeral I ever saw; for there were none cried but dogs, which the soldiers hooted away with a barbarous noise, drinking and taking tobacco in the streets as they went."[69] Reading Evelyn's account provokes the comment that if the army did not mourn the general who had led them from victory to victory, the funeral was a futile gesture. If in any way intended as a demonstration in favor of the Protectorate, it seemed to have failed. Maybe those responsible for the lying in state and procession were troubled by no misgivings, but felt that no magnificence was too great for the leader of Puritanism. But if Oliver did not live in the hearts of Englishmen, all the trappings of death were in vain. The one reward he would have valued was the continuation of his work, and this was to be denied.

[67]*Defensio Secunda,* in *Works,* VIII, 225.

[68]Nov. 23, Thurloe, VII, 528.

[69]Under October 22, a slip which shows that Evelyn wrote up his diary from time to time, and did not always make daily entries. The soldiers may have known they were only seeing the Protector's effigy and behaved less reverently accordingly.

CHAPTER IV

Parliament and the Constitution

EVEN BEFORE Oliver's funeral there had been speculation that the want of money would compel the summoning of a parliament.[1] The formal decision to hold a general election for a parliament to meet on January 27 was taken on December 3,[2] but the Council had so resolved a few days earlier, when after "much to do" it was voted that Scotland and Ireland should be represented in the same manner as formerly. Thurloe, ever cautious, told Henry Cromwell that the reasons were that parliaments had always been summoned at the beginning of every prince's reign, that the need of grants was urgent, that Richard enjoyed the good opinion of people in general, and that there were other considerations suitable only to be communicated by word of mouth. There would be, Thurloe prophesied, keen contests for seats. The Commonwealthsmen had their daily meetings to decide what kind of a government they would establish, taking it for granted they could pick and choose, and they hoped to prepare a part of the army to fall in with them, wherein the writer trusted they would be deceived. "I must needs say, I like not the aspect of things, and my fears are greater than my hopes."[3] Perhaps what Thurloe felt but was unwilling to trust to the post was that to call a parliament in order to counterbalance the army's overweening pretensions was a last resort. His experience of parliamentary intransigeance may also have made him fearful of a fresh appeal to the electorate. Thurloe outlined the program the civilian Commonwealthsmen had adopted—that all voting in Parliament should be by "a ballatinge box," judging that there would be many "a Nicodemite" there who would vote with them if he dared. Then they meant to dispute parts of the Humble Petition and Advice, in order to subject the House of Lords and the Council to approval by the House of Commons. Lastly they intended to raise the question of the succession, hoping thereby to establish a commonwealth. He also spoke of a remonstrance which officers had proposed in order to justify their recent actions but which they had been persuaded to lay aside.[4] But any advantage the government may have gained by this was offset by an open quarrel at

[1]Bordeaux, Nov. 17/27, Nov. 22/Dec. 2, Guizot, I, 260, 262, 264.

[2]Council Register.

[3]Nov. 30, Thurloe, VII, 541; Thomas Clarges to Henry Cromwell, ibid.; Fleetwood to the same, undated, ibid., p. 550.

[4]Undated, Thurloe, VII, 550. Among the leading Republicans Thurloe mentioned Scot, Weaver, Neville, and Ludlow.

the Council board when Disbrowe charged Mountagu with conspiring with Fauconberg to kidnap him and Fleetwood. As the accusation was based on a letter which Disbrowe refused to produce, the Protector naturally sided with the accused.[5]

Meanwhile the eyes of all were fixed upon the approaching elections. The Petition and Advice contained the provision that "in all other particulars" (i.e., not concerned with the disqualification of Royalists and Roman Catholics) "which concern the calling and holding of Parliaments, Your Highness will be pleased, that the Laws and Statutes of the Land be observed." The Council interpreted this to mean that, so far as England was concerned,[6] the ancient laws should be followed, not the electoral reform embodied in the Instrument of Government, according to which the two Parliaments of Oliver had been elected. The difference was great. By the Instrument seats had been redistributed and the county franchise fixed at real or personal estate to the value of £200. The smaller boroughs had been disfranchised and additional seats allotted to the counties. Thus by the new constitution Bedford had one seat and Bedfordshire five, whereas by the old system, now readopted, Bedford returned two members and the county two. Cornwall, so long a glaring anomaly in parliamentary history, recovered its forty-four members, instead of fourteen, but Yorkshire had only twenty-two instead of thirty-two, and so forth. Ludlow, ever inclined to suspect the worst, attributed the decision to return to the old electoral divisions to the courtiers'[7] hope that "mean and decayed boroughs" could more easily be corrupted than populous counties and towns.[8] It is true that the counties in 1656 had returned many opponents of the court, and that in 1659 they sent to Westminster several pronounced anti-Cromwellians, including Republicans like Okey and Bradshaw, and Royalists (or men about to become so) like Booth, Falkland, Howe, and Townshend. However, the Protectorians had no monopoly of small boroughs because Ludlow, Scot, Vane, and Weaver all sat for such constituencies. Ludlow also charged that the government officials could bring great pressure to bear on the Cinque Ports and, indeed, on all seaports, because obstreperous individuals could be pressed for service in the fleet. Sheriffs, generally picked for their pliability, could help to secure the return of courtiers by disposing of the

---

[5]Bordeaux, Dec. 6/16, Guizot, I, 271; *Clarendon Calendar,* IV, 118, 122. According to Hyde's correspondent, Ingoldsby was also named by Disbrowe.

[6]Scotland and Ireland, however, were represented by members chosen for the same places as under Oliver. The Instrument of Government had merely provided that the distribution of members in each country should "be agreed upon and declared by the Lord Protector and the major part of the Council." *Acts and Ordinances,* II, 816.

[7]"Courtiers" included supporters of the Protectorate as well as office-holders at court.

[8]*Memoirs,* II, 48. Bordeaux agreed with Ludlow; Guizot, I, 274.

writs to whom they pleased, and by their decisions on the qualifications of voters. Officials seem to have been negligent of their opportunities at the ports, but a few sheriffs were thought guilty of sharp practices.

Charges were made both in the House and in print that Thurloe and others had unduly influenced the elections. The Secretary, noticing the insinuation that eighty members had been returned as a result of his recommendations, denied that he knew of more than three thus chosen. Henry Howard, later sixth Duke of Norfolk, was accused of boasting that he had nominated twenty-four members, but the Committee for Elections never presented its report on his case. He was concerned in the contests at Castle Rising and other places, but not to the extent of his alleged boast.

Little is known about the actual campaigning. There was almost no propaganda by pamphlets and public meetings—or little trace of either method has survived. Hythe is possibly unique inasmuch as we know what the electors were concerned about—Henry Oxinden's alleged participation in the rising in Kent in 1648 and his attitude toward tithes. His record placed him at the bottom of the poll. Local prominence or connections were advantageous in all kinds of constituencies. Nicholas Lechmere and a Foley[9] were returned for Worcestershire, though their expenses for entertainment at Worcester alone cost £614. In Newcastle-on-Tyne Mark Shaptoe, the recorder, and Thomas Lilburne, a cousin of the better-known Robert and John, were chosen. Sir Wilfred Lawson sat for Cumberland, and a son and son-in-law for Cockermouth. In not a few constituencies the candidates bore names familiar in local annals for many years. However, the medieval rule in boroughs that members should be "resident and free" had ceased to have much validity. According to one member, if the rule was held to be still in force the elections of three hundred might be questioned. Whether the franchise in certain boroughs was restricted to freemen was disputed, but no general principle was established.

Although little is known about electioneering there is ample evidence that seats were eagerly sought for. Perhaps the best proof is the number of pluralists elected, eighteen—there is no way of determining how many members chosen for one constituency had wooed another unsuccessfully. Thurloe and Maynard were elected in three places. Vane lost at Hull and Bristol but won at Whitchurch. Scot was defeated at Aylesbury but prevailed at Wycombe. How many candidates contested a two-membered constituency is unknown, but there were often four, or, as at Hull, five.

[9]Although I have failed to establish the identity I believe this to be the Thomas Foley who owned the important ironworks near Stourbridge. See *DNB*, s.v. "Foley, Thomas."

If contemporaries were puzzled at the outcome of the election, a modern student cannot be very certain. One difficulty is that more than half the members were newcomers to Westminster, and many of these were young men. A second is that in Parliament, as in the nation, between the Cromwellians and Commonwealthsmen there were many moderates, to use the contemporary phrase. A third is the dilemma which confronted a crypto-Royalist. He wished neither to strengthen the Protectorate nor exchange it for a republic. Of the alternatives he preferred Richard to the Rump. Hyde in exile complained that "our friends in the house do not make a clear judgement of the parties and so oft mistake their votes," but he never gave definite instructions as to which side they should support. The result was that sometimes they voted with the courtiers, at others against—on one occasion Townshend and Hesilrige were tellers together. There was much cross-voting, but on one issue—the army—little or none. The majorities in favor of recognizing the House of Lords or the other house were very narrow because so many swordsmen had been nominated to sit in it. This anti-militarism was revealed both in debates and resolutions. Thurloe completely failed to defeat a motion to impeach the unpopular Major General Butler. Reminders of how dangerous it might be to provoke the army fell on deaf ears when the release of victims of arbitrary imprisonment was in question. The majority of members hated the thought of military rule. A protectorate limited by the Humble Petition and Advice was preferred to a republic, a republic to the sword.[10]

On January 26, 1659, the day before Parliament met, Richard issued a commission to John Thurloe and forty members and officials to administer to members of Parliament the oath provided in the Humble Additional and Explanatory Advice. Members were called upon to swear to maintain the true, Protestant, Christian religion, to be true and faithful to the Lord Protector, and to endeavor to preserve the rights and liberties of the people. Next morning eight commissioners, attended by the deputy clerk of the Commonwealth in chancery, who brought with him a book containing the names of the members elected, sat at a large table at the door of the House and tendered the oath to members as they arrived. Later, the congestion becoming acute, several groups of commissioners were formed to expedite the swearing in.[11] Then the members were free to enter the House.

Meanwhile the Protector was coming to open Parliament as ceremoniously as his father had on former occasions. Attended by his Privy

[10]For a more elaborate account of the election with full references, see the *English Historical Review*, LXIII (Oct., 1948), 488-501.

[11]*Commons Journals*, VII, 593-94.

Council, the officers of state, of his household, and of the army, he embarked in a new galley and landed at the Parliament stairs. Thence he passed to the House of Lords. After an interval for rest he passed in solemn procession[12] to Westminster Abbey, where in company with the Lords and Commons, he heard Thomas Goodwin preach on the text, "Mercy and truth are met together; righteousness shall look down from heaven."[13] Thomas Burton, the parliamentary diarist, supplies an adequate summary, "inciting to unity, and to mix mercy and truth, righteousness and peace together: to give liberty for erroneous consciences; but not so much encouragement as to true professors, &c."[14] The Protector then went to the House of Lords, where the peers took their places. The correct procedure would have been for the Commons to assemble in their own chamber and there await a summons to the other house. But whether from ignorance or contempt for convention, members of the Commons had already scattered themselves about the House of Lords and some declined to leave.[15] When Black Rod summoned those members sitting in the Lower House to hear the Protector's speech, only a handful responded and some one hundred fifty remained where they were, presumably because they refused to recognize the House of Lords.[16]

Richard began by reminding his audience that few of them, some months ago, would have expected a parliament to meet in peace. After a decent tribute to his father who had left the three nations in great honor abroad and full peace at home, he declared that the trust laid upon him and his own principles alike induced him to govern by the advice of the two Houses of Parliament. He then complimented "the best army in the world" for its patient endurance of great arrears of pay which reduced many soldiers to dire necessities but which Parliament would now relieve speedily and effectively. The war with Spain, carried on by the advice of Parliament, should be vigorously prosecuted. The dispute about the Sound involved several countries and among them were "The Emperor of Germany" and other Popish states. England should, therefore, be on her guard lest her interests be prejudiced. Leaving a fuller explanation of foreign relations to the Lord Keeper, Fiennes, he concluded by recommending to his hearers the care of the people of God, the work of reformation in manners and the administration of justice, the Protestant cause abroad, and love and unity among themselves.[17]

[12]Described in *Mercurius Politicus*, pp. 197-98.   [13]Psalm XXXV, 10.

[14]Burton, III, 1-2.   [15]Burton mentions "Colonel Matthews, etc."

[16]Slingsby Bethel, *A True and Impartial Narrative of the most material Debates and Passages in the late Parliament* (1659), reprinted in *The Interest of the Princes and States of Europe* (1694), and in *Somers Tracts*, VI, where the present reference is to p. 479; Burton, III, 2.

[17]Reprinted in the old *Parliamentary History*, XXI, 265-69.

The Lord Keeper started with the wise man's question, "What can the man do that cometh after the King?" The answer was, "Even that which hath been already done." Though he spoke three times as long as the Protector, verbosity rather than fresh material mainly accounts for the increased length. He did introduce into his eulogy of Oliver mention of his care for universities and schools. He referred to the Humble Petition and Advice, which, though looked upon by some with prejudice, exactly defined spiritual and civil liberties. He also exhorted to unity and declared that if a spirit of division ran through the principal parts of the government they would end by falling upon each other. The situation in the Baltic might require them to stake their wooden walls there this spring, and both defensive and offensive measures should be taken promptly. A brief reference to finance merely asserted that, had the revenue voted by the last Parliament been up to estimate, the debt inherited from the Commonwealth would not have been much increased, if at all.[18]

Assembling in their own chamber the Commons then elected Chaloner Chute, the elder, and a lawyer, as their Speaker, John Smythe as clerk of the parliaments, Ralph Darnall as clerk assistant, and Edward Birkhead as sergeant-at-arms. The following day, Friday, February 4, was set apart as a day of humiliation and seeking the divine blessing upon the endeavors of the House. Four ministers were chosen to assist but the order in which they should be named provoked a discussion. Eventually this order was decided upon: Reynolds, Manton, Owen, and Calamy. As General Lambert was in favor of giving Owen the precedence over Calamy, and a leading civilian Republican, Sir Arthur Hesilrige, proposed the opposite, it may not be fanciful to suggest that Owen was still in close touch with the army leaders and so was obnoxious to the survivors of the expulsion of the Rump in April, 1653. The incident is noteworthy only as revealing one of the cross currents in the House.

The place for the religious exercises was also debated, some arguing for the House itself and others for St. Margaret's. Hesilrige was for the first although there would be "less room here, and crowding, and want of air." He felt that formerly at St. Margaret's when the public was admitted, the ministers either refrained from rebuking the faults of Parliament, or, if they did speak out, their criticisms had been used to reproach members. This argument carried the day. A proposal to thank Goodwin for his sermon found no seconder for two reasons: he had addressed the Lords and it was for them to thank him, and no proper accommodation had been assigned to members.[19]

[18]Ibid., pp. 269-81.
[19]Burton, III, 11-13, including the note from the unprinted diary of Guibon Goddard. On the other hand, the four ministers were thanked for their services on the fast day and desired to print their sermons. *Commons Journals*, VII, 599.

The official newspaper praised Richard's speech as "excellent" and his deportment as "gracious and princely."[20] Others less biased also spoke well of the address. It deserved at least some of this praise; compared with his father's speeches, it was briefer, better arranged, and more lucid, but it lacked the fire, the intensity, and the conviction that marked Oliver's utterances.[21] So far as can be discovered it had no effect at all. No vote of thanks for it was ever passed, perhaps because of resentment at the failure to provide adequate room for members when it was being delivered.[22]

The early discussions in the House foreshadowed those to come. Most of the topics that were to be debated at tiresome length were glanced at, no matter what the business before the House. Thus the reference to the Commons of a law case in which Henry Neville sued William Strode, sheriff of Berkshire, for failure to return him as a member for that county in 1656, provided the occasion for Hesilrige to declare to the Speaker, "I look upon you as the greatest man in England; the Speaker of the Parliament of England or Commons"—a remark which must have recalled the position from Charles I's execution to the eviction of the Long Parliament when the Speaker was first in dignity.[23] A debate on a Major Lewis Audley who was said to have called one of the successful candidates for Gatton "a base rascal" in order to provoke a duel, evoked recriminations, officers defending him and civilians condemning him. Veiled insinuations against the army eventually provoked Colonel Okey to exclaim: "I see it will be a crime to be an army man. Is the expense of our blood nothing?"[24] When a member called attention to Ludlow who sat although he had not taken the oath, much irrelevancy was introduced. Some members argued that they were assembled because the Petition and Advice gave the Protector power to summon parliaments, but Scot asserted that they owed their position to the people's choice. Another asserted that but for the Petition and Advice they would not be sitting there at all. Yet, he added, they had been elected not in accordance with that act but with the old laws. Weaver, a Republican like Scot, contrived to slip in a reference to the exclusion in 1656 of a hundred and twenty members—"a dishonourable act." He and others of like mind asserted their right to bring into question all the provisions of the Petition and Advice.[25]

[20]*Mercurius Politicus*, p. 199. For other comments see the notes in Burton, III, 7, 11.
[21]One member commented upon the "sweetness" of Richard's voice and language. Burton, III, 124.
[22]Burton, III, 35-36.
[23]Burton, III, 18. See *Commons Journals*, VII, Feb. 3, 1659, for a record of the case, furnished by the Lord Chief Justice.
[24]Burton, III, 43. Audley was sent to the Tower but released after a few days' confinement. A motion to strike him off the panel of justices of the peace was defeated in the first division taken. *Commons Journal*, VII, 597.
[25]Burton, III, 72-73, 76.

But the real bone of contention was the bill entitled an Act of Recognition of his Highness' right and title to be Protector and Chief Magistrate of the Commonwealth. In introducing it Thurloe urged that it followed precedent and was necessary to warn all who were trying to create divisions in the state that members were of one mind in Parliament in their determination to uphold the constitution. After some protests from the Republican leaders which boded ill for unity, the bill was read a first time but when the attorney general moved that the second reading be the next day, the opposition was too strong, and further debate was postponed until February 7—some six days later. This initial failure to carry the bill through all stages promptly was of the greatest importance, because delay was ruinous to the Protectorate. The unpaid army could not be restrained indefinitely.

The bill declared that immediately after Oliver's death, Richard became his lawful successor, to the joy of the people, as witnessed by their general consent and by addresses from the armies, navies, counties, cities, and boroughs. This bill would remain a testimony to posterity of the affection of the two Houses of Parliament and of their recognition of his Highness' just right to succeed to the government. In the name of the people all allegiance was renounced to Charles Stuart and other issue of the late king, Charles I. Attempts to restore or aid any members of the Stuart family were to be adjudged high treason.[26]

One point of cardinal importance should be kept in mind while studying the debates on the bill of Recognition—that the Republicans deliberately prolonged them[27] in the hope that failure to secure parliamentary approval of the Protectorate would open the door to drastic changes in the constitution. Though they were in a minority even when reinforced by crypto-Royalists, they had the best, as well as the most verbose speakers and not a few old parliamentary hands. Their tactics were admirably suited to an assembly containing so many new and young[28] members whose inexperience exposed them to the beguiling oratory of their seniors. Moreover, time was on the side of the opposition. The Parliament had been summoned because the need of money was so crucial, and the more weeks that were wasted in speechifying, the greater the unrest among all whose pay was in arrears. If the armed forces grew too impatient and upset the Cromwellian applecart, the Commonwealthsmen might come into their own.

[26]The only text of the bill seems to be in Thurloe, VII, 603.

[27]Ludlow claimed that time was gained to infuse sound principles into young members (*Memoirs*, II, 55), and Slingsby Bethel that slavery was averted by the delays (*Somers Tracts*, VI, 486).

[28]Chaloner questioned whether some were old enough to take an oath. Burton, III, 76. Hesilrige was taken to task for his frequent comments on the many young men in the House, ibid., p. 49.

Sir Arthur Hesilrige started this filibustering campaign when the bill of Recognition was read a second time. He spoke for two or three hours. Beginning with a general sketch of English history from the Heptarchy to the end of the Middle Ages, he became more detailed as he proceeded. His purpose seems to have been to demonstrate how the country was rescued from tyranny by the Long Parliament, and how, after the execution of the King and the abolition of the House of Lords, trade flourished, the City of London grew rich, the navy was never so powerful and the army never stronger. But in 1653 Cromwell turned out the Long Parliament and acted as if all power had devolved upon himself. Hesilrige then dwelt upon the Instrument of Government and Cromwell's becoming Protector, the two Parliaments from which members including himself were kept out by pikes, and upon the Petition and Advice. "And these must be the fruits, all we must enjoy, after the spilling of so much blood and so much treasure!"

This had been the work of a lame, imperfect Parliament. We have now the "freest, the clearest, and most undoubted representatives that ever were since the dissolution of the three estates. . . . We can do here whatsoever is for the good of the people. We have power over their purses and persons; can take away whole laws, or part of them, or make new ones. I will tell you what we cannot do. We cannot set up any power equal to the people, either in one person, or another House. . . . Let not us set up what God has pulled down."[29] Recently the nation has not prospered, trade and glory have diminished, the Council has been bewildered, acts of Parliament have been made without Parliament,[30] habeas corpus has been denied, attorneys have been sent to the Tower for asserting Magna Charta,[31] things of which no king was ever guilty. Lovable as the Protector was, his recognition should not precede agreement upon the foundations—the civil liberties of the people—and the powers he should be trusted with.[32]

Hesilrige's speech has been summarized to illustrate the wide range of the debate on the simple question of whether Richard should be recognized as "chief magistrate," a phrase repeatedly used in preference to

[29]Later Hesilrige admitted that the people cared not what government they lived under, so long as they could plough and go to market. Burton, III, 101, 257. A pamphlet, *Some of the Arguments*, explained that the Civil War had started over the militia, but later "a higher Providence" had introduced the abolition of the hierarchy, House of Lords, and King.

[30]I.e., the ordinances the Protector had been empowered to issue by the Instrument of Government before Parliament met.

[31]George Cony, a London merchant, refused to pay customs duty on the ground that there was no legal authority authorizing its collection, being levied under ordinances only. His counsel were sent to the Tower. Wilbur C. Abbott, *Writings and Speeches of Oliver Cromwell* (Cambridge, Mass., 1945), III, 498-99, 719; S. R. Gardiner, *History of the Commonwealth and Protectorate* (1903), III, 299-301.

[32]Burton, III, 87-105. Sankey reported to Henry Cromwell that Hesilrige described Richard as "without guile or gall." Lansdowne MSS, Feb. 8, 1659.

Protector. It is not surprising that the Speaker, after listening for several days to similar effusions, should have declared, "We are indeed in a wood, a wilderness, a labyrinth," or that a member should complain, "The chair ought to direct us to keep to the point."[33] Leadership was lacking because spokesmen for the government were silent. Whether they were conscious of their inability to cross swords with the opposition speakers or whether they abstained in the hope of expediting proceedings by their self-denial is uncertain. At any rate, the main debate was between the Commonwealthsmen and the Presbyterians, with army officers and backbench Cromwellians intervening. Most speakers professed their willingness to declare Richard the chief magistrate. First, however, the Republicans wished to lay down a foundation on which civil and religious liberty would be based. In particular, they wished to deprive the Protector of "a negative voice" or power of veto, and of control of "the militia," or navy and standing army. Though the "other house" was not the subject of debate, some were unwilling to recognize it because it was mainly composed of officers and not representative of property. Two members at least, Neville and Baynes, showed that they were disciples of Harrington's *Oceana*. The former, for example, called for a single person, senate, and popular assembly.[34] Whereas until Henry VIII "all depended on the Lords," now "the balance is in the gentry. They have all the land." They must not return to the government of the Long Parliament, because that had been an oligarchy, and they must not accept the Petition and Advice, because that conferred kingly authority. Therefore, let Richard be declared "the chief magistrate, under such rules and limitations as you shall agree upon."[35]

Two army officers—Packer[36] and Lambert—made lengthy speeches, the former apologizing for being one of those guilty of "irruptions of the privileges of this House in 1653" because he had then felt that the great work of the reformation and establishment of freedom of conscience would not be accomplished by Parliament. He said all was well until the Petition and Advice was introduced and passed. If Richard had become Protector by his father's death, his title had become hereditary. As for the addresses acknowledging Richard, he (the speaker) laid little stress on them, because if Charles II had landed at Dover he would have got as many. People were like a flock of sheep. What was needed was a bill

[33]Burton, III, 269, 270.

[34]"Nothing of this kind has been gratefully received." Thomas Clarges to Henry Cromwell, Feb. 8, Thurloe, VII, 609.

[35]Burton, III, 132-35.

[36]Packer was soon afterward deprived of his seat and his opponent at Hertford declared elected. *Commons Journal*, VII, 619.

of recognition for the army, forty weeks' pay behind, he was informed. Then followed a familiar description of his opposition to the other House, how Oliver had "told me I was not apt, I that had served him fourteen years, ever since he was captain of horse, till he came to this power, and had commanded a regiment seven years: without any trial or appeal, with the breath of his nostrils I was outed. . . . Five captains under my command, all of integrity, courage, and valour, were outed with me, because they could not comply; they could not say that was a House of Lords." In settling the militia, care should be taken that a single person should not have power to blow all the officers away by one breath. Moreover, the grant of an annual income made it possible for a Protector by ending the war with Spain or retrenching the cost of the army to live without parliamentary grants.[37]

Lambert began by giving his version of the cause and course of the Civil War. His exposition had the merit of simplicity. They had defended the people from the "exorbitances of an old monarchy." On the one side were "all debauched people," on the other, "an honest, sober, grave people that groaned under oppressions, thirsted after grace [and] got together an army, fit for God Almighty to do miracles withal." Now, too much dependence should not be placed in a chief magistrate, because the best man was but a man. As for the other house, originally it had acted as a brake on the royal power, as a balance, which was good. Now, though many of the members were estimable, they had a veto on the proceedings of the Commons, which was dangerous because they were of necessity close to the Protector. Therefore, though there should be another house, it should be reconstituted.

The most extreme speech was delivered by Thomas Scot, an ardent Republican. In words that were to be quoted against him after the Restoration in his trial for regicide, he denounced Charles I as a man that delighted in bloodshed, the instigator of the war in 1648, the contriver of more mischief than a thousand kings could remedy. Justice demanded a sacrifice. "We did not assassinate, or do it in a corner. We did it in the face of God, and of all men." He defiantly added that he wished his epitaph to read: "Here lies Thomas Scot who adjudged to death the late King." He then proceeded to brag of the achievements of the Long Parliament which, but for its interruption, might have brought the Dutch to "oneness with us" and made us "masters of the whole world."[38]

Major Beake, one of the few courtiers to speak or be reported at any

[37]Burton, III, 165-69.

[38]Burton, III, 109-12. Barwick reported to Hyde that Scot alone spoke reproachfully of the late King. Thurloe, VII, 616. For the use made at his trial after the Restoration of this rash speech, see *A Complete Collection of State Trials*, eds. T. B. Howell and T. J. Howell (1816), V, 1063-64.

length, energetically refuted Scot's extravagant claims for the Long Parliament. In his opinion during the years of its ascendancy "all errors, opinions, and blasphemies . . . levelling principles, Agreement of the People, nothing monstrous but that time produced."[39] The main criticism of the Long Parliament came, however, from Presbyterian members who had been victims of Pride's Purge in 1648. One described how he and others had been stopped from entering the House by pikes and muskets, kept in confinement without food, carried to inns, and thence to prison.[40] Colonel Birch, another secluded member, claimed that at the time of the outrage a large army was maintained at small cost, and money was abundant.[41] John Maynard, the famous lawyer, pointed out that less violence was done to the Parliament which passed the Petition and Advice than to the Parliament which, when purged, ruled England from 1648 to 1653.[42] Some speakers looked "in the dark backward and abysm of time" and saw that commonwealths had always been tyrannical, citing Sir Walter Raleigh's *History of the World* for proof. Others asserted that throughout the ages the wisest men had favored monarchs, to whose credit were all the great achievements of mankind. From here to the duty of building up again the old fabric of the constitution was an easy step, an unknown speaker making the point that the assertion that the government rested in the hands of the Commons and power in the people was unfounded and could not be proved by any records.[43]

After a week's spate of oratory the House at last went to a division. The first motion, to recognize Richard as Protector, was carried by 191 to 168, but the second, to recognize him as "undoubted" Protector, was negatived without a vote. Two later divisions showed the majority of courtiers increasing each time. Finally, it was resolved without a division that it be part of the bill to recognize and declare Richard to be Protector, but that before the bill be committed, such additional clauses be added as might set bounds to the chief magistrate's power and secure the privileges of Parliament and the liberties of the people.[44] Secretary Thurloe is said to have been alone in raising his voice against the second resolution, so it should apparently be regarded as the almost unanimous wish of the Commons.[45] Perhaps many of its supporters had no intention of rewriting the constitution and merely acquiesced in a pious resolution.

[39]Burton, III, 113-14.
[40]Bulkeley. Burton, III, 106.
[41]Ibid., 58.
[42]Ibid., 184.
[43]Ibid., 123, 128, 158, 222.
[44]*Commons Journals*, VII, 603.
[45]*Somers Tracts*, VI, 481. Robert Beake, a Cromwellian, remarked on the great heat engendered by the Republicans, who were opposed by the Presbyterians. Lansdowne MSS, Feb. 15.

Possibly as a diversion after so much history and constitutional lore, the Commons next dealt with a petition originally offered on February 9. Then such Republicans as Neville, Weaver, Baynes, and Vane had urged that the petitioners—"all have honest old faces"—should be welcomed, and they were supported by such malcontents as Lambert and Okey. But the decision was to postpone consideration of the petition until the present debate was finished. Members were well advised not to act precipitately, because this was the same petition which had seemed so dangerous in February, 1658, that Oliver had preferred to dissolve Parliament rather than allow it to be discussed there.[46] Promoted by men like Hesilrige, Scot, and Weaver, it was intended as a Republican manifesto—that it addressed the House of Commons as "the Parliament of the Commonwealth of England" would suffice to prove this.[47] Its contents were even a surer guide to its origin.

This petition began with a short recital of the tyrannous acts of Charles I, and proceeded to remind its readers of the army's declaration and the Agreement of the People as providing a foundation for right, freedom, and justice. Parliament was then requested to provide: A constant succession of free parliaments duly chosen, to which the supreme power and trust should be given by the people (the original of all just power) in order to make laws, constitutions, and officers for the government and to call to account all justices and ministers of state; a militia to be settled so that none might be able to use it against the people or parliaments; a revenue solely dependent upon common consent in parliament; guarantees that none should be imprisoned except after legal trial; security for officers and soldiers that none should be cashiered except by court-martial, so that "the military power may be preserved in the hands of such who are not merely mercenary, neuters, or disaffected"; and encouragement of all sincere professors of religion that no tender consciences may be oppressed. After these clauses came a virulent attack upon the Protectorate because under it "the territories of the great Turk may as properly be called a free commonwealth as the islands of Great Britain and Ireland."

The petition was artfully framed to attract all opponents of the Protectorate, except the Royalists. The first clause, which implied the destruction of the constitution as established by the Petition and Advice and a return to an omnipotent House of Commons, satisfied all who

---

[46]Burton, III, 152-55. Francis Aungier to Henry Cromwell (Lansdowne MSS, Feb. 15) described the petition as emanating from "those of Prayse God Barebones gang" and another letter (ibid., Colonel Thomas Gorges to Dr. Gorges, Feb. 15) as from Commonwealthsmen, Levellers, and Fifth Monarchy men.

[47]Thurloe, VII, 617; *Clarke Papers*, III, 180.

accepted the notion that Oliver had betrayed the good old cause. The reorganization of the militia gratified the civilians who resented military intervention in politics. Parliamentary control of revenue would abolish the provision in both Cromwellian constitutions of an annual income of £1,300,000. The provision for a legal trial appealed not only to victims of arbitrary imprisonment—and the Royalists may be included here—but also to the many who had fought to establish the supremacy of law. The fifth clause giving security of tenure to all officers would please those who had been summarily dismissed for political nonconformity or who feared they might be so dismissed. The last clause might include within its ample folds all who disapproved of a national church and a public confession of faith as contemplated by the Petition and Advice. Though the extreme sectaries and Quakers opposed tithes, the petition made no mention of this grievance, presumably because its insertion would have alienated many Puritan ministers with rich livings. Taken as a whole, here was a standard under which all enemies of the Protectorate could rally. As a program for an opposition it was admirable, provided that no thought need be taken for what would happen if the Protectorate fell. Its supporters were to find that, though they could unite to destroy, their unanimity soon vanished when they were forced to build.[48]

The petition was presented on February 15, 1659, by many citizens, headed by Samuel Moyer, who had been one of the representatives nominated for London in the Barebones' Parliament. Burton states that Moyer was allowed to utter "a great deal of cant language" for almost an hour. Hesilrige, Neville, Vane, Lambert, Scot, and others moved a vote of thanks to the petitioners, but a resolution was passed, by a majority of ninety, that they should be told the House had already considered some parts of their petition, would consider such others as were fit, and would expect the signatories to acquiesce. It is not surprising to learn that they "were scarce well satisfied."[49]

The majority is likely to have been actuated both by dislike of the petition and by the knowledge that the army was again restless. Fauconberg informed Henry Cromwell that the factious parties of the army, headed by Disbrowe openly and Lambert covertly, were renewing their old practice of remonstrating and, but for disagreement about the wording, another address would soon have startled Whitehall and Westminster. Probably Lambert and the under officers were prepared to adopt Moyer's

[48]For the earlier history of the petition, and for admirable comments on it, see Firth, *Last Years*, II, 30-34.

[49]Burton, III, 288-96. Mabbott commented to Henry Cromwell that the petitioners were not a little troubled that they were not thanked by the House. Lansdowne MSS, Feb. 15.

petition while the leaders were against so Republican a document. Richard's intervention and admonition to be prudent may have influenced the field officers. The upshot was that Fleetwood and Disbrowe appointed a committee to draw up "some heads," in case it might be seasonable to offer something to Parliament. Its composition did not augur well for the Protector. The French ambassador thought Richard's attempts to court the army by such gestures as attending when regiments were paid did not improve the situation.[50] Nevertheless, the assaults of both civilian and military Republicans were temporarily repulsed.

The debate on the other house was very protracted. The sittings devoted to it were many and long and almost to the end of the session opponents, defeated on the main question, raised every kind of obstacle to recognition, and conceded it only in the most grudging fashion.[51] The discussion really began on February 17 and lasted three weeks—apart from a few interruptions. In spite of almost endless repetitions and both true and false antiquarian lore, the debates are of great significance. Of course, the result proved to be unimportant, because Parliament was dissolved too soon for the recognition of the Upper House to have any practical effect. Nevertheless, the differences of opinion about the past, present, and future of the Commonwealth are worthy of analysis, inasmuch as they afford the best guide to the divisions that had developed in the Puritan party. For the only time in ten years a free parliament indulged in a free debate on a subject wide enough to reveal how fundamental the disagreements were between the groups that had developed since the beginning of the Puritan Revolution. To assert that the history of the next year could have been foreseen by an auditor in the House of Commons may be extravagant, but no great powers of divination would have been required to tell that a great conservative reaction had set in, that anti-militarism was strong and growing stronger, and that Republicanism could not present a united front.

The general principle that there should be a second chamber was ac-

[50]Mabbott's newsletter of February 17 supplied some of the names. *Clarke Papers*, III, 182-83; Lansdowne MSS. Mabbott's newsletter of Feb. 15; Guizot, I, 321, 324, 345; Fauconberg to Cromwell, Feb. 15, Thurloe, VII, 612. According to Bordeaux Richard told the officers he would resort to extreme measures rather than allow their petition to be presented. Bordeaux added that the petition would reduce Richard to the position of a Doge of Venice—and that it had almost the same objects as Moyer's. Guizot, I, 304-305, 307. A Royalist wrote that Richard said that he would part with the generalship and his life together, and another that, if the petition were drawn up, Parliament would soon have no significance. The Protector, he thought, relied more on the chief officers, and the Republicans on the under officers, than upon votes. *Clarendon State Papers*, III, 425-26; Thurloe, VII, 615.

[51]On April 14, Mr. Grove, by a vote of 144 to 100, was deputed to carry the declaration for a fast to the other House, and directed to return without staying for an answer. *Commons Journals*, VII, 639. The long sittings seem to have been responsible for the Speaker's death (Burton, IV, 56, 90-91, 150, 203, 430). His temporary successor, Sir Lislebone Long, became so ill on March 14 that Thomas Bampfield was named to take his place on March 16. He was formally chosen Speaker on news of Chute's death.

cepted on February 19 without a division. On the previous day a motion that the power of the negative voice be determined before the question whether there should be two Houses of Parliament had been defeated by 217 to 86.[52] The size of the majority indicated that members fully shared Oliver Cromwell's dislike for the arbitrariness of single-chamber government.[53] The Commons was much more evenly divided, however, on the composition of the other house. Many speakers denounced the present body on several grounds. The first was that the single person would always be upheld by his own creatures. The versatile Sir Anthony Ashley Cooper agreed with the staid William Morice that the nominees would merely be their creator's echo. Sir Arthur Hesilrige phrased the objection rather differently, saying that the present members had really chosen themselves, because they had chosen the single person (in 1653) and he them. The second objection was much more serious. Member after member rose to revile a house consisting of officials and swordsmen. No office-holder should be a member, urged one. It was not fit that paid servants should lord it over their masters, asserted another, who demanded a new self-denying ordinance. Others scorned to recognize a House of Lords composed of mean persons without property or interest. But the gravest charge was that there were twenty or more officers in the other house, besides the lieutenant of the Tower and naval commanders. Members of the Long Parliament showed by their anger that they had not forgotten or forgiven the outrage on the House in 1653, when swordsmen had evicted them and helped the Speaker out of his chair. If we recognize the other house, cried Hesilrige, we shall next vote canvas breeches and wooden shoes for the free people of England. These men, Ludlow shouted, have been guilty of all the attacks upon the liberties of the people. Additional arguments against reorganizing a chamber with so large a military element were that the sword could not be controlled by any constitutional limitations, and that it would be useless to expect agreement when any bills to reduce the size of the army were before Parliament.

While the debate was in progress an incident occurred which must have exacerbated anti-militarism. Richard Knightley, member for Northamptonshire, having obtained leave to withdraw, returned to complain that on his way home "one met me and said: If this vote pass in the negative, you shall be dissolved tomorrow." Passing through Scotland Yard he was stopped by soldiers. As soon as they learned that he was a

---

[52]*Commons Journals*, VII, 605; Burton, III, 316-45.

[53]Cromwell's speech on April 2, 1657, in Abbott, *Writings and Speeches of Oliver Cromwell*, IV, 484-97, especially 488-89.

member of Parliament, their officer, Shaftoe, expostulated with him. He perceived, he said, "they begin to look with an ill face upon us." Sir Henry Vane at once improved the occasion by remarking that if soldiers stopped a member leaving, it would be interesting to see whether they stopped all tomorrow from entering.[54] A Royalist, Mordaunt, was as prompt as Vane to see the possibilities of the situation. He reported to Hyde that he had at once sought out Knightley and had "blown him up all I can, and he is naturally choleric, so that I am sure such things may prove well, and the trying them cannot prejudice us."[55]

The resentment of soldiers at the slurs upon them was not unnatural. From 1647 onward they had prided themselves on this above all, that they were not a mere mercenary army. Yet a member made the sneering remark that if the soldiers had ventured their lives, they had been paid well, whereas he had fought and lost £10,000.[56] Moreover, the defenders of the army were few and feeble. True, one member asserted that they had the best army and the best officers in the world, and another that he had heard no great complaint against major generals in his county. No speaker for the government ventured to defend the officers responsible for Pride's Purge—Pride had been named a lord but died October 23, 1658—or for the ejection of Parliament in 1653. Thurloe deprecated reflections upon what officers now in the Upper House had done under extreme necessity. Colonel Gorges claimed that an honest cobbler was better than a hundred old lords, and Colonel West that service in the army was the best test of fidelity. Nicholas Lechmere acknowledged that the persons Oliver had nominated might lack high birth and long pedigrees, but the Romans had always preferred virtue to other qualifications for senators. But these voices were unheard in the chorus which proclaimed that to recognize the present other house would be to enslave the nation.

The torrent was too strong to be resisted directly. There is every sign that if a division had been taken on recognizing the Upper House composed only of the Cromwellian nominees the "noes" would have triumphed. The voices demanding the admission of the old lords were many and their arguments diverse. Some called for the reading of the

[54]Burton, IV, 75-76.

[55]*Clarendon State Papers*, III, 433. Another version is in a letter of March 11, 1659 (British Museum Add. MSS 15750, ff. 46-47), where the soldiers are reported to have told Knightley that unless members did what they were summoned for they would not sit much longer.

[56]Sir Thomas Wroth, Burton, IV, 17. As Sir Thomas was a "near kinsman" of Henry Wroth, who had disarmed Major General Packer and Captain Gladman on the highway, the gratuitous insult must have been the more galling. Burton, III, 436-37; IV, 2-7. A letter of March 11 stated that the talk of the town was that if the sixty members from Scotland and Ireland were removed, the Commonwealthsmen would provoke the Protector and his redcoats to dissolve Parliament. Ludlow and Lambert were said to have bitterly reproached the army leaders with imposing a perpetual slavery upon the people. Add. MSS 15750, ff. 46-47.

act to prevent the dissolution of Parliament and of the Triennial Act in order to prove that the House of Lords could not legally be abolished. Others, more numerous, tried to show how from Magna Charta to the present the barons had always fought for freedom. One member asserted there had been a House of Lords since William I, while another delved into the storied past and thought he found that, from the time of Brute, through the Roman, Saxon, and Danish eras, barons and nobles had been in all councils and assemblies.[57] Even so rigid a Republican as Hesilrige said that he preferred the old lords to swordsmen. There were nineteen regiments, divers garrisons, and the Tower of London represented in the other house, averred one member, who continued that members had learned by experience the mischief of the sword. "The little fingers of major-generals have I found heavier than the loins of the greatest tyrant kings that went before." Another member raised the number of regiments represented to twenty-two. Republicans of the Harringtonian school argued for a second chamber but chosen either by the people or by the House of Commons. The duty of the second chamber would be to bar the sudden and precipitate enactment of laws. When the argument was raised that to admit the old lords would be paving the way for the return of Charles Stuart, the answer was that the admission should be confined to the faithful lords. The government spokesmen were prepared to go as far as this, but even this concession hardly overcame the general aversion to the military complexion of the Upper House. The decisive divisions on March 8 showed majorities of only nineteen and seven in favor of recognition even when accompanied by the addition "that it is not intended to exclude such peers as have been faithful to the Parliament from their privilege of receiving a summons to the other house."[58]

The next constitutional issue was the presence of the representatives from Scotland. The debate began on March 8 and did not end until March 21. It affords a striking example of the time-consuming tactics of the opposition because the arguments, for and against, were few and capable of precise definition. In favor were the following considerations: that when the English armies had entered Scotland they had proclaimed their intention to free the land; that a union had been made; that Scotland had been given representation in the English parliament by the Instru-

---

[57]This remarkable antiquary was Colonel Terrill. Burton, III, 513-15.

[58]*Commons Journals*, VII, 611-12; Burton, IV, 11; Sankey to Henry Cromwell, Mar. 8, 1659, Lansdowne MSS. According to the tract *England's Confusion* (1659), the supporters of the upper House came from the court and the army, those in favor of the admission of the faithful lords were the "moderate honest patriots" (*Somers Tracts*, VI, 516). A correspondent of Henry Cromwell reported that under the cloak of the old peerage "some carry Chas: Stewart" (Sankey to Henry Cromwell, Mar. 8, Lansdowne MSS).

ment of Government, and that no member had protested against their presence in 1654 or 1656; that the Petition and Advice provided for Scottish members; and that the present Parliament had already claimed to speak in the name of the three nations and must, therefore, represent all three.

Opponents were mainly content to point out that if the Protector could have thirty members introduced from Scotland he could equally well have three hundred, and that, whatever the number, it meant a decisive addition to the ranks of government supporters now that questions were being settled by small majorities. As one orator put it, including the Irish members, there were now sixty that voted at the Protector's nod. Vane's subtlety discovered a grave constitutional inconsistency in the whole composition of Parliament. He pointed out that whereas the English members were elected from the old constituencies, the House of Lords and the Scottish and Irish members sat by virtue of the Petition and Advice. Another speaker raised an issue of a very different kind, whether the Scots were truly represented by members nominated by the government who had never seen Scotland except on a map.[59] Finally, on March 21, a motion that the Scottish members should sit was carried by 211 to 120.[60]

During the debate on the Scottish members an interlude most unwelcome to the government had occurred in the appearance of Colonel Robert Overton. On February 3, his sister had presented a petition on his behalf, and the House had ordered that he be brought to Westminster in a frigate, and now, on March 16, he was in attendance. Asked by the Speaker what he had to say about his imprisonment, he tactfully acknowledged that after three years' confinement, following fourteen years in the service of Parliament, he was granted the favor of a hearing. All he asked was that he might hear the charge against him in order that he might answer it. When he withdrew, the warrant, signed by Oliver, was read. It simply ordered the governor of the Isle of Jersey to detain the bodies of Overton and three others until he received further orders.[61] Immediately hatred of military rule found vent. "Such a warrant was never, since William came in," declared Hesilrige. He should have reparation as well as release, said Vane, for no free man should be imprisoned without cause shown. "The military act it all now," deplored Captain Baynes. Crypto-Royalists joined in the attack on Oliver Crom-

[59]Members were grossly inconsistent on this point, for another objected to Scottish members as foreigners. Burton, IV, 87, 128-31.

[60]*Commons Journals*, VII, 616; Burton, IV, 219.

[61]Burton, III, 45-49; IV, 151. For Overton's alleged participation in the plot named after him, see Gardiner, *Commonwealth and Protectorate*, III, ch. xxxvii.

well's arbitrary acts, thus following Hyde's instructions to them.[62] In vain Major General Whalley warned members that Overton had been confined as a soldier, not as a civilian, that the government durst not set forth the reasons for his imprisonment, because they would have revealed the sources of their intelligence. Release men like Overton, and "you will lay all your officers in the army liable to actions" for false imprisonment. Thurloe pleaded in vain that in time of danger soldiers could not observe forms. He did not venture to divide the House on the motion that Overton should be discharged without paying any fees.[63]

Several incidents occurred about this time, all of which infuriated the army officers. The first was the famous altercation between Richard and a cornet in Ingoldsby's horse who complained of his major's wickedness. The Protector is reported to have exclaimed:

"You article against your major because he is for me? You are a company of mutineers (meaning the officers who often met to seek the Lord and bewail their apostacy from the good old cause), you deserve a hundred of you to be hanged; and I will hang you and strip you as a man would strip an eele; you talk of preaching and praying men, they are the men that go about to undermine me." And clapping his hand upon Colonel Ingoldsby's shoulder, said, "Go thy way, Dick Ingoldsby, thou canst neither preach nor pray, but I will believe thee before I will believe twenty of them. And he says to the cornet, you never owned my father; you have lost your commission, and shall never ride more in this army."[64]

Ludlow comments that

from this time all men among them who made but the least pretences to religion and sobriety, began to think themselves unsafe whilst he governed, and thereupon soon formed a resolution to use their utmost endeavours to divide the military from the civil power, and to place the command of the army in Lieutenant-General Fleetwood.[65]

A private quarrel between Whalley, appointed judge advocate in Ireland, and Colonel Ashfield about the Upper House was significant because so many officers took sides that the outcome came to be regarded as a sort of trial of strength. The details are obscure, but Ashfield seems to have dared Whalley to strike him, whereupon the superior officer appealed to the Protector who, as commander in chief,

[62]*Clarendon State Papers*, III, 436, 454; *Nicholas Papers*, IV, 75; *Clarendon Calendar*, IV, 141, 157. A Royalist noted a remark of Sergeant Maynard's apropos of the Cavaliers and Republicans voting together, that C. Stuart had more friends in the House than the Protector. Ibid., 166.

[63]Burton, IV, 151-61.

[64]*A Second Narrative of the Late Parliament*, pp. 30-31. This account is in a "postscript" not included in the reprint in the *Harleian Miscellany*, VI (1810). The same version is quoted from *A Second Narrative* in *A True Catalogue*, p. 53, except that the parenthesis mentions "some of the honest officers who often met at the Mews, etc. to seek the Lord and bewail their apostacy." According to another report Richard said, "Here is Dick Ingoldsby who can neither pray nor preach, and yet I will trust him before ye all" (Ludlow, *Memoirs*, II, 63).

[65]Ibid., p. 63.

ordered Ashfield either to apologize or stand his trial at a court-martial. The colonel was very popular with the Anabaptists, and a deputation from their churches waited on Richard to urge him not to cite their hero before a court martial. When Richard refused, Ashfield was represented as a martyr to court favoritism. Monck, to whose army Ashfield's regiment was attached, urged that he and Lieutenant Colonel Gough, who was involved in the quarrel, should be sent down to Scotland. "If they were heere, these two could signifie but a little, as little as any two officers in Scotland; . . . There are no forces can be quieter then these are, and shall be satisfied with any thinge His Highnesse and Parliament shall settle."[66] Why Richard neglected to follow this excellent advice is unknown. Possibly he feared to provoke a crisis, and showed by not having Ashfield court-martialed that he preferred to trust to the policy of conciliation and leniency he had pursued from the beginning of his protectorate. Almost certainly, he missed an opportunity of ridding himself of a determined opponent and of demonstrating, by a striking example, that he meant to be obeyed.

A third source of annoyance and anxiety to officers was the questioning of the legality of all that had been done from the day of Pride's Purge to the expulsion of the Long Parliament. During the debate on the admission of the Scottish representatives, a member[67] rather casually remarked that the union had been made "by the fag end of the Long Parliament" and so had no legal basis. Another member, in a fiery argument with Hesilrige, used the same phrase and the same argument that nothing transacted then had any legal force. Hesilrige, full of self-righteousness, was not the man to bear patiently reproaches for the great deeds that had been accomplished by the attenuated House of Commons—abolition of the monarchy and House of Lords, the conquests of Scotland and Ireland, the war with Holland, and the sale of confiscated lands, royal, church, and delinquent. The parliamentary diarist noted that "this was presently noised abroad, and very ill resented by the army. I doubt it may breed ill blood; for every man that acted begins to say, 'What did I do in that fag-end of Parliament, and how shall I be indemnified but by my sword? We will not give the cause away.' Never did two words work such an alteration in one day in the face of affairs."[68] The reason why this simple

[66]Monck to Thurloe, Mar. 22, 1659, Thurloe, VII, 638; Ashfield's account is in Hist. MSS Comm., *Leyborne-Popham MSS* (1899), pp. 114-15; Anthony Morgan (whose informant was Whalley himself) to Henry Cromwell, Mar. 8, 29, and Whalley to Cromwell, Mar. 15, Lansdowne MSS; Ludlow, II, 61-62.

[67]Mr. Boscawen, Burton, IV, 209.

[68]Burton, IV, 221-23, under date Mar. 21.

phrase caused such a commotion was twofold—it threatened the very basis of the existing regime, and it menaced the estates which many officers had acquired through the sale of lands. Therefore, they feared that their principles and properties were in danger if so fundamental an issue was raised. But if the rift widened between an anti-militaristic majority in Parliament and the army, probably it helped reconcile the Republican minority and the officers, both of whom felt that the acts of the Long Parliament must be upheld at all costs.

The next issue to be raised was whether the Irish members should continue to sit. The debate was short and to the point. Speakers in favor argued that the thirty members were all Englishmen and represented Englishmen who should not be taxed without representation. Voters in Ireland naturally claimed a voice in making the laws by which they were governed. The opposition conceded the last point but urged that the right course was to give Ireland her own Parliament, not to bring her representatives to Westminster to impose laws on England. The division was 156 in favor and 106 against.[69] Perhaps the explanation for the comparatively brief debate is to be found in Burton's comment: "The chair behaves himself like a Busby amongst so many schoolboys, as some say; and takes a little too much on him but grandly."[70]

On March 25, a debate, damaging to the government, occurred on a petition from seventy Royalists sold as slaves to Barbados for their alleged share in the rising planned at Salisbury in 1655.[71] The petitioners alleged that many of them had never seen Salisbury or borne arms, and had been either acquitted by juries or untried. After a year's imprisonment they were shipped to Barbados, and sold for 1,550 lbs. of sugar apiece as the goods and chattels of Martin Noel, Major Thomas of London, and Captain Hatsell of Plymouth. They were used for grinding, attending to the furnaces of sugar mills, or digging. They were whipped at their masters' pleasure and housed worse than hogs in England.[72] Those responsible appear to have made a very feeble defense. Sir John Copplestone, then high sheriff for Devon, claimed that one of the chief petitioners, Marcellus Rivers, had undoubtedly been engaged in the insurrection, but had to acknowledge that he had been acquitted. Noel admitted that he transported men from Bridewell and other prisons to work in the plantations, and that he "had to do in sending" the petitioners though only by recommenda-

[69]*Commons Journals*, VII, 619; Burton, IV, 225-43.
[70]Burton, IV, 243.
[71]Gardiner, *Commonwealth and Protectorate*, III, ch. xxxix.
[72]Burton, IV, 255-58.

tion. He then stated that the transported usually served five years and and then were paid wages. They worked only twelve hours a day with four stops for refreshing. He wound up by an appeal to the mercantile interests—the island was "as grateful to you for trade as any part of the world."[73] Others sought to divert the attention of the House by claiming that the petition was a breach of privilege inasmuch as it concerned members. More to the point was the fear expressed by Thurloe and others that to consider a petition from Royalists would endanger all that had faithfully served the Commonwealth and force them "to look to themselves." "I doubt," said Colonel Birch, "you will raise such a flame as you will hardly quench."[74]

Naturally, Republicans and Royalists did not miss this golden opportunity of blackening the Protectorate. Vane denounced the violation of the liberties of free-born Englishmen, and appealed to those who condemned the tyranny of the late king to denounce equally those who trod in his footsteps. Captain Baynes avowed he had been too zealous against Cavaliers until he saw how his friends were illegally treated. Major General Browne, by now a Royalist, recounted how in spite of fighting for Parliament he had been expelled without a hearing, and kept in prison five years without a trial. In vain army officers pointed out how evil the effect of such debates would be, how the Cavaliers would be heartened, and silenced ministers encouraged to preach openly. "I doubt the next petition will be from Charles Stuart."[75] On this occasion, at least, Hesilrige spoke to the point and briefly. He declared that the Cavaliers' case may be the Roundheads' a year hence. "Our ancestors left us free men. If we have fought our sons into slavery, we are of all men the most miserable."[76] Perhaps it was as well for the courtiers that the chair was vacated without putting the question. Later in the day a vote was carried to void the vote of December 4, 1649, disabling Browne from being an alderman of the City of London, and a committee was named to consider what debts were due to him.[77] Nothing was done, however, for the Royalists in Barbados, perhaps because later revelations showed how deeply another petitioner, Rowland Thomas, had been involved in Royalist plots.[78]

On March 28 the decisive vote was taken on the motion that the House would transact with the persons now sitting in the other house

[73]Ibid., pp. 258-59.
[74]Ibid., p. 262.
[75]Major General Kelsey, ibid., pp. 267-68.
[76]Ibid., pp. 271-72.
[77]Ibid., p. 276; Commons Journals, VII, 621.
[78]Burton, IV, 301-308.

as a House of Parliament, "not intending thereby to exclude such ancient Peers as have been faithful to the Parliament." Members were plainly tired of the subject—"We have been two months windbound," said one—and declined to accept one amendment that the recognition should be only for the present Parliament,[79] and another that the members of the other house must be approved by the Commons. The vote on the main question was 198 to 125, the tellers for the ayes being Sir Walter St. John and Sir Charles Coote, and for the noes, Sir George Booth and Sir Arthur Hesilrige.[80]

After this troublesome constitutional issue had been settled the House turned to finance. A member introduced a bill, leaving blanks for the number of years and months, to abolish the excise and new impost after .... years, and customs, tonnage and poundage .... months, after the Protector's death.[81] An acrimonious discussion followed. Opponents detected in it an acknowledgment that the acts of the Protectorate were legal or an attempt to give the Protector an income for life. Vane argued that those who supported the bill, having spent two months in establishing tyranny and slavery, were now ready to endow their settlement. Supporters urged that necessity was responsible for taxes: the Protector could not live on air alone. If the levying of these taxes was unlawful, then free quarter, "the greatest grievance," must follow. The House did nothing effective, however, because it turned aside to consider the declaration for a fast.

Discussion of a declaration for a fast to be held May 18 was partly factious. Inasmuch as the other house was now recognized, it was a pure waste of time to protest against the title—A Declaration of the Lord Protector and both Houses of Parliament—or to try to add a proviso that the Declaration should not interfere with the right of the Commons to set bounds either to the single person or other House.[82] Nevertheless, the language used in the Declaration raised justifiable alarms that toleration, which most Independents and sections of the Army prized so highly, was in danger. The framers had not been content to bewail in general terms the causes of God's displeasure, as in-

[79]William Dougal Christie in his *Life of Anthony Ashley Cooper, First Earl of Shaftesbury* (1871), I, app. iv, accepts the attribution to his hero of *A Seasonable Speech made by a Member of Parliament*, but cites no evidence. It would not suit the occasion on which Mr. Christie supposes it to have been delivered—the amendment above—and it reads like a Republican pamphlet.

[80]*Commons Journals*, VII, 621; Burton, IV, 277-93. According to Barwick's letter to Hyde, Apr. 9 (Thurloe, VII, 647), "the moderate party (as they are called) were so jealous of the starting up of a commonwealth, as they joined with the Whitehall men in bringing in not only the Scotch and Irish members, but the other house also." This explains the relatively large majorities.

[81]Burton, IV, 296. The blank spaces were in the bill.

[82]On April 5 the first motion was defeated by 135 to 96 and the second by 123 to 73. The final division was in favor of the declaration by 94 to 34—figures which suggest that many members, bored with the debates, had left the House.

duced by "the great mortality upon man and beast . . . besides the decay of trade and the just dearth which is amongst us," but had been specific. "These nations are overspread with many blasphemies and damnable heresies against [the Trinity and] against the word of God, the only rule of faith and life, by denying the authority thereof, and crying up the light in the hearts of sinful men as the rule and guide of all their actions; besides many other abominable errors . . . with the growth of gross ignorance, atheism, and profaneness . . . the great scandal given by professors, and the sad divisions amongst them." The civil magistrates, entrusted with the maintenance of public service, with purity of doctrine and the punishment of sins, were chided for their remissness and connivance in permitting the growth of these abominations. All ministers were required to read the Declaration to their congregations on the Sunday before the day of public fasting.[83]

Vane and others who believed in complete religious freedom denounced "this imposition upon consciences" as a surrender of the cause for which they had fought. "All is lost," he exclaimed. The Marquis of Argyle protested that Scottish ministers would not meddle in civil affairs and could not lawfully read the Declaration. Most of those who favored it avoided the issue of toleration, though one member indicated his desire for the suppression of Quakerism.[84] A long wrangle preceded the decisions that members of the Commons only should carry messages to the lords and that messages from the other house should not be received unless brought by members of that House. This, Burton noted, "was the first question that ever the Republicans got."[85] These acrimonious debates were all in vain because Parliament was dissolved before agreement between the two houses was reached. Yet the threat to toleration profoundly stirred the army and Republicans, and gave them a common cause to defend. It also widened the divisions among Puritans. Instead of being an olive branch to unite, the Declaration proved a sword to divide.

[83]Old *Parliamentary History*, XXI, 321-23.
[84]Burton, IV, 328-45, 351-59, 370-78.
[85]Ibid., p. 378; *Commons Journals*, VII, 632.

CHAPTER V

The Fall of the Protectorate

AN EXTRAORDINARY FEATURE of Richard's Parliament is that, although called to grant money, it had made little attempt hitherto even to examine the financial situation. In his opening speech Richard had called attention to the great arrears of pay, and Fiennes who followed him had promised "a particular account . . . of the state of the public revenue and of the forces both by sea and land."[1] Not until February 17 did the House refer the public accounts to a committee. Four days later, without waiting to hear the state of the national finances, the members approved sending a very considerable fleet to sea after Thurloe had stated that the cost would be a million pounds.[2] Finally, the committee mentioned above presented its report on April 7. The total annual income of England was £1,517,000, of Scotland £144,000, and of Ireland £208,000. The expenditures were for England £1,548,000, for Scotland £307,000, and for Ireland £346,000. Taking the three nations together expenditures exceeded revenue for the year by more than £333,000. In addition, there were debts inherited by Richard from his father, and arrears due to the army and navy, "besides what may be due to the forces in Flanders, of which there is no account to be had."[3] The main sources of revenues for England were the monthly assessment (£420,000), the customs (£392,000), the custom of sea coal (£20,000),[4] the excise on imports (£197,000), the excise on domestic commodities (£58,000),[5] the excise on beer and ale (£33,000), the tax on new buildings in London (£30,000), and the sums received from papists' and delinquents' estates (£54,000).[6] The largest issues were: for the army in all three nations £1,244,000, for the navy £418,000, for his Highness' household £100,000. Unfortunately the figures are given in such a way that no precise estimate is possible of the debts Oliver bequeathed to his successor. Probably they were in the neighbor-

[1] The old *Parliamentary History*, XXI, 267-68, 279.

[2] Ibid., pp. 290, 313.

[3] The report is printed in *Commons Journals*, VII, 627-31, and in the old *Parliamentary History*, XXI, 327-38. The debt was reckoned to be £2,474,000 but this included £394,000 for the navy up to November 1, 1659. How much of this was due by the end of the fiscal year which for the army terminated on March 29 does not appear—probably either nothing or a small proportion only.

[4] Both in farm to Martin Noel.

[5] In farm to various individuals, whose names are given, *Commons Journals*, VII, 635.

[6] Details about the revenue for Scotland and Ireland are given in the chapters devoted to those countries.

hood of £1,500,000, which had increased by the end of March, 1659, by over half a million.[7]

A deficit that amounted to little more than a year's revenue seems trivial in these days, but in April, 1659, when no Englishman had conceived the notion of funding the debt, it appeared disastrous. "I see an incurable disease, unless you apply a cure presently," was one comment in the House of Commons. Another was: "You are in an incurable consumption. You are not bound to pay the debts that are accrued without your consent . . . whatever any Parliament contracted, let us set our shoulders to pay it."[8]

Other points emphasized were the costliness of the war against Spain and the distress of the country. Hesilrige declared that at least 1,200 ships had been lost and few now put to sea. Also, he claimed that no rents were paid by tenants, who had become very scarce.[9] Vane said merchants "break every day, ten at a time."[10] Colonel Birch affirmed that in Herefordshire ready money had almost disappeared. He also complained of extravagant salaries and the cost of levying the excise, whereby merchants were losers and knaves gainers. He proposed a second self-denying ordinance.[11] Another moved to examine what land had been bought by officers and office-holders contrary to their trusts, and a committee for this purpose was named.[12] Naturally enough, the farmers of the excise were soundly denounced, and ordered to pay promptly the amounts they owed the Treasury. Their excuses reveal how unpopular the impost was. According to them, "all possible means are used to dispute the laws." The brewers of London had even refused to brew for some time rather than pay. The officers employed by the farmers were perpetually under arrest, but they themselves could get no justices of the peace to issue warrants on their behalf. When they got judgments the fines were ridiculously small.[13]

One feature of the debate is truly remarkable. Although the meanest intellect should have seen that the existing taxes were inadequate even to meet current charges, much less pay debts, no one ventured to suggest the obvious remedy—to restore the monthly assessment to the old rate

[7] £2,474,000 minus £394,000 (due to the navy to November 1, 1659) plus £80,000 for additional arrears to the armed forces which seem not to be included in the report. The last sum cannot be guaranteed and may be too small. After making my own calculations I found that Sir Charles Firth estimated the debt at Oliver's death to be £1,500,000 and at the beginning of April £1,900,000 (Firth, *Last Years*, II, 265-66). On April 16 the Committee submitted a corrected report by which the debt "at present, and before the year end, is, and will be" £2,222,000.

[8] Burton, IV, 363-64.

[9] Ibid., p. 364. Thurloe in his reply said the loss of ships was exaggerated but gave no alternative figures (ibid., p. 366). A petition of mariners and seamen for their great loss of shipping by the late wars was read on April 8, but not printed (ibid., p. 379).

[10] Ibid., p. 365.

[11] Ibid., p. 384.

[12] Ibid., pp. 385-86.

[13] Ibid., pp., 394-97, 416-20.

of £120,000 a month, instead of the present £50,000. Presumably the courtiers feared defeat from a coalition of all other groups in the House. The Republicans objected to the Protector's having a fixed annual revenue, and hoped, by denying him necessary funds, to render him unpopular. Insofar as they had any plans for increasing the revenues and paying debts, they are said to have relied upon the recovery of some grants made (illegally in their opinion) to favored individuals since 1653 and upon a composition with the chief creditors who would receive half of what was due.[14]

Little was done, therefore, to appease the army but much to irritate it. Men of such different principles as Vane and Thurloe urged the need for paying the soldiery—the first added, "else you may be in the destruction before you are aware."[15] Nevertheless, the only practical step toward that end was the attempt to secure the prompt receipt of what was due from farmers of the excise. But a declaration for this purpose was recommitted after a close division, because it contained a clause which restricted it to "the sitting of this present Parliament"—apparently a Republican proviso which ignored the other house and the Protector, and which was tantamount to legislating by a declaration.[16] All that was accomplished was to instruct a committee of the whole House on April 16 to consider how expenses could be diminished and how arrears due to the army and navy could be satisfied.

The attack on William Butler (or Boteler), who had been major general for the counties of Northamptonshire, Bedford, Rutland, and Huntingdon,[17] was bound to prick the army officers in a very sore spot—their individual responsibilities for any illegal actions performed under the orders of their superiors. The main charge against Butler concerned the famous manor of Holdenby (or Holmby) in Northamptonshire. Sir Thomas Hatton, holder of the lease, let part to Lawrence Manley, whose executor was Robert Manley. When, in 1657, the executors of Sir Thomas obtained a judgment against Robert Manley for arrears of rent, his sheep were taken in execution by the sheriff, and his cattle distrained when the demesne he had rented was reclaimed. His misfortunes did not end here because he became a delinquent and fled. Butler intervened at this point. He resisted the sheriff's execution, seized the estate, and imprisoned a

[14]Letters of Apr. 5 signed T. L. (who may be Thomas Lynch), Lansdowne MSS.

[15]Burton, IV, 365, 383. The pay for three months (of 28 days) for the army in England was about £ 90,000. It is significant that the estimate (ibid., p. 387) was only for England. This unfair discrimination against the forces in Scotland and Ireland (whose arrears of pay were the greater) may be one reason why these two bodies ultimately opposed the army in England.

[16]This is how I interpret Thurloe's remark that the committee which drew up the declaration "have decided this question, that the legislative is wholly in this House." Burton, IV, 436.

[17]His commission is printed in Abbott, Writings . . . of Oliver Cromwell, III, 845-50.

shepherd who had sold stock for Manley until he agreed to deposit the money with Captain Baynes, from whose house it was forcibly removed.

Butler justified all these proceedings "by colour of his late Highnesses' letter commanding him so to do."[18] His defense served but to aggravate his crimes. Member after member demanded his immediate punishment. Resolutions to strike him out of the commission of the peace and to restore all properties he had illegally seized were easily passed, but a motion to disable him from all employment was contested by Cromwellians, Republicans, and army officers. Few ventured a complete vindication, though Anthony Morgan, a correspondent of Henry Cromwell, argued that a soldier could not dispute his superiors' orders. Thurloe, while asserting that Butler had served "faithfully and honestly and valiantly," went no further than to request that he should be heard before so severe a sentence be passed.[19] Eventually the House listened to the secretary's reminder that, according to precedent, witnesses should be heard and an impeachment drawn up and sent to the other house, so a committee was named to proceed against the obnoxious major general.[20]

Conscious that its baiting the army imperiled its own existence, the House of Commons at long last gave practical effect to its recognition of the other house. After a motion had been defeated that Mr. Grove, selected to carry thither the declaration for a fast, should not wait for an answer, he appeared at the bar of the other house, accompanied by about fifty members. After an exchange of bows, he delivered his message without giving his auditors any title: "The Knights, Citizens, and Burgesses, assembled in the House of Commons, have commanded me to present the declaration for a public fast to you, wherein they desire the concurrence of this House." He then retired but being called in again received an answer. Fiennes, apparently confused by the novelty of the situation, began, "The Lords," but quickly changed to, "This House will return an answer to you by messengers of their own."[21]

According to Ludlow,[22] the other house was unanimous in its eagerness to receive the declaration but revealed sharp differences about its

[18]The relevant passage from *Commons Journals* (Apr. 12) is printed in Burton, IV, 403-404; Thurloe, VII, 653.

[19]Thurloe was especially concerned to defend Butler because he had been chosen major to replace Packer in Oliver's, now Richard's, horse. A life of Butler, not in *DNB*, is in *Huntington Library Quarterly*, XI (1947-1948), 1-11, written by Paul H. Hardacre.

[20]Burton, IV, 403-12.

[21]Journal of the Protectorate House of Lords, printed in *The Manuscripts of the House of Lords, 1699-1702* (1908), pp. 560-561; Burton (who was present), IV, 427; Ludlow (*Memoirs*, II, 60-61), says Grove was accompanied by "divers young gentlemen, and many of the Cavalier-party . . . attending like so many lackeys." On the other hand, one prominent Royalist, Lord Falkland, had been a teller in favor of the motion mentioned above. The Protectorate House of Lords is the subject of Appendix G in G. E. C.'s *Complete Peerage*, IV (1916), ed. Vicary Gibbs et al.

[22]Ludlow, *Memoirs*, II, 60-61.

contents. "Mr. Cromwell's party and the Presbyterians fell violently upon the Independents and some of the army, concerning some clauses therein inserted, as they said, by those of their party." That the House did not unanimously accept the declaration is proved by the references to it in the Journal, but whether the debates were precisely as Ludlow stated is doubtful. It is likely that courtiers and Presbyterians attacked extreme sectaries and the army, but defended "some clauses" obnoxious to believers in complete freedom of worship.

During the four months that had elapsed since the decision to call a parliament the army had been fairly quiescent, probably waiting to see what would be the outcome. On March 22 Thurloe wrote to Henry Cromwell: "It is a miracle of mercy that we are yet in peace, considering what the debates are, and what underhand working there is to disaffect the officers of the army: but for ought I can perceive, they remain pretty staunch, though they are in great want of pay, for which no provision is at all made, nor do I see that we are likely to have any yet."[23] But this was the calm that precedes a storm.

Ludlow, who now penetrated into the center of politics, analyzed the military groups. The Commonwealthsmen were headed by Colonels Ashfield, Lilburne, and Fitch, Lieutenants-Colonel Mason, Moss, and Farley, Major Creed, and the inferior officers in general. At the head of the Wallingford House party—so called because Fleetwood's residence was their meeting place—were Fleetwood, Disbrowe, Sydenham, Clerk, Kelsey, Berry, and others of the higher officers. The third group adhered to the Protector and included Colonels Ingoldsby, Goffe, Whalley, Howard, and Goodrick, with many of the officers in the armies in Scotland and Ireland.[24]

That there should be factions in the army was no novelty. Indeed, they had existed in one form or another since the formation of the New Model Army. At the end of the first Civil War, the quarrel between Parliament and the army had led to the expulsion of many supporters—mainly Presbyterians—of the former. The execution of Charles I, the invasion of Scotland, the creation of the Protectorate, various policies of Oliver, as Protector, and the Petition and Advice had all caused dismissals or resignations. The most obvious feature that was new was that Richard did not, like his father, command the loyalty of the army as its general. Probably the officers were little influenced by the sophism that Oliver Cromwell had exercised the command of the armed forces as their general and not as Protector, and that the civil power had been entrusted to

[23]Thurloe, VII, 636. A week later Fauconberg thought the outlook improved. Mar. 29, Lansdowne MSS.
[24]Ludlow, II, 61.

him not because he was the general but because of "the reputation of his personal virtue." More significant was that "many of the officers only call R. Cromwell *the young gentleman,* and say that he never drew sword for the Commonwealth."[25] His lack of influence and his failure to adopt strong measures to purge dissentients immediately after his succession when his short-lived popularity was at its height had permitted the existing divisions in the army to grow deeper, and the personal ambitions of its leaders to become overweening. Furthermore, the parliamentary attacks on the army, and the neglect to vote supplies to pay it promptly, touched all in their pride and their pockets. Their leaders were becoming convinced that the Protector intended to rely on Parliament and to form a party whose unquestioning obedience he could trust, to the diminution of their own influence.[26]

The Wallingford House party, therefore, made overtures to the civilian Republicans, and Ludlow agreed to meet the army leaders. Judging from his account—and there is no other—the difficulties in the way of any agreement were serious. As uncompromising as ever, Ludlow began by pointing out that the officers were responsible for the present situation because they had (in 1653) elevated a single person to rule when they might instead have established English liberties. He then conceded that it might not be too late even now if they would join the Commonwealthsmen in the army and restore the government "which had cost the nation so much blood to establish"—i.e., the Commonwealth from 1649 to 1653.[27] To prove their sincere reconciliation with the Commonwealthsmen he proposed they should defend Colonel Ashfield. Ignoring the first part of Ludlow's discourse, the army leaders claimed they had already done what they could for the colonel, but professed their unwillingness to go so far as to ruin some of their friends who supported the Protectorate, including Whalley. To this Ludlow replied that no one would recognize them as saviors of their country if they were governed by "private interests and engagements." When they expressed a desire to see Vane and Hesilrige, Ludlow said these two Republicans were too prudent to appear at Wallingford House until its occupants had proved their sincerity. After the meeting had broken up Ludlow acquainted Vane and Hesilrige with what had happened. They approved and promised to assist "in all things tending to the public service" as soon as sea-

[25]*Clarendon Calendar,* IV, 100; *An Expedient for the preventing any Difference between His Highness and the Parliament* (Thomason's date, February 26).

[26]Ludlow's language is: "Richard Cromwel, who having cast off those that had taken the pains to advance him, joined himself to men that were more suitable in his inclinations." *Memoirs,* II, 61.

[27]It never seems to have occurred to Ludlow and those who agreed with him that during the first Civil War when most blood was shed, none of the leaders had any thought of establishing a republic. They did intend to try Charles I if they won the second Civil War, but never announced what form of government they would establish.

sonable. Ludlow then saw Sydenham, informed him what the two had said, inquired what the army leaders intended to do next, and learned that they planned a meeting of the general council of officers.[28]

The most significant point of these preliminary discussions was the complete absence of any definite program. Such vagueness was to characterize all the negotiations between the Republicans and the army leaders. There was, of course, no real unity of purpose, except of a negative kind. Both sides were dissatisfied with the present state of affairs. The one had plainly demanded the re-establishment of the Commonwealth, but the other had no wish to see an omnipotent, oligarchical House of Commons ruling the three nations. Fleetwood and his associates had quite a different form of government in mind. Evidently they hoped to utilize the Republicans to advance their own ends and then to ignore them. The sequel was to show that they underestimated the strength of the Commonwealthsmen in the army. But in the immediate future they were successful.

They caught Richard off guard and secured his consent to a meeting of the general council of officers. It met on April 2 and agreed upon the heads for a petition, soliciting their arrears and future pay, indemnity for their past actions in arresting Cavaliers and in preserving the peace, and for measures against Royalists.[29] The selection of the committee to incorporate these heads into a petition led to an animated scene. The aristocratic Fauconberg was angered to hear the under officers ("for all the rabble were present") applauding Lilburne, Ashfield, and their kind when they produced a draft much worse than the petition finally adopted. It was discussed clause by clause and the Cromwellians with difficulty got some changes made but it remained "hardly credible."[30]

The preamble to the Humble Representation and Petition of the general council of the officers of the armies of England, Scotland, and Ireland asserted that the officers, having often solemnly declared that they were not members of a mercenary army, and being careful to avoid the suspicion, which enemies had tried to cast upon them, of a desire to meddle in "Matters not relating to an army," had hitherto refrained from any appeal to his Highness with regard to "the crying Necessities of the Armies for want of Pay." But now, finding that all they had fought for was in danger of ruin and that his Highness, by the sitting of Parliament, was able to provide against the approaching danger, they made

[28]Ludlow, II, 63-65.

[29]*Clarke Papers*, III, 187.

[30]Apr. 12, Lansdowne MSS. Bordeaux reported that at the meeting the Protector's friends were in a majority but that the others, who boldly declaimed their views, were sure of the support of most subaltern officers. The second clause is truer than the first. To Mazarin, Apr. 7/17, Guizot, I, 351.

four representations. The "good old cause" was frequently and publicly derided and reproached by its implacable enemies, who began to appear in places where "that Cause was wont to receive its chiefest countenance and shelter." Secondly, many Cavaliers had crossed from the Continent, met frequently, and affronted and assaulted faithful servants of the Commonweath. The names of the judges of Charles I were scattered in the street as if they were marked out for destruction. Suits were initiated at common law against soldiers for acts committed under orders from their superiors, and the "famous Actions of the Parliament, his late Highness of Blessed memory, and the Army in and since the year 1648" were vilified.

Thirdly, the armies were in "great extremities for want of Pay," and, although their condition had been pointed out, no effectual remedy had been applied. Consequently, officers' purses had been "generally emptied" by loans to soldiers and their credits to the victualers stretched to the utmost, the poor soldiers had been obliged by want of bread to sell for ready money their expected pay much below its face value, and the great mortality among horses had compelled many troopers to buy twice over.[31] Fourthly, they were resolved to assist his Highness and the Parliament "in plucking the wicked out of their places" wherever they should be found, and in reforming the "Law and Manners." The conclusion reiterated the above but added a request that "Good and well-affected people" might repair with freedom to their places of worship, "of late much violated by Indicting and Imprisoning many of their persons."[32]

The sober Whitelocke, one of the commissioners of the Great Seal, judged the petition "the beginning of Richard's fall, and set on foot by his relations," Fleetwood and Disbrowe and others of their party.[33] A Cromwellian M.P. felt that the army had put such a damp upon the members of his party that they trifled away time and hardly knew what they were doing. The vote against Butler, pressed by the Commonwealthsmen in order to make the army dissatisfied with Parliament, had alarmed many officers as guilty as Butler. From the chaos likely to ensue the enemies of the Protectorate hoped to profit. Arthur Annesley,

[31]Troopers had to provide their own mounts. For the price of horses see C. H. Firth, *Cromwell's Army* (1921), pp. 242-46. In the *Calendar Venetian* (pp. 6-7) is a reference to the loss of hundreds of cavalry horses.

[32]The petition seems not to have been published separately, but is printed in the official newspapers and reprinted in the old *Parliamentary History*, XXI, 340-345. A comparison of the latter version with that in the *Publick Intelligencer*, April 11/18, shows that the paragraphing has been changed. The newspaper of this date explained that it reprinted the Representation because previously it had been very erroneously printed. Ibid., p. 355.

[33]*Memorials*, IV, 342. See Whitelocke's life in *DNB* for a description of how the *Memorials* were compiled.

author of *England's Confession* and one of the best-informed pamphlet-eers of the time, compares the petition to "lightning before thunder, both to the Protector and the House." It made, he wrote, "some seeming fair professions" but in such "canting equivocating language, whereof the sword was like to be interpreter, that the sting was easily visible through the honey." The past record of the army's intervention in politics rather than their present utterances seemed the best clue to their intentions.[34]

The petition was doubtlessly intended to be a challenge to the civil authorities. The army leaders had failed to gain the ascendancy in Parliament and the Privy Council. Blind as their arrogance rendered them to many of the signs of the times, they must have perceived the antimilitarism evinced so often in the Commons, most notably in the proceedings against Butler. They saw the House was determined to regard them as its servants, and found this position intolerable.[35] Their sinister hint that they would help "pluck the wicked out of their places" implied an early purge of all who withstood their pretensions. They profited by the unwisdom of Parliament in neglecting the material grievances of the army, because, by emphasizing arrears of pay,[36] they gained the soldiers' support. They apparently never considered whether they were raising hopes they might not be able to satisfy. Forgetting all else in their resolve to rule the state they also forgot that they might ruin it, and be involved in its ruin.

The petition was presented to Richard on the evening of April 6. He received it, according to *Mercurius Politicus*,[37] "with a very great affection and respect to the whole body of officers which presented it, using many expressions of tenderness and endearment to them, as the old friends of his renowned father, and the faithful servants of the publick interest of these nations, in the maintenance whereof he resolved to live and die with them &c. In a word, so great a satisfaction appeared on either side at this meeting that it speaks nothing less than a vigorous asserting of the present government, to the terror and confusion of the common enemy." The next day Bordeaux reported that the Court party was full of optimism.[38] If so, it is conceivable that had Parliament promptly acceded to the main demands of the petition, the crisis might have been postponed.

[34]Thomason's date is May 30. Reprinted in *Somers Tracts*, VI, 518.

[35]"They took them still to be their servants," is the phrase in *England's Confusion* (*Somers Tracts*, VI, 518).

[36]In the preamble, main body, and conclusion of the petition.

[37]P. 352. The account written on April 8/18 by the Venetian ambassador is very similar. He adds that the Protector must now consider how he can satisfy the soldiers so that further delay of pay may not provoke them. *Calendar Venetian*, p. 7.

[38]Guizot, I, 360.

Richard sent a letter with a copy of the petition to each House on April 8. The other house decided to consider the petition on the following Monday (April 11), but in the Commons no resolution followed its reading.[39] The explanation of the omission is that both communications were very unwelcome.[40] However dilatory and irrelevant the debates, members had taken pride in the freedom they enjoyed. They were not likely to submit to outside coercion, especially in a matter which involved increased taxation.

Meanwhile the army was getting more and more out of hand. Anyone who recalled the crises of the past twelve years might have foreseen the worst when a day[41] was devoted to a fast and prayer meeting, at which Hugh Peters, John Owen, John Griffith, and perhaps another preached.[42] The next day over five hundred officers met and heard Disbrowe propose a new test of loyalty—that every officer should swear that he believed the late King's execution to be just and lawful. His motion was greeted with shouts of "well moved." But Broghil, a staunch Cromwellian, proposed as an alternative an oath to defend the government as established with a Protector and Parliament. This adroit proposal checked Disbrowe and his adherents and, after consulting together, they suggested that both tests should be dropped, to which Broghil agreed.[43] Probably the officers were momentarily content with vague declarations against Charles Stuart and for Richard and the Parliament that all present could accept.[44]

After Thurloe and Disbrowe, a strange combination, had failed to win over the Republican leaders, Hesilrige, Scot, and Vane, a meeting may have taken place between Thurloe and other councillors and lead-

[39]*House of Lords MSS, 1699-1702*, pp. 557-58. *Commons Journals*, VII, 632. Unfortunately the Protector's letter was not entered in either place.

[40]The French ambassador was correct in the fact but incorrect in asserting that the reason why the communications were "ill-received" was that the letter "termed the Parliament the House of Commons." From both *Journals* it is evident that it did nothing of the kind.

[41]April 13.

[42]*Mercurius Politicus*, April 7/14; *Clarke Papers*, III, 189; Guizot, I, 362-63; Lansdowne MSS. Mabbott, April 19. Peters, in a letter printed in *England's Confusion*, claimed that when he addressed the officers he had no idea of their intentions. The letter is worth study as a severe indictment of the army leaders (*Somers Tracts*, VI, 525-26). Willam Orme (*Memoirs of John Owen* [1820], pp. 276-79), discusses and minimizes Owen's responsibility, while the *DNB* ignores it altogether. Perhaps Richard's replacing Owen as Vice-Chancellor of the University of Oxford may have influenced the divine who is stated to have "gathered a church" which Fleetwood, Disbrowe, Sydenham, Berry, Goffe, and other officers attended (Letter of Arthur Annesley, March 15, Lansdowne MSS). Baxter states (*Reliquiae*, p. 101) that at the church at Wallingford House "it was determined that *Richard's* Parliament must be dissolved." This is not improbable, but the evidence for it is rather weak. Some particulars of correspondence between the church at Wallingford House and the Congregationalists at Yarmouth are given in John Stoughton, *History of Religion in England* (1881), III, 28-29. Certainly it was no accident that William Allen, once an agitator, published on April 27 his account of the most remarkable of all the army's prayer meetings—that at Windsor in 1648 which decided to try Charles I.

[43]*A Collection of the State Letters of Roger Boyle, the first Earl of Orrery*, ed. Thomas Morrice (Dublin, 1743), I, 55-57; Thurloe, VII, 662.

[44]G. Mabbott, April 19, Lansdowne MSS.

ing officers. The councillors are said to have proposed that Richard should assume the generalship of the army, dissolve Parliament, and devise means of paying the soldiery. The officers were divided: Whalley and Goffe in favor, but Fleetwood and Disbrowe against the proposals as too hazardous except in the last extremity.[45] Whether this sounding, for it is unlikely to have been more, preceded or followed a meeting between Richard and his adherents, cannot be ascertained.[46] At this meeting on April 16 or 17, Fauconberg, Goffe, Howard, and Ingoldsby and other officers swore in the usual formula "to live and die" with Richard, and offered to seize the leaders of the Wallingford House party. He was dissuaded from this violent step by Thurloe and others, but consented to order the council of officers to disperse.[47]

The House of Commons was now determined to bring matters to a head. On April 18, although the business should have been financial, a debate started about the meetings of officers and in a surprisingly short time two most important votes were passed. The one was that during a parliamentary session no general council of officers should meet without the consent of Protector and both Houses of Parliament.[48] The second was that no one should hold any command in the army or navy who refused to pledge himself not to interrupt the free meetings of Parliament. The concurrence of the other house was sought for both votes. A notable feature of the debate was that the opposition came from Commonwealthsmen.[49] The strange sight was seen of Republicans like Hesilrige, Scot, and Vane urging that the army be courted and that a conference be held with the other house; but the recent negotiations with the army leaders explain the inconsistency.

The Protector had now to take sides either with or against the army leaders. Why he abandoned the policy of conciliation which had been evident on April 6, and perhaps at the later meeting between Thurloe, Fleetwood, and Disbrowe and others, is not clear. There are several likely explanations. He may have become convinced that the army was determined not to accept him as its commander[50] which he regarded as a

[45]Thurloe, VII, 660-661. The sole authority seems to be Joseph Bampfield, a former Royalist and now one of Thurloe's spies. His informant, "young Mr. S.," was one of Thomas Scot's sons. If Bampfield is correct, the incident reveals Thurloe's naïvete.

[46]According to a letter from Berwick to Hyde, dated April 20 (Thurloe, VII, 662), the meeting was on April 16.

[47]Baker's Chronicle, p. 659. Baker puts the meeting on the day before the vote of the Commons against the army council which was on April 18, though Baker gives the date as April 19. It is possible, of course, that the seizure was discussed on several occasions right up to Richard's surrender.

[48]This was carried by 163 to 87, the tellers for the majority being, or soon becoming, Royalists, and for the minority a regicide and a Republican.

[49]Burton, IV, 450, 453-55.

[50]The Venetian ambassador, in a letter of April 22/May 2, reported that the officers were saying openly everywhere that Richard was incompetent to be their general, had shed no blood for the cause they protected, and they would not have him. Calendar Venetian, p. 10.

sine qua non to any agreement. He probably learned that Fleetwood and Disbrowe were negotiating with the Republican leaders. He may have doubted whether the army would adhere to the Wallingford House party and have hoped that the soldiery would be patient a little longer now that the Commons were bestirring themselves about pay. But all that is known beyond dispute is that Richard, probably before the above votes had been passed by the Commons, summoned the officers to White-hall and told them that as Parliament was considering the petition there was no longer any need for them to meet. Therefore, he declared the general council dissolved and ordered officers to rejoin their regiments. He justified his action further on the grounds that many members of Parliament disliked such meetings, and that the Cavaliers were arming for a new insurrection. Disbrowe replied he wondered that any honest man should be offended at their meetings to regulate disorders among themselves. His Highness affirmed his first orders and withdrew. Disbrowe and divers others went out with him towards his chamber, and as they went Disbrowe said to his Highness, "But Sir, the meeting is not dissolved for all this for they adjourned themselves to a meeting at Wallingford house and not to this place." His Highness replied, "Sir, I say they shall not meet there nor any where else." Colonel Ashfield stepped up and said, "Sir, this sudden order will put us to great inconveniences, and when we come to our soldiers without mony wee shall not know what to say to them besides there are divers officers but newly come to town." His Highness replied, "Sir, you of all men have least reason to except against this order having been two years from your command, and I believe those who came lately to town will be willinger to returne then those who have been longer here."[51] In defiance of this order, the officers met again and protested that they would meet whenever they pleased until they received satisfaction, and openly announced they desired the dissolution of Parliament.[52] Matters had now reached a crisis, and nothing but a *coup d'état* could save the situation.

[51]Anthony Morgan, April 19, Lansdowne MSS.; *Clarendon Calendar,* IV, 184. Morgan states definitely that the Commons' votes were passed between the time Richard summoned the officers to his presence and his telling them to disperse. Therefore, the Protector must have known of the resolutions beforehand, and, presumably, approved of them. Cf. *Clarke Papers,* III, 191, 212; Guizot, I, 363-64; *Clarendon Calendar,* IV, 184. On the other hand, *Publick Intelligencer* (pp. 375, 383) twice dated the meeting on April 17. If correct, this date would suggest that the Commons' votes may have been the result of the officers' defiant attitude. None of these accounts confirms the narrative in the *State Letters of Roger Boyle,* I, 57-58, where Broghil is credited with the advice to dissolve the council of officers and with the composition of the speech delivered there. However, he may well have given the advice and helped with the speech.

[52]*Calendar Venetian,* p. 11. Probably John Harris in his *Peace and Not Warre* ([1659], pp. 24-25), interprets the view of the army in the complaint that Parliament began "to impose upon the army, by denying them the liberty of meeting together to consult their affairs either as Englishmen, or soldiers." This distinction between the army's rights as Englishmen and as soldiers had been very prominent in 1647.

A deceptive calm prevailed on April 19 and 20. On the former the Commons sent the Lords their votes of the previous day. The Lords resolved to take them into consideration without permitting any other business, but only after a hot debate and by one vote.[53] The advocates of a Commonwealth were not idle. The officers were incited to put an end to the slavery that prevailed by their sufferance. They were asked why they talked of the good old cause when it was voted out of the House of Commons by courtiers and Cavaliers? Was it because they were so weighed down by the spoils and oppressions of the people that they could not stir? Would Cavaliers fear to encounter those who allowed cowards and courtiers to triumph over them? "Let it never be said that you who once ventured for the Golden Fleece of Publique Liberty, have now exchanged it for the asses ears of servitude and slavery."[54] On April 20 the officers of the trainbands of the City of London presented an address to Richard in which they associated themselves with Fleetwood and the army officers.[55]

The events of the following day, a Thursday, were decisive. In spite of representations from Fleetwood and others to the Protector not to permit Parliament to discuss the command of the army, a debate took place on it in the Commons, though the nominal subject under discussion was the control of the militia. The debate had only an academic interest, because, as Scot said, "This looks like Hezekiah's will, 'put thy house in order, for thou shalt die and not live.'"[56] These proceedings enraged the army, which believed that Richard had broken a promise to Fleetwood and Disbrowe by exerting all his influence to have Parliament declare him general, and that his supporters had joined with the Cavaliers to this end. Thereupon, even the common soldiers cried out against what had happened and begged their officers to remember the cause for which they had so often shed their blood.[57]

Meanwhile, Richard was conferring with his leading supporters as to whether to dissolve Parliament. Whitelocke reports that most were in favor of a dissolution but that he himself was opposed to it, especially now that the Commons had begun to consider how to raise money which would reconcile the soldiery. He says that the reasons which swayed the

[53]*House of Lords MSS, 1699-1702*, p. 563; Thurloe, VII, 658; Burton, IV, 465; *Clarke Papers*, III, 192.

[54]*An Invocation to the Officers of the Army . . . presented to them on 20 April* (1659).

[55]*Publick Intelligencer*, Apr. 18/25. According to some members of Parliament the majority was only one, and a number of officers were not consulted (Burton, IV, 474-75). A newsletter (*Clarke Papers*, III, 192) states that the Lord Mayor and aldermen of the City of London presented a petition to Richard on April 21, promising to stand by him and Parliament. I have not found any other reference to a petition, but Dudley Loftus wrote that Richard's order to the officers was generally approved, especially by the City (April 19, Lansdowne MSS).

[56]Burton, IV, 478.   [57]*Clarke Papers*, III, 212.

majority were the present great dangers threatened both by Parliament and by the Cavaliers who were flocking to London and secretly fomenting a division.[58] Either then or later Richard seems to have agreed to the arrest of Fleetwood and the army ringleaders. A messenger was sent to request Fleetwood to come to Whitehall. On his refusal, Richard ordered some of his bodyguard to seize him. They asked to be excused such a task. When Fleetwood called a general rendezvous of the army at St. James's, Richard appointed a counter-rendezvous at Whitehall, but the colonels who supported him found that their regiments disobeyed their orders and were persuaded by their own officers to cast in their lot with their fellow soldiers at St. James's. According to one report, seven colonels could not muster more than three companies and two troops out of their regiments to support Richard. It is apparently to this critical stage that the following passage in Baker's *Chronicle* should be assigned:

In the evening many of his [Richard's] friends encouraged him to take horse, and appear in the head of some troops that were ready to receive him. While this was doing, the other party had drawn up some men in the several avenues to Whitehall, and in Saint James's Fields, yet it was believed, if he had appeared with vigor and courage amongst them, respect of his person would have prevailed much with the common soldiers; but he was fearful and unresolved,[59] of a spirit unbecoming the quality he assumed; and many of those about him were as irresolute as he, some advised one thing, some another, wasting their time in contradictions; and, as it happens in the consultations of fearful people, they debated many things fit to be done, till the time was past to put them in execution.[60]

To a fanatical Republican, "this night was the brightest appearance of the Lord that has been in our age."[61] Other chroniclers gave a more mundane explanation of the Protector's desertion by the rank and file—namely, that it had been instilled into them that he intended suddenly to disband them and trust to a militia commanded by the nobility and gentry in order to restore the Stuarts and to destroy the liberty of the Gospel for which they had fought so long.[62]

[58]*Memorials*, IV, 343. Whether the majority gave disinterested advice or were trying to curry favor with the army is a moot question. Rumor asserted that Thurloe had made his peace with the army and even that he betrayed the son of his great benefactor, but he may have done no more than express his conviction that the Protectorate could not stand without the army's support—a truth self-evident to a collector of intelligence like himself. *Calendar Venetian*, pp. 13, 17-18; *Clarendon State Papers*, III, 442, 448, 452-53.

[59]Perhaps some of those present remembered the scene on Corkbush Field, in November, 1647, when Oliver quelled singlehanded an incipient mutiny in two regiments led astray by the Levellers.

[60]P. 641.

[61]*Clarke Papers*, III, 213.

[62]Baker, *Chronicle*, p. 641. A pamphlet, *Fast and Loose* (1659), p. 5, probably is merely repeating what many soldiers thought: "that which gave the army a motive hereunto, was because this Parliament had a purpose of securing the nation by militia and trained bands, as in former times, and so to disband this army being a very great burden."

That evening Disbrowe and others went to Whitehall and told Richard that if he would dissolve Parliament the officers would take care of him, but if he refused they would act without him and leave him to shift for himself. For a while he resisted stoutly, because he wanted first to consult some of his council, but this was denied him. Eventually his resolution gave way to the threats Disbrowe did not hesitate to utter. Some time during the night, he signed a commission for the dissolution of Parliament.[63] Therefore, Fiennes, the lord keeper, formally ended the session the next morning, Friday, April 22.[64] A section of the Commons, knowing what was to happen, declined to obey the summons to the other house and voted to adjourn until Monday. According to a pamphleteer, before the adjournment Hesilrige and others moved that the House should declare it treason to put force upon any members of the House and that any votes passed by some members of Parliament while the rest were excluded should be null and void.[65]

Richard's Parliament, like that of 1614, was "addled." It did not succeed in passing a single act. Slingsby Bethel claimed that "such were the great Abilities of the Country Party, that even by the strength of their parts and reason, they did for three months together keep the Courtiers from setting the stamp of Parliament upon anything to the prejudice of the Nation."[66] The Republican leaders owed much, of course, to crypto-Royalists, whose aim was to discredit the existing government. Both groups took every advantage of the license then allowed to speakers, and reiterated their denunciations of the arbitrariness of the Protectorate in all debates, no matter what was normally under discussion. By protracting debates on the Bill of Recognition they prevented consideration of financial necessities, and thus ruined all hope of conciliating the armed forces by the payment of arrears. This antimilitarism at last forced Richard upon the horns of a dilemma—he must either support Parliament against the army or the army against Parliament, and both choices were fraught with the direst peril.

In striking contrast to the skill of the Republicans was the ineptness of the courtiers. Both their strategy and tactics were bad. The introduction of the Bill of Recognition was an obvious blunder. It provided an

[63]Public Record Office, S.P. 78, Vol. 114, fol. 230 (letter from De Vaux, in French [not in cipher, as stated in *Calendar Domestic, 1658-1659*, pp. 335-36]); *Clarke Papers*, III, 192-93, 213. For later rumors of what happened this night, see p. vi of "The Life of John Howe," by Edmund Calamy, which is prefixed to *The Works of John Howe* (New York, 1838); T. M., *The History of Independency: The Fourth and Last Part* (1660), pp. 38-39; George Bate, *Elenchus*, p. 246; Roger Coke, *A Detection of the Court and State of England* (1694), II, 78-79.

[64]*House of Lords MSS, 1699-1702*, p. 567.

[65]*England's Confusion*, Somers Tracts, VI, 519.

[66]*A Brief Narrative*, appended to *The Interest of the Princes and States of Europe* (second edition, 1681), p. 356. This passage is not in the reprint in the *Somers Tracts*, VI.

ideal occasion for all who wished to challenge the Protectorate and the Humble Petition and Advice. Had it ever been passed there is not the slightest reason to suppose that it would have strengthened Richard's position. The fact that the House had recognized him did not weigh a feather in the minds of those responsible for his fall. Indeed, after he had been proclaimed with so much enthusiasm, to try to underprop him by the bill seemed not only futile but also stupid as likely to cast doubts upon his succession. Tactically the courtiers erred in permitting debates to be so protracted and so restricted to the past. An occasional speaker urged an oblivion for the past but this sensible view was not generally accepted, even by Richard's supporters. They had no leaders to indicate the right road. Indeed, a perusal of a debate often fails to discover who were the exponents of the official policy, and even whether there were any.[67]

Nevertheless, although the Parliament did not fulfil the hopes of those responsible for its calling, it did help to clear the air. Its short history reveals more clearly than any other evidence the incompatibility of the army and a House of Commons freely chosen by all political elements except acknowledged Royalists. Two features, so conspicuous in earlier parliaments, are now found more rarely—religious enthusiasm and zeal for the reformation of manners and morals.[68] Throughout, except for the utterances of men like Packer, a mundane spirit prevails. In these respects, as well as in its divisions, the Commons faithfully mirrored the constituencies, except that the conservative reaction was stronger outside than within the House. Yet at the time Wariston probably expressed the opinion of most Englishmen: "There was not so much difference of good between one forme of government and another as worth to purchase it at rate of blood."[69] Anthony Morgan, unlike Wariston, a Cromwellian, reported: "I can not say here is a generall satisfaction but all men seem so or att least strangely indifferent who governs."[70]

[67]Bethel stated that several tables were kept at Whitehall to corrupt members by lavish entertainments. *Somers Tracts*, VI, 481. If this is more than a Republican libel, the money thus spent was wasted because the Cromwellians never appear to have been well organized.

[68]The House of Lords, with much time at its disposal, did name committees to consider whether the laws against swearing, breach of the Sabbath, drunkenness, and stage plays and the opera were defective. The committees seem not to have reported. *House of Lords MSS, 1699-1702*, appendix, pp. 529, 533, 537. For the revival of plays, disguised as moral representations or opera, see Arthur H. Nethercot, *Sir William D'Avenant* (Chicago, 1938), ch. xvii.

[69]*Diary of Sir Archibald Johnston of Wariston*, III (ed. James D. Ogilvie, 1940), May 1, 1659.

[70]May 10, Lansdowne MSS.

CHAPTER VI

The Restoration of the Rump

THE MILITARY *coup d'état* which had forced the Protector to dissolve Parliament was bloodless. Richard, abandoned by all and bewildered at the turn of events, lingered at Whitehall until July, reluctantly acquiescing in whatever was demanded of him and failing to communicate promptly with his brother in Ireland or with Monck in Scotland. His silence may have been due to his belief that his relatives Fleetwood and Disbrowe would induce the army to stand by him and thus redeem the promise made to him during the night of April 21-22. He may well have expected to retain the title of Protector though shorn of all power.[1] Fleetwood soon proved that he was too weak to control the movement he had greatly helped to start. In a disingenuous letter to Monck he explained that the Royalists' flocking to London compelled action.[2] The Protector had dissolved Parliament and the army had upheld him. Now if the forces in England and Scotland would unite, they would serve his Highness and preserve the good old cause.[3] The suggestion that the Protectorate and the good old cause could benefit equally from the *coup d'état* demonstrates the writer's foolish optimism rather than deliberate deception.

Changes in the army soon revealed the prevailing wind. The expulsion of the more prominent of Richard's supporters and their replacement by officers Oliver had cashiered showed how vain were any hopes of maintaining the Protectorate. Richard lost his three regiments, one of horse being given to Sanders and the other after some delay to Packer, and his foot immediately to Fleetwood. Ingoldsby was replaced by Okey, Fauconberg by Lambert, Smith by Overton, and Mill by Sydenham, who was thus rewarded for his intrigues with the Republican leaders. The Major Babington, whom Richard had upheld when he made his unhappy comment to Ingoldsby, was arrested, and a few captains were

---

[1] A dispatch in *Calendar Venetian*, p. 14, states that since April 25 the Protector had frequently met Fleetwood and Disbrowe. The extreme bitterness Richard expressed in the two letters (see below) he wrote his brother on or about May 12 and 17 was no doubt due to his conviction that Fleetwood and Disbrowe had betrayed him by false promises—"I could not have beleved that relation religion and selfe interest wold have deceved me." According to Edmund Calamy's "Life of John Howe" (*Works*, I [1838], vib), when Fleetwood was reminded of his promise to Richard, his excuse was that he had thought his influence with the army greater than it proved to be. A Royalist letter of May 6 (*Clarendon Calendar*, IV, 197) mentioned an intercepted letter from Richard to Henry Cromwell. I regret that I cannot trace it and that its contents remain unknown.

[2] Perhaps in order to bolster up what became the official excuse for the act of April 22, a proclamation was immediately issued for the banishment of nonresident Catholics and Royalists from London until June 10. *Mercurius Politicus*, Apr. 23.

[3] Letter of Apr. 23 in *Clarke Papers*, III, 194, and in *Leyborne-Popham MSS*, pp. 115-16.

dismissed. Further changes took place when all commissions were reviewed by the restored Long Parliament.[4] Unanimity stopped here and for a fortnight no one knew what form of government would be imposed on the three nations, or whether the armies in Scotland, Ireland, and Flanders, and the navy in the Sound under Mountagu, would accept dictation from London.

The army was not united, though the dispersal of the Cromwellian party removed one dissentient group. Most of the field officers adhered to Fleetwood and Disbrowe, who wished to retain Richard as nominal Protector, pack the Privy Council, and control the government themselves: there is no evidence that at first they contemplated a parliament, the necessity for which their shallow minds may have overlooked. A letter from the officers in England to those in Scotland did not mention the recall of the Rump or the summoning of any alternative representative body.[5] The Commonwealthsmen in the army, comprising a few field officers and most of the captains, met at St. James's and determined to end the Protectorate. The rank and file were unorganized, but they also began to signify their adherence to the good old cause. The meanest redcoat, wrote a contemptuous Royalist, was clutching at the reins of government. The knowledge that soldiers were contending "for reducing all to the Rump (as they call it) of the Long Parliament" and the fear that they might elect agitators as in 1647 were factors of great importance.[6] As early as April 8 the under officers and soldiers of the regiment lately Pride's had addressed Fleetwood, and the noncommissioned officers and privates of Goffe's now followed suit. Among their demands the recalling of the "good old Parliament" figured prominently.[7]

Civilian groups, composed of Republicans, first in and around London and then in the provinces, petitioned for the Rump's restoration. The arguments employed were many and varied. No other visible, legal authority existed which could provide for the great necessities of the army and navy and pay off the vast debts. No Parliament of the type prescribed by the Petition and Advice would indemnify the army and promote the good old cause. Because the army and the Long Parliament were equally responsible for the King's execution and the establishment

[4]Baker's *Chronicle*, p. 660, and *Clarke Papers*, III, 195-96. The succession of colonels can be traced in the lists printed at the beginning of Firth and Davies, *Regimental History*. A Royalist letter of June 3 reported that some scores of officers from colonels to captains had been cashiered and Levellers and Quakers restored to their old commands (*Nicholas Papers*, IV, 151-52).

[5]*Clarke Papers*, IV, 4-6.

[6]*Nicholas Papers*, IV, 122-23; Sharp to Douglas and others, April 28, *Register of the Consultations of the Ministers of Edinburgh*, ed. William Stephen, II (1930), 177. Corporals, quartermasters, and privates are said to have had their meetings at the Nag's Head Tavern, once infamous in ecclesiastical controversies. *Clarendon Calendar*, IV, 191, 193.

[7]April 26. A good extract from the petition from Pride's regiment is in Burton, IV, 388-89.

of a free state, they must act together or both fall. If the army failed to recall the Long Parliament, the late *coup* would seem to have been dictated by the desire to advance the chief officers higher and to establish military rule. Members of the old Parliament were, thanks to their long experience, best fitted to cope with domestic distractions and the dangers from abroad likely to arise now that France and Spain were at peace. They would also know how to restore trade, "much damped by the late turne."[8]

The clique at Wallingford House was slow to respond to the manifestations in favor of the Rump's recall. They had raised a spirit they knew not how to lay. They were reluctant to lose "the sweetness of power and profit" they had enjoyed during the Protectorate.[9] Dr. Owen used his influence to overcome their reluctance. At first he had shared their hopes of retaining a titular Protector and of gaining parliamentary approval for the plan. When this proved impossible, he sought to reconcile them to an appeal to the Rumpers to sit again, presenting a list of a hundred and sixty members who had attended at Westminster since Pride's Purge in 1648.[10] Fleetwood and his associates may have been thus convinced that the Rump would not be insignificant numerically. More important, however, was the realization that money must be raised for the army and navy. They canvassed the notion of imposing taxes without parliamentary authority but shrank from so arbitrary a course.[11] Therefore, on or about May 2, Lambert and other officers, including Colonels John Jones, Kelsey, and Berry, met the Republican leaders, Vane, Hesilrige, Ludlow, and Major Salwey.[12]

The officers propounded four conditions for acceptance by the civilians likely to be leaders in the restored Parliament. They required an act of indemnity to cover any illegalities soldiers might have committed, and the civilians readily consented that "something of that nature should be done." They also agreed that Richard's debts should be paid and an income secured to him, but refused to listen to any plea that he should

[8]*Some Reasons Humbly Proposed . . . for the Speedy Readmission of the Long Parliament*, dated by Thomason April 28. Other tracts repeat much the same arguments. For the titles of a dozen or more petitions, etc., see *Catalogue of the Pamphlets . . . Collected by George Thomason* (1908), ed. G. K. Fortescue, under dates from April 25 to May 5.

[9]*Nicholas Papers*, IV, 124; Ludlow, II, 74. The rumor (*Calendar Venetian*, p. 19) that a proposal to recall the King was defeated by six votes only in the army council seems incredible. If the rumor had any substance, it indicated the field officers' distrust of the Rump.

[10]*Diary of Wariston*, III, 107-108. As late as May 3, Wariston mentions a conversation with Owen, who hoped to retain the Protector and to secure a "good" council, another house or senate, and a new representative.

[11]Whitelocke, *Memorials*, May 5.

[12]Wariston gives the same names as Ludlow except that he substitutes Sydenham for Kelsey (*Diary*, III, 108). Salwey's majority was probably acquired during the first civil war when he fought in Worcestershire. See *Diary of Henry Townshend*, ed. J. W. Willis Bund (1920), I, lix, etc. Annesley (*England's Confusion*, p. 10) called him "a smart prating apprentice newly set up for himself."

retain a semblance of power. They made no difficulty about the reform of "whatsoever should appear to be amiss in church and state." The fourth proposition, that the government should rest in a representative house and a select senate, was the crux of the negotiation.

Ludlow, finding that his colleagues ignored the question in the hope, apparently, that the officers would assume that their silence gave consent, refused to allow their compliance to be taken for granted. He stoutly denied that he would support any permanent senate on an equality with the house of representatives, but he averred he approved of such a body as a useful expedient while an equal and just Commonwealth was being established. After some hours of discussion, Lambert agreed to report proceedings to the council of officers. A day or so later, the same delegates met again when the officers declared that the council was resolved that the Long Parliament should be restored.

Ludlow, the only person present who described the negotiations, is not the clearest or the most reliable of writers. Not only is the language of his report extraordinarily vague—"something" should be done, and "whatsoever should appear to be amiss" should be reformed—but he makes no mention of arrears of pay or of any agreement about the composition, duration, or powers of a senate. So far as is known, no discussion took place on the questions that had caused the expulsion of members in 1653—how long Parliament should sit and whether the present members should retain their seats and merely fill vacancies or whether a new Parliament should be elected. This omission is the more striking in that Lambert and other officers had been exasperated by members' breach of faith in 1653. Why officers who knew all about events six years before should expect Vane and his colleagues to be more straightforward in 1659 is an insoluble mystery. Perhaps they felt the pressure to restore the Long Parliament to be so strong that if they delayed they might be swept aside. Rumors of a plot to be headed by Broghil may have given them an excuse for their surrender.[13] Certainly to wait until Parliament had met before formulating their demands was pure folly.

Agreement to restore the Long Parliament was reached on or before May 5 when it became generally known.[14] The next day a declaration of the officers announced that they had invited "the members of the Long Parliament who continued sitting till the 20th of April, 1653, to

[13]Wariston, *Diary*, May 4; *Register of Consultations*, II, 182. Annesley (*England's Confusion*, p. 9) seems alone in asserting that fifteen articles were agreed on by the officers and the civilians, who "over confidently undertook for the rest [of M.P.'s]."

[14]*Calendar Domestic, 1658-1659*, pp. 340-341. Sharp thought that the army leaders had made up their minds to restore a commonwealth by May 1 (*Register of Consultations*, II, 178). Wariston "heard for newes that the Long Parliament men and the officers" were agreed on May 4 (*Diary*, III, 108).

return to the exercise and discharge of their trust." The officers began by acknowledging that they had contributed to the existing state of affairs by wandering from the path of righteousness so that now the good old cause had become a reproach. Recalling that members of the Long Parliament had been eminent asserters of that cause, they restored them and promised their utmost assistance.[15] With this declaration in hand a deputation of officers either preceded or joined a group of members at Lenthall's house, and asked him to summon the survivors of the Long Parliament to meet next day at Westminster.[16] The old Speaker, swayed alternately by timidity and vanity, urged one flimsy excuse after another until his auditors bluntly informed him that they would go ahead without him. They then ordered messengers to summon all members within reach. The following day, Lenthall, as soon as he heard that members were assembling in the House of Lords, hastened to join them.[17] The difficulty of making up a quorum was met, it is said, by sending for Henry Marten and Lord Munson out of gaol, and for Whitelocke and Lisle from the law courts. With the Speaker at their head, the forty-two members walked in procession to the House of Commons. A prejudiced report mentioned that they entered in pairs like the beasts into the ark.[18]

Had the members of the Rump been disinterested framers of a new constitution and not, as their critics asserted, ambitious seekers for some scheme that would perpetuate themselves in authority, they could not have satisfied their adherents. As a pamphleteer commented, although it might not be true that every member had in his pocket a model of the government he thought best, certainly every bookseller's basket or shop had some new plan for a popular government.[19] He then mentioned *A Model of a Democraticall Government*, which advocated a senate, to have the sole power of debating and proposing laws, and a representative, the sole function of which was to pass or reject them. The novel feature here was the composition of the senate. The three hundred senators chosen by the people were to decide who should sit for one, two, or three years, the hundred retiring annually to be replaced by a similar

[15]The old *Parliamentary History*, XXI, 367-68.

[16]Whitelocke, *Memorials*, IV, 344-45, printed the declaration and listed the names of the officers. The *Publick Intelligencer*, under May 6, reported that M.P.'s visited Lenthall after the officers' departure.

[17]Ludlow, II, 77-79.

[18]Annesley, *England's Confusion* (*Somers Tracts*, VI, 520-521). This tract lists the 42, adding opprobrious adjectives. A newsletter states there were between 50 and 60 M.P.'s. *Clarke Papers*, IV, 8; *Nicholas Papers*, IV, 134.

[19]*The Grand Concernments of England Ensured*, p. 43, dated by Thomason October 25, but mostly written before October 13. I cannot insist too strongly that the schemes for reform cited in the text should be regarded merely as specimens. To analyze all would require a whole volume. For a general treatment see Margaret James, *Social Problems and Policy during the Puritan Revolution, 1640-1660* (1930).

number due to retire from the representative, a third of the members of which would be chosen by the people every year—"the people" for this purpose not including the Royalists. The senate would be the supreme administrative body and would name a council of state consisting of five members from each hundred or fifteen in all. Councillors would retire at the same time as the hundred senators from whom they had been selected. The councillors would name a council of war, three out of each group of five. The system of rotation was also applied to the three army leaders, the commander in chief being replaced after a year's service by the lieutenant general from Scotland, and he by the major general from Ireland.

This constitution adopts James Harrington's view on the necessity of a senate, a third of which should retire annually, but differs in most other respects. The author of *Oceana* put forth several tracts during 1659. His idea was that the people of England, although perhaps twenty to one for monarchy,[20] were deceived by the name, having of late been more arbitrarily governed than formerly. Therefore, when they called for the restoration of monarchy they were really expressing their wish "not to be at the will of men, but [to] return unto the Government of Laws."[21] The problem was to make this government by laws a reality and not to set up an unequal commonwealth which would permit domination by the few. At present the obstacle to an equal commonwealth was oligarchy. If a council of state summoned a parliament and failed to pack it, the council would be ruined, and if parliament was packed, then the same kind of oligarchy would exist as under king and parliament. The only way around this dilemma was to choose a senate of three hundred and a popular assembly of a thousand and fifty, each for three years with a third retiring annually. An election was a most complicated affair. A hundred parishes each chose every fifth man, who joined the fifth men from nineteen other hundreds similarly chosen. These electorates, fifty in all, would each nominate two senators and seven assemblymen every year. This method, concluded Harrington, would erect "an equal commonwealth, a work [that] never was nor can be done any otherwise."[22]

Outside the Harringtonian circle the advocates of a senate were mostly senior officers. They wanted a second chamber as the guardian of certain fundamental laws which would guarantee, among other essentials,

[20]Harrington thought there were not "fewer then fifty thousand of the more active and knowing that drive vigorous at a Commonwealth." *Pour Enclouer le Canon* (which Harrington dated May 2), p. 3.

[21]That government should be by laws and that all men should be equally accountable to the laws were two fundamentals of the Levellers' program. See *The Leveller: or, the Principles & Maxims concerning Government*, dated by Thomason February 16, 1659.

[22]Ibid., p. 8.

their own continual existence. Most writers, however, favored a single house, to be limited in power by a written constitution. Their schemes were many and varied. There was less unanimity about the origin of a constitution than about its contents, especially in the provisions dealing with economic and social reforms. One tract called upon the Rump to draw up a new Magna Charta and submit it to the people of every parish on a Sunday for their subscription. The writer was optimistic enough to believe that "the most part of the good people" would certainly sign a charter which promised so much for their freedom and benefit. The signatories having chosen a new representative to confirm the charter, it would become an unalterable law, and anyone trying to change it would be adjudged a traitor and punished as such. The proposal that Parliament, elected by all except the disaffected and dissolute, should sit for one year only out of three embodied the general dislike of a perpetual session. Before its dissolution Parliament would elect a council from among its members to administrate for the next two years.[23]

More usual than popular subscription was parliamentary adoption of a new constitution. The Quaker, Edward Byllynge, wished a parliament to be chosen by hundreds, each hundred to consist of ten united parishes. Religious persecutors were disqualified both as members and electors for the first parliament but delinquents and persons "subservient to a foreign state"[24] permanently. This parliament would establish the fundamental laws, and any future member who questioned them *ipso facto* expelled himself.[25] Like all the framers of constitutions at this time, Byllynge failed to provide for two contingencies—that the people or their representatives might be unable to agree or, to use the phrase of Rousseau, there might not be any general will, and that the constitution might require amending. The need for some provision to permit alteration should have been obvious. Recently both the Instrument of Government and the Humble Petition had failed to gain popular support. The optimism which inspired the drafters of a third constitution rested on no solid basis. They had only to read each other's proposals to see how far apart they were.

Perhaps reformers were nearer unanimity when dealing with the law and its administration than with any other subject. They agreed that it was incomprehensible to the layman and that its administration was too

[23]*Speculum Libertatis Angliae Rerestitutae: or the Looking-Glasse of Englands Liberties Really Restored*, dated by Thomason July 13.

[24]Presumably Roman Catholics.

[25]*A Mite of Affection, Manifested in 31 proposals*, dated by Thomason October 25. For identification of the author, analysis of contents, and comment on its author's contribution to the constitution of West New Jersey, see *Children of Light*, ed. Howard H. Brinton (New York, 1938), ch. v, by John L. Nickalls.

centralized, costly, slow, and uncertain. They wanted few laws and these to be equal for all conditions of men and readily understood by everyone. Trials should take place in local courts, but appeals to metropolitan courts were allowed, provided the appellant posted a bond which was forfeited if he failed to win his case. The judge should propound the law applicable to each case, and every man should be allowed to conduct his own cause. The court of chancery found no defenders, but some would permit ordinary courts to take into account equity and conscience. The land laws should be freed from all Norman accretions such as servile tenures and copyholds, which enslaved their victims to lords or, rather, tyrants of manors. All suits about property rights should be held within the county and should be publicly registered. The existing treatment of debtors was generally abhorrent. One writer would allow no imprisonment for debt, and another only if the debtor was suspected of an intention to decamp, and even he was to be given by his creditor three shillings for each day he was in gaol. The extraordinarily severe penalty proposed for unjust imprisonment for debt—five pounds an hour— suggests this was a real grievance. One proposal was to free the debtor from all further claims as soon as he had paid up all he had. Another offered the creditor alternative procedures: he could take all the debtor owned and lose all claims for the future, however rich the debtor might grow, or he might leave his victim a reasonable proportion of his assets and retain the right to collect the rest of what was due if the debtor prospered. The state of the prisons was roundly condemned. Byllynge called for the dismissal of harsh gaolers and the erection of strong, warm, and decent gaols with no dungeons or "little easies," or other nasty holes.

As for the poor, some writers were content to urge that no one should be allowed to suffer want or compelled to beg, but the able-bodied should be found work and be paid well for it, and the impotent provided for in a Christian manner. Others referred to specific grievances and remedies. An elaborate plan began with the erection in every market town or large parish of free-schools for the instruction of poor boys and girls, at least in reading, after which they were to be placed in service. Then no corporation was to enact any laws or enforce any usages which would deny to a free-born Englishman two liberties: to follow any trade or occupation anywhere he wished, whether he had served an apprenticeship or no; and to reside with his family in any place where he found work without running the risk of being returned to the place of his legal settlement or of being obliged to give security that he would not become chargeable to the parish.

As regards trade, the policy of the Navigation Act of 1651 was clearly popular. One "J.S." proclaimed it "that never to be forgotten Act . . . the Glory and Top of their [Rump's] Great Advice; if it had been continued and duly Executed, *England* had been the most happy, and most rich People this day upon the face of the whole Earth: they had been the Ware-house of the World."[26] On the other hand he denounced the war with Spain as destructive of trade. Another writer repeated the clause in the Act against the importation of merchandise in foreign bottoms unless it was the genuine product of the country to which the importing ships belonged. He also approved of the English claim to the sovereignty of the narrow seas, and demanded the encouragement of fishing which was of "vast benefit to the Hollander." He was against monopolies of trade or farming of taxes as being tyrannous, oppressive, and vexatious.[27] A third pamphleteer argued that trade had never flourished under the kings of England. Under their rule a gentleman preferred his son to be bred up for the gallows rather than dishonored by a trade. It had always been a maxim with monarchs to keep the unruly plebeians from being "over pursey, least their wits should increase with their wealth, and they should begin to contend for their Privileges," but projectors and patentees were encouraged to "eat out the heart and keep the Merchant as bare as my nail." Under the Commonwealth, however, gentlemen's sons had been apprenticed and "the best gentry of England, are very desirous, and do daily match their Daughters into the City." This remarkable change had happened although recently trade had been so "miserable bad" that it had afforded a comfortable livelihood to a third only of those engaged in it.[28] Among suggestions to improve domestic trade were that weights and measures should be uniform and free trade be established between England, Scotland, and Ireland.[29]

What to do with the army was an awkward problem. Harrington felt that while a commonwealth was being formed a standing army was essential but when the government and the militia were established, then the army should be disbanded and given half pay for life.[30] Others conceded the necessity of an army but would limit it to ten thousand or so. The Levellers, however, denounced all mercenary soldiers and advocated a kind of universal military training. Although the cost of the

---

[26]*The Continuation of this Session of Parliament, Justified* (pp. 11-12), dated by Thomason May 16. The author does not indicate how Cromwell failed to enforce the Navigation Act, but he may have had in mind the system of licenses which did weaken it.

[27]*Speculum*, p. 17.

[28]*The Grand Concernments*, pp. 16, 34.

[29]Byllynge, *A Mite of Affection.* Proposals 23 and 28.

[30]*Aphorisms Political* (2d ed., 1659), Nos. xcv-xcviii. I have assumed that the phrase "the Military and Provincial Parts" means the militia, but Harrington's meaning is not very clear. The *Oxford English Dictionary* dates the first use of the term half pay as 1664.

army was responsible for the great increase in taxation few pamphleteers seem to have traced cause and effect. Considering how heavy the burden of taxes was, there were surprisingly few suggestions of how to raise them in a more equitable manner. One writer did propose to levy them only on those best able to pay, whom he defined as possessors of ample or at least adequate means. The exceptions he made were customs and excise, to be levied only on strong drink. One visionary wanted all taxes and excise to be abolished and never reimposed, and free trade for all victuals, ammunition, and materials imported and for all manufactures exported. Another of his proposals was: "To indeavour a maintenance for souldiers that have been for the Good Old Cause, without Taxes or Oppression of the People."[31]

As for toleration, practically all Republican writers favored it, though most excepted the Roman Catholics. The Church of England was generally proscribed because its members were Royalists. One writer was willing that Anglicans and Presbyterians should enjoy liberty of conscience only if they refrained from attacks on the Commonwealth. He referred approvingly to No. XLI of Harrington's *Aphorisms*: "Where the minor part taketh away the National Religion, there the major part is deprived of the Liberty of Conscience by the minor." Therefore he supported a state church and the maintenance of ministers by tithes, which many sectaries wanted to abolish.[32]

Since such Utopian ideas engrossed the minds of its supporters, the restored Long Parliament faced a most difficult position. To prepare themselves for their ordeal, members fasted on Sunday, May 8, and listened to a sermon by John Owen. He took his text from Isaiah 4:5, and compared members to the very small remnant that preserved the Jews from the fate of Sodom and Gomorrah, to a brand plucked out of the fire, and to those that were left after great trials and desolations. "All is blessed and prosperous for their sakes." But he then went on to lament that the nation was being overwhelmed by a profane, wicked, carnal spirit, contemptuous of all the work of reformation that had been attempted, so that in many places the very profession of religion had become a scorn while in others the old forms and ways were taken up greedily. "I pray God we lose not our ground faster than we won it."[33]

In the biblical language of the time, Owen pointed his finger at an insurmountable obstacle—the conservative reaction that had set in. What was most serious was that the Republicans had to encounter not

[31]*The Declaration and Proclamation of the Army of God* (1659), p. 4.
[32]*Speculum*, p. 14.
[33]*The Glory and Interest of Nations Professing the Gospel* (1659). This sermon, not reproduced by Orme, proves how Owen had identified himself with the destruction of the Protectorate.

only the active hostility of Royalists and of many erstwhile Parliamentarians, but also the indifference or passive resistance of a large class of Englishmen alienated by the efforts to enforce what was generally called the work of reformation. At the dawn of the Puritan Revolution members of this group had lent a sympathetic ear to the preachers' exhortations, but in its twilight they had grown skeptical. They had become irritated by intrusive Puritan morality, by its interference with their daily habits. They had not yet reached the point of open revolt. Indeed, their aloofness from the political arena was marked. Yet once there was a prospect of more "cakes and ale," the voice of the people would be heard on every side. But the members of Parliament that now assmbled at Westminster seem to have been troubled by no misgivings.

At their first meeting (May 7), they read the declaration the army had issued the previous day and then drew up one of their own. It contained three promises: to establish a commonwealth without a king, single person, or house of lords, to carry on the reformation, and to secure a godly magistracy and ministry. They appointed a committee of safety[34] for eight days, subsequently extended until the council of state was established, and then adjourned. As a shrewd observer noted, Parliament and council of state contained such a diversity of interests and complexions that no harmony was likely to prevail.[35] The next meeting on May 9 was disturbed by the attempt of William Prynne, Sir George Booth, Arthur Annesley, and other secluded members to take their seats. According to Prynne's list[36] there were 213 members still alive who had been shut out of the House at one time or another. The victims of Pride's Purge outnumbered the Royalists previously expelled by about two to one. Although the indomitable Prynne caused some embarrassment by taking his seat on May 9, he and the rest were shut out by the rule that those who had not sat since 1648 and had not subscribed the Engagement to be faithful to the Commonwealth should not sit. But if he could not raise his voice in Parliament to protest against the claim of the Rump to represent the people, he used his pen to expose its absurdity.[37]

The Long Parliament at once took steps to increase its members. The

[34]May 7. The original members were Hesilrige, Vane, Ludlow, Sydenham, Salwey, and John Jones. On May 9 the committee asked that Lambert, Disbrowe, and James Berry be added. The House agreed but included Scot. In dealing with transactions in the Commons, the insertion of the exact day saves any other reference to the *Journals*.

[35]Sharp's letter of May 12. *Register of Consultations*, II, 180.

[36]Reprinted in the old *Parliamentary History*, XXI, 372-75.

[37]For his pamphlets see *Thomason Tracts* under May 7, 13, 30, 31. David Masson's contemptuous description of Prynne as "a rhinoceros in blinkers" is very superficial, because he delivered many shrewd blows at the restored Long Parliament, and rallied public opinion to the cause of the secluded members and the old constitution.

Speaker addressed letters[38] to all survivors who had taken the Engagement and had not been disqualified by the present Parliament, but the response is unknown. Masson, after a careful scrutiny of the membership of committees recorded in the *Journals* and of lists published at the time, came to the conclusion that about 122 took their seats at one time or another.[39] Of these, about one third were original members and two thirds "recruiters"—members elected, often irregularly, to fill vacancies. The greatest number known to have been present on any day is seventy-eight,[40] but it is likely that the average attendance was not more than sixty and may well have been about fifty.

The House passed a resolution that all in positions of trust should be persons fearing God who had given testimony of their fidelity to the cause of the Commonwealth. One committee was appointed to examine the state of the public revenues and how they might be improved,[41] and another to consider what persons were imprisoned for conscience sake and how they might be discharged.[42] An act was passed to empower justices of the peace and sheriffs of May 6 to continue the exercise of their functions, and to provide that legal proceedings should be carried on in the name of the keepers of the liberties of England by authority of Parliament.[43] Seven were appointed to nominate officers for commissions in the land forces, and Fleetwood was made lieutenant general and commander in chief of the armies in England and Scotland.[44] The House then received and read a petition from the army presented by Lambert and other officers. The petitioners were thanked for their good affections but were not told that all they asked would be granted.[45]

The petitioners began by referring in general terms to their determination to recover and secure some of the fundamentals of their good old cause. They felt it their duty, therefore, to represent what they had in mind when they opened the way for the return of the Long Parliament. Then followed fifteen separate requirements. Seven of these were accepted by the House in the very words of the petition. These dealt with the establishment of a free commonwealth; regulation of law and courts of justice; protection for all who believed in the Trinity and

[38]A specimen is in *Commons Journals*, VII, 645, and the old *Parliamentary History*, XXI, 378.

[39]David H. Masson, *The Life of John Milton*, VI (1894), 453-54. The list is elaborately annotated to show the previous parliaments in which members had sat, who were regicides, etc.

[40]May 14. Under the date June 1, the *Weekly Intelligencer* printed a list of "all those Honourable Personages who do now sit in this present Parliament." They numbered 114.

[41]May 9.

[42]May 10.

[43]May 11.

[44]May 12. The seven were Fleetwood, Lambert, Hesilrige, Disbrowe, Berry, Vane, and Ludlow.

[45]May 12. The petition is reprinted in the old *Parliamentary History*, XXI, 400-405.

accepted the Scriptures as "the revealed or written word or will of God," provided they were not prelatists or papists or disturbers of public worship; maintenance of a godly and "painful Gospel-preaching ministry"; reformation of universities; reservation of public positions to supporters of the good old cause; and a succession of parliaments.[46] The third clause was not discussed inasmuch as its subject matter had already been covered by an order to bring in a bill of indemnity. Clauses four and five, proposing that all laws passed and all debts incurred since April 19, 1653, should be recognized as valid, were referred to a committee for examination and recommendation. Clause nine, which requested the removal from office of Royalists and ungodly people, was to be considered by a grand committee of the whole House. Clause twelve was ignored as Fleetwood had already been named commander in chief. Clauses thirteen to fifteen were reserved for discussion by a grand committee. Clause thirteen sought to place legislative power in a House chosen by the people and a select senate, "co-ordinate in power, of able and faithful persons, eminent for godliness and such as continue adhering to this cause." Clause fourteen concerned a council of state which was to be the "executive power of government." Taken together, these two clauses constituted the minimum provisions for curbing the arbitrariness of the Commons the army would accept. The fifteenth and last clause proposed the payment of Richard Cromwell's debts, the settlement of £10,000 upon his heirs forever, and £8,000 upon his mother. The House agreed to appoint a committee to investigate the debts. A committee was named to consider the condition of Richard, described as "the eldest son of the late Lord General Cromwell." At the same time the decision was taken to sell Whitehall and Somerset House to help pay the arrears due to the army. Some Quakers would have bought Somerset House to hold meetings in, but George Fox prevented them, "for I did foresee the King's coming in again at that time."[47]

The House intended Richard to evacuate the palace and become a private gentleman. He hesitated for some days, hoping that the forces in distant parts would remain loyal to the Protectorate and telling his brother Henry that he had heard nothing from Scotland or Dunkirk or the fleet.[48] But Richard had allowed the time for intervention on his

---

[46]May 21. The above clauses were numbered 1, 2, 6, 7, 8, 10, and 11.

[47]*Journal*, p. 355.

[48]Two undated and unsigned letters written to Henry are in the Lansdowne MSS and printed in the *American Historical Review*, VIII, 86-89, ed. Ralph C. H. Catterall, who dated them May 12 and 17. When Henry received them is uncertain but on May 23 he declared he had not heard from Richard "for some time before the last parliament was dissolved." Thurloe, VII, 674. Richard was declared exempt from arrest for debt for six months, told on July 5 to leave Whitehall within six days, and given £2000 on his removal to his father-in-law's house at Hursley. Register, July 2, 5, 6.

behalf to pass. Possibly if he had appealed to Monck, Lockhart, and Mountagu before he dissolved Parliament they might have responded. As the champion of parliamentary liberties he might have been supported by parts of the armies in Scotland and Ireland and by the ships under Mountagu, but few, if any, would have fought merely to retain him as a nominal Protector. Some six months later a Royalist correspondent told Hyde that Monck had said: "Richard Cromwell forsook himself, else had I never failed my promise to his Father, or regard to his memory."[49] Apparently, about the time of the dissolution of Parliament Richard listened to overtures from Royalists. His attitude led John Mordaunt to believe that he was going to order Mountagu to sail to Dunkirk, embark the garrison with Lockhart's consent, and make for Portsmouth, where Colonel Norton would cooperate. He was also expected to direct his brother Henry to declare for the King in Ireland. But either his courage failed, as all Royalists assert, or he could not lend himself to an attempt to undo his father's work, and he refused to sign the letters Broderick had prepared.[50]

Assurances were soon forthcoming that the armed forces outside England would accept the Rump.[51] On May 18 Vane reported from the Committee of Safety that Lockhart had promised his utmost endeavors to defend Dunkirk for the Commonwealth, and to keep the garrison there, together with the three English regiments in the French service, in obedience to the present government. Lockhart also utilized the opportunity to request that the soldiers' "subsistence" should be continued, the officers' spirits refreshed by payment of arrears, and his own salary as ambassador, of which nearly £5,000 was owing, be given him. He also announced that he should observe the truce between France and Spain, which had started on May 1, until further orders. The House referred his report to the Council of State.[52] More important than Lockhart's acceptance of the *coup d'état* was Monck's announcement to the House

[49]Broderick to Hyde, December 16, 1659, *Clarendon State Papers*, III, 628. Thomas Gumble, in his *Life of General Monck* (1671), p. 97, stated that Monck "had certainly marched" into England if Richard had not dissolved Parliament, not to support the Cromwellians but to restore the Stuarts. The first part of the sentence is probably true but not the second. Cf. Pepys, *Diary*, June 21, 1660.

[50]Mordaunt to the King, May 11, and Broderick to Hyde, May 23, *Clarendon State Papers*, III, 469, 477-78. On April 30/May 10 Hyde wrote that he was not sorry Cromwell had refused Sir William Waller and his friends the commissions they desired, because the writer had no proof that Cromwell would serve the King. A possible inference from these statements is that Richard declined to cooperate with Royalists so long as there was any chance of remaining Protector, was then tempted, but after hesitation decided to acquiesce in his own downfall.

[51]As early as May 9 letters from Monck and from Ireland were read in the House of Commons, showing that the forces in Scotland concurred with the English army, and that some at least of the officers in Ireland were in favor of the good old cause. *Journals*, VII, 647.

[52]*Commons Journals*, VII, 657; Lockhart's letter to the Committee of Safety, May 17, describing his officers' acceptance of the new government is in Thurloe, VII, 670-671.

the same day.[53] The general and his officers addressed a letter to Fleetwood and the general council of officers which expressed the joy felt at the late proceedings of the army in England which had after so many years returned to its former engagements. They besought their fellow soldiers to lay aside any private interest and advance men of holy, strict, and religious conversation, to see that provision was made for Richard and his family, to maintain, as free-born Englishmen and not mercenaries, the just liberties of the whole people, and assert the freedom and privileges of their representatives, the members of the restored Long Parliament.[54]

By this time Richard saw the end had come, so he signed a declaration drawn up by the committee named above and at the same time submitted a schedule of his debts.[55] In the former he asserted that he valued the peace of the Commonwealth above his own interests and intended to live peacefully under the present government. The debts he inherited from his father or incurred for affairs of state amounted to £29,000. As to the family property, estates yielding £2,000 had been settled on Henry, £1,200 on Frances, leaving £4,100 for himself, but this was charged with annuities to the amount of £2,800, including £2,000 to his mother. His private debts amounted to £3,000. The House accepted Richard's declaration, which may be regarded as his formal abdication, agreed to assume his public debts, voted him £2,000 immediately, and named a committee to consider a comfortable subsistence for him.[56]

[53]For some particulars about the mission of Henry Monck, sent to his uncle in Scotland by Henry Cromwell to sound the general, see *Clarke Papers,* IV, ii.

[54]May 12, Thurloe, VII, 669-70. Whether the last sentence was intended as a hint that the army in England should refrain from any further interference with a parliament there is no means of telling.

[55]A Royalist wrote unkindly: "Tumble downe Dick hath kissed the tayle" (*Nicholas Papers,* IV, 148). Other slighting phrases applied to Richard in the rude verses of the time were "Queen Dick" and "a very Dick." The caricature, a copy of which is at Worcester College, Oxford, of him as an owl, reproduced in *Clarke Papers,* III, was on sale by June 24 (*Nicholas Papers,* IV, 160).

[56]Richard's declaration was undated but accepted by the Commons on May 25 and printed in the *Journals,* along with the schedule of debts.

CHAPTER VII

The Rump in Power

ONE of the first tasks confronting the Rump was to form an administration. Apart from such authority as it delegated to the Council and committees, it combined both legislative and executive functions. The Speaker was again first in precedence as he had been nominally from 1649 to 1653. Distrust of a single person can be seen in the reluctance to entrust individuals with power. Thurloe, the Cromwells' Secretary of State, was not reappointed and no one took his place.[1] The great officers of state were replaced by committees and commissions. Of these bodies the most important was the Council of State established by an Act of May 19, 1659. There were thirty-one members, twenty-one were M.P.'s and ten outsiders. The first group was chosen by ballot after much debate, Hesilrige, Vane, and Ludlow heading the list. That three staunch Republicans secured more votes than any of the army malcontents was significant. Of the seven outsiders nominated without ballot, the inclusion of Fairfax was a useless compliment because he withdrew to Yorkshire and never took his seat. Lambert, Disbrowe, and Berry were rewarded for the part they had taken in upsetting Richard Cromwell. Bradshaw, not long for this world, may have owed his position to his defiance of Oliver Cromwell in 1653. His first attendance was at the afternoon session of July 22. A surprise motion when the House was on the point of rising was said to be responsible for the nomination of Sir Anthony Ashley Cooper and Sir Horatio Townshend. The former had already showed that he was no stickler for principle, while the latter, a cousin of Fairfax, was a Royalist who sought Charles II's permission to sit.[2] The best known of the three outsiders chosen by ballot was Archibald Johnston of Wariston. He had opposed the recall of the Rump, but was nominated by Vane, who reminded members that Wariston, in the other house, had protested against the bill to recognize Richard as Protector. Inasmuch as the House declined to recognize the Cromwellian union with Scotland and directed their members who sat in the Council to consider the question, a Scottish representative was obviously needed.[3]

[1] See his life in *DNB* for the various duties he performed for the Cromwells.

[2] *Publick Intelligencer*, p. 432; *Clarendon Calendar*, IV, 204; Ludlow, II, 83; Masson, V, 456, for an annotated list. The Minute Book of Proceedings of the Council of State from May 19 to August 10 is in the Bodleian Library, Rawlinson MSS C. 179, and a film of it in the Huntington Library. It shows that Townshend never attended, and that Cooper attended with fair regularity until July 8 but not afterwards.

[3] Wariston's *Diary*, III, 106, 113; *Commons Journals*, VII, 658.

A perusal of the membership of the Council at once suggests two characteristics. The presence of twenty-one M.P.'s, including the Republican leaders who had so skillfully led the opposition to the court party in Richard's Parliament, more than a third of the number of members usually present in the House, meant that the Council's recommendations were likely to be accepted by the Rump. The second feature is that members who firmly believed in the subordination of the military to the civil power were in the majority. Men like Hesilrige and Ludlow, Scot and Bradshaw, who had braved the wrath of Oliver Cromwell, were never likely to submit to dictation from Fleetwood or Lambert. Fixed in their conviction that they represented the people of England,[4] they would never stoop to conciliate the military. The officers realized that they had been outmaneuvred or outvoted, and did not hesitate to show their chagrin at the composition of the Council. According to Ludlow, they seldom came to the Council and when present, behaved with perversity and insolence.[5] As the first part of this charge can be disproved by the record of attendances, the second may be exaggerated. They did boggle at subscribing to the oath to maintain the Commonwealth "as it is declared by Parliament without a single person kingship or house of peers," but they took advantage of the permission of Parliament and substituted a declaration of the same tenor as the oath.[6]

The act constituting the Council of State gave it very extensive powers and instructions. Among its many duties were the suppression of Royalist revolts, to which end it could direct the militia and the armed forces by land and sea. It could administer an oath to anyone, imprison all who were disobedient to orders issued in pursuance of its instructions, and prevent any meetings it might judge dangerous. It was entrusted with the encouragement of trade and the conduct of relations with foreign powers. It was authorized to charge the public revenue with the expenses of foreign negotiations, intelligence, and the salaries of such subordinate officers as it might employ. In addition, it could consult about anything concerning the good of the Commonwealth and advise Parliament about the same, and should carry out such further orders as it might receive from Parliament from time to time.[7]

The Council appointed its chairmen for short periods, often extended. Its clerk was Captain Richard Dean, with whom Henry Scobell was later

[4]For a very trenchant criticism of this claim, see Masson, V, 457-59.

[5]Ludlow, II, 84-85. Actually out of 114 possible attendances, Berry made 51, Disbrowe and Fleetwood 52, Lambert 59, and Sydenham 44. Considering the military duties officers performed at the time of Booth's rising, their attendance was much better than the figures suggest.

[6]Register, May 25 and later dates. For a speech, probably by Wariston, against the oath, see *Clarke Papers*, IV, 11-15.

[7]*Acts and Ordinances*, II, 1272-76.

associated. It carried on its business through committees, some *ad hoc*, some permanent. A report that Royalists designed a general insurrection led to the appointment of four to examine a London gunsmith, arrested on suspicion of furnishing arms to the enemies of the Commonwealth. Two days later Fleetwood, Salwey, Scot, Sydenham, and Vane were named as a committee to discover plots and to manage intelligence both foreign and domestic, the contemporary description of the modern secret service.[8] Six members were to consider all matters concerning the English plantations in foreign parts.[9] Eight, headed by Wariston, were to prepare drafts of acts pertaining to the union with Scotland and the administration of justice there.[10] One committee is conspicuous by its absence—for foreign affairs. From time to time members were required to interview the representatives of the United Provinces, Denmark, and other powers or to peruse their communications, but they were not always the same individuals. On one occasion, Algernon Sidney, Scot, Whitelocke, and Honeywood were detailed to meet Nieuport, the Dutch ambassador, and on another Vane, Lambert, Wariston, and Honeywood.[11] Seven were directed to meet from time to time with the Swedish envoys.[12] When the Council received definite information that a rising was planned, it set up two standing committees: one, including Bradshaw who had not previously attended but who emerged from retirement (probably due to ill health) now that the republic was in danger, to examine all apprehended on suspicion of complicity; and the other, consisting of members who were army officers, to act as a committee of safety to execute the Council's orders for the preservation of the public peace.[13]

The Council differed from a modern cabinet in many ways. It had no prime minister; none of its members headed departments of state, although some belonged to commissions that controlled such departments; not all members sat in Parliament; parliamentary votes rejecting conciliar advice led to no resignations; and collective responsibility was not recognized as essential. Some of the most important subjects of which the Council took cognizance are discussed elsewhere—foreign relations, Scottish and Irish affairs, and the precautions taken against insurrection. Among the significant topics that troubled the Council from the start was the lack of money. On June 18 the Council ordered Hesilrige to re-

[8]Register, May 22, 24.
[9]Ibid., May 30. The six were: Chaloner, Scot, Sydenham, Honeywood, Thompson, and Berners.
[10]Ibid., May 31, afternoon. There was also an Irish committee of fifteen named the same day.
[11]Ibid., May 20, June 2.
[12]Ibid., June 23.
[13]Ibid., July 23, 29.

port to Parliament how the conduct of business was greatly hampered by want of money, the army and navy both in great need, and the weekly income disproportionate to the constant charge. But the sole remedy the Council proposed was the speedy collection of the very great sums owing the Commonwealth said to be in private hands. The delusion that any substantial amount could be extracted from farmers of taxes and other individuals perhaps reconciled members to the postponement of the evil day when either new taxes would be imposed or the state would go bankrupt. To tide the government over the immediate crisis the Council tried to borrow £30,000 from the East India Company on the security of the monthly assessment. Perhaps to influence the merchants concerned, frigates were ordered to ply between the latitudes of 49 and 50 degrees to protect shipping from Barbados and the East Indies. Public credit being bad, the Company lent only £15,000 and this to be repaid out of its "own growing customs." At the same time it petitioned for reparations for injuries suffered in the Indies and for "a free trade in all places there."[14] An appeal to the City of London for a loan of £15,000 seems to have elicited no favorable response.[15]

One feature of the Council Register is the complete absence of any reference to the work of reformation. The recommendation to Parliament that horse races, cock fighting, hurling, cudgel playing, football, and other unlawful assemblies should be forbidden was inspired by the wish to prevent meetings for recreations from being used by Cavaliers to plot treason. The recommendation was not followed by a proclamation to enforce it.[16] Whereas the Privy Council of Richard had devoted much time to improving ministers' stipends by uniting adjacent benefices, no evidence shows that its successor ever spent a minute for this purpose. Almost the only entries in the Register of an ecclesiastical nature refer to John Rogers, granted £50 to furnish him with necessaries for his journey into Ireland to preach the gospel there.[17] There are two items of literary interest: one shows that Andrew Marvell had lodgings in Whitehall, and the other is a petition from John Denham for leave to come to London for the cure of his lameness.[18] Among the entries of an economic or social nature are an order prohibiting the export of "any frames or engines for knit-workers of silk stockings," a description of Liverpool as "an open small market town,"[19] and a long list of the articles to be supplied from Whitehall for the service of the commissioners to Sweden and Denmark. Abundance of plate was described, including ten

[14]June 21, 30.
[16]May 28, July 12.
[18]July 14, 16, 18.

[15]June 30.
[17]July 13, 16.
[19]June 14, 15.

tumblers "to shut together."[20] The pieces of tapestry included seven of the naked boys, six of Samson and Delilah, six landscapes ("landskips"), and five of the five senses. Kitchen utensils were in profusion, especially for cooking meat and fish.[21] Two orders earn the gratitude of historians: one for an inspection of the state paper office in Whitehall to see what repairs were necessary to keep it dry, and the other for a grant of £50 for presses for the records of Parliament.[22]

So far as any conclusion can be drawn from a perusal of the respective Registers, the Council of State was more important than Richard's Privy Council, dealing with more significant topics and meeting oftener. Indeed, members who also had parliamentary duties must have toiled daily from morn to night. They met early so as to be free to take their places in the legislature, and not infrequently they sat in the Council chamber again in the afternoon. In addition, they often served on committees both parliamentary and conciliar. It is small wonder that they seem to have acted at times like tired, irritable men.

In addition to setting up the Council of State, the Rump passed other acts to make provision for the service of the state. Commissioners were named to bring in the arrears of revenue due since April 20, 1653.[23] Twelve M.P.'s, colonels, and merchants were appointed to manage the affairs of the admiralty and navy. They could issue warrants for the repair and equipment of vessels, prepare lists of captains and other officers, together with the salaries they recommended, for parliamentary approbation, and dismiss any officers under the rank of captain. They were to furnish Parliament with an account of all ships belonging to the navy, remove all corruptions and abuses, and prevent waste or embezzlement of stores.[24] A third act appointed Fleetwood commander in chief under the Parliament of the armies in England and Scotland. His authority was circumscribed by his subjection to the orders of Parliament or Council of State. He was not given the right to commission or promote army officers.[25] Indeed, the Rump had already associated Lambert, Hesilrige, Disbrowe, Berry, Vane, and Ludlow with Fleetwood as commissioners to nominate officers.[26] Later, Parliament amended a bill appointing the commissioners by rejecting a clause which had empowered Fleetwood to grant commissions and inserting instead a clause that all commissions

[20]The first example in *OED* of tumbler meaning a drinking cup is dated 1664.
[21]June 29.
[22]July 6, 8.
[23]*Acts and Ordinances*, II, 1276-77, May 26.
[24]Ibid., pp. 1277-82, May 31.
[25]Ibid., pp. 1283-84, June 7.
[26]*Commons Journals*, May 13. The statement in *Calendar Venetian* (p. 24) that Lambert was responsible for the nomination of commissioners in order to prevent Fleetwood from attaining the position to which he (Lambert) aspired is improbable.

should be signed by the Speaker and should run as follows: "The Parliament of the Commonwealth of England do constitute and appoint you [name] . . . colonel [or other rank]."[27] It is noteworthy that in the commissions, obedience to Parliament or Council of State was placed before obedience to a superior officer.

These proceedings were intended as a warning that henceforth the army was to be subordinate to the Parliament. A minority in the Rump, including Vane, Salwey, and Ludlow, opposed the clauses certain to be disliked by the army leaders, but Hesilrige, Algernon Sidney, and Neville prevailed. At first it looked doubtful whether the grandees of the army would yield. At a meeting at Disbrowe's house, Lambert voiced the general discontent and denounced the affront to the army implied in the proviso making the duration of a commission depend upon the pleasure of Parliament, contrary to the promises made before the recall of the Rump. The reply was that the promises bound individuals only, not the House as a whole, and that the officers concerned had been continued in their commands. It was urged that the actions of Parliament should be judged in the most favorable light, especially as members had voted on June 6 that the House should be dissolved not later than May 7, 1660, thus showing that they did not intend to perpetuate their power. Another argument was the need for unity because the sole hope of their enemies was in their divisions. The meeting apparently closed with Disbrowe's challenging remark that the commission he already had was as good as any the Parliament could give.[28] The next day apparently brought calmer moods. Hacker and his officers appeared in the Commons and each received his commission from the Speaker. The example was generally followed and for weeks the House often spent part of the day in witnessing the delivery of commissions. But most of the officers had first to be scrutinized by the seven commissioners and, if they survived this ordeal, to be approved by Parliament.

Some minutes of "the committee of safety and for nomination of officers" are among the state papers. Though incomplete, these are full of interest because they sometimes indicate the motives which moved the members to grant favors to some and to cashier others. The first day's proceedings to be recorded are for June 16. Then consideration was given first to the officers of the Irish army now in England and to those cashiered "irregularly." Five were named to command regiments.[29] Matthew

---

[27]I have never seen the text of this bill but its contents are clear from *Commons Journals*, June 6 to 8. Like commissions were to be used for the navy.

[28]Ludlow, II, 89-90; *Clarke Papers*, IV, 17.

[29]Thomas Cooper, Richard Lawrence, John Clark, and Alexander Brayfield, foot, and Hierome Sankey, horse.

Alured, one of the three colonels who were cashiered by Cromwell in 1654, was to be offered a regiment of foot in England or of horse in Ireland—eventually he commanded a regiment of horse in England. Overton, who had lost his command when implicated in the plot against Cromwell which bears his name, was to have his regiment of foot back and to be governor of Hull. John Mason was offered the governorship of Jersey or Inverness or a foot regiment, and chose the first. When the officers of Packer's regiment[30] were discussed, one cornet was replaced as "old and scandalous" and another for "playing at table Lord's day." The quartermaster was accused of keeping a woman and giving her £3 a month. Of the six officers dismissed by Cromwell for disaffection early in 1658, four were reinstated. Rich, reappointed to his old regiment which he had lost at the end of 1654 on account of Fifth Monarchy sympathies and which had been lately led by Richard Ingoldsby, seems to have had satisfactory officers, except for a quartermaster alleged to have been "much for the last Parliament."[31]

On June 17 a lieutenant, William Thomlinson, claimed that he had been turned out because he was not of his colonel's opinions, but Colonel Sanders asserted he had resigned in 1650, pleading he was lame and unable to take part in the invasion of Scotland. He was not readmitted to the army. The Committee could not agree about Captain Thomas Pride, so it made no recommendation to Parliament. Captain Charles Duckett, who had left the army in 1647 and been later reinstated, was now recommended for a captaincy, testimony being brought that he had fought valiantly at Newbury and against Middleton in Scotland, that he had responded promptly to the order to bring his troop into St. James's Fields last April, that he was a changed man and had often complained of the corruptions of Cromwell's court.[32] When Barkstead's regiment's turn came, one officer was accused of drinking and horse racing, a second of keeping company with naughty women, a third of being a drunkard, a fourth of not being "very well affected," and a fifth of being cashiered for drinking though subsequently named an ensign. The charges against three of the five seem to have been judged as proved.[33] The most surprising recommendations were those of William Butler (or Boteler) as quartermaster general, because this was the unpopular major general whose impeachment had been voted in the last Parliament, and of Ed-

---

[30]This was originally one of the two regiments formed from the Ironsides, and Packer had been its major until his dismissal in 1658.

[31]*Calendar Domestic*, pp. 375-76.

[32]Ibid., p. 378.

[33]Ibid., pp. 384, 395. Barkstead was replaced both as colonel and as governor of the Tower by Thomas Fitch, a stout Republican and protégé of Hesilrige.

ward Whalley, a staunch Cromwellian. Perhaps Hesilrige, Ludlow, and Vane were outvoted: they can hardly have supported either officer.[34] When Butler's case was debated in the House, a paper was read entitled "A Short relation of the unjust and arbitrary dealing of William Butler . . . one of the late major-generals . . . towards Wm. Lowell of Harding-ton in the county of Northampton." This recital was fatal to Butler's chances of appointment. The proposal that Whalley be colonel of horse was negatived by twenty-nine to twenty-two votes, Vane and Neville being tellers for the majority. The regiment was given to Alured.[35]

How many officers were discharged during the six months between the dissolution of Richard's Parliament and the ejection of the Rump in October is unknown. In an unsigned letter of June 14 the statement is made that about 160 officers, ranging from colonels to quartermasters, had been put out "without hearing, without charge, without tryall."[36] Most of these were Cromwellians, expelled by the army itself, the seven commissioners having had little time to act when the letter was written. But some officers lost their commissions because they were not recom-mended by the commissioners or because Parliament declined to accept the recommendations. After the breach with Parliament the general council of the officers bitterly complained that the resolution that all commissions should be handed out by the Speaker opened a way "to cast out whom they pleased, without so much as [a] hearing. . . . What fac-tions hereupon grew up in the army, what new moulding, changing and transforming thereof (to the discomposure of the whole) how parties were made, headed, and encouraged by divers members sitting in Par-liament, and strengthened, not only by bringing divers persons into com-mand of prejudiced mindes, but by removing faithful officers into remote parts of this Commonwealth, without any cause shewen, or consultations had with the Commander in Chief thereupon, was not onely notoriously known by those, who are concerned in military affairs, but obvious to common observations."[37]

A vigorous reply to this declaration asserted that in reality the army leaders were responsible for "modellizing" the regiments, because as they alleged, Hesilrige, Ludlow, and Vane were strangers to the whole army. Parliament always accepted the lists the commissioners sent it, provided five of the seven set their hands to the lists.[38] The only excep-

[34]Ibid., p. 384.

[35]*Commons Journals*, July 4, Aug. 5.

[36]*Clarke Papers*, IV, 21.

[37]*A Declaration of the General Council of the Officers of the Army*, Oct. 27, p. 6.

[38]The need for five signatures seems rather inconsistent with the previous statement that the four soldiers prevailed.

tions were Whalley, Butler, and Captain Goffe.[39] Moreover, though there were serious charges against Colonels Kelsey and Gibbons and Major Daborn (or Daberon), the House gave way. As to the charge that faithful officers were sent into remote parts, there were only four captains who refused to own Fitch as Lieutenant of the Tower,[40] probably because they were unwilling to change places with officers from Fitch's regiment stationed at Aberdeen.

Though the *Journals* afford proof that the Rump made a few more changes than its defender would allow, the point at issue was not one of mere figures. The plain fact was that the army leaders had lost the struggle they had been waging ever since Richard had succeeded his father as Protector. They had sought in vain two concessions, that Fleetwood should be given the authority to commission officers which Essex, Fairfax, and Cromwell had enjoyed,[41] and that officers should not be cashiered unless found guilty by a court-martial. That they accepted their defeat, although with bitterness and reluctance, was due to a consciousness that the inferior officers and the rank and file had more confidence in the Rump than in them, and that there was no alternative to the Rump except the naked rule of the sword or a Stuart restoration. The antimilitarism of Richard's Parliament had shown that to appeal from the Rump to the electorate would be to jump from the frying pan into the fire.

The Rump itself, however, entirely failed to appreciate its peculiar position. It was indispensable only to a relatively small fraction of the nation—the Republicans. A free election or the readmission of the members excluded earlier by Pride's Purge would immediately place the Rumpers in a hopeless minority. The day that the military guard was withdrawn from its door, the House would contain a majority hostile both to the English army leaders and to the Republicans. Therefore, to ensure the continuance of the present régime, an alliance between army and Rump was essential. Vane perceived this self-evident truth, and Ludlow sometimes saw it, but Hesilrige, Scot, Neville, and their adherents never realized it.[42] They had insisted on a course of action certain to anger the English army leaders, and they now proceeded to affront the officer who of all others was most likely to respect the civil authority.

[39]The William Gough, major in Monck's regiment of foot, who was recommended for a captaincy in Whalley's regiment of horse.

[40]*The Declaration of the Officers of the Army Opened, Examined & Condemned*, by E. D., pp. 20-22. Thomason did not date his copy but mine has written in it "3 10 1659," and 6d. The author, E. D., I regret I cannot identify.

[41]Firth, *Cromwell's Army*, p. 48.

[42]They were faced with the difficulty that the army leaders were growing more and more determined to be the predominant partner.

When General Monck heard that Parliament was making changes among the officers, he addressed a request to it through the Speaker that it would not alter any of the officers in Scotland because they had at once acquiesced in the establishment of a Commonwealth and were very faithful to it. If the House declined to grant his request for all his regiments, he particularly asked that his own two regiments and Talbot's should be left alone.[43] A brusque reply was returned. Monck was told that it was of "high concernment for the settlement of the nation" to ensure that officers would be "really faithful to the Commonwealth." During the late changes "great discoveries of men" had been made, and "peradventure, such things are known to the Parliament that are not to yourself." The letter ended with the assurance that he was looked upon as the faithful servant of Parliament which would be mindful of his fidelity.[44]

Monck replied in words that grew the more significant as time passed. After disavowing any intention of protecting the scandalous or disaffected he protested that he was not one of those who aspired to greatness, having served his military apprenticeship in the service of the United Provinces, where soldiers received and obeyed the orders of civilian authorities but gave none to them. "Obedience is my great principle," he continued, "and I have alwaise, and ever shall, reverence the Parliament's resolutions in civill things as infallible and sacred." As for his request that changes should not be made in the army he commanded, he knew that Parliament was guided by the information it received, and felt that he was as good a judge of his men as individuals "who may act their own passions under pretense of publique safety."[45]

The letter was not without effect at Westminster. The seven commissioners, the septemvirate as they were called by the unrepresented army in Scotland,[46] proposed more extensive remodeling than Parliament would sanction.[47] A Robert Glynn, cashiered in 1655 for disaffection, was now restored, but this was the only change in the captains of Monck's regiment of horse. In his regiment of foot the company commanders were all retained except Abraham Holmes, now promoted to be a lieutenant colonel, and destined to attract Macaulay's notice by his courage at his execution for participation in Monmouth's rebellion.[48] The explanation which Monck's chaplain gave for the few changes—that in

[43]June 2, 1659. *Clarke Papers*, IV, 16-17. The letter was read on June 9, when Hesilrige was deputed to draft the answer—an unhappy choice.

[44]*Commons Journals*, June 10.

[45]June 18, *Clarke Papers*, IV, 22-23.

[46]Gumble, *Life of Monck*, p. 99.

[47]*Clarke Papers*, IV, 39-40.

[48]For further particulars, see G. Davies, *The Early History of the Coldstream Guards*, pp. 88-89.

the General's regiment of foot "they could not have put in more violent persons hands than many of these were"—was to be justified later.[49]

As for Talbot's regiment of foot, the septemvirate allowed their itch to interfere full scope. A new lieutenant colonel, Wroth Rogers, a protégé of Lambert's, was introduced, displacing Henry Pownall who was demoted to major, the former major, John Hubblethorne, becoming a captain. Various other changes were proposed among the captains. Monck remonstrated strongly and apparently effectively. He urged that the officers of his own regiment of horse be left unchanged and that Major Hubblethorne, "a very good officer," be retained in Talbot's regiment. He continued that he would have acquiesced without protest in the decisions of Parliament if the country had not been "in such a distemper, that it's a miracle of Mercy that they are not running into Blood." The officers whose good conduct he guaranteed stood for a commonwealth against a single person and none of them had been "active in these late Miscarriages and Declensions of the Armie." He reaffirmed emphatically his devotion to the Parliament. "I blesse the Lorde I have learned Obedience, and desire to expire with that Principle." This letter had some effect because the list of officers recommended by the commissioners was merely read in the House but not passed.[50] But the House agreed to the supersession of Colonel William Daniel, a Cromwellian and enemy of Quakerism, by his lieutenant colonel, John Pearson, an Anabaptist, then engaged in expelling ungodly officers from the Dunkirk garrison.[51]

Fortunately for the Rump not a few of the changes it adopted on the commissoners' recommendations were made too late to affect materially the composition of Monck's army. When the crisis came in October, the new officers had either failed to appear in Scotland or arrived when time was lacking for them to establish themselves in their regiments. It is not surprising that the commissioners, the army leaders being in a majority, should have countenanced officers who acted with the army against the Rump in October. What is amazing is that the Rump was so ill-informed about the politics of officers. The claim to be able to judge better than Monck the character of his officers was proved unfounded, and the Rump was to be saved in its own despite.[52]

The only other forces to be considered were abroad, in Flanders or

[49]Gumble, p. 102. For the lists of Monck's horse and foot regiments see *Commons Journals*, Sept. 19 and July 30.

[50]Zachary Grey, *An Impartial Examination of the Fourth Volume of D. Neal's History of the Puritans* (1739), App., 160-161. The date given, Sept. 2, is hard to reconcile with the phrase "late Miscarriages . . . of the Armie," but it appears to be correct. *Commons Journals*, VII, 789 (Sept. 29, misprinted 26) and Hist. MSS Comm., *Portland MSS*, I (1891), 685. *Commons Journals*, Sept. 27; Firth and Davies *Regimental History*, II, 467.

[51]*Regimental History*, II, 494-95.

[52]The forces in Ireland are described in the chapter devoted to that subject.

Jamaica. Now that there was every prospect of peace between France and Spain, the English contingent that had fought under Turenne was not wanted in the field. The three regiments at Amiens were recalled to Dunkirk. This reinforcement was most welcome at Dunkirk as the garrison there was much depleted by sickness and too feeble to repel a determined attack if the Spaniards and their Royalist allies should choose to ignore the truce. Moreover, many officers fell short of the high moral standard required by the Rump. A small commission, composed of two colonels and a lieutenant colonel[53] sent over to investigate after the discovery of a plot to plunder the town in default of pay, found "that profaneness and wickedness . . . do sadly abound," and recommended the appointment as governor of "an honest, godly, faithful and able person."[54] But the Rump had its hands full at the time with Booth's rebellion, and sent for the three regiments that had been with the French army. In England, after the rising had been suppressed, many officers of these regiments were cashiered. No other change of importance occurred until the end of the year.

The forces in Jamaica were too few and too remote to affect or be immediately affected by events in England. On July 30, 1659, Parliament listened to a report on the island from the Council of State. It was mainly concerned with the six frigates supposed to be stationed at Jamaica, but rather incidentally mentioned that the army, according to the latest musters received, amounted to 2,230 officers and men, "but whether effective, they have reason to suspect." A petition from the forces there was then read, and referred to the Council of State.[55]

Among the first topics to which the Rump turned its attention was the bill entitled "An Act of Indemnity and Pardon for what hath been acted or done during these late times." It passed its first reading on May 23 and its second the following day, when it was referred to a grand committee.[56] The time spent on it suggests that it excited great opposition.[57] Because the original bill as introduced does not exist and no divisions in committee are recorded in the *Journals*, little can be learned about the reasons for the protracted discussions. The figures for three divisions only are recorded. The first, carried by thirty-six to twenty-eight, in-

[53]Packer, Ashfield, and Pearson. Their instructions are in the Register, June 29.

[54]Thurloe, VII, 695, 714. During Lockhart's absence on a diplomatic mission to the French court, Colonels Arnop and Lillingston were in command. An anonymous informer said that the former thought religion useless in military discipline and that the latter was an enemy to religion and godliness. Quoted in C. H. Firth, "Royalist and Cromwellian Armies in Flanders," in *Transactions of the Royal Historical Society* (1903), pp. 112-13.

[55]*Commons Journals*, VII, 740-741.

[56]Ibid., 662-63.

[57]Ibid., 667, 669, 671, 681, 685, 692, 694, 697, 699, 705-706. The bill was reported from the grand committee on July 8 (p. 707).

serted the word "necessary" in the clause which stated that "all moneys already paid for necessary salaries and allowances . . . shall be . . . allowed, and the persons who received the same, discharged and indemnified." This was substituted for a proposal, hotly debated though finally rejected, that everyone should refund any public salary or gift received during the Protectorate.[58] The second, defeated by forty-three to twenty-four, proposed a fee of forty shillings for every pardon. The third, defeated by thirty-one to twenty-eight, proposed to exclude from pardon any public officer guilty of maladministration, or anyone who had, to the injury of another, done what was contrary to due course of law.[59] In addition to the clause about salaries, the act, as passed, stated that after the violent and illegal interruption of Parliament many things had been done contrary to the interest of the Commonwealth and contrary to law, but that all who had proceeded under color of the authority of Protector or reputed Parliaments should be pardoned. All legal proceedings and decisions since April 19, 1653, should not be questioned for want of legal power in the judges, but all titles of honor granted since that time should be null and void. Grants of office since that day were not confirmed. Farmers of the excise who neglected to pay arrears were excluded from the benefit of the act. All who claimed a pardon must first subscribe a declaration to be true to the Commonwealth without "a single Person, King-ship, or House of Peers."[60]

The day after the act was passed Lambert met Ludlow and bitterly denounced it because, though there was no security given officers for what they had done, yet they were liable to be called in question for what they had received.[61] Ludlow ignored the first point but replied to the second. He argued that soldiers were indemnified for what they had received and that Parliament would never penalize any except those who had enriched themselves by the ruin of the Commonwealth and had opposed Parliament's recall. At this moment Hesilrige came up—he is likely to have been responsible for the insertion of the vital word "necessary," the great stumbling block because capable of a wide interpretation. He argued that the act was full and comprehensive, but Lambert answered that it signified nothing and left them still at mercy. " 'You are', said Sir Arthur, 'only at the mercy of the Parliament, who are your good friends.' 'I know not', said Lambert, 'why they should not be at our

[58]July 11 (p. 712); Wariston's *Diary*, 119-20, 123. Whether certain individuals like Thurloe and Barkstead should be excepted by name led to much discussion. *Calendar Venetian*, p. 38; *Nicholas Papers*, IV, 165.

[59]July 11 and 12 (p. 714). The bill passed July 12.

[60]*Acts and Ordinances*, II, 1299-1304.

[61]The indemnity seems to have been granted only for acts "in reference to the several changes in government," 1653-1659, and for "necessary salaries."

mercy as well as we at theirs.'" His startled hearers were outraged at such threatening words. Ludlow suspected a design once again to over-awe or eject the Parliament and Hesilrige told him that if Lambert had not already been given two regiments, he would never have got them with his [Hesilrige's] consent.[62] As for the other army leaders, their feelings were adequately set forth later. They complained that the Act of Indemnity, after hanging long in suspense, came forth "imperfect and ineffectual," because officers were liable both to be ruined at the pleasure of Parliament and to be molested at law for "acts done for the publick service, as well during the time of their former sitting, as under other succeeding governments."[63]

The Act of Indemnity, instead of calming the troubled waters, intensi-fied the storm and, together with a bitter quarrel between the higher officers and some Rumpers, nearly led to another ejection of Parlia-ment.[64] To aggravate the crisis were feuds between individuals. Fleet-wood and Vane exchanged passionate words, probably because the gen-eral accused the Parliamentarian of breaking the conditions agreed upon when the Rump was recalled. Then Hesilrige and Vane differed about the future constitution, the one advocating a "pure republic"—unfor-tunately not defined—and the other wishing to entrust the government only to "pious and holy persons" because the masses were mad. Both the French and Venetian representatives in England believed that Lam-bert sided with Vane, and that the Rump might be turned out at any time, but they did not quite agree on the reason why the soldiers hesi-tated to act. Bordeaux thought the explanation was that the subalterns were against Lambert and Vane, but Francisco Giavarina that the offi-cers considered that they must first agree among themselves what form of government to substitute before they upset the Rump. A main cause of disunion in the army was the senate. The leaders not only wanted a senate but also to be the senators, but a faction in Parliament was excit-ing the junior officers against any such other House. The noncommis-sioned officers are said to have had their caucus and they apparently demanded a single chamber. Some Rumpers were against any kind of senate but others hoped to satisfy the army leaders with a senate elected annually. No M.P. appears to have found a senate of swordsmen accept-able.[65]

Although the army council never pronounced the reform of the

[62]Ludlow, II, 100.
[63]*A Declaration of the General Council of the Officers of the Army*, dated Oct. 27, p. 5.
[64]At the beginning of June wagers were being made that Parliament would not last another fortnight. *Nicholas Papers*, IV, 152.
[65]Wariston's *Diary*, III, 123, 125; Guizot, I, 391, 407, 412, 424, 426; *Calendar Venetian*, pp. 44-45, 50.

militia a grievance, yet its members viewed the determination of Parliament to create a rival organization with misgivings. As early as May 9 the House had named a committee to prepare a bill to settle the militia of London, though the act itself was not passed until July 7. It named many commissioners, the Lord Mayor, aldermen, regular and militia officers, and citizens including Isaac Penington, twice Lord Mayor at the beginning of the Civil War, Praise-God Barebones, and Slingsby Bethel. They were empowered to assemble all able-bodied, well-affected citizens, arm and form them into regiments, to assess persons for the provision of horses and weapons according to their estates, and to nominate all officers, who, if approved by Parliament, would receive commissions signed by the Speaker. A similar measure was passed on July 26 for the countries of England and Wales.[66]

The Rump was unfortunate in one respect at least, that it could not hope to win over the rank and file of the army by an increase of pay or even by the settlement of arrears. The utmost that Parliament could manage was to give the private soldiers on duty in London and Westminster one penny more a day for the foot and threepence for the horse. Thus these troops received the same amount as before the cuts in 1655, but all others continued at the same rate, 2/3 for the horse, 1/8 for the dragoons, and 9d. for the foot.[67] As to the debts to the armed forces, three estimates were presented to Parliament at different times. On May 20, the debt due to the army up to March 29 was said to be £800,000, chiefly made up of £224,000 owing to the forces in England, £95,000 to the forces in Scotland, and £371,000 to the forces in Ireland. The total amount was rather less than four-fifths of a year's pay or about four-ninths of the annual revenue. The cost of the army and navy together was reckoned to be about £100,000 more than the total revenue after deducting the cost of collection. On June 8 it was estimated that by June 20 the army would be owed £601,000, and the navy £693,000 May 28. Clearly the land forces had gained at the expense of the sailors. The amount of additional revenue needed to balance the books by the end of the year was £1,042,000. Most significant is the entry "Ready Cash there is none."[68] On July 28 Vane presented another statement which purported to show that the amounts owing to the forces in England, Scotland, and Ireland to July 18 were £189,000, £167,000, and £333,000—the last representing thirteen months' arrears. Taking the two last sets of figures the debt to the army had increased by about

---

[66]*Acts and Ordinances*, II, 1293-98, 1320-1342; Guizot, I, 432, 434; *Nicholas Papers*, IV, 164, 167-78.

[67]Firth, *Cromwell's Army*, pp. 185-87.

[68]*Commons Journals*, VII, 660, 675.

£88,000—that is to say, it had not been paid for the last month—but to the navy by about £10,000. From Vane's report it appeared that £723,000 additional revenue would be required by December 1, but only £20,000 if the debt to the navy to July 1 was ignored—the debt to the army had not been included in the £723,000, why is not apparent. But this figure had been obtained by including the whole year's monthly assessment, though customs and excise only to December 1, after which date the arrears would increase again.

Perhaps the House found Vane's report as unsatisfactory as a modern historian does, though fairness to Sir Harry demands the condemnation of all financial statements of this era as arbitrary, confused, and incomplete. The only action taken was a request to the Council of State further to consider the estimate and to present a report in time for a debate on the morrow.[69] The Register of the Council shows no sign of any compliance with this request, the attention of members being concentrated on the expected insurrection. The measures taken to increase the revenue were wholly inadequate, because they consisted merely of two acts to quicken the collection of arrears,[70] and an act of assessment, which did no more than direct prompter payment at the old rate.[71] In the absence of any guide to the financial policy of the Rump, inferences are dangerous, but the aim seems to have been to gain time and defer the evil day for the return to heavier monthly assessments. There is not the least likelihood that Rumpers were deterred from imposing heavier taxation by any acknowledgment of their unrepresentative character, though they were no doubt conscious how unpopular new levies would be. Moreover, to lay additional burdens on the three kingdoms in order to support the armed forces was abhorrent to the antimilitarist. Apart from sentiment, the bad times[72] through which the country was passing were unfavorable to new taxes. The Rumpers may have hoped that with the end of the war with Spain in sight trade would revive, prices fall,[73] and revenue become more buoyant.

The Rump was in a dilemma. It was doomed to send away empty the soldiers upon whom its very existence depended. Yet any attempt to provide means of paying the arrears due to the army was likely to anger some of its most ardent civilian supporters. Since the ejection of the

[69]Ibid., 737-38.

[70]Acts and Ordinances, II, 1276-77, 1286-87.

[71]Ibid., 1284-86. The first half of the assessment was to be paid by August 1, the second by October 10.

[72]Almost any pamphlet contains a reference to the bad times and decay of trade. See also William Robert Scott, The Constitution and Finance of . . . Joint Stock Companies (Cambridge, 1912), I, 466. Here the years 1659-1660 are considered to mark a crisis.

[73]Sir William Beveridge's Prices & Wages in England (1939), I, shows that 1658 and 1659 were dear years as 1655 had been a cheap one.

Rump in 1653 the armed forces, and especially the grandees, seemed to some Republicans the real enemy. The antimilitarism is well illustrated in a letter to Milton written by Moses Wall, who has been called "a scholar and Republican opinionist."[74] Replying to Milton's lament of the nation's backsliding in liberty and religion, Wall asked what could poor people do when held fast in chains by the very men they had advanced to power—the soldiers, true descendants of those who had watched the holy sepulchre to keep Christ from rising. But like most reformers he had no financial panacea to suggest, but only changes in the economic and social spheres. To rouse people from their dejection and servility, he contended they must be given "a comfortable subsistence" by improving "our manufactures, our fishery, our fens, forests, and commons." But these long-term remedies, however necessary, would afford no immediate relief to an impoverished treasury.

With the national finances in such a parlous state, any remission of taxes was unthinkable. That meant the retention of the hated excise. The impost, levied on food and drink and many commodities in daily use, had been established in 1643, and its collection was always liable to cause a riot.[75] It had been denounced as a burden upon the poorer classes in *The Case of the Army*[76] and in many Leveller tracts.[77] It was now as unpopular as ever, if the sentiments expressed in some verses published on July 2 can be accepted as generally felt. *A Dialogue betwixt an Excise-man and Death* represents the former as a night bird seeking its prey and as an officer in public service to fill his own pocket and confident of protection by the state against all complaints. But at last, convinced that Death had a warrant for him, he breaks down and confesses:

> With horror I behold my secret stealing
> My Bribes, oppression, and my graceless Dealing.

Another grievance of the time was inclosures. Item 12 in *The Humble Petition*, a Leveller manifesto of 1648, which listed the things expected of Parliament, ran: "That you would have laid open all late Inclosures of Fens, and other Commons, or have enclosed them onely or chiefly to the benefit of the poor."[78] That the century-old hatred of inclosures had not yet vanished was proved by a report to Parliament that on May 3, 1659, "Divers rude people, in tumultuous way," had broken down fences

[74]Dated May 18. Masson, V, 601-603.
[75]An earlier example, in 1647, is given by S. R. Gardiner, *History of the Great Civil War* (1911), III, 216.
[76]Oct. 15, 1647.
[77]See the index to The *Leveller Tracts*, eds. William Haller and Godfrey Davies (New York, 1944), for a score of references.
[78]*Leveller Tracts*, p. 152.

in the Forest of Dean, carried off gates, and turned in their cattle. But the Rump evinced no sympathy for the commoners and ordered the local authorities to suppress all tumults of this kind.[79] A few weeks later the Council learned that at Enfield a rough multitude had thrown down the hedges and ditches of the inclosure there and threatened to tear down a house. The Council was no more sympathetic than Parliament. The local justices of the peace were directed to suppress the tumult, and two troops of horse were dispatched to their assistance.[80]

As to religious matters in which so many of its supporters were vitally interested, the Rump began by appointing a strong committee of its members to investigate the case of those imprisoned for conscience sake and how they might be discharged.[81] According to the testimony of Quakers, the committee examined causes of detention very fully and released a number of them. Among those freed was James Nayler, the central figure in the messianic entrance into Bristol in 1656.[82] The next step was an attempt to define the limits of toleration. On May 21 Parliament resolved that all men who believed in the Trinity and in the Scriptures as the revealed word or will of God should be encouraged and protected equally, provided they were not disturbers of others' worship, papists, or prelatists, or such as practiced licentiousness or profaneness under the profession of religion. In addition, a gospel-preaching ministry was to be maintained, and universities reformed so that they might become nurseries of piety and learning.

The attitude of the Rump toward the freedom of the press and religious liberty deserves wholehearted praise. The historian must acknowledge with gratitude, even though his burden becomes heavier, that neither Parliament nor the Council of State imposed any shackles on the press. Thomas Mabbott, in a newsletter of May 3, remarked that "Westminster Hall is filled with papers to this purpose [recall of Long Parliament]; every day new sheetes come out."[83] This statement is confirmed by the figures given by G. K. Fortescue in his introduction to the *Thomason Tracts*. Whereas there were 282 tracts collected by Thomason for 1658, there were 652 in 1659. The two official newspapers which were published during the Protectorate—*Mercurius Politicus* and the *Publick Intelligencer*—were joined by a third in April, 1659, by four more in May, and two more in June, all the additions being unofficial. Nine was the total for the rest of the year, though the news-

[79]*Commons Journals*, VII, 648.
[80]Register, June 1, 1659; *Weekly Intelligencer*, July 19-26; James Heath, *A Chronicle of the Late Intestine War* (1676), p. 423.
[81]*Commons Journals*, VII, 648.
[82]W. C. Braithwaite, *The Beginnings of Quakerism* (1912), pp. 273, 457-58.
[83]*Clarke Papers*, IV, 3.

papers for any one month are usually not identical with those for the preceding or succeeding month. One of the most interesting of the new-comers, *The Weekly Post*, which began May 3-10, declared that it was printed "for the general satisfaction and information of the PEOPLE," perhaps the first time such a claim had been advanced.

The liberty of the press was not welcomed by all. A leading article in the *Weekly Intelligencer* for June 14-21 vehemently denounces the license then practiced: "Not a day which brings not forth many Pamphlets laden with as much impudence as ignorance, and the onely Querie now is, when they will make an end of their Queries and Libels. A strange thing it is that Christians should write, and commend those things written and printed, which even the Heathens themselves do abhor to think on. We live in a wild Age in which Impudence doth pass for wit, the patience of the State hath been such, that with much silence they have passed by the rudeness of these pens, hoping at the last they would either be weary or ashamed: but finding their Insolence to inc[r]ease with their lenity, they are now taking a course to suppress them."

On the whole, toleration may have been more general during the five months when the Rump sat than at any other time since the Civil War began. The French ambassador informed his government there was no need to worry about the English Catholics, because Parliament showed no intention to persecute them.[84] Certainly most sectaries had little to complain of so far as molestation by officials was in question. The Quakers, however, were less fortunate. Their refusal to take off their hats before magistrates or to pay tithes often led to their imprisonment, sometimes prolonged indefinitely by their unwillingness to pay the fees their gaolers tried to extort. Even if they escaped legal pains and penalties, they were liable to have their meetings interrupted by mobs or soldiers and to be cruelly beaten and kicked. Throughout the seventeenth century law enforcement against mob violence was generally ineffective: at this time little or no effort was made by the guardians of the peace to afford Quakers the protection of the law. But though on many points nearly every man's hand was against them, there was one sentiment at least that they shared with Anabaptists, Fifth Monarchy men, and other extremists—their dislike of a state church and the payment of its ministers by tithes. On both points they were supported by one of the greatest of all Puritans.

John Milton had addressed to the Parliament of the Commonwealth of England *A Treatise of Civil Power in Ecclesiastical Causes.*[85] The first

---

[84]Guizot, I, 440.   [85]*Works*, VI, 1-41.

sentence gives the substance of the little tract: "Two things there be which have bin ever found working much mischief to the church of God, and the advancement of truth; force on the one side restraining, and hire on the other side corrupting the teachers thereof." The author would have left men free to worship as they pleased and to choose whatever pastors they cared to pay. Each congregation would have been a unit in itself, and its shepherd subject to no supervision save of his flock.

The opponents of the existing form of church government concentrated their attacks on tithes, a tangible grievance which, if removed, would be likely to inflict upon a state church the rapid loss of any means to pay ministers. On June 14 the House received "The Humble Representation and Petition of many well-affected Persons in the Counties of Somerset, Wilts, and some Parts of Devon, Dorset, and Hampshire."[86] After the petitioners had been thanked, a resolution was moved that a committee should consider "how a more equal and comfortable Maintenance may be settled for the Ministry, and Satisfaction of the People, than by Tythes." The division was a tie, seventy-six members voting. The Speaker then declared for the Yeas, so the business was referred to a grand committee.

Thereupon the enemies of tithes redoubled their efforts, the Quakers in particular supporting a petition from the freeborn people of the Commonwealth, and appointing men at each of their meetings to collect subscriptions and, in Kendal, even to canvass from house to house. By the time the petition was presented to Parliament it had more than 15,000 signatures.[87] It was read, but now the House was less inclined to listen to its arguments. Possibly the knowledge that the Presbyterians were likely to rise in arms may have influenced some members to try to conciliate them by opposing the abolition of tithes. The prominent share the unpopular Quakers had taken may have moved others to change their minds. Opponents of tithes may have been absent or caught unawares.[88] Whatever the explanation, the House carried a resolution that to encourage godly, preaching, learned ministers, tithes should continue to be paid as at present, unless Parliament should find some better way to maintain them. Moreover, in order that the public should know the attitude of Parliament the vote was to be printed and recited by judges on their circuits.[89] Parliament had some days before shown that it had no intention of accepting the "voluntaryism" in church

[86]This petition was not printed but others like it were. See Fortescue, *Thomason Tracts*, II, 241, 243; *Weekly Intelligencer* under June 22.

[87]Braithwaite, I, 458.

[88]Louise F. Brown, *Baptists and Fifth Monarchy Men*, p. 184.

[89]*Commons Journals*, VII, 694.

organization which Milton and others of like mind advocated; it had ordered that a bill should be brought in for the ejection of scandalous ministers, and that the committee for plundered ministers should be revived.[90]

Prynne seized the opportunity to write one of his tracts for the times. It is entitled *Ten Considerable Quaeres concerning Tithes* and is a curious mixture of plain, factual argument, abstruse learning, and absurdities. His first two points were probably the most effective—that nine out of ten of the present petitioners were poor, mechanical persons who never paid tithes, and that they hoped by abolishing tithes to abolish Protestant ministers, being instigated by disguised Jesuits and other Romish emissaries who controlled most congregations of Anabaptists and Quakers. He questioned whether for every tithe-payer who felt the charge a grievance, a hundred did not desire to continue this maintenance of ministers. Other queries asked whether tithes were not protected by Magna Charta, whether there were any scriptural texts against them, and whether a few giddy-pated innovators of the present age were not presuming to condemn the practice of most Christian churches at all times?[91]

Milton entered the fray again with his tract, *Considerations touching the likeliest means to remove Hirelings out of the church*, published in August. It has an address to the Parliament which is of greater interest to an historian than the main argument based on scriptural texts. He calls upon "the authors and best patrons of religious and civil libertie, that ever these Ilands brought forth" to take their stand with "the many thousands best affected both to religion and to this your returne," and not to try in vain to satisfy the covetousness of hirelings whose disaffection "ye well know both to your selves and your resolutions."[92]

Neither this tract nor further petitions induced the Rump to rescind the obnoxious vote. In this matter, as in those concerning army arrears, the excise, the wrongs of commoners or copyholders, Parliament had not satisfied the hopes of its more extreme supporters. There must have been a feeling of disillusionment spreading over the land. Whether men sought a new Jerusalem or an earthly paradise, they were alike doomed to disappointment. The change from a single person and two Houses of Parliament to an omnipotent House of Commons had done little to remedy the religious grievances and social evils denounced by Ana-

[90]Ibid., 689.

[91]Dated by Thomason June 27.

[92]*Works*, VI, 43-100. Probably the preface at least was written after news of Booth's rising reached London.

baptists and Levellers and a host of other small but vociferous groups. Not a single act had been passed to carry on the work of reformation. Except for a resolution that the existing Parliament should not sit after May 7, 1660, nothing had been done to meet the demand for "an equall distribution of Elections in the Representatives of this Common-wealth, and for a definition of the qualifications of electors and elected."[93] The Rump had satisfied some individuals by restoring them to the commands or offices they had forfeited during the Protectorate, but it had lost the support of most Cromwellians, and those who remained in its service, like Monck or Mountagu, were or soon became out of sympathy with its oligarchical self-sufficiency. It had not gained the loyalty of the army leaders and it was gradually forfeiting the devotion of the under officers who had been mainly responsible for its recall.

[93]The resolution was passed on June 6.

CHAPTER VIII

Sir George Booth's Rising

THE FALL of the Protectorate and the recall of the Rump had seemed to Royalists "to be the most dismal change that could happen, and to pull up all the hopes of the King by the roots."[1] Of the opponents of the House of Stuart, the Republicans were the most determined. Their virulent hatred of a single person and House of Lords was not to be overcome. Once they were firmly established in power, hopes of a Stuart restoration would fade. The problem the Royalists had to solve was whether to wait and trust to a gradual disintegration of their enemies, or to try to overthrow the Parliament by force at once. There were plausible grounds for either course.

The older Royalists generally favored patience. Since about the beginning of 1654 they had formed a council known as the "Sealed Knot." They had advised against Penruddock's rising in 1655 as premature, and its easy suppression justified their caution.[2] Two results had followed the unsuccessful rising, the reorganization of the militia and its payment by means of the decimation tax. The one provided in each county a force which could quickly stifle an insurrection at birth, the other further crippled the Royalists financially.[3] No wonder the Sealed Knot became apathetic. Their attitude reflected the prevalent mood. The Cavalier and Roman Catholic Blundell wrote in June: "I cannot perceive any great satisfaction to many in the late change of government, yet they would rather suffer a worse than a new war; which is the only thing now we do all abhor."[4] Hyde lamented this defeatism, but was well aware of the futility of isolated risings. After he had learned of the dissolution of Richard's Parliament, but before he learned of the recall of the Rump, he had warned John Mordaunt of the great danger from "any unseasonable attempt of hot headed men, which would gratify Thurloe with a plot, and presently unite the contending parties, at least the heads of them."[5] Royalists' hopes sprang from the many factions in the Rump, the army, and in the Republican party in general. As one of them put

[1]Clarendon, *Rebellion*, XVI, 13.

[2]Gardiner, *Commonwealth and Protectorate*, III, 117, 276. The adjective usually applied to the Sealed Knot by the more active Royalists was "wary." There are many examples of its use in Mary Coate's volume, *The Letter-Book of John Viscount Mordaunt* (1945), valuable alike for its documents and its notes.

[3]Gardiner, *Commonwealth and Protectorate*, III, ch. xl.

[4]*Cavalier: Letters of William Blundell to His Friends*, ed. Margaret Blundell (1933), p. 90.

[5]May 9, 1659, *Clarendon State Papers*, III, 463. The writer did not know that Thurloe ceased to be Secretary of State after the Rump's recall.

it, "chaos was a perfection in comparison of an order and government, the Parties are like so many floating islands, sometimes joining and appearing like a continent, when the next flood or ebb separates them that it can hardly be known where they will be next."[6] This picture, though overdrawn, was accurate enough, but it omitted one essential element. The divisions were not yet so deep that union was impossible in face of a common danger, such as an invasion by foreign troops to restore Charles II or even a revolt in his favor. The increasing distrust of their leaders by both the subalterns and the rank and file had not yet produced open disaffection or desertion, but the longer the army was without active service, the greater the opportunity for grievances to be nursed.[7]

Unfortunately for the Royalists, lack of unity was not confined to their opponents, because they also had their own differences. Personal jealousies were rife, both in England and at the little court Charles II maintained abroad.[8] Some of the Royalists exalted the Duke of York above his brother, and their wives and daughters also took sides.[9] There was no agreement on the old question of whether foreign aid should be sought. Hyde, claiming that Charles II was "the most an Englishman and the most a Protestant," felt that the King should owe his restoration more to his own subjects than to foreign princes who would always have their own interests in mind. Therefore, the work should begin at home.[10] Mordaunt thought assistance from abroad "a sad cure for an ill disease, when more nobly wee may do it ourselves."[11] Yet even he acknowledged that either France or Spain must supply men and ships in order to secure some port.[12] But it was recognized that, before either power would help, the present armistice must first be converted into a treaty of peace, so the prospects of immediate aid from the Continent were bad. When they were at amity, the two powers might co-operate to re-establish the King. Meanwhile, without financial assistance from Spain, the King was too poor to think of transporting the forces he had in Flanders to England.

In England co-operation between Anglican and Presbyterian was

[6]June 3, Ibid., p. 479.

[7]Major Wood, in the letter just quoted, was premature only in stating that Fleetwood, Lambert, and Disbrowe were "not much reverenced" by the soldiers who knew their own strength and would "set up for themselves."

[8]See, for example, Clarendon State Papers, III, 434, 452; Eva Scott, The Travels of the King (1907), pp. 382-85.

[9]Clarendon State Papers, III, 457, 462, 470, 475, 526; Eva Scott, pp. 383-84.

[10]To Mordaunt, June 10/20, Clarendon State Papers, III, 496.

[11]Hist. MSS Comm., Tenth Report, VI, 192.

[12]Ibid., pp. 200-201. Hyde estimated the Royalist forces in Flanders as 3,000, but he believed that a port must be seized before a force from abroad could venture to cross the seas. Clarendon State Papers, III, 471-72.

hard to arrange because each expected different benefits from a restoration. The Cavaliers hoped for the unconditional return of the King, and the restoration of the Anglican church to its former position. The "new Royalists," as the Presbyterians were sometimes called, though they were not all of one mind, wanted the King to imitate his father and assent to the articles of the Isle of Wight.[13] These articles provided for the establishment of Presbyterianism and the Directory in place of Episcopacy and the Prayer Book, and for control of the militia by Parliament for twenty years.[14]

The most eager of the Royalists for action was John Mordaunt. In June, 1658, he had been acquitted on a charge of treason by the High Court of Justice only by the casting vote of its president, but his ardor for the royal cause was in no way lessened by his narrow escape. He tried to form an alliance with the Presbyterians, and urged upon the King the need of an accredited leader. On March 1, 1659, the King did issue a commission to Mordaunt, Lords Belasyse and Loughborough, Colonel John Russell, Sir William Compton, and Sir Richard Willis. They were styled "the Trust." They were empowered to negotiate with any rebels (the regicides excepted) and to promise them that if they would change sides the King would pardon them, and even reward those who performed any remarkable service, such as handing over a town or fort.[15] On the same day Charles wrote two "instructions for my friends." In one he expressed his confidence in the Earl of Oxford and his willingness that Lord Willoughby of Parham, Sir William Waller, and Major General Browne should be given commissions as soon as they were willing to receive them, together with Andrew Newport. The first three would have helped cement the alliance between Royalists and Presbyterians, because they were former Parliamentarians, but only the first joined the six and not until June, when Newport followed suit.[16] The King went on to explain that he was not by nature revengeful and would reward the services of those who returned to their loyalty, but that he was against general promises which might give a legal title to those in possession of crown or church lands or the confiscated lands of his faithful subjects. He left to the discretion of those who rose in arms whether they should declare at once that they were fighting to restore the monarchy, or whether they should merely assert they took up arms to secure

---

[13]Hist. MSS Comm., *Tenth Report*, VI, 205.

[14]These articles were submitted to Charles I in September and October, 1648. Gardiner, *The Great Civil War*, IV, 217 et seq. The negotiations are sometimes called the "Treaty of Newport." The term "new Royalists" had also been applied by Republicans to the Cromwellians.

[15]The title and a summary are in Coate, pp. 3-4, and the text is in Hist. MSS Comm., *Tenth Report*, VI, 189-90.

[16]Coate, p. 3 note.

themselves from violence and to vindicate the laws of the land.[17] Here is the authority for the declaration Sir George Booth was to issue five months later.

The second set of instructions was for the six commissioners. After asking them to consult together for his service, he averred his intention to join them as soon as a rising took place, "or sooner if you shall advise it." He hoped none of his friends would take offense at not being included in the commission because those only were mentioned with whom he had most correspondence. He realized that there were many who, out of apprehension of their enemies and hesitation to engage until success seemed probable, would be slow to start but who would afterwards venture as freely as the rest. To them he would consider himself as much beholden as to others. The six and "those who have always consulted together"[18] would fill in the blank commissions sent, and distribute them so that there would be leaders in the counties "without any emulation or particular contention upon commands."[19]

Inasmuch as all of the six except Mordaunt had been "wary gentlemen," the issuance of this commission did not lead to prompt action. The great need was still for leadership. Mordaunt, though fearless and optimistic, was not the man to form a united front from the discordant ranks of the King's adherents. He was jealous, suspicious, and "alternately self-distrustful and overbearing." His resentment of criticism impaired his value as a colleague, and his personal feelings too often dictated his attitude toward others.[20] His judgment both of situations and of people was very defective. Granted that he could not foresee the series of blunders which were to split the Republicans into fragments, he should have perceived that because they were strongest on the battlefield and weakest in the council chamber, a military rising would attack them where they were invulnerable. His own letters prove that he knew his opponents were at sixes and sevens, but he was unable to grasp that time was necessary before a breach would open up and grow irreparable. The wisest policy was Hyde's—to induce friends in Parliament to provoke the army, and friends in the army to affront Parliament, because a rude dissolution of Parliament would be advantageous to Royalists.[21] Precipitation would lead only to the sacrifice of the most ardent Royalists, and, as Mordaunt had realized earlier, "an unseasonable attempt will only

[17]*Clarendon State Papers*, III, 437-38. This document seems designed to be shown to likely converts.
[18]No doubt the Sealed Knot.
[19]Hist. MSS Comm., *Tenth Report*, VI, 189-90.
[20]To this point I have followed Miss Coate's characterization of her introduction, pp. xviii-xix.
[21]To Mordaunt, May 25/June 4, *Clarendon State Papers*, III, 481. The same advice was frequently given. See Ibid., 487-88, 494, 499, 501.

settle them and ruin us."[22] Caution was essential in the spring of 1659 because the Rumpers were on their guard.

The Lord Protector had been induced on April 23 to issue a proclamation commanding all Papists and Royalists to leave London within three days and not return before June 10.[23] Inasmuch as an alleged, impending rising was to be the excuse of the army council for coercing Richard into dissolving Parliament, the restored Rump at once accepted a report from the committee of safety that Charles Stuart intended a speedy invasion, that many of his adherents had crossed the sea, including Captain Titus and Colonel Massey, and that royal emissaries were trying to seduce some of the army from their loyalty to the Commonwealth. The previous night a search had been made but Titus and Massey had escaped, though some malignants from Flanders had been apprehended.[24]

As soon as the Council of State was appointed, it began to investigate the alleged preparations for an insurrection, and ordered the arrest of Sir Henry Moore, James Sharp, Colonel Adam Brown, son of Sir Ambrose Brown of Surrey, Mr. Kidwell of Kingston, Titus, and Massey, and the seizure of any horses and arms found in their possession. John Grubham Howe was summoned to attend the Council. The shops of Herman Barnes and other gunsmiths were to be searched. Fleetwood was authorized to call out of Scotland such regiments of foot as he thought necessary to secure the north, and to send from London regiments to keep the peace in "the midland part" of the country. Packer, the commanding officer at Oxford, and Crofts, captain of the militia troop in Gloucestershire, were warned to search all suspected houses. The commissioners of the navy were to fit out ships for a summer guard in the Channel. Four other Royalists, including Thomas Armstrong[25] and Charles Gerrard,[26] were to furnish bonds for good behavior. These various orders had very little result. Sharp was first ordered not to leave London, and then to return home and not meddle with politics, and Howe duly appeared and was dismissed. The other Royalists seem to have eluded arrest. On June 6 the various militia troops, lately employed,

[22]To Hyde, April 14, *Clarendon State Papers*, III, 452. Curiously enough, I have not noticed any suggestion that in time soldiers would begin to share the sentiments of the people among whom they lived. If most people wanted a Stuart restoration, the soldiers would also ultimately want it. This happened before very long. There is a parallel case in 1688 when the army, which James II formed on Hounslow Heath to overawe London, came to feel as Londoners felt.

[23]It is strange that two proclamations were issued with the same date. The first permitted Papists and malignants to return by May 12 but they were then to stay within a five-mile limit. The second was as above. Steele, *Tudor and Stuart Proclamations*, Nos. 3106-3107.

[24]*Commons Journals*, May 9.

[25]To be executed in 1683. His father, Sir Thomas, was already in prison.

[26]Whether this is the later Earl of Macclesfield (see *DNB* s.v. "Gerrard, Charles") is doubtful. In the Council Register, July 19, reference is made to the informations of Charles Gerrard and others.

were to disperse to their homes.[27] The relaxation of precaution allowed the Royalists to go ahead with their plans for an insurrection, and their messengers to cross and recross the seas in security.[28]

Whether all the Royalists ever agreed upon a strategic plan is doubtful. They may have meant to rise in various parts of the country, to seize a port or ports where the King could land with, it was hoped, a small army, and thus to entice the Republican forces from London. When the capital was denuded of troops, Sir Richard Browne and the Presbyterians there would rise. All depended on capturing the seat of government, and thereby paralyzing the enemy. However, if the bulk of the army was kept in London, then the provinces could be overrun and time gained to consolidate strongholds which would act as rallying points for those who had hung back at first.[29]

The members of the Trust met with many disappointments in organizing a series of simultaneous risings. For several months they cherished the illusion that the armies outside England would aid them, but the adherence of the forces in Scotland, Ireland, and Flanders to the Republic shattered these hopes. Richard Cromwell had proved a broken reed, and Mountagu, in command of the fleet in the Sound, though disgusted by the turn of events in England and willing to listen to royal agents, was not yet prepared to cast all on a single throw and declare openly for the King.[30] Then the expected breach between the army and the Rump did not take place and the dissensions in the army did not lead to mutiny. There was little prospect that the King could land bringing with him either the small Royalist army in Flanders or a foreign army.

In the circumstances the Sealed Knot was unwilling to rise, but Mordaunt and other enthusiasts were determined to try their luck. Even in England, however, they met with much discouragement. Cornwall and Devon would rise only after a force from abroad had landed.[31] Every confidence was expressed that Bristol and Gloucester would fall into the hands of Sir Edward Massey, the former defender of Gloucester against Charles I, but even here difficulties arose. Massey was dissatisfied with John Grubham Howe, than whom Mordaunt thought no one more powerful and wealthy in Gloucestershire.[32] The help of Alexander Pop-

[27]Council Register, May 22 to June 6.
[28]Clarendon, *Rebellion*, XVI, 27.
[29]No Royalist set forth this plan as definitely as it is stated above, and it has been pieced together from many references in Royalist correspondence. *Clarendon State Papers*, III, 455, 470, 537; Hist. MSS Comm., *Tenth Report*, VI, 199, 206.
[30]See Frank R. Harris, *The Life of Edward Mountagu, First Earl of Sandwich*, ch. iv.
[31]Coate, p. 18. A few days later the report was that the two countries would act their part. Ibid., p. 22. The earlier report was to prove the more correct.
[32]*Nicholas Papers*, IV, 115-16; *Clarendon State Papers*, III, 433, 478, 517.

ham, brother of Edward, the Parliamentary general at sea, was judged necessary, but he laid down two conditions to be fulfilled before he would take up arms—that Bristol should first be secured, and that the King should land in the west with 500 horse. Later he yielded to his wife's alarms and withdrew.[33] The faint hope that Sir Anthony Ashley Cooper would bestir himself in Dorset was soon abandoned, and he was pronounced "rotten."[34]

In South Wales assurances were given that Chepstow Castle would be secured with the magazine there.[35] In North Wales, Sir Thomas Middleton, a former Parliamentarian, was ready to join Sir George Booth, who had undertaken to raise Cheshire and Lancashire, though conscious that now that Henry Cromwell had submitted he was liable to be threatened at short notice by troops from Ireland.[36] The north presented a problem that was never solved. Early expectations had been that Lords Belasyse and Manchester, a nice combination of an old Cavalier and a Parliamentarian, would act together, but both proved disappointing. Belasyse, though one of the Trust, was "shy, having been often in prison." He intended to rise on August 1 but both he and the Earl of Middlesex were arrested the night before.[37] His nephew, Lord Fauconberg, though he sent money to the King, did not take up arms when the day came.[38] Manchester had been approached by the King and was expected to engage Lords Warwick, Saye and Sele, and Robartes in the royal cause, but they may have been among the Presbyterian lords who were said to fear that if the King was restored by an insurrection, he would be more absolute than his father when his prerogative was highest.[39] Lincolnshire was to be secured by Edward Rossiter, a colonel of horse in the New Model until 1647 when he lost his command for supporting Parliament, Lord Willoughby of Parham, and others.[40] Great importance was attached to Norfolk and especially to King's Lynn, a possible landing place for Charles II. The influence of Sir Horatio Townshend, and the anticipated treachery of James Whitelocke, a son of Bulstrode Whitelocke and a captain of horse, seemed likely to gain the county and the

---

[33]*Clarendon State Papers*, III, 449, 455, 476, 485, 505, 510, 516-17.

[34]Ibid., pp. 478, 490, 512.

[35]Ibid., III, 509; Coate, pp. 19, 24.

[36]Clarendon, *Rebellion*, XVI, 26; *Clarendon State Papers*, III, 477, 489, 517.

[37]His recent marriage to Sir William Armin's "young widow" may also explain his backwardness. *Clarendon State Papers*, III, 528. He was arrested in Lincolnshire. Register, August 5; Hist. MSS Comm. *Ormonde MSS*, N.S. II, 398-99.

[38]Coate, pp. 3, 8, 28-29; *Clarendon Calendar*, IV, 20, 130, 169.

[39]*Clarendon Calendar*, IV, 235; *Clarendon State Papers*, III, 490, 527. They were alleged to have changed their minds next day (ibid., p. 529), but they did not rise.

[40]*Clarendon State Papers*, III, 490.

port.[41] In the Midlands, Lord Byron intended to capture Newark,[42] and Sir Charles Wolseley answered for Staffordshire.[43]

Kent, Sussex, and Surrey were to be associated south of the Thames, and the Earl of Winchelsea aspired to the chief command. When his claim was opposed, the possible co-operation of his father-in-law, the Marquis of Hertford, was lost.[44] Moreover, Kent was reputed willing to second, but not to begin, unless the King first sent troops thither. Mordaunt, Willoughby of Parham, Sir John Boys, and Sir Thomas Peyton met to perfect the association, probably with the result that Peyton was to be the leader in Kent, and Mordaunt in Surrey and perhaps Sussex.

These plans Mordaunt no doubt explained when he visited Charles II at Brussels. The King agreed to leave Brussels on July 11/21 and make his way with all secrecy to Calais, and to arrange that the Duke of York should be near at hand. As soon as news of a successful start was received, the King would proceed to one port in England and the Duke to another.[45] The die was now cast, because it was decided that the rising should take place on the appointed day even if the government in England learned about the insurrection and made arrests. This proviso was due to the fear that Sir Richard Willis, one of the Sealed Knot, was a traitor.

A certain G. Paul[46] claimed in 1663 to have rifled the study of Samuel Morland, employed by Thurloe, and to have found out that Willis was the "Thomas Barrett" who supplied Thurloe with information about plots to have posted Willis as a traitor,[47] and to have converted Morland.[48] Be this as it may, there is no doubt that Morland supplied the evidence, including "a great number of his letters,"[49] that convinced the King, Hyde, and others that Willis was in the enemy's pay.[50]

Back in England at the beginning of July, Mordaunt found that the members of the Sealed Knot had done nothing themselves for the royal cause, and had discouraged others. Under these conditions, he was confirmed in his opinion that Charles II should not move until he heard

[41]Ibid., pp. 473, 484; Coate, p. 18.

[42]Alfred C. Wood, *Nottinghamshire in the Civil War*, pp. 176-77.

[43]Coate, p. 24.

[44]*Clarendon State Papers*, III, 472, 482-83, 490, 534; Coate, pp. 24, 34.

[45]Clarendon, *Rebellion*, XVI, 27; *Clarendon State Papers*, III, 519-20; cf. ibid., pp. 523-24, for Jermyn's letter that Mazarin had agreed with the Queen that if Henrietta Maria asked for a pass for her son Charles it was to be refused. This is confirmed by Mazarin's letter of June 25/July 5, *Lettres du Cardinal Mazarin*, IX, 163.

[46]Possibly the George Paul who became involved in a dispute over half the land he and a Royalist, Samuel Clarke, had leased from All Souls College, Clarke having died while his lands were sequestered.

[47]On July 3 a notice was set up in the Exchange. *Clarendon State Papers*, III, 518.

[48]G. Paul to Charles II, *Clarke Papers*, IV, 304-306.

[49]Clarendon, *Rebellion*, XVI, 30. The letters would be those sent to Thurloe by "Thomas Barrett."

[50]See note on Willis at end of chapter.

again from England.[51] Nevertheless, on July 9, Mordaunt, Willoughby, Grenville, Massey, Peyton, Newport, and Titus met and decided on August 1 as the date for the rising, although some present thought that a nearer day would be better. Ominous was the belief that "one White" had informed the government of the King's intention to set out. Well might Mordaunt wish that the King's journey "could be so carried that no flesh could know when or where" he would land—a vain wish equally applicable to all other Royalist plans.[52] As the day approached, mixed news reached the leaders. Although Colonel Richard Ingoldsby, his major, Babington, and one of his captains, Elsmore, engaged to seduce two troops of his former regiment at Chichester and Lewes,[53] the opposition to the Republic was still divided, and few arms or horses were available for the insurgents. Yet the more resolute were determined to persevere, in spite of a passionate negative harangue by Willis. He declared that if he encouraged action which must cause bloodshed and miseries, he would be neither a Christian nor an Englishman, alleging as his sole reason the approaching harvest, although he had for three months opposed the rising as totally Presbyterian, and in the hands of "rash, vaine, giddy people."[54] The reason for this eleventh-hour protest may have been his consciousness that he had already betrayed the plans of the conspirators to the government.[55]

When the Council of State learned of the conspiracy is uncertain. Judging from the instructions recorded in its register, it appears that the Council's members not only realized by the beginning of July that a rising would take place shortly, but soon acquired much precise information. Together with its committee of intelligence, the Council seems to have adopted precautionary measures *pari passu* with the Royalist preparations. Early in July orders were issued to search houses in London and to seize all horses there, those which belonged to dangerous persons were to be kept, the others restored. Some six hundred were secured, which were later used to mount six companies as dragoons. Cavalry horses out at grass were to be brought near at hand. Ludlow and his subordinates were required to go to their commands in Ireland, and

[51]*Clarendon State Papers*, III, 517-18; cf. pp. 518-19. The date of Mordaunt's return is fixed by a reference to the libel against Willys, set up in the Exchange on July 3, in his letter of July 26 where he says this happened the day before his arrival. Coate, p. 32.

[52]Mordaunt to Charles II, July 11, *Clarendon State Papers*, III, 524-25; Coate, p. 26; Mordaunt reported that Lord Northampton arrived late but concurred in the decision. The Sealed Knot was invited but neither came nor sent. Probably the White mentioned was Ignatius White mentioned in Scot's account of his activities as intelligencer, of which more later. *English Historical Review*, XII, 122.

[53]*Clarendon State Papers*, III, 489; Coate, p. 33.

[54]Mordaunt to Baron, July 26, Coate, p. 31. Another Royalist thought the date badly chosen because peasants would rather work at harvest time for 2/ or 2/6 a day, "such is now their price in most counties," than fight for nothing. Broderick to Hyde, July 16, *Clarendon State Papers*, III, 527.

[55]See note at end of chapter.

officers of the forces in England and Scotland soon received the same order. One bill required householders to supply particulars of their lodgers' horses and arms, and another made incitements to soldiers, to desert or mutiny, acts of high treason.[56]

During the next days the Council must have received more definite information. Its orders became more specific. Vice-admiral Lawson and a squadron were to put to sea for the purpose of watching the Flanders coast and gaining intelligence of forces said to be assembling at Ostend. Infantry regiments were to be recruited to 800 men, cavalry troops to 60, and Ashfield's regiment was to march from Newcastle to Newark and Nottingham.[57] Letters were sent to the commanders of the militia troops of horse in thirty counties or divisions of counties.[58] The officers were to prevent all assemblies, seize weapons and horses beyond the customary number in the possession of delinquents, and secure any strangers that might be emissaries of Charles Stuart. All the recently named captains of militia troops were warned to take command of their forces. Care was taken to safeguard three of the places the Royalists expected to seize, Chepstow, Chichester, and Arundel, the troops of horse at Chichester and Lewes being replaced by others more trustworthy. All ships entering Yarmouth, a port the Royalists hoped to capture, were to be searched. All former enemies of the Commonwealth were to return to their homes, and not travel five miles from them. Arms and equipment were issued from the Tower to the seven regiments of foot in London so that they might be ready to take the field.[59] On July 14 England and Wales were divided into eleven areas and officers named to command the regulars and militia in them, most being colonels of the army. The defenses of Coventry, Bristol, and Gloucester were to be put in order, and volunteer companies recruited at the last two places. And, "at the desire of Colonel Sydenham," warrants were issued for "Lady Elizabeth Willoughby," Colonel William Legg, Andrew Newport, and John Mordaunt. Legg and Newport were captured and sent to the Tower but Mordaunt escaped.[60] The sequel to her ladyship's arrest is to be found in Scot's confession made after the Restoration: "I had some [sayes & alarms of Sir George Booths business] from one called by Lady Willoughby, a Catholick, by the meanes of Coll. Sydenham. Shee spoke very exactly of the intended day of Rising, and of some meetings the King's party had

[56]Register, July 9.

[57]Register, July 8.

[58]Register, July 9/13. It is significant that among the counties omitted were Cheshire and Lancashire, where Booth's rising originated.

[59]These were the regiments of Fleetwood, Lambert, Morley, Hewson, Sydenham, Moss, and Fitch (the Tower regiment).

[60]Council Minutes, July 14.

neare Grayes Inne, and that Sir Rich. Willis was one, but suspected by them."[61]

The Council now knew enough about the rising to take ample counter measures. Among those arrested were Sir John Grenville, released on parole, Philip Howard, bonded for £1,000, Sir Hugh Middleton and Howe in custody at Gloucester, Lady Mary Howard, Broderick and Colonel Blake, and warrants were issued for Major General Browne, Major Babington, Captain Elsmore, and Sir William Russell.[62] On July 25, Disbrowe, just returned from the West, was authorized by the Council to pay £100 to a person unnamed if he redeemed his promise to apprehend Massey. He was captured on July 31, but escaped the same evening.[63] In addition to the arrest of prominent conspirators the Council was able, thanks to the intelligence it received from informers and intercepted letters, to reinforce the army in districts where Royalists planned to rise. New companies of volunteers were enrolled at Bristol and Gloucester, Colonel Okey was required to make Gloucester his headquarters and to be informed of what Scot had lately learned—doubtlessly the day fixed for the rising—and more troops of horse were sent into Kent and Surrey. Every care was taken to prevent a rising in London. All the highways were patrolled, and barges stationed in the Thames to prevent suspicious persons' crossing. Travelers had to obtain passes or were liable to arrest on sight. On the eve of the insurrection orders were given to recruit troops of horse to eighty, or one hundred in case of an actual rising, and foot regiments to 1,200. Many additional companies of volunteers were authorized. Lawson was now to change his station and watch Boulogne, Calais, and Dieppe. Five hundred horse and 1,000 foot were sent for from Ireland. Finally, on July 30, Salwey was asked to announce to Parliament that the Council had lately received letters from Neville and Blagrave "discovering the intentions of the enemies

[61]*Eng. Hist. Rev.*, XII, 123. Scot also named Colonel Bampfield as giving information he obtained from his Presbyterian acquaintances. The only Lady Willoughby seems to be Elizabeth, the wife of Willoughby of Parham, who was deeply involved in the Royalists' plot. If she was the lady concerned, it is curious that her husband was not summoned to attend the Council before August 6. It is even more astonishing that no Royalist seems to have become aware of her revelations until after the Restoration. In fact, the identification is extremely improbable, but I can suggest no alternative.

[62]*Register*, July 15/31. Lady Mary Howard is said to have arrived in England recently with commissions from Charles II and to have been in treaty with "a grand officer," probably Lambert. *Clarke Papers*, IV, 29. Ludlow (II, iii), asserts that Mrs. Lambert was approached by Royalist agents, and that Lambert acquainted Vane with their propositions.

[63]*Minutes*, July 25; *Clarke Papers*, IV, 36; *Mercurius Politicus*, No. 582, Aug. 4/11. Lord Herbert, taken at the same time, failed to escape. According to Clarendon, *Rebellion*, XVI, 31, Willis betrayed Massey and his design on Gloucester, but this charge may be unjust in view of what is stated above and the "Narrative of Events at Gloucester" in *Clarke Papers*, IV, 34-37, which implies that intelligence was obtained locally about July 25. A letter from Thomas Pury and his son, also Thomas, shows that they expected an attempt to seize Gloucester on July 27. They had enrolled three hundred musketeers from citizens, poor men who cheerfully left their occupations to serve. Bodleian Library Tanner MS. 51, f. 97. In the same volume (f. 140) are some particulars of Massey's place of concealment.

of this commonwealth to raise new commotions . . . and the time of their intended insurrection." This was duly announced the same day.[64]

But there was one area in which no special precautions were taken—Cheshire, Lancashire, and North Wales. The assumption appears safe that the Council remained completely in the dark about the plans of Sir George Booth and his associates until they were about to rise or possibly until they had risen. This ignorance is hard to explain except on the hypothesis that the informers who revealed so much of other plans had never learned those of Booth. The Presbyterian leaders had distrusted Willis and kept their designs from him, and may have been equally careful with others.[65]

In spite of every discouragement, some Royalists rose, but in general the arrest of so many of their leaders, and the many signs of the Rump's preparedness, deterred them.[66] There was no movement in the West. In Cornwall, Sir John Grenville, and in Gloucestershire, Sir Edward Massey, were irreplaceable. In Dorset a score or so of persons talked of taking up arms, but neglected to do so.[67] In London, the situation was so hopeless that the few ready to embark on a forlorn hope preferred to try to make their way to Tunbridge Wells or Redhill.[68] Most seem to have been arrested on the way, among the captives being Edward Penruddock, whose father had perished on the scaffold in 1655, and Elsmore, upon whose influences over his former troop in Ingoldsby's horse much reliance had been placed. A trooper, John Atkinson, who was taken at Reigate with a dozen Cavaliers, was promptly court-martialled and condemned to death for desertion, though subsequently pardoned. Some fifty Royalists are said to have been taken in Kent, among them being two apprentices to "one Prince a goldsmith and a papist living in Covent

[64]Register, July 30; Commons Journals, VII, 741. In a letter to Gloucester, Whitelocke, then taking his turn as president of the Council, reported that Neville and Blagrave had intercepted letters in Berkshire on July 28 about the rising fixed for August 1. Calendar Domestic, 1659-60, p. 55.

[65]See Marjory Hollings, "Thomas Barret: A Study in the Secret History of the Interregnum," Eng. Hist. Rev., XLIII, p. 55. But if Willis failed to betray Booth through ignorance, what becomes of Clarendon's general accusation that Willis "poured out" information about Presbyterians (Rebellion, XVI, 31)? Judging by arrests made or ordered, someone betrayed as many Cavaliers as Presbyterians.

[66]Clarendon (Rebellion, XVI, 36) mentions that on July 31 there was excessive rain, which continued next day with high wind, so that persons hastening to their rendezvous were "infinitely dismayed," and some lost their way. Adam Martindale (Life, p. 136) gives the foul weather as one cause for the failure of the rising.

[67]The local authorities at Plymouth declined to assist a constable who wanted to post up a proclamation against the rebels, but beyond this passive resistance they did not venture to go. Tanner MS. 51, f. 125; Hist. MSS Comm., Portland MSS, I, 686; A. R. Bayley, The Great Civil War in Dorset (Taunton, 1910), pp. 383-85.

[68]The Rump had about the equivalent of seven regiments in or near London and as many militia—an overwhelming force. In addition, three English regiments from Flanders were on their way home, arriving at Dartford, Kent, before or on August 10. Mercurius Politicus, August 4/11. Each man was to receive on arrival a red coat, grey breeches of broadcloth, a shirt, a pair of stockings and of shoes. Register, July 25. These articles were collectively called a suit. Ibid., July 27. Part of the lifeguards prevented a rendezvous at Redhill. Tanner MS. 51, f. 107.

Garden."[69] In the eastern counties, arms were seized at Norwich and a few arrests made, but otherwise there was little to report.[70] The same statement holds for the Midlands so far as August 1 was concerned. In view of the faint-hearted response by Cavaliers the leaders of the rising may well have approved a poem entitled *The New Litany*, dated by Thomason September 22:

> From such as in Drink rout Men and Horse too,
> From those that can prate, yet nothing dare do,
> From a ranting, swearing, drunken crew.
> > Libera nos Domine.

The one momentarily successful rising was headed by Sir George Booth, a rich Presbyterian who had fought valiantly for the Parliamentary cause in the first Civil War. Immediately after "the latter [afternoon] sermon" on Sunday, July 31, the drums beat to arms at Warrington.[71] Supported by the Earl of Derby, Viscount Kilmorey, and other local magnates, Booth got together perhaps 500 on the appointed day. Then he received a royal message and a communication from Mordaunt about the King's readiness to cross to England.[72] Losing no time, the party advanced to Rowton Heath where a general rendezvous had been appointed. Being assured that the citizens of Chester would open their gates to them, Booth and his adherents took possession in the early morning of August 2. The castle was held against them by Thomas Croxton,[73] and, as they had no great guns, they could only blockade it and trust that a lack of food would compel surrender. Two appeals for support were issued on this day, a third a week later.

The first appeal, *The Declaration*, stated that Englishmen were without any "settled foundation of religion, liberty or property." With the legislative power usurped and condemned at pleasure, and the armies first raised for their defense now misled into unwarrantable actions by ambitious officers, they had no one man or council lawfully constituted to whom popular grievances could be properly addressed. They had

[69]*Mercurius Politicus*, No. 581, July 28, August 4. It would be interesting to discover if this "Prince" was the Miles Prance who figured so prominently in the Popish Plot. See John Pollock, *The Popish Plot* (1903), pp. 120, et seq.

[70]*Clarendon Calendar*, IV, 304, 308.

[71]*Clarke Papers*, IV, 31. Cf., ibid., p. 33, for Colonel West on the "horrible things" said from the pulpits. Gilbert Burnet (*History of My Own Time*, sec. 66-67) states that when Willis' treachery became known, two messengers were sent to Booth to tell him not to rise but both were arrested, so that the rising took place. I know of no confirmation of this and doubt it.

[72]Baker's *Chronicle*, p. 668.

[73]Thomas Birch claimed that, on a Quaker's information of the rising, he warned Croxton. Letter to the Speaker, Aug. 2, Tanner MS. 51, 108. According to evidence before the county committee for sequestration on September 27, a Mr. Playward, one of the sheriffs, opened the gates to Booth, who was received with shouts of joy and whose *Declaration* was proclaimed. News of the brief rising at Derby evoked cries of "God Save the King." *Calendar Committee for Compounding*, ed. M. A. E. Green, I (1889), 751-52.

taken up arms, therefore, in vindication of the freedom of Parliament, and in support of the known laws, liberties, and properties of the good people of the nation, now groaning under illegal, arbitrary, and insupportable taxes unknown to their ancestors. They promised arrears and increase of pay to the army and security against impositions on men's consciences.[74]

Together with this declaration was printed *A Letter from Sir George Booth to a Friend*. Though it repeats the substance of the first appeal and lays down the same objectives, it is permeated by a class consciousness likely to attract the nobility and gentry. It begins with the claim that the writer and gentlemen who are engaged with him, being "considerable members of our countrey," have "more sober and couragious thoughts in time of extremity than other men have." It asserts that the newly constituted militia subjected them to "the meanest and most fanatick spirits of the nation," and it prophesies that if the rising is defeated, a "mean and schismatical party must depresse the nobility and understanding commons." It ends with the promise to lay down arms if those in authority would either admit the old members to both Houses of Parliament or call a new and free Parliament.[75]

The third manifesto, *An Express*, is as democratic as the second was aristocratic. Addressed to the citizens of London and all other freemen of England, it embodies sentiments that the Leveller and Anabaptist could approve. It professes that as Englishmen, of whatever station or fortune, they are all heirs to the same birthright, not only according to nature, which gave all "a common and equal bond of freedom and unity," but also according to laws and customs, "general, equal and impartial to all, without respect of persons, rank, quality, or degree." But these rights have been torn from them and in their stead are arbitrary imprisonment and taxation, monopolies, excise—all contrary to Magna Charta and the Petition of Right. This oligarchical tyranny has been established solely in the interest of some few, ambitious grandees, who never observe their solemn engagements, protestations, or oaths and were not restrained by the law of God or man, conscience or reason. No just man can shed his blood for such creatures, and if he sheds the blood of others, it will surely be required of him.

Having sought to deter the soldier from resistance, this appeal next deals with religion. All coercive power in religion is denounced in the

---

[74]*The Declaration of the Lords, Gentlemen, Citizens, Freeholders, and Yeomen of this once happy Kingdome of England*. The only copy I have seen is printed in the top half of a broadside which also contains Booth's *Letter to a Friend*.

[75]The broadside is dated Chester, August 2, 1659. Booth's *Letter* is reprinted in *Tracts Relating to the Civil War in Cheshire*, ed. James Augustus Atkinson (Manchester, 1909), pp. 185-87.

strongest terms, and the promise made that all however "differenced from us" shall be protected and "made equal to our selves." Then follows a long list of the reforms that will ensue if the existing tyranny be overthrown: annual elections of all officers and magistrates, constant succession of Parliaments, trial by jury only, abolition of the excise and other new taxes and of monopolies and patents, the protection of the commons for the poor, and the restitution to them of all commons wrongfully seized.

After an exhortation to the "gathered separate churches" not to be fearful but to join with them to protect the laws and liberties of Englishmen, the declaration closed with a proposal that the militia, army, and whole nation should unite to secure the speedy election of a free Parliament, to whose authority all should submit.[76]

There is no evidence that this long, democratic appeal influenced the Rump's supporters, or deterred anyone from opposing Booth. Indeed, a Leveller or Anabaptist who possessed and compared all three appeals might well have suspected the sincerity of the sponsors, so striking were the differences between them. Nevertheless, as will be seen later, the *Express* set a pattern for later, and more successful, propaganda designed to alienate soldiers from their officers. At the time of its appearance, the *Declaration* gave offense to some. Adam Martindale, a Presbyterian minister who detested the Rump and all its ways but did not take part in the rising, complained that the *Declaration* promised universal toleration "which must be either a perfect cheat . . . or else a serious promise of that which I utterly abhorred." He noted also that endeavors were made to raise recruits by spreading rumors that the Quakers were up in arms, and concluded that a rising would not prosper when its foundation was laid in "lying and deceit."[77] Other Lancashire ministers were less sensitive or more courageous. According to *Mercurius Politicus,* in order that the *Declaration* "might not want the old cover of all treason," it had "the shadow of religion to countenance it," because on the previous Sunday [July 31] ministers read it to their respective congregations.[78] The afternoon service was followed by a call to arms.[79]

From Chester, Major General Egerton marched with a party to

---

[76]*An Express from the Knights and Gentlemen now engaged with Sir George Booth; To the City and Citizens of London, and all other Free-men of England.* It is not surprising that *The New Litany* prays to be delivered from "Cheshire lyes."

[77]Martindale's *Life,* pp. 137, 139. Newcome confirms the rumors about the warlike Quakers. Henry Newcome's *Autobiography,* II, 109. *Mercurius Politicus* (p. 692) notes that ministers round Derby called their opponents Anabaptists and Quakers. For a good article on the political activities of Friends at this time see James F. Maclear, "Quakerism and the End of the Interregnum," *Church History,* December, 1950.

[78]Under August 5, p. 649. The *Declaration* was thus read the day before the rising was to take place.

[79]Newcome's *Autobiography,* I, 109.

Chirk Castle, where Sir Thomas Middleton joyfully received them and, leaving his son in command, hastened to Wrexham where he boldly proclaimed the King.[80] He may have been precipitate and caused misgivings among Presbyterians that an unconditional restoration was intended, whereas some at least wished first to receive the King's promise to accept the Isle of Wight articles.[81] Apart from Colonel Ireland's securing of Liverpool, and a few trifling captures in North Wales, no other success attended the rising. According to a hostile pamphlet, a council of war at Chester determined that Booth should march to York and Middleton return to Wales. The one made little progress, perhaps because his levies were unwilling to leave their houses unprotected,[82] and the other's rear guard was routed by two troops which Major Creed had dispatched from Shrewsbury.[83]

Royalists in the Midlands and elsewhere once again tried to rise but with no success. Lord Byron and Colonel Charles White were joined by sixty or eighty persons in Sherwood Forest, but, on the approach of local militia, fled hastily through Nottingham to Derby, where they caused an uproar in the market place, some crying "A King," others, "A Free Parliament." The tumult ceased on the arrival of the militia, both horse and foot, from Leicestershire and Nottinghamshire. Thence White fled to Uttoxeter, where he read Booth's *Declaration*. Whereupon all shops were shut, the horses of the militia seized, and many of the militia, headed by a Captain Doubty, changed sides. Colonel Sanders appeared, was offered but refused the leadership, and was permitted to depart. But this sudden enthusiasm cooled overnight, and no sign of a Royalist force appeared on the morrow.[84] The Earl of Stamford assembled a small force, including Major Babington, drank the King's health, and then quietly submitted to arrest at Leicester.[85] The indomitable Mordaunt, with the Earl of Lichfield and thirty others, was active again in Surrey, during

[80]Baker's *Chronicle*, p. 668. Reports received by the Council state that the Cavaliers drank healths to the King on their "bare knees." Register, August 9.

[81]Cf. Mordaunt's account in *Collection of Original Letters . . . of Ormonde Papers*, ed. Thomas Carte, II, 196, with the story of a gentleman's meeting forty ministers in Northampton (printed in *Mercurius Politicus* under August 11) where an argument ensued whether "capitulations" were necessary before a restoration. Many are said to have cried, "We have been for a King, and will live and die for a King." According to Martindale (pp. 136-37), some Cavaliers refused to stir because the leaders did not rise for king and church.

[82]This account conflicts with a letter from officers left behind at Chester, probably to besiege the castle. They professed to be amazed at hearing that Booth had advanced as far as Northwich. Tanner MS. 51, f. 128. Colonel Robert Lilburne with a regiment of post-New Model Horse was on the fringes of Yorkshire, and Colonels Francis West and Thomas Birch were said to be active in Lancashire, and Major Creed at Shrewsbury. Before long, Booth's rear was threatened by the Irish Brigade, dispatched by Ludlow about the middle of August (Ludlow, II, 220, n. 1). Booth was hemmed in, and could do little except await the attack. Thomas Birch is to be distinguished from John Birch whose arrest the Council approved August 9.

[83]*A Bloody Fight between the Forces of Sir George Booth and the Parliaments* (1659).

[84]*Mercurius Politicus*, No. 583, under Aug. 11/12; Tanner MS. 51, f. 144.

[85]Ibid., pp. 671, 686; *Clarendon Calendar*, IV, 325-26.

the weekend of August 13-15, but meeting with no success, made his way by water to London where he took refuge with Alderman Robinson.[86]

Meanwhile the Republicans were extremely active. As soon as the Council of State received word of the insurrection, it ordered the Admiralty to send ships of war to prevent any provisions reaching Booth at Chester by sea. The two companies of dragoons were to be made up to six and placed under the command of Tobias Bridge,[87] and no less than fourteen new regiments of foot were to be raised in different parts of the country, and more were authorized later. A sign of the emergency was that the colonels were given the right to nominate their own officers, a privilege hitherto denied to colonels of the established army.[88]

The immediate need, however, was for a striking force to confront Booth. The Rump, after some hesitation, nominated Lambert to be commander in chief, apparently influenced by his revealing that his wife had been approached by Royalist agents. In the commission he received from the Council on August 5, he was empowered to direct military operations in the counties from Chester to Lincoln and in the six northern counties, to command his own regiments of horse and foot, Lilburne's Horse, and Hewson's and Biscoe's Foot (the last being scattered in garrisons in the eastern counties), to summon to his aid any other forces he might need, and to grant commissions to such as he deemed faithful to raise additional regiments, troops, or companies. At the same time, Disbrowe was to take command of the forces in the southwest, South Wales, and Gloucestershire and Worcestershire.[89]

Lambert reached Nantwich on August 15 and received reinforcements of four companies of Biscoe's regiment of foot and a troop of his own horse. Three days later he set out for Chester, but learning that the enemy, "four or five thousand horse and foot," were advancing to Northwich, altered his route to meet them, spending the night at Weaverham. The next day he found the enemy in front of Northwich. He had under his immediate command from 1,200 to 1,500 horse and about 3,000 foot.[90] A skirmish, rather than a battle, ensued. The ground was too broken up by hedges to use the horse at first but the foot, mainly Hewson's, drove their opponents over Winnington bridge and secured it so that the horse could

[86]*Clarendon Calendar*, IV, 333, 341; Baker's *Chronicle*, p. 668.

[87]"Colonel Bridge" is the former major of Okey's Dragoons.

[88]Council Register, Aug. 4.

[89]Register, Aug. 5. Of Lambert's small army part of his horse was already near Booth under Major Creed, Lilburne's was in Yorkshire, and Biscoe's foot had to be assembled. A small train of artillery was provided but whether it ever reached the battlefield is doubtful—which is also true of the dragoons under Bridge. In addition, Lambert either brought, or was joined en route by Swallow's horse. For some details about parts of various regiments joining Lambert at Drayton and Nantwich, see his letter reprinted in *Tracts Relating to the Civil War in Cheshire*, p. 168.

[90]See *Clarke Papers*, IV, 38-39 n., for the regiments present at the battle.

pass over. Then ensued a brief fight performed by the horse "on both sides like Englishmen." Lambert's men prevailed and soon Booth's army was scattered in all directions, most escaping in the enclosures where horse could not follow. Lambert is reported to have diverted the pursuit from Booth's infantry, saying, "Alas! poore men, these are forced and hired." He may well have wished to avoid the odium which a massacre of peasants would have attached to him.[91] The casualties were trifling— one killed and three seriously wounded of the victors and thirty killed and 300 captured of the losers, according to Lambert's calculation—but the affray was decisive. Chester surrendered next day without resistance and Lambert was able to divide his army, sending part to Lancashire to take Liverpool and part to secure Chirk Castle. Both forces easily accomplished their missions.[92]

Various criticisms were passed on Booth's conduct. According to Mordaunt a great mistake was the failure to secure at all costs the castle at Chester, and thus gain the arms and ammunition needed for the men who flocked to join Booth. The same critic stated that the supply of match, powder, and ball they had was in Chester and not available on the battlefield, so that both foot and horse retired without fighting. Looking back, after the Restoration, Clarendon blamed the decision to fight a battle instead of retiring to Chester, which he thought might have been successfully defended.[93] These charges have little validity. Booth might no doubt have kept the field a week or so longer by avoiding an engagement, but without hope of ultimate success. His half-armed volunteers could not face Lambert's veterans, and delaying tactics were futile when all prospects of help from risings elsewhere had disappeared. Perhaps the capture of Booth in woman's clothes at Newport Pagnell was a fitting end to what had been from the first rather an amateurish affair.[94] Lodged

[91]Martindale's *Life*, p. 140.

[92]Lambert's dispatches of August 20 and 21 and other letters and a narrative are reprinted in *Tracts relating to the Civil War in Cheshire*. Mordaunt's account is in *Ormonde Papers*, II, 194-200; and in *Clarendon State Papers*, III, 552-55, where all the cipher is deciphered. Hist. MSS Comm., *Portland MSS*, I, 684. Booth's prompt defeat may have deprived the royal cause of two powerful supporters. Mountagu's unexpected decision to bring the fleet back from the Sound, although lack of provision justified it, may have been partly due to his desire to be on the spot to aid a Royalist insurrection. As he did not arrive until early in September, he found the rising at an end, and was allowed by the Council of State to retire to Hinchinbroke. Whether Monck was preparing to intervene when news arrived of Booth's defeat, may never be known. To induce him to change sides, Charles II wrote him a letter not only reminding him of the great benefits he might confer on the country and himself but promising as well to be guided by his advice. The letter was entrusted to the general's younger brother Nicholas, who carried it to Scotland. George Monck is said to have refused to receive it, though allowing Nicholas to tell him its contents. He is also reported to have been about to declare for a free parliament when he learned of Booth's defeat. Gumble and Price concur on the point, but neither indicates what military preparations were started. The complete absence of any sign of the kind of measures Monck took in the following October must render his biographers' account suspect. The evidence about Mountagu is to be found in Mountagu's life by Frank R. Harris, and about Monck in the *DNB*.

[93]*Rebellion*, XVI, 41.

[94]Booth complained that he had been "basely deserted." Newcome, *Autobiography*, p. 110. A letter of August 25, in *Clarke Papers*, IV, 47, stated that Booth was captured "yesterday."

in the Tower and examined by Hesilrige, Salwey, and Vane, he denied that he was responsible for the proclamation of Charles II or that he had had any correspondence with the King, though he admitted he had met Mordaunt often in London.[95] He was never brought to trial and escaped all punishment.

The Rump, with all its faults, was not bloodthirsty, and none of the participants in the rising was executed.[96] But the need of money was great, and here was a splendid opportunity of filling the empty treasury. On August 27 an act appointed seven commissioners to sequester the estates, real and personal, of the leaders, Randolph Egerton, Robert Werden, Booth, and Middleton, and of all others who since May 7, 1659, had been in arms or plotted or concealed plotting against the Commonwealth. All those who since January 30, 1649, had promoted the cause of Charles, "son of the late King," were to suffer the same penalty unless they had already made their peace with the government.

The commissioners drew up rules for the county committees and named members of them. Very little was accomplished. The county committees found their powers imperfect and required their instructions to be amended. Some of the nominated declined to serve and time was lost finding substitutes.[97] In Leicestershire two were allowed to be a quorum. The most serious handicap, however, was that the commissioners could authorize the county committees only to seize, but not to sell or let, delinquents' estates, and could not permit the payment of any agents. A sentence from London to the Lancashire committee is probably of general application—"We can come to no result that satisfies you." Local men had no wish to serve a cause whose future looked so uncertain and eagerly sought for excuses for doing as little as possible. Those who were active seized estates and amassed evidence against their owners, and some collected rents. The expulsion of Parliament by the army on October 13 seems to have stopped or delayed proceedings in many places. The committee for Durham asked on October 31 for new instructions because "those strange revolutions doth put a great amazement upon most men." They were not alone in their bewilderment.[98]

[95]Ibid., p. 48. Prynne in *A Plea for Sir George Booth* argued that the baronet was no worse than the army leaders who had accomplished what he had failed to achieve—the ejection of Parliament.

[96]For an amusing account of how Grenville so pleased Vane and other councillors by abusing Oliver Cromwell that they released him, see *Clarendon State Papers*, III, 543. Many of the insurgents had to wait until the new year before obtaining their freedom.

[97]*Acts and Ordinances*, II, 1347-49. A curious petition is printed in *Publick Intelligencer* under August 6, complaining that many thousand families, tenants of malignant landlords, had been ejected from their holdings, and praying that those who assisted in suppressing Booth's rising might hold their tenements, themselves and their heirs forever, and pay only the ancient rents. Newcome (*Autobiography*, I, pp. 116-17) describes the obstacles the sequestrators encountered at Manchester.

[98]*Calendar Committee for Compounding* summarizes the imperfect records, I, xxii, 745-75.

Note on Sir Richard Willis

Miss Marjory Hollings subjected the evidence against Willis to minute scrutiny (*English Historical Review*, XLIII [1928], 33-65) and placed students of the period under a heavy debt of gratitude, whether they accept or reject her main conclusions. The chief obstacle to her spirited defense of Willis against the accusation that he was in Thurloe's pay from 1656 onwards is Willis' own defense (printed in *Notes and Queries*, 12th Series, X, 123), which is singularly unconvincing. It is, however, difficult to understand because it was apparently taken down by someone examining Willis and written without regard to the antecedents of pronouns.

After describing how at the end of 1656 or the beginning of 1657, Thurloe explained to Willis that he (Thurloe) did not intend to destroy Willis if he would reconcile Thurloe to the King when the time came, and that until then the royal cause should speed the better for Thurloe, the statement continued: "Which he is very confident has been effected by his management in preserving many of them (and that the most eminent) both in their lives and fortunes, preventing many from, and delivering others out of, restraint." Miss Hollings assumed that "his management" meant Thurloe's, but it is more likely that Willis meant his own. Otherwise Willis made nonsense of his own statement by adding that Thurloe had offered him £1,000 to betray Ormonde who visited London on the King's behalf in February, 1658. Surely Willis cannot have expected his accusers to believe that Thurloe wanted to have Ormonde arrested in order to show his devotion to the royal cause, or to gain credit for releasing him later because, of course, such an eminent Royalist's fate would have rested with Cromwell and his Council and not with Thurloe alone.

To Miss Hollings' comments on Morland's charge that Willis, on the eve of Booth's rising, tried to get the King to land in Kent at a certain place and time, and thus deliver him to his enemies, I have one addition to make—that Scot, one of the alleged confidants of Willis, said nothing about the existence of such a plot in 1659 but did acknowledge that such an offer to trepan Charles II had been made "manie years since" to him by one Jansen (See Scot's statement in *English Historical Review*, XII [1897], 116-26). This happened some time during 1649 to 1653 when Scot was intelligencer. Inasmuch as he was writing when a prisoner in 1660 and had a chance to save his life if he made a full confession, it is extremely unlikely that he would have omitted the Royalist's treachery reported by Morland if it had any foundation.

Miss Hollings conceded that Willis was in the pay of the government from June to October, 1659. There is, therefore, no point in re-examining the evidence on this point. What Willis revealed is nowhere stated, but, as I have shown, the sources of most of the information can be traced. In the Council Register are three references that deserve notice. On June 13, "Mr. Willis" is called upon to attend the Council tomorrow. On July 22, mention is made of the imposition of a bond for £6,000 on "Richard Willis Esq." as the condition for accepting his parole for his peaceful behavior. The Clerk of the Council sometimes was careless about titles and the two entries may refer to Sir Richard. It is difficult to find another Richard Willis from whom so heavy a bond would be exacted. On July 29, the Council ordered a letter to be written requiring the attendance of "Sir Richard Willis." By then the Council knew the date set for the rising and many particulars, so the summons is likely to have been sent to a suspect rather than to a spy.

I regret that D. E. Underdown's suggestive article, "Sir Richard Willys and Secretary Thurloe" (*English Historical Review*, LXIX [1954] 373-87), appeared too late for me to use it.

CHAPTER IX

The Army and the Rump

AFTER THE DEFEAT of Booth's rising in August the republic seemed more firmly established than ever. Henceforth for the Royalists to overturn it by force was unthinkable. The danger came from the unsolved problems which had already provoked a crisis which the rising merely postponed. The relations of the army and Parliament were still inimicable, and no agreement about the future constitution was in sight. The arrears of pay were far from satisfied and could not conceivably be settled permanently so long as the Rump shrank from imposing additional taxes. Confiscations of the property of Royalists engaged in the late insurrection might ultimately yield a windfall, and the device of collecting all the monthly assessment for the year in six months might give temporary relief, though it left prospects for 1660 darker than ever.[1] Failure to give the soldier his due had two very serious consequences: he was alienated from Parliament and in the mood to listen to any plan which promised him his pay; and he had to live at free quarters which he disliked and which his unwilling host disliked still more.

As for the form of government to be established, there were many schemes. The army leaders would have preferred a nominal Protectorate with themselves collectively playing the rôle of mayor of the palace. This being impossible, they were determined not to submit to the rule of a single house. They demanded the creation of a senate to safeguard fundamentals, including toleration and the continuance of the army. The junior officers wanted fundamental laws, but did not agree that a senate, in which their seniors were likely to form the majority, was the ideal body to preserve these laws. Their panacea was a rigid, written constitution. The rank and file were very slowly becoming aware that they were being used as pawns by their superiors. They did not find leaders, and the occasional rumors alleging that they had chosen agitators as in 1647 were false. Yet signs were not lacking that the soldiers' patience might be nearing its end. After Booth's defeat, the orders from the Council to disband the militia regiments or smaller units raised to put down the Royalists met with resistance whenever pay was not forthcoming. The common soldiers seized the militia commissioners at various centers and threatened to detain them until they received what was due to them.[2]

[1] On June 23 the Commons voted to send a letter to the commissioners of assessment for each county telling them to collect half the amounts by August 1 and the other half by October 10.

[2] Hist. MSS Comm., *Portland MSS*, I, 686-87; *Calendar Domestic*, p. 179.

The commissioners seem to have been able to raise enough money to induce the soldiers to go home peacefully. If militiamen, whose arrears cannot have been greater than for two months or so, took such drastic action, the regular soldiers, with longer arrears, were not likely either quietly to endure privation indefinitely or to disband unless paid in full.

The Rump, like the army, was divided. The number of swordsmen was not inconsiderable, but the officers that attended did not form a solid phalanx. Had Fleetwood been able to give them an inspiring lead so that they would have voted together, they could often have formed a majority in the thin Houses of the time, but he was ineffective and his occasional activity did more harm than good. In most divisions officers, past and present, voted on opposite sides. Similarly, civilians were divided in opinion. A small group, headed by Neville, was permeated with the theories enunciated by Harrington. A larger body usually followed Hesilrige, who carried most weight in domestic politics, but his character was ill-suited to the leadership of a majority. Stiff-necked and narrow-minded, prolix in public but morose in private, he could not assay either men or measures. Though he had not disdained to lay hands on confiscated church property, he was a rigid guardian of the public purse and failed to realize the popular appeal of well-timed generosity. He, like Scot, preferred a unicameral government untrammeled by either senate or written constitution. Both were determined to induce the army to unquestioned obedience to the civil authority. Impetuous and passionate, Hesilrige did more than any other individual to alienate the army from the Rump. Vane presented a contrast to him. His major interests were foreign affairs and theology. He was an adroit politician and a mystic, clear-headed in politics if cloudy in religion. Of first-rate ability, with a sense of humor all too rare among his colleagues, great industry and scrupulousness in financial transactions, a willingness to compromise and tolerance of ideas alien to his own, he was the man from whom Cromwell prayed to be delivered and of whom Charles II wrote that he was too dangerous a man to be allowed to live if he could honestly be executed. George Fox found him "vain, and high, and proud, and conceited."[3] To have alienated three men of such varied characters, Vane must have been a very unusual politician, perhaps an inferior Gandhi. Rightly or wrongly, his subtlety seemed to contemporaries to approach lack of principle. In his tract, *A Healing Question*, published in 1656, he had advocated a convention elected by the people to draw up inviolable "fundamental constitutions." Then "the supreme power" would be a

[3]*Journal*, p. 336; Burnet, *History of My Own Time*, I, 286, n. 2. Those who have tried to understand Vane's religion may agree with the bishop: "I have sometimes taken pains to see if I could find out his meaning in his books; yet I could never reach it."

single chamber. A Republican, whom Milton had once praised as "young in yeares, but in sage counsell old," Vane soon espoused the side the poet denounced. Thus the army and the Rump had many divided interests as well as a mutual antipathy.

When the need for unity was greatest, violent quarrels between Hesilrige and Vane enlivened debates in Parliament and the Council. The immediate occasion was a new engagement obliging militia officers to denounce Charles Stuart and to promise to be faithful to the Commonwealth without a single person and House of Lords. On September 3 the House ordered the clerk to write this engagement on parchment so that all members could subscribe to it on the sixth. When that day came members veered round and, instead of subscribing, sent the engagement to a committee from which it did not emerge. Wariston states only the facts that the debate was very heated and that angry words passed between Hesilrige and Vane. Yet the surmise is easy that Hesilrige favored this purely political test and that Vane opposed it. The two men differed about far more serious issues than whether members should take one more oath. For the moment, the most serious cause of dissension was the attitude towards the army. The one wished to do no more than recruit the House, regardless of what the army wanted, the other thought that the form of government should be settled with the army's consent.[4] Whether either would obtain his desires was soon to be seen.

Lambert's dispatch announcing his victory was received by the Council the next day (August 20, 1659). A motion in Parliament that he should be promoted to the rank of major general was defeated by Hesilrige, though he supported the grant to Lambert of £1,000 rather than £500. The sum of £500 was voted to be divided between Lieutenant Colonel Duckenfield and Major Creed, who brought the report of the victory to London. £12,000 in cash and £2,000 in assignments were scraped together to pay the men. Lambert distributed his gift among his soldiers. One of the innumerable queries that got into print asked, when he "melted it [£1,000] into liquor, and bestow'd it upon his Janizaries, whether the Army drank more for the Rump, or *Lambert*?"[5] He showed his chagrin at the refusal of promotion by ignoring an invitation of the Council to attend its sittings until September 21.[6]

---

[4]Wariston's *Diary*, Sept. 6, 7, 22; Oct. 3.

[5]*The Game Is Up: or, XXXI New Quaeries*, No. 3 (dated by Thomason November 5); *Calendar Domestic*, pp. 132, 134, 145; *Commons Journals*, VII, 766, 769; Guizot, I, 464. Ludlow (II, 114-15) asserts that Fleetwood moved the promotion knowing that it would be rejected and hoping that Lambert would be provoked enough to join the army leaders in their "detestable design" of destroying the Parliament. Whether such a design existed at this time is doubtful, but certainly the grandees meant to control events if they could.

[6]*Calendar Domestic*, pp. 147, 157, 160, 168, 213.

Creed, on his return to the army, met Colonels Axtell, Sankey, and others unnamed, and they considered how they might improve the occasion of their victory. The sequel was that about the middle of September some fifty officers of the expeditionary force at Derby assembled in order to turn their victory to the greater glory of God and the good of the nation.[7] To this end they appointed Colonels Mitchell and Sankey and Major Creed to draft a petition, which they did. They are said to have acted without consulting Lambert, who tried to suppress their petition before and after his return to London.[8] As it seems improbable that these officers took the initiative on their own account, some correspondence is likely to have been exchanged with members of the army council in London.[9]

This Derby petition, as it was called, was the spark which started the conflagration that destroyed the Commonwealth. It was addressed to "the supreme authority of these nations, the Parliament of the Commonwealth of England." The preamble recites that "we, with others who desire to fear the Lord . . . have been again saved by the Lord, and have had a late view of his appearance as of old." Having claimed that success in battle proved that Providence was on their side, they professed that they trembled lest the fruit of victory might not be garnered. Therefore they presented for consideration five proposals: that the Wallingford House petition[10] should be given life as the only expedient yet presented for securing the civil and spiritual liberties of the nation; that the unity of the faithful army be preserved and the efforts to divide it into factions be frustrated by the permanent appointments of Fleetwood as commander in chief, Lambert as second in command, Disbrowe as chief officer of the horse, and Monck as chief officer of the foot; that all be removed from their employments, civil and military, who recently assisted the enemy or remained neutral; that corporations be regulated by removing the disaffected and replacing them by persons well qualified to serve the Commonwealth; and that magistrates, ministers and all others who lately provoked men to rise in arms should be proceeded against.[11] Lambert arrived in London on or about September 20. His army, "a little flushed" with the late victory, followed within a few days, being quartered in Westminster and the City. He and his chief officers

[7] A *Declaration of the General Council of the Officers*, p. 8; *A True Relation*, by E. D., which is listed by Fortescue under October 11, but which describes events leading up to the history of October 11 and 12, and what occurred on those days.

[8] Mitchell to William Clarke, Sept. 24, in *Leyborne-Popham MSS*, p. 123. According to Baker's *Chronicle*, p. 672, the officers first met on September 16.

[9] It is so stated in Baker, p. 672, but no letters are known to survive.

[10] Presented to Parliament on May 12.

[11] To be found printed only in Baker's *Chronicle*, p. 673.

held daily meetings at Wallingford House, in which Fleetwood, Disbrowe, Barrow, Berry, Cobbet, and Ashfield participated.[12] There was, therefore, no reason to doubt that the Derby petition or another based on it would be supported by the army in England, but whether it would be equally acceptable to the rest of the army was by no means clear.

A copy of the petition was sent to Monck with a commendatory letter, urging him to signify his approval to Duckenfield or Creed, who were being sent from Derby to the general council of officers in London. On the contrary, Monck informed his leading subordinates that he had always opposed petitions to Parliament in general, and was still of the same opinion. Therefore, he ordered them not to allow those under their command to sign any petitions without his consent. He also wrote to the Speaker a letter which has not survived but which is said to have encouraged members to resist the army's importunities. He was assured by the Speaker's reply of the high esteem Parliament had of his valor, prudence, and faithfulness.[13]

In England the course of events was different. Fleetwood let the cat out of the bag and showed Hesilrige the petition.[14] The latter brought the matter up in the House in the morning of September 22, raged against Lambert, and proposed sending him to the Tower.[15] Calmer counsels prevailed, however, and a vote passed without a division that Colonels Pearson, Ashfield, and Cobbet should bring the petition to the House that afternoon, that Fleetwood should also produce his copy, and that he should inform the three officers of the order. In the afternoon Fleetwood produced a letter addressed to Ashfield, Cobbet, and Duckenfield by many persons in the army asking them to present the Derby petition to Fleetwood, and the petition itself. The debate was adjourned until the morrow, when a resolution was passed that "this debate be kept under secrecy." Then a motion was carried without a division that to have any more general officers was "dangerous, chargeable, and dangerous to the Commonwealth," but another motion was defeated by 31 to 25 that the petition was unreasonable and of dangerous consequence. Finally, Fleet-

[12]Thomas Rugge, "Mercurius Politicus Redivivus, or a Collection of the most Material Occurrences and Transactions in Publick Affairs, 1659-1672," p. 8. This diary is in British Museum Add. MSS 10116-17, and a photostat of it is in the Huntington Library. It is a compilation from newspapers with a few personal entries.

[13]*Clarke Papers*, IV, 57-59. For Monck's letter of October 13 declining to sign the petition of October 5 see *Weekly Intelligencer*, pp. 194-95; Hist. MSS Comm., *Portland MSS* II (1893), 98-99.

[14]Ludlow, II, 134. According to *A Declaration of the General Council of the Officers* Fleetwood, to avoid giving offense to Parliament, showed the petition to Hesilrige and proposed a conference with Vane and Salwey. Hesilrige agreed, but "contrary to expectation and ingenuity [i.e., ingenuousness]" brought up the matter next day in the House and prejudiced members against Lambert and other officers.

[15]Ludlow, II, 135, 143; *Calendar Venetian*, p. 74. In the official *Army's Plea for their Present Practice* ([1659] p. 16) it is stated that members demanded that some of the chief officers of Lambert's brigade should be hanged.

wood was directed to communicate the vote to the officers, admonish them for their irregular conduct, and prevent any similar proceedings.[16]

For nearly a fortnight a pall of silence descended upon the relations of Parliament and the army. The council of officers was persuaded to abandon the Derby petition on condition that another should be substituted. The Rump began to cultivate the City of London and to reconsider their vote that John Ireton should continue as lord mayor for a second year. They received a petition from the common council in which the government of the City was said to depend upon its customs and its charters, according to both of which the lord mayor was chosen by the citizens. The House was reminded of the many occasions when it had formally acknowledged its indebtedness to the City. A vote was promptly passed to permit the free election of the lord mayor, and Thomas Aleyne (or Allen or Allin) was chosen.[17] The size of the majority, 38 to 13, Fitch and Salwey telling for the minority, suggests that members were becoming conscious of the need of outside support. The heavy fines, ranging from £100 to £5, imposed on absentees imply a consciousness how few members were settling the affairs of the nation—they may also reflect a desire to punish those suspected of disaffection or the chronic shortness of money.[18] On October 4 a resolution was passed that arrears of pay of officers and soldiers should be met from half the money raised by the sale of the land of delinquents participating in the recent insurrection and from half of the proceeds of the sale of forests and chases, the New Forest and the Forest of Dean being excepted.[19] The obvious drawback to this scheme was that before it became effective the soldiery might grow impatient.

The silence which had prevailed in military circles since September 23 was broken on October 5 when Disbrowe headed a group of officers who presented another petition which, though styled "humble" and containing much about faithfulness to the Parliament, was a very stiff document. It began with a reference to Fleetwood's report of the parliamentary votes and an assertion that to all unprejudiced minds the actions of the council of officers and of their brethren at Derby would not have appeared improper. To prove their innocence and to frustrate the hopes of those who expected to profit by dissensions they declared that they were opposed to setting a single person in supreme authority; that they

[16]*Commons Journals*, Sept. 22-23. The tellers for the majority were Fleetwood and Hesilrige, for the minority, Neville and Scot.

[17]Ibid., Sept. 2 and 28; the petition is summarized in R. R. Sharpe, *London and the Kingdom* (1894-95), II, 355. The City authorities responded by inviting members and high officers to a dinner at Grocers Hall on October 6.

[18]*Journals*, Sept. 30.

[19]Ibid., p. 791. The other halves were earmarked for the navy and for the redemption of debts incurred on the "publick faith."

had not changed their principles which led to a well-regulated Commonwealth and that they prayed to God to make the Parliament instrumental in founding a government that would secure liberties and rights to posterity; that the Derby petition and its reception by officers in London had no sinister end; and that they had been misrepresented to Parliament and publicly admonished. They prayed therefore for nine concessions, of which the most important were: the second, that whoever cast scandalous imputations in Parliament upon the armed forces should be brought to condign punishment; the third, that members of the army should be allowed their rights as freemen to petition Parliament; the fourth, that speedy consideration be given to the necessitous condition of the poor soldiers and of widows and orphans; the sixth, that no officer or soldier be cashiered except by court-martial; the seventh, that as Parliament had thought fit to appoint a committee of nomination, henceforth no officer should be appointed without the committee's approval; and the eighth, that Parliament should consider that the commander in chief's commission would expire in a few months and reach a decision "as may prevent our fears, and the hazard of leaving the Army to confusion."

The deputation was thanked by the House and informed that attention had already been paid to the relief of widows, orphans, and maimed soldiers and to the satisfaction of arrears. The rest of the petition would be taken into consideration on Saturday, October 8.[20]

The discussion in Parliament of the army's petition began on the eighth and continued on the tenth and following days. The nine points were answered separately. The responses to the second and third were that it was the duty of all citizens to inform the House of whatever concerned the public safety and the right of the House to receive information and resolve as it thought fit; and that soldiers, as freemen, had the right to petition Parliament, but ought to seek nothing that might disturb the Commonwealth and to acquiesce in the judgment of Parliament. The fourth point having already been answered, the House agreed to the fifth, an innocuous plea for the encouragement of all who had proved faithful during the late insurrection. But on the same day, the eleventh, the House passed through all its stages a bill declaring it high treason to levy a tax not imposed by common consent in Parliament and to make void all "patents, grants, acts, and ordinances" passed since April 19, 1653, which had not received the approval of the present House. Moreover, the bill was to be printed and published.

[20]The petition is printed in *A True Narrative of the Proceedings in Parliament, Councell of State, General Councell of the Army and Committee of Safetie: From the 22 of Septemb. untill this present* [November 16]. This official defense of the army was published by John Redmayne, and has valuable documents. Hereafter cited as Redmayne.

The reason why such an act was passed in haste was exactly the same as had prompted a similar measure in April—fear that the army was about to expel the Parliament. Members had learned that Lambert, Disbrowe, and other high officers had been soliciting by letter additional signatures to the petition already presented.[21] One of these letters addressed to Colonel Okey was read on the twelfth, and determined members to put all to the test. They may have been angered at this attempt to tamper with a regiment upon which they relied, and they probably believed that the letter was intended to stir up the army against themselves,[22] so they decided to try to forestall these efforts to have all the armed forces present a united front. They may have suddenly grown tired of sitting under the sword of Damocles and preferred to mend or end an intolerable situation. Their action was bold because it was certain to promote a crisis. By the unusually large majority of 50 to 15 they revoked the commissions of the nine officers who had signed the obnoxious letter—Lambert, Disbrowe, Berry, Kelsey, Ashfield, Cobbet, Creed, Packer, and Barrow. At the same time they annulled Fleetwood's commission and enacted that henceforth the army should be governed by seven commissioners—Fleetwood, Ludlow, Monck, Hesilrige, Walton, Morley, and Overton.[23]

In virtue of this act, Hesilrige, Walton, and Morley ordered the regiments of Morley and Moss to occupy Westminster Hall and the parts adjacent.[24] The two regiments obeyed and took up their stations with muskets loaded and match burning. Lambert at once accepted the challenge and called together the officers concerned, and they decided to expel the Rump. They gained an important advantage immediately. The parliamentary guard of horse of 160 picked men at 3/– a day under Major Arthur Evelyn at first did its duty in Palace Yard but when its leader was approached by Lambert, he tamely submitted, dismounted,

[21]A specimen of a circular letter, dated October 5, is in Thurloe, VII, 755, and the similar letter to Monck is in Redmayne, pp. 13-14. The letter addressed to Okey upon which Parliament acted I have not found, but it was probably similar to the above.

[22]This design was imputed to the English army leaders by the council of officers at Edinburgh. Redmayne, p. 39.

[23]At some future time Fleetwood explained that his conscience would not allow him to become one of the commissioners. Hesilrige and others from Portsmouth sent him a pointed rejoinder to the effect that it was strange that he could accept from private men [i.e., Lambert and his associates] what he declined from Parliament. Thurloe, VII, 795.

[24]Commons Journals, October 12; Redmayne, p. 19. According to the Weekly Post, p. 195, and The Weekly Intelligencer, p. 189, the commissioners sat all night in the Speaker's chamber, but the latter added that there were five, which seems impossible as Ludlow, Monck, and Overton were not in London, and Fleetwood was opposed. In A Declaration Moss is not mentioned, no doubt because he soon joined the army faction. This official statement adds that Okey led three troops into the City to join the militia there but found no support, and that orders were given to Hacker's regiment in Leicestershire and to other forces in remote parts to march on London. The commissioners for the militia of London on November 3 or 4 by a majority of one decided to send a letter to Monck approving Lambert's coup d'état. The letter and the names of those voting for and against are printed in Redmayne, pp. 64-66. The failure to act on October 13 is thus explained.

and saw Creed take his horse and command. His lieutenant, Cathness, helped to persuade his men to change sides, which they did, waving their hats in their hands.[25] Okey did his best to bring his regiment to the defense of Parliament but most of his dragoons deserted him.[26] The rest of the forces in or near London rallied to Lambert. The soldiers, according to the *Weekly Intelligencer*, were much discontented that a general who had performed remarkable service for his country and received many wounds on its behalf should be cashiered by those he had served so faithfully.[27] A less charitable motive was supplied by Ludlow—that the soldiers had either forgotten their trades or refused to return to an industrious life, and supported their officers in order to prevent their own disbandment.[28]

The regiments adhering to Lambert, including his own horse and foot which had now returned from Cheshire and Derbyshire, formed a ring round those guarding Westminster, and also manned boats to make the blockade complete. They turned back members trying to reach the House, among them the Speaker. When he was stopped at the gate into Palace Yard he asked who was detaining him. The answer was, "an officer of the army." He replied, "Then know, I am your General, and return unto your duty." But he was told the officer acted under express orders, and was obliged to turn back. At Wallingford House he was stopped again, but, on refusing to enter, he was suffered to return home.[29] During the livelong day the two forces faced each other, sometimes maintaining a surly silence and sometimes indulging in arguments. Lambert tried to induce first Morley's regiment and then Moss's to betray their trust but they stood firm. After asking some men under Moss whether they would suffer nine of their old officers who had shed their blood for them and with them to be ruined and their families too, he received the colonel's reply that better nine families should be destroyed than the civil authority trampled under foot.[30] Each side gained some deserters, but the outcome was uncertain until news spread that the Council of State had ordered all troops to return to their respective quar-

[25]*Calendar Venetian*, p. 79; *Weekly Intelligencer*, p. 190; Firth and Davies, *Regimental History*, I, 56, and the authorities there cited. The cornet was young Henry Vane but whether he took any part in the scene is not stated.

[26]*Weekly Intelligencer*, p. 189; Ludlow, II, 136.

[27]*Weekly Intelligencer*, p. 190.

[28]*Memoirs*, II, 138.

[29]*Weekly Intelligencer*, p. 192; Ludlow, II, 139-40 (who states that the officer was Lt. Col. Dunkenfield). Hyde, writing to Ormonde, embroiders the above by adding that when the Speaker claimed to be their general the soldiers replied "they knew no such thing; that if he had marched before them over Warrington-bridge, they should have known him" (*Ormonde Papers*, II, 266).

[30]Ludlow, II, 138-39. Though Ludlow did not arrive in London from Ireland until October 29, he tells us that from conversations with Fleetwood and others he became "fully acquainted with the grounds and causes" of this crisis.

ters till further orders. Thereupon both parties marched away, firing many volleys to show their joy at the bloodless end of a very trying day. As Moss's regiment was departing, Lambert rode through the ranks and was saluted with volleys of shot "in the acknowledgment of so brave a soldier."[31] He did not neglect to leave two or three companies at Westminster as a guard.

There are two accounts of the Council's meeting by members. Whitelocke states that Lambert, Disbrowe, Hesilrige, Morley, and others had a "long and smart debate," but at last all parties, to avoid bloodshed, agreed that Parliament was not to sit. He adds that the council of officers undertook to preserve the peace and to cause "a form of government to be drawn up for a new parliament to be shortly summoned, and so to settle all things." Finally, the Council of State in the evening sent orders to the soldiers of the opposing forces to go to their several quarters.[32] Wariston, who claims that he and Salwey had the chief part in persuading the councillors to send the orders, does not mention any agreement that the existing Parliament should not meet or that the officers should be responsible for a new Parliament. Instead, he relates that at a second meeting at night councillors learnt that Lambert had set two companies at the doors of the House "which imported the dissolution of the Parliament." The next day he found the councillors still uncertain whether Parliament and Council would be dissolved.[33]

These narratives cannot be reconciled. Wariston's is likely to be the more correct. An examination of the names of the eighteen councillors present prompts the inference that the majority would never have acquiesced in the conditions Whitelocke outlines. None of the pamphlets defending the coup d'état urges that the Council had agreed to the dissolution of Parliament. The refusal of men such as Hesilrige and Scot to listen to any proposals for a reconciliation with the army leaders may well have resulted from a conviction that Lambert had been guilty of a breach of faith.

However well-intentioned, the Council's intervention was fatal, because the army leaders were given time to undermine the loyalty of pro-parliamentary regiments and to replace their officers by others more compliant. The next day, the fourteenth, the Council ordered the officers to withdraw the guards round the Houses of Parliament, but no one paid

[31]*Weekly Intelligencer*, p. 191 [misprinted 179]; Redmayne, p. 20.

[32]*Calendar Domestic*, p. 251. There were eighteen councillors present, including Hesilrige and Scot. Whether they were outvoted or acquiesced in the order apparently cannot be determined. Hesilrige attended for two more days, Scot until the end. The Venetian ambassador goes so far as to assert that Lambert and some of his supporters at Whitehall issued the order "in the name of the council of state." The parliamentary forces accepted it as genuine. *Calendar Venetian*, p. 80.

[33]*Diary*, Oct. 13.

the slightest attention. The sergeant-at-arms sent to Westminster to deliver the order brought back the laconic reply from the corporal—no higher officer being present—that the guard would remain where it was until ordered to withdraw by its superior officers.[34] The Council continued to sit until October 25 and transacted only the most routine business. Some of the debates, however, were very significant. A fundamental issue was immediately raised. "I found at Counsel," wrote Wariston, "some asserting the Parliaments absolut authority, some that it was limited [so as] not to be prejudicial to the cause." This one sentence explains not only why Hesilrige and Vane quarreled—a relatively unimportant matter—but why the army and its few civilian supporters insisted on some safeguard, a senate or a written constitution, against the arbitrary rule of a single chamber. A grave difficulty confronted those who believed that the cause was all important; for who should define it, when Levellers, Fifth Monarchy men, grandees, and subordinate officers—to name a few of the groups within the Republican fold—all had different notions? Those, like Vane, who thought the *melior pars* should prevail over the *major pars* were in much the same quandary.[35] What kind of test would separate the sheep from the goats?

An incident at one of the Council's last meetings deserves remembrance. Sydenham was justifying the army's proceedings on the old, familiar ground that it was bound to answer "a particular call of the divine Providence." Bradshaw, now with one foot in the grave, could no longer stomach such a claim and indignantly interrupted the colonel, "declaring his abhorrence of that detestable action, and telling the council, that being now going to his God, he had not patience to sit there to hear his great name so openly blasphemed." He withdrew from public affairs and died on October 31.[36] Exulting ballads prove the popular detestation of the president of the court that had condemned Charles I, but these last recorded words are very creditable to him. It was time indeed that they were uttered because the army leaders' contention that success on the battlefield proved that Providence was on their side had already been used, by Cromwell as well as by his subordinates, to justify all kinds of constitutional innovations and disorders and, if accepted, would lead logically to rule by the naked sword.

One who had tried to defend the sentence which had made Bradshaw

---

[34]Redmayne, p. 22; *Calendar Domestic*, pp. 252-53. According to a newsletter the council of officers refused to support the Council of State when it ordered the guard to withdraw. *Clarke Papers*, IV, 62.

[35]Wariston's *Diary*, Oct. 14, June 18. The second reference is to a debate between Vane and Neville on *melior pars vel major pars*.

[36]Ludlow, II, 140-141. As Bradshaw was last present on October 15, the incident probably occurred on that day.

and his fellow judges so hated now took up his pen to denounce the military coup d'état. Milton, after learning from a friend[37] the inwardness of the state of affairs, wrote him a letter which is most revealing about his political opinions. He acknowledged that he was overjoyed when the army, "under the working of God's holy Spirit, as I thought," restored the old famous Parliament which they had unjustly dissolved. He was persuaded that God was pleased at its restoration, because his approval was shown by the victory gained when a great part of the nation was striving to return to its Egyptian bondage. But now for no other cause than "the discommissioning nine great officers" upon notice of their intentions against the Parliament there had occurred what was "most illegal and scandalous, I fear me barbarous, or scarce to be exampl'd among any Barbarians, that a paid Army should . . . thus subdue the Supream Power that set them up. . . . Which will undoubtedly pull down the Heavy Judgment of God among us, who cannot but avenge these Hypocrisies, Violations of Truth and Holiness." In the existing anarchy a senate or council of state must be established on two conditions—liberty of conscience and abjuration of a single person. The only cement to unite a Parliament or Council to the army was "a mutual League and Oath . . . not to desert one another till Death."[38]

Living in that age Milton should not be singled out for censure for assuming divine sanction for actions pleasing to himself and divine punishment for those unpleasing. He should not be blamed for his assertion that the Rump had set up the army, because many others were as forgetful as he of the fact that but for Pride's Purge—a military coup—the Rump might never have existed. That he should have accepted a state position after a majority of members had been excluded from Parliament in 1648 but be so vehement when the remnant was expelled in 1653 and 1659 in no way marks him as more inconsistent than the Rump itself. But it is surprising that one so ardent in the defense of a free conscience should propose an oath to unite army and Council. It is more surprising that one who had seen many oaths taken and broken since 1641 should still retain so firm a belief in their efficacy. But here again he was no more fallible than the Rump—the army leaders had become skeptical.[39]

Another Republican, unfortunately anonymous, denounced the army as fiercely as Milton. He pointed out that all the officers had received

[37]Masson (V, 618) suggests Vane or some other councillor of state. If Vane was the friend, his adherence to the army might explain why the letter was not published at the time.

[38]"A Letter to a Friend," in *Works*, VI, 101-106, dated Oct. 20. The letter was not printed for half a century, but was designed to be handed round to his friend's friends.

[39]*A Narrative of the Causes and Events of Civil-War* (1659), by F. M., attempted to prove from historical parallels from classical as well as English history that oaths were efficacious. At the end is the assertion that laws might be repealed but oaths remained binding.

their commissions from the Speaker and one by one promised obedience, naming Packer and Lambert as great sticklers for the Parliament. Officers had claimed to be saints but were liars. As for the Fifth Monarchy men who were flocking to Wallingford House, "Upon my word, these were fit to live *and reign with Christ a thousand years*, who cannot keep Faith an hundred dayes. . . . With flattering lips, and with a double heart do they speak." The officers' senseless action was a benefit only to the Cavaliers, while their inconstancy had introduced a facetious proverb to Europe—"as certain as England." What did they now intend? Was the army to be the representative of England, its general the archon or sole legislator, the council of officers the senate, and the inferior officers the people? Why not a corporation of the navy too, because this would be every jot as reasonable? Look at the army's record. They first "Declared against a Single Person: Then routed the Parliament: Then set up a Mock-Parliament: Then pulled it down: Then made their General Protector for life; Then made him to beget a Protector: Then broke this Government: Then suffered the Parliament to sit again. Now they have broken them again. What comes next? That which they will break again ere long." The author concluded with an application of the account of St. Paul's voyage to Rome to the position in England. The officers had expelled the best pilots. Unless they recalled them they could not be saved.[40]

The army council on October 14 suspended Morley, his lieutenant colonel, and Evelyn, from their commands, and directed Colonels Sanders, Okey, Markham, and Alured to withdraw. These officers signed *The Humble Representation of Some Officers*, November 1, which is a very able indictment of the army leaders as valuing the nine officers above the welfare of the nation.[41] Before long fifteen field officers had been turned out.[42] The council ordered Cobbet to go to Scotland and Barrow to Ireland to expound the army's case to the troops there, and nominated Fleetwood as commander in chief. The choice was more or less inevitable. Fleetwood, a pliant reed, provided a convenient shelter for Lambert's ambition. Just as in the revolution that had overthrown Richard Cromwell he had left the decisive action to Disbrowe, so he now left it to Lambert. As a figurehead he divided the army less than any other, but was incapable of inspiring affection in the soldiery. He was told to his face by Wariston of three faults which proved his incapacity

[40]The above is from an addition made after October 13 to one of the best tracts that appeared in 1659, *The Grand Concernments of England Ensured*.

[41]*The Lord General Fleetwoods Answer* is a fiction. See *Mercurius Politicus*, November 10-17.

[42]According to Redmayne (p. 21), their dismissal would be decided by court-martial. The names of fifteen are given in *The Declaration of the Officers of the Army Opened*, p. 29. The author, E. D., I regret I cannot identify.

for leadership: "No good friend and no ill foe; slow to come to a determination and suddenly to break it; and doe things by privat suggestions."[43] He could use the scriptural phraseology of the time, but was incapable of penning a popular appeal. His letters to Monck, for example, are among the least convincing that were written. To assert that the army was following direction from on high seemed sufficient to him.[44] If he had any ideas about the future government now that the Rump was ejected, he left little trace of them. Except for the appearance of his name on committees and councils little more can be recorded about him.

The next day the army council chose ten persons, five soldiers and five civilians, to consider how to carry on the government. The first were obvious selections, Fleetwood, Lambert, Disbrowe, Sydenham,[45] and Berry; the second probably represent a Hobson's choice, because few Rumpers attained any pre-eminence and fewer still adhered to the army. They were Whitelocke, who contrived to serve all masters; Vane, who exulted at the imminent appearance of the kingdom of God;[46] Sir James Harrington, a former member of Oliver Cromwell's Council and of the Council of State; Salwey, a steady supporter of the army; and Johnston of Wariston, whose diary provides a valuable account by a participant in the proceedings of the ten. He found that the officers were adamant against allowing the Rump to sit again, rejecting Vane's proposal that another session should be opened, on December 1, perhaps to draw up a constitution or to approve one drafted by the Council of State. As to the latter body, the military leaders required that councillors should first engage to act with the army, and long debates ensued whether to continue the existing Council or appoint another. They decided in favor of a committee of safety, nominated the existing ten, then three, and finally another ten. Wariston records with pride that he was chosen unanimously and not by plurality, as were Vane and Salwey. The Fifth Monarchy men and Quakers were reported to have proposed, though unsuccessfully, the names of the Earl of Pembroke, Major General Harrison, and John Carew.[47] The newcomers were Steele, lord chancellor of Ireland; Ludlow, the commander in chief there, though now in England; Walter Strickland, a former ambassador to Holland in 1651; Lawrence,

[43]Wariston's *Diary*, III, 149.

[44]The letter of October 18, to Monck (*Clarke Papers*, IV, 63-64) is a good specimen of his epistolary style. Lambert was thought to use Fleetwood as Cromwell was alleged to have used Fairfax as a figurehead to conceal the ambition of the second in command. *Calendar Venetian*, p. 86; Coke, *Detection of the Court*, II, 81.

[45]The Colonel Denham in Redmayne's list (p. 21) is an error for Sydenham.

[46]Wariston's *Diary*, II, 149.

[47]Ibid., pp. 145-48.

a councillor under Oliver and Richard Cromwell; Ireton and Tichborne, both former lord mayors and now aldermen of the City of London; Henry Brandrith, a London clothworker; Robert Thomson, a navy commissioner;[48] Colonels Hewson, Clerk, Lilburne and Bennet, and Cornelius Holland, a very minor politician.[49] The original ten had all been members of the Council of State, together with Ludlow.

As if further to emphasize the military origin of the committee of safety, it was directed to consult with the general council of officers "as occasion shall require," and to exercise such authority as that body delegated to it. In general it was to have all the power previously held by the Council of State, to call delinquents to account for the recent insurrection and to sell their estates, to indemnify all persons who had acted for the Commonwealth since 1641, to treat with foreign nations, to call out the militia which would be commanded by Fleetwood, and to dispose of all public officers, removing those who were scandalous.[50]

By the end of October all chance that the military coup d'état would be accepted by the forces in Scotland had vanished. Perhaps for this reason Vane was able to use his influence on Lambert to arrange a conference between the army leaders and himself, Ludlow, and Salwey. The discussion is most enlightening. Lambert at once explained that he had no intention to interrupt Parliament until self-preservation obliged him to act when Hesilrige thirsted after his blood. Then we are told the officers declared they would "do great things for the publick good," and pressed the three to attend the committee of safety. They demurred, preferring to wait until the common cause should be secured to the satisfaction of the godly. When all had agreed that they should meet again, they went their several ways.[51] A student of history may conclude that if the grandees felt that a purely selfish motive was a sufficient justification for ejecting Parliament, any attempt at a compromise was doomed to failure. If he inquires what "great things" were about to come to pass, all he can discover is a report that the army council had been considering the abolition of tithes and the court of chancery—reforms, if reforms they were, desired by the under officers—and that a subcommittee of the committee of safety had been named to draft a constitution, and that Vane had consented to serve on it.[52]

[48]His brother was Colonel George Thomson, member of the Council of State, and he himself was often addressed as colonel or major.

[49]Redmayne, p. 41, dated their appointment October 26.

[50]*Weekly Intelligencer*, pp. 202-203, under October 26.

[51]Ludlow, II, 143-44.

[52]Guizot, II, 284.

In spite of the discouraging outlook Ludlow persevered. He met a few Rumpers. Scot demonstrated that he had no thought of reconciliation with the grandees, and urged Ludlow to speak out against them and in support of Monck. But Ludlow argued that if either the army or the Parliament prevailed entirely, both would be ruined because each was indispensable to the other—the Parliament to vote taxes to pay the soldiers and the army to help establish a new government.[53]

The army leaders and the civilians associated with them did not rely only upon private conferences or mediations. They appeared before the common council of the City of London to plead their case. Whitelocke spoke first on the danger of another civil war and the havoc it would cause in the City where Monck, he said, hoped the citizens would rise. The present commotions, he urged, were really the work of the old enemy who, under Booth, had tried to establish tyranny and slavery. A few sentences will reveal the essence of Fleetwood's speech: "You know this poor Army the Lord has been pleased to make use of as an Instrument to preserve our Peace. . . . I dare say our Design is God's Glory: We have gone in untrodden Paths, but God hath led us into Ways, which, if we know our own Hearts, we have no base or unworthy Design in." Disbrowe enlarged upon the theme that the army had always valued peace as the greatest of blessings. If the citizens disturbed it, "an inconvenience" would befall them. They must not cast dirt at the army but wait until they saw the result of its actions before judging it. He ended by telling them not to meddle with affairs beyond their spheres but to follow peace and holiness.[54] What the citizens thought of these orations is unknown. Two reflections they can scarcely have avoided—that no explanation of the recent coup d'état was accorded them and that not the least hint was dropped of what form of government they might expect. The moral they were expected to draw was: Trust the army and all will be well.

For a brief period the citizens may have been too thankful that no street-fighting had taken place to think about the morrow. This indifference to how they were going to be governed soon gave way to anxiety at the prospect of military rule. A minister heard the bellman singing as he went his rounds:

---

[53]Ludlow, II, 144-46. For a conversation with Hesilrige, who thought the recall of the Rump the only remedy for the present confusions, see ibid., pp. 155-56.

[54]The speeches are reprinted in the old *Parliamentary History*, XXII, 10-17. One of Hyde's correspondents told him (*Clarendon State Papers*, II, 601) that one object of the visit to the City was to borrow £30,000. I have ignored this statement because none of the speeches mentions such a purpose, and Whitelocke (*Memorials*, IV, 370) and other authorities are equally silent. Hyde's correspondent also stated that on their return the citizens shouted for a free Parliament.

Whilst you securely Sleep, I ring my Bell,
Which lately hath Rung out your Freedoms Knell.
Your Souldiers, now, your Sovereigns are become,
Your Laws and Liberties command by sound of Drum.
Nor is it strange, for they read no Commission,
Regard no Bonds, but prosper by Transgression.
By Pride and Perjury, these Saints most rude,
Have Cut off the King, and Parliament subdu'd.
Your eyes have seen't, vile Slaves, yet in this season,
You are Rid like Asses, and not Rul'd by Reason.[55]

No strong imagination is required to picture the citizen turning uneasily in his bed as he heard this rude verse. He may well have concluded with the minister that the return of the King offered the only escape from an intolerable situation.

Meanwhile, the forces around London adhered to Lambert and the eight officers cashiered by Parliament. This is not to be explained only by their popularity, though this was a factor, but also by the sympathy their subordinates felt for their cause. The Rump had repeated Richard's error in allowing over two hundred officers, including a high percentage of the field officers, to remain in London attending the army council. This had become a sort of training school for military politicians and induced the conviction that it was the sole guardian of the "good old cause." It was coming more and more to regard itself as the proper judge of what was good for the people and to disregard what the people wanted. They may have been deceived by the indifference of the public to the events of October 13. But the apparent apathy was deceptive. Many Englishmen at first thought of the issue between the Rump and the army as a mere choice of evils, and it must have been difficult in October to see that the restoration of the Rump was an essential preliminary to the return to parliamentary government. This became clearer when the committee of safety proved incapable of agreeing upon any substitute. One serious obstacle to any agreement among Republicans was the prevalence in their ranks of visionaries, well versed in the Scriptures but uninterested in the practical questions of the day.

One of the best examples of the religious enthusiast was Robert Overton, governor of Hull and one of the commissioners Parliament had appointed to command the army. He put forth a tract entitled *The Humble and Healing Advice* which is a perfect example of the unworldliness of men of his type. Addressing himself to Fleetwood and Monck and their inferior officers, he claimed that all, whatever their preferences in respect of forms and constitutions, civil and religious, aimed to serve the

---

[55]*Englands Repentance* (1659), p. 3.

Lord. This is the sole reference he made in six pages to the vital problem, how England was to be governed. Amid many remarks on "the new creation" about to be formed, and on the expectation of the Saints, "the true royal heirs," now that in the fullness of time they must take the kingdom and possess it, are interspersed some critical comments worth noting as coming from a leader of an important section of Republicans. He rebuked the officers of the English army for their past apostasy and warned them against "advantaging and greatening" themselves and of mixing politic, time-serving trucklers with men of public spirit. Monck, he felt, he could not support, because his religious principles were weak and his face turned against the dispensation of God, "though it be clouded with the weakness and failings of the instruments." Therefore Monck should agree with his brethren in England and not widen the breach. Finally he announced that if fighting started, he would try to keep Hull in peace.[56] Probably there were not a few Saints unwilling to fight because they were uncertain what they would be fighting for.

One of Overton's captains, Robert Scrope, who with four companies was in Scotland, shared his colonel's reluctance to intervene in the impending struggle. In a very straightforward letter without any of the mystical or scriptural language of his superior, he told Monck that though he could not justify the interruption of Parliament, yet he felt unable to fight against his old comrades—"we which have prayed together, took counsel together, fought together, obtained victories together, and rejoiced so often together," could not now destroy each other which the common enemy never did but was always defeated. He had served seventeen years, sixteen as an officer, so no one should attribute his scruples to cowardice. Therefore, he asked that he might be ordered to march to Hull.[57] No doubt others shared the scruples of this honest man. Some there were, too, who pondered the text: "Had Zimri peace, who slew his master?[58]

[56]Thomason failed to secure a copy. Mine has next to the year 1659 on the title page "2 ber 9" written by a contemporary in ink. I presume this meant November 2.

[57]*Leyborne-Popham MSS*, pp. 126-27, where the name is printed "Scrape."

[58]E. D., *A True Relation*, p. 12. The author closed this sharp attack on the English army with a Latin quotation, *Nulla fides pietasque viris qui castra sequuntur.*

CHAPTER X

Monck and the Army in England

Ews that the army had again expelled the remnant of the Long Parliament reached Monck on October 17 or 18, 1659.[1] He cannot have been surprised, because recent events had cast their shadows before them. Fully prepared for such an emergency, he did not hesitate for a moment in taking his stand on the side of the Rump. He called together the few he trusted of those near at hand—Colonel Wilkes, Lieutenant Colonel Clobery of Reade's foot, Major Hubblethorne of Talbot's foot (whom he had managed to retain in his rank after Parliament had proposed to demote him), Captain Jeremiah Smith of his own horse, John Miller of Henry Smith's foot, Ethelbert Morgan, senior captain of his foot, and his chaplain and biographer, Thomas Gumble. Agreement having been reached to declare for Parliament and against the army in England, it was essential to ensure that the forces in Scotland should be of one mind. Therefore, all officers likely to oppose the daring resolution taken must be dismissed.

In Edinburgh were two foot regiments. Luckily the colonel of one, Thomas Talbot, was in England, because after vacillations he was to throw in his lot with Lambert. This regiment, regarded by Monck as most trustworthy, was ordered to parade in battle order with lighted match, powder, and bullets. The other regiment, Monck's foot, was full of politicians and extremists, though Lieutenant Colonel William Gough, who had had a minor part in Richard Cromwell's downfall, and Major Abraham Holmes, were both absent. The regiment went on parade with no ammunition, and was obliged to submit to a most drastic purge. Including the officers who were absent and never returned or who deserted Monck later, the lieutenant colonel, major, four captains, seven lieutenants, four ensigns, the quartermaster, and nine noncommissioned officers were displaced. Either before or after the purge Monck addressed the regiments and told them of his determination to oppose the factious party of the army in England which had interrupted the Parliament and of his expectation that they would stand by him. He was careful to add that he would satisfy all arrears of pay. Whereupon he was applauded by shouts and volleys. The displaced officers were secured in Tantallon Castle, and most were soon given passes to return to England. Their successors were

[1] Baker's *Chronicle*, p. 681; Daniel Mackinnon, *Origin and Services of the Coldstream Guards* (1833), I, 73.

all promoted from within the regiment, though for some unknown reason the position of major was left vacant.[2]

Monck then proceeded to Leith where Wilkes's foot was stationed. The colonel was thought reliable. His services at the time of Overton's plot had won Oliver Cromwell's warm approval for "standing by and sticking to your honest general Geo. Monck, who is a simple hearted man." Wilkes remained staunch four years later, and his foot needed little immediate change. The major, William Knowles, whom Parliament had promoted, was cashiered and Thomas Hughes, whom Parliament had reduced to a captaincy, became major once again. Two lieutenants and two ensigns lost their commissions now but other officers were displaced later.[3] Monck then dealt with Ralph Cobbet's foot, which, like his own, was full of Anabaptists of violent principles. Sending for Lieutenant Colonel Young, he had him arrested on arrival. In all, this regiment lost its three field officers, five captains, six lieutenants, and two ensigns.[4] Cobbet himself was arrested at Berwick and imprisoned in Edinburgh Castle. He was a dangerous man, credited with the intention of spreading disaffection and even of seizing Monck himself. His colonelcy was left vacant, but two captains who had been displaced by Parliament became respectively lieutenant colonel and major.[5] Other regiments lost some officers but not so many as Monck's and Cobbet's. Occasionally privates were dismissed as well as officers. Thus Robson, promoted to command Sawrey's foot, was obliged to get rid of twenty-four soldiers as well as six corporals, being all "Captain Spencer's people of that church" —presumably one of the "gathered" churches.[6]

According to the lists published in the newspapers early in December, in all nearly one hundred and fifty officers and noncommissioned officers were dismissed or deserted—including ten from the garrison at Berwick. An examination of the names shows that Parliament had displayed gross ignorance of the politics of officers in the summer of 1659. Not a few of those who supported most eagerly the latest military coup d'état had recently been promoted, and some who stood by Monck most firmly when he emerged as the defender of Parliament had been demoted or even dis-

---

[2]Davies, *Coldstream Guards*, pp. 91-93; *Weekly Intelligencer*, pp. 210-211. In the long and valuable letter quoted in Mackinnon, *Coldstream Guards*, I, 75, it is stated that Nicholas became major and Winter captain of Holmes's company. I believe this to be an error.

[3]Firth and Davies, *Regimental History*, I, 395. According to the list of those who from first to last deserted Monck, the regiment lost its colonel, lieutenant colonel, four captains, three lieutenants, an ensign, and five noncommissioned officers. The list was printed in the newspapers, e.g., *Publick Intelligencer*, Nov. 28/Dec. 5, pp. 913-14.

[4]Ibid., II, 474. Whether Young was seized at Glasgow or at Monck's headquarters is disputable. Cf. Baker's *Chronicle*, p. 682, and Mackinnon, I, 74.

[5]*Regimental History*, II, 473.

[6]*Clarke Papers*, IV, 160-161.

missed. The civilians on the committee for the nomination of officers and the Rumpers, had sometimes been both misled by their military advisers in London and victimized by the crudest rumors. The officers in London represented the ambitious politicians, many of them long absent from their regiments and out of touch with opinion in the army. Either they were at least half blind or they would have realized that the forces in Scotland and Ireland would not necessarily follow their lead. Monck, like Cromwell before him, saw that a cashiered officer had little or no influence with his late regiment, provided that the remaining officers did not share his views.

Having taken measures to ensure the fidelity of his army, Monck sent three letters to London, all dated October 20. The first to Fleetwood was a very adroit indictment. It began with a reminder that the part of the army which had just ejected the Parliament had recently recalled it and owned it, promising obedience and repenting of its apostasy in turning it out in 1653. If Fleetwood refused to restore Parliament to its freedom to sit, then he (Monck) was resolved to prosecute its just cause to the last drop of his blood. His army was unanimous, and if any officers declined to honor the commissions they had received from the Parliament, he would use the authority bestowed upon him as one of the seven commissioners appointed by act of Parliament and substitute others. The justice of his intentions was plain. God had already appeared against raising money without the people's consent and against any control of the army except by Parliament. Let Fleetwood beware lest he ruin the nations in order to gratify private ambitions. His own sole purpose was to establish the authority of Parliament and the laws which their ancestors had purchased with so much blood. The letter to Lambert contained a severe warning that England would never submit to any arbitrary government and that true Englishmen in the army would also oppose it. The third letter to Lenthall, the Speaker, asserted Monck's determination to uphold the Parliament. It also conveyed the news that he had already cashiered such officers "as would not act according to your Commission."[7]

Two official apologies were issued for the army in England, the longer on October 24 and the shorter, more or less an abridgment, three days later. The first starts with some generalities which are maxims in democracies today, such as that governors were made for the people and not the people for them, and that when they sought only their own interests and neglected the common safety they forfeited their right to allegiance and obedience. When Charles I and his adherents so acted,

[7]The letters are reprinted in the old *Parliamentary History*, XXII, 4-7, and elsewhere. The last sentence proves how promptly Monck had acted.

the Parliament was justified in executing him, abolishing kingship, and episcopacy, and the House of Lords, and setting up extraordinary courts of justice to put to death notorious enemies, although such actions were contrary to the existing laws. Parliament had raised an army by means of appeals published in places of public meeting which, together with the dictates of common reason, had instructed the soldiers that resistance to authority might be necessary to preserve the natural rights of the people. The army had constantly upheld the good cause and would never desert it. When Parliament annulled the commissions of Fleetwood and nine officers without hearing a word in their defense, the intention to destroy the army or to transform it was evident. Seeing, therefore, what slender hope remained that the liberties of the nation would escape destruction, the army was compelled to defend the cause for which it had fought and to put an end to the Parliament. It was true that the officers had promised obedience when they received their commissions from the Speaker, but only because of the implied condition that Parliament would preserve the people's liberties. When that condition was broken, the officers were as free of its obligation as members of Parliament had felt they were free from the Solemn League and Covenant, which had pledged them to defend the King, when they executed him. The minority in Parliament had welcomed the exclusion of the majority by the army eleven years before and allowed the army then to be judge of the case. The same members should not now deny the army's right to judge what was necessary. The people should stop their ears to all unreasonable suspicion and believe that the army would defend their persons, property, rights, and interest.[8]

Perhaps an impartial judgment on this defense is that the army or, rather, its officers, had a fair case against the Rump; its main weakness, however, was the failure to produce evidence to prove that the Rump, when it cashiered Lambert and the rest, was threatening the people's liberties. From the point of view of the man in the street, the army had no case at all. To the question, "who made thee a prince and a judge over us?," there was only the reply that Providence, by granting so many victories, had evidently smiled upon the army. To interpret signs of divine approval by the ordeal of battle was unlikely to satisfy many civilians. Now that the army was divided, which half could claim divine sanction? All the talk about liberties was idle when Englishmen were denied the right to select their own form of government.

Compared with the number of its critics the army found few pam-

[8]The above is an abstract of the thirty-page tract, *The Army's Plea for their Present Practice*. The other defense, *A Declaration of the General Council of the Officers*, has nineteen shorter pages.

phleteers on its side, and these are likely to have done it more harm than good. The most extreme defense, *The Armies Vindication of This Last Change,* claimed to be published "by special command." The author set out to prove that the army was "the principal body of the people" and much superior to the Parliament that had raised it. His chief argument was that the army had conquered its enemies. Therefore, he claimed, the privilege of rule belonged to it. To the objection that in the previous May the army had owned Parliament as the supreme authority and received commissions from it his answer was that Parliament was the supreme authority only so long as the army consented. What it had raised up, it could pull down. Now Parliament was a broken idol, having outlived its usefulness. The army, "with the good people in the condition of conquerors," would discard the law of the land and privileges of parliament, "old and rotten customes not regarded." It would not summon a free parliament because the temper of the people was such that they would return malignants and neutrals. The best government would be mixed, having something of Christ and his kingdom and something of a worldly concernment. The army must unite with the faithful and reform the law, purge the courts of justice, break every yoke, ease all burdens, banish all profanity, release the prisoners, and relieve the poor. How far this program could be carried out was now to be seen.

One answer to the *Army's Plea* was remarkable for its boldness. John Evelyn published his tract, *An Apology for the Royal Party,* as he claimed, in a time of danger when it was a capital offense to speak or write in favor of the King. "It was twice printed; so universally it tooke."[9] A thoroughgoing Cavalier pamphlet, it sets forth the sentiments which many concealed until Charles II was firmly seated on his throne. No one who reads it is likely to be surprised at the severity of the Clarendon Code. Evelyn began by pointing the finger of scorn at the Scots, who had been rewarded for selling their King and betraying his son by a slavery worse than Egyptian and an infamy as unparalleled as their treason and ingratitude. In England the Presbyterians had suffered as badly under Cromwell, "the most infamous hypocrite and proflegate Atheist of all the Usurpers that ever any age produc'd." All the confiscations and intolerable taxes had been squandered away to gratify a few covetous and ambitious wretches whose appetites were as insatiable as the grave. The pretended reformation of religion had produced a thousand different

---

[9] *Diary* under November 7. The tract is dated October 27. Baker (*Chronicle,* p. 722) credits it with three editions and claims that it won more proselytes for the King than any other pamphlet. In a postscript Evelyn explained that his censure of the Presbyterians did not apply to those who were now conscious of their errors. Evelyn sent a copy of his tract to Jeremy Taylor, who praised it highly and wished every Englishman could be obliged to read it twice. *The Whole Works of . . . Jeremy Taylor,* ed. Richard Heber (1828), I, xciv.

kinds of blasphemy and atheism. Booth's rising, wholly managed by some Presbyterians the Rump had disobliged, had brought a calamity upon them which their former actions had deserved. The poor Cavaliers had been innocent but were seized for want of other prey. The sectaries had covered "all this Hydra of Impostures with a mask of Piety and Reformation while breathing nothing but oppression and lying in wait to deceive." The fate of the Eastern Empire was before their eyes. A happy and blessed people had been suddenly overspread by a horrid barbarity because of "the giddiness of a wanton people, the schisms and heresies in the church, and the prosperous successes of a rebellious *Imposter*." England had one course only to avoid a similar disaster—to recall the King. He had never evinced the least inclination for revenge, so every rebel, however crimson his sins, would find a ready pardon. He and his brother were a fraternity spotless in their honor, pure from the exorbitances of youth, and conspicuous for temperance, magnanimity, constancy, and understanding. Let the King be recalled and trade would immediately recover, tender consciences be considered, purchasers of confiscated lands satisfied, and the soldier paid.

About the beginning of November, Monck's prospects did not seem very bright. Except for the possible neutrality of the garrison at Hull, he might have to face all the army in England, superior in numbers, and especially in cavalry, to his own, and contingents from Ireland and Dunkirk. His appeal to the fleet in the Downs was unsuccessful.[10] Though some Republican and other officers had condemned the recent affront to Parliament, no mutinies had followed.[11] So far the forces south of the border presented a united front to the public, however much they might bicker in private. Monck had three tasks to perform: to ensure that his army would follow him, to enlarge the divisions in his opponents' ranks until paralysis resulted, and to rouse public opinion in England. Probably at least nine out of ten Englishmen were cursing the army but so long as they confined their discontent to words they would be as ineffective as those Cavaliers who confined their loyalty to drinking to the King.[12] Monck could not adopt a slogan like "the people versus the

[10]Gumble, *Life of Monck*, p. 136.

[11]See, for example, the long letter addressed to Fleetwood and printed in Redmayne (pp. 55-62). Included among many telling points were the quotations that "all they that take the sword shall perish with the sword," and that Parliament had never raised soldiers to the law-makers but as a defense against law-breakers. Three of the signatures were Alured, Okey, and Sanders, regarded as Republican martyrs for their opposition to the Protectorate and dismissal by Cromwell. The letter is also in Thurloe, VII, 771-74. More impressive was *The Remonstrance of the well-affected people of London . . . against those officers who interrupted the Parliament*. It was dated November 16 and signed by, among others, Fairfax, Skippon, Vice-Admirals Lawson and Goodson, the lord mayor and common council of London, Ashley Cooper, John Wildman, and Colonels Overton, Whetham, Sanders, Streeter, Alured, Moss, Hacker, Rich, John White, William Rainborough, and Okey.

[12]In *A Letter to . . . Lambert* by S. L., October 14, is the statement that a secret ballot would prove that nine out of ten Englishmen would vote for the old constitution.

army," because he would have united all sections of the army against him. But he could use an indirect approach and bring the weight of public opinion to bear upon the rank and file until these came to share the views of citizens. If the soldiers could be convinced that by continuing to support their ambitious commanders they would become mercenaries, holding down their fellow countrymen like a garrison in a conquered nation, then they might desert or refuse to obey orders.

The task of undermining the soldiers' loyalty to their officers was rendered easier by material grievances. When ready money was not available to pay the soldiers, debentures were issued stating the amount of arrears due. A long interval might intervene before the debenture was redeemed. Therefore, the needy soldier often sold his debenture at a discount, frequently to an officer. Because the debentures were sold at the highest at twelve shillings in the pound and at the lowest at one shilling, the soldier lost heavily.[13] What made his plight even harder to bear was to see his colonel becoming a landed proprietor at his expense. Even before a definite attempt was made to induce the English soldier to refuse to fight to gratify his officer's ambition, bitter complaints had been uttered against "the grandees of the army (who have sufficiently already gotten by the poor soldiery, in putting a necessity on them to sell their arrears to you for a matter of nought)." Thomas Clarges in a tract, *Hypocrites Unmasked*, argued that the grandees treated the inferior officers and soldiers like menial servants, to whom they gave housing, food, and clothing, and in return expected all their quarrels to be espoused by their retainers.[14]

Other grievances were boldly stated in print. At the end of the civil wars they expected liberty to flourish, wrote a former captain who now professed to be a private, but they saw their poor country more cheated than formerly. They dared not complain to Parliament of the tyrannies they suffered "because of self-seeking men set over us, who by our means were raised from the meanest Mechanicks to Lord-like Inheritances." If they informed Parliament, for which they had expended their lives and fortunes, they were "enjailed, beaten, and abused by our officers, in a most barbarous manner."[15] Another very striking statement began by declaring that their landlords were grumbling at the taxes which should be

[13]These are the two extremes noted in Firth's *Cromwell's Army*, pp. 203-207.

[14]William Cole, *A Rod for the Lawyers . . . and a Word to the Army* in *Harleian Miscellany*, VII. Thomason dated the tract July 12, 1659. For the authorship of Clarges' tract see Hist. MSS Comm. *Leyborne-Popham MSS*, p. 137.

[15]*The Sentinels Remonstrance or, A Vindication of the Souldiers to the People of this Commonwealth*, by W. B. The initials are the same as William Bray's, who narrowly escaped death in 1647 for his share in the mutiny of Robert Lilburne's regiment. Inasmuch as another pamphlet with W. B. on the title page is signed William Bray, his authorship of the tract analyzed above is reasonably certain.

enough to satisfy all the soldiers' arrears and of which they hoped Parliament would call for an account. Without their pay the soldiers could not buy bread and drink for their wives and children, having sold and pawned what they had to satisfy their hungry stomachs and racking landlords. Those who had families were obliged to eat at cooks' shops and victualers where their officers provided them with credit of sixpence a day. They had to be content with what these tradesmen provided or starve. If they were paid they could buy their commodities at the cheapest rates, whereas now the sutlers grew rich and the army was being ruined.[16]

In standing forth as the upholder of the parliamentary authority Monck had to meet two main charges: that deliberately or accidentally he was promoting the cause of Charles II and that he aimed at dividing the army and thus was abandoning all that it had fought for. To the first he protested that to maintain the Commonwealth was his sole purpose. The Parliament was the main support of the Commonwealth and those who expelled the one were ruining the other. Moreover, the Parliament had justly suspected a design to set up a single person when it had cashiered the nine officers. As to the second charge, the council of officers in London, in its ambition to make the army a corporation independent of the civil authority and distinct from the people by whom it must live, was trying to enslave the three nations to the army, the armies of Scotland and Ireland to the army in England, and the army in England to nine or ten[17] persons or, perhaps, in a short time to one person.[18]

After his first remodeling of his army, Monck set to work to instill into all who remained with the colors a knowledge of what was at stake. Careful to avoid any appearance of autocracy, he used a great council of all commissioned officers to discuss policy. "It was a pleasant sight," wrote Gumble, "to see the General at the end of a Table . . . putting the question . . . and then an Ensign to make a long speech to the contrary (who was last started from a Corporal the other day)."[19] No doubt participation in these debates provided a liberal education for the many promoted officers. Perhaps Monck wished those present to mark the contrast be-

---

[16]*To the Right Honourable, the Supreme Court of Parliament, the Humble Petition of the Sentinels in the Regiment formerly belonging to Major General Goffe*. Thomason's date is June 10.

[17]That is, the nine officers cashiered by Parliament plus Fleetwood.

[18]The letters from Monck or from his officers setting forth arguments like the above are too numerous to cite individually. One of the best is Letter IX in *A Collection of Letters Written by . . . Monck*, reprinted in 1714. Letters were printed separately or in small batches, and many can be found in the *Clarke Papers* and in Redmayne.

[19]Gumble, *Life of Monck*, p. 140. According to *Mercurius Politicus* (Nov. 16), when Monck declared his intentions to a general council of officers Captain Poole of Fairfax's foot proposed an enquiry into proceedings in England first, whereupon Monck had him clapped up. Poole was an extremist (Price, p. 722) who was discharged and, therefore, unlikely to have attended many, if any, general councils of officers. George Fox (*Journal*, p. 325) states that he and his wife became Quakers.

tween his great council and the council of officers in London, rarely attended by subalterns. He used a small committee of officers to reply to declarations and letters from other branches of the army. For propaganda in his own forces he caused to be printed a gazette written by an officer "who was guilty of a little wit."[20]

Five issues of this newspaper, which was called *Mercurius Britanicus*, appeared from December 3 to January 4. They contained favorable news,[21] the justification of Monck's proceedings, and criticisms of English officers and their journal, *Mercurius Politicus*. One incident was referred to several times, the riot in the City of London by the apprentices who were petitioning the common council for a free parliament.[22] It is noticeable that the first issue mentioned two or three of the City slain and a lieutenant and four soldiers wounded. In later issues the civilian casualties grew—three or four killed and twenty or thirty slashed; six or seven killed—but the reference to the military casualties disappeared.[23] Next to an exaggerated version of the riot came a paragraph that soldiers were so vilified, scorned, and hissed in London that they were ashamed to march, and that officers when they went into the City dared not wear swords for fear of affronts.[24] A curious anecdote is that Oliver Cromwell's widow sent a gentleman to Fleetwood to remind him of her husband's dying words, that Fleetwood would never leave his whimsies till he had put the nation in blood. It is very interesting that this newspaper thought worthy of insertion a saying of the Protector.[25]

Other propaganda took the form of tracts and broadsides. The pamphlet, *A Conference between two Souldiers*,[26] is of value because it purports to reproduce a discussion between one of Monck's men and one of Lambert's. Inasmuch as so very little is known about the views of the rank and file it is worth examining to see what kind of argument Monck's propagandists thought would influence privates. After the soldier from Scotland denied the stock accusation that the forces to which he belonged were starting a new war, both found that they agreed about the origin of the civil war—to defend Protestantism, the King's person, parliamentary privileges, and the laws and liberties of the subject. They agreed too about the King's execution—kings were made for the people and not vice versa; men were freeborn with none having a hereditary right over oth-

[20]Gumble, p. 141.

[21]Not infrequently derived from newsletters printed in *Clarke Papers*, IV.

[22]See below, p. 181.

[23]*Mercurius Britanicus*, pp. 26, 32, 34.

[24]Ibid., p. 35.

[25]Ibid., p. 35; cf. *Clarke Papers*, IV, 167.

[26]It is called the first part, though no second is known, is dated November, and is said to have been printed at Newcastle, which may be doubtful.

ers; all power was in the people and entrusted to kings only conditionally; and the House of Lords was inconsistent with the people's liberties. They were of one mind about Pride's Purge and the expulsion of the Long Parliament in 1653, because the good old cause required them. But the recent expulsion was the bone of contention. Whereas the soldier from Scotland constantly reiterated that the army in England had restored the Rump, acknowledged it, and taken its commissions and its pay, the soldier from England claimed that the army was as much master as servant, that it was not composed of mercenaries but of freemen "who now stand not bound in Duty and Conscience to any assembly of men" and who represented the people just as well as the Rump. When the one asked whether rule by the sword was to be perpetual, the other could reply only until a form of government was settled. To the remark that only a parliament could approve a constitution the reply was that a free parliament would destroy all they had fought for. Monck's soldier accepted this but used it as a reason for recalling the Rump, whereupon his opponent went on in the old familiar fashion to claim that those to whom God had given the victory must establish a fundamental constitution.[27]

For those who might prefer a terser appeal a broadside was issued, *Information from some Souldiers of the Parliaments Army in Scotland.* It stated that they meant to restore the Parliament, for which the English soldiers had fought, and from which they must expect their pay. Parliament had been expelled in the interest of a few ambitious and selfish officers who rather than lose their places would destroy the nation. They were supported only by Anabaptists, who through the committee of nominations had caused hundreds of officers to be turned out last summer. Because Parliament stopped the design to put Anabaptists in all places, the soldiers must now live at free quarters, and lose their pay and arrears. They talked of a parliament but only to deceive, because no parliament would ever act with them. Let the English soldiers join Monck and they would have present pay and secure their arrears.[28]

In order that propaganda might exert its full influence, time was essential. Fortunately for Monck his opponents in England provided such an interval. In a letter of October 25 Fleetwood had urged Monck, if dissatisfied with what had been done in England, to send some of his officers in whom he most confided to confer with representatives of the

---

[27]Extracts from this tract are quoted in Davies, *Coldstream Guards,* pp. 130-134. My attention was first called to this and other tracts in Worcester College Library by Mr. C. H. Wilkinson, who has added to my obligations to him by facilitating the filming of some of the Clarke manuscripts in the college.

[28]The copy of this broadside at Worcester College seems to be unique. It is reproduced in Davies, *Coldstream Guards,* pp. 137-38.

English army. The bearers of the letter were Colonel Talbot and Dr. Clarges, both of whom Monck was very glad to see.[29] Somewhat inconsistently the committee of safety, after requiring Monck to release the officers he had cashiered and restore them to their commands, threatened that if he persisted in his errors he would be constrained by force.[30]

Replying to Fleetwood's letter, Monck defended Hesilrige, Walton, and Morley for endeavoring to protect Parliament and condemning its interruption, and proposed that three representatives from each army should meet. The overture must have been very welcome, because it would postpone if not avert the danger of an armed clash with the forces Lambert was beginning to lead to the border. An onlooker saw him depart from the City on November 3. Addressing some of the men, he said that they did not look as if they would hurt Monck. "Noe, Sir, you may swear it," was the soldiers' response.[31] However, on paper at least, Lambert's army was formidable—perhaps numbering as many as 12,000, though he never assembled all at his headquarters at Newcastle which he had reached by November 23.[32] As Monck could hardly muster two-thirds of this number for an invasion of England, clearly he must gain time by negotiation. Besides, the notion of one section of the army fighting another was so generally abhorrent that every effort must be made not to lend plausibility to the rumor that the army in Scotland was about to wage war on the army in England. Even now he could not depend on the loyalty of all his men. As late as November 23, Captain Robinson brought a complete troop over to Lambert, and Captain Williams at St. Johnston (Perth) attempted to take two companies by sea to England but was surprised, and escaped with about twenty men only.[33]

A council of war at Edinburgh on November 3 approved negotiations with their counterpart and named Wilkes, Clobery, and Knight as its commissioners. An *ad hoc* committee drew up instructions that were signed the next day. At York the commissioners saw Lambert, who seemed content with all they had to ask except the restoration of the Long Parliament. Arriving in London on November 12, they reached agreement by the fifteenth, but not without yielding important points. The two essential articles in the instructions had been the return of

[29]*Clarke Papers*, IV, 73-74, 85.

[30]Ibid., 80-81.

[31]*Clarke Papers*, IV, 92.

[32]According to W. H. Dawson (*Cromwell's Understudy*, p. 361), Lambert had 3,500 horse and 4,000 foot. A Captain Southwell, writing from Durham on November 30, states that Lambert had about 3,000 horse and 5,000 foot at Newcastle (*Clarke Papers*, IV, 155). To these should be added the Irish brigade, nominally 1,500 strong and some regiments already in the north as Lilburne's. The figure 12,000 is given in Baker's *Chronicle*, p. 685. For Lambert's arrival see *Publick Intelligencer*, p. 908.

[33]*A Narrative of the Proceedings of the Northern Armies*, which Thomason dated December 5. It was written by H. G. from Durham, November 24.

Parliament and its uninterrupted sitting until May 6, and the recognition of its right to determine the future constitution. In the agreement no constitution was to be determined by any part of the army without the approbation of a general council of officers of the whole army and navy, in which should sit two commissioned officers chosen from each regiment by commissioned officers, governors of garrisons, and ten representatives of the navy. A parliament was to be speedily summoned in such form as the above council agreed, and the qualifications of members fixed by a committee, in which members of the committee of safety would be in a majority, though the Irish army was to be represented by three persons named, and the Scottish by three to be appointed and by the three commissioners. Another significant article provided that the cases of officers displaced since October 11 were to be decided by fourteen commissioners, seven from the English and seven from the Scottish armies.[34] Why the commissioners from Scotland made what amounts to a complete surrender is not wholly clear. Wilkes, described as a former tailor and member of Feake's church, betrayed their instructions to the opposing party.[35] Blamed by Clarges for their precipitancy, their excuse was that to continue to differ would not benefit either the English or the Scottish army but only the common enemy.[36] Later, they pleaded in extenuation that the article about a parliament did not necessarily exclude the Long Parliament, possibly because they expected the grandees in London to succeed in collecting a quorum of Rumpers to sit again and pass an act for an assessment of £100,000 a month.[37] They may have been overawed by their associates who included Fleetwood, their former commander in chief, or frightened by rumors that Monck's men were deserting fast.[38] Whatever the cause, their compliance was a sad blow to their comrades across the border.

Both Monck's chaplains described the receipt of news of the agreement at Edinburgh. Price speaks of the dejection of officers at the thought that if the agreement was accepted the recently promoted must sink, a colonel into a captain, a captain into an ensign, and an ensign into a sergeant. Besides, their hopes that by marching southward to restore the Rump they would be going homeward would be blasted.[39] Gumble describes the officers' gloom that their own and the nation's safety would

[34]The instructions are printed only in *Clarke Papers*, IV, 97-99; the agreement is to be found in a number of places including Baker's *Chronicle*, pp. 689-90.

[35]*Clarke Papers*, IV, 299-300; *A Letter sent from General Monck*, Dec. 29.

[36]Baker's *Chronicle*, pp. 688-89. The commissioners' letter in *Clarke Papers*, IV, 116-17.

[37]This is a mere surmise. *Clarke Papers*, IV, 125-26, 133-34.

[38]Gumble, *Life of Monck*, p. 167; *Clarke Papers*, IV, 134.

[39]Price's *The Mystery and Method of his Majesty's Happy Restauration* was printed in 1680 and reprinted by Francis Maseres, *Select Tracts* (1826), II. References are to the reprint, here to pp. 741-42.

be destroyed and that the tyranny of the English army would continue. Monck was "very melancholy and dark," but at length exclaimed that if the army would stick to him he would stick to them. Whereupon all swore they would live and die with him.[40]

For the Scottish army summarily to have rejected the agreement would have been unwise, because the longer a clash of arms was avoided the less the likelihood that it would ever take place. The council in Edinburgh, therefore, was content to assert that their commissioners had overlooked parts of their instructions and misunderstood others. To correct these errors it would send new commissioners with fresh instructions to join the three then in London. It also required that the new treaty should be negotiated at York, or, better still, Newcastle.[41] Probably in order to spin out time Monck requested from Fleetwood a safe conduct for the two new commissioners. He added, perhaps as a conciliatory aside, that he had now released all the officers he had imprisoned except Cobbet and requested that those officers of his detained in England should be allowed to return to their commands.[42]

Monck's dilatory proceedings evoked a sharp protest from the officers under Lambert at Newcastle. They complained that the waste of time would enable France and Spain to complete their obvious preparations for an invasion in concert with the Royalists in England. They asked whether any reason existed for believing that they were not equally concerned with the officers in Scotland in the prosperity of their native land and in the liberties of Christian men. To disavow the agreement signed by fully empowered commissioners was contrary to the practice of a declared enemy, much more of brethren. Nevertheless, they had desired Lambert to give the safe conduct and to consent to Newcastle as the place for negotiation. But they had advised their general that "nothing in the agreement may bee parted from, nor new matter or further explanacions admitted which are not consentaneous to what is already concluded." The meeting of the general council of officers must take place on December 6 to approve a constitution.[43] Whether any reply was returned to this peremptory note is unknown. Perhaps not, because events were now taking place which made the continuation of negotiations unnecessary.

Unofficial mediators had been no more successful than official. The officers of Monck's army had addressed a declaration to the Churches of Christ in the three nations, in which amid much laudation of both pas-

[40]Gumble, pp. 151-53.

[41]To the commissioners in London, November 24. *Clarke Papers*, IV, 126-29, where the signatures are all printed.

[42]*Clarke Papers*, IV, 129-31.

[43]Ibid., 143-46. Newcastle, Nov. 29. All the signatures are printed.

tors and people occurred the sentence: "We own and assert the Authority of this present Parliament which is now through sad mistakes and misapprehensions interrupted."[44] Nearly twenty ministers eagerly clutched at this opportunity of intercession and dispatched two pastors, Joseph Caryl and Matthew Barker, and two former Cromwellian officers, Whalley and Goffe.[45] The deputation was received at Holyrood by Monck, Colonels Fairfax and Syler, Barrow, the judge advocate, Gumble, and Collins. Caryl delivered a set oration, claiming that while the interruption of Parliament could not be justified, yet Monck had no call to intervene, his business being only to keep Scotland quiet. He then said that if brethren hitherto at one, now divided, the Royalists would benefit from this quarrel and "the people of God (for so he called his own party)" be endangered. Whatever happened would be laid at Monck's door as the beginner of the war. The general answered warmly that Lambert and his adherent had begun the war by their violence to the Parliament which granted their commissions. He condemned their restless instability which prevented any stable government at all, citing their declarations and their actions. If they continued in their present course, he declared, he would lay them on their backs. The debate grew calmer but ended inconclusively.[46] Further correspondence between Monck and the congregated churches led nowhere.[47]

John Owen not only sponsored this deputation but also engaged in a very instructive correspondence with Monck. The divine demonstrated more clearly perhaps than any other disputant what he and men of like mind felt. Compared with the awful possibility of a Stuart restoration, the differences between the armies of England and Scotland were trivial. The one thing needful was to preserve the rule of the Saints threatened with destruction by multitudes. Better the Rumpers were banished to the ends of the earth than that the armies should fight. A commonwealth could be settled without bringing back the Rump. Indeed, if allowed to sit again, imagination could not conceive that the members would be willing only to look forward and forget the past. Now that the commissioners of both armies had signed an agreement, Monck by accepting it could be "instrumentall in putting a perfect issue and perpetuall oblivion to the late breach and division." Monck's reply can be summed up in a few sentences. He dared not sit still and see the laws and liberties of Englishmen go to ruin but was obliged in honor and conscience to free

[44]Redmayne, pp. 25-28. It is said to have been written by Collins, chaplain to Wilkes's foot. *Clarke Papers*, IV, 67n.

[45]*Clarke Papers*, IV, 81-82.

[46]Baker's *Chronicle*, p. 688. Gumble (pp. 142-44) gives rather a different account but agrees that Caryl angered Monck.

[47]*Clarke Papers*, IV, 184-85, 212-15.

his country from the intolerable slavery of government by the sword. The only legal foundation for a free state was Parliament, either the existing body or a newly elected one. As to the Cavaliers, none had opposed them more or would continue longer to oppose them to the last drop of his blood than himself, but nothing had given them greater encouragement than the interruption of Parliament.[48]

This controversy between the general and the dean of Christ Church reveals a deep cleavage of opinion. Owen was willing to sacrifice the laws and customs of England in order that the Saints, a small minority, might be preserved. To this end he was willing to submit to military dictatorship. He must have recognized that not the slightest chance existed that Englishmen would elect a parliament in accordance with his wishes. The most he could have looked forward to was another nominated parliament, though even this travesty of representation might be unacceptable to the council of officers which could no longer stomach any kind of equal, much less a superior. He acknowledged that one of the great dangers to the good old cause came from fanatical, self-seeking persons among his party. Yet he was ready to perpetuate the rule of these very persons in order that the work of reformation should be carried on. That the majority of people hated the interferences with their daily habits that were inflicted under the specious name of reformation apparently mattered little. A perverse generation must be coerced into the paths of righteousness marked out by a small group that had arrogated to itself the sole right to interpret godliness. He had so abandoned his mind to cant that he could not see the writing on the wall—a great conservative reaction which opened the eyes of Monck and many others to the necessity of a free parliament.

The propaganda issued in Scotland and measures taken to intercept any propaganda from England had done much to consolidate Monck's army. Probably of equal importance was prompt pay. Monck had managed to get £20,000 from England on the plea that, although Parliament had ordered a year's assessment to be paid, half in August and half in October, a longer time was necessary for its collection in Scotland. He now required the Scots to pay up, and the money he then received, plus the sums from customs and excise, furnished pay for some months.[49] The time gained during the negotiations with the English army provided the interval required to gather together the forces he intended to take into England. On December 8 he established his headquarters at Coldstream on the Tweed some nine miles from Berwick. This little village gave its name first to Monck's army, the Coldstreamers, and then to the only

[48]Ibid., 121-24, 151-54.   [49]Baker's *Chronicle*, p. 685.

regiment of it which is still represented in the British army, Her Majesty's Coldstream Regiment of Foot Guards. There he had within easy reach all four regiments of horse—his own, Knight's (late Sanders'), Clobery's (late Twistleton's), and Morgan's (formed out of four companies of dragoons)—and six regiments of foot—his own, Reade's, Hubblethorne's (late Talbot's), Lytcott's (late Cobbet's), Charles Fairfax's, and Morgan's (late Daniel's). If the regiments were up to strength the horse numbered 2,400 and the foot 6,000, but it is doubtful if they were.[50] Monck had difficulties in finding officers and troopers to take the place of the disaffected. Major General Morgan and Adjutant Jeremiah Smith were employed, according to Price, as "itinerant reformers" dismounting suspected troopers and mounting foot soldiers who could buy boots.[51] For officers, many promotions were made. Lieutenant Colonel Clobery and Major Knight becoming colonels, Smith and Captain Thomas Johnson, who had secured Berwick, majors, while lieutenants became captains, cornets lieutenants, and quartermasters cornets.[52] Even so, there was still a shortage of officers, and Clarges was directed to try to get some in London and ship them by sea to Scotland.[53] Vacancies in the foot were also filled by promotions, and, in the case of privates, Scots were enlisted in small numbers, much exaggerated by propagandists in England. It is said that Monck increased his pikemen to equal his musketeers so as to be better able to withstand a cavalry charge. Another reason may be that pikes were cheaper and easier to make than muskets.[54] Letters which Monck sent urging a rising in the west and the seizure of Exeter were intercepted, but a few English volunteers were forthcoming elsewhere, the Ogles raising two troops in Northumberland and the Howards of Naworth promising a hundred gentlemen.[55]

Far more important than the adhesion of these small forces was the promise of assistance in Yorkshire, in Lambert's rear. Monck was fortunate in finding as a collaborator one whose fame as a victorious general was still gratefully remembered and whose influence was strong in Yorkshire. Thomas, Lord Fairfax, commander in chief of the New Model from its formation until he resigned, rather than conduct the invasion of Scotland in 1650, had quarreled with Oliver Cromwell when his son-

---

[50]Ibid., p. 695, gives the figures, probably correctly, as 2,000 horse and 5,000 foot.

[51]Maseres, Select Tracts, II, 739.

[52]For examples in Monck's horse, see Firth and Davies, Regimental History, I, 139-40, and in Clobery's, ibid., 170-172.

[53]Baker, p. 693. The chronicler notes that the Scots declined to provide Monck with horses.

[54]Clarke Papers, IV, xxii; Baker, p. 693.

[55]Two letters of Colonel John Pearson dated November 1 and 5 describe the contents of the intercepted letters. They are printed in Mackinnon, Coldstream Guards, I, 77-78, and in General Monck's last letter to . . . Fleetwood, and are summarized in Weekly Intelligencer, p. 215; Baker, p. 693; Clarke Papers, IV, 79, 90, 119, 128, 179; Gumble, p. 194; and Maseres, II, 744.

in-law, the Duke of Buckingham, was imprisoned. During Richard's Parliament he had acted with the opposition and sat next to Hesilrige, as the latter was proud to point out. He did not share Sir Arthur's Republican views but was actuated by dread of military government. When the army leaders recalled the Long Parliament in May, 1659, he was chosen one of the Council of State but he never sat in it. He belonged to the constitutional, Presbyterian party. At the end of the first Civil War he was shown a copy of Magna Charta and exclaimed that this was what they had fought for. To a man with a belief in the historical evolution of the English constitution the crude attempts of the council of officers to frame an entirely new model of government must have been abhorrent. To him news that Monck was prepared to oppose the army in England was doubtlessly most welcome.

Fairfax is said to have been persuaded to appear in arms by a letter from the King, delivered by Sir Horatio Townshend.[56] He made known his intention to a Dr. John Troutbeck and Major General Thomas Morgan, who had returned from Flanders where he had gained great distinction as second in command of the English expeditionary force. They brought with them Monck's declaration against Lambert's ejection of Parliament. When Fairfax read it, he remarked that if Monck had any other design than to restore the Parliament to its old freedom and re-establish the ancient government, he would oppose him, but otherwise he would heartily join with him.[57] Troutbeck accompanied Morgan to Edinburgh. The latter had been laid up with gout at York and dissembled his sympathies with Monck in order to induce Lilburne, the governor, to let him join his former general as soon as his health permitted. Gaining the required permission he set out and reached Edinburgh late in October or nearly in November.[58] Morgan greeted Monck with the question whether he would lay down his arms and be friends with Fleetwood and Lambert. The reply was that if they would restore the Parliament there was little more to say. Morgan explained that he had promised to ask the question and now felt free to join Monck in whatever he did. The short dialogue is significant. It reveals how the leaders of the English army viewed the issue on personal grounds, and how Monck felt that for the present the restoration of the Long Parliament was the one thing necessary. Morgan showed the attitude of the professional soldier

[56]Clarendon, *Rebellion*, XVI, 117.

[57]Hist. MSS Comm. *Sixth Report*, p. 466.

[58]"About the seventh or eighth of November," according to Baker, but the account of Clarges' subsequent itinerary makes this too late. Clarges took part in the discussion with Morgan, rode to York, had an accident on the way to Lincolnshire which detained him ten days and yet reached London the evening of the day the Agreement of November 15 was signed—clearly an impossibility if he was at Edinburgh on November 7 or 8.

as contrasted with the politico-religious enthusiast—that his duty was to obey orders.

Morgan had brought a letter from Edward Bowles, an influential minister at York and known to enjoy the confidence of Fairfax. It asserted that Fairfax and others in Yorkshire were willing to join with Monck but that they disapproved of his declaration in that it called only for the restoration of the remnant of the Long Parliament and not of the excluded members and that it supported only a commonwealth. Monck's response was said to have been that what was printed in his name was not to be regarded as representing his own views but as drafted by others. Until he had consolidated his authority he could not contradict what was issued. Even now, all that was written could scarcely persuade the army that he did not intend to re-establish kingship. The outcome was the dispatch of Clarges to Fairfax, Rossiter, and others.

Clarges met Bowles in York and convinced him of Monck's rectitude, whereupon the minister consented to negotiate with Fairfax, Bethell, Smithson, and others and brought back the good news they would rise in January. Bowles asked Clarges what other expectations of support he cherished and was told that Whetham at Portsmouth; Hacker, Hutchinson, and Hesilrige, in Nottingham and Leicestershire; and Okey in London would all assist. Bowles at first demurred at such aids but accepted Clarges' reasons for relying upon men of their principles.[59] Clarges then started for Lincolnshire to see Rossiter, but fell from his horse near Doncaster and was laid up for ten days. A messenger he sent to Rossiter reported that the former colonel in the New Model would join Fairfax. Resuming his journey, Clarges learned that Hesilrige was disinclined to act for fear that the Royalists might seize upon the opportunity of a division in the army and rise. But Clarges urged him and other members of the Council of State to meet in London, with the results to be described later.[60]

A messenger Fairfax sent to Monck was intercepted, so Brian Fairfax, his lordship's cousin, was dispatched in disguise to say that Fairfax would join Monck against Lambert "who was against all Parliament[?s], and oppressed the counties where he lay by for quarters and contributions." He would rise on January 1, and asked that if any of Lambert's army marched back to Yorkshire, Monck would advance and watch

[59] Baker, pp. 685-86. Hugh Bethell had fought in Yorkshire under Fairfax and later, but had left the army in 1649. Smithson was at this time a major in Robert Lilburne's horse. It is most unfortunate that Monck's letter to Fairfax is missing, because its exact wording might help solve the difficult question of whether Monck's secret intentions differed from those publicly declared. He must have been aware that his intervention might lead to the King's recall and may have hoped that it would, but that he was at this time deliberately planning the Restoration is extremely doubtful.
[60] Baker, pp. 687-88. There is no other evidence to confirm the above, based no doubt upon Clarges' own account which may exaggerate his achievements, perhaps especially with regard to Hesilrige.

them. After many adventures, Brian Fairfax arrived at Coldstream, delivered his message, and returned to Fairfax with the assurance that Monck would watch Lambert as a cat watches a mouse.

Events in the south of England were becoming as significant as those in the north. Nine members of the Council of State had no intention of acquiescing in their supersession by the committee of safety. Scot was chosen president and associated with him were Hesilrige, Neville, Wallop, Berners, Reynolds, and the two colonels, Morley and Walton. Anthony Ashley Cooper, whose slippery nature had prevented his adhering long to any party since his first appearance as a Royalist early in the first civil war, now became one of the most active of the nine, of whose proceedings he has left a memoir.[61] They managed to arrange a meeting with Monck's three commissioners, but not until the day after they had signed the agreement with the English army leaders. Ashley Cooper argued powerfully against an agreement between Monck and Fleetwood. If Monck stood firm he would be sure to become generalissimo of all the forces in the three kingdoms, but if he yielded the best he could expect would be dismissal and ruin. Cooper claimed for the nine "a great correspondence and interest with the inferior officers and common soldiers of every troop and company" about London, and assurances that Portsmouth would declare for them and that Ireland would be secured by Sir Charles Coote. Lawson, who commanded the fleet in the Thames, and Fairfax, still the idol of the soldiery, could be counted on. These considerations are said to have convinced Clobery and Knight, but not Wilkes, who threw in his lot with the English officers.

The nine soon passed from words to acts. A letter[62] to Monck, praising his faithful actions and promising to stand or fall with him, was followed by a commission appointing him commander in chief of all the forces raised and to be raised in England and Scotland and empowering him to appoint such officers as he judged faithful. According as the service of Parliament demanded, he should march into any part of England or Scotland and destroy any forces hostile to Parliament. He was to obey any orders he might receive from Parliament, the Council of State, or a group of five—himself, Hesilrige, Walton, Morley, and Overton.[63]

The nine sent Hesilrige, Walton, and Morley to Portsmouth. The governor was Nathaniel Whetham, a Presbyterian who had fought for the parliamentary cause from 1642, a member of the council of state for

---

[61]Printed by Christie, *Life of Shaftesbury*, I, ch. vii. Cf. Louise Fargo Brown, *First Earl of Shaftesbury* (1933), pp. 82-85. As Christie remarked, Cooper's account may be a "portion of the autobiography of Shaftesbury's old age." It may magnify Cooper's share in events.

[62]Baker, p. 691. This letter is signed by the nine.

[63]Commission printed in Clarke, IV, 137-39. The five were the same commissioners appointed by the Rump just prior to its ejection except for the omission of Fleetwood and Ludlow. Baker, pp. 678-79.

Scotland in 1655 and a friend of Monck's and Cooper's, and governor of Portsmouth in succession to Norton whom the Rump had suspected of discontent in May, 1659. Whetham gave the three a hearty welcome on their entry on December 3. The magistrates and townsmen, assured that winning Portsmouth for the parliamentary cause might facilitate the treaty on foot between the armies in England and Scotland, gave all the support they could. Officers suspected of disaffection were promptly seized, and reinforcements raised within the town and received from without, though a party Colonel Fagge was bringing from Sussex was stopped on the way. Soon the leaders felt strong enough to send a letter to the City of London, suggesting that if Parliament could not safely meet at Westminster it should sit at Portsmouth. The situation became even more satisfactory when the forces sent to besiege Portsmouth joined hands with the garrison on December 20.[64] Then Hesilrige and his associates marched on London with the equivalent of two and a half regiments of horse and a regiment of foot. Although the progress of events in the capital made these troops unnecessary, Portsmouth is entitled to full credit for being the first town in southern England to cast off the military yoke.

London had now shaken off the political apathy so noticeable during the summer. Some citizens refused to pay taxes, and nearly killed two soldiers for assisting in their collection.[65] The demand for a parliament became daily more menacing. The committee of safety, therefore, drew up a proclamation prohibiting the collection of signatures to petitions, because the peace of the commonwealth was thereby endangered.[66] The Lord Mayor did his best to check disorder by directing each alderman with the constable of his ward to go from house to house to charge all heads of families to see that their sons and servants did not engage in any unlawful designs.[67] On December 5 the apprentices defiantly presented a petition[68] to the common council, and then attacked a troop of horse that escorted Dendy, sergeant at arms, when he posted the proclamation against petitioning at the old Exchange. Showers of tiles from roofs and lumps of ice from the gutters forced the troop to withdraw, but

[64]C. D. and W. C. D. Whetham, *History of the Life of Colonel Nathaniel Whetham* (1907), ch. ix; *A Letter from Sir Arthur Hasilrigge in Portsmouth* (1659). There is a list of other authorities in a note in *Clarke Papers*, IV, 169-70, where Sunday, December 3, should be Saturday. A letter from Portsmouth dated December 20 is printed in *Publick Intelligencer*, pp. 957-58. The pamphlet, *A Remonstrance or Declaration touching the Re-establishing and Sitting of the Parliament* (1659), states that Rich's horse and some of Berry's horse, nine troop in all, and several companies of Lagoe's foot deserted and joined the Portsmouth garrison.

[65]*Clarke Papers*, IV, 301.

[66]Dated Dec. 1, and printed in *Publick Intelligencer*, pp. 919-20.

[67]Dated Dec. 3 and printed in *Publick Intelligencer*, p. 924.

[68]The petition is summarized in the *Weekly Intelligencer*, pp. 241-42. It demanded either a new election or the return of the Rump.

soon reinforcements appeared—some horse under Disbrowe and a regiment of foot under Hewson. All shops were shut, Hewson was hailed by cries of "A cobbler, a cobbler," and any soldiers that straggled were disarmed and kicked by apprentices. Growing bolder, the lads kicked a football among the soldiers, and stoned them as the proclamation was read aloud. At last the soldiers' patience gave way and, apparently at Hewson's orders, they fired into the angry mob that contemned them. Some apprentices were killed, and more wounded by bullets or swords, and at length the crowd dispersed. The soldiers stood on guard all night at the gates but were withdrawn next day, perhaps after a deputation of aldermen and common councillors to the committee of safety had excused the riot and denied any share in it.[69]

This affray was magnified by enemies of the English army and fanned the antimilitary sentiment everywhere. Propagandists seized on the occasion to ask whether soldiers were paid to murder citizens. It was in vain for spokesmen for the army to ascribe the riot to Royalist agents, because most citizens did not require any outside solicitation to induce them to reveal their detestation of Fleetwood and his supporters. Even the trained bands, though carefully sifted, had done nothing to suppress the riot, but had been content, according to Pepys, to exchange sour looks with Hewson's men. But, in spite of great discontent, the Londoners were not yet prepared to take decisive action. They preferred to wait and see whether the army would not disintegrate from internal stresses.

The nine members of the Council of State hoped to profit from the dissension. Cooper was given a commission to command the forces he and his colleagues expected to revolt in London, but he was arrested before he could accomplish anything. Brought before Fleetwood, he found that he was supposed to be going to raise the west and so was able to swear that he had no such intention. He declined to give a pledge not to act against the army leaders but promised not to depart from the City without permission. He was released, managed to evade a second arrest, and took part in the abortive effort to seize the Tower.[70]

Four of the nine councillors—Scot, Cooper, Berners, and Weaver—cooperated in this attempt. The Lieutenant of the Tower, Colonel Fitch, readily fell in with their scheme which was that he would have the gates opened early on the morning of December 12 ostensibly to allow his

---

[69]Though there are many accounts of this riot the exact number of casualties and the sequence of events are hard to ascertain. The most vivid picture is drawn by Pepys in a letter to Edward Mountagu, first printed by C. H. Firth in *Macmillan's Magazine* for November, 1893. It is reprinted in *Letters and the Second Diary of Samuel Pepys*, ed. R. G. Howarth (1932), p. 15. A later letter (p. 17) states that the coroner's verdict was one of murder against Hewson who gave the order to fire. See also Sharpe, *London and the Kingdom*, II, 358; *Clarke Papers*, IV, 165-69; *Publick Intelligencer*, p. 930.

[70]Christie, *Life of Shaftesbury*, I, 196-98.

coach to take him to the City. Okey with four companions was to use the opportunity to surprise the guard and seize the fortress. But the Lord Mayor learned of the plan and warned the army leaders who dispatched Disbrowe and Salmon to the Tower where they arrested Fitch and put Lieutenant Colonel John Miller in charge.[71] Scot and his associates promptly addressed a letter to Fleetwood in which they boasted that they had tried to gain possession of the Tower. They also severely arraigned the nine army leaders whose ambition had denied the poor soldiers their arrears and future pay, made the whole nation their enemies, and exposed them to the dangers of a new, unnatural war. But Providence had raised up a deliverer, General Monck, who was standing firm against the rebellious party in the army and the common enemy. They concluded with a denunciation of the "strange new parliament"[72] whose meeting and debating must be at the pleasure of the army.[73]

The defeat of the attempt to surprise the Tower was more than offset by most ominous news from the fleet in the Downs. Vice-Admiral Lawson and his captains addressed a letter to the Lord Mayor, aldermen, and common councillors of the City of London on December 13. In it they demanded that the Rump should be permitted to sit again, threatened that if this could not be accomplished in a friendly manner, they were ready to use force, and desired the City authorities to assist. They also issued a declaration which they hoped Parliament would adopt when restored. Its seven points were: a general indemnity, just foundations of government, freedom of worship, a godly ministry maintained, navigation and trade encouraged and excise removed as soon as possible, no impressment for service by land or sea, and provision for maimed seamen, widows, and orphans, and employment for the poor.

The fleet then sailed toward the capital. On the way first Scot, Okey, and Streater, and then Vane, Salwey, and two others were taken on board, the first group representing the Council of State and the second the army and the committee of safety. Vane at once urged Lawson to anchor but he declined until he was off Gravesend. There he assembled a council of war, to which both groups were admitted, together with Colonels Salmon and Barrow, who came to assist Vane and his party. After Lawson had read the declaration and his letters to Fleetwood and the Lord Mayor a most interesting debate ensued.

To the argument that the Long Parliament recalled in May had effected nothing for the good of the nation, the reply was that the army

[71]A full account is in *Publick Intelligencer,* pp. 945-46, a summary in Ludlow, II, 169-70.
[72]The reference is to the declaration of the council of officers on December 10 that a Parliament should meet in February.
[73]The letter is printed in Thurloe, VII, 797-98; Christie, I, app. v, and elsewhere.

had always obstructed members and so overawed them that they had done things unpopular with the people. If so, a free parliament, or at least one chosen under limitations on the right to vote at elections, was necessary. Not at all, was the reply. The Long Parliament by the act of 1641 was the only legal authority. Any other parliament, whether chosen freely or under limitations, would owe its origin to the army which would thus be the supreme power. The device of a free parliament was a transparent trick. If it declared for Charles Stuart the army would dissolve it and claim that parliaments, the idol of the people, were hopeless. If it did not do so, it would be certain to be overruled by the twenty-one conservators of liberty nominated by the army, and would not their interests overbalance regard for the public welfare? But, urged Vane's party, the army must see that what it had fought for should not be lost in a breath. The response was that Parliament had striven for the public interest whereas the army had set itself up as a distinct corporation above the people, and must be brought under the civil power. Any promises it might make to submit to a parliament of its own calling were useless because the record proved that it had never kept any covenant, engagement, or declaration. Lawson and his captains all agreed with Scot's party rather than Vane's. They sent a second letter to the City fathers, similar to the first, but now recommending precautions against the Cavaliers.[74] A letter Fleetwood addressed to Lawson arrived too late. In it, the general explained that the council of officers had resolved to call a parliament to sit on January 24. The council, he continued, could not agree to the recall of the Long Parliament because Lambert and his officers had been promised that such a step should not be taken without their consent, which they had refused to give. But the new parliament must be chosen upon qualifications which should be designed to prevent any danger to the cause they all had at heart and which representatives of the navy should help to determine.[75]

The general council of officers and the committee of safety had done little to avert their approaching doom. A group of officers and civilians had been named on November 1 "to prepare a form of government," but its deliberations were productive of little except acrimonious debate.[76]

[74]The two letters are in the *Publick Intelligencer*, pp. 967-68, the second having the signatures of Lawson, twenty-one captains, and a lieutenant attached. The discussion is reported in *A Narrative of the Proceedings of the Fleet* (1659), by M. H., probably Captain Mark Harrison, one of the officers who carried the second letter to the Lord Mayor. This tract is printed in Granville Penn's *Memorials of Sir William Penn* (1833), II, 186-91. The two letters are also printed there but the second is dated in error December 29 instead of 21. The declaration is summarized in the *Weekly Post*, pp. 266-67.

[75]Dec. 21. Printed in *Memorials of the Civil War*, ed. Robert Bell, II (sometimes referred to as Vol. IV of the *Fairfax Correspondence*), 148-49.

[76]Redmayne, pp. 62-63, where the names of members are given. For a few details about the deliberations of this body see Wariston's *Diary* for November and early December.

Vane and Wariston became the opposing leaders in a wrangle about the extent of toleration and the maintenance or disestablishment of the church. The party in favor of a new parliament prevailed over Ludlow and the champions of the Rump. But time was running out, and the council of officers seems to have taken matters into its own hands. At last its members perceived that the ground they stood on was cracking under their feet. By the middle of December they saw arrayed against them Monck's army, soon to be supported by Fairfax in Yorkshire, the forces in Portsmouth, about to be joined by the horse and foot sent to besiege them, and the fleet in the Thames. Had they known it, the army in Ireland had suddenly reversed its stand and come out for the Parliament.[77] The people of England were almost to a man against the grandees. Against this combination of enemies, Fleetwood could oppose almost literally no one. No help could be expected from Lambert. His men a month before had been heard to say they would not fight but would make a ring for their officers to fight in. He tried to prop up the falling fabric in London by sending Disbrowe's horse southward, but it soon proved that it was no more reliable than other regiments. When they reached St. Albans, the horsemen decided to throw in their lot with the regiments in London and restore the Long Parliament.[78] Another alarming symptom was the growing indiscipline of garrisons. At Exeter, for example, soldiers were living at free quarters or obliging householders to purchase exemptions from billeting at the rate of five shillings a week per man.[79]

What was now called by a terminological inexactitude "the general council of officers of the armies of the three nations and of the fleet" could do nothing to stop the adverse tide. Notices were inserted in the newspapers on December 13 that the council had agreed upon seven unalterable fundamentals. These were: no king; no single person; the army to be continued, maintained, and conducted and not be disbanded or its control altered "but by consent of the Conservators appointed"; no imposition on the conscience of the people that feared God; no House of Lords; the legislative and executive powers to be distinct and not exercised by the same persons; and two assemblies constituting a parliament to be elected by duly qualified people of the commonwealth. This announcement was followed by another—that the council of officers had made known to the committee of safety its desire that a parliament should be summoned speedily in accordance with its intention "of setting

[77] The revolution of December 13 in Dublin was announced in the London newspapers under the twenty-fourth.
[78] *Clarke Papers*, IV, 300; *Publick Intelligencer*, p. 972; *Weekly Post*, p. 271 (misnumbered 278).
[79] See a letter from Exeter, dated Dec. 19, in the *Weekly Post*, pp. 269-70.

up the civil authority, and being subservient thereunto," and that the committee had declared that writs should be issued for a parliament to meet on January 24. A few days later came the news that the council of officers were considering the qualifications of the persons who were to choose or be chosen members of parliament "as also the manner of making the elections" which the militia was to supervise.[80]

Unlike the council of the army in 1647 the latter body left no record of its debates, and only a few scraps of information, plus some rumors, can be collected about its proceedings. Wariston records how the decision to summon a parliament consisting of two houses reversed a previous vote, and how the resolution that the senate should not be nominated now by the army but elected later was carried by officers who wished to please the people because they had acquired considerable estates and were loath to hazard them.[81] Little can be discovered about the conservators except that they were to number twenty-one and be the especial guardians of the army's interests. Wariston thought they were also to protect all the fundamentals and not merely the third, and he was almost certainly correct. Ludlow, who claimed to have proposed that conservators of liberty should be appointed to determine any dispute that might arise between parliament and the army about the fundamentals, submitted a list of twenty-one persons he thought suitable for that purpose. To his dismay he soon found that the officers voted for their own supporters and warmly denounced them for their intention "to carry on a faction, and to govern the nation by the sword."[82] In view of the officers' record Ludlow's indignation is hard to understand. He was an obtuse man wholly blind to his inconsistency in condemning others for wishing to rule the country by a faction when he hoped to accomplish the very thing himself. True, his faction was larger than theirs, but the Republicans, even if united instead of being split into fragments, constituted a small minority of Englishmen.

Suddenly their eyes were opened to their situation. On December 21, when Wariston and others were wrangling whether representatives from Scotland and Ireland should sit in the new parliament, they were suddenly called to Wallingford House. There they learned that the troops

[80]*Publick Intelligencer*, No. 207, under Dec. 13, 14, 15. Steele, *Tudor and Stuart Proclamations*, No. 3139. A tract with the suggestive title, *The Great Cheat*, pointed out that, if the officers permitted the election of parliament "under qualifications," the concession was delusive because they would decide the qualifications. Another tract, *Ten Quaeres upon the Ten New Commandements* (December 22), questioned whether, in view of their past record of perjuries, the officers' professions could be trusted.

[81]*Diary*, December 9, 10.

[82]*Memoirs*, II, 172-74. See C. H. Firth, *The House of Lords during the Civil War* (London, 1910 [pp. 266-68]) for proof that the Harringtonians had anticipated Ludlow. According to Bordeaux, those chosen were all from the council of officers except Fairfax, Overton, Lawson, Harrison, and another Fifth Monarchy man. Guizot, II, 316.

sent to besiege Portsmouth had changed sides and joined the garrison. Cries of woe sounded on all sides—the soldiers everywhere were likely to mutiny for want of pay and were refusing to fight against the Long Parliament. The officers present abandoned all hope but threatened to betray the committeemen to their adversaries. Dr. Owen, Sydenham, and Disbrowe bewailed that all was lost, and that nothing remained but to treat, if the triumphant army at Portsmouth would consent to treat. Despair was in every voice. The "under-officers and sojours would not stand be their superiors nor us. These things astonished us." To add to the gloom Vane and his faithful henchman Salwey entered and related that the City of London had elected a common council full of malignants.[83] Staggering under these blows the decision was taken to withdraw their fundamentals before the ink on them had well dried.

According to the Venetian ambassador the fundamentals were all unpopular.[84] They are significant only as the officers' last dying effort to perpetuate themselves as well as their ideals. The complacent self-sufficency of the representatives of the English army—less than half the total army—is fully revealed in this attempt to prescribe the main lines of an unalterable constitution. They had heard from Oliver Cromwell that what was for the people's good, not what pleased them, should be the aim of a government. They had certainly ignored what the people wanted, and thought of their own good, not the people's. At the last moment they substituted for their fundamentals ten articles which should be the basis of the future government—a Republic without a single person or peers and with an executive distinct from the legislative, an indemnity to cover all that had occurred since October 1, and an army constituted as on October 9. The next day (December 23) the general council of officers met and approved the articles for which they would live and die.[85] Then they dispersed, "unwept, unhonoured, and unsung."

The officers did not voluntarily abandon the dominant position they had occupied for about ten weeks. Menaced from every side by hostile forces, they found discord within their own ranks. The soldiers began to demonstrate for the recall of the Rump in spite of their colonels' efforts. Those at the top failed to set an example of constancy. Fleetwood, the nominal commander in chief, was in a state of maudlin perplexity. While the general council of officers was drawing up fundamentals or articles, he was negotiating with a deputation from the City and promising that a parliament would be summoned which should be free from military

[83]Wariston, *Diary,* December 21.

[84]*Calendar Venetian,* p. 103.

[85]Steele, *Tudor and Stuart Proclamations,* No. 3141; *Weekly Post,* p. 269.

interference. Simultaneously he listened to a suggestion that he should be instrumental in restoring Charles II. Whitelocke relates how on December 22 Lord Willoughby, Major General Browne, and several influential Londoners urged him to go to Fleetwood and advise him to send to Charles II at Breda and offer to restore him "upon good terms" and thus forestall Monck, who, after hoodwinking Hesilrige and the Rump, intended to gain the credit of the King's restoration. Whitelocke accepted the mission and proposed alternatives to Fleetwood. The first was to draw together all the soldiers and if, as seemed likely, the number proved small, to take possession of the Tower and then, with the probable assistance of the City fathers, declare for a free parliament. The second was to offer to restore the King upon such terms as Charles would agree to. Fleetwood asked Whitelocke whether he could undertake to go to the King and he said he would. As he was leaving he met Vane, Disbrowe, and Berry on their way to see Fleetwood. In a quarter of an hour Fleetwood joined him and passionately declared twice "I cannot do it." He explained that his three visitors had reminded him that he had engaged not to do any such thing without Lambert's consent.[86] That Fleetwood should throw away his last chance of leadership in deference to a personal obligation is typical of his career. That he should change his mind on such a vital issue twice within so short a time is one more proof of his instability. That he should remain loyal to an individual though he had been false to the Cromwellians and to the Rump shows defects which wholly unfitted him for the position he coveted. His rash ambition had led him to a great height but he lacked the firmness to maintain a footing there. He was fond of the Scriptures and should have remembered the text, "Unstable as water, thou shalt not prevail." One of his last recorded utterances was that "God had spit in his face"[87]—his way of describing the changing favors of Providence which so perplexed Milton in *Samson Agonistes*. His last significant act was on December 24—to send the keys of the Parliament House to the Speaker with notice that the guards were withdrawn so that members might take their places. Except for his mention among those incapacitated from holding office under the crown he passed into utter oblivion, dying in 1692. Cromwell had called him a milksop in 1658 and the epithet seems to have clung to him.[88] The disappointed Whitelocke rejected overtures from Ingoldsby and Howard, two former Cromwellian colonels who were now Royalists.

[86]Whitelocke, *Memorials*, IV, 380-383.

[87]*Clarendon State Papers*, III, 633, 647; Baker's *Chronicle*, p. 694. The phrase even appeared in a ballad, *Rump: or an exact Collection of Poems 1639-1661* (1662), II, 24.

[88]Ludlow, II, 203; Abbott, *Writings . . . of Oliver Cromwell*, IV, 728; John Tatham, *The Rump* (1660), act 1, sc. 1.

He still clung to the hope that a free parliament might be summoned and sealed writs to that end, and sent one to the Lord Mayor and one to the sheriffs of London. However, the direction of affairs was now to pass to other hands.

On December 23, the members of the Council of State, together with Speaker Lenthall, ordered the forces in London to rendezvous on the morrow in Lincoln's Inn Fields under Okey and Alured. Little is known of the meeting except that all "with one consent resolved to live and die with the Parliament, using many high expressions in declaring their resolution." They then marched in good order down Chancery Lane, stopping at the door of the Speaker's house and sending in word that they waited his pleasure. When he appeared the officers lamented their great defection in the late interruption and promised strict obedience for the future. The soldiers, recognizing him as the representative of Parliament, hailed him as their general and the father of their country. He issued orders where they should be stationed to keep the peace until Parliament met and gave them the watchword for the night. They showed their approval by volleys of shot.[89] After a visit to the City the Speaker, together with Cooper and three other councillors, waited on the Lord Mayor and reached an agreement about the meeting of Parliament. They then went to the Tower where Miller delivered from the garrison a declaration of adherence to the Parliament. The Speaker, after distributing money to the soldiers, departed, leaving Cooper, Weaver, and Berners to execute the lieutenancy for the present.[90] Perhaps the Speaker, the citizens of London, and all who had learned of the end of military tyranny celebrated their Christmas, certain that this year at least their kitchens would not be searched and their dinners confiscated by soldiers engaged in the "work of reformation." Perhaps some of the celebrants pondered the question whether they had more to hope or to fear from the Rump once again in authority.

[89]Whitelocke, IV, 388; *Publick Intelligencer*, p. 971, and *Weekly Post*, p. 270. The newspaper accounts are identical. *A Remonstrance . . . touching the Re-Establishing . . . of Parliament* names Packer's and Okey's horse and Hewson's, Fleetwood's, and Lambert's foot together with the rest of the forces in London. Alured is said to have commanded Packer's horse.

[90]*Publick Intelligencer*, p. 972. Morley was named governor of the Tower on January 7. For Evelyn's attempts to induce him to declare for the King, see *Diary*, Dec. [probably a mistake for January] 10 and 12, Jan. 12; "Evelyn and Colonel Herbert Morley in 1659 and 1660," by E. S. de Beer (Sussex Archaeological Collections LXXVIII, 177-83); and Arthur H. Nethercot, "New Marginalia by John Evelyn on Morley, Monck, and the Restoration," *Huntington Library Quarterly*, I, 439-46.

CHAPTER XI

Foreign Relations

AT OLIVER'S DEATH English prestige was higher on the Continent than at any time since the Armada or even Agincourt. "His greatness at home," said Clarendon, "was but a shadow of the glory he had abroad." The extent of his influence seemed incredible.[1] Stepping into his shoes, Richard might seem to have had no more to do than to follow in the same direction. His task was, however, by no means so simple. His father's plan for a Protestant league had already proved an empty dream. The secular interests of the Protestant powers around the Baltic were stronger than their religious affinities. The war Oliver had started against Spain, though now very successful in Flanders, was most unpopular, because it was expensive and destructive to commerce. However, it appeared to be drawing to a close. By the treaty of March 23, 1657, renewed for another year on March 28, 1658, England had furnished France with an auxiliary force of 6,000 men for service in Flanders. After the battle of the Dunes, June 4, 1658, Dunkirk had surrendered and, in accordance with the treaty, had been immediately handed over to an English garrison. Four regiments under Major General Sir Thomas Morgan remained in the field with the French army under Marshal Turenne. The Spaniards and their Royalist allies were too weak to fight a pitched battle, and one after another the Flemish fortresses surrendered. Bergues, Furnes, and Dixmude were taken in July, Gravelines in August, and Oudenarde and Ypres in September. The campaign had resulted in the capture of most of Flanders before the Anglo-French troops took up their winter quarters.

Oliver's death did not affect military operations but it did render the English alliance less valuable to France. Cardinal Mazarin, who had never favored the grandiose schemes of the late Protector for the advancement of the Protestant cause on the Continent, had now become anxious to crown his career with as glorious a treaty as that of Westphalia which was regarded as a monument post mortem to Richelieu. He had not succeeded in preventing the election of Leopold as Emperor, but by lavish bribery he had induced the electors to impose on Leopold various conditions, including pledges to observe the treaty of Westphalia, and to give no aid to the enemies of France or her allies, or to the enemies of the princes and electors of the Empire. Furthermore, in

[1] *Rebellion*, XV, 152-53.

August, 1658, he formed the League of the Rhine by which certain German potentates, the King of Sweden, so far as he was a German prince, and the King of France agreed to protect each other and the territories they had acquired at the close of the Thirty Years' War.[2] The Austrian branch of the house of Hapsburg having been rendered powerless for the time being, the task of concluding peace with the Spanish branch should be easier. France was weary of a war that seemed eternal —it had started in 1635. The price of victory in Flanders—the cession of Dunkirk to the English—had startled many Frenchmen who hated the Protestant republic. To them Dunkirk seemed a potential second Calais, so long a thorn in their side. Moreover, at last a marriage between Louis XIV, now twenty, and the Infanta, Maria Theresa, might be arranged because Philip IV had become the father of a male heir in 1657.[3] Because the Salic law did not operate in Spain, the danger that their empire might pass to France induced the Spaniards to refuse an offer of a marriage treaty on favorable terms in 1656, but now they were better disposed toward one. Before the end of the year 1658, Mazarin, who had been profuse in promises to uphold the house of Cromwell in England in every eventuality, informed his representative, Bordeaux, in London, that a Spanish agent, Pimentel, had let him know that Spain was now willing for the Infanta to marry Louis XIV on conditions that would lead to peace.[4]

In northern and central Europe, English diplomacy achieved no success comparable to the military gains in Flanders. The reason is explained in a sentence Thurloe wrote in 1657: "The protector in all these cases governes himself by the Protestant cause, and he thinkes a peace betweene the two northern crownes is best for that, if it may be had."[5] The historian of the war between Denmark and Sweden stated that England had a great interest in the Baltic because she wanted a free and undisturbed commerce and, being at war with Spain, wished Sweden to keep the Austrian branch of the Hapsburgs in check.[6] Perhaps to see in Charles X of Sweden a successor to Gustavus Adolphus, the great Protestant hero, was a natural error, but it was the mistake which ruined the Cromwellian plan for a Protestant league. Charles X, though a Protestant, did not hesitate to wage war against Protestant states such as Denmark and Brandenburg. His aim was to convert the

[2]James Breck Perkins, *France under Mazarin* (New York, 1886), II, 311-17.

[3]This son, and a second, died young, leaving as heir the future Charles II.

[4]Letters to Lockhart, Sept. 12/22, and to Bordeaux, Dec. 3/13, 1658, *Lettres du Cardinal Mazarin*, IX.

[5]Letter of Oct. 2, Thurloe, VII, 547.

[6]Sir Roger Manley, *The History of the Late Warres in Denmark* (1670), p. 3.

Baltic into a Swedish lake, not to assail the Emperor as a Catholic power. He had taken a huge stride towards the achievement of his ambitions when his crossing both the Little Belt and the Great Belt on the ice had compelled Christian IV of Denmark to accept the treaty of Roskilde at the end of February, 1658.

Meadowe states that he tried to moderate the terms of the Swede without appearing pro-Danish, and to safeguard English interests. He claimed two successes. Charles X was persuaded to be content with Trondheim and Bohus. To have allowed him to tear from Denmark the whole of Norway would have prejudiced England, according to Meadowe, because Sweden would then have possessed all the chief materials such as "masts, deals, pitch, tar, copper, iron, &c. needful for the apparel and equipage of our ships, too great a treasure to be entrusted in one hand." The other concession secured was the insertion in a proposal that both Sweden and Denmark should jointly bar from the Baltic all foreign men-of-war of the adjective "inimical," a significant modification.[7] However, the Swedes soon found that a treaty dictated by force was durable only so long as the force lasted.[8]

When one Protestant power had made peace with Sweden, Oliver deemed it expedient to try to aid the conclusion of a treaty with another. Accordingly, he commissioned Meadowe as envoy extraordinary to Charles X, with the special task of attending the conference at Brauns-berg where, if he found Charles X bent upon the acquisition of East Prussia, he was to use his best endeavors to persuade Poland to agree. Though the Elector of Brandenburg would thus lose the territory he had acquired from Poland, Meadowe was to try to reunite Frederick William and Charles X. With both potentates he was to insist upon the total exclusion of the Emperor from the treaty.[9] Another envoy, William Jephson, tried to persuade the Elector's councillors that neither his religious nor his secular interests would benefit from an alliance with the enemies of Sweden or from a vote in favor of Leopold as Emperor. He found, however, that the Elector, as a Calvinist, was so embittered by the exclusion of his co-religionists from most offices in Sweden, a Lutheran state, that any argument about a common Protestantism fell on deaf ears.[10] Moreover, to expect that the Elector would change sides and voluntarily relinquish Prussia, the acquisition of which was his dearest ambition, was absurd, particularly as no compensation was in

[7]Philip Meadowe, *A Narrative of the Principal Actions Occurring in the Wars between Sweden and Denmark* (1677), pp. 58-62.

[8]Ibid, pp. 73-74.

[9]Abbott, *Writings . . . of Oliver Cromwell*, IV, 779-82. Brandenburg had deserted Sweden in 1657 and joined Poland, her enemy.

[10]Jephson to Thurloe, Apr. 30, 1658, Thurloe, VII, 106-107.

sight. An alliance with Poland, Jephson was informed, was "grounded upon the unseparable interests of these two princes." The response to the proposition about the choice of an emperor was equally disappointing. The Elector had determined to cast his vote for Leopold, though, as already indicated, he had no objection to the conditions imposed on his titular superior.[11]

Charles X was proving intractable. Hardly had the treaty of Roskilde been signed than he found it insufficient. He was determined to acquire the island of Hveen (Huen in Meadowe's spelling) in the Sound by a right called in France *"le droit de bienséance,"* if no better claim could be advanced. He was also resolved to keep Swedish troops on Danish soil "to the inexpressible burden of the people albeit the time prefixed by the treaty for their marching of[f] be lapsed a good while since."[12] The English envoy noted, too, that the Swedes had a maxim that the Dane will never want the will to hurt them and so must be deprived of the power.[13] Denmark alone could not be a formidable adversary, but she might become dangerous in conjunction with the other enemies of Sweden, especially if the United Provinces joined them. Meadowe thought that the Dutch representative, Conrad van Beuningen, a regular firebrand, was trying his utmost to embroil the United Provinces and Sweden. As early as April the arrival at Elsinore of a thousand foot soldiers levied in the Low Countries was observed, and more were expected.[14] That the Dutch should view with alarm the progress of the Swedish army was natural. Their share in the Baltic trade was easily the largest—two-thirds of the traffic through the Sound.[15] They had two reasons to fear Swedish aggrandizement, that if Sweden acquired control of the Sound she might levy what dues she wished or even exclude Dutch ships altogether, and that if she conquered East Prussia she might hamper or forbid Dutch commerce in that area.

A similar interest in the Baltic trade might have made England and the United Provinces allies, but actually they were rivals. As Manley wrote, "the trade of the Baltic and free passage of the Sound, exclusive each to other, was the ground of their jealousie, and the design of their arms."[16] This rivalry was by no means confined to the Baltic. The Dutch

[11]To Thurloe, June 21, 1658, ibid, 188-89.

[12]Meadowe to Thurloe, May 31, 1658, *Eng. Hist. Rev.,* VII (1892), 731-32. The Isle of Hveen lay off the port of Landskrona and might in the hands of an enemy impede its trade. Therefore, argued Charles X, the island should properly belong to Sweden.

[13]To Thurloe, June 29, 1658, ibid., p. 737.

[14]To Thurloe, Apr. 21, 1658, ibid., p. 730.

[15]Charles E. Hill, *The Danish Sound Dues and the Command of the Baltic* (Durham, N.C., 1926), pp. 155-56.

[16]Manley, *History of the Late Warres,* p. 62.

declaration of war upon Portugal as a result of an old dispute about the possession of Brazil was inconvenient to England and France because they wished the entire strength of Portugal to be free to act against Spain—the war of independence which had started in 1640 still continued. However, some consolation was found in the reflection that if the Dutch fleet was busy in Portuguese waters it would not be available for action in the Baltic. The seizure by the Dutch East India Company of English ships at Bantam provoked loud protests, and the utmost efforts of George Downing, sent in January, 1658, to represent England at the Hague, were being exerted to secure restitution. A more permanent English grievance was the covert assistance given the privateers, nominally Spanish but really Netherlandish, and especially the sale of captured goods in Dutch harbors. Mountagu, in command of the fleet off Flanders, voiced his indignation at the way in which the Netherlands had become "a nest to shelter rogues that interrupt our tradinge. They receive the enemies men of warr in, with their prizes, and suffer them to sell them, and refitt and mann themselves, and to sea againe, and convoy all the Spaniards money and goods for Flanders."[17] For their part the Dutch, the great protagonists of the doctrine that free ships make free goods, could complain of the way the English exercised the right of search. They were alarmed at the easy progress of the allies in Flanders and at the prospect that in a possible war, they would find Dunkirk in the hands of a strong naval power and not of effete Spain. They also blamed English support for the dangerous hegemony Sweden was establishing in the north, to which the only reply that Downing could give was that they were really responsible, because they had hindered the conclusion of peace between Sweden and Denmark.[18] The chances, therefore, of a hearty co-operation in the north were slim.

An agreement with Sweden was equally beyond Oliver's diplomacy. His financial weakness, the greater after his quarrel with Parliament which ended in its dissolution in February, prevented his paying the subsidy of £30,000 he had promised Charles X in November, 1657. His defaulting was most prejudicial. Without the money, wrote Meadowe, "my negociation wil avail nothing. The levies of England which are sent over hither signify little. They find not things answer promise or expectation which makes them mutiny or run away to the dishonor of our nation."[19] In addition to an empty exchequer, other obstacles prevented an alliance. Because Charles X was unwilling to hand over Bre-

[17]To Thurloe, July 21, 1658, Thurloe, VII, 284-85.
[18]Ibid., 245-46.
[19]To Thurloe, *Eng. Hist. Rev.*, VII, 737.

men, because it might become a key to north Germany as Dunkirk was expected to be to western Europe, no sufficient inducement could be offered for English intervention. The futility of expecting Charles X to abandon his hopes of conquest and become a disinterested champion of militant Protestantism was now made clear. In the middle of August he suddenly attacked Denmark with the intention of annexing her. As Meadowe foresaw, if Denmark was lost, Norway would follow, and then the King of Sweden could gratify his ambition and sign himself as "The King of the North."[20] Oliver Cromwell's death on September 3 left to Richard and his councillors the question as to what policy to adopt.

For the first two months of his Protectorate, Richard and his Council allowed the northern war to proceed without any interference.[21] They may have thought or hoped, like Monck, that the Swedes would capture Copenhagen. The Danish agent's plea for assistance was not granted and the Council advised negotiation for a treaty with Sweden. But some of the councillors are likely to have become conscious of the dilemma stated by Downing with his usual bluntness—that if the Swedes captured Copenhagen they would be "very formidable" and if the Dutch relieved it they would be "insupportably insolent." The necessity for action was soon apparent. A Dutch fleet under Opdam sailed north, defeated a Swedish squadron, relieved Copenhagen from the blockade by sea, and landed two thousand troops, thus averting any danger of the Swedes storming the capital. The union of the Dutch and Danish fleets at once gained a decisive superiority at sea, and made feasible the transport of the Brandenburg and Imperial forces in Holstein to Zealand.[22] When to these hostile forces were added the Poles, the odds against Sweden were great. These considerations induced the Council to listen to a plea from the French court to send an English fleet to succor Sweden. Two advantages might be gained—the Dutch might be deterred from sending a second auxiliary force they had equipped, and the Brandenburgers be kept from landing in Zealand. The Privy Council on November 11 agreed that a fleet should be sent to the Sound to offer mediation between Sweden and Denmark and that Vice Admiral William Goodson should be in command.[23] The English then raised the question what would be the French attitude if the dispatch of the fleet led to hostilities with the Dutch, and received from Mazarin a promise that in such an eventuality France would immediately declare war on

[20]Aug. 16, 1658, ibid., p. 742.

[21]In a letter dated October 15, Thurloe explained to Downing that "we being but in the beginning of our government are not very ripe to consider foreign affairs." British Museum, Add. MSS 22919, f. 54.

[22]Thurloe, VII, 408-409, 415, 421, 440.

[23]Council Minutes; Guizot, I, 247, 249, 254, 260, 263, 272.

Holland and not make peace except in conjunction with England.[24] At the same time some three hundred naval recruits under Sir George Ayscue were to be transported to Sweden. Goodson was most unlucky in the weather he encountered. Starting from Aldborough Bay on November 18, he was driven back again on the twenty-second. After repairs he set out again on December 3, reached the northernmost point of Jutland, the Skaw, but could not round it on account of adverse winds. Twelve days later Goodson made up his mind to return, but a gale severely damaged his ships, though all eventually reached home ports. Ayscue's little force, reduced from three to two hundred, did not land in Sweden until the spring.[25]

On November 20/30 Downing, on behalf of England, and de Thou, on behalf of France, presented a memorial to the States General. In his, Downing represented that, having received the resolution of the States General that their intention in intervening in the war between Sweden and Denmark was solely in order to re-establish peace, England and France were ready to co-operate with the United Provinces to that end. A joint offer of mediation for a separate peace between these two countries should not embrace any other subject. The Protector, wrote Downing, was the more earnest to propose this to the States General because he had heard that a Dutch fleet was to help the imperial forces now in Holstein, which assistance would not restore peace but hazard putting the command of the Baltic into the hands of the house of Austria. The Dutch were, therefore, asked not to furnish additional assistance to any belligerent. The French memorial advised the Dutch not to send reinforcements or pretend to make a general peace, but to make propositions jointly with England to end hostilities between Sweden and Denmark.[26]

Downing claimed that "these two unexpected thunderclaps coming thus both together" startled the States General. The two representatives conferred with John de Witt, the Grand Pensionary of Holland, who did not appreciate the idea of a separate peace unless the strength of Sweden and Denmark should be brought more nearly equal. He felt the basis for mediation ought to be the treaty of Bromsebro, 1645, thus depriving Sweden of her recent gains. De Thou thought this a ridiculous proposition and Downing backed him up vigorously. On one point all three seemed to agree—to abolish the stipulation in the treaty of Roskilde that

---

[24]*Recueil des Instructions . . . Angleterre*, I (1648-1665), ed. J. J. Jusserand (Paris, 1929), pp. 226-27. The promise was given after Goodson had sailed.

[25]List of the ships in *The Journal of Edward Mountagu First Earl of Sandwich*, ed. R. C. Anderson, for the Navy Records Society, 1929, p. xiv; *Nicholas Papers*, IV, 90.

[26]Both memorials are in Thurloe, VII, 520-521. In a letter of November 16, Thurloe emphasized to Downing that a separate peace must be made between Sweden and Denmark without intermixing the interests of other states which would render peace impossible. B. M. Add. MSS 22919, f. 61.

hostile fleets might be excluded from the Baltic.[27] Soon the States General were expressing their pleasure at the willingness of England and France to contribute toward the pacification of the north, and announcing that they would send ambassadors extraordinary to the two belligerents to cooperate with the representatives of England and France.[28] England and France next proceeded to sign a treaty which bound them to mediate between Sweden and Denmark and, if peace were concluded and then broken, to take part against the defaulter. In the event that mediation involved either England or France in war with a third nation, the other would automatically become her ally.[29] At this point the English government thought fit to test the opinion of Parliament on its foreign policy.

On February 21 a most interesting debate was started by Thurloe. After a survey of the antecedents of the northern war, he proceeded to argue that its continuance would hamper trade and, if the Sound was controlled by an enemy, would ruin English shipping because hemp, pitch, tar, cordage, and masts all came from the Baltic lands. Experience during the late war with the Dutch, when the Danes prohibited English shipping from passing the Sound, proved that point. The Emperor was now as likely to command the Baltic as the King of Spain commanded the western seas. When the Emperor had achieved his aims in the north, he and his confederates would pour into Flanders and thence into England to restore the house of Stuart. The Protestant cause was in great danger. Therefore, England should reconcile Denmark and Sweden and, in alliance with France, induce the United Provinces and Brandenburg to cease their attacks on Sweden, and try to make peace between Poland and Sweden. The Dutch had already sent naval and military assistance to the Danes but had stopped reinforcements when informed that the English were sending a fleet to the Sound. Though this fleet had been obliged to return, owing to the unseasonable frost, it had preserved the status quo from October to now. But spring was the time for action. The States General wanted peace, but showed it did not rely solely upon diplomacy by preparing a large fleet. England was as much concerned as the United Provinces and should also strengthen her diplomacy with a fleet. Its preparation was well forward, and he was informing the House in order that members should advise what was fit to be done.[30]

When Thurloe sat down, a deep silence lasted for a good while, to be broken by Vane whose subtle mind at once detected that the secretary

[27]Thurloe, VII, 522-25.
[28]Ibid., 543-44.
[29]Jan. 24/Feb. 3, *Recueil des Instructions . . . Angleterre*, I, 227-28; Guizot, I, 284-88.
[30]Burton, *Diary*, III, 376-84.

had significantly omitted to mention who was responsible for the renewal of the war between Denmark and Sweden. To have acknowledged that Sweden had begun hostilities would have fatally weakened his case, so Thurloe had to be content to say that the Protector was still in the dark. He and others contended that the English were not concerned about the cause of the war but only about its effect upon their interests. Though not a few felt that the Protestant cause was at stake and would be lost if Sweden was defeated by her numerous enemies, many more feared that the Dutch would gain direct or indirect control of the Sound and thus monopolize the Baltic trade. Jealousy of their commercial rivals inspired many speakers. Some of the statements about the Dutch were: They have already excluded us from Bantam and will soon deny us all trade; we are islanders, and our life and soul is traffic. Your cloth trade will be lost. Remember Amboyna; I believe the quarrel between the Dutch and us is irreconcilable because we are rivals for the fairest mistress in all Christendom, trade; and he that is master of the Sound is master of all the trade of Europe. Another grievance against the Dutch lay in the help they gave the Spaniards in the war now being waged. "It is rather a Dutch war, under the Spaniard's name," said Maynard. This war found no defenders but many assailants, who claimed that 1,200 or even 1,500 ships had been captured at sea. The figure 1,200 may have been derived from a tract entitled *The Merchants Humble Petition and Remonstrance* (1659). Richard Baker signed the preliminary matter and was probably the author. According to this pamphlet the losses were both direct and indirect. Among them were £500,000, the value of the goods, etc., when the Spaniards seized English property in Spain and her territories after they heard of the attack on San Domingo in 1655; another £500,000 a year because fish from Newfoundland could no longer be imported to Spain; the carrying and coastwise trade, now in the hands of the Dutch; 1,200 captured ships which with their cargoes were worth £4,000 apiece or £4,800,000 in all; and the loss of a profitable market in Spain for manufactured goods, especially woolen, and for colonial produce like sugar and tobacco which had been imported "incovertly." No doubt Baker exaggerated, but his tract is valuable for the details he gave of the trade with Spain, including insurance.[31]

The Cromwellians and the crypto-Royalists agreed that Sweden must be supported, but while the former, or some of them, expected that

[31]*The Merchants Humble Petition* was warmly praised in a tract, *Englands Settlement*, dated by Thomason Sept. 2, pp. 6-7. It also emphasized the heavy taxes compared to the far lighter ones to which people objected when raised by Charles I. Evelyn (*Diary*, Nov. 15, 1659) recorded that the Dutch ambassador "did in a manner acknowledge" that his nation thought only of profit and for this reason gave aid to Denmark but none to the exiled Charles II.

armed mediation would suffice, the latter may have hoped that a war with the United Provinces would ensue. None was disposed to deny that the Dutch were dangerous rivals, but by no means all were in favor of the control of the Sound passing from the Danes to the Swedes. In general, the Republicans were suspicious of Sweden. Brandenburg, Holland, and Denmark were as good Protestant countries as Sweden, said Neville, and to give the Sound to the last was like giving both the door and the house, whereas the status quo would retain for Denmark only the door. The weaker country would not try to engross all trade in the Baltic but the stronger would be so potent that we should trade by his courtesy. As for the Emperor, danger from him was remote—he had his hands full with the Turks. Scot introduced a red herring in asking that the question of the control of the armed forces ought first to be settled, otherwise members would be no more than purse-bearers and would, in effect, tell the Protector that if he declared war, he could rely on them to find the money to pay for it. Hesilrige emphasized the cost of a war and the risk of an invasion headed by Charles Stuart. Later he talked like a nineteenth-century Little Englander, and argued that Christianity forbade the seizure of the Sound from the Danes to whom it belonged, and that God had blasted their attack upon the dominion of Spain, perhaps forgetting that success at Jamaica had followed failure at San Domingo. Vane raised two issues: how was the £1,000,000 needed for the fleet to be paid and who was to command it? He and members of like mind wanted to dictate foreign policy and nominate the commanders of the forces needed to enforce it. They also wished to name commissioners who would take over the administration of the navy.[32] Thus it happened that there was a unanimous vote for sending a large fleet to sea for the safety of the Commonwealth and the preservation of trade and commerce, but a prolonged debate and division before the resolution was carried that the Protector should put the unanimous vote into effect, "saving the interest of this House in the militia and in making of peace and war."[33] As the Solicitor General commented, this was "to shake off a single person and another house."

The debate, apart from its significance as a guide to public opinion on foreign affairs, is noteworthy for its disorderliness, though not to a greater extent than others. No matter the subject under discussion, the Republicans managed to condemn Oliver's policy—in this instance for concluding peace with the Dutch in 1654 and for attacking Spain—and to ignore the constitution as established by the Petition and Advice. But

[32]Burton, pp. 386, 392, 394, 399, 387-91, 396, 457-58, 461, 492.

[33]*Commons Journals*, Feb. 24. The vote was 176 to 98.

possibly the most remarkable feature of the debate is that, though the cost of setting forth a fleet was mentioned, nobody proposed any way of meeting it.

During the winter the question of peace with Spain came to the fore. At first Mazarin was unwilling to agree to a suspension of arms because it might enable Spain to apply her main strength to the conquest of Portugal, but he informed Pimentel, the Spanish agent, that England and France would examine any propositions Spain might offer. Mazarin several times urged the Protector to empower a representative to discuss joint terms but the months slipped by without any favorable response. Bordeaux approached Thurloe often but could not obtain any satisfaction. He surmised that the Protector did not send Lockhart back to Paris because his presence at Dunkirk was essential to keep the garrison there loyal at a time when the army in England was threatening political intervention. He believed that the English were afraid that if France and Spain were at peace they would together aid the exiled Charles II. The continual postponement of any decision whether to strive after a joint peace or not was partly due to the causes Bordeaux alleged, but more to the general paralysis of the Protector and Privy Council as tension between the court and army increased. There was also a grave difference of opinion in the Council and outside it about foreign policy in general. Thurloe explained to Bordeaux that the Protector thought the present was a most inopportune time for a pacification which would allow Spain to re-establish her power and achieve the universal monarchy at which she aimed. In Germany, the Emperor and his allies would crush the King of Sweden, and endanger the United Provinces. If the war was continued for a few more years, her neighbors would never again have cause to be fearful of the greatness of Spain. These ideas were not shared by Richard's opponents or by the country at large, which wanted to end the war with Spain.[34] If peace was not made, the shipping interests wished for a prohibition of all Spanish imports, including wine, grapes, figs, tobacco, and wool—a fitting retaliation for the closing of all Spanish ports to English goods. The agreement between France and Spain for a truce, signed on April 27/May 7, was reached without English aid. The suspension of arms applied to the two towns the English garrisoned, Dunkirk and Mardyke, but did not end the war at sea, where the losses continued, to the great vexation of merchants.[35]

[34]*Lettres du Cardinal Mazarin*, IX, 112-14, 133-40, 144-46; Guizot, I, 313, 318, 337, 342, 353-54; *Calendar Venetian*, pp. 2-4, 31. The Venetian ambassador agreed with his French colleague about the fear lest peace would lead to a joint invasion of England by French and Spanish armies. Ibid., pp. 18, 52.

[35]Jean Dumont, *Corps Universal Diplomatique du Droit des Gens* (Amsterdam, 1726-31), VI, Part II, 249.

English shipping interests had many grievances against the Dutch. Some were general, some particular; some old, some new. The jealousy of the Dutch carrying trade, which had inspired the Navigation Act of 1651, was as rife as ever. Indeed, it had been intensified during the Anglo-Spanish war, which was a gold mine to Holland. One of the most serious consequences of the dangers English ships encountered at sea was that merchants were beginning to trade in Dutch bottoms. If they continued, Thurloe was told, "in a shorte time we shall have noe ships of our owne."[36] The English, like the French, refused to acknowledge the Dutch theory of international law, that the flag covered the cargo, and insisted on the right to search ships trading with Spain for contraband. The Dutch had another cause of complaint—that ships captured by vessels commissioned by, or pretending to be commissioned by, the King of Sweden, were detained in French or, more often, English harbors for months while the prize crews consumed all the provisions aboard.[37] The King of Portugal also issued commissions to English captains, whose seizures of Dutch vessels were brought by Nieuport to the attention of the Privy Council at Whitehall.[38] Englishmen who could prove they had suffered material loss from the Spaniards were granted letters of marque to recoup themselves. Security had first to be given "for observing such rules as are usually required in cases of like nature."[39]

A dispute Richard Cromwell inherited from his father was about the Bantam ships, as they were called. These ships did not belong to the English East India Company, but had been seized by its Dutch rival on the ground that they had violated a legal blockade and had supplied munitions to the natives of Batavia in revolt against the Dutch. On the contrary, the English asserted, the ships were engaged in peaceful trading. Downing thought he had prevailed and gained an order for the restitution of the ships and their goods at the end of July, 1658, but the dispute continued about compensation. In February, 1659, Downing secured a promise of £50,000 to be given the owners of the three ships. In return he seemed to have assured the Dutch that this payment would cancel all other claims. Inasmuch as the East India Company received nothing for their losses at sea, protests were promptly made to the Protector, but without effect. Unfortunately for amicable relations,

[36]Thurloe, VII, 582.

[37]See for examples Nieuport's memorandum to Thurloe (VII, 637). Those sailing under Swedish commissions were not particular about the nationality of the ships they seized. See Council Register for an order of December 30 to the authorities at Dunkirk to secure a Captain Welsh who had captured several Eastland ships laden with naval stores for England. Cf. ibid., Oct. 15, 25, 1658.

[38]Register, Jan. 4. Cf. Thurloe VII, 62, for earlier examples of "Portugall prizes."

[39]Register, Jan. 11. Grant to John Jeffreys, captain of the "Fortune." The stipulation was in accordance with Article xxv of the Treaty of Westminster, 1654.

privateering in waters nearer home soon led to fresh charges and countercharges, among which were the many injuries the Dutch had suffered near Barbados and the Caribbees.[40] Even Downing, whose forceful advocacy of the English case neglected no point, thought that his task would be easier if a ship, the "Vrede,"[41] which Penn had captured on the high seas in 1655 was released.

The greatest grievance was the friendly reception accorded Spanish privateers, called Ostenders, and their prizes in Dutch harbors, especially those in Zealand. Downing continually complained that the Dutch "enjoyed perfect peace in all the havens of England, and the English from day to day [were] undone in the havens of the United Provinces." He asserted there were many score of English ships brought into Dutch ports by Ostenders and there "unladen, sold, and disposed of."[42] The answer to his many remonstrances was sometimes a *tu quoque*, but reading the charges and countercharges leaves the impression that both governments wished to act in accordance with the articles of the treaty of 1654. Yet even with the best will in the world, long and perhaps ruinous delays ensued between the illegal capture of a ship and its ultimate release. In England proceedings would begin by a complaint from the Dutch ambassador that a ship was being illegally brought into a harbor. The Privy Council appointed a committee which found it necessary to request a report from Dr. Walker, judge advocate of the Admiralty Court. When Walker's report was available the committee considered it and advised the Privy Council, which would then inform the Dutch ambassador. If the facts of the case were in dispute, a decision by the Admiralty Court might be sought. Meanwhile the crew would be living as best they could at their owner's expense or their own, lucky if their cargo was not embezzled. In the United Provinces, Downing would hand in his complaint to the States General, which referred it to the admiralty of the province concerned. Any action taken would be indirect —the States General would issue a *placaert* or proclamation, defining the law, and trust the local admiralty court to enforce it.[43] If Downing's protests were valid, too often the English owners found that the delays had enabled the privateers to exact ransoms from the officers, sell the cargoes, and to disappear before the port authorities bestirred themselves.

---

[40]Thurloe, VII, 296. He told Downing that "the eyes of all the Nation are upon" the East India business. Jan. 7. B.M. Add. MSS 22919, f. 72. *A Calendar of the Court Minutes etc. of the East India Company, 1655-1659*, ed. Ethel Bruce Sainsbury (Oxford, 1916), p. xxxi.

[41]Thurloe, VII, 457-58, 499, 504, 515. Foreseeing difficulties ahead Thurloe tried to get the compensation paid promptly. B.M. Add. MSS 22919, f. 75 (Feb. 4). Soon there were complaints by merchants of other injuries for which the agreement provided no compensation. Ibid., p. 81.

[42]Ibid., VII, 465.

[43]Ibid., VII, 465.

To decide which side suffered the greater injustice would require "a Daniel come to judgment." The English believed they were victimized and anti-Dutch feeling grew apace.

Richard determined to send a strong fleet to the Sound. Mountagu was put in command of it and was ready to sail by the end of March. His instructions were complicated because they had to provide for so many possible situations. The most important would arise if the King of Sweden or the King of Denmark refused the proposed invitation to begin negotiations. Mountagu was ordered to deal very seriously with Charles X, and to explain that aiding him might lead to war with Holland, which England was in no condition to engage in and which Parliament did not wish. If he would not agree to peace, England could not help him. If the King of Denmark refused terms based on the treaty of Roskilde, he should be told that England would help Sweden. In that event Mountagu was directed to deny a passage to the Brandenburgers to the Danish islands, to defend the Swedish fleet if it should be attacked, maintain the blockade of Copenhagen, and keep the new Dutch fleet separate from the old, by force if necessary. But first Mountagu should induce Charles to sign the treaty of assistance, which gave England freedom from Sound dues and the exclusion of her enemies from the Baltic. A further instruction was that if Charles X proved the obstacle to peace, then Mountagu was to try to gain for England the same advantages of trade and commerce as the Danes gave the Dutch.[44] Mountagu at once discovered that far from any negotiations for a peace being under way, both Sweden and Denmark had "an utter aversion thereto." He also learned that Charles would never agree to the clauses in the treaty of assistance about closing the Baltic to the enemies of England because this would involve him in a perpetual war with Holland.[45]

To oblige the northern kings to make peace, England, France, and the United Provinces signed a treaty at The Hague on May 11/21. The treaty of Roskilde was to be the basis of the new pacification, but its third article, providing for the exclusion of unfriendly navies from the Baltic, was henceforth to be omitted. Three weeks were to be allowed for the two kings to accept the mediation, during which time neither the Dutch nor the English fleet would commit any hostile act. If at the end of three weeks no peace had been concluded, the three mediating powers would all refrain from aiding whichever country was at fault. Other clauses provided that all three mediators should enjoy the status of the

[44]These instructions, apparently undated, are summarized in Sandwich's *Journal*, App. I.
[45]Mountagu to Thurloe, April 11, Thurloe, VII, 652.

most favored nation, and that they would do their best to make a good treaty between Sweden and, first Poland, then Brandenburg. The English and French were to try to secure the ratification of the treaty of Elbing.[46]

Meanwhile in England the Protectorate was ending and the Long Parliament was in power. The Republicans were less friendly to Sweden than the Cromwellians had been and more anxious to improve relations with Holland. They agreed to ratify the treaty of May 11/21 but were disposed to listen to Dutch suggestions that Denmark should receive some compensation for the unprovoked attack of the previous August. However, a report of a proposal to his representatives in London that he should cede Trondheim and Bornholm drew from Charles X the boast that he would never yield them so long as he had a sword at his side and a soldier behind him. At the same time the King of Denmark declined to consider a peace apart from his allies, and so was technically the "refuser" and liable to lose Dutch aid.[47] The period for waiting was prolonged from three to six weeks but the belligerents were no nearer an accommodation.

Thurloe thought that Goodson's brief voyage had deterred the Dutch from sending further reinforcements to the Danes, a withdrawal which Downing attributed to the memorials which he and the French ambassador had presented. He was soon able to forward to Thurloe a resolution of the States General expressing "extraordinary satisfaction" that England and France were ready to cooperate with the United Provinces to secure peace in the northern parts. But there were considerable differences between the terms the English and Dutch preferred. The former wished to restrict the mediation to Sweden and Denmark and to reach a settlement on the basis of the treaty of Roskilde, the latter to include the other combatants, Austria, Brandenburg, and Poland, and to go back to 1645, the treaty of Bromsebro, for the basis.

The Council appointed three additional commissioners to the Kings of Sweden and Denmark—two of its own members, Algernon Sidney and Sir Robert Honeywood, and Thomas Boone. Joining the three to Mountagu was a sign that councillors did not trust him. He had been too faithful a Cromwellian to please the Republicans, and too bitter an opponent of the grandees, especially Disbrowe, to be trusted by them. At one time the notion was entertained of replacing Downing at The Hague by Rich, but the colonel asked to be excused, so Downing received

<hr>

[46]Dumont, *Corps Diplomatique*, VI, Pt. II, 252-53. By the treaty of Elbing, 1656, Sweden had granted the United Provinces the status of the most favored nation. An interesting letter from Downing to Mountagu on the English requirements is in Carte MS. 73, f. 272, dated May 12/22, 1659.

[47]Meadowe to the Council of State, June 11/21, Thurloe, VII, 688.

fresh credentials.[48] He was very busy negotiating what the Council called the "concept of an additional and explicatory treaty" or "elucidation of the treaty" of May 11. This amending, or supplementary agreement was signed on July 12/22 at The Hague. By it England and the United Provinces were bound to use their utmost endeavors to bring about a good treaty between Sweden and Holland on the basis of the "formula" of Roskilde except that now Trondheim was to be restored to Denmark. In the event of failure to arrange a pacification, then both commonwealths would give aid and succor to the king who accepted the terms and "effectively constrain" the one refusing them. The two kings were allowed only a fortnight to accept or reject the terms offered them.[49] A further elucidation was signed on July 25/August 4, but did little more than fix the day from which the fortnight should be reckoned, provide that the Dutch and English fleets should act together in conformity with the plans the ministers of the two powers should judge most effectual, and agree that each should have sufficient forces to carry out the agreement of July 12/22 and that the remainder should return home.[50]

The commissioners from England did not join Mountagu until July 20. They found the King of Denmark unwilling to enter into negotiations directly with Sweden because he feared that his allies, the Emperor, King of Poland, and Elector of Brandenburg would at once desert him, but he was willing that the English and Dutch commissioners should "go between, hear the pretences of both parties, and terminate the differences between them." After this satisfactory response, they visited the Swedes in turn but met with a different reception. At first Charles X declined to meet them after an exchange of courtesies, and the senators he deputized refused to offer more than that Swedish commissioners should be named to hear whatever the English commissioners might have to communicate. In vain these urged that Charles X should state categorically whether he would accept the treaty of Roskilde or, if not, what exceptions he wished made to it as the basis for a new treaty. When at length they and their Dutch colleagues were admitted to an audience, Charles X told them he received them as mediators not as arbitrators. He would not accept a project of a treaty nor negotiate with any but the King of Denmark. Turning to the Dutchmen, he said he looked upon them as his enemies and would not admit of their mediation. England and Holland, he boasted, "made projects upon our [i.e., their] fleets,

[48]Council Register, June 8, 27.
[49]Dumont, *Corps Diplomatique*, VI, Pt. II, 260-261. The Council Minutes for July 16, two days after the agreement was signed, show that the English wished to have inserted a clause that the Sound dues should never be raised higher than they were in 1600.
[50]Council Minutes, Aug. 9.

and he laying his hand upon his sword, had a project by his side.”[51]

At this stage the situation was suddenly altered because the commissioners were deserted by their colleague, Mountagu, and the English fleet. Mountagu seems to have been very concerned about the requirement in the instructions that the English fleet or the major part of it should be free as soon as possible to sail homeward, and secured his colleagues' assent to a proposal that the English and Dutch should each leave a squadron sufficient to master both the northern kings' fleets and send the rest home. The Dutch agreed in principle, but wished the ratio of ships to be twenty-five or thirty to fifteen whereas the English wished equality. There was the further difficulty that the Dutch declined to move until the States General had named the ships to return. This would entail a serious delay because the admiralties of the different provinces would have to be consulted.[52] In these circumstances the four English commissioners debated at length whether the whole fleet should return or whether fifteen ships should be left behind as the English contingent in the joint fleet which, according to the second agreement at The Hague, should coerce whichever king should be unwilling to make peace. Among the arguments used in favor of leaving an English squadron in the Sound were that the Council of State had directed that part of the English fleet should remain, that if no English ships were left English influence in the settlement of the northern war would be slight, and that a withdrawal would be a breach of faith with the Dutch. On the other side were the weakness of a squadron of fifteen ships in the event that the Dutch did not play fair, and the probability that, if it were used at all, the English would be committed to action against Sweden, whose king was likely to be judged guilty of declining conditions of peace— the English commissioners being themselves divided on this point, Mountagu being pro-Swedish and Sidney pro-Danish. Also, winter was close at hand and victuals were hard to come by, no money being available and the fleet having hardly more provisions than would suffice for the voyage home. Three of the commissioners were in favor of sending the whole fleet back to England, and the flag officers when consulted by Mountagu concurred. Sidney was inflexible and said that if he consented he would deserve to lose his head. He accused Mountagu of favoring Charles X because that monarch was against a commonwealth, and told him that the people of England no longer felt toward Sweden as they had done in Cromwell's day. To this Mountagu's reply, that the inter-

[51]Thurloe, VII, 725-26, 732-34, 736.

[52]In reply to a remonstrance from Nieuport, Lenthall as Speaker asserted that the want of provisions which compelled Mountagu to sail home would have been less acute if the Dutch had agreed "to a timely settlement of a joint fleet" to remain in the Sound according to the agreement of July 25/August 4. Council Minutes, a letter endorsed as read September 21 and delivered the twenty-third.

est of England required support of Sweden regardless of the form of government, is an early plea for continuity of foreign policy. In the end the three commissioners, Sidney dissenting, ordered the whole fleet home, adding that there were only a month's provisions on board. On August 24, the fleet under Mountagu weighed anchor.[53]

The influence of the English commissioners in the Sound was much weakened by the fleet's departure. Though the Dutch afforded help to the Danes and all along the north German coast the enemies of Charles X were active, hoping to capture Bremen and the Swedish possessions in Pomerania and Prussia, he would not yield. He was persuaded that England and France would never suffer him to fall and nothing Sidney could say disabused him of this notion.[54] The failure of the Commonwealth to send back any ships to the Sound soon convinced all concerned that the English did not intend to carry out the treaty and agreements signed at The Hague. Lambert's ejection of the Rump totally extinguished all hope of an English fleet. Sidney, who stayed in Copenhagen until after the Restoration, believed that since the return home of the English fleet, Charles X had become convinced that England would never use force against him. "A few shot of our cannon would have made this peace," but they could not be fired.[55] When the death of Charles removed the great obstacle to peace, the treaty of Copenhagen (May 27/June 6) was guaranteed by England, France, and Holland. Denmark received back Trondheim and Bornholm plus the Sound dues less 3,500 rix-dollars per annum. A month before a French threat of armed intervention had forced the Emperor, the Great Elector, and the King of Poland to sign the treaty of Oliva (April 23/May 3) with Sweden.[56]

As for Anglo-French relations, first Richard and then the Rump were inexplicably slow in sending Lockhart back to Paris. Notwithstanding the urgent representations of Bordeaux, Lockhart did not reach Paris until March and then without proper instructions.[57] Richard and his Council were unwilling to treat with Spain "by the way of France," but wanted a three-handed negotiation at some neutral place. Nothing had been arranged when the Protectorate ended.[58] Not until July 2 did Parliament formally approve Lockhart's credentials. Then the Council of

[53]Mountagu wrote out an elaborate account of these discussions on August 30 on his way home. *Journal*, pp. 47-67.

[54]Thurloe, VII, 741-42; *Sydney Papers*, ed. R. W. Blencowe (1825), pp. 163-68.

[55]*Sydney Papers*, p. 172.

[56]*Recueil des Instructions . . . Suède*, ed. A. Geffroy (Paris, 1885), p. xlix.

[57]Guizot, I, 312, 322, 326, 352, 361, 380.

[58]Thurloe's account of relations with France and Spain which he drew up after the Restoration. Thurloe, I, 762. According to the same account, an unofficial Spanish agent suggested these terms as possible conditions of peace: Dunkirk to remain in English hands unless sold to Spain; Jamaica to be sold back to Spain; a limited trade by license permitted with Spanish colonies; and an assurance that Englishmen should not be molested by the Inquisition. Charles II was not to live in Spain or Flanders but receive a pension to reside elsewhere.

State woke up to the consequences of the long delay, and even regretted the ceremonious reception accorded Lockhart in Paris because it prevented the ambassador from immediately pursuing Mazarin, on his way to Bayonne to finish the negotiations with Don Luis de Haro, the Spanish minister. Thus England was not represented either at the cessation of arms or at the preliminaries of peace signed on May 25/June 4. These contained the essentials—that Louis XIV should restore some of his conquests if his marriage to Maria Theresa, the eldest daughter of Philip IV, was arranged. The treaty of the Pyrenees, October 28/November 7, contained the marriage contract which was to trouble European diplomats for nearly half a century—that Maria Theresa, on receipt of a dowry of half a million gold crowns, should renounce all claim to the Spanish empire. Lockhart was treated courteously enough but exercised no influence at all upon the settlement at any stage.[59] Indeed, the Council of State was far more concerned about the journey of Charles II to Bayonne in the hope of gaining support from both France and Spain. England was left at war with Spain, and French aid to Portugal was now at an end. If England wished to help Portugal to regain her independence she must act alone.

Mazarin had no intention of embroiling France and England, no matter what government prevailed in that restless country. He disapproved of Turenne's attempt in August and September to provide from the army under his command an expeditionary force which James, Duke of York, should lead across the Channel. But news of Booth's defeat and capture arrived when James was about to embark, so the plan was abandoned. Mazarin declined to see Henry Bennet who had been Charles II's representative in Madrid since early in 1657 and who accompanied Don Luis to Fuentarabia. Similarly, Charles II himself, who arrived on the scene in October, was refused an audience. His only reward for his long journey was a gift of twenty thousand crowns from Don Luis—a poor exchange for the failu.e of the Spaniard to pay his forces in Flanders since the cessation of arms.[60] When the Restoration was seen to be near

[59]*Commons Journal*, July 2, Oct. 11 (for Lockhart's summons home); Council Minutes, July 21, 25; M. Mignet, *Négotiations relatives à la Succession D'Espagne* (Paris, 1835), I, Pt. I. The provision for the disbandment of Condés' army, in Spanish service, deprived Charles II of a possible force for the invasion of England.

[60]A fortnight after Lambert had dismissed the Parliament, Mordaunt had urged that Charles II should "engage the public ministers of France to demand the King's restoration" of the army officers and then similarly appeal to Spain. The letter arrived too late to have influenced the King's decision, but it is significant that so prominent a Cavalier as Mordaunt thought foreign assistance indispensable. To Ormonde, Oct. 28, 1659. Carte MS. 213, f. 389-90. The relevant documents are cited in Scott, *Travels of the King*, ch. xvi, and Violet Barbour, *Henry Bennet, Earl of Arlington* (Washington, 1914) ch. iii. Eventually Mazarin did give interviews to Ormonde and Bennet but nothing resulted therefrom. I regret that F. J. Routledge's *England and the Treaty of the Pyrenees* (Liverpool, 1953) reached me too late for more than this reference to it. I agree with his conclusion (p. 108) that France and Spain were too suspicious of each other's political designs to launch a Catholic crusade in either Great Britain or Ireland.

at hand, both Spain and France tried to persuade Charles II to spend his last weeks on the Continent on their soil. But the King, having anticipated an order for his detention at Brussels by his escape to Breda, declined to return. He also rebuffed his mother's favorite, Jermyn, who came with a pressing invitation to Paris, or, if the capital seemed too remote, to Calais. He realized that if he joined his mother at either place the suspicion that he had fallen under her baleful influence would prejudice him in English eyes. His presence at the French court might invite the belief that he still hoped to marry Hortense Mancini, the Cardinal's niece, whose hand had already been refused him. A marriage to a Roman Catholic would have allowed the opponents of the Restoration to beat the Protestant drum still able to stir up the unreasoning hatred of Rome which was so fatal to the Stuarts.

The relations with Holland did not improve, whoever was in authority in England. During Lambert's brief supremacy Nieuport commented that the merchants, while very eager for peace with Spain, were "possessed with extraordinary malice against the United Netherlands. . . . It is better to be envied than pitied."[61] Of this malevolence Downing was a fitting mouthpiece. To the very eve of the Restoration his memorials to the States General are full of complaints of the reception of privateers and their prizes in Dutch harbors, and, in one instance at least, of the condemnation by the admiralty at Amsterdam of the "Sun," with corn from Lubeck by a London merchant, which was captured first by the Danes, then by the Swedes, and finally by Dutch warships. Nieuport presented many countercharges, mainly concerned with the welcome accorded in English ports to ships commissioned by Sweden which brought in Dutch prizes. Downing, of course, blamed the Dutch for the prolongation of the northern war, though he felt that its continuation helped English trade in the Baltic. Another grievance was that English wool was imported into Holland in such quantities that, if unchecked, the English cloth trade on the Continent would be ruined.[62]

English foreign policy since Oliver's death had met with no striking success. A Protestant league was not so much as mentioned after the Protectorate ended. The pacification of the north accorded well enough with the terms agreed upon in May, 1659, and Downing was right in attributing to the agreements then made the mild concessions Sweden was obliged to make at the treaty of Copenhagen, but the influence of France was noticeably stronger than England's, both there and at Oliva.[63] In spite of many attempts by England and the United Provinces

[61]To De Witt, Nov. 11/21, Thurloe, VII, 783.   [62]Ibid., VII, 845, 811, 848.

[63]Ibid., VII, 874. Cf. p. 837, where Downing opined that French pro-Swedish policy somewhat balanced the death of Charles X.

to stop the piracies at sea, the intense rivalry at sea and commercial competition were very threatening. Only the future would reveal whether the enthusiastic and generous reception Charles II enjoyed just before sailing to England would serve to lessen the animosity between English and Dutch.

There were other countries with which England maintained or tried to maintain diplomatic or commercial relations. In the Baltic no progress was made in healing the rupture with Russia. Although the Parliamentarians had assiduously courted Gerasime Dokhtourov when he arrived in London in November, 1645, to announce the succession of Alexander as Czar, they had failed to make a favorable impression on him. On his return to Russia in June, 1646, an ordinance was passed which took away the most important privilege of the Muscovy Company, their exemption from payment of duties. The Czar may have wished to penalize the merchants of a revolutionary country, but he was also gratifying his own merchants who complained of the privileged situation members of the Company had enjoyed. Three years later a ukase banished all English merchants from Russia and forbade their trading with any Russian town except Archangel. This decree remained in force until after the Restoration. The Czar received an envoy from the exiled Charles II, Lord Culpepper, and made a loan which consisted of furs and corn to the value of about 40,000 rix-dollars. He also gave interviews to William Prideaux in February, 1655, who brought two letters from Cromwell. This ambassador asked that the ancient liberties of the Company should be reestablished, that the English should not be held collectively responsible for individual debts, and that the agents and merchants of the Company should be authorized to live in the vicinity of the court. The Czar sent a friendly letter to Cromwell but did not relax the ukases of 1646 and 1649.[64]

At Hamburg, the English resident, Richard Bradshaw, now back from an abortive mission to arrange peace between Russia and Sweden, was useful in buying powder and masts there, and in victualing a warship.[65] He returned to England before the end of 1659 and was not replaced. Perhaps one reason for not filling his position was the decay of trade. The two regulated companies, the Merchant Adventures and the Eastland Merchants, were languishing from want of capital which was not likely to be forthcoming so long as Parliament favored free trade. In Oliver Cromwell's last Parliament a committee of trade had voted that

[64]Inna Lubimenko, *Les Relations Commerciales et Politiques de L'Angleterre avec La Russie avant Pierre Le Grand* (Paris, 1933), ch. xiv.

[65]His instructions, c. April, 1657, are in Abbott, *Writings . . . of Oliver Cromwell*, IV, 450-451; *Calendar Domestic 1658-1659*, pp. 142, 224, 452.

Englishmen might trade with Germany and the Netherlands, though without prejudice to the mart at Dort. On October 12, 1658, a committee of the Privy Council, because of the "naval commodities" imported from the Baltic, such as "hemp, flax, pitch, tar, cable yarn, &c.," proposed a new charter for the Eastland Company which would have conferred a monopoly of the trade with Norway, Sweden, Poland, parts of Prussia and Pomerania, and Copenhagen and Elsinore, and certain adjacent islands.[66] Why this charter was not adopted or why the Council of State failed to act is not explained in the records of the two Councils.[67]

English relations with Portugal were governed until after the Restoration by the Treaty of 1654. Cromwell severely penalized the Portuguese for their tolerance of Prince Rupert and his small Royalist fleet in the Tagus when ships, money, and goods of English merchants had been seized. Ample compensation for these losses was provided. A valuable concession was the right to trade with all Portuguese colonies, although certain exceptions were made in the case of Brazil where the Portuguese-chartered company had a monopoly in certain merchandise. Englishmen in Portugal were to enjoy freedom from arrest unless the conservator, or English judge, had first given permission or when the culprit had been taken in the very act. The custom duties were never to exceed twenty-three per cent. The net result of these concessions was to give Englishmen a preferred position over the King's own subjects. Such harsh terms were obtained because Portugal, being engaged in a war of independence against Spain and in a struggle against the United Provinces for Brazil, could not face a third enemy, especially one so powerful at sea as the English Protectorate.[68]

Thomas Maynard was appointed consul at Lisbon in 1655 and remained there until superseded by Sir Richard Fanshaw in 1661. Just before the Restoration, Sande, the Portuguese ambassador in London, signed a treaty with the Council of State authorizing the enlistment in Britain of 12,000 infantry for the King of Portugal's service. Although the treaty was never ratified, it did prepare the way for a more modest arrangement after the Restoration.[69]

Within the Straits a fleet of about ten frigates under John Stoakes

[66]Burton's *Diary*, I, 308-310; Register of the Privy Council. The Council named seventeen individuals who were to be admitted to the company gratis.

[67]The minutes of the Council for June 13, 1659, mention a petition from the Eastland Company and its reference to a committee but nothing further. G. Maud Sellers, *Acts and Ordinances of the Eastland Company* (1906), pp. xlvii-xlviii.

[68]Edgar Prestage, *Diplomatic Relations of Portugal with France, England and Holland from 1640-1668* (Watford, 1925), pp. 118-41; V. M. Shillington and A. B. Wallis Chapman, *Commercial Relations of England and Portugal* (1907), ch. iii.

[69]Prestage, *Diplomatic Relations*, p. 139; Guizot, II, 390-400.

remained to exercise English sea power. The admiral had concluded treaties with Tetuan and Tunis, both providing for free trade and immunity from capture at sea of the ships of the respective parties.[70] But Oliver's death removed the chief deterrent, and soon the Barbary pirates were resuming their seizures of ships, goods, and crews. Robert Browne, the English consul at Algiers, wrote that "these people tell me that the peace with us has lost them many millions, not only by transporting of their enemies' goods, but all nations whatsoever carry English colours." Therefore they were determined to search all ships, which, Browne thought, "will cause a breach on both sides." For reasons which are not stated but may have been economic, political (as soon as the truce was arranged between France and Spain English men-of-war were no longer welcomed at French ports), and strategic (the need to strengthen the naval forces in home waters when a fleet was maintained in the Sound), Stoakes was ordered home in June and arrived in the Downs in September. In the following February, Robert and Thomas Browne, described as consul and agent of Algiers and Tunis, were directed to return to England.[71] In October, Jonas Poole was appointed to command three frigates to convoy merchantmen to the Straits, and then to proceed to Genoa and Leghorn and guard any ships found there to the Levant. His highhanded proceedings in capturing two Spanish ships from Messina and in resisting the demand that he must submit to "pratique" (quarantine) for forty days at Zante aroused the hostility of the Venetians. When their resident in London complained, the only redress he obtained was a reference of his complaint to the admiralty.[72] Thus the dominant position in the Mediterranean won by Blake had not been wholly abandoned on the eve of Restoration.

English trade in the Near East was in the hands of the Levant Company, with its ambassador, Sir Thomas Bendish, at Constantinople. Among his duties at this time were protests against the importation of false French louis and measures to stop the factors from combining with ship masters to cheat the company of its consulage, a levy to maintain consuls or agents.[73] A consul[74] was maintained at Aleppo, but the importance of this factory was diminishing. Had Shakespeare been writing half a century later, the master of the Tiger might have been

[70]The treaties, dated August 9, 1657, and February 8, 1658, are printed in Abbott, *Writings . . . of Oliver Cromwell*, IV, 919-21.

[71]*Calendar Domestic 1659-1660*, pp. 135, 485; A. C. Wood, *A History of the Levant Company* (Oxford, 1935), pp. 63-64.

[72]*Calendar Domestic*, pp. 243, 374, 386; *Calendar Venetian 1659-1661*, pp. 120, 133, 147, 150.

[73]*Calendar Domestic 1659-1660*, pp. 266, 432.

[74]Henry Riley who retired late in 1659 when Benjamin Lannoy was appointed in his stead. Ibid., p. 267.

sailing to Smyrna, the most important of the company's factories at this time.[75] Among its comparatively recent exports was cotton, which was also shipped from Cyprus and Syria.[76]

Relations with Venice were largely dictated by the presence in Turkey of the Levant Company. A conversation between Giavarina and Oliver Cromwell in November, 1657, demonstrates how mercantile interests were guiding the Protector's foreign policy. The Venetian resident, after showing how the Turks were aided in their operations against Candia by the munitions supplied by English traders, pleaded that an English fleet should join the Venetian and crush the infidel. Cromwell replied that it was unreasonable that Christians should provide the Turks with arms to destroy other Christians, but he held out no hope of naval assistance. "Your Excellencies would understand," he argued, "the loss this nation would suffer, which has such treasures scattered about the chief places of the Turkish empire, if he sent ships directly against the Ottoman. It would be followed immediately by the confiscation and spoiling of all this precious capital, the imprisonment of the English dwelling in those parts, and the total ruin of the numerous families which are supported by that trade."[77] In these circumstances the duties of the two representatives, John Hobson at Venice and Giavarina in London, were confined to such matters as the payment of English ships in Venetian service. Commercial intercourse had fallen greatly. Venice had long ceased to be the *entrepot* of Mediterranean trade. To some extent Leghorn had usurped her place as a port of transshipment, and an English consul, Charles Longland, was in residence there. Even the trade in currants, for which the English appetite had seemed insatiable, was being transferred from Venice to her dependency Zante, where another consul, William Womble, was maintained.

A comparison between the worldly policy pursued at the end of the Puritan Revolution and the idealism which some had expected would govern foreign relations is most significant. In his *Oceana* Harrington puts into the mouth of the Archon his views of the proper policy for his ideal republic. A true commonwealth, he asserts, is not created to serve selfish ends but to be "a minister of God on earth, to the end that the world may be *govern'd with righteousness.*" To provide a "stock of liberty" and "a sanctuary for the afflicted," and to propagate civil liberty

[75]William Prideaux was the consul.

[76]Particulars of the English factories and exports and imports are given in Lewis Roberts, *The Merchants Map of Commerce* (1700). Though Roberts described the trade of the early Stuarts, conditions had not substantially changed by 1660. His accounts of Smyrna, Aleppo, and Constantinople will be found on pp. 92, 102, 269.

[77]*Calendar Venetian, 1657-1659*, pp. 136-37.

and liberty of conscience—these "will stand, and last for ever."[78] In his Horatian ode on Cromwell, Marvell had set forth his high hopes:

> As Caesar, he, ere long to Gaul,
> To Italy an Hannibal,
>   And to all states not free,
>   Shall climactèric be.

To a limited extent the Puritan Revolution did witness a turning point in European history, but the turn was not in the direction the Puritan enthusiast desired. Not Protestant crusades but wars for territorial aggrandizement or colonial empires were in store for Europe. England herself was soon to be engaged in the most commercial of all wars, and against another Protestant country.

[78]*The Oceana and other works of James Harrington*, ed. John Toland (1771), pp. 180, 188-89.

CHAPTER XII

Scotland

THE PROTECTORATE was in no danger from the Celtic fringe. Both Scotland and Ireland lay helpless at the feet of their conquerors. After a series of bloody defeats each found the raising of another army an impossible task. Probably superior leadership and greater resources would have enabled England to prevail over a united Scotland or Ireland. Actually, in both kingdoms the Cromwellians had been aided by acute divisions in the ranks of their enemies. In Ireland the utmost efforts of Ormonde could not bridge the gap between the Anglo-Irish, the native Irish, and the Ulster Scots: similarly, in Scotland Charles II failed to combine Montrosians, Engagers,[1] and the stricter Covenanters to resist the hated southron.

At the time of Oliver's death Scotland was enduring an uneasy peace, not negotiated between equals but imposed by force. In 1654 an ordinance had united the two kingdoms and swept away the Scottish Estates, but thirty members were supposed to represent the northern kingdom at Westminster—in reality they represented little more than the English interest.

The administration was predominantly English. At its head was George Monck (1608-1670), a professional soldier. He had fought against the Spaniards at Cadiz in 1625, the French at La Rochelle in 1627, the Spaniards again while in Dutch service from 1629 to 1637, the Scots at Newburn in 1640, the Irish in 1642 and 1643, and the Parliamentarians at Nanturich in 1644 when he was captured. Released in 1646 he served again in Ireland until 1649, and the next year Cromwell gave him a regiment, the ancestor of the Coldstream Guards. He accompanied Cromwell to Scotland and when the main army marched south in pursuit of Charles II, he was left behind as commander in chief. Often as he had changed sides, he had invariably been faithful to the cause he was serving. The guiding principle of his life was obedience to the government from which he held his commission and by which he was paid. Seven years after the Restoration, Pepys described him: "I know not how, the blockhead Albemarle hath strange luck to be loved, though he be, and every man must know it, the heaviest man in the world, but stout and honest to his country."[2] "A dull, heavy man" is the

---

[1]Those who accepted the Engagement of December, 1647, by which Charles I agreed to the establishment of Presbyterianism in England for three years and to the suppression of Independency.
[2]*Diary*, Oct. 23, 1667.

diarist's comment on several other occasions. Seth Ward, the bishop of Sarum, who preached his funeral sermon, explained the taciturnity which Pepys misunderstood as stupidity: "He was a man *great* of *performance*, *little* of Speech, no lover of wast words, or fine composed orations, but a great affector of what was *short* and *plain, easie* and *inaffected*."[3] This gift of silence was of the greatest importance in 1659, when it concealed his designs and allowed all but the extremists to hope he was on their side.

He was not far-sighted and probably did not speculate about the ultimate consequences of his break with the army leaders in the autumn of 1659. His step-by-step advances in 1660 seem to have been admirably timed. Though he learned to use the extravagant and sanctimonious language with which his contemporaries clothed, and sometimes clouded, their thoughts, he had no trace of fanaticism in his religion. He was a Presbyterian, an advantage to the head of the government in Scotland, though more moderate and Erastian than most of the Scots. He took a genuine interest in the welfare of the country and realized that she was overburdened with taxes. Although he had to uphold the hated union, he was not personally disliked, because of confidence in his fairness and in his firmness in maintaining strict discipline in his army. His nickname "Black George," due to his swarthiness, supports other evidence of his popularity with his soldiers.[4] He understood the value of propaganda, gauged public opinion correctly, and was willing to accept it as his guide. Like some other generals of his age, he was ambitious but, unlike them, he never recklessly strove for self-advancement at all costs. His marriage to Anne Clarges may have been irregular, and she may have been, as Pepys thought, "a plain homely dowdy" or even "the veryest slut and drudge," as Mountagu called her.[5] Yet Monck was a faithful husband to her, and Ward is justified in his comment that "they *twain* were loving in their Lives, and in their *Deaths* they were not *divided*." Whatever influence she exercised was in favor of the restoration of the monarchy.

Of the original nine members of the Council[6] established in 1655, William Lockhart and John Swinton were the only Scots, and the former was soon too busy as Oliver's and Richard's ambassador to France to pay much attention to the affairs of his native land. Broghil, an Irishman who had won Oliver's confidence, was president, and succeeded

[3]*The Christians Victory over Death. A Sermon*, April 30, 1670.
[4]Ward asserted that his soldiers looked upon Monck as their father and were ready and ambitious to live and die with him.
[5]Pepys' *Diary*, Mar. 8, 1660; Feb. 25, 1666. See the index to Wheatley's edition for the grudge Mountagu bore her.
[6]Firth, *Scotland and the Protectorate* (Edinburgh, 1899), p. 306.

in winning the confidence of Scots to a remarkable degree. Five of the rest were soldiers, and the last, Samuel Disbrowe, was the younger brother of Major General John Disbrowe. The Court of Session was replaced by commissioners whose number varied but had increased by the summer of 1659 to ten.[7] Their impartial administration of justice won general approval in spite of such handicaps as the ignorance of the English members of Scottish laws and the absorption of members in their work as councillors or in other capacities.[8] The interruption of sessions after Oliver's death, presumably for want of members, was such a national grievance that in April, 1659, Monck wrote to Thurloe to urge that three of the judges, Wariston, Swinton, and Lawrence, be spared from their parliamentary duties in order to hold sessions in June when they usually began, lasting four months.[9]

The institution of justices of the peace at the end of 1655 was a successful innovation. Like their English equivalents, they were given administrative as well as judicial powers, including the fixing of wages. The work of reformation was not forgotten and severe fines were to be imposed on cursers and profaners of the Lord's Day, and much more severe on fornicators.[10] Even the Highlands were reduced to order, and robbery and cattle-stealing became rare offenses. Samuel Disbrowe boasted in a debate at Westminster on the admission of Scottish members to the English Parliament that the Scots "submit unto all things. A Man may ride all Scotland over with a switch in his hand and £100 in his pocket, which he could not have done these five hundred years."[11] The peacefulness of Scotland, however, was not due solely, or even mainly, to impartial justice, but to the presence of a powerful army.

George Monck, commander in chief of the English forces beyond the border from 1651 to 1652 and again from 1654 to 1660, had at his disposal in 1658 five regiments of horse, four companies of dragoons, eleven regiments of foot, and an odd company or two.[12] The total strength, including officers, would be about 1,550 horse, 210 dragoons, and 8,060 foot. The foot regiments were distributed in garrisons of very varied strength. Strong citadels were built at Ayr, Leith, Inverness, Perth, and Inverlochy, and about a score of smaller garrisons were established

[7]Samuel Disbrowe was president. Among his colleagues were Sir Archibald Johnston of Wariston, Alexander Brodie (who had accepted office in 1658 after maintaining for years that aloofness from the government was the only course for an honest man) and James Dalrymple (better known as the first Viscount Stair).

[8]Scotland and the Protectorate, pp. 385-86.

[9]Thurloe, VII, 656; Scotland and the Protectorate, pp. 391-92, where is printed a paper entitled "The hurt and prejudice sustained by the subjects of Scotland for the want of justice."

[10]A summary of the instructions to the justices is reprinted in Scotland and the Protectorate, pp. 403-405, from the Publick Intelligencer.

[11]Burton, Diary, IV, 168.

[12]See the establishment of December 21, 1657, in Firth, Scotland and the Protectorate, pp. 373-81.

throughout the country.[13] The advantages of this system of garrisons were great: any suspicious gathering could hardly fail to be noticed by one or the other of the local commanders and dealt with at once; the justices of the peace or loyal Scots could always find support near at hand; and the fortified posts could be held by relatively few men so that a field force was always available. The disadvantages were the remoteness of many of the military centers, the costliness of building and supplying them, and the hardship and unpopularity of service in them. The infantry regiments in the army of Scotland were not changed, as the cavalry were, so many soldiers lived in a kind of perpetual exile, mitigated in the case of married men by permission to have their wives to live within the fortifications.

The condition of Scotland during the enforced union has been variously judged. Contemporaries differed as much as modern historians. Robert Baillie, one of the most learned Scots of his generation and versed in public affairs since 1638, has two very revealing passages in letters written in 1658: "For our State, all is exceeding quiet: A great armie, in a multitude of garrisons, bydes above our head, and deep povertie keeps all estates exceedingly at under; the taxes of all sorts are so great, the trade so little, that its marvell if extreme scarcitie of money end not, ere long, in some mischief." A little later he complained: "The Countrey lies very quiet; it is exceeding poor; trade is nought; the English hes all the moneyes. Our Noble families are almost gone: Lennox hes little in Scotland unsold; Hamilton's estates, except Annam and the Baronie of Hamilton, is sold; Argyle can pay little annuelrent for seven or eight hundred thousand merks; and he is no more drowned in debt than publict hatred, almost of all, both Scottish and English; the Gordons are gone; the Douglasses little better. . . . Many of our chief families [e]states are cracking; nor is there any appearance of any human relief for the tyme. What is become of the King and his family we doe not know."[14]

Some of Baillie's statements are unassailable. The nobility was assuredly almost powerless. The confiscation of the estates of the more prominent leaders of Glencairn's rebellion, and the imposition of ruinous fines upon others left them without resources. Heavy bonds kept the rest in order. The Highland chiefs were crippled by the abolition of hereditable jurisdiction, and the substitution of the court baron. A license was required to possess or carry arms, and when granted usually was restricted to an individual. Noblemen or Highland chiefs might be

[13]Firth, *Last Years*, II, 87-90; Firth, *Scotland and the Protectorate*, xxxix-lii; Davies, *Coldstream Guards*, ch. iv, describes the conditions under which Monck's regiment lived.

[14]*Letters and Journals of Robert Baillie*, ed. David Laing (Edinburgh, 1841-42), III, 357, 387.

allowed a few fowling pieces for recreation and a few weapons to defend their homes against "broken men" or disbanded soldiers, but never enough to equip a clan. In return for the concession a chief was held responsible for the misdeeds of his clansmen, just as in the Lowlands each village was responsible for the crimes of its inhabitants and on the Border each county for the depredations of mosstroopers. Both crime and disaffection were rendered more difficult by the passes which all travelers and strangers had to obtain from the military authorities.

The causes of the poverty to which Baillie and others allude were both permanent and temporary. Among the former were the climate and the soil. Judging from entries in contemporary diaries, the 1650's seem to have been remarkable for floods at harvest time and unusual snows and frosts in the winters. The harsh comments of English travelers on their experiences suggest a lower standard of living north of the Border. In the century before the dawn of the age of secular interests, absorption in theological disputes diverted the national energies from the pursuit of wealth. No reliable data exist for a calculation of the casualties the Scots suffered in their heroic struggle to enforce the Covenants, but if to the known losses in battle are added as many more who died or were disabled by sickness, the total would probably be a staggering percentage of the manhood.[15] Similarly, the proportion of the national wealth consumed—cost of armies, destruction, and devastation by the Scots to hamper the invaders and by the English to starve out the defenders— must have been very high. Scotland needed a period of peace to recuperate, but unfortunately for her, peace could only be had at a great price —the loss of national independence. The hope of the English was that the material benefits of the Union would suffice to counterbalance the affront to patriotism. In 1652 "A Declaration of the Parliament of the Commonwealth of England, concerning the Settlement of Scotland" announced that, "for the advancement of the glory of God, and the good and welfare of the whole Island," Scotland would be incorporated with England into one Commonwealth.[16] When the declaration was read in Edinburgh, an Englishman noted that "so senseless are this generation of their own goods that scarce a man of them shewed any sign of rejoicing."[17] This ingratitude seems to have persisted to the Restoration.[18]

The great benefit the Scots were supposed to derive from the Union

[15]The population of Scotland in 1755 is said to have been 1,265,380 (James Gray Kyd, *Scottish Population Statistics* [Edinburgh, 1952], p. xv). It is not likely to have been much above a million a hundred years before.

[16]*The Cromwellian Union*, ed. C. Sanford Terry (Edinburgh, 1902), pp. xxi-xxii.

[17]The bonds imposed at the time of Sir George Booth's rising are printed in *Clarke Papers*, IV, 26-28; C. H. Firth, *Scotland and the Commonwealth* (Edinburgh, 1895), p. 41.

[18]An exception was the proclamation of Richard at Inverlochy in October, 1658. Firth, *Scotland and the Protectorate*, p. 384.

was freedom of trade with England and the dominions, but any goods not permitted to be exported from, or imported into England were under a similar prohibition in Scotland.[19] The first stipulation certainly helped one Scotch industry, the salt trade, and was denounced in the Parliament of 1656 as ruinous to the English salt-works.[20] But the second was harmful inasmuch as the prohibited exports included raw materials that the Scots had long sent to the Continent, such as wool, hides, and skins, and because there were no facilities for manufacturing these at home, and no capital to create them, these raw materials must either be sold to the English or not at all. On the whole it is possible that England gained more than the Scots from the economic clauses of the ordinance of union.[21]

Two other disadvantages the Scottish trade suffered from the Union were the Navigation Act and involvement in the war. Scotland had few ships and the new prohibition to use Dutch bottoms as carriers was a hardship. The Anglo-Dutch War deprived her of her best Continental market, and the Anglo-Spanish war exposed her scant shipping to the Ostend privateers because she had no navy to guard home waters or to provide a convoy. The provost and baillies of Aberdeen recommended the use of men of war for these purposes, because, as Monck was informed, "it is a shame that we ar put to imploy Dutchmen."[22] However, if foreign trade remained so unsatisfactory, the domestic market improved during the era of peace that followed the suppression of Glencairn's rebellion. At least, the rapid increase in the revenue from the excise suggests an improvement. Also the burghs, and especially Glasgow, appear to have benefited. The mere fact that they provided whatever support the government found implies their acquiescence in the economic order, though another factor was undoubtedly the freedom they were allowed in their choice of magistrates.

The attitude of the two Scottish factions is well defined by Broghil: the Resolutioners "love Charles Stuart and hate us" while the Protesters "neither love him nor us."[23] Some of the latter, however, became reconciled. Wariston, their lay leader, came to the conclusion that Cromwell without the malignants was preferable to Charles with them,[24] and accepted his old office of Chief Clerk Register. This was not the general attitude. Soon after Richard's accession Thurloe was informed that the

[19]*Acts and Ordinances*, II, 873.

[20]Burton, *Diary*, II, 57.

[21]Theodore Keith, *Commercial Relations of England and Scotland* (Cambridge, 1910), ch. iii.

[22]*Aberdeen Council Letters*, III, ed. Louise B. Taylor (1952), 297.

[23]Firth, *Last Years*, II, 95.

[24]*Diary*, p. 91.

Scots daily prayed for their king in such transparent terms as that the Lord would be merciful to all in exile or in captivity, and that he would deliver them from the yoke of Pharaoh or the Egyptian bondage.[25]

The Protesters naturally found favor with many of the English leaders, especially the military. In Scotland, Monck at first thought them more trustworthy than the Resolutioners, although Broghil was an ardent advocate of the latter. In England, Cromwell began by preferring the Protesters, but experience of their narrow-mindedness changed his attitude. No doubt the extremely skillful advocacy of James Sharp, the agent of the Resolutioners in London, was a factor in converting first Cromwell and then Monck.

The accounts of Sharp and Wariston of the attitude of prominent Englishmen they encountered in London are most valuable. It is true that meetings of representatives of the two Scottish factions with Cromwell, with the English Council, and with a committee of officials and divines all failed to reach agreement. The one positive result of this effort to enlist English support in this Scottish controversy was that the Protesters secured the insertion in the Humble Additional and Explanatory Petition and Advice that those who had invaded England in 1648 under Hamilton were debarred from serving as members of Parliament. The division in the House of Commons was close, and might have gone the other way had not Broghil been disabled by gout from attending.[26] Much more significant was the light this struggle between Scottish factions throws upon the divisions among the Cromwellians.

On the Protesters' side were almost all the swordsmen,[27] headed by Fleetwood, Lambert, and Disbrowe. With them were associated Dr. Owen and other Independent divines. The Resolutioners could count upon Thurloe, Wolseley, and Philip Jones, and Presbyterian ministers like Simeon Ashe and Thomas Manton. The Scottish issue was, therefore, a trial of strength between the two parties that contended for Oliver's ear and were to contend for Richard's. Lambert's dismissal and Owen's loss of favor were heavy blows to the Protesters and a proof that their cause was losing ground at Whitehall. The reaction from the extreme sectarianism of 1653 is clearly to be traced in this contest, and the increasing reliance upon moderate Presbyterianism is discernible. Also, the cleavage which led to the downfall of the Protectorate in April, 1659, is already noticeable.

At home, although the breach between the Protesters and Resolu-

[25]Thurloe, VII, 416.

[26]*Acts and Ordinances*, II, 1183; Wariston's *Diary*, June 17, 1657.

[27]Fleetwood's phrase recorded in Wariston's *Diary*, June 15, 1657.

tioners was not healed in spite of pious attempts at reunion, and although the General Assembly was not allowed to meet, the Kirk retained much authority. Synods continued to excommunicate sinners, who sometimes tried to ignore the sentence but who in the end were obliged to submit penitently.[28] The successful translation of the Shorter Catechism into Gaelic prompted attempts to translate first the Psalms and then the whole Bible, but by 1660 only fifty Psalms were printed in Gaelic.[29] A difficulty the Kirk encountered arose from the establishment from time to time of days of fasting or rejoicing. As these were declared by the civil government, ministers declined to participate, a defiance to which Monck turned a blind eye.

A new element in the religious life of Scotland was provided in the 1650's. Quaker missionaries in Scotland found that their seed often fell on what George Fox called a "thick, cloddy earth of hypocrisy" which nourished a "dark, carnal people."[30] The two great obstacles were Presbyterianism and a hatred of all things English. Sectarianism, especially the extreme forms, did not have many adherents north of the Border and Quakers found few of the groups there which supplied adherents in England. The number of converts in Scotland was in no way commensurate with the great missionary effort made during the first decade. Many of the most famous Friends came to Scotland, some more than once. Among them were George Fox, James Nayler, who preached on the morrow of Dunbar where he had fought, Edward Burrough, James Howgill, and William Caton. In all, some fifty came from England to spread the light. Though here and there a few individual Scots received their message, ministers and congregations, and magistrates and mobs, were generally hostile. Attempts by Friends to speak in churches after the service was over, to question ministers, or to denounce them as hirelings, led almost without exception to their expulsion, sometimes with unnecessary violence. Not infrequently they were protected by soldiers, sometimes through approval of attacks on "priests," a term applied to all salaried ministers, sometimes, perhaps, because they believed in toleration or stood up for their fellow countrymen. Insofar as the persecution of Quakers had a legal basis, the vagrancy Act of 1657 supplied it. This act provided that wanderers from their usual abode without sufficient cause should be adjudged rogues, Vagabonds, and sturdy beggars, and punished within the Elizabethan statute which enacted that

[28]For some interesting comments and examples see *Minutes of the Synod of Argyll, 1652-1661,* ed. Duncan C. Mactavish (Edinburgh, 1944).

[29]Ibid., pp. vii-xii.

[30]*Journal,* pp. 331, 326; *Journal of the Life of Will. Caton* (1689), p. 32, where it is stated that Friends found lodgings with difficulty at Sterling because they were taken for straggling soldiers.

such offenders should be whipped and returned to the parish where they were born. The verdict of the historian of Quakerism in Scotland is that "cruel advantage was taken" of the Cromwellian act.[31]

English soldiers were more receptive of Quakerism than native Scots. Among the converted officers was Captain Lieutenant Davenport.[32] His colonel, Daniel, complained bitterly that Davenport, after nearly fourteen years of service was now so besotted that it was as useless to speak to him as to a wall, and that when his men saluted him he bade them put on their hats because he expected no such distinction. Daniel told Monck that Quaker principles were undermining all discipline because "liberty with equallity is so pleasing to ignorance that proselytes will be dayly brought in, . . . where all are equalls I expect little obedience in government." Monck shared these sentiments and Davenport lost his commission.[33] Another convert was Cornet Ward of Berry's horse who gave great offense at Aberdeen both by his open support of John Hall, a Quaker preacher, and by his own sweeping condemnation of all ministers as being, without exception, "upholders of the kingdom of Satan and of darkness; . . . because they taught not absolute perfection here even in this world." He and two troopers were given passes to England and troubled the army no more.[34] In Lilburne's horse a captain and a lieutenant were cashiered and another captain retired of his own volition.[35] Among civilians a distinguished convert was Swinton, who nevertheless retained his official positions until the Restoration.[36]

Monck was not a persecutor of Quakers, but he regarded their principles as inimical to discipline. He supported his colonels who wished to eliminate Quakers from their regiments but there seems to be no evidence that he "determined to clear all Quakers and other sectaries out of the Scots army" in the autumn of 1657.[37] When the great purge happened in the last months of 1659, religious affiliations did not provide the yardstick, though the religion of a man and particularly his views on ecclesiastical organization often determined his politics.

[31]George B. Burnet, *The Story of Quakerism in Scotland, 1650-1850* (1952), p. 29; *Acts and Ordinances*, II, 1098-1099; Joseph R. Tanner, *Tudor Constitutional Documents* (Cambridge, 1930), pp. 484-88.

[32]Ashfield, a colonel, favored Quakers, and his wife was converted. He followed suit but not until after the Restoration.

[33]Firth and Davies, *Regimental History*, II, 493-94. According to Fox (*Journal*, pp. 328-29), Davenport was dismissed for not putting off his hat and for saying "thou" and "thee" to his superior officers.

[34]Firth and Davies, II, 247-48.

[35]Ibid., I, 272.

[36]He is said in *DNB* to have joined the Friends in 1657, a fact which deprives Sir Walter Scott's jest about his maternal ancestor of most of its point—that "if he had not *trembled* [at the danger he was in at the Restoration] he would not have *quaked.*" *The Letters of Sir Walter Scott, 1811-1814*, ed. H. J. C. Grierson (1932), p. 312.

[37]Burnet, *Story of Quakerism*, p. 42.

Apart from this sterile controversy the history of Scotland is singularly barren. Letter after letter from Monck merely recorded that all was quiet. What news there was related mainly to the English army and officials. The Anabaptists were thought to be disaffected and boasted that they had the army on their side but not Monck.[38] Arrears of pay were very serious—the captains are "nine months pay behind, and like to be more." This grievance was the harder to bear because the forces in Scotland were further in arrears than those in England or Ireland. "All we ask is that we have equal shares of money proportionate to our numbers."[39] Nevertheless Monck would not permit his troops to petition or hold meetings to discuss their material needs or political aspirations.[40]

The election of members to sit in Richard's Parliament caused little excitement in Scotland. The members of the council at Edinburgh, now reduced to four plus Monck, obviously thought that whoever they nominated would be chosen. Disbrowe casually inquired of Thurloe whether he had two or three in mind he would like chosen. The Secretary named five and Monck thought he could find seats for them, though he warned that they must not expect their constituents to pay them. To his chagrin he learned that Argyle and others were exerting themselves to get Scots elected. Inasmuch as Sharp did his utmost to get the Resolutioners to support the government[41] it is likely that Argyle was supported by the Protesters, but absence of particulars renders this an inference only. The returns came in slowly with the result that there were only twenty-one Scottish M.P.'s chosen when Parliament met on January 27. But at least two others[42] are known to have sat in Westminster, so there is no good reason to doubt that Scotland had her full quota of thirty members, though they may not all have taken their seats before the dissolution on April 22. Of the known members, two-thirds were either officers or officials. The most notable of the rest was Argyle, though he did not take his seat until March 24.[43] John, Earl of Tweeddale, had been a Cromwellian but was now, or was soon to become, a Royalist.

The return of the Rump to power in May, 1659, had important constitutional results in Scotland in that the disappearance of the Cromwellian House of Lords deprived her of her three representatives, while

[38]*Clarke Papers*, IV, 41.

[39]John Barwick to Charles II, Thurloe, VII, 415; letters of Langley, ibid., pp. 371-72, 403-404, 554; letter of Thomas Lilburne, ibid., p. 436.

[40]Monck to Thurloe, Aug. 3, Dec. 2, 1658, Thurloe, VII, 363, 545; ibid., VII, 452, 545, 616-17.

[41]Thurloe, VII, 555, 574-75, 583-84, 600, 607-608.

[42]Major Knight (*Cromwellian Union*, p. lxxix) and the Earl of Linlithgow, who acted as a teller with Thurloe on March 23.

[43]*Aberdeen Council Letters*, p. 341.

in the Rump she had no members, and in the Council of State Wariston alone could speak for the northern dominion. Office-holders as of May 6 were confirmed in their places. The ordinance of union of 1654 was not expressly repealed, but the Rump did not treat it as valid. The Rump, like Charles II later, refused to build according to Cromwellian models. It first directed members who belonged to the Council of State to prepare a new act, then to consider the bills under consideration in the interval between the conquest of Scotland and the establishment of the Protectorate, and once again to prepare a new bill, perhaps after hearing Vane's report of the committee of the council.[44] By July 20 the bill was ready to be presented to Parliament.[45] Meanwhile Parliament had received two petitions from Scotland. The one, from the deputies who had in 1652 consented to a union, asked that Scottish representatives should be consulted about the new bill, the other, from the "gathered" or Independent congregations in Scotland pressed for the inclusion in the Act of Union of a promise to guarantee that they and others of like mind should enjoy the same toleration as "the truly Godly in England content for, and expect to be received in by you."[46]

The bill was introduced on July 27, given a second reading, and referred to a committee of the whole House. Although discussed on eleven days, it never emerged from the committee. The delay was caused by grave difference of opinion about toleration, the amount of the assessment ("cess") Scotland should pay—the former amount or a thirteenth of England's contribution—the enforcement of English law beyond the Border, and an English or Scottish judiciary.[47] When Lambert ejected the Parliament on October 13, the position was as Wariston had described it on the fourth: "In the meantyme poor Scotland lyes desolate without law, justice, gouvernment or settlement of publick or privat interest, religious or civil."

When in October Monck determined to uphold parliamentary government and possibly lead an army into England, he had first to settle affairs in Scotland. His chief opponent, Lambert, asked, if the armies of the Commonwealth came to blows, would not Scotland, which cost England a dear price, fall into the hands of Royalists? Therefore, Monck

[44]*Commons Journals*, May 18; June 13, 25; Council Register, May 31; June 23.

[45]The late Sanford Terry (*Cromwellian Union*, p. xci) was misled by an entry in the *Calendar Domestic* into thinking that the Council had two bills for a union before it on July 19. The Register (July 20) shows one bill was for a union and the other for a free pardon.

[46]*Cromwellian Union*, pp. lxxxix-xc; *Clarke Papers*, IV, 50-55; Wariston's *Diary*, III, 116; *The Life of Mr. Robert Blair . . . and Continuation by William Row*, ed. Thomas McCrie (Edinburgh, 1848), p. 338.

[47]Wariston's *Diary*, pp. 133, 136, 138, 141; *Register of Consultations*, II, 185. The English Council was willing that Monck should collect the assessment in as easy a way as he could devise but unwilling to reduce the amount. *Clarke Papers*, IV, 42-43.

could not risk what would have been a catastrophe at that time and likely to cause his own forces to desert him as well as close up the ranks in England. Accordingly, he proceeded cautiously. He sent circular letters to the noblemen, gentlemen, and magistrates of the burghs and the shires and desired them to send representatives to meet him at Edinburgh on November 15. They duly appeared, the noblemen choosing as their president the Earl of Glencairn, whose name had been given to the rising of 1653, and the burghs, Sir James Stewart. Monck seems to have made a short speech and then distributed it to those present in the form of a letter—or, possibly, reversed the order. He declared he had received a call from God and his people to march into England to maintain the liberty of Parliament, the ancient constitution, and the rights of the three nations against tyrannical usurpations upon their consciences, persons, and estates. He called upon them to preserve peace in their shires, to abstain from any correspondence with Charles Stuart's party, and to be faithful to the Parliament. He promised to procure from it an abatement of the assessment. He requested an answer whether they would comply with his desires, to which he added that they should be in readiness to pay the last four months' assessment whenever it should be called for.[48] The commissioners thanked the general for his resolution to relieve their burdens, and promised to concur with his desires, but asked how they were to prevent tumults in their several shires. They wished precautions to be taken to prevent raids from the Highlands.[49] When Monck asked what proposals they felt would accomplish these ends, they submitted five. The first, that he should appoint in each shire a committee to carry out his commands, he approved with the proviso that members should engage to do nothing to the prejudice of the Commonwealth or in favor of Charles Stuart. To the request that each shire should raise a small force of horse, the reply was that the counties adjacent to the Highlands might have forty men in arms. The third proposal was that if the treaty now on foot with the English army leaders failed, he would authorize the shires to arm for his assistance and their own defense, but all Monck said in reply was that he would answer when the issue of the negotiations was known. To achieve the third proposal, the commissioners wished arms to be made available, but were told that arms would be supplied when they were in danger. Finally, permission was granted for noblemen and gentlemen to wear swords and for four servants of the former and two of the latter to be armed.[50]

[48]*Clarke Papers*, IV, 78; 78-79; 113n; 114-15, and n; the speech or letter is printed in *Aberdeen Council Letters*, III, 298.

[49]*Clarke Papers*, IV, 115-16.

[50]Ibid., pp. 190-191.

The decision not to allow the Scots to arm and join Monck's forces had been reached only after an animated debate between the general and some of his chief advisers. The clinching argument was that, even if Scots were mingled with the English regiments and not permitted to form independent units, their presence would cause much desertion. To have called the Scots to arms at this time would have been disastrous. A Quaker missionary reported Scotland to be in "a mighty uproar." Many Scots would gladly have risen, ostensibly to assist Monck but really to expel the English. Monck's old soldiers, he continued, "go from him, them that doth remain they say they will not fight against Lambert and his forces, but they will fight against the Scots if they do rise."[51] Monck himself thought that he had enough foot and that, if the Scots would provide horses so that that he could strengthen his cavalry, in which he was very inferior to Lambert, all would be well. But the Scots refused to be so obliging, being disappointed at the refusal to allow them to make levies. Some Scots were enrolled in the foot, but not many. Otherwise, as has been remarked, it was "to the goodwill rather than the active assistance of the Scots," that Monck owed his freedom from anxiety about his base.[52]

Monck began his march south on January 1, 1660, and reached London unopposed a month later. Ministers who were Resolutioners eagerly welcomed the turn of events, and a group in Edinburgh including David Dickson, Robert Douglas, and James Wood, gladly complied with Monck's request that Sharp be sent to join him in London. Sharp's instructions were to endeavor to obtain for the kirk of Scotland the freedom established by law, to represent the sinfulness of the present lax toleration, to have rectified the abuses of vacant stipends so that they be applied to pious uses by presbyteries, to see that ministers had the benefit of the act abolishing patronage, and, if a commission should be appointed for settling and augmenting ministers' stipends, to try to get named to it faithful and well-affected men.[53] Sharp arrived in London on February 13, saw Manton and then Monck who recommended him to Sir Anthony Ashley Cooper and Weaver. The general replied to the ministers in Edinburgh, promising to do his utmost to preserve the rights of the church of

[51]The second statement should be discounted to some extent, because a Quaker would be likely to derive his information from Anabaptists, almost his only sympathizers in the English army, and they were admittedly hostile to Monck. The above quotation from a letter of George Collinson [Nov.] 20, [1659] is derived from "Early Quaker Letters from the Swarthmore MSS. to 1660," calendared by Geoffrey F. Nuttall, p. 499. This unpublished calendar has been very generously distributed to the leading libraries in the United Kingdom and in the United States and not only reproduces passages omitted in the letters previously printed but also corrects misreadings, wrong dates, etc.

[52]Baker's *Chronicle*, pp. 692-93; *Clarke Papers*, IV, xxii.

[53]Robert Wodrow, *The History of the Sufferings of the Church of Scotland*, ed. Robert Burns (Glasgow, 1828-30), I, 5.

Scotland and their afflicted country. Sharp reported his own activities in a series of valuable letters which showed that his counsel helped to persuade Monck to readmit the secluded members which "ministers and good people" regarded as the only expedient for securing religion and dashing the hopes of Cavaliers and sectaries alike. He added that Monck had spoken in favor of "presbyterian government not rigid." Douglas at once took exception to the last word and protested that it sounded harsh to the ears of all honest men to hear "presbytery, the ordinance of Jesus Christ, reflected upon by the epithet of rigidity." Here was again appearing the division between the English Erastian Presbyterians and their more thoroughgoing brethren across the Border which had been so significant fifteen years earlier. Later letters suggest that Sharp was becoming immersed in politics and did not worry much about his instructions. He claimed that he had been instrumental in securing the release of the Earls of Crawford and Lauderdale from Windsor, and that he was pointed at by Cavaliers as the Scottish presbyter who "stickled to bring in the secluded members, to undo all by the presbyterian empire." Of the two chapters of the Directory referred to a committee by Parliament, he said no more than that they were likely to stick there till the new Parliament sits. And yet these two sections anent discipline were to a Scot of the essence of the confession of faith. The revival of the Covenant consoled Douglas who concurred with Sharp in denying slanders on Charles II's behavior in Scotland and asserted that when in Scotland the King had told him that by advice of Parliament and a synod of divines he would try to bring about that unity in religion which the Solemn League and Covenant prescribed for the two kingdoms. He and his colleagues indignantly repudiated the calumny that they stood for a commonwealth.

Sharp related how Monck had sent his coach for Calamy, Ashe, and himself, how they had warned him that a commonwealth was impracticable, and how he had refuted their notion of keeping the present Parliament so as to settle the government on terms. Douglas, having received an appeal for cooperation from Ulster, suggested that Sharp or his brother cross to Ireland and enclosed a paper on the power to settle the government and the form of the government to be settled. As to the first, it lay in the Parliaments of the three kingdoms, not in the English Parliament alone. As to the second, the recall of "the righteous heir" was as essential as the establishment of Presbyterianism. He also urged Sharp to secure a warrant for a meeting at Edinburgh to choose commissioners to look after the national interests. As the days passed Douglas received little comfort either as a patriotic Scot or a stout Presbyterian. Sharp told him that Monck was surrounded by Englishmen who "incline to keep

Scotland at under, and either incorporate, or make us distinct, as they shall find most serviceable to their interest." Douglas may have drawn some consolation from Monck's determination that no remonstrant should have a position of trust. However, just before Parliament met, Sharp reported that the Council had drawn up the terms of a treaty with the King to be laid before Parliament: "No notice is taken of Scotland in the treaty: We shall be left to the King, which is best for us."[54] In England the Solemn League and Covenant would be neglected, he prophesied, and moderate episcopacy accepted as the fairest settlement. Other Scots saw the need for unity. "What use the Lord may yet have of Scotland we know not, but certainly without entire union among those who intend Scotland's libertie, Scotland shall never be considerable."[55] Events went to prove that a divided house could not stand.

In Scotland the Restoration was mainly accomplished by alien hands. Though she had sacrificed her sons freely for a covenanted king, she had little voice in his recall. Yet in none of the three kingdoms was his return more ardently desired than in the land of his ancestors, and, it may be added, in none was loyalty so ill rewarded. The Scots were so eager to cast off their yoke that they scarcely paused to inquire what the future had in store for them. James Kirkton, who lived to regret the Cromwellians because there were never greater purity and plenty of the means of grace than in their time, ascribes the unpopularity of the English rule to a variety of causes. Their governors were men of social inferiority and the garrisons maintained to hold the Scots in check laid heavy burdens on the land which were the more odious because imposed by those who called themselves patrons of the people's liberty. Toleration encouraged the vilest blasphemies. Moreover, the high character given Charles II made his return seem a remedy for all ills. Those who had suffered in the wars to restore him expected not only "compensations from his justice, but a gratuity from his bounty." Indeed, men believed that with the King would come a golden age for all.[56]

This confidence in the King was unshaken by evidence of the hostility of Cavaliers. A most interesting tract entitled *A Message Sent from the King of Scots . . . to the Lord Douglas*, signed by C. Culpepper and dated at Brussels, November 6, conveyed a clear warning. Douglas was asked to look upon the Scots who, instigated by the crafty Cardinal Richelieu, imposed a Babylonish tyranny upon church and state. Their reward for

[54]Ibid., 7-20.

[55]*Lauderdale Papers*, ed. O. Airy (1884-85), I, 9. For a futile attempt at reconciliation see *Life of Blair*, p. 343.

[56]*The Secret and True History of the Church of Scotland*, ed. Charles K. Sharpe (1817), pp. 55, 58-60.

deceiving their brethren, selling their king, and betraying his son was to become a conquered nation. Yet Charles II was prepared to forgive all sins, however crimson. His virtues and modesty were not excelled even in the most refined families. If he should be restored, merchants would be secure, trade recover, laws flourish, tender consciences be undisturbed, present purchasers [of forfeited lands] satisfied, soldiers paid, and Christianity and charity revived.[57]

The Scots labored under grave disadvantages. They had no recognized leader, Argyle being wholly inacceptable to both Charles and Monck. Neither the Estates nor the General Assembly was permitted to come together. Monck allowed the convention of the royal burghs to meet at Edinburgh at the beginning of February and the noblemen and gentlemen of the shires to sit at the same time. The two bodies each appointed five of their number to draw up an address to be presented to the lord general for redressing the grievances of the nation. He was asked to stay all proceedings with respect to Scotland until commissioners from the two bodies should wait on him to ask that assessments, excise, and customs should be made proportional to the levies in England, and that quartering of soldiers should be regulated as in England. Further demands were that a way should be discussed for uniting the nations, trade should be encouraged and a naval force sent to guard against Swedish privateers, the extraordinary imposition on coal and salt moderated, a mint be taken into consideration, the nation governed by Scottish laws, and judges appointed of integrity and knowledge of the laws of Scotland. Three additional clauses were added—that annuities of tithes and gifts in favor of whatsoever person or persons be revoked, that prisoners of war be released, and that vacant stipends be put to pious uses.

The conventions did not agree on all points with their joint committee. The representatives of the shires objected to the clause about the union, those of the burghs to the clause staying all procedures and to the revocation of gifts. The former wanted an extension of the moratorium on debts but the latter altogether dissented therefrom.[58] No agreement

[57]The *Message*, printed at Aberdeen, bears the direction that Douglas was to transmit it to Colonel Brown and the rest of the nobility and gentry in the Scottish nation. As I cannot believe that Charles thus insulted the Scots, I have cited this tract only as evidence of the rancor Cavaliers felt.

[58]*Extracts from the Records of the Convention of the Royal Burghs of Scotland, 1615-1676*, ed. J. D. Marwick (1878), pp. 490-503; John Nicoll, *A Diary of Public Transactions . . . Chiefly in Scotland*, ed. David Laing (Edinburgh, 1836), p. 272. A commission from Linlithgow to Sir Archibald Stirling, January 27, is printed in Sir William Fraser, *The Stirlings of Keir* (Edinburgh, 1858), and the summons to Glencairn to go to London with the rest of the commissioners, February 26, in Fraser, *Memoirs of the Maxwells of Pollok* (Edinburgh, 1863). Monck directed William Ross, commissary of Dunfries, to tell the representatives of the shires and boroughs that he [Monck] was going to ask the English Parliament to treat Scotland on an equality with England. He also requested the prompt payment of any "cess" due. Sir William Fraser, *The Book of Carlaveroch* (Edinburgh, 1873), II, 53-54.

being possible, the burghs named William Thomson, their "generall clark," to repair to London to treat with Parliament and General Monck. His instructions were similar to the above proposals, except that the clause about the union was omitted, and several more were added, including one for license to export skins, hides, and wool until manufactories be set up.[59]

Unfortunately no hint is recorded of the reasons why the shires objected to the proposal for a union and why the burghs silently dropped it in Thomson's instructions. Its initial insertion supports the suggestion already made that the burghs had benefited from the Cromwellian union and wished it continued in a more equitable form. Otherwise the main interest of these proposals lies in the light they cast upon the prevalence of a mundane spirit. The Covenant is not even mentioned, and the clauses which may be judged ecclesiastical refer to property, not to creeds or disciplines. The stress on economic questions suggests that but for the intolerance displayed on both sides—Episcopalian and Covenanter—at the Restoration, what the late P. Hume Brown called " the age of secular interests" need not have been delayed until the eighteenth century.

Even among the unco guid traces of worldliness can be found. A leader of the Protesters, Wariston, was now convinced that he had turned aside from the path of righteousness in order to worship an idol—the position of Lord Clerk Register. Friends like James Guthrie had warned him against co-operating with the English but he had even supported the army leaders and sat on the Committee of Safety. When the Rump was restored he was obliged to retire to Scotland after some unworthy overtures to Sharp. Monck was now his enemy, denouncing him as an incendiary who divided the Presbyterians and incited the Protesters against the Parliament. When he returned to his own land he found he was universally hated. He was accused of raising the prices of all writs and oppressing the poor, afflicted people. He realized that men cried for his blood, but still he tried to oppose the King's restitution. In Scotland, as in England, he chose the losing side. His day was now ended.[60]

The Resolutioners might reasonably expect the royal favor because of their loyalty. Yet their ministers were to be grievously disappointed. Indeed, the maintenance of a form of Presbyterianism seems today to have been so natural that satisfactory explanations for the establishment of episcopacy are hard to find. Therefore, some have stressed two points,

[59]See *Lauderdale Papers*, I, 9.

[60]Wariston's *Diary* from Dec. 31, 1659, to the following May 20 when it ends. This is a most valuable source both for the characters of the English leaders with whom he associated and for his own character, a psychological problem. See also Nicoll, *Diary of Public Transactions*, p. 279.

that Charles II told Lauderdale Presbyterianism was no religion for a gentleman,[61] and that James Sharp by his metamorphosis from the agent of the Resolutioners into the Archbishop of St. Andrews became the Judas of the Kirk. No doubt the royal saying is true if the King be accepted as a gentleman. His manner of life was utterly incompatible with Presbyterianism, but so it was with any religion that required the observance of a moral code. The determination of Charles II not to go on his travels again was stronger than his dislike of any creed or discipline. He could, and did, stay away from his northern kingdom for the rest of his life, and rarely showed any consistent interest in Scottish affairs. There is no convincing evidence that his personal feelings were directly responsible for the course of events.[62]

As for Sharp, he undoubtedly yielded to temptation, but it cannot be demonstrated that he deliberately plotted from the start the ruin of the church to which he belonged. His apostasy was a gradual process. Like Monck he seems to have expected that a moderate, not a rigid, Presbyterianism would be established in England and Scotland, although the phrase annoyed his chief correspondent at Edinburgh, Robert Douglas. The Erastian attitude of the English Parliament after the readmission of the secluded members, called forth protests from Scots like Baillie against a decree that "Christ may be allowed no spirituall government of his Church." To this minister the sole remedy was to bring home "our sweet Prince." Like other Scots he clung to the hope of reclaiming England and proposed the compilation of a corpus of the writings of living Episcopalians to show how bitter they were against Covenant and Presbyterians and how ardent for Arminianism and most of Popery.[63] Sharp judged the prevalent temper in England more justly and soon recognized that not even a moderate Presbyterianism would be established. He was wrong in his belief that a moderate episcopacy would satisfy Anglicans, but to foresee the Clarendon Code in the spring of 1660 would have been as difficult as to foresee the "drunken" administration or the "killing time."

[61]Gilbert Burnet, *History of My Own Time*, I, 107, 131.

[62]In an address of April 6, N.S. to the King, the noblemen and gentlemen of Scotland complain that they received no commands from him. So far as I know no instructions were sent, probably because the King had not made up his mind. *Clarendon Calendar*, IV, 620. A valuable letter from Charles II to the presbytery of Edinburgh, dated August 10, 1660, stated that he was resolved to maintain the government of the Church of Scotland as settled by law and to countenance all ministers who lived peacefully. The acts of the General Assembly at St. Andrews and Dundee in 1651 were to be recognized until another assembly met. Sir William Fraser, *The Melvilles and the Leslies* (Edinburgh, 1890), II, 23-24; Burnet, I, f. 109.

[63]Letters to Sharp, March 10, April 16, 1660, in *Letters and Journals of Robert Baillie*; Wodrow, i, 28. See the letter cited in the previous note. Sharp was, of course, soon convinced that the chances of establishing Presbyterianism in England were nil, and in that sense he was guilty of treachery to those who still expected the provisions of the Solemn League and Covenant to be enforced.

By reverting to the policy of the Solemn League and Covenant the Scots had gone far to ruin their cause. Their consistency was admirable but not practical politics. Moreover, they persisted even when they recognized that the Covenant no longer excited enthusiastic support at home. Both Wariston and Douglas, who agreed on scarcely anything, testified to the general dislike of the Covenant. The former heard from his friends that there were now as many men against it as there had been for it in 1643, and that the bulk of the nation was now Montrosian and against the work of reformation and Presbyterian government, hating the instruments thereof.[64] Douglas wrote that a new generation had arisen which was ignorant of the work of reformation. "You will not believe," he told Sharp, "what a heart-hatred they bear to the Covenant and how they fret that the parliament should have revived it." Yet he urged Sharp that he, Lauderdale, and Crawford see that the League and Covenant be settled "as the only basis of the security and happiness of these nations."[65]

Perhaps along with this hostility to the political policy entailed by the Covenant went a revolt against clerical domination. The causes which had united nobleman and minister in 1638 had little strength in 1660. Even after allowance has been made for Kirkton's exaggerations and prejudices, there is much truth in the picture he supplies of Scotland at the Restoration, when men became "not only inebriat but really intoxicate, not only drunk but frantic."[66] Drunkenness and debauchery seemed proofs of loyalty. But the writer is in error in blaming these social evils on the King's return. That provided only the occasion for the coarse jollity that had been artificially and superficially driven underground. The remedy was not to be found in covenants or episcopacy, and the alternative to puritan austerity was not necessarily evil living. Thirty unhappy years were to pass by before these truths found general recognition.

[64]*Diary*, April 21, 28.

[65]Ibid., March 31; Wodrow, I, 15.

[66]Ibid., pp. 65-66. Nicoll (*Diary of Public Transactions*, pp. 283-84) describes how wine flowed freely, healths were drunk, dancing took place round the bonfires, etc.

CHAPTER XIII

Ireland

THE HISTORY OF IRELAND during the twenty-one months that preceded the Restoration is mainly concerned with the English interest there. The native or "mere" Irish were in the same condition of subjection as the Britons during the Roman occupation. They had been decisively defeated by an army more powerful in every respect except numbers. The confiscation of the property of all who had, or were thought to have, taken part in the massacre of 1641 or had been in arms since then had transferred more than half the land fit for cultivation to alien landlords—adventurers who had advanced money for the reconquest of Ireland or officers and soldiers who had accomplished it and who received their arrears of pay in the form of land grants.[1] Many of the soldiers seem to have sold their debentures or claims to lands to their officers, no doubt for a small portion of their value because they needed ready money.[2] The result was that the future "ascendancy" class of landlords was largely derived from adventurers and officers but not, usually, privates. Most of the land had changed hands before Oliver Cromwell's death though some outstanding claims remained and some individuals were dissatisfied with their shares. The corollary to the confiscations, the transplantation of Irish rebels to Connaught, had been carried out with less thoroughness. The estates of the new landlords needed laborers, and only the native Irish could provide them. Therefore, with or without licenses, many former tenants remained to till the soil for their new masters.[3] They not unnaturally looked upon their dispossessed landlords much as the Scottish clansmen

[1]The question of what proportion of the land in Ireland was confiscated is most difficult, and depends on an interpretation of Petty's figures given at the beginning of his work entitled *The Political Anatomy of Ireland*, written in 1672, published in 1691, and edited by Charles Henry Hull in *The Economic Writings of Sir William Petty* (Cambridge, 1899). Petty computed that there were in Ireland 10,500,000 acres, of which 1,500,000 could not be cultivated at all and another 1,500,000 were very coarse and unprofitable, leaving 7,500,000 "good meadow, arrable and pasture." He reckoned that of the 5,230,000 acres confiscated, the Papists had recovered by 1672, 2,360,000 acres, the Protestants 2,400,000 plus 470,000 acres of the poor land. Therefore, the fraction confiscated would seem to be 5,230,000 divided by 9,000,000 or, roughly five-ninths. If the good land only is to be counted the fraction would be 4,760,000 divided by 7,500,000, or about three-fifths. According to these figures the Roman Catholic Irish recovered about one-fourth of the 9,000,000 acres. Since they are said (pp. 154, 156) to have owned two-thirds of the land before the war, their permanent loss would be two-thirds minus one-fourth or five-twelfths. Sir Charles Firth in his work *Last Years* (II, 138) gives for the total confiscation the fraction as two-thirds which seems rather too large.

[2]John P. Prendergast, *The Cromwellian Settlement of Ireland* (1865), pp. 95-108. Petty stated in *Political Anatomy* (p. 152) that in 1653 debentures were freely sold for 4 s. and 5 s. the pound, and that a pound purchased on the average two acres. He thought the 9,000,000 acres were worth annually 2s. an acre, a figure Sir Richard Cox felt was too low by a third.

[3]For a specimen of an application for a license, see *Ireland under the Commonwealth*, ed. Robert Dunlop (Manchester, 1913), II, 694-95.

regarded their chiefs in exile after the '15 and '45. A James Byrne was caught when he returned to Wiklow, as he alleged, "to look after some gratuities from some of that county, who were formerly his tenants and acquaintances, and now poor labouring people there."[4] According to a letter from Cork, "the great Dons of the transplantable persons" returned to their old homes every quarter to receive contributions from the inhabitants of their former estates.[5]

How many were transplanted is a problem. There are, however, some census returns for 1659 which, when supplemented by calculations for the areas for which returns are missing, give the following figures for the population of the four provinces: Leinster, 155,534; Ulster, 103,923; Munster, 153,282; and Connaught, 87,352. The total population is 500,091. The census divides the people into English, Scotch, and Irish but the totals given are open to question. In Ulster the English and Scotch were in a minority of two to three and in Leicester of two to eleven. In the other two provinces no Scotch are recorded, and in both the Irish outnumbered the English ten to one. The only place of those cited where the English exceeded the Irish was Dublin, the figures being 6,459 to 2,321, but in the county 3,323 to 9,724.[6] If the total population is too low, as has been argued, the mistake may be due to some obscure systematic error rather than to occasional lapses from accuracy.[7] If this suggestion is true, then the figures for the different provinces may be relatively correct. In that case the transplantation would seem to have been on a smaller scale than is generally thought. That the proportion of English to Irish is the same for Munster and Connaught confirms the inference.

However, even if Petty's arithmetic is open to question, the general picture he paints of the condition of the Irish is almost certainly true. Six out of eight of all the Irish, he wrote, "live in a brutish nasty Condition, as in Cabins, with neither Chimney, Door, Stairs nor Window; feed

<hr>

[4] Ibid., II, 703-704.

[5] Sir John Percivale to ——, Oct. 16, 1658, Hist. MSS Comm. *Egmont MSS* (1905), I, 600.

[6] "Observation by W. H. Hardinge on the earliest known manuscript census returns of the people of Ireland," in *Transactions of the Royal Irish Academy*, XXIV, Antiquities, Part IV (Dublin, 1865) pp. 325-26. The returns are printed in full in *A Census of Ireland, circa 1659*, ed. Seamus Pender (Dublin, 1939), with elaborate indexes of places and names. See the Introduction, p. xiii, for Dr. Erin MacNeill's opinion that the classification of the English, Scottish, and Irish is untrustworthy.

[7] Sir William Petty, calculating from the number of hearths, made the population 1,100,000 with 200,000 families in 1672, or 1,200,000 (*Economic Writings*, ed. Hull, I, 141, 272). Of the first figure he gave 200,000 to the English, 100,000 to the Scotch, and 800,000 to the Irish. The population in 1652 he reckoned at 850,000. The increase in thirteen years is too great for these totals to be correct if the census is reliable. Sir Charles Firth (*Last Years*, II, 144 n.) suggests that the figures for certain towns represent the male inhabitants only. However, if the suggestion is applied to the total population and allowance made for women and children, the new figure would in probability be higher than Petty's, considering that the casualties during the war and the victims of transportation beyond the seas were largely men. A more likely surmise is that the 500,091 were adults, but speculation is rather idle. Petty's calculations and inconsistencies do not inspire confidence.

chiefly upon Milk and Potatoes." Therefore, he concluded, though they outnumbered the Protestants by eight to three, the Roman Catholics were not likely to take up arms again.[8] This passage refers to 1672 but if it errs at all for a description of the condition of the Irish about 1658, the error is not likely to lie in the use of over-dark colors.

The bitterness the Irish felt at their terrible economic losses was greatly aggravated by the proscription of their religion. Though after the war Roman Catholic priests were liable to the penalties of high treason if they remained in Ireland, they were usually punished by banishment to the West Indies. A reward of £5 was offered for the apprehension of a priest and a substantial number suffered transportation or imprisonment. Nevertheless, others, from Spain it is said, took their places. Laymen were not suffered to remain undisturbed. The provisions of an act passed by the Parliament at Westminster in 1657 for "convicting, discovering and repressing of Popish Recusants" applied to Ireland as well as England and Scotland. Its main provision empowered grand juries to present at assizes all persons from the age of sixteen upward who were suspected to be Papists. A person so presented was convicted and forfeited two-thirds of his estates or he took an oath to which no conscientious Roman Catholic could possibly swear. He was required not only to renounce the papal supremacy and power of deposition, but also to deny that the Church of Rome was the true Church, and to affirm his disbelief in transubstantiation and purgatory. No convicted recusant was to be permitted to take the oath unless he had for six months frequently attended approved services.[9] This act naturally filled the Irish with alarm. Realizing that the Irish would never take the oath, the government in Dublin was also fearful of its effects, and, as Henry Cromwell pointed out, to require the denunciation of foreign jurisdiction was reasonable but to include matters of doctrine was a mistake. Actually, he rarely or never enforced this act, but its very existence *in terrorem* was probably harmful and likely to render the Irish desperate.

By the act of July 7, 1659, passed by the Rump, the commissioners named to govern Ireland were authorized to execute laws in force in England for the punishment of, among other offenders and offenses, popish priests and Jesuits, and the use of the Book of Common Prayer.[10] The order of September 13, 1659, recommended the justices of the peace to suppress the celebrations of saints' days.[11]

The history of the Church of Ireland during the Puritan Revolution

[8]*Economic Writings*, I, 156.
[9]*Acts and Ordinances*, II, 1170-1180.
[10]*Acts and Ordinances*, II, 1298-99.
[11]Dunlop, II, 712.

consists of a catalogue of individual sufferings. Of the hierarchy Ussher took refuge in England and Bramhall on the Continent, but some bishops remained in Ireland and accepted pensions or grants out of their diocesan incomes from the Cromwellian government. One bishop, Henry Jones of Clogher, went much further than his brethren in recognizing the new regime because he acted as scoutmaster-general to the English forces, and drew up a declaration of the rebels' cruelties in Leinster and Munster with a view to inducing the largest possible confiscation of land there. At the Restoration he changed sides and, for services not easy to detect, was promoted to Meath. Of the lower clergy, some perished in the massacre of 1641. Of the survivors, a number formally joined the Presbyterians while others took the Covenant when it was imposed on Irish Protestants.[12] Jeremy Taylor, who went to Ireland in 1658, was arrested the next year apparently because he used the cross in baptism.[13] He seems soon to have been released. Thus the members of the Irish Church had all men's hands against them.

The position of Presbyterians in Ireland affords some parallels with that of their coreligionists in Scotland, except that they had had to face the Irish rebellion of 1641. They welcomed the Solemn League and Covenant and the enforcement of the Covenant, but, like their brethren across the Irish Channel, they opposed the execution of Charles I. With the triumph of the Cromwellian forces, they were even threatened with the transplantation of their leaders from Down and Antrim to Munster. Nothing came, however, of this scheme to impair communication between northeast Ulster and southwest Scotland. A more moderate policy was adopted by Henry Cromwell than his brother-in-law, Fleetwood, had pursued. Ministers were persuaded to accept a salary from the state, the prevailing argument being that the government fund from which they were paid was derived from the tithes which legally belonged to them. Difficulties arose from their unwillingness to observe the prescribed fasts or thanksgiving days, because such a recognition would violate their consciences. Here again, Henry Cromwell showed his good sense and listened to Colonel Cooper, the governor of Ulster, who found that the ministers "may with more ease be led than driven." The government at Dublin seems to have permitted the discipline of the Presbyterian Church to be established, because mention is made of a synod attended by ministers and ruling elders. Curiously enough, the move-

[12]James Seaton Reid, *History of the Presbyterian Church in Scotland*, ed. W. D. Killen (Belfast, 1867), II, 211, n. 15.

[13]Dunlop, II, 706; Taylor to Evelyn, June 4, 1659. Life by Reginald Heber prefixed to *The Whole Works of Jeremy Taylor* (1828), I, lxxxix; Conway to Rawdon, June 14, in *Conway Letters*, ed. Marjorie Hope Nicolson (1930), p. 159.

ment toward uniformity of doctrine between Independents and Presbyterians, already noted in England, also produced a declaration of faith in Ireland.[14]

Most of the other religious groups were represented in the army. These sectaries formed the "new" Protestants in contrast to the "old" Protestants who had been in Ireland before the landing of Cromwell's forces. While Fleetwood was Lord Deputy, he had favored the more extreme sectaries, the Anabaptists rather than either the Independents (Congregationalists) or the Presbyterians who comprised most of the "old" Protestants.

An entirely new group appeared in Ireland which, though often linked in popular writing with the Anabaptists or fanatics, had little in common with them except for a joint dislike of tithes and an established church. The founder of Irish Quakerism was William Edmundson, who had fought under Cromwell in Scotland, married and left the army about 1651, and listened to the appeals of his brother, a soldier in Ireland, to go thither. Having settled in Antrim and disposed of the goods he had brought with him, he returned to England for more in 1653. This time he heard James Nayler, was converted, and went back to his family determined to testify to the truth as he saw it. He and his brother formed the first settled meeting of Friends in Ireland in 1654. Other Friends came from England, including Edward Burrough and Francis Howgill. The first of these related how he visited Baptist meetings at Fleetwood's home and concluded that officers in the hopes of promotion had bowed down to the idol of adult baptism, but that, though formerly fashionable, it now was withering. Howgill made a missionary journey and found, within fifty miles of Dublin "the desolatest places that ever any did I think behold, without any inhabitant except a few Irish cabins here and there, who are robbers and murderers that lives in holes and bogs where none can pass." He claimed that the word had been sowed in the principal towns within a hundred and twenty miles of the capital. The receptions these Quakers met with varied. Colonel Phayre, the governor of Cork, later a Muggletonian, attended meetings and said the Quakers were doing more than all the priests had accomplished in a hundred years. The number of converts the Friends made in the army alarmed Henry Cromwell who feared they would ruin discipline. He began to have their preachers arrested, including Burrough and Howgill who were sent back to England. Some colonels, like Henry Ingoldsby, turned out of the army any Quakers who refused to obey orders, but in spite of their efforts the movement progressed slowly among the Protestants but

[14]Reid, II, 210-211, 236-37, 227, 220, 231, n. 45.

not apparently among the Roman Catholics. In all one hundred and one Quakers are said to have suffered imprisonment in Ireland during the Protectorate, and to have lost £86 13 s. 6d.[15]

The main difference between the groups that composed the Protestant party was not only religious but also political and economic. While the Anabaptists wished to give priority to soldiers' claims for land in compensation for their arrears of pay, the others were more willing that all to whom the government was indebted should be treated on an equality. When Henry Cromwell arrived in Ireland, first as commander in chief and then as lord deputy, he preferred the second of these policies, having particular regard to the old proprietors. There was another issue—that many of the field officers, especially those promoted when Fleetwood was lord deputy, were Republicans at heart who had unwillingly accepted the Protectorate in 1653 and disliked still more its modification by the Humble Petition and Advice.

It is impossible to be certain of the attitude of the privates, but the payment of their arrears by debentures cannot have contented the majority of them. Even those who retained their debentures until they received land in exchange are not likely to have had the capital necessary to start small holdings in a country so completely devastated as Ireland had been, and must have become either tenants or hired laborers of the new landlords. They were isolated in a strange land, far from their relations. In spite of regulations to the contrary they married Irish women, especially in Connaught and County Clare. Apparently, also, some recusants had remained Roman Catholics at heart.[16] Sectarian ministers seem to have displayed little of the zeal of the priests because there are complaints that many parts of the country were without Protestant services. Though Henry Cromwell tried hard to secure a godly ministry and to prevent, by grants to favored individuals, the diminution of the revenue from bishops' lands which provided the fund out of which ministers' stipends were paid, his success was not striking.[17] The failure to attract ministers would by itself go far to explain why the Irish were not converted, even if their brutal treatment by the English had not already erected a bar to the adoption of their conquerors' religion.

However, the immediate issue in Ireland during the years from Cromwell's death to Charles II's restoration was the attitude of the army. In 1658 there were in Ireland six regiments of horse, one of

[15]These figures are on p. 345 of Thomas Wight's *A History of the . . . Quakers in Ireland*, ed. John Rutty (1800). The paragraph above is based on this work and on Braithwaite, *Beginnings of Quakerism*, pp. 210-222.

[16]Dunlop, II, 711-12. Declaration of September 9, 1659.

[17]See the interesting protest to Oliver Cromwell against such grants in Dunlop, II, 692-93. For a grant to William Goffe of bishops' land of the annual value of £500, see ibid., p. 694.

dragoons which, by an order of January 2, 1658, was to be paid like the horse,[18] and eleven of foot. The total number of officers and men, including "loose," or unregimented troops and companies, was about 15,000 or 16,000. The politics of the colonels can best be illustrated by noting which of them lost their commissions after the Rump returned to power in the spring of 1659. Naturally, the Protector lost his horse with his position, and his brother Henry, like his brother-in-law Fleetwood, both horse and foot.[19] Redman was deprived of his horse, became a Royalist, and was named, at the end of December, 1659, the commander of the Irish brigade which had been sent to England to help put down Booth's rising. He was knighted by Charles II for his staunch support of Monck. Thus, of the horse, two colonels only, Hierome Sankey and Henry Pretty, together with Abbott of the dragoons, were judged to be Republicans. The changes in the foot were fewer. Apart from the substitutions of Ludlow for Henry Cromwell and Axtell for Fleetwood, the only immediate change may have been Robert Barrow for Henry Ingoldsby. Either in July or a little later, Hewson seems to have been replaced by Markham, though when he left Ireland to assume command of his foot in England is uncertain. When he emerged from obscurity, he earned great unpopularity by his severity against the London apprentices in December, 1659. Not all the colonels who kept their commissions were Republicans, the most important exception being Sir Charles Coote, president of Connaught. Events in 1659 were to demonstrate that the Irish army was divided in its politics and, like its counterpart in England and Scotland, was to undergo several purges before the Restoration.

One reason why the army was never harmonious was that its pay was always in arrears. Even after the reduction in strength after the war ended, the cost remained constant at about £28,000 a month or £364,000 a year.[20] But the total revenue was £70,000, half coming from the lands reserved to the government and half from indirect taxation, plus the monthly assessment which should yield £108,000, or £178,000 in all. To this could be added a remittance from England of £8,000 a month. Thus Henry Cromwell could count as a maximum on a revenue of £274,000 for all governmental expenses. Allowing £35,000 for civil expenses, the sum required was over £100,000 more than the income, and this result does not take into account arrears of pay to the soldiery. Devices like farming the indirect taxes might furnish about a third of this sum. If quitrents could be extracted from

[18] To the authorities in Firth and Davies, II, 621-22, add *Clarke MSS* xxx, 1b.

[19] Fleetwood retained his English regiments and no doubt the Rump thought these, together with his position as commander in chief, sufficient for one man.

[20] The "month" was a lunar month.

adventurers and soldiers—they had been exempted from this charge until June, 1659—another £24,000 might be obtained.[21] The only way to make both ends meet was to reduce the army. Henry wished to cut down the number of officers while retaining all the men, but was obliged by the Council in England to adopt the opposite plan. Yet he was not provided with the necessary funds to pay off the men it was proposed to disband. Whether the size of the army was materially changed is doubtful but the dissatisfaction of soldiers, with their pay steadily falling behind and with the possibility of disbanding for some of them, is likely to have increased.[22]

At the head of the Irish government was Henry Cromwell, the second surviving son of Oliver. In spite of his comparative youthfulness—he was born in 1628—he was already well versed in Irish affairs. He had served in the field under his father in 1650, and returned to Ireland in 1654 to feel the pulse of the army leaders with regard to the recently established Protectorate. He was back again in 1655, having been nominated commander in chief and a member of the Council. He succeeded his brother-in-law Fleetwood as lord deputy towards the end of 1657, but had had much influence during the previous two years because Fleetwood had retired soon after his arrival. He had been a very able administrator with statesmanlike views, but had made enemies. That officers showed they were aggrieved at his substitution of civil government for their arbitrary sway was inevitable and no blame attaches to him on this account. But he allowed his dislikes to influence him unduly. Very early his father warned him that "time and patience" might convert his opponents, especially if they saw his "moderation and love" towards them. Soon the father felt obliged to counsel the son to avoid "making it a business to be too hard for the men who contest with you." In spite of these exhortations Henry continued to be too severe. He had a lieutenant colonel Alexander Brayfield brought before a court-martial which condemned him to be cashiered. This heavy sentence Henry allowed to stand in spite of his father's remonstrance, because Brayfield was a critic and intriguer belonging to the faction in the army led by Hewson which used to deride Henry as "Absalom."[23]

The Lord Deputy was very sensitive, too inclined to view opposition as a personal slight. He was also unduly suspicious, among others, of Fleetwood, though his father assured him his suspicions were groundless. A querulous note runs through his letters and suggests that he was

[21]Henry Cromwell thought £2,000 a month the utmost that could be raised in this way.

[22]This paragraph is mainly based on Firth, Last Years, II, 164-73.

[23]Letters of Nov. 21, 1655; Apr. 21, 1656; Oct. 13, 1657; Abbott, Writings . . . of Oliver Cromwell, IV, 26-27, 146, 646-47.

rather a disappointed man. During his brother's protectorate he complained that he was kept in the dark and that all the information sent him he could learn from the newsbooks. A perusal of his correspondence rather confirms this charge, but he should have borne in mind that the post was unsafe and that he did receive oral communications whenever a trusty go-between was available. The prime cause of his discontent was the failure to summon him to sit in the Council in London. The reasons given for keeping him at his post were that Ireland would not be safe if he left, that his presence and command of the army there were stout props for the Protectorate, and that, in England, he might be seized by the army leaders. A comparison of the two brothers reveals that Richard lacked the great administrative ability and strong convictions of Henry, who in his turn was without the amiability that made the Protector generally liked. Whereas the one was deserted at a crisis because his easy-going ways inspired no confidence, the other alienated possible allies by his proneness to take offense. Had Oliver nominated Henry instead of Richard as his successor, the Protectorate might well have ended more quickly but not so bloodlessly.

News of Oliver Cromwell's death reached Dublin on September 10. The same afternoon Richard was proclaimed his successor with as much joy and satisfaction as in the best-affected places in England. Henry Cromwell caused an address to Richard to be circulated throughout the Irish army, which he intended to be "a witness against the treachery and falshood of any officer of this army, that may hereafter in the least manner warp from his due obedience."[24] At the same time he complained bitterly of his Council, the majority of members being antagonistic to whatever he proposed. In particular, they had undertaken to reduce the army by rules which made him odious and were preposterous —retaining the officers but diminishing the number of men. He asked, therefore, that he might be allowed to cross to England in order to confer with the Protector, a favor he often sought but never obtained from his brother.[25] He may have deemed his elevation to the higher dignity of lord lieutenant a poor compensation for the retention of his former councillors.[26] He distrusted William Steele, the chancellor, both on public and on private grounds. He thought that Steele was dissatisfied

[24]The text of the proclamation, with the signatures, is in Thurloe, VII, 383-84; the letter of Henry Cromwell with the comment cited above, ibid., p. 400.

[25]Letter of Sept. 18, ibid., pp. 400-401.

[26]On September 28 the Council advised Richard to renew Henry Cromwell's commission by the title of Lord Lieutenant, and on October 5 the committee for the affairs of Ireland was directed to prepare a draft of instructions, but no record of it is in the Register. Henry's formal appointment was dated November 6. *The Fourteenth Report of the Deputy Keepers of the Public Records in Ireland* (Dublin, 1882), Appendix, p. 28.

with the course of events, though willing to accept a single person at the head of the government of the three nations so long as he was Oliver Cromwell, and particularly at the discouragement of the Anabaptists and others professing godliness. Discovering that the chancellor wished to dictate maxims of state and rules for the management of the Council, Henry put an end to confidential intercourse, whereupon Steele tried to influence the godly against the government. In these intrigues Colonel Matthew Thomlinson, also a councillor, was the main instrument employed. A third councillor, Miles Corbet, chief baron of the exchequer, was another opponent. The remaining two, Richard Pepys, chief justice of the upper bench, and William Bury, a Lincolnshire squire, were supporters.[27] The dissensions in the Council and in the army continued as long as the Protectorate lasted.

After the English army leaders had forced Richard to dissolve Parliament he was so bewildered that he neglected even to inform his brother what had happened. Accordingly, Henry Cromwell looked in vain for any instructions. A month afterward he wrote to Richard to explain that he and the officers had been "in a waiting frame to see what God or our superiors would command us," and that they remained in the same condition.[28] He was now sending to England three very good friends to acquaint Richard with proceedings in Ireland. He concluded: "I am glad, at least, that our dear father went off in that glory, which was due to his actings. I pray God bear up your highness's spirit, and that we may be encouraged to do our duties."[29] By the time this letter reached its destination Richard had shuffled off the public stage and the Rump was in control. Its decision was soon made. On June 7 the resolution was passed that Ireland should be governed by commissioners nominated by Parliament and not by a single person, and that Henry Cromwell should be so informed and directed to repair to Westminster and report. At the same time three of the five commissioners were named, the Council of State being asked to nominate the other two.[30]

There should have been no doubt that Henry would obey the orders of Parliament once his brother had abdicated, because he had often

[27]Henry Cromwell's letter of June 23, 1658, to Thurloe about Steele is a fine example of the writer's suspicious nature.

[28]May 23, Thurloe, VII, 674.

[29]According to Ludlow (II, 72) Henry at first contemplated armed support of his brother in conjunction with Broghil and Sir Charles Coote, but found the council of officers unwilling to act.

[30]*Commons Journals*, VII, 674. Colonel John Jones, William Steele, and Robert Goodwin, an "adventurer" and former member of the Irish Council were named. The proposal to nominate Miles Corbet was at first rejected. An act of July 7 nominated five commissioners, the above three together with Miles Corbet and Colonel Matthew Thomlinson. *Acts and Ordinances*, II, 1298-99. Their authority was restricted to three months and was not renewed so technically, if the adverb can be used about these revolutionary times, Ireland had no legal government after October.

expressed his abhorrence of using the army in politics. It was equally certain that he would not try to restore the Stuarts because he regarded that as the worst extremity that could happen. Overtures were made to him in the King's name by Fauconberg, once again a Royalist, and, perhaps, by Broghil, though whether the last named had changed sides yet is uncertain. In spite of Sir Edward Hyde's positive statement that Henry had promised to declare for the King but at the eleventh hour lacked the necessary courage, it is most improbable that any such assurance was ever given.[31] His letter resigning the government of Ireland has a ring of sincerity that compels credence. He described how he was left to learn of events in London from rumors, and how, after hearing of the dissolution of Parliament, he had taken steps to prevent Cavaliers or native Irish from profiting by the opportunity. After receiving a letter from the committee of safety commending the security of Ireland to his care, he communicated it to his officers, promising to transmit to England their thoughts upon it.[32] He sent to England an account[33] of "such things, as the granting thereof (as is conceived) would much settle the minds of people and army here, whose case and concernments are very different from those of England and Scotland." Meanwhile he was expecting instructions from the Protector, to whose authority he owed his position. Now that Richard had submitted to the change of government, he also would acquiesce, although he could not promise as much affection to the late changes as others very honestly might. He hoped that the army leaders who had acknowledged their fault in turning out Parliament in 1653 would never repeat their error. The army in Ireland would concur with their brethren in England and would obey rather than overawe Parliament. For himself, the change of government from the form which had raised his father and then his brother to the head of the state rendered him unfit to serve any longer. He thanked God that he had resisted "the great temptation, wherewith I have beene assaulted to withdraw my affection from that cause, wherein hee lived and dyed." He would yield up his charges to any whom Parliament should send to receive it.[34] In another communication he announced that he had received from Westminster a letter instructing the two commissioners on the spot to administer the government and that he intended at once to hand over the reins to them and to sail for

[31]Hyde's letter of October 25 is printed in *Clarendon State Papers*, III, 589 (cf. p. 500) and in *Ormonde Papers*, II, 242-44. Cf. John Barwick to Hyde, June 21, Thurloe, VII, 686-97.

[32]Probably this is the basis for Ludlow's accusation already mentioned, that Henry sounded his officers.

[33]By Bury, Jones, and Lawrence.

[34]June 15, Thurloe, VII, 683-84. Much of this letter is quoted in Masson, *Life of Milton*, V, 461-62.

England. He concluded with satisfaction that he was leaving Ireland in tranquility and with good wishes for his successors.[35] About the same time the council of the army of Ireland sent an address to Parliament full of assurance of their expectations of the blessings they would enjoy and of their own obedience.[36]

Having provided for the government of Ireland, the next step of the Rumpers was to scrutinize the army upon which its existence depended. On paper at least, the force was formidable, comprising six and a half regiments of horse, one of dragoons, and eleven of foot, plus some ten loose companies. Ludlow, named commander in chief, was not permitted to choose his own officers any more than Fleetwood and Monck were, but he was named colonel of a regiment of horse that had been the Protector's and of a regiment of foot formerly the lord lieutenant's.[37] As for the other colonels, their past records were debated by the committee of nominations. Some of the results of their deliberations are noteworthy. Daniel Redman was dismissed because of his "zeal to the usurpation of Cromwell"[38] and replaced by the fanatical William Allen, author of the well-known tract on the fateful meeting at Windsor in 1648 when the officers determined to bring Charles I to trial.[39] Sir Charles Coote's name was retained on the list, perhaps because the evidence was conflicting, though he was alleged to have prevented Dublin from being immediately secured for the Rump. Henry Ingoldsby had ensured his dismissal by the remark that he would withstand the Parliament "to the wearing out of his old shoes."[40] Henry Flower was cashiered because he had been sent by Coote to secure Ulster for the Protector in the spring.[41] He was succeeded by Daniel Axtell, a regicide who had been pre-eminent even in those bloodthirsty times for his ferocity against the native Irish. Many changes were proposed among officers below the rank of colonel, but absence of complete records prevents any estimate of the number actually made.[42]

[35]To the Speaker, June 22, *Mercurius Politicus*, p. 544. The two were William Steele and Miles Corbet.

[36]Ibid., pp. 541–42.

[37]Ludlow, who was also named lieutenant general of horse in Ireland, lost the colonelcy of a regiment in England which he hoped Vane would now have, but the Presbyterians in the House insisted on naming Herbert Morley instead (*Memoirs*, II, 95 and n. 1). For two of Ludlow's commissions, see Hist. MSS Comm. *Eighth Report*, p. 6.

[38]Ludlow, II, 203.

[39]*Somers Tracts*, VI.

[40]*Calendar Domestic, 1659-1660*, p. 19. He sought refuge in France and was replaced by Robert Barrow.

[41]Ludlow, II, 72. Why Flower was thus punished when Coote was exonerated is not clear.

[42]A surprising nomination was Nicholas Kempson as major in Ludlow's horse. As Kempson had been a volunteer for Ireland in 1647 it is strange that the army leaders consented to his nomination. Also, as Ludlow was his brother-in-law, it would seem that the commissioners were not above jobbery. Ludlow, II, App. I.

On or about July 19, Ludlow, accompanied by Colonel John Jones, set out for Ireland. On that day he wrote a letter to the Speaker, pointing out that since Parliament had refused to recognize the validity of transactions since its expulsion in 1653, a bill to confirm the grants of Irish land made during the Protectorate should be passed promptly in order to allay the anxiety of the adventurers, soldiers, and others who had been paid by grants of forfeited lands. That such an act was never passed seems to have made no obvious difference, though probably the failure to enact it disquieted English landowners and made them suspicious of the Rump.

The only act passed which concerned Ireland gave the five commissioners powers to levy the taxes voted by Parliament, to imprison anyone deemed dangerous, and to apply all the laws in force in England to suppress treason, Anglicanism, and Roman Catholicism, and to punish moral offenses.[43] The army was not even mentioned, so its control rested solely with the commander in chief. There was no sign of any conflict of authority. Indeed, Ludlow found the commissioners too obliging because they asked him to sit with them next to the chairman, and at all other times to take precedence of them, a compliment he declined on the characteristic ground that the military should submit to the civil powers. Soon after his arrival Ludlow addressed the officers. He extolled the Rumpers "who as they are called the fathers of the country, so they have the tenderness and affection of parents for all who take care to deserve their kindness and affection." He thought his audience well satisfied, perhaps as much by the knowledge that £30,000 was forthcoming for their pay as by his words.[44] Almost immediately the news of Booth's rebellion obliged him to call upon the Irish army to send first a hundred men to augment the garrisons of towns on the Welsh coast and then five hundred horse and a thousand foot to Chester or other available ports to help suppress the insurrection. Landing about the middle of August, the Irish brigade under Hierome Sankey assisted in the capture of Chirk and was then ordered back to Ireland. But it never returned thither, staying to play a notable if minor part in later events in England.[45]

When Lambert closed the doors of Parliament to the Rump on October 13, 1659, the attitude of the army in Ireland was at first doubtful. Ludlow relates how copies of the Derby petition were sent across the Irish Sea by Sankey together with letters requesting that they should

[43]*Acts and Ordinances,* July 7, 1659.

[44]Ludlow, II, 105-106. However, in a letter to the Speaker of September 14, he stated that the army was fourteen months in arrears (ibid., p. 448).

[45]Ibid., pp. 107, 110. *Calendar Domestic, 1659-1660,* pp. 179-81, 310, 500, 587.

be circulated to the officers and their signatures obtained. But Ludlow summoned as many officers as were in or near Dublin and urged them to refuse to sign the petition. He argued that pay had been prompt when the Long Parliament had exercised authority but in arrears since 1653, that the restored Parliament must soon settle a form of government as the date of dissolution was next May, that the nation would never consent to be governed by the sword, that Lambert's forces had been amply rewarded, that Fleetwood's commission sufficed in practice, and that more general officers were unnecessary and dangerous. These views prevailed and Ludlow was able to write to Hesilrige that the army in Ireland acknowledged that the supreme authority rested in Parliament which it would support.[46]

Meanwhile Ludlow had nearly completed a list for new modeling of the army in Ireland, having already removed such officers as he suspected and replaced them by those he judged trustworthy.[47] Before leaving for England he had to decide whom to leave in command, after having been dissuaded by Fleetwood from naming the parliamentary commissioners. Sankey was the senior colonel but he was disqualified by his share in promoting the Derby petition. Hardress Waller, though a regicide, was too much of a time-server. Sir Charles Coote seemed too engrossed in his presidency of Connaught and in retaining his regiments of horse and foot. Ludlow selected Colonel John Jones, a regicide, a member of Parliament, and a commissioner, but nonetheless he was a very poor choice. He had seen very little active service, and to pass over Sankey and Waller in his favor was to inflict a marked slight upon them. He soon showed both his disloyalty and incapacity.

Barrow, sent to Ireland by the council of the English army, could not at first secure the approval of the Irish officers for Lambert's coup d'état.[48] However, Jones, Corbet, and Thomlinson were accused of acting hand in glove with Fleetwood, of suppressing a letter from Monck asking them to join him in supporting Parliament, and Jones of publishing his reply to Monck.[49] The reference in the last phrase is to the letter which Jones, Waller, Cooper, and four other officers sent to Monck in reply to a communication from him now lost. They expressed their surprise and trouble that he was going to engage the three nations in war, thereby

[46]Ludlow, II, 119-21.

[47]The seventeenth article of Ludlow's impeachment (to be noticed later) asserted that he cast out of the army without examination or consultation the Parliament's friends and faithful servants (Ludlow, II, 468). John Jones feared that the many officers deprived of their commands and the many more expecting their dismissal, would revolt or divide the Irish army (letter of Oct. 30 to Barrow, *Transactions of the Historic Society of Lancashire and Cheshire 1860-61*, pp. 271, 278-79).

[48]Ludlow, II, 141-42.

[49]The three were impeached along with Ludlow (*Memoirs*, II, 464-70).

opening a sure way for the common enemy to destroy their joint interest as men and Christians. They refused to countenance any setting one part of the army against the rest, and declared they would do their utmost to prevent the same.[50] The council of officers at Dublin, the same day, November 4, chose Major John Barrett, to go as their representative to Monck in order to dispose their friends in Scotland to a peaceful frame of mind after they had been undeceived.[51]

It is clear, however, that the forces in Ireland were by no means solidly behind Jones and his adherents. The colonel himself realized that the army's Declaration had a mixed reception. According to its critics it was badly worded, and couched in too general language without mentioning specifically the peculiar blessings the nation expected. He saw also that there were unquiet spirits abroad, mostly former Cromwellians alienated by the fall of the Protectorate. Among them were Colonel Thomas Cooper and Major Edward Warren. The Royalists were, he thought, delighted at the course of events and expected their king to be proclaimed in Scotland.[52]

The English army leaders soon alienated powerful individuals in Ireland by a systematic purge, so that of forty field officers all but a very few belonged to their faction. Rightly or wrongly, they conveyed the impression that they meant to transform Ireland into a place of refuge if distressed in England. Their opponents in Ireland, therefore, seized their instruments there.[53] On December 13, Dublin Castle was captured by a ruse and the three commissioners for the government of Ireland— Jones, Corbet, and Thomlinson—were seized.[54] The prime movers in this coup were Sir Theophilus Jones, Colonel Bridges, and the Warrens. Sir Hardress Waller, the senior officer in Ireland, was persuaded to act as the figurehead of the movement. Sir Charles Coote and his three brothers secured Connaught; Broghil, Munster; and Colonel Thomas Cooper, Ulster; and soon the only town that held out was Duncannon, which was besieged by a force under Thomas Scot, the son of the councillor. The besiegers' profanities were compared by the garrison to the bad language formerly ascribed only to Cavaliers.[55]

[50]*Transactions of the Historic Society of Lancashire and Cheshire 1860-61*, pp. 272-73.

[51]Ibid., p. 274. Baker's *Chronicle*, pp. 686-87, where it is stated that Barrett was expelled from Scotland for trying to seduce the soldiery. In a letter dated Nov. 8 and printed in *Publick Intelligencer*, pp. 889-90, Jones, Corbet, and Thomlinson bewailed at great length their past deviations and protested their future rectitude. To this end they were establishing a weekly day of humiliation and prayer.

[52]Ibid., pp. 276-77; Ludlow, II, 147.

[53]John Bridges, Edward and Abel Warren, *A Perfect Narrative of the Grounds . . . moving some officers . . . to the securing of the Castle of Dublin* (1660).

[54]*Mercurius Politicus*, Dec. 29-Jan. 5.

[55]The authorities are given by Richard Bagwell, *Ireland under the Stuarts* (1909-16), II, 366, 369.

The reasons why the Irish forces suddenly changed sides varied. Though they were the professed champions of the Rump, it is improbable that most of the chief actors felt or, indeed, had any reason to feel, any deep attachment to that body. Almost certainly the officers who started the ball rolling on December 13 were animated more strongly by anger at the slights put upon them by Ludlow and the commissioners than by constitutional scruples, even if they did assign disloyalty to the Parliament as the main reason for refusing to let Ludlow land at the end of December and for the articles of impeachment they drew up against him and the commissioners.[56] Ludlow had favored the former opponents of Henry Cromwell at the expense of his supporters and they now had their revenge. Men like the Cootes and Broghil were not Republicans at heart. They had been perfectly ready to serve a protector who ruled with a strong hand and, after Richard's downfall, to pay lip service to the Rump so long as they were left alone to govern their provinces or garrisons. They knew that the army council in London and Ludlow in Dublin were likely to revert to the policy Fleetwood had pursued when deputy, and to reserve the plums for their staunch supporters, the Anabaptists. But mingled with selfish ambitions was genuine concern at the extinction of parliamentary government. The rank and file were willing enough for another change. They seemed forgotten and neglected by those in authority in London. Service in Ireland had never been popular, and arrears of pay made it more obnoxious. Probably many of them had never been Puritans. If they had, some were forgetting their earlier ideals, as their seeking wives among the Irish Catholics and their cursing prove.[57]

For a couple of months semblance of unity was preserved. Waller and the council of officers set forth a declaration which is remarkable even in that age for its hyperbole. It claimed that Providence had prevented the ruin of their religion and liberties, notwithstanding the mountains raised to hinder the work of reformation. Romish emissaries and engineers of darkness had divided them, and the powers of Hell had laid the very necks of magistracy and ministry upon the block of direful anarchy and arbitrary rule. God's own people had been guilty of apostacy and hypocrisy, of unfaithfulness and breach of covenant. They were hastening to the Munster desolations, threatened by the like fanatical spirits, when they were rescued by the miraculous patience and bounty of

[56]See Ludlow, II, App. II.

[57]A letter from Warren, Jones, and others, dated Dec. 24, stressed the importance of the adherence of the common soldiers and inferior officers to the Rump. Hist. MSS Comm. *Portland MSS*, I, 688-89. Cf. ibid., 693. An order of September 9 stated that soldiers had married Irish Papists and that some, perhaps natives, had been formerly popish recusants and only pretended to be Protestants. Dunlop, *Ireland under the Commonwealth*, II, 711-12.

God.[58] The reference to the German Anabaptist, communist, disorders at Munster in 1534-1535 suggests that Presbyterians were in the ascendant in the council of officers. The Rump seems to have recognized this because, of the commissioners nominated for the management of Irish affairs, Sir Charles Coote, Sir Hardress Waller, and Henry Markham were Presbyterians. The fourth, Robert Goodwin, was no fanatic, but the fifth, John Weaver, was an Independent and Republican. The English Council of State was directed to prepare instructions for the commissioners, but no trace of them has been found.[59] Of the councillors, Annesley is said to "steer" Ireland, but one of the few signs of his activity is the proposal to the Commons that the assessments of Scotland and Ireland should be abated or more time allowed for their payment. The Commons agreed to the second but not the first suggestion.[60] Ludlow and his colleagues were ordered to attend the House and answer the articles of impeachment which Bridges had brought from Dublin. The impeachment was not, however, proceeded with. A list of Irish officers was referred to the English Army Commissions for consideration, but the outcome is unknown.[61] However, the commissioners were divided on a political rather than a religious issue. Waller was a rigid Republican and staunch supporter of the Rump, while Coote was now a Royalist who sent Sir Arthur Forbes to seek instructions from Charles II in February.[62] For the present he was content to act hand in glove with Monck, having dispatched James Cuff to the general to keep him informed on Irish factions.[63]

Meanwhile the council of officers had carried out an intention expressed during the suspension of the English parliament and had summoned a convention consisting of two representatives from each county and borough. It met on February 7, and its composition may be judged from its choice of a chairman, Sir James Barry (afterwards Lord Santry), who had served Strafford faithfully.[64] Eight days later Waller, possibly suspecting a design by Coote to supersede him and certainly

[58]Dated Dec. 28 and printed in *Mercurius Politicus* on Jan. 14. A good extract is given in White Kennet, *A Register and Chronicle Ecclesiastical and Civil* (1728), pp. 24-25. Similar references to the Munster Anabaptists occur in other pamphlets, as in Daniel Featley's *The Dippers Dipt* (January, 1660).

[59]See *Commons Journals*, Jan. 19, for the appointment and for the revocation of the powers granted to Ludlow, John Jones, Corbet, and Thomlinson. Whether the new commissioners also superseded the commissioners named on January 13 to govern the Irish army, I do not know.

[60]Carte, *Ormonde Papers*, II, 316; *Commons Journals*, March 12.

[61]Ludlow, II, App. III; *Commons Journals*, Jan. 5, 19; Feb. 8, 15.

[62]Carte, *Ormonde Papers*, IV, 6.

[63]Baker, p. 703. For a note on Cuff see Dunlop, II, 524.

[64]*Mercurius Politicus*, Mar. 21 (No. 612); Carte, *Ormonde Papers*, IV, 5-6, where it is stated that the English Council of State in vain ordered its dissolution. As there is a gap in the Irish *Journals* from 1648 to 1661, no official record of proceedings exists.

disapproving of a declaration by the council of officers in favor of the secluded members, suddenly seized Dublin Castle. He found so few supporters that three days later he was obliged to capitulate.[65] Imprisoned for a short time at Athlone but allowed to return to England at the request of his cousin, Sir William Waller, he took no further part in politics. Coote and his adherents now subjected the Irish forces to a drastic purge. Particulars are lacking, but Ludlow, who complained that everything Monck did in Ireland was "coloured with the name of Sir Charles Coote," was substantially correct in asserting that Coote gave himself two regiments, his brothers Chidley, Richard, and Thomas, and his cousin St. George, one apiece.[66] Henry Ingoldsby, returned from exile, could assure Lenthall that the Irish army was so modeled that rebellious and unruly swords were laid aside, and the most obedient servants of Parliament placed in command.[67]

While Coote had been active in Dublin, Broghil had been busy in Munster. He and his officers issued a long declaration. It denounced Pride's Purge as destroying the foundations of public life. Since then, though they were fighting for liberty and religion, they had almost lost both. The universities and schools had been poisoned and many employed to teach who should have been taught instead, while ministers had been appointed to preach who could better have been paid to keep silent. Never had taxes for the army and navy been so heavy, yet never had arrears been so great. While many were unrepresented in the legislature, few were likely to obey the law. If it was right to declare in favor of restoring a minority of members of parliament, it was even more right to declare for restoring all members. Yet eminent persons who petitioned for the restoration of secluded members were sent to the Tower. After a passing reference to the signers' having fought against the pretended king as long as any others and so ought to fear his return as much as others, they pledged themselves to join with their brethren in the three kingdoms "who disdain to be made slaves." Among the advantages they expected from a just settlement were, of course, the payment of arrears and the plantation of Ireland by adventurers, soldiers, and other English protestants.[68] Probably Broghil, a former Royalist, was not at this time in direct communication with the exiled court, and was sincere in pressing merely for the readmission of the secluded members, though

[65]*Leyborne-Popham MSS*, pp. 152-53.

[66]*Memoirs*, II, 209, 229-31.

[67]Feb. 1, 1660. Zachary Grey, *An Impartial Examination*, IV, App., 142-43.

[68]Feb. 18. Thurloe, VII, 817-20. No doubt Broghil wrote the declaration, perhaps the most readable of many similar documents issued at this time. The address of May 7 is printed in *Mercurius Publicus*, pp. 314-15.

he may well have regarded this as a necessary step towards the Restoration. The whole army sent an address to Monck on May 7, expressing its joy at the light now breaking through the darkness which had overspread the land ever since the violence committed against Parliament in 1648. The signers had read the royal Declaration from Breda and would obey whatever orders they received.[69] This is the last political manifesto that emanated from the Irish forces.

Meanwhile civilians had not been idle. Although many of the members of the Convention were Royalists and prelatists at heart, they felt it prudent to dissemble their real sentiments. They began by choosing as their chaplain, Samuel Cox, one of the soundest of Presbyterians, and by summoning two orthodox ministers from each of the four provinces to advise them on a religious settlement. The convention accepted a list of 160 ministers of sound principles named by the eight, and gave them a legal right to the tithes of the parishes in which they resided. Simultaneously, they degraded and deprived of their stipends all ministers whom the eight designed as Anabaptists. Yet a suggestion to renew the Solemn League and Covenant at once aroused so much animosity that it was never formally made in the Convention, the chairman avowing that he would leave the chair and denounce such a proposal. Moreover, as the leaders perceived the steady drift towards monarchy, they began to court the few surviving bishops and to give them their tithes. The committee on religion named by the Convention, which at the beginning had accepted the recommendations of the eight, now began to plead on behalf of "divers old prelatical men who were corrupt in their doctrine, and immoral in their lives." Before the King's return to England commissioners had been sent to him urging the restoration of the former system of church government and worship.[70] In view of the above it is not surprising to find one of Hyde's London correspondents reporting that the English Presbyterians have become more moderate, especially on the news from Ireland.[71]

As regards politics, to differentiate between the work of the Convention, the commissioners, and individuals like Coote and Broghil is impossible in the absence of state papers. The arrest of John Cook, whose conduct of the proceedings at the trial of Charles I had been rewarded by his appointment as a judge of the upper bench in Ireland, preceded

[69]The draft of a letter from the King, dated March 21/31, suggests no prior communication, though Edward Villiers had already been in touch with him on Charles's behalf. *Clarendon Calendar*, IV, 582, 610. Broghil, like Coote, was in touch with Monck who on January 27 urged him to discountenance Irish petitions for the readmission of the secluded members. Hist. MSS Comm. Various, VI, 438-39.

[70]This paragraph is based on Patrick Adair's *A True Narrative of the Rise and Progress of the Presbyterian Church in Ireland*, ed. W. D. Killen (1866), pp. 233-36; Thurloe, VII, 909.

[71]Apr. 6. *Clarendon Calendar*, IV, 639; Thurloe, VII, 911.

the securing of regicides in England. This action, and various rumors such as an alleged offer to send 7,000 or 8,000 men to England if Scotland would co-operate, and a false report that the King had been proclaimed in Ireland, may account for the anxiety felt at the English council board, which is said to have asked Broghil to suspend ("forbear") the Convention and to send Cook and other prisoners to England. If such an order was sent it was ignored.[72] The Convention claimed full legislative authority and passed an ordinance to raise money to supply the army and to defray other public charges by means of a poll tax. All over fifteen years were to pay amounts graduated according to social rank, beginning with a levy of twelve pence for those under the quality of a yeoman and ending with eight pounds for a marquis.[73] At some unknown time the Irish commissioners were changed once again. Patrick Adair names three, Broghil, Coote, and William Bury, whom he calls "a religious sober man."[74] But a letter indicated that there may have been two more, Sir John Clotworthy and another.[75] The same authority is partly responsible for the view that there was rivalry between Coote and Broghil.[76] Coote received about the middle of March a letter from Charles II, confessing his inability to prescribe the method of effecting his own restoration because ignorant of Coote's supporters. He sent Coote two commissions, one in which he could insert the names of those he trusted, and the other in which he could insert only his own name if he thought the work to be done required more rigorous action than the many would be likely to concur in.[77] Though which commission to use was left to his own discretion Coote used neither. He preferred to imitate Monck in England and, while waiting, to place control of the army in the right hands. Broghil was more hesitant or more uncertain what would be the outcome and, in several letters to Thurloe, repudiated the notion that Ireland would let the King in by the back door. So late as April 24, he told Thurloe that there were odd plots concerning the King but that he had secured his province, Munster, against any that should be for the King, and that the like was true of Ulster and some of Leinster. "I do monstrously dread the Cavalier party, and if the parliament should be of such, God only knows what wil be the evills." A week or so later he was

[72]*Clarendon Calendar*, pp. 582-83, 586, 596, 610, 639.

[73]The ordinance is printed in *A Census of Ireland*, ed. Pender, pp. 610-627.

[74]Bury had been an adventurer and one of Henry Cromwell's Council. He was knighted by Henry July 21, 1658, and by the lords justices in Ireland, January 26, 1661.

[75]Major Rawdon to Viscount Conway, Mar. 17: "Four of the Commissioners or Councillors are here; yet Sir John Clotworthy is in England. . . ." *Calendar State Papers Ireland*, p. 719.

[76]Clarendon says that Coote "expressed great jealousy" of Broghil (*The Life of Edward, Earl of Clarendon* [1857], I, 377).

[77]Carte, *Ormonde Papers*, IV, 7.

expressing his alarm at a report from England that there was to be a union with the King on condition only of an act of indemnity and a few things of that nature. "We will hope those pretious rights we have soe longe, and we thinke justly contended for, will not be exposed but provided for." In the same letter he enclosed the declaration in which the Convention denounced in the strongest language possible the execution of Charles I, which the English House of Lords promptly ordered to be printed. In another week he received the votes passed by the Convention at Westminster, which "did not a little amaze me." He dwelt, not upon the King's return, now inevitable, but upon "our whole settlement."[78]

Broghil and others like him who had acquired large estates as a reward for their part in the Cromwellian conquest obviously had hoped that before the Restoration a promise should be obtained to safeguard the owners of confiscated lands. The Convention had tried to get this question settled and had sent two of its members, Sir John Clotworthy and William Aston, to England on March 30. They were instructed to ask that the transplantation of the Irish to Connaught and County Clare might be good and effectual, that the decrees granted to transplantable persons and dispositions of land and all decrees made on behalf of such as had manifested their constant good affection to the English interest might be ratified, and that the Roman Catholics of Cork, Yonghal, and Kinsale, who had not aided the late rebellion might be exempted from personal transplantation. Much more significant was the instruction to obtain confirmation of the grants made to adventurers by the act 16 Charles I, and of the land given officers and soldiers under the Act of Satisfaction, September 26, 1653, and to Broghil, Coote, Michael Jones deceased, Henry Jones, and to the children of the late Charles Coote.[79]

This request for confirmation of the settlement which had transferred much of the land to new owners and established an alien landlordism was not then granted, but substantially it was ceded at the Restoration. No one in England had the necessary authority to give a legal guarantee to the landlords. The King, as the Irish commissioners pointed out in an address to Parliament, did not mention Ireland in his letters to the Houses or in his Declaration from Breda. They, therefore, asked that he be advised to summon a parliament to meet there because, owing to the late bloody rebellion, great disorder and confusion obtained which required speedy remedies. Both Houses agreed to advise the King to call

[78] Mar. 17, Apr. 24, May 2, 8; Thurloe, VII, 859, 908, 911-12. The declaration is printed in *Mercurius Publicus*, pp. 290-291.

[79] The above articles are to be found in Hist. MSS Comm. *Eighth Report*, 1, 49. The full text is not known to survive. The two acts mentioned are in *Acts and Ordinances*, I, 70; II, 722. 16 Charles I is in *Statutes of the Realm*, V, 176-77.

an Irish parliament to consist of protestant lords and commons. They also concurred in a most important declaration which Charles II issued as a proclamation on June 1.[80]

The King was proclaimed at Dublin on May 14 in the form prescribed by the English parliament.[81] His restoration was legally as unconditional in Ireland as in England. Yet the proclamation contained a very significant, implied condition. It began by asserting, without any strict adherence to the truth, that many native Irish, guilty of the rebellion of 1641, had recently been robbing and murdering English Protestants and taking possession of their estates by force. Therefore, being conscious of the innocent blood of many thousands slain by these barbarous rebels, all of them were to be proceeded against as traitors. Adventurers and soldiers, occupying on January 1 any lands of the aforesaid rebels, were to remain in undisturbed possession of them until the King should, by the advice of Parliament, give further directions or until they should be ejected by due process of law.[82] This policy was followed after the Restoration with exceptions in favor of individuals. Thus the native Irish were condemned to be hewers of wood and drawers of water on land they regarded as rightfully their own. The ascendancy class which dominated Ireland for more than two centuries was being created.

---

[80]See the *Journals* of both Houses from May 11 to 29. Steele, *Tudor and Stuart Proclamations*, England, No. 3220, and Ireland, No. 620; Carte, *Ormonde Papers*, IV, 9-10; Bagwell, *Ireland under the Stuarts*, III, 6.

[81]Old *Parliamentary History*, XXII, 275-76.

[82]Already the Irish estates of regicides were being seized. *Mercurius Publicus*, p. 357.

CHAPTER XIV

The Rump and Monck's March to London

THE LONG PARLIAMENT sat for its last session from December 26 to March 16. Its history may be conveniently divided into two parts by Monck's arrival in London on February 3. Until that day members had six weeks in which to deal with many problems—the army, revenue, and the future constitution being the most urgent. During that time they occupied a more advantageous position than during the previous summer because they were no longer in danger from the English army, which had repudiated its leaders to recall the Rump. The armies in Scotland, Ireland, and Flanders, and the navy, were, or were about to be, pledged to their support. But their position was stronger in appearance than in reality. In spite of promises, the armies were unlikely to render unconditional obedience because their loyalty to the Rump was steadily being undermined by the almost universal cry for a free Parliament. As soon as men began to breathe normally after the excitement of the English army's submission, their enthusiasm for the Rump quickly evaporated. Its short-lived popularity had rested upon no other foundation than that the alternative governments seemed to be the Rump or the sword. When the menace of the sword disappeared, the Rump soon ceased to be regarded as indispensable. Indeed, members had scarcely taken their seats before Bordeaux concluded that London and the country liked Parliament no better than the army. A tract dated on the anniversary of the execution of Charles I boldly stated that the Rump was "generally *hated*, very little either *loved* or *feared*."[1]

The center of disaffection was London. Recent elections to fill vacancies in the court of aldermen had returned some pronounced Royalists, several being knighted at the Restoration.[2] The court of common council, chosen annually, was elected this year on December 21. A newspaper reported that many members of the previous council, having proved themselves to be of great experience and integrity, were again chosen.[3] Probably the former members, who were thought to be Royalists at

[1]Guizot, II, 324. A Royalist agreed with the Frenchman, *Clarendon Calendar*, IV, 493; *No Droll, but a Rational Account* (1660).

[2]A. B. Beaven, *The Aldermen of the City of London* (1908), II, 89-90.

[3]My copy is defective but I think it belongs to the *Weekly Intelligencer*, No. 33, p. 261. The electors of the councillors were urged not to vote for anyone who had sat on a high court of justice, or on sequestration committees, or who had been farmers of excise, or customs, purchasers of forfeited estates or officers of the present army. *An Admonition of the Greatest Concernment* (1659). Cf. *The Resolve of the Citie*, Dec. 23. The reader will notice that similar appeals were issued to electors of the Convention.

heart, were now joined by councillors more open in their attachment to monarchy. On January 4, 1660, the court decided to settle the trained bands of the City. A strong committee was named to confer with Hesilrige and other members of Parliament about filling up the House of Commons by admitting the secluded members and new elections in the place of persons deceased. Furthermore the committee was instructed to discuss the calling of a free parliament. Nothing definite is known about the result of this conference, but the large Royalist element among the City representatives and their demand for a free parliament are likely to have convinced Hesilrige and the other Rumpers that no agreement was possible and that coercive measures against the City were imperative. At or about the same time orders were given that the gates of the City should be strengthened and chains and posts set up in the several precincts.[4] A clean sweep was made of the militia officers appointed by the army as recently as the previous month. Men like John Ireton, Owen Rowe, William Kiffin, and Robert Tichborne soon gave way to Royalists like William Wale, William Vincent, and John Robinson.[5]

A petition to Parliament was drafted and called for the admission of the secluded numbers, but its presentation was postponed.[6] The City had another way of proclaiming its desires.[7] The military precautions adopted by the City alarmed the Rump and a deputation headed by Hesilrige went to confer with the Lord Mayor and aldermen. Hesilrige reported that the City fathers did not mean to set up posts and chains in the streets, and those already in position would be taken down. He also claimed that they owned the Parliament and promised obedience to its authority.[8] He was silent on the calling out and reorganizing of the trained bands. If he expected the common council to pause and await Parliamentary directions, he was disappointed, because it ordered the settlement of the trained bands to proceed. At the same time its committee was directed to press for a full and free Parliament.[9] It could not seize the initiative without a revolutionary innovation, because, by recent precedents, to the aldermen belonged the first perusal and approval (or disapproval) of any petition addressed to the common

[4]Sharpe, *London and the Kingdom*, II, 360-361; *Clarendon Calendar*, IV, 493, 495-97, 500. This information is derived from the records of the common council, a film of which has been acquired by the Huntington Library from the Corporation of London Records Office through the courtesy of Philip E. Jones, the deputy keeper. I regret the film did not arrive in time for me to use it for the whole period with which I am dealing.

[5]*Publick Intelligencer*, No. 203, Nov. 16. Bordeaux wrote that the colonels were very Royalist and that Presbyterians were not considered zealous enough (Guizot, II, 323).

[6]Sharpe, II, 363.

[7]See below, p. 266, for the letter to Monck.

[8]*Journals*, Dec. 31, Jan. 2.

[9]Sharpe, II, 364.

council.[10] The aldermen were not likely to assume the lead in upsetting the Republic because, according to Mordaunt, nineteen out of the twenty-four had purchased crown and church lands "which, with other mercenary motives, makes them a corrupt court."[11] During January, therefore, the civic authorities took no decisive steps. Citizens waited with painful anxiety to learn whether Monck would take his stand with the City or with Parliament. Pepys, who recognized this antithesis, also noted belief that the common council would not levy any taxes at the Rump's order. Time was to show that he was premature by little more than a month.[12]

Smaller cities were as restless as London. Some of them were now forced to pay the soldiers stationed in their midst to prevent free quarters or plundering. Risings or, rather, tumults were not infrequent, some of the rioters varying their cries for a free Parliament by shouts of "Charles Stuart." But the presence or arrival of regular troops soon dispelled the crowds.[13] The whole country was seething with discontent. The soldiers, who had been denounced as janissaries for interrupting the Rump, were now cursed as its mainstay and as the bar to a free Parliament.[14] Actually, a section of the army preferred a free Parliament to the Rump, as the mutinies in London were to demonstrate.

The really important issue which the Rump could not dodge for long was constitutional. In its simplest terms it was whether the remnant of a Parliament elected in 1640 would repeat its tactics of 1653 and try to perpetuate itself in power by merely filling vacant seats or would dissolve itself and leave the determination of how England should be ruled to "a free and full Parliament, which is at present the desires, and the hopes, and expectation of all."[15] There was the further question whether the Rump would try to bind the hands of future parliaments by a written

[10]The late A. B. Beaven stated that the aldermen assumed the same attitude towards the councillors as the English Parliament to the Irish under Poyning's law (Aldermen of London, II, xlvii).

[11]To the King, Jan. 20, 1660. Clarendon State Papers, III, 650. A broadside entitled satirically, The Humble Petition of Richard Cromwell, complained that the mayor and aldermen preferred perpetual bondage to hazarding their vast estates for the purchase of their freedom.

[12]Jan. 5, 13.

[13]For riots at Bristol, see John Latimer, Annals of Bristol in the 17th Century (Bristol, 1900), pp. 290-291; and at Exeter, Mercurius Politicus, under Jan. 17.

[14]Complaints and Queries upon Englands Misery, by E. D.; The Northern Queries from the Lord Gen: Monck (both about October or November, 1659); The Red-Coats Catechism (dated by Thomason February 9, 1660). In the last tract occurs: "I believe in Sir Arthur Hasilrigge the whole number of Sectaries and Conventicles, the Council of State, the Act of Oblivion, the resurrection of my Lord Lambert, and the continuance of our power to everlasting." One verse of a ballad sums up the popular opinion of the army:

When our Masters are Poor, we Leave 'em
'Tis the Golden Calf we bow too;
We kill, and we slay,
Not for Conscience, but Pay;
Give us That, wee'l fight for you too.
(Rump: or an Exact Collection, II, 9)

[15]The quotation is from the brief introductory note Pepys prefixed to his Diary.

constitution. The answers to these questions should explain why a body cheered by citizens and soldiers alike when it began its last session became the object of almost universal derision on the night of the roasting of the Rump.

The Speaker and about forty members[16] assembled at Westminster on the evening of December 26. The accusation was made at the time that they met at such an unusually late hour, after Lenthall had secretly summoned the Rumpers to convene first at Whitehall, in order to prevent secluded members entering simultaneously. To the same end they are reported to have hastened to the House early the next morning. But they had not sat for long before twenty-two secluded members appeared at the entrance. They prevailed upon Colonels Okey and Alured to admit them into the lobby but they got no further. All their demands to see the orders for excluding them elicited only the response that the orders were verbal. At length the sergeant at arms informed them that the House had voted, in effect, that on January 5 the business of the absent members would be taken into consideration. After this "disdainful affront" they departed, and some of them at once took pen in hand to inform Englishmen of the treatment their representatives had received.[17] On January 5 a vote was passed that the members discharged from sitting and voting in 1648 and 1649 were now expelled and that writs should be issued to elect new members in their places. Four days later musketeers were sent to seize the secluded members who were meeting at Arthur Annesley's house to draw up a declaration of their "unjust and anti-parliamentary exclusion," but the birds had flown. Prynne, therefore, took up their defense alone and produced *The Case of the Old Secured, Secluded, and now Excluded Members,* one of the best of his many pamphlets. He outlined the story of Pride's Purge, vindicated freedom of speech in Parliament, and showed how absurd was the indignation of a quarter of the members (i.e., the Rump) at their expulsions by Cromwell and by Lambert, when they themselves were excluding by force three-quarters of their number.[18]

[16]The highest number of members present was on December 30, when sixty-two appeared to ballot for the Council of State. *Journals,* VII, 800. In the early divisions less than fifty, sometimes less than forty, voted.

[17]The source used is A *Brief Narrative,* published by some of the secluded members. It gives the names of the twenty-two, including Sir William Waller, Arthur Annesley, Sergeant Maynard, and William Prynne, who was probably a co-author. It also lists forty-two Rumpers, among whom were Vane, Salwey, and Sydenham, now required to make a quorum but later expelled or suspended. One noteworthy point is the frank statement that on January 5, 1642, "upon a small breach of privilege, in comparison to this, made by the late King, in demanding only five Members of the House of Commons, after a particular impeachment of high Treason, without secluding any," the House voted the same a high breach of the rights and privileges of Parliament. "Whereas above 200 of us living stand still secluded, without the least offer of an impeachment."

[18]The pamphlet is the authority for the vote of January 5 which does not appear in the *Journals,* having been obliterated according to the order of February 21.

The most urgent business before the House was the army. Until three or more of the seven commissioners appointed on October 12 should arrive in London and take charge, a new committee of seven was named for the purpose. At the same time a month's pay was ordered for the private soldiers, and two days later officers under the rank of captain and noncommissioned officers were included in the vote.[19] All forces raised without Parliamentary authority, except by Monck, were to be disbanded. Regiments in the north of England were to repair to such quarters as the army commissioners should direct. To provide for the urgent need of money acts to continue customs and excise to March 1 and to authorize a loan of £20,000 were speedily passed.[20] Later an act for a monthly assessment of £100,000 was passed.[21] Votes of thanks were extended to the leaders of the movement that restored Parliament. The officers promoted or commissioned by Monck were confirmed in their respective ranks, and his removal of others was approved.[22] A Council of State was chosen by ballot. Following precedent, twenty-one were to be members and ten non-members. Of the twenty-one, twelve had belonged to the earlier body, but three only of the non-members. Hesilrige again received the most votes, a tribute to his staunchness in upholding the rights of Parliament as represented by the Rump. He became the unacknowledged leader of the House and one of the most important men in England for the next two months. The omitted members were far more significant than the recruits. No doubt Colonel Fagge and John Weaver deserved some reward for their recent services, and Henry Marten could be trusted to enliven proceedings by his jests. The others carried little weight and compared very unfavorably with men of the caliber of Vane, Ludlow, Salwey, Algernon Sidney, and Whitelocke. Ashley Cooper and Berners were the first chosen of the non-members, of whom the only important new members were Monck and Lawson, the rejected including Lambert, Disbrowe, Berry, and Johnston of Wariston. The nomination of several citizens of London suggests a desire to cultivate the City.

After these early votes Parliament gave great attention to the army. The three commissioners, Hesilrige, Morley, and Walton, on their arrival from Portsmouth on December 29, were ordered to appoint officers to command regiments.[23] A sweeping vote on January 2 indemnified for life and estate all officers in commission on October 11 and all

[19]Dec. 26 and 28.
[20]Dec. 27.
[21]Jan. 16, 23, 24, 26 .
[22]Dec. 29.
[23]Dec. 31.

other officers and soldiers in the "late defection," provided they had submitted or should submit before January 9 to Parliamentary authority. But they were to be "disposed of" by the Council of State, the army commissioners, or General Monck. By twenty-eight to eighteen votes Lambert was included in the indemnity, but a proposal that all should be guaranteed liberty as well as life was defeated by twenty-eight to fifteen.[24] Lambert, Disbrowe, and the other seven officers cashiered in October were ordered to repair to whichever of their residences were farthest from London. Vane's regiment was disbanded. The army commissioners soon got busy and from January 11 onward lists of officers were given the House and each name was voted upon individually. Approved officers came and received their commissions from the Speaker. There were many new faces, but how many it is difficult to reckon. Ludlow speaks of "fifteen hundred old officers" as removed from their commands but this figure is impossible because there were not so many officers in the regiments concerned.[25] The total army then consisted of about twenty-four regiments of horse and thirty-seven of foot, of which four of the one and eleven of the other were under Monck and so excluded from the new purge. The lists printed in the *Journals* allow twenty-four officers for a regiment of horse and thirty-four for one of foot, a total of 1,364 in all.[26] An examination of Disbrowe's horse shows that it lost its colonel, major, three captains, two lieutenants, an ensign, and a quartermaster.[27] In the regiment of which Richard Moss was colonel, three captains, five lieutenants, four ensigns, and the surgeon's mate disappeared.[28] If these regiments may be taken as typical, the fraction that was discharged was, therefore, about three-eighths, or more than five hundred. If account is taken of the Cromwellians cashiered the previous summer, perhaps more than half the officers were new to their positions. No wonder cohesion was lacking during the winter and spring of 1660.

The cleavage between the two main sections of the Republican civilians was emphasized by the expulsion from Parliament of members who had sided with the army. Vane was a natural choice as the first victim. He was also ordered to repair to his house at Raby Castle in the county

<hr>

[24]In the first division the tellers were Hesilrige and Neville for the ayes and Weaver and Colonel Hutchinson for the noes; in the second Hesilrige and Rich told for the minority and Fagge and Hutchinson for the majority.

[25]*Memoirs*, II, 204.

[26]The total includes the Dunkirk regiments, one of horse and six of foot (of which three were now in England). The 24 officers included 4 for each troop, the infantry 30 for 10 companies plus 4 regimental officers.

[27]See *Journals*, July 4, 1659, and Jan. 12 for the lists compared.

[28]*Journals*, July 1 and Feb. 1.

of Durham, and to remain there during the pleasure of Parliament.[29] The Presbyterians in the House wished to seize the opportunity of expelling other sectaries as guilty as Vane, but were opposed by Hesilrige.[30] Yet on January 17, Sydenham and Salwey were both discharged from their membership and the latter sent to the Tower. The *Journals* state that he declined to try to justify himself or to extenuate his fault but submitted to the judgment of the House as one sensible of his errors. Whitelocke heard that Scot had threatened he should be hanged with the great seal about his neck, observed for himself "a great sharpness" in Parliament toward all who had served on the committee of safety, and prudently retired to the country.[31]

On January 23, a whole day was devoted to a Declaration which after sundry amendments was ordered to be printed. It began with a statement how Parliament had established the Commonwealth and enumerated various benefits it would have bestowed upon the people had it not been so often interrupted. Then a paragraph was devoted to current misrepresentations—how the present members meant to perpetuate themselves, to govern by force, to abolish tithes, and to encourage fanatical principles. The rest of the Declaration consisted of six articles. The Commonwealth, without a king or house of lords, was to be established so that the people would be governed by representatives chosen by themselves, and the army made obedient to the civil authority. The administration of the law should not be interfered with by Parliament. Ministers would be supported by tithes. Universities and schools would be encouraged to promote godliness, learning, and good manners. Trade, now greatly decayed, would be restored. Every care would be taken to ease the people of their present burdens.[32]

Pepys's comment on this string of platitudes was that Parliament declared "for law and gospel, and for tythes; but I do not find people apt to believe them."[33] There was no reason why people should give credence to the Declaration. There had been so many similar documents in the past, mostly waste paper. Insofar as this particular example had any distinction, its interest is in its omissions rather than its contents. Nothing is said about the work of reformation this time, and the silence

---

[29]Jan. 9. Bordeaux (Guizot, II, 329) asserts that an intercepted letter showed that Vane had kept up an extensive correspondence with Lambert. If so, it seems to have perished.

[30]Guizot, II, 331. Ludlow (II, 204) complains that Hesilrige was so "elevated" that he could scarcely discern his friends from his enemies.

[31]*Memorials*, IV, 384, 386. His wife burnt many of his official papers "which makes the present relations the less perfect." The rest of his *Memorials* is little more than a digest of newspapers.

[32]Reprinted in the old *Parliamentary History*, XXII, 58-62.

[33]*Diary*, Jan. 24.

can hardly have been accidental.[34] In the absence of evidence, the conjecture may be ventured that Hesilrige, Ashley Cooper, and politicians of this type realized how unpopular the attempt to make men moral—as precisionists understood morality—by legislation had been. They disavowed "fanatical principles," and among these they may have included Puritan asperities. But more important to contemporaries was the neglect to indicate the form of government proposed. Here no speculation is needed. The reason is evident. The members could not agree.

All members of Parliament had taken the Engagement to be faithful to a commonwealth. However, a proposal to add to it a clause renouncing Charles Stuart and promising resistance to the setting up of any single person or house of lords met with strong opposition. Tried with the newly chosen Council of State, it was at first taken by twelve only and later by one other. Inasmuch as Ashley Cooper swallowed the Engagement,[35] the renunciation must have been what he could not stomach, and his reluctance to pledge himself to oppose a restoration is likely to have been shared by others.[36] The bill for exacting an oath abjuring Charles Stuart from every present and future member of Parliament was introduced on January 3 and given a first reading only by twenty-four to fifteen. Hutchinson, a teller for the minority, is reported by his adoring wife to have thought it ridiculous "to *swear out* a man when they had no power to defend themselves against him," and to have declared how the oaths formerly imposed had multiplied the sins of the nation by perjuries.[37] How many members were swayed by fear they might cause England to sin and how many by a desire not to appear as out-and-out opponents of a Restoration there is no means of telling, but the wordly wisdom of men like Cooper is unmistakable. There were certainly enough of both kinds to prevent the passage of the bill.[38]

Progress was slow on the question which agitated all men's minds, the future composition of Parliament. It was easy to resolve that vacancies by death should be filled, but more difficult to decide the qualifications for members and electors. Not until the day after Monck's arrival in London was the resolution taken that the House should be "filled up to 400 members, that the distribution of seats should be as in 1653, and that a committee should decide which seats were vacant and how the

---

[34]Mayors and justices of the peace were enjoined to see that all laws for the strict observance of the Lord's day were observed. *Journals,* Jan. 7.

[35]On taking his seat as member for Downton on January 7.

[36]See the list of attendances prefixed to the *Calendar Domestic, 1659-1661,* where Mrs. Lomas gives only thirty names instead of thirty-one, forgetting that there were two Loves, one an M.P. and the other an alderman. Cf. Guizot, II, 332.

[37]*Life,* p. 317.

[38]Bordeaux (Guizot, II, 329) stresses the bitterness of this debate.

House should be filled up."[39] Two days later Pepys noted graphic if vulgar illustrations of the general contempt in which the Rump was held "among all the good and bad." The phrase, "filled up," twice repeated in as many lines, showed that the Rumpers had learned nothing from their ignominious experiences. They were arrogating to themselves the right to sit as long as they lived after the new elections, for which they omitted to set a date. They would be in a large minority, but they may well have expected to have exercised over the newcomers an influence wholly disproportionate to their weight because of their long experience of parliamentary tactics.[40] Meanwhile they had yet to settle who might elect or be elected. As the French ambassador saw, to ensure that the new members would favor the present government was difficult because the people were so alienated. Yet the time for debating was brief, and the need for action urgent because civilians and soldiers alike were losing patience.[41]

At Coldstream Monck was now ready to undertake the greatest enterprise in his life. He was well known to his fellow countrymen for distinguished service in Ireland, Scotland, and at sea, but his one appearance on an English battlefield had been most unhappy. He had joined the army Ormonde sent from Ireland to fight for Charles I, had been captured at the battle of Nantwich by the Parliamentary forces under Fairfax in January, 1644, and confined in the Tower for two years. Sixteen years later he was about to cross the Tweed to co-operate with Fairfax in re-establishing parliamentary government. The son of Devonshire gentlefolk, he was now fifty-one years old. During more than thirty years he had been practicing the art of war. His experience of civil government had been limited to Scotland, where he had been content to execute the orders he received from London. Alone of Cromwell's lieutenants he had so conducted himself as to win the esteem both of soldiers and civilians. Now he was emerging from his subordinate position. He was appearing on a larger stage and playing the leading part. He was fortunate at the start because he could count on a diversion in the rear of the opposing army under Lambert.

Fairfax had kept his promise and the handful of men he started with was soon swollen by the adhesion of Royalists and Presbyterians. The burden of maintaining Lambert's men and their insolence had alienated the north countrymen. Fairfax was troubled at the prospect of bringing

[39]See *Journals*, Jan. 3, 11, 31; Feb. 4. Presumably the need of guidance on how the House should be filled up was because the sitting members represented constituencies that would no longer exist according to the Instrument of Government of 1653.

[40]As already stated, this was the case in Richard's Parliament.

[41]Letter of Feb. 6/16, Guizot, II, 341.

his volunteers face to face with old soldiers, but there was to be no fighting. Smithson brought over four of the six troops of Lilburne's horse, so all immediate danger vanished. Then the Irish brigade joined him at the rendezvous on Marston Moor and presented him with a declaration against government by a single person. He tore it up and placed himself at the head of his own troops. Though in poor health, he seemed to an observer to become another man, "his motions so quick, his eyes so sparkling, giving the word of command like a General, that I took heart." His resolute attitude sufficed, and the Irish brigade ceased to try to be politicians. Meanwhile, Sir Philip Monckton and others secured York.[42] The garrison Lambert had left there under Lilburne admitted Fairfax, partly because the citizens all shouted "A Fairfax" and "A free Parliament" and partly because Monckton promised it the same terms that had been offered to the Irish brigade and the troops of Lilburne's horse which had changed sides—payment of arrears and also a reward. If the second reason was the more potent, the soldiers' dislike of living at free quarters is a sufficient explanation. Lambert's army melted away and Monck had no other obstacles to his march south than the snow and ice.[43]

> George and his Boyes (as Spirits do, they say)
> Only by walking scare our Foes away.[44]

Monck was as punctilious as Fairfax in observing the agreement they had reached and began his celebrated march on London on Sunday, January 1. He had just heard that the forces in London had repented once again and permitted the Rump to return to Westminster. He sent Knight on ahead with some troops of horse, and the infantry to follow. He himself crossed the Tweed the next day with the rest of the cavalry. He had with him all his four regiments of horse and six regiments of foot. He soon divided his army into two brigades, one comprising his own and Knight's horse, and his own, Fairfax's, and Lytcott's foot, the other Morgan's and Clobery's horse, and Morgan's, Reades's, and Hubblethorne's foot.[45] The going was hard in the very wintry weather with

[42]Brian Fairfax, "Iter Boreale," a narrative printed in Bell, *Memorials of the Civil War*, II, 151-74; "The Monckton Papers," ed. Edward Peacock, in *Miscellanies of the Philobiblon Society*, XV (1877), 24-42. At first the officers of Lilburne's horse objected to the presence of Cavaliers, but seem quickly to have acquiesced in their helping Fairfax to secure Yorkshire. Hist. MSS Comm. *Fifth Report*, p. 193b. Another account ascribes to Bethel the opposition to old Cavaliers. *A Letter from a Captain of the Army*, dated Tadcaster, Jan. 2. A messenger from Monck reported in London that he had passed through Northallerton and found Lambert there with fifty horsemen only, the rest of his army having declared for the Parliament as Lambert had also done. *Mercurius Politicus*, under Jan. 4.

[43]For outrages committed by Lambert's forces see *Life of Hutchinson*, pp. 313-15; and for an article on why the rank and file acquiesced in the Restoration, see *Journal of the Society of Army Historical Research*, XXXII (1954), pp. 26-29.

[44]Robert Wild, *Iter Boreale*, printed on St. George's Day, 1660, by George Thomason.

[45]Gumble, *Life of Monck*, p. 192; *Clarke Papers*, IV, 238.

frost and snow so continuous that, according to Price, "I do not remember that ever we trod upon *plain earth* from Edenburgh to London." The men stepped out bravely because, after an absence of ten years, they were marching towards their homes.[46]

Whether the rank and file were conscious of the importance of their mission is unknown. Perhaps the safest surmise is that they were content to obey orders and to march in support of a Parliament to which they looked for their maintenance. Now that the politico-religious enthusiasts, both officers and cavalrymen, who had shown a greater interest in politics than infantrymen from the beginning of the war, had been weeded out, Price was justified in saying that the soldiers did not trouble their heads about religious parties but fought for their pay.[47] Monck, a better authority than his chaplain on such a point, informed the Speaker just before starting that his army was "very cheerfull and unanimous, willing to endure any hardship for your Service." Of the newly appointed or promoted officers he said they were very honest, "ready to die for your Service, or disband at your Command."[48]

The first day's journey brought Monck to Wooler where he received a kind letter from the Speaker, informing him of the readmission of the Rump but saying nothing about his marching south. This, we are told, "increased his jealousy."[49] Two days later he reached Morpeth where he met William Man, the sword-bearer of the City of London, who at long last brought an answer to his letter of November 12. The explanations of this delay were doubts of its authenticity, which caused the imprisonment of its bearers, Colonels Samuel Atkins and Henry Markham, and possibly dislike of its contents.[50] Monck's letter had affirmed the writer's intention to restore Parliament to its former freedom and authority and the people to their rights and liberties. It called upon the City to do its part in the south while he faced the army in the north, an appeal he was confident no Englishmen would ignore. The reply was most cordial. It claimed that the City had contributed to check the presumptions of those who had interrupted the Parliament, and referred him to its declaration for proof how entirely they complied with him. He answered with many compliments, reiterations of his determination to restore the Parliament

[46]Maseres, *Select Tracts*, II, 749. Though the horse had been regularly changed, the foot had not been relieved.

[47]Maseres, II, 712.

[48]A *Letter sent from General Monck Dated at Coldstream, Dec. 29.* Monck wrote a letter to the Speaker containing a similar phrase from Wooler, *Clarke Papers*, IV, 238-39.

[49]Maseres, II, 750. Gumble (pp. 196-97) thought the letter "as cold as the night." Actually the Speaker wrote Monck two letters of similar content, probably to ensure that one reached him. *Clarke Papers*, IV, 222-23. Neither mentions a march southward but both fully acknowledge that the restoration of Parliament was due to Monck and his army.

[50]*Leyborne-Popham MSS*, pp. 136-37; Whitelocke, *Memorials*, IV, 375.

as it sat on October 11, and added that his forces would not count their lives "too precious to hazard for your welfare."[51]

Gumble wrote that Monck, as soon as his army was on the march, dispensed with general councils of officers with whom he had hitherto conferred. The ostensible reason was that they were no longer necessary but the true one was that "publike assemblies were not agreeable to his Designs."[52] From Durham, Sir Joseph Douglas, one of Monck's Scottish intimates, was dispatched to Ireland to get into touch with Sir Charles Coote in order that the forces there, which had just overthrown the faction that had supported the English army leaders, should declare for a free parliament.[53] At Newcastle the inhabitants begged Monck that the militia might be entrusted to safe hands, the officers who adhered to Lambert reduced, and no Anabaptists or Quakers admitted to places of trust, civil, or military. This concern was unnecessary as the General had already appointed new commissioners for the militia.[54]

Five days were spent at York. By this time all danger of resistance from Lambert had vanished. His army disintegrated, some, perhaps most, of it going to quarters designated by Parliament and some stealing off whither they would go. No doubt Parliament found a special pleasure in depriving Lilburne of his regiment because when he heard that his friend Lambert had expelled the Rump he exclaimed "that he hoped never a true Englishman would name the Parliament again, and that he would have the house pulled down where they sat for fear it should be infectious."[55] He had been foremost among Monck's opponents but his hour had passed. Because no opposition was now to be feared, Monck sent two regiments back to Scotland, whither he intended Morgan should return as acting commander in chief, and left Colonel Fairfax with his foot regiment to garrison York. Naturally Monck called on Lord Fairfax but no satisfactory account of the interview survives. That written long afterwards by Brian Fairfax asserts that Monck offered to resign his command to Fairfax, who declined the offer but frankly stated that only the restoration of monarchy and a free parliament would constitute a satisfactory settlement. Monck himself, however, at the time assured John Weaver that Fairfax had agreed in a private conference to join with him if needs be in opposing Charles Stuart.[56] Certainly Monck

[51]The old *Parliamentary History*, XXII, 46-52.
[52]Gumble, p. 202.
[53]Maseres, II, 751.
[54]*Leyborne-Popham MSS*, p. 139.
[55]*Calendar Domestic, 1659-1660*, p. 295.

[56]Brian Fairfax did not write his narrative, printed in *Memorials*, ed. Robert Bell, II, 168-69, until 1699, and Price (Maseres, II, 753) who confirms him to some extent, not until 1680. Monck's letter is in the *Clarke Papers*, IV, 250-251.

was careful to disavow any intention of doing more than support the Parliament and cudgeled an officer publicly who said he was going to restore the King.[57] Before leaving York he received the parliamentary resolution that he should come to London.[58]

Little of importance happened until he established his headquarters at Mansfield on January 18. Here he received the report of Gumble whom he had dispatched from Newcastle with letters of credence to Parliament, the Council of State, the commissioners of the army, and Fairfax, but also with private instructions. Gumble was received by Parliament on January 12, voted £100, and heard that Monck's "taking up" horses and marching into England were approved. The brief references in the *Journals* say nothing of Gumble's message which according to his own account contained some veiled criticisms. Parliament was urged not to trust persons of seditious or unsettled principles but men of sober judgment, to prevent the scandal caused by the intrusion into pulpits of many mechanical persons, to reward Scotland for its devotion in the recent crisis, and to confirm the commissions Monck had granted. The conclusion Gumble reached after being questioned was that Parliament "neither dares to trust, nor yet openly distrust the General, and perhaps they had reason." He never met the Council of State or commissioners of the army formally, and refused to divulge his instructions to individuals or unofficial groups. They seemed most fearful that Monck was a Royalist at heart, but Gumble merely upheld that such suggestions emanated from their own jealousies and fears. When they asked him to go to interview Fleetwood he flatly refused. The most satisfaction he received was at conferences at the Speaker's lodging where all the lawyers and men that had any spark of honor or honesty met and approved Monck's proceedings. He also consulted Robinson and other prominent citizens and found them all "expectants of Deliverance from the General." They were assured that he would do their business if they would give him time. Gumble also reported that the House of Commons was divided between the abjurers and non-abjurers, and that those who opposed the proposed new oath against Charles Stuart were Monck's friends.[59]

At Nottingham Monck paused to allow the infantry in the rear to catch up, and utilized the time in writing letters. To the Speaker he justified his march into England as a pursuit of Lambert whose forces had not then dispersed, and he explained that he had secured the northern

[57]Maseres, II, 753.

[58]Passed January 6.

[59]Gumble, pp. 204, 207-21.

counties the best he could in so short a time and taken care of Scotland. The troops there would suffice until replacements could be sent from the south. He had put out some militia captains that had done the Parliament disservice. He had ordered the Irish brigade to march into Cheshire, having first named six honest officers whom he trusted would be confirmed in their new positions. He praised Redman and Brett, now in command. He adhered to his appointment of Colonel Hugh Bethell to Lambert's horse, although he had heard that the commissioners in London had named Twisleton. He had acted by virtue of the letter the Speaker and others had sent him on December 23.[60] His other correspondence is chiefly of interest as showing whom he reckoned his friends —Chief Justice St. John, whom he praised for his noble resolution to promote a settlement which would avoid "those two rocks of the Malignant and fanaticall interests," Weaver, Ashley Cooper, Widdrington, and Colonels White and Thompson. One incident at Nottingham deserves mention. A proposal was made that the army should subscribe a paper "that we should be obedient to the Parliament in all things, except the bringing in of Charles Stuart." This was answered by the argument that such a declaration would imitate the errors committed by the English army, by constituting the signers judges and consequently masters of parliamentary actions.[61] Perhaps the anxiety thus shown helps to explain the emphatic letter which Monck addressed from Leicester to the gentlemen of Devon in answer to a letter they had sent to the Speaker. The signers were, he said, his friends and relations, so he was telling them his views of the present situation. He argued that several interests now existed which had been unknown in the former monarchical government in church and state. There were on the one hand, Presbyterians, Independents, Anabaptists, and sectaries, and on the other, the purchasers of the forfeited estates of the King, bishops, deans and chapters, and Royalists, and all who had fought against Parliament. Therefore, the restoration of monarchy was impossible "because its support is taken away" and because it was incompatible with the newly created interests, which only a republic could protect. Consequently, to admit the secluded members, very many of whom supported monarchy and the abolition of all laws passed since their expulsion, would be likely to continue the civil war rather than end it. For this reason he counselled submission to the present Parliament "who have resolved to fill up their

[60]This letter is missing. See *Clarke Papers*, IV, 217-18, n. 1. For the letters from Nottingham, see ibid., 247-58. In this last Monck mentioned that he had received the commission from the Council of State of November 24, making him commander in chief of the forces in England and Scotland. The commission was approved by Parliament on January 26.

[61]Maseres, II, 754.

House, determine their Sitting, and prepare a way for future Succes-
sions of Parliament."[62] In a private letter, sent like the above to Robert
Rolle, he urged that the gentry should meet again and declare their
acquiescence in "this Parliament's proceedings." The only sop of comfort he conveyed was that though in the public letter he had seemed to
provide even for "the giddy interests," yet he did not mean to entrust
them with military or civil positions but only to secure their rights as
men and Christians.[63]

Price explained that Monck, to allay any suspicions (possibly aroused
by the stifling of the declaration against Charles Stuart), consented that
the above letter should be sent in his name.[64] If this is true, Monck may
have smiled sardonically when he saw the argument used against the
King because, in the popular literature of the day, no class was damned
more frequently than the purchasers of confiscated property. But he
may well have been anxious to dampen the enthusiasm of his native
county. He knew better than any of those who sent or presented addresses in favor of the secluded members the misgivings in his own
army. Any false step, any precipitate act, might alienate his small army
and give the numerically superior English army a rallying cry. He was
accomplishing the avowed purpose of his intervention in politics—the
freeing of Parliament from military dictation. "Let that suffice for the
present" may well have been his rule as he approached London. Unless
the hypothesis be accepted that he planned the Restoration as soon as he
heard that Lambert had expelled the Rump, there is no reason to regard
him as farsighted; but within his limited range he saw clearly. Hating
rule by the sword, he meant to give the Rump every opportunity to effect
a settlement. Unless it obviously failed, he need take no thought for the
morrow. He was what a contemporary might have called a waiter on
Providence, or, in modern parlance, an opportunist. He had little choice,
because the foundations on which the Commonwealth rested were cracking in all directions. He could scarcely be expected to know how soon
external pressure and internal decay would cause the Republic to
collapse.

The gentlemen of Devon returned a most trenchant reply to Monck.
They asserted that the reasons against a monarchy were that those who
had swallowed up the revenues of the crown were against it, that the
army would never endure it, that a restoration would start a new war,

[62]*Collection of Letters*, pp. 50-52. Monck seems to have been misinformed because there is no evidence that the Rump had settled the date of dissolution.

[63]*Clarke Papers*, IV, 258-60. He also wrote to the same effect to his cousin William Morice, Secretary
of State after the Restoration.

[64]Maseres, II, 754.

and that the nation can never be united except in a republic. Since the King's death the nation had been ruled by force, as a prey to the strongest. "It is a feeble argument against monarchy that we have never been happy since we lost it." If a republic is held necessary, a free parliament ought to introduce it or is it to "exclude a considerable in favor of a small interest?"[65] When arguments of this nature were introduced into addresses, Monck probably welcomed the opportunity of leaving the task of replying to them to others. Henceforth he allowed two parliamentarians to wrangle with those who insisted that only a free parliament would content the people. Before he reached Leicester, Monck met Scot and Robinson who had been delegated by Parliament to go to congratulate and thank him. They were able to tell him of a resolution that £1,000 a year in land should be settled upon "Commissioner" George Monck.[66]

The nearer Monck got to London the greater became the resemblance of his journey to a triumphal march. The ringing of bells and the applause of the multitude greeted him at every town. Many addresses were handed him for a full and free parliament, but his acknowledgments were the briefest possible. He gladly allowed the Parliamentary representatives to answer those who presented the wishes of the various counties.[67] The most vigorous argument between addressers and Scot seems to have been at Stony Stratford. Sir Richard Temple, a former Cromwellian, had urged the gentlemen, ministers, and free-holders of Buckinghamshire, to sign a petition for restoring the secluded ministers, and now presented it in such outspoken language that Colonel Lytcott told him "he would fain hold a trencher again to a single person, as he had done to Oliver, but it must not be." And Scot was so angered that he exclaimed that old as he was he would first take up the sword before the petitioners' demands should be granted. The Rump shared Scot's indignation and committed Temple to the custody of the sergeant at arms, but this and other similar examples failed to stifle the almost universal call for a free parliament.[68]

[65]*Calendar Domestic,* January 28.

[66]*Journals,* Jan. 16. On the next day Scot was formally made Secretary of State, though the duties of this office had been assigned to him on the tenth. Collins in his curious narrative in *Leyborne-Popham MSS* (p. 207) states that Hesilrige could not bear to hear Monck spoken of as General, but the titles in the *Journals* vary, and include General as well as Commissioner and Commissioner General.

[67]Gumble (p. 223) remarked that Norfolk, Devon, Northampton, and Buckinghamshire were the first and boldest counties to demand a free Parliament. These and other addresses were all printed separately. They can be traced in *Thomason Tracts* under the dates: January 13, Leicestershire; 23, Gloucestershire; 24, Northampton; 28, Devon; 30, Suffolk; 31, Norfolk; February, Buckinghamshire and Kent. Not all of the above were addressed to Monck. There were also some general manifestoes. Many addresses can be found in whole or in part in Kennet's *Register,* and some in *Mercurius Politicus.*

[68]See G. Davies, "The Political Career of Sir Richard Temple," in *Huntington Library Quarterly,* IV (1940), 50-51.

The most defiant of the addresses was presented, not to Monck, but to Parliament. *The Declaration of the Gentry of . . . Norfolk*, handed to the Speaker on January 28 by Lord Richardson, Sir John Hobart, and Sir Horatio Townshend, roundly asserted that unless the secluded members were admitted and vacancies filled—and without any oath or engagement—the people of England could not be obliged to pay any taxes. This courageous manifesto, unnoticed in the *Journals*, appears to be the first of its kind which its authors openly acknowledged. Soon more influential areas were to imitate this bold precedent.[69]

Meanwhile the relations between the Rump and the City had rapidly deteriorated. The City, with only a single M.P. to represent it, Alderman Atkins, had been disappointed with Monck's reply to the letter the swordbearer had carried him because he had professed no more than his intention to maintain "this present Parliament, as it sate on October 11."[70] A friend of Pepys informed him that Monck's letter was "a cunning piece" in which the citizens placed little confidence. The same source related how on January 12 Hesilrige and Morley at the Lord Mayor's denounced the City and claimed that it had forfeited its charter and were answered by the chamberlain who told them how greatly they had formerly been indebted to London. The diarist also heard on January 13 that the citizens were resolved not to address Parliament again or pay any taxes until the secluded members were admitted or a free parliament chosen. A new deputation was sent to Monck but the outcome has not been recorded.[71] The general impression seems to have been that Monck was resolved to "stand to the Parliament and nothing else."[72]

An incident at St. Albans deserves a passing notice. February 1 was a fast day and Hugh Peters delivered one of his characteristic sermons on the text: "He led them forth by the right way, that they might go to the City where they dwelt." He explained how, though the distance from the Red Sea to Canaan was a march of only forty days, the Israelites spent forty years in the wilderness in "the Lord's right way, who had led his People crinkledom cum crankledom."[73] After this familiar touch, which helps to explain why his enemies thought him a hypocritical jester and also why many found him a popular preacher, he applied the Biblical story to the present, when the Lord's people were not yet come to the

[69]The bearers of the declaration are said to have been threatened with the Tower, but not sent thither, and to have presented the declaration to Monck at St. Albans, who did not receive it cordially. Hist. MSS Comm. *Fifth Report*, 153a; *Mercurius Politicus*, where the declaration is said to have been given the Speaker on January 28.

[70]Jan. 6, *Collection of Letters*, p. 49.

[71]Sharpe, *London the Kingdom*, II, 364-65.

[72]Pepys, *Diary*, Jan. 30.

[73]I.e., zigzag.

City of Habitation but were still being led in the right way. Price, a listener of very different principles, later claimed that he had thought Peters was preaching his own funeral sermon, though perhaps this recollection was tinged by the knowledge that the preacher had been executed after the Restoration.[74]

From St. Albans Monck sent Lytcott with a letter to Parliament. In it he explained that he was bringing with him three regiments of horse, each 600 strong, and four of foot, each numbering 1,000.[75] He asked that with the exception of the regiments of Fagge and Morley (which he trusted) all the forces in London should be sent to the quarters he assigned to them in lists which he enclosed. The lists assigned widely scattered quarters to the troops or companies of each regiment so that any concerted action would be well-nigh impossible. A typical disposition is provided by Hesilrige's horse which had been one of the two regiments formed from Cromwell's Ironsides. Two troops were now to be quartered at Oxford and one each in Reading, Gloucester, Worcester, and Hereford.[76] To reassure Parliament, Monck pointed out that his regiments contained as many soldiers as the four horse and six foot he wished to be displaced.[77]

Parliament promptly approved the lists Monck had sent for the distribution of the forces that were to leave London and ordered the army commissioners to see that the soldiers went to the assigned quarters.[78] A month's pay was to be given them at the time of their removal. At the same time Monck's trusted brother-in-law, Thomas Clarges, was named commissary general of musters, and £10 a day was voted for a table for the army commissioners, to begin as soon as Monck arrived in London. This hospitality the Speaker is said to have advised Monck to decline, because it was a device of Hesilrige's to keep the general under surveillance and a slave to the rest of the army commissioners.[79]

At first grave difficulties were encountered in inducing the soldiers

[74]Maseres, II, 756-57.

[75]Either Monck or the printer erred in stating that he brought only two regiments of horse, though later in the letter the number is given as three. *Collection of Letters*, pp. 53-54. The colonels of horse were Monck, Knight (late Sanders), and Clobery (late Twistleton); and of foot, Monck, Read, Hubblethorpe (late Talbot), and Lytcott (late Cobbet).

[76]Baker's *Chronicle*, p. 702.

[77]*Collection of Letters*, pp. 53-54. According to the lists in Baker (p. 702) the following were the regiments which were to leave London: horse, Hesilrige, Ashley Cooper (Fleetwood), Rich, and Okey's Dragoons; foot, Streeter (Hewson), Fitch (Fleetwood), Twistleton (Fitch), Moss, Eyre (Lambert), and Markham (actually John Lenthall had now become colonel in place of Markham who had displaced Sydenham). See *Journals*, Feb. 2.

[78]*Journals*, Jan. 30 to Feb. 1. Monck was voted the custody of St. James's Park. Ludlow asserts (II, 211-12) that Monck's letter about the distribution of the regiments in London was contrived by Hesilrige's enemies in Parliament in order to render him impotent. There may be an element of truth in this assertion, but the mutinous conduct of the forces in London soon justified Monck on other grounds.

[79]*Leyborne-Popham MSS*, p. 213.

in London to depart. One regiment was drawn up in St. James's fields to receive orders to march next day. An officer struck a soldier for some insolence and was knocked senseless by the butt end of a musket. The incident started a mutiny. The soldiers refused to mount guard, some crying "let us hang up our officers" and others, "let's tear their clothes from off their backs and strip them naked." All were united in their determination not to leave London without their money. Their colonel eventually appeased them by promises of pay.[80] The example was followed the next day by the regiment lately given to the Speaker's son and stationed at Somerset House and Salisbury Court. When the order to march was given the soldiers refused to stir, tore up their colors and beat and kicked a captain who remonstrated with them. Their pay was fourteen or fifteen weeks behindhand.[81] By night many of them were drunk and shouted sometimes for a free Parliament and sometimes for King Charles the Second. They had been encouraged and treated by apprentices who hoped to gain them as allies in a rising they had planned that night. But the apprentices who assembled at Leadenhall or in the streets were set upon by a party of horse. Those taken prisoners were brutally handled and nearly stripped before being lodged in gaol.[82]

Parliament, at its wits' end for funds, scrutinized payments made during its interruption and demanded the repayment of £8,500, including nearly £7,000 for black cloth for Oliver Cromwell's funeral. The repayments, or personal loans on the strength of them, seem to have brought in enough to satisfy the soldiers who then obeyed orders and departed.[83] The ringleaders of the mutiny had been secured and on February 18 a sergeant and eight soldiers were brought to Charing Cross, four having been sentenced to death and five to be lashed on their bare backs. The four were permitted to cast lots, the two losers being hanged on the spot. The sergeant was given forty stripes, three men thirty-nine, and the others twenty-one. In addition to mutiny, some of these soldiers had been guilty of highway robbery.[84]

[80]Rugge, "Mercurius Politicus Redivivus," p. 56; Pepys, Feb. 1. Rugge describes the regiment as "once Lord Lambert's" and Pepys as formerly Fitch's. I believe the latter is correct because the next day Twistleton's regiment was ordered by Parliament to be paid. George Twistleton had succeeded Fitch.

[81]L'Estrange drew up a paper, "The Sense of the Army," which purported to be the soldier's declaration. It has survived apparently only in Roger L'Estrange, *L'Estrange His Apology* (1660), p. 63. Cf. Massey's letter to Hyde, Feb. 3, Bodleian Library, Clarendon MS. 69, ff. 55-57; Thomas H. Lister, *Life and Administration of Edward, first Earl of Clarendon* (1838), III, 83.

[82]Rugge, pp. 57-58; Pepys, Feb. 2, 3; *Mercurius Politicus*, Feb. 4. Five companies of the regiment formerly Sir Brice Cockran's also mutinied when ordered to march to Gravesend to be transported to Dunkirk, whence the regiment had come the previous August. *Journals*, Feb. 4, 8.

[83]*Journals*, Feb. 2 and 3. The Royalist report that Hesilrige borrowed £30,000 from the City was false. *Clarendon Calendar*, IV, 543. A list in Mackinnon, *Coldstream Guards* (I, 88-89), names four regiments of horse and six of foot as leaving London.

[84]Rugge, p. 70.

During the meeting of Lenthall's regiment, the Council of State had sent Scot hurriedly to Monck at Barnet to urge him to march instantly. But the general, imperturbable as usual, declined to alter his plans for entering the capital on the morrow.[85] Probably he was not sorry that the Rump had been taught, if capable of learning, that it could not rely unconditionally on the soldiers outside Monck's army. It could not reasonably expect to balance the forces from Scotland by the English army. As both bodies were similarly composed, lack of pay might soon cause trouble in Monck's army. Whether the Rump could raise the necessary money was soon to be decided.

[85]Maseres, II, 757. The statement in Rugge that Parliament sent a messenger thrice to Monck to hasten his entry into London is probably an exaggeration if not a complete error. The same compiler noted that five regiments left London.

CHAPTER XV

Monck and the Long Parliament

THE SITUATION as Monck approached London at the end of January, 1660, was obscure. Nominally, the remnant of the Long Parliament was able to exercise an uncontrolled supremacy. The English army was incapable of a united opposition. It was, or was soon to be, scattered, here a troop and there a company. More significant than its separation into small units was its internal divisions. Grandees, subalterns, and privates could no longer agree on a common platform. Monck and his forces, together with the armies beyond the seas and the navy, were pledged to uphold the Rump. Members of Parliament still retained their old belief in their indispensability. Whether they possessed the substance, or merely the shadow, of power was soon to be put to the test.

On February 3, 1660, Pepys watched the Coldstreamers march to Whitehall and noted that they were "in very good plight and stout officers." Monck himself had been greeted with many calls for a free parliament but little other welcome. In the Strand he had met the Speaker and saluted him as representing the sovereign authority. He then took up his quarters at Whitehall where most members of Parliament visited him, rested the next two days, and, we may surmise, gave anxious thought to the speech he was to deliver to Parliament on Monday (February 6).[1] He may have anticipated the approbation of most members because in his letter to the gentlemen of Devon he had adhered to the present body and not supported the admission of the secluded members or a new parliament. Yet he knew that some members, especially Hesilrige and his clique, were suspicious of him for two reasons—he had received addresses in favor of a free parliament, and he commanded the only unified army in England and was certain to be supported by the other forces in Scotland and Ireland. To continue in power and to render the military subordinate to the civil authority seemed the ruling passions of a majority of Rumpers. Monck may well have pondered how he would fare at the hands of such men.[2]

He was escorted to Parliament by Scot and Robinson. A chair was provided for him within the bar, and there he heard the Speaker compare his appearance with his army to the little cloud which Elijah's

[1] Maseres, *Select Tracts*, II, 758; Gumble, *Life of Monck*, p. 228.
[2] Cf. *Clarendon Calendar*, IV, 544, 546.

servant saw at Carmel and which refreshed the whole nation. After hearty thanks to Monck and his officers and men, Lenthall yielded him the floor. The general began in the style then current and attributed the peaceful restoration of Parliament to God alone. He himself had done no more than his duty and was unworthy of the honor now bestowed upon him. He described the addresses he had received en route, desiring a free and full parliament and a date fixed for the dissolution of the present Parliament, a gospel ministry, encouragement of learning and universities, and the admittance of the secluded members without any previous oath or engagement. To the addresses he had replied that Parliament was now free and laws already passed would soon make it full, that the duration of the session had already been settled, and that a decision had been reached about the secluded members. To admit members to sit without any previous engagement was never done in England, but he added what he had not said to the addressers but now ventured to say to members, the fewer oaths the better. He urged that members should seek to enlarge, not to restrict, the boundaries of their party, relying on the sober gentry but excluding from all share in power both Cavaliers and fanatics. He concluded with pleas that Ireland should be gratifed by an act to secure the estates of adventurers and soldiers, and Scotland rewarded with the confirmation of the union and a reduction of taxes so as to make them proportionate to those in England.

The general's admiring biographer, who may well have been present, commented with the understatement that the discourse was "not over-pleasing to many Members of the House, who censured it upon many accounts, but did not think fit to take any notice of it."[3] However, although the *Journals* do not record Monck's speech, it soon found its way into print. The sole response from the Rump was indirect: the next day the arrest was ordered of a number of individuals who had presented addresses to the Parliament or to Monck. Then proceeding with the report of its committee on the qualifications of members and electors of future parliaments, the Rump decided that forty-shilling freeholders should have the vote in counties and that all who had abetted the Irish rebellion and all Roman Catholics should be permanently incapable of being elected or of voting at elections.[4]

February 8 was memorable not for the proceedings at Westminster but for those in the City. On that day the householders and freemen

[3]Gumble, pp. 230-234. Gumble reprints the speech which is also available in the old *Parliamentary History*, XXII, 88-90, and elsewhere. Scot and his party were said to object to the speech as too confident of the Irish army's support, holding out hopes to the Royalists that they might be admitted to offices, and threatening the fanatics with exclusion from power. Baker's *Chronicle*, p. 706.

[4]On the eleventh a resolution was passed disqualifying as electors or elected all who had assisted Charles Stuart since February 1, 1649.

addressed a petition to the Lord Mayor and common council asking them not to submit to any authority that could not rightfully claim the legislative power of the nation or assess or levy any money on petitioners unless voted by such a lawful authority. They were also asked not to cooperate with any other power or person that should impose any law or tax "until the authority thereof may be derived from a full and free Parliament, as being the rightful representatives of the people, by whom every individual doth consent." Then, and then only, might there be a hope of reviving languishing trades and enlarging hearts and purses to a cheerful contribution. The minutes of the common council do not enter the petition but merely state that it would be taken into consideration so far as concerns the court. The persons who presented the petition were thanked "for their respect and long patience."[5] That rumor should magnify this harmless resolution into a vote to pay no taxes until a full Parliament voted them is not surprising, because a similar rumor had been spread a month before.[6] The episode merely epitomized the hostility between the City and the Rump in the strongest way. Whether the citizens formally or individually refused to recognize as legal the Rump's decrees made little difference. The challenge was unmistakable. It must be accepted without delay. Unless the Rump could coerce the citizens into obedience their example would prove infectious and the whole country would soon resound with the cry of no taxes unless levied by a representative parliament. Without a division the House adopted a series of orders Scot recommended from the Council of State: that the army should be used to reduce the City to obedience, to take away the posts and chains, unhinge the gates and wedge the portcullises, and to apprehend eleven citizens.[7] This invidious task was imposed on Monck. Why his friends in the House did not force a division is unknown. Did they perceive that Hesilrige and his supporters were about to cut their own throats and think the sooner the better?

Monck marched into the City, made the arrests except of two persons

[5] See Corporation Records for the terms of the vote of the common council on February 8. At a previous meeting on January 30, a petition from divers inhabitants and freemen of the City was ordered to be handed back to the person who delivered it. Probably this snub was administered to the bearer of the petition presented to the House of Commons less than a fortnight later and described below. The petition of February 8 was printed with the title *To the Right Honourable the Lord Mayor . . . the Humble Petition of divers well-affected householders and freemen*; Pepys, Feb. 9; Roger L'Estrange, (*Apology*, p. 57) claimed to have printed on January 24 a paper entitled "A Plain Case," in which occurred these sentences: "Suppose the City should refuse the Tax [assessment of £100,000 a month]: (the *Countries* are resolved upon't) How *Certain* and *Inevitable*, is their [Rumpers'] *Ruine*?" I regret that I have failed to find this paper as a separate publication. Previously, on January 3, L'Estrange had proposed that no levies of men or money should be suffered (ibid., p. 54).

[6] Pepys, Feb. 9, Jan. 13.

[7] At the same time the army commissioners were authorized to seize any of the nine officers ordered to leave town. Curiously enough, no account seems to name which gates were to be destroyed or which were destroyed. Almost certainly, the House of Commons wished to render useless the defensive measures the common council had recently ordered. See *ante*, p. 257.

not to be found, and ordered the work of destruction to proceed. His officers protested and offered to resign their commissions. They said that they had ventured their lives for their country and adhered to him, but they did not want to affront the City. If they were to be used as scavengers, let them begin at Westminster and make that house clean. Monck paused and sent a letter to the Speaker, urging that, having taken away the posts and chains, he might be excused from the rest of his task lest he exasperate the City. He had good reason to expect that the assessment would be levied if the common council was allowed to meet the next day. Therefore, he had suspended the execution of the remainder of their commands and recommended to their consideration the release of the common councillors arrested by their orders.[8]

Meanwhile the Rumpers had been listening to a petition presented by Praise God Barebones and others in the name of the well-affected persons of London and Westminster. The petitioners, after praising the good old cause, asserted that its restless enemies, in the disguise of a moderate party, had succeeded in getting the subtlest of their friends into many places of trust and command, both civil and military. Owing to the encouragement of these men "a general boldness hath been taken to plead a necessity of returning to the Government of King and Lords . . . or, which is all one, for a Return of the justly-secluded Members, or a Free Parliament, without due Qualifications." Therefore, the petitioners asked that no one should be admitted to a future parliament or council of state or allowed to hold any office, preach, or instruct the youth, who did not denounce Charles Stuart. Anyone who advocated the return of Charles Stuart or a single person or House of Lords or a coercive power in matters of religion should be adjudged guilty of high treason. Here was the price which must be paid to maintain the good old cause. Its enemies, and they had become legion, were once again reminded of the oligarchic conditions essential to its survival. Yet the petitioners were thanked for their constant devotion to Parliament.[9]

In the afternoon the Rumpers reassembled and sent a curt reply to Monck that he was now to destroy the gates and portcullises, whereas formerly he was only to render them useless. They also ordered that the common council elected for the year should be declared null and void, and appointed a committee to draft an act for another council to be elected under such qualifications as the Parliament should think fit. Perversity could not go further. The confidence in Monck's obedience upon which such decisions must have rested appeared at first to be

[8]The old *Parliamentary History*, XXII, 92-93. In a postscript Monck urged that the House would "hasten your qualifications that the writs may be sent out" which would pacify the country.

[9]The old *Parliamentary History*, XXII, 95-97; *Journals*, Feb. 9, morning session.

justified. The gates were destroyed and the portcullises rendered useless, but the soldiers showed plainly how they hated the task set them. They told the citizens "that they came from Scotland where their enemies loved them, and now they were employed to oppress their best Friends." At Newgate one officer gave his men pieces of the broken gates to take the place of the medals the Parliament was alleged to have promised when they took the field against Lambert. Murmurs were even heard that Lambert had been right in ejecting the Rump, and that his example would have to be followed again.[10] The citizens for their part seemed stupefied at the course of events. In Pepys's graphic phrase, "the City look mighty blank, and cannot tell what in the world to do." But their hour of deliverance was at hand.

While soldiers were grumbling and officers proposing to resign their commissions Monck "was dark, and chewed his tobacco."[11] He had a momentous decision to make. He can hardly have been unconscious that, if he broke with the Rump, the Restoration would follow as certainly as the night the day. But he decided still to proceed cautiously. He was fully conscious of his men's disgust at the unworthy task set them. He received assurances from Morley, now lieutenant of the Tower, that the regiments he and Fagge commanded would support any action he might start. Many and anxious consultations occupied the next day when the general returned to Whitehall. Civilians and officers pressed upon him their discontent at the proceedings in the City and argued that he was discouraging his friends and strengthening his enemies. As his custom was, he patiently listened to all and sundry, but the decision that the moment had come to curb the enormities of the Rump was reached at a conference with a small group late on the tenth.[12] At first Monck was against immediate action, but was persuaded by Clarges, Barrow, and two other officers unnamed that delay was dangerous. After he had consulted with Clarges, Thompson, Sanders, and Barton, the last being two of his officers known to favor the admission of the secluded members, they agreed that the Coldstreamers should march into the City the next day, but found it difficult to decide on the explanation to be given Parliament. The decision was finally reached to give none, but to summon a meeting of the chief officers for 6:00 a.m., to whom a letter to the Rump should first be submitted. After agreement had been reached on the main heads Monck retired and left to the four officers the composition of the letter. Next morning Monck and fourteen of his chief officers

[10]Gumble, pp. 241-42. The only other reference I have found to the promise of medals is in Nicoll, *Diary of Public Transactions*, p. 56.

[11]Maseres, II, 672.

[12]Gumble, p. 243.

signed the letter which was committed to Clobery and Lytcott to be delivered to the Rump.[13] Then the general drew up his forces in Finsbury Fields and awaited word from Clarges who had been sent to the City to acquaint the authorities with the intention to quarter the army there. The Lord Mayor was very reserved but Alderman Robinson and others were more forthcoming. On hearing from Clarges, Monck at once entered the City and arrived at the Lord Mayor's. Not unnaturally, he was told that the City was full of apprehension at his sudden return after the recent violence. He answered that he hoped to make the citizens of another mind in a few hours. He was unwilling to commit himself further until he learned what kind of reception the Rumpers had given his letter. But the news of its dispatch was already spreading. Pepys heard it by noon and observed how men's countenances changed from gloom to joy in half an hour. Probably many recognized that when Monck and the City joined hands the Restoration would soon follow. "And this in truth," wrote Baxter, "was the Act that turned the Scales and brought in the King."[14]

About the same time the Rumpers were listening to the letter from Monck and his officers. It began with a reminder that the Scotch army had been instrumental in the restoration of the Parliament and had obeyed its commands even in the work of destruction in the City, "which was something grievous" to them, and which recalled to their minds that they had declared their intention not only to restore the Parliament but also vindicate the liberties of the people. Officers now feared the opportunity afforded by the unparalleled deliverance was being neglected because men impeached by treason and members of the late committee of safety were permitted to sit in the house, Lambert and Vane allowed to remain in London, and dangerous officers retained in the army. They perceived men trying to enact a new engagement who had had the least (if any) conscience in keeping engagements already taken. They resented the petition recently presented which would exclude many sober men from public employment. They found that the great cause of the present dissatisfaction in the nation was the unrepresentative character of Parliament. Therefore, they were constrained to desire that writs to fill vacancies might be issued before Friday the seventeenth so that the suspicion that Parliament meant to be perpetual might be removed and

[13]Among the claimants to the merit of having persuaded Monck are Clarges, whose narrative (in Baker's *Chronicle*, pp. 707-708) I have mainly followed, Collins (*Leyborne-Popham MSS*, pp. 217-18), and Ashley Cooper (Shaftesbury's narrative mentions that in the evening "his [Monck's] lady, Sir Thomas Clarges, myself, and some other of his friends prevailed upon the general." Christie, *Life of Shaftesbury*, I, 208).

[14]This is the verdict of Baxter, *Reliquiae*, p. 105. Gumble's comment (p. 250) was that "all *England* (almost) put together, did not more contribute to the King's Restoration" than London.

the people assured of a succession of parliaments, "which is the undoubted right of the English nation." The better to wait for full parliamentary acceptance of their desires they would quarter their forces in "that great City, formerly renown'd for their resolute adhering to Parliamentary authority."[15]

Concealing their anger, members within the House passed a resolution thanking Monck for securing the City and assuring him that filling up the Parliament was under consideration before the receipt of his letter and would be dispatched in due time. This resolution was entrusted to Scot and Robinson to deliver to Monck. Outside the House, men perceived that the Rump was doomed. As Hesilrige left the House in anger, Byllynge the Quaker seized him by the arm and exclaimed: "Thou man, will thy beast carry thee no longer? Thou must fall!"[16]

In the City Scot and Robinson received no satisfaction from Monck and were forced to listen to some very plain speaking from others. When Scot sought to placate Monck with compliments, Colonel Bridges interrupted and said the general had no reason to believe their fair speeches because their words and practices did not correspond. He himself had come from Ireland to impeach Ludlow and Jones but was put off from day to day while Barebones, presenting a seditious petition, was heard the moment he appeared at the door of the House. Clobery added that the members were clearly trying to create a counterbalance to Monck and his forces out of the former enemies of Parliament. Therefore, the Scotch army must provide for its own safety. Monck ended the discussion by saying that all would be well if Parliament took the advice given in the letter.[17]

The Rump at once demonstrated that it was not going to follow the path of prudence. During the afternoon of February 11 an act was introduced to make Fleetwood commander in chief of the army and, although its passage is not recorded in the *Journals*, was presumably passed immediately.[18] Then five army commissioners were named to take the place of the seven. Four were soon chosen, Hesilrige and Walton with Monck and Morley. To which party the majority would incline depended on the fifth. Monck's friends proposed Ashley Cooper but were defeated by thirty to fifteen. Then Alured was named. Three were to

[15]*Collection of Letters*, pp. 61-67.

[16]Pepys, Feb. 11. One wonders whether Hesilrige recalled that in 1650 his regiment had furnished five companies to the regiment then formed for Monck?

[17]Baker, p. 708.

[18]The *Journals* show that it was repealed on the 24th. According to Ludlow (II, 223) Monck was first proposed as commander in chief, but the majority "chose rather to perish by the hands of an enemy, if Monck should resolve to be so, than by the delusions of a pretended friend." Ludlow continued that to avoid giving Monck "the least just cause of discontent" he was named first of the commissioners. So far as I can tell the above represents the sentiments of the majority most accurately.

constitute a quorum. The motion that Monck should be one was rejected, seemingly without a division.[19] It is not surprising to read that when news of this ingratitude reached the general "he could not avoid expressing much indignation at it." While in this mood he met the Lord Mayor and common council. His employment in the City, he said, had been the most displeasing to him that he had ever undertaken, and if there had been any way of avoiding it except by resigning his commission he would have refused it. But to have resigned would have placed authority in the hands of others less inclined than he to a settlement. He had that morning sent to the Parliament to issue out writs to fill vacancies within a week, and not to sit after May 6 as the date when a full and free parliament would be summoned.[20] The glad tidings spread rapidly through London. The scene that followed can be described only by Pepys: "I went alone to Guildhall to see whether Monck was come again or no, and met with him coming out of the chamber where he had been with the Mayor and Aldermen, but such a shout I never heard in all my life, crying out, 'God bless your Excellence.' . . . And indeed I saw many people give the soldiers drink and money, and all along in the streets cried, 'God bless them!' and extraordinary good words. . . . In Cheapside there was a great many bonfires, and Bow bells and all the bells in all the churches as we went home were a-ringing. Hence we went homewards, it being about ten o'clock. But the common joy that was every where to be seen! The number of bonfires, there being fourteen between St. Dunstan's and Temple Bar, and at Strand Bridge I could at one view tell thirty-one fires. In King-street seven or eight; and all along burning, and roasting, and drinking for rumps. . . . Indeed it was past imagination, both the greatness and the suddenness of it."[21]

The news that Monck had demanded a free parliament was equally welcomed in the provinces. As L'Estrange wrote when Monck and his army became one with the City, they simultaneously "contracted a nearer Alliance with the Nation." At Bristol the apprentices shouted, "A free parliament, a free parliament," and then "a full parliament, pull out the Rump, cut the Rump, oh, burn the Rump." Others cried out, "A king, Charles II." Yet a marked difference between the rejoicings in London and in other places was discernible. The citizens of London

[19]Baker, p. 709. Ludlow (II, 223-24) recorded that Overton was first considered but laid aside, because the knowledge that Overton was at odds with Monck would cause his defeat, so Alured was substituted. Ludlow also stated that he persuaded Marten to move that the Irish army should be governed by the commissioners.

[20]Baker, p. 709.

[21]John Aubrey (*Brief Lives* [Oxford, 1898] II, 73-74) is unusually eloquent on this theme. A correspondent of Hyde's compared London in the morning of the eleventh to a deflowered virgin lamenting the rape committed on her the day before, and in the afternoon to a bride hastening to her wedding. *Clarendon State Papers*, III, 681.

treated the soldiers as friends, but elsewhere the old enmity between the inhabitants and the garrisons still persisted. Soldiers were used to extinguish bonfires and to stop the ringing of bells in some towns because cries for a free parliament were mingled with shouts of "a King."[22]

After the excitement of February 11, the next few days seem rather an anticlimax. Monck stayed in the City and declined all invitations to join the Council of State so long as members were required to subscribe to the engagement.[23] Some 7,000 fanatics and persons disaffected to the Parliament possessed arms, he averred, and until the weapons were returned to the stores he would remain where he was. When Alured came from the Council, Monck stressed the continued failure to enforce the orders given Lambert and Vane to leave town and asserted, probably unjustly, that Hesilrige corresponded with both.[24] Another visitor was Ludlow who sought to remove the prejudices Monck appeared to have against him, because he favored the fanatical party in Ireland. When Ludlow stated that a man's religious beliefs ought not to disqualify him from office if he was zealous for the public good, Monck replied: "Yea, we must live and die together for a Commonwealth." Thus encouraged, Ludlow warned Monck that the secluded members, whose return he was thought to support, might wish to restore the King. The answer he received was: "It may be they will attempt it, but they say they will not; and I assure you, though I bear as much respect to Parliament as any man, yet if I should observe a Parliament to be about such a thing, I would interrupt them therein."[25]

By the time he wrote his *Memoirs* Ludlow had come to hate Monck as the perjured apostate who betrayed the republic, but there is no reason to question the account of the above interview. There is plenty of evidence that Monck tried to lull his opponents by deception. He was to contradict himself often during the ensuing weeks. Probably some sentences Shaftesbury wrote in his old age correctly describe the general's hesitations and tergiversations: "Neither was General Monck without his apprehensions that matters might go too fast for him and overset him. . . . He treated at the same time with all sorts of men, and appointed a select number of several sorts to confer together, and consider what they had to offer concerning the present posture of affairs; intermixing them as he thought fit, sometimes two, sometimes three

[22]See L'Estrange, *Apology*, p. 73. *Mercurius Politicus*, p. 1126, under February 17 and 18, for celebrations at Yarmouth and Bristol and in Herefordshire; Rugge, "Mercurius Politicus Redivivus," pp. 69-70, for events at Bristol.

[23]The letters from the Council are in *Calendar Domestic*, pp. 358, 360, 365, 367, 370, 372, and two from Monck in *Clarke Papers*, IV, 261-63.

[24]Hesilrige wrote to Monck on February 12 to deny holding conferences with Lambert and Vane. *Clarke Papers*, IV, 260-261.

[25]Ludlow, II, 226-27.

parties together, keeping the world in great uncertainty, and (if myself and others that were nearest him were not mistaken) himself too." As Gumble wrote, Monck displayed great dexterity and cunning in making use "of all tempers for his present occasions. . . . All parties visited him, and all endeavoured to promote their own Ends, either of their Safety or Advantage; and in this he was not backward, to send them away laden with Promises."[26] Probably the simplest explanation is correct— that Monck was determined not to commit himself openly and irrevocably until Parliament proved it was incapable of a deathbed repentance.

The Rump made some half-hearted gestures by directing the sergeant at arms to convey Vane from London, Lambert to attend the Council of State on Thursday, and the members of the committee of safety to appear before Parliament a week hence. A month's pay was ordered for the forces in and around London, but only £5,000 was available at the treasury out of the £16,600 needed.[27] Perhaps this proof that the Rump could not pay them was not without influence upon the soldiers. The oath for councillors was changed to a simple promise to be faithful to the Commonwealth without a king, single person, or house of lords. But the most important question before the House concerned the qualifications of members. Because no text of the bill, whether as introduced or as finally passed, has been found, knowledge of it is limited to the amendments, and their meaning is not always clear as the clauses they amend are not cited. However, there was a formidable list of persons disqualified: all who had advocated any single person as supreme magistrate, were guilty of blasphemy, were married to Papists, denied the Scriptures to be the word of God, were drunkards, were the sons of sequestrated fathers (to disqualify sons for no offense except their parenthood was new), and attempted to bribe a corporation or individual to secure election. Anyone voting at an election when disqualified was to forfeit a year's value of his real estate and a third of his personal estate, and any member unlawfully elected who should take his seat in Parliament was to be subject to a penalty of £1,000. A last-minute amendment apparently empowered the sheriff to tender the conciliar oath to a successful candidate. If he refused it he was automatically debarred from taking his seat.[28] Finally, on February 18 the act was ordered to be printed and published.

[26]Christie, I, 210; Gumble, pp. 246, 258.

[27]*Journals*, Feb. 3 and 16.

[28]The last two sentences are inferences only from the brief note in the *Journals*, Feb. 16. A letter from Broderick to Hyde says that a proposal to disqualify all who had signed declarations in favor of an open parliament was defeated by a single vote. *Clarendon State Papers*, III, 682.

On the vital question of filling up the House, a resolution was passed on the fifteenth that writs should be sent to counties, cities, and boroughs "as anciently accustomed." But an unexpected obstacle was raised by the Speaker's refusal to sign a warrant to the commissioners of the Great Seal to send out the writs. If he signed the warrant, he said, he might be sued at law by each of the secluded members in whose place another should be elected. In vain he was told that his position required his obedience to the orders of the House. Rather than obey, he asserted he would prefer to be sent to the Tower. Ludlow failed to persuade his fellow-members to replace the Speaker by someone more compliant, so an act was passed to allow the clerk to sign the warrant. The incident is significant only as proving the low estate to which Parliament had fallen if a timid time-server like Lenthall could defy it with impunity. He doubtlessly thought his imprisonment would be very short because he now knew the secluded members were to be admitted to Parliament.[29] The Rump, by its persistence in the device of filling vacancies in its membership and in preventing the secluded members from taking their seats, was deliberately flouting public opinion.

A startling proof that the City rather than Parliament represented the general will was now forthcoming from the north. On February 10, some lords, knights, gentlemen, and ministers of Yorkshire met and subscribed a declaration that, having no representation to express or remedy their grievances, they desired, if the Parliament elected in November, 1640, was to be continued, the members excluded in 1648 to be readmitted and all vacancies filled up. Otherwise they asked that a new parliament be elected without any other qualifications than those in force before 1648. Until one or other proposal was adopted, they felt no obligation to pay taxes, being denied the fundamental right of Englishmen to express their consent to laws through their representatives.[30] Among the signers of this memorable document were Fairfax, Fauconberg, Sir Thomas Wharton, Sir Christopher Wyvell, Sir Henry Cholmley, and other names familiar in the annals of Yorkshire. Copies were sent to Monck and to the City, accompanied by letters. The City was informed that the Yorkshiremen had noted its vigorous assertion of "our common freedom as Englishmen, too much of late violated" and were now impelled to set forth similar resolutions, to which they intended firmly to adhere.[31]

[29]Ludlow, II, 233-34; Pepys, Feb. 20. Ludlow claims to have suggested that members should adjourn to the Tower. Had he forgotten that the lieutenant was Morley, a confederate of Monck's?

[30]A summary is in *Calendar Domestic*, p. 356. The text was printed in York and London. See *Thomason Tracts*, Feb. 13 and 16.

[31]*Calendar Domestic*, p. 356.

Fairfax himself wrote to Monck to explain that the promoters of the meeting had been careful to confine it to those who had not borne arms against the Parliament because Morgan and Charles Fairfax, Monck's local commanders, might otherwise have interfered. But the declaration was not contrived by a few but by many and these "for quality, estate and callings the most interested in the country [county], with the concurrence of many thousand more." He urged Monck to be the happy instrument of restoring the just rights of the nation.[32] In his reply Monck reported the Parliament to have "condescended" that their numbers should be filled up, for which purpose writs would be issued the next day, and to have established no qualifications which would prevent secluded members from being re-elected. He acknowledged that this was not exactly what Fairfax and his colleagues had proposed but he hoped they would be satisfied.[33]

This letter, dated February 18, is significant because it proves that Monck still judged it expedient to profess his hope of co-operating with the Rump. Forty-eight hours later his attitude changed. Perhaps the more he pondered, the greater the significance of the recent events in the City and Yorkshire appeared, and the more likely it seemed that their example would be speedily followed throughout the length and breadth of the land. Most of the county addresses demanded the recall of the secluded members, to be followed by a free parliament, not the mere filling of vacancies. Having so many examples of the extreme perversity of the Rump before his eyes, he can scarcely have expected it to mend its ways at the eleventh hour. Yet he hesitated, maybe because he remembered his pledges to uphold the Parliament, maybe because he still felt uneasy about the reaction of the army if the secluded members were allowed to sit. Their restitution would be a long step towards the recall of the King. Indeed, Monck almost certainly thought it inevitable now, and his anxious pauses between each fresh advance may be explained by his determination to avoid a third civil war. What is beyond conjecture is that he lingered behind public opinion because he must carry his soldiers along with him.

Perhaps with this end in view he tried to bring the Rumpers and the secluded members to some acceptable compromise. The first meeting he arranged of representatives of the two groups was on the fourteenth. He was encouraged by the "free and civil discourse" which took place and invited Hesilrige to bring Scot and Colonels White and Morley, and St.

[32]*Leyborne-Popham MSS*, pp. 149-50. The alarmist letters of Morgan and Charles Fairfax showed they did not understand what was going on until they received Monck's letter of February 11 to the Rump. This they had distributed widely. Ibid, pp. 146-49, 153-54.

[33]*Leyborne-Popham MSS*, pp. 154-55.

John to bring Ashley Cooper, Carew Raleigh, and Reynolds to a meeting at his quarters on Friday evening.[34] No record of the proceedings at this meeting has survived, but it may have been adjourned until the next day, the eighteenth, when a larger group assembled. The Rumpers present were St. John, Hesilrige, Morley, Thompson, Ashley Cooper, Weaver, White, Feilder, Hutchinson, and Raleigh. Among the secluded members were Arthur Annesley, in whose house they were wont to meet, Colonels Popham, Harley, Norton, and John Birch, Sir John Evelyn, Sir Gilbert Gerrard, and John Crew. In Baker's *Chronicle* is the statement that no conclusion was reached because the Rumpers could not undertake for the rest of the House, but that all present seemed well satisfied with the moderation displayed.[35] Other accounts, however, do not leave the impression of harmony. Annesley is said to have made such indecent reflections upon the proceedings of Parliament since Pride's Purge that Hesilrige left the meeting in a rage.[36] Perhaps the best reason for doubting the possibility of any agreement between the two factions is that Monck, apparently after toying with the idea of leaving the Rumpers in sole possession of the House, decided without worrying about their consent to admit the secluded members.

Cooper's story is that he learned from Monck himself that he had come to terms with Hesilrige and Scot and meant to return to Whitehall from Alderman Wale's house in the city, support their interest and obey their commands, they having promised that he should be named the sole general of the armies. Cooper, uninfluenced by Monck's promises that he should be protected, went immediately to Mrs. Monck, urged her to send for her brother, Clarges, while he summoned Clobery and Knight. The four argued with the general until three o'clock in the morning before he was convinced and agreed to admit the secluded members that very morning, which was Tuesday, February 21. Accordingly, Clarges and Cooper gathered the secluded members together to Annesley's house, whence they went so secretly to the prince's lodgings at Whitehall, Monck's quarters, that Hesilrige and his faction had no knowledge of what was going on until they called on the general and found him in the midst of a large number of secluded members. Thereupon, Hesilrige, pale and in a furious temper, exclaimed to Cooper that it was his doing and would cost blood. "His own if he pleased," was the cool reply.[37]

[34]Monck to Hesilrige, *Clarke Papers*, IV, 264; Pepys, Feb. 17; in *Mercurius Politicus* a list of those present is given, but no information about the result is supplied.

[35]Baker, pp. 709-10; Gumble, p. 260; Maseres, II, 770-771.

[36]Ludlow, II, 228; Collins (*Leyborne-Popham MSS*, pp. 219-20) questions the moderation and mentions Colonel Hutchinson as opposing the readmission. The certificate in Hutchinson's favor, signed on June 26, 1660, by Ashley Cooper and others, claims that he supported the readmission (*Life*, p. 450).

[37]Christie, I, 211-12.

The writer was not a modest man and in his old age may have exaggerated his influence at this critical moment. Yet it was very considerable. James Sharp, sent to London by the ministers at Edinburgh in response to Monck's appeal, recorded that on the day of his arrival (February 13) the general recommended him to Cooper and Weaver. In a letter written on the day the secluded members re-entered the House, Sharp reported that on the eighteenth he had interviewed the general and secured his agreement that some of the most prominent of them should apply to him, and that on the twentieth four of them sent him with some propositions to the general, to which he brought back a favorable answer. But, he added, "with no small difficulty the general was brought to admit the secluded members, which was kept very close till this morning," when seventy-three entered the house to eighteen Rumpers.[38]

These propositions Monck incorporated in the written declaration he read to the members who assembled in Whitehall preparatory to their readmission. Although he asserted that he wished to impose no conditions and to leave them in perfect freedom, he reminded them that the old foundations were broken beyond repair. If a long and bloody war against the King should end in his restoration, then he might certainly rule as he pleased and dispose of parliaments as he wished because the people would not rise in arms again. The interests of London, "the bulwark of Parliaments," must lie in a commonwealth which alone can make it "the Metropolis and Bank of Trade for all Christendom." The best settlement of the church would be the establishment of a moderate Presbyterian government, with liberty for consciences truly tender. He then stated the four propositions: to settle the three armies in the way most conducive to their harmony; to raise funds to pay the forces by land and sea and to carry on the government; to appoint a council of state which should issue writs for a new parliament to represent the three nations, to be elected by the constituencies of 1654 and to meet on April 20; and to establish a commonwealth without a king or house of lords, and to dissolve themselves. When he had finished, the members promised to create him commander in chief by sea and land. Then Adjutant General Miller, a captain in Monck's own foot, escorted members to the House. Seeing them enter with the Speaker arriving last, Pepys thought it strange that the affair was managed so covertly that the Rumpers heard nothing of it until they saw members, secluded no longer, in their seats. He noted also Prynne's arrival with an old basket-hilt sword on,

[38]Wodrow, *Sufferings of the Church of Scotland,* I, 5-6. *Mercurius Politicus,* p. 1122, states that about four score of the formerly secluded members were present.

and the applause which greeted him. This sword provided a touch of comedy because it got entangled in Sir William Waller's short legs and threw him, at which the crowd laughed—good-humoredly we hope, because both these champions of parliamentary liberties deserved well at the hands of their fellow countrymen.[39]

The same day Monck assembled the officers in and about London to draw up and sign a letter which, with the declaration, was sent to all regiments and garrisons. It explained that no better way had been available to satisfy the good people of the Commonwealth than the readmission of the secluded members in order that they should dissolve the present Parliament and issue writs for a new one. There followed some vague assurances that dearly purchased liberties, civil and spiritual, would be preserved. The present Parliament would not repeal any of the acts concerning the sale or disposition of lands forfeited to the state, and the new parliament would be pressed to confirm the same. Any disturbers of the peace in favor of Charles Stuart or other pretended authority were to be secured. Finally, the forces were promised supplies of money, not the least of the motives that prompted the readmission having been to facilitate the raising of money for the pay and arrears of pay for the army and navy, "which would not otherwise have been done (if at all) but with effusion of Blood." Monck, eleven colonels, and other officers signed this appeal.[40]

The readmission was most welcome to the vast majority of civilians, and London celebrated that night again with bells and bonfires. Celebrations in the provinces were without restraint. At Bury St. Edmunds, for example, Charles II was proclaimed and, in spite of the local commander's orders to the contrary, bonfires were lit in every street. Soldiers carrying off the fuel were stoned and taunted that the citizens would soon be strong enough to declare for King Charles and end the rule of rogues like the soldiers.[41] Few seem to have worried their heads about the conditions imposed. Rumpers thought them dishonorable, and waited on the general to hear him explain his actions. He avowed that he wanted to free himself from the secluded members' importunities and would prevent them from doing any harm. Asked if he would join the old members against the Royalists, he declared he would oppose to the utmost Charles Stuart, a single person, or a house of lords.[42] Whether

<hr/>

[39]Price, in Maseres, II, p. 772; Aubrey, *Brief Lives*, II, 175. The Parliament did not implicitly follow the declaration. The new Parliament did not meet on April 20 or represent Scotland and Ireland, and was not chosen by the constituencies of 1654. Probably the declaration was designed for propaganda as well as a guide to M.P.'s.

[40]Baker, pp. 710-711.

[41]Rugge, pp. 88-89, 91.

[42]Ludlow, II, 236-37.

these protestations were sincere may be doubted. Monck must have recognized, as Whitelocke did, that the reason why the readmission was so popular was that people thought it the best way to restore the King. If he looked ahead, he should have foreseen Charles's return. Even if he did, he was still determined not to be precipitate—to soothe the Republicans with words pleasing to their ears until they were powerless. That would happen only when adherents of the good old cause had been removed from the army.

On February 20, Pepys and a friend went to the Coffee Club and found Harrington, the Earl of Dorset, and an unnamed peer discussing another meeting place for the famous debating society, the Rota. "After a small debate upon the question whether learned or unlearned subjects are the best, the Club broke up very poorly, and I do not think they will meet any more." No later meeting is known. That the end of the Rota and the readmission of the secluded members should have coincided so nearly in time was very natural. Henceforth men's minds would be too full of hope that the old constitution would be restored to leave room for speculations about utopias, new models of government, or even written constitutions, though there is plenty of evidence that Harrington's *Oceana* had attracted attention and made converts. The proceedings at the Rota, established in November, 1659, did not influence events except negatively. As Burnet remarked, the knowledge of the schemes of government the few were proposing made the many conclude that the King's recall was necessary "that so matters might again fall into their old channel."[43] Otherwise the nightly meetings at the Rota provided entertainment rather than instruction. Aubrey thought parliamentary speeches flat compared with the discourses of Harrington's disciples, and found the coffeehouse crammed every evening. Pepys dropped in and heard "very good discourse" on "the balance of propriety" at Rome but judging from his account the conclusions reached on successive nights were self-contradictory.[44] Wits both in prose and verse continued to jest about the Rota after its dissolution and equated membership with light-headedness, but their humor should not hide the lasting importance of Harrington's theories, especially in the future United States.

The turn of events alarmed John Milton. He had finished, or nearly finished, his tract, *The Readie & Easie Way to Establish a Free Commonwealth*, when he learned of the readmission. He prefixed a new paragraph and then sent the tract to the printer. It appeared on or before

[43]*History of My Own Time*, I, 151.

[44]H. F. Russell Smith, in *Harrington and his Oceana* (Cambridge, 1914), quotes Pepys (Jan. 17) as writing "balance of prosperity," which is incorrect unless a deliberate correction of the text. This is a very slight flaw in a very good book.

March 3, when Thomason secured his copy. He also wrote a letter to Monck, not published until 1698. He may well have been prompted by the declaration which the general read to the secluded members immediately before they took their seats, and which Milton mentioned as a warning against the restoration of a monarch "not to be trusted with the power of Revenge."[45] In both letter and tract a parliament or, preferably, a grand or general council of the nation was to be charged with the armed forces ("under the conduct of your Excellency," the letter adds), foreign affairs, general laws, and peace and war. The novelties were two: the council, once elected, was to be perpetual, and the constituencies were to be cities, or large towns promoted to be cities, each with a competent territory adjoining. The tract demonstrated two points very clearly: Milton dreaded frequent elections because of the rude multitude, even if the electors were submitted to "a third or fourth sifting"; and he distrusted any central authority, even one of his own devising, and preferred to entrust spiritual and civil liberty to the "counties and precincts" he proposed to endow with ample authority. The local bodies, he said, would have only themselves to blame if they did not have a few laws to expect or fear from the general council—and these few they might assent to, or dissent from, within a limited time, but yielding to the wishes of a majority of cities.[46] To make the people fittest to choose, and the chosen fittest to govern, education must be adapted to teach "faith not without vertue, temperance, modestie, sobrietie, parsimonie, justice; to bring men up not to admire wealth or honour; to hate turbulence and ambition, and to place every one his privat welfare and happiness in the public place, libertie and safetie." The obvious criticism is that if Milton's scheme required such a state of perfection it was self-condemned. On every hand were signs that men had rejected the work of reformation insofar as it had attempted to impose on them a moral standard not of their own choosing. The last sentence in the tract lamented "the general dejection of a misguided and abus'd multitude."[47] And this was after nearly two decades of Puritan rule.

[45]It is curious that Milton should write of the qualifications of future M.P.'s as decreed but not yet repealed, unless he wrote on the evening of February 21 or was uninformed of the proceedings on the twenty-second, when a new committee to prepare qualifications was set up. The intention clearly was to ignore the bill dealing with the matter passed on the eighteenth. L'Estrange's gibe (*Apology*, p. 85 [86]) that Milton had just finished his model of a Commonwealth when Monck spoiled it by allowing the secluded members to take their seats, reverses the order of events, at least as far as publication of the *Readie & Easie Way* is concerned.

[46]Perhaps a modern analogy would be a parliament of restricted authority and county and municipal councils of greatly enlarged scope with a power of veto by a majority of councils.

[47]Perhaps the author of *A Character of the Rump*, dated by Thomason March 17, had not troubled to read Milton's tract, otherwise he would hardly have used the phrase, "But *John Milton* is their [Rumpers'] Goos-quill champion." It is interesting to note that the anonymous writer thought Milton and Nedham ought to be hanged together.

Some ninety members took their seats in Parliament on the morning of February 21. They at once rescinded various resolutions passed from December 18, 1648, to January 5, 1660, which had declared about 150 members incapable of sitting and named a small committee, including Prynne, to search the records for similar resolutions. The main result of this labor of love was to expunge the votes against Denzil Holles and other Presbyterians accused of treason by the army in 1647 and 1648. Major General Browne was admitted to his seat. The Speaker was to write to sheriffs to summon members to attend. Thanks to these measures there were 116 members present on February 23 and 150 before the brief session ended, probably about two-thirds being secluded members and a third Rumpers.[48]

The majority was on the whole magnanimous towards its enemies, while not neglecting its friends. Certain individuals were deprived of their offices—Hutchinson and Croke of their shrievalties of Nottinghamshire and Oxfordshire, Adam Baynes, Luke Robinson, John White, and James Harrington of minor offices, and Owen of the deanery of Christ Church. A few field officers lost their commissions by direct Parliamentary action but their cases will be described below. Naturally, all petitioners for a free Parliament like Sir Robert Pye[49] and Sir Richard Temple were released. Perhaps more surprising were the orders to set free Sir George Booth, though under £5,000 bail at first, and other prominent supporters of his rising, including Sir Thomas Middleton. Their sequestrations were first suspended and then the two acts of sequestration passed against those who had risen the previous August were repealed.[50] Parliament delved into the past and set at liberty the Earls of Crawford and Lauderdale, imprisoned since 1651, and Bishop Wren, first confined in the Tower in 1641 and then continuously since 1642 though never brought to trial.

Monck, of course, received every consideration. At once he was appointed commander in chief of all the land forces of England, Scotland, and Ireland, and an attempt to insert in his commission some proviso against Charles Stuart was defeated.[51] A bill to settle upon him the manor of Hampton Court was introduced, but ultimately he was granted no less than £20,000 instead, though being named steward. He was accused of having proposed the first grant in order to lull members to sleep (because if he intended the King's restoration he would not want

[48]Ludlow (II, 235-36) and Neville were the chief Rumpers who declined to sit.

[49]For his attempt to sue for a habeas corpus and its refusal by Richard Newdigate, see Ludlow, II, 232-33.

[50]*Acts and Ordinances*, II, 1423.

[51]*Journals*, Feb. 25. The commission seems not to have survived.

royal lands), but his friends prevailed in securing him the second.[52] He and Mountagu were named generals at sea, the latter to go forthwith to the fleet. The joint appointment may have aroused his resentment, on the ground that this was a violation of his agreement with the secluded members.[53] The City of London was conciliated by orders for the re-erection of its gates and chains at the public expense, by the cordial reception given to its deputation, and by the immediate acceptance of a list of officers for its militia presented by the deputation. In presenting an address Alderman Fowke explained that his brethren "found some Persons for a Monarchical, some for a Comonwealth, some for No Government at all: The last they did dislike: For the other, they would not presume to direct; but should acquiesce and submit to the Determination of Parliament." That a petition which openly placed monarchy as an alternative to a republic received no rebuke but hearty thanks was a sign which way the wind was blowing.

To carry on the government two essentials were money and an executive. As regards the first, Parliament did not interfere with the act for an assessment of £100,000 a month passed on January 26, and found it necessary to continue the customs and excise for four months beyond the end of February when they expired under the existing act. The changes were in the commissioners and in the exemption from duties of woollen and woollen mixed with linen stuffs exported to Ireland for use there.[54] As there was a crying need for ready money, a committee was sent to the City and reported that notwithstanding the great decay of trade and the poverty, £60,000 would be advanced. Later, the City agreed to lend £27,000 upon the security of the assessment on itself. Such sums would be a present help but could not lessen the arrears of pay already due. An estimate of the naval debts amounted to nearly £700,000 but no similar estimate was made for the army.[55]

The House showed some originality in establishing an executive. Once again a council of thirty-one was chosen, Monck unanimously and the rest by ballot. Apart from the general, all were M.P.'s whereas only twenty-one had been in the previous body.[56] About eighteen were

[52]Ludlow, II, 245. Price (in Maseres, II, 780-781) asserts, on the contrary, that Rumpers craftily proposed the grant.

[53]Ludlow (II, 237) so alleges, I think wrongly. Gumble (pp. 261, 264-65) mentions both the agreement that Monck was to be general at sea and the joint appointment but implies that Monck was not resentful.

[54]*Acts and Ordinances*, II, 1353-55; 1416-17.

[55]*Journals*, Feb. 23, Mar. 2, 5; Sharpe, *London and the Kingdom*, II, 372.

[56]Masson (*Life of Milton*, V, 544) also exempts Fairfax, but he and Nathaniel Rich had been declared members for Cirencester February 17, 1649 (*Official Returns* [1878], I, 489). Cooper had been admitted to sit when a disputed election was decided in his favor after eighteen years, as Ludlow (II, 205) bitterly complained.

original members of the Long Parliament, the others recruiters (elected to fill vacancies). Seven had been Rumpers, and owed their nominations to the part they had played in the negotiations preceding the readmission. Three of the seven—Cooper, Morley, and Thompson—had belonged to the council chosen the previous May and, with Fairfax, Monck, Weaver, and Widdrington, to the council elected by the Rump in December. There were several former officers of the New Model, like Mountagu and Rossiter. Most were Presbyterians, including not a few who had been prominent in opposition in Richard's Parliament to recognition of the Protectorate. There was one strange omission—William Prynne. Perhaps the ingratitude of the secluded members to their tireless champion may be explained as due to a feeling that the vast but ill-digested learning of "Marginal" Prynne would be more valuable to Parliamentary committees than to the executive. With few exceptions, they wished to see a king once again at Whitehall; but some, perhaps most, hoped to impose conditions. All were moderates, as the position at the head of the list of men like Pierrepont and Crew proves. Indeed, there was not a fanatic. John Thompson and Thurloe were appointed secretaries of state. The latter soon opened negotiations with the exiled court but many doubted his sincerity.

Whether the Council ever formally drafted terms which the King should be asked to sign as the conditions of his restoration is uncertain. In April it was said to have drawn up "the most sticking part" of the articles to be laid before Parliament for a treaty with Charles II—those dealing with an indemnity for past offenses and with the disposal of confiscated land that had been sold.[57] Individual councillors and prominent Presbyterians who were not councillors certainly busied themselves with this question, but they were divided as to whether a protector or king should become the head of the state. At first Mountagu, St. John, and Thurloe were reported to favor Richard Cromwell's recall. The last two remained Protectorians (St. John being described as "the most deadly enemy the King has in England"), but Mountagu soon abandoned this cabal and joined Crew, his father-in-law, and Pierrepont who desired a conditional restoration. The Earls of Manchester and Northumberland and, perhaps, Bedford were expected to head the group in Parliament which aimed at fettering the prerogative. They were very confident, according to Royalists, and had already divided up the great offices of state among themselves. To achieve their ends in the new parliament or convention, which was to be summoned, they must exclude from the House of Lords not only the Cavalier peers but also

[57]Wodrow, i, 20b.

the "young Lords" (those who had been minors during the Civil Wars), and from the Commons any Royalists that might be elected. Royalists even as late as the beginning of May seem to have assumed that some conditions would be laid down but to have hoped that they would be easy and honorable.[58] But whether the Presbyterians could thus override the popular demand for a free parliament depended on Monck's attitude. Before the Convention met he was thought to support these oligarchic measures, but whether he would maintain this position remained to be seen. All that was really known was his insistence that Parliament should decide whether to recall the King and, if so, upon what terms, if any.[59]

A strange omission of the Presbyterians was their failure to take into consideration Charles's probable attitude towards a conditional restoration. Stranger still, the royal attitude is uncertain. In November, 1659, Hyde had told Barwick that "all discourses of the Treaty at the Isle of Wight trouble me little; though it comes mentioned sometimes to us by those, who pretend no Disaffection to the Church; and who pretend all shall be repaired again afterwards. But as I am confident, the King will never endure it: so if he should consent to it, it can never be reduc'd into Practice, or a Peace to be establish'd in the Kingdom by it."[60] This passage is open to the cynical interpretation that if the King accepted the treaty before his restoration he would repudiate it afterwards. Nothing in his previous career rules out such an interpretation. But Hyde may well have been thinking that if the King was restored and a free parliament elected, the majority would refuse its consent to the most important article of the treaty—the establishment of Presbyterianism for three years. He may already have contemplated adding to any articles the King might sign the saving clauses so skillfully used in the Declaration of Breda—"We shall be ready to consent to such an Act of Parliament. . . ." Some months later, when the Royalists' prospects were much brighter, Hyde preferred to cultivate individuals among the moderate Presbyterians by promises to satisfy their appetites for public offices rather than to try to win over the whole party by concessions at the expense of the Anglican Church.[61] George Morley, later bishop of Winchester, was sent on a mission to England to parley with the Presbyterians. He was an excellent choice because, like theirs, his theological views were Calvinist. He was also charged to moderate the rising pas-

---

[58]There are several letters to this effect in Bodleian Library, Clarendon MSS 72, f. 114 and fol.

[59]C. H. Firth, *The House of Lords during the Civil War* (1910), pp. 276-82; *Clarendon Calendar*, IV.

[60]*Life of Barwick*, pp. 465-66.

[61]*Life of Barwick*, pp. 515, 525.

sions of Anglican divines whose rash utterances were thought to be imperiling the royal cause.[62] Whether he was instructed to offer more than vague asurances of the King's constancy to Protestantism and of his kindly feelings towards Presbyterians is doubtful. As Hyde told Barwick that the King would be "very tender" of parting with the revenues of the Church, Morley probably could offer no more material advantages to Puritan divines than promotion within the Anglican Church.[63]

The majority in Parliament at once showed its religious preferences by the nomination of Calamy and Manton to conduct the thanksgiving services on February 28 for what was called "the Union of the Parliament." It soon passed a series of acts and resolutions leading in the same direction. One act ordered the laws against Jesuits and priests to be put into execution.[64] Another named a new set of commissioners to approve all persons presented to benefices or lectureships. Among the judges of the fitness of ministers were Reynolds, Calamy, Manton, Ashe, Case, and Spurstow, all of whom would be likely to see that nominees would perform all their duties according to the Directory established by Parliament on January 3, 1645, and now prescribed.[65] The ordinance of August 29, 1648, for dividing the counties of England and Wales into classical presbyteries was to be put into force.[66] Another act provided that a minister in possession of a benefice on March 14 should be the lawful incumbent and be entitled to tithes. An ejected minister, however, if neither he nor his wife possessed real estate of the value of £30 per annum or personal estate worth £500, might be granted by justices of the peace an allowance out of the income of his former benefice not exceeding a fifth part.[67] In addition, Parliament adopted the Confession of Faith presented to it by the Westminster Assembly of Divines on September 25, 1646 (excepting the thirtieth and thirty-first chapters which dealt with ecclesiastical censures and synods) as the public confession of faith of the Church of England.[68] The Solemn League and Covenant was to be published and forthwith read in every church, and

[62]Morley seems to have arrived in March. Ibid., pp. 513, 517-18.

[63]Ibid., p. 524. Morley was also to see whether anything could be done to avert the possibility that the episcopal succession would cease—there were ten bishops only left alive at this time. For Morley's mission as a whole see Robert S. Bosher, *The Making of the Restoration Settlement* (New York, 1951), pp. 105-14.

[64]Mar. 12, *Acts and Ordinances*, II, 1425.

[65]*Commons Journals*, Feb. 27; Thurloe, VII, 897-98.

[66]Mar. 14, *Acts and Ordinances*, II, 1459.

[67]Mar. 16, ibid., II, 1467-69.

[68]Mar. 2, 5. *Journals*, pp. 858, 862. On the later date the act for this purpose was ordered to be printed.

hereafter read once a year: it was also to be set up in the House itself.[69]

Nearly a year ago that staunch Presbyterian Robert Baillie had written when he heard of the recall of the Rump: "I doe conceive our Church and Land was never in so great hazard to be hurt by the Sectaries and Remonstrators as this hour." Now he was troubled at the omission of the two chapters from the Confession of Faith by Parliament so that "the world may know, within their jurisdiction, Christ may be allowed no spiritual government of his Church." A little later he feared a greater evil—the restoration of episcopacy, Arminianism, and "the farre most of Poperie."[70]

The army received attention from the legislature, executive, and commander in chief. The act for settling the militia repealed the act of July 26, 1659, and vacated the powers and commissions granted in pursuance thereof. Many changes were made in the list of commissioners to execute the act. Practically a clean sweep was made of all concerned in the ejection of Parliament the previous October, and not a few were omitted who had then opposed the army but who had since showed their hostility to the readmission or were suspected as likely to oppose the restoration of kingship. Among the victims were Okey (Bedfordshire), Marten and Neville (Berkshire), Disbrowe (Cambridgeshire), Lambert (Yorkshire), Salwey (Herefordshire), and Fleetwood, Whitelocke, Barkstead, Kiffin, and James Harrington (Middlesex)—the list might be almost indefinitely extended. More surprising than the omissions were the inclusions. Whenever possible the panel for a county was headed by peers, baronets, and knights, and the rest were substantial gentry or citizens. Perhaps the most remarkable addition made by the House itself was Sir George Booth, until lately a prisoner in the Tower as a rebel.[71]

Before the bill passed through all its stages, there was a possibility of military interference. The precise course of events is obscure, but at least it is clear that at the beginning of March officers were viewing the future with anxiety. They required assurances on several points—confirmation of the sales of confiscated property, payment of arrears, and a general indemnity for all past actions. The militia bill may well have provoked agitation because the army had always been touchy on this subject. On Wednesday, March 7, the officers assembled with a remonstrance ready for printing. Okey is said to have delivered a long speech about the inundations of evils breaking in upon them to invade their

[69]Mar. 5, ibid., p. 862.

[70]*Letters and Journals*, III, 395, 398, 400.

[71]*Journals*, Mar. 10. At the same time Scot was rejected as a commissioner for Surrey. The text is in *Acts and Ordinances* under March 12.

civil and religious liberty. If great care was not taken, Charles Stuart would be introduced. Therefore, they should oblige Parliament immediately to declare for a commonwealth without king or house of lords. If Parliament refused, they must adopt such a remedy as God would put into their hands to save the nation from destruction. Clarges answered that he thought Okey's fears groundless. If Parliament was addressed in the manner proposed, the response was not likely to be agreeable. Their past history showed that members were not likely to be intimidated. Upon such an address they would probably dissolve themselves and leave the country without a government. Then officers must set up a single person, Richard Cromwell, and so expose themselves to his vengeance for the indignities they had put upon him and his family. As for General Monck, he would not assume the government, having already declared that he would rather be torn in pieces by wild horses than thus betray the nation. Monck then said that Parliament was too near its end to do the ill some of them feared. The new parliament he did not doubt would give them greater satisfaction than the present body. They should remember that none could be elected who had borne arms against Parliament. He confirmed what Clarges had stated—that if an address led to a dissolution he would not take upon himself to govern the country. Then an officer said that the qualifications for the new parliament were useless because the members to be elected would be judges of the returns and a majority of them might not be properly qualified. Monck ignored this unanswerable argument, and brought the meeting to a close with some plain speaking. He told his officers "he brought them not out of Scotland for his, nor the Parliament['s] Council; that for his part he should obey the Parliament and expected they should do the same." He may have added that it would be easier to find officers in the room of those who remained obstinate than for them to find regiments if Parliament denied pay. Possibly as a concession a meeting was arranged for the next day between ten members of Parliament and ten officers.[72]

The conference between officers and M.P.'s ended indecisively. Apparently the civilians were unwilling to give the assurances the military required about indemnity, sales, arrears of pay, the militia, and the

[72]I have followed Baker's *Chronicle* (p. 716) in the main, but have taken the two concluding sentences of Monck's from two Royalist letters in *Clarendon State Papers*, III, (pp. 696-97), both written on March 9. None of the three authorities is definite about chronology, and possibly something of what I have attributed to this meeting may have occurred at the conference of officers and M.P.'s the next day, or similar remarks may have been made on both occasions. Bordeaux, in a letter of March 8/18, clearly dated the meeting of officers the seventh, and attributed their excitement to the Parliamentary vote about the Covenant. Francisco Giavarina, on March 9/19, placed this meeting on the seventh, and, even more clearly than Bordeaux, assigned Monck's blunt speech to this occasion. For these reasons I am convinced that Guizot (II, 162) was wrong in placing Okey's remonstrance as late as he did.

future government, and based their refusal on the ground that the present Parliament could not legally pass on these matters. The officers were obliged, therefore, to be satisfied to have their demands referred to the next parliament.[73] These two days were judged to be decisive, and *Mercurius Politicus* announced that on the ninth, Monck had required all officers to repair to their commands.[74] This measure, if obeyed, would effectively prevent any more general councils of officers. Parliament now felt free to proceed with the militia bill, and added to the commissions a number of territorial magnates whose sympathies were well known to be Royalist. On the thirteenth it took an even bolder step and voted that the engagement to be true to the Commonwealth as now established be taken off the file. Once again the officers in London took alarm, and talked of a declaration against the king, nobility, and militia. Bordeaux thought the danger acute because the officers, when aroused, had never deferred to their seniors—perhaps he was thinking of the events of early May and late December, 1659.[75] But the storm soon passed, perhaps calmed by Monck's promise to write to Parliament about the militia.

Monck's letter has not been preserved, but apparently requested the suspension of the Militia Act. Parliament on the contrary had been annoyed by the delay in printing it, and authorized Prynne and two others to interview the printers, to give directions for its speedy printing, and to inquire if there was any obstruction. The next morning he reported that there had been no undue delay. Then Monck's letter was read, and Morice, Annesley, and Holles were asked to wait on the general and give him satisfaction. Naming Morice, Monck's confidant, may lend countenance to the suspicion that the letter was only an idle gesture to calm the army and that its writer really wished the act to be published.[76]

While Parliament was passing the militia bill it took measures to insure the loyalty of the standing army. On March 6 it read and approved a report from the Council that Lambert, having declined to give security in £20,000, had been committed to the Tower. The same day it deprived Overton of the governorship of Hull and a colonelcy of foot. The colonel's conduct had been ambiguous from the time of Lambert's coup d'état.

[73]*Calendar Venetian*, p. 129; Guizot, II, 379; *Nicholas Papers*, IV, 201.

[74]*Mercurius Politicus* (p. 1165) said that Monck issued the direction in accordance with a Parliamentary order.

[75]To Mazarin, Mar. 15/25, Guizot, II, 380.

[76]This is the opinion of Ludlow (II, 248-49), though he places the receipt of the letter before Prynne's visit to the printer, instead of after it, and of an anonymous correspondent of Thurloe (VII, 861). According to Ludlow, Monck protested that the appointment of disaffected commissioners "might erect such a power in opposition to the army, as might be sufficient to bring in Charles Stuart." Cf. Guizot, II, 382; *Calendar Venetian*, p. 131; *Journals*, Mar. 15, 16; *Mercurius Politicus*, pp. 1163, 1174. The newspapers have many notices about the reorganization of the militia in various counties, and some lists of officers including those for the London trained bands (*Mercurius Politicus*, p. 1205).

He had then declared his opposition to the readmission. More recently he permitted or inspired a remonstrance of the garrison at Hull, addressed to Monck but distributed to the troops at York, which expressed fears at recent events and determination to adhere to a commonwealth against Charles Stuart. Monck ordered Charles Fairfax to take command at Hull, and the Council directed Overton to appear before it immediately. He obeyed, arrived in London about March 18, and then disappeared from history except as a suspect imprisoned after the Restoration.[77]

Hesilrige's was an awkward case. Until lately he had been one of the most influential men in England, and he still retained his command of a regiment of horse and one of foot and his governorship of Berwick, Carlisle, Newcastle, and Tynemouth. On March 7, after Parliament had received a report from the Council about him, he stood up and denied that he was guilty of anything wherewith he was charged. The House referred the matter back to the Council. On the nineteenth the Council accepted his promise, together with Disbrowe's and Kelsey's, to submit peacefully. He lost his military positions, his regiment of horse being given to Fauconberg and his regiment of foot to Meyer.

Another member who stood up in Parliament to defend himself was Colonel Rich, whom the Council had committed.[78] His regiment of horse had been sent from London before Monck's arrival and distributed in the eastern counties. The colonel and most of his officers resented the readmission. At Bury St. Edmunds, according to the quartermaster's report to Monck, great dissatisfaction resulted from attempts to persuade the soldiers that Parliament intended to recall Charles Stuart. Some troopers mutinied at Ipswich, and a general rendezvous was held at Bury to which five of the six troops came. Rich is said to have refused to recognize Monck as commander in chief and to have tried to induce the foot at Colchester to join him. His men were by no means unanimous, however, and at least four score declined to march, probably towards Colchester, with him and his major, Breman. The news of this disaffection seemed the more serious because reports came to hand that Lambert, Fleetwood, Kelsey, and others were busy about Newmarket and Cambridge. Though this intelligence was false at least as regards the first two, the danger was real. Monck acted promptly and on February 26 sent Richard Ingoldsby to take command. The latter, a man of action, at once ordered the regiment to return to Bury and to bring the officers as prisoners if they would not come of their own accord. Rich tried to gain

[77]*Clarke Papers*, IV, 245, 265-66; *Leyborne-Popham MSS*, pp. 163, 170-171; *Mercurius Politicus*, p. 1157; Firth and Davies, *Regimental History*, II, 559-60.

[78]*Commons Journals*, Mar. 7.

time, but when confronted with the need for immediate decision, gave way, laid down his commission, and suffered imprisonment until released by the Council.[79] His regiment was reconstructed, only the loyal troop retaining its captain. Former officers like Babington and Elsmore were reinstated, though they had taken part in Booth's rising.[80] That the new purge was effective was soon to be demonstrated.

The officers of the navy required some attention but less than those of the army because seamen, unlike soldiers, had not thrust themselves into politics on all occasions. Their intervention on behalf of the Parliament in December was the more decisive because unexpected. The fleet Lawson commanded remained in the Thames during the ensuing weeks, and he was named a member of the Council of State, and received the thanks of Parliament and its approval of his appointments of certain officers to command frigates. He was also given a pension of £500 for his fidelity to the Parliament.[81] At St. Albans he and some of his officers met Monck who entertained them courteously.[82] After the readmission of the secluded members Lawson's stock fell. He was not one of the new Council of State and he ceased to command the fleet, although remaining a vice admiral. Parliament named Monck and Mountagu severally and jointly to be generals of the fleet, the latter being requested to join it forthwith[83] He confided in Pepys that there were "great endeavours" to restore Richard as Protector but even if successful he would not last long, "no, nor the King neither (though he [Mountagu] seems to think that he will come in), unless he carry himself very soberly and well. Everybody now drinks the King's health without any fear, whereas before it was very private that a man dare do it."[84] Mountagu had now to solve the problem how to insure that the navy would acquiesce in the restoration of monarchy nearly every civilian desired. The main obstacle seemed to be Lawson, regarded as a staunch Republican. Agents of the King had already won over Bremes, and he persuaded Lawson to follow Mountagu's lead.[85]

As soon as Lawson heard of Monck's and Mountagu's appointment he wrote to express his pleasure at it and his gratitude for his own nomination as vice admiral, "and trust I shall aprove my self faithfull in my

[79]Ibid., May 17.

[80]Firth and Davies, II, 156-58.

[81]*Commons Journals*, Jan. 2, 9, 21.

[82]Arthur W. Tedder, *The Navy of the Restoration* (Cambridge, 1916), p. 27, quoting *Publick Intelligencer*, Jan. 23-30, p. 1052.

[83]*Commons Journals*, Mar. 2; Pepys, Feb. 29, where Mountagu is said to have been appointed by the Council.

[84]*Diary*, Mar. 6.

[85]*Clarendon State Papers*, III, 652, 706. I am not sure that "Bremes" was the Arnold Brahams of Kent knighted by Charles II on May 27, 1660.

Imployment under your Lordships." He also returned thanks for an addition of a pound a day to his salary and for the settlement of the £500 a year previously granted by Parliament. He then proceeded to recommend that Captain Dakins be commissioned as rear admiral, and others as commanders of ships in accordance with an enclosed list which had been approved by the commissioners of the navy. In reply the two generals at sea assured him that his advice would be weighed, but they added that when they found able and faithful commanders formerly employed, they would continue them in their position.[86] When they came to revise the list, the "Naseby" was assigned to Mountagu as his flagship with Roger Cuttance as captain—his name did not appear at all in Lawson's list. Consequently Lawson had to shift to the "London," whence Stayner moved to the "Swiftsure," replacing Dakins who was not given any command.[87]

Mountagu joined the fleet on March 23 accompanied by his secretary, who began to realize his new importance when he received a letter addressed to Samuel Pepys Esq., "of which God knows I was not a little proud." Mountagu had to proceed warily because there were rumors that some of Lawson's captains were dissatisfied and threatened to oppose him, but Lawson denied the reports.[88] In a letter to Monck, Mountagu explained that he took no notice of some commander's "unhandsome passages" because he did not want to stir up animosity. But Dakins, now of the "Worcester," was an Anabaptist, "much discontented & busy in stirring up others, & in the river very weak and undutiful." Dakins expected to command a squadron sailing as a convoy to the Straits but whether he should be trusted to that extent needed consideration. Another of the same principles, designs, and humors was Captain Newberry of the "Plymouth," whose way of governing his ship was "very discontenting & wearisome to his men that are not of his way." Mountagu rather timidly proposed that a member of the Council should move their removal and so "take off any unkindness from me towards them." He then mentioned a Captain Algate of the "Oxford," guilty of "very undutiful speeches" about Monck, and suggested that his ship should be given to Cuttance's son.[89] None of the suspected captains commanded ships in the fleet that weighed anchor to fetch the King home from Scheveningen.[90] Having weeded out disaffected captains, Mountagu felt

[86]Bodleian Library, Carte MSS 73, 355, 449, the letter to Lawson being an unsigned copy. The enclosed list, dated February 22, is ibid., f. 222.

[87]The revised list is dated March 7, ibid, f. 231.

[88]Pepys, Mar. 29.

[89]Copy of this letter to Monck, dated April 12, in Carte MSS 73, 399. As Mountagu was not certain about Cuttance's loyalty, the suggested offer to his son was an indirect bribe (Pepys, Apr. 11).

[90]Granville Penn, *Memorials of Sir William Penn*, II, 220-221; Pepys, Apr. 15, 17.

he could relax the discipline imposed by Puritan austerity. Pepys records that the evening of April 23 was "the first time we had any sport among the seamen, and indeed there was extraordinary good sport after my Lord [Mountagu] had done playing at ninepins." How the times had changed may be judged from Mountagu's singing a ballad upon the Rump. There are too many ballads on the Rump to admit of a guess at the one the admiral sang, but they are all extremely derogatory and usually very indecent. A verse in one of the few quotable runs as follows:

> Our Lawes, Lives, Lands, Liberties, were upon sale,
> By this everlasting *Rump*, Fag-end or tail,
> Yea to save our very souls, they refus'd to take bail,
> Which no body can deny.[91]

Parliament had been winding up the session in a very dilatory way. Some of the readmitted members seem to have caught from the Republicans the itch to rule. Popular impatience at the delay was summed up in a comment of March 1: "Rumpe Maior begins to smell as ranke as Rumpe Minor."[92] When at length on March 8 a bill to call and hold a parliament on April 25 was introduced, many amendments seem to have been proposed, the most important being to debar from voting at the general election all who had been in arms for the late King or his son. This was defeated by 93 to 56, the tellers for the minority being Marten and Scot.[93] A delaying proposal to refer the bill to a grand committee was only defeated the next day by 84 to 66, and an exciting debate ensued. Prynne boldly asserted that the Parliament had been dissolved on the King's death, but if not, then they were a part only of the House of Commons and in either case they could do nothing without the King and the House of Lords. He and other lawyers there present, he argued, had drawn up a bill against Laud, archbishop of Canterbury, for endeavoring to subvert the constitution which had cost the archbishop his life, but the bill now introduced would destroy all the fundamentals of law and government. Blind old Edward Stephens seconded Prynne, frankly stating that the only way to save the dying kingdoms was to call home the King. Annesley replied that he could not contradict what had passed but, the ship of state being ready to sink, they must steer the course necessary to save her, even though they departed from the right and

[91]*Rump: or an Exact Collection*, II, 120. Thomason's date was March 1, 1660.

[92]*Memoirs of the Verney Family*, III, 469-70. One of the few tracts in favor of prolonging the session was *No New Parliament*, dated March 12. The argument was that a new Parliament would be hostile to the old cause.

[93]March 13. Marten and Scot were said to have returned to the House on the eighth.

legal way.[94] The debate was adjourned to the next day. The awkward question in whose name the writs should run was solved by the adoption of the old formula—in the names of the keepers of the liberties of England by authority of Parliament. The right to sit was denied to anyone who had abetted the rebellion in Ireland, was a Papist, or had assisted in the war against the Parliament, or whose father had done so, unless father or son had since manifested his good affection to the Parliament. No qualifications at all were imposed on electors except those provided in statutes.[95] At the eleventh hour a proviso was added, which suggests that Prynne's words had not fallen on deaf ears: "That the single Actings of this House, enforced by the pressing necessities of the present times, are not intended to infringe, much less take away, that Ancient Native Right which the House of Peers (consisting of those Lords who did engage in the Cause of the Parliament, against the Forces raised in the name of the late King, and so continued untill One Thousand six hundred and fourty eight) had and have to be a part of the Parliament of England."

Before the dissolution a disorderly and apparently irrelevant debate took place about the execution of Charles I. John Crew moved that before they separated for the last time members should bear their witness against "the horrid murder." One after another rose to deny their concurrence in it. Then Scot bravely defended the execution and hoped he would never repent of it and desired that on his tombstone might be inscribed: "*Here lies* Thomas Scot, *who adjudged to death the late King.*"[96]

Macaulay twice described the Long Parliament. "In November 1640 met that renowned Parliament which, in spite of many errors and disasters, is justly entitled to the reverence and gratitude of all who, in

---

[94]This is a Royalist account in *Clarendon State Papers,* III, 696. Another Royalist thought that Prynne's bold language for the King earned him the title of "the Cato of this age." Carte, *Ormonde Papers,* II, 312; Thurloe, VII, 855. According to Price (p. 782), Prynne was admonished for his boldness by Monck. A letter dated March 9 attributed the remarks of Stephens to the debate on restoring the Covenant (*Nicholas Papers,* IV, 199). He may have used similar language on two occasions. Prynne and his supporters shared Hyde's opinion that to summon another Parliament was "the farthest way about" to restore the King, and to have wished to reserve that honor for the sitting House (*Life of Dr. John Barwick* [1724], pp. 507-508).

[95]Though it is not specifically stated, I think there is no doubt that by "statutes" Parliament meant acts which had received the royal assent.

[96]There are several versions of this sentence. I have followed the one in *An Exact and Most Impartial Accompt of the Indictment . . . of Nine and Twenty Regicides,* 1660, p. 86. Cf. Ludlow, II, 249-50, and note 1; *Memoirs of the Verney Family,* III, 473. A ballad-writer (*Rump: or an Exact Collection,* II, 45) thus rendered the sentence:

> That precious Saint *Scot*
> Shall not be forgot,
> According to his own desires
> Instead of Neck-Verse
> Shall have it writ on his Herse,
> *Herr hangs one of the Kings Tryers.*

305

any part of the world, enjoy the blessings of constitutional government." In March, 1660, "that memorable Parliament, which had, in the course of twenty eventful years, experienced every variety of fortune, which had triumphed over its sovereign, which had been enslaved and degraded by its servants, which had been twice ejected and twice restored, solemnly decreed its own dissolution."[97] It is well to recall the great achievements of its early sessions which time has not impaired. Even towards the end its stout fight against military dictatorship should be remembered to its credit. Though, as one present confessed, the Parliament expired only "after many sad pangs & groanes" from its members,[98] yet to contemporaries its most popular act was its last. Pepys, noting the joy in Westminster Hall as the Speaker passed through without his mace, made the significant comment: "And now they begin to talk loud of the King." He then heard how the previous day at 5 p.m., a man had taken a ladder to the Great Exchange and obliterated the inscription on the statue of Charles I—*Exit tyrannus, Regum ultimus, anno libertatis Angliae, anno Domini 1648, Januarie XXX.* Then a large bonfire was kindled and people shouted "God bless King Charles the Second."[99] The work of the Rump was soon to be swept away but the work of the Long Parliament which had received the royal assent was destined to endure.

---

[97]*History of England,* ed. C. H. Firth, I, 87, 129.

[98]*Memoirs of the Verney Family,* III, 473.

[99]For the identification of the man as Michael Darby, "now painter to the company of mercers," see *Mercurius Publicus,* Aug. 16-23, 1660.

CHAPTER XVI

The Election of the Convention Parliament

THE ROYALISTS' position at the end of 1659 seemed as hopeless as in May after the first recall of the Rump. The prospect of foreign aid had vanished. Charles II had returned to Brussels on December 16 from his fruitless journey to the Pyrenees with no more likelihood of support from France and Spain now that they were at peace than when they were at war. Indeed, the peace had cut the ground from under his feet, because Spain no longer required his aid against France. The best he could expect was permission to remain in Flanders "with a narrow assignment for his bread, which was a melancholic condition for a king."[1] The Rump's resurrection seemed to be proof that Providence approved its usurpation. There was a faint, very faint, hope that Monck's march into England might produce some change for the better.[2]

To Royalists in England Monck was a sphinx. Mordaunt was unable to foresee his intentions but feared the worst. He regarded the general as the only possible bulwark against a restoration and apprehended he would prove a devil. "Monck is so dark a man," he complained, "no perspective can looke through him, and it will be like the last sceane of some excellent play, which the most juditious cannot positively say how it will end."[3] Hyde, the recipient of these opinions, thought the prospect of affairs melancholy, because if Monck proved obstinate a foreign army only could recover the kingdom.[4] In the instruction for the King's commissioners in England they were urged to add Northampton and Chesterfield to their number, if the earls were willing to join the trust; to preserve unity; to name two at the least for every county who in their turn should pick others to serve with them and issue commissions for regiments and governorships; to restrain unseasonable insurrections and not to take up arms until the King should appear in their midst, unless an opportunity for seizing a good port should facilitate his coming; to raise money; and to ascertain what arms Royalists possessed. Mordaunt and Sir John Grenville were to make it their particular care to find the

---

[1]*Clarendon Calendar*, IV, 485, 489-90; Clarendon, *Rebellion*, XVI, 75, 112. George Morley wrote on January 31/February 10, that not a penny had reached the King from Spain so that the court was never in greater want. *The Correspondence of John Cosin* (Surtees Society, 1869), Part I, p. 292.

[2]Clarendon, *Rebellion*, XVI, 111, 114.

[3]Coate, *Letter-Book of ... Mordaunt*, pp. 155, 166-67, 174, 176, 180.

[4]*Clarendon Calendar*, IV, 545.

speediest way to let Monck know the kindness and good opinion the King had always had for him.[5]

Monck, however, consistently declined to receive Royalist agents, who remained as much puzzled as before about his intentions. The reports of his activities and plans, as well as the interpretation Royalists placed upon them, varied almost from day to day. When he first arrived at London he was thought to favor the Rump and filling up its vacancies rather than the readmission of secluded members or a new parliament, which the Royalists preferred. His initial severity against the City was judged tyrannical and a proof that he supported the commonwealth.[6] His sudden change of front raised hopes that the tide had turned against the Rump and made a great impression at the exiled court. A better prophet than most, William Howard foresaw that if a full Parliament voted for monarchy Monck would acquiesce. Bets were reported on February 17 that three days hence the Rump would sit as the Rump no longer but would be swamped by the secluded members. On the day they were admitted Mordaunt wrote to the King: "Hee that made you our King has restored your Majesty to your crownes," but even this optimist advised some things to be done, namely to persuade guilty opponents that if they supported the King their offenses would be forgiven. Another writer thought that the most potent argument to unite all parties was the royal constancy to the Protestant religion.[7]

Hyde felt that Royalists should be patient with Monck, and rely on the influence of Clobery, now an active Royalist. The readmission of the secluded members, he thought, was great news, but he could not see how they could call a new parliament after they had dissolved this, and he wondered why they did not begin a treaty with the King upon the terms discussed at Uxbridge at the beginning of 1645.[8] Hyde no doubt had in mind two of the propositions Parliament presented to Charles I as conditions of peace—that the King should take the covenant, agree to the substitution of Presbyterianism and the Directory for episcopacy and the Prayer Book, and consent to the control of the army and navy by parliamentary commissioners.[9] Parliament did try to re-establish Presbyterianism as the national religion, but without any negotiations with Charles II. Those Presbyterians who endeavored to lay down conditions for the King's restoration preferred the terms actually accepted by Charles I at Newport which were less stringent. Curiously enough, in view of the great importance attached to control of the militia in

[5]Coate, *Letter-Book of . . . Mordaunt*, pp. 157-60.
[6]*Clarendon Calendar*, IV, 544-46, 549, 551-52, 555-56; Hist. MSS Comm. *Fifth Report*, p. 194.
[7]*Clarendon Calendar*, IV, 560, 563, 565, 567, 569, 573.
[8]*Clarendon Calendar*, IV, 577-78, 600.
[9]Gardiner, *Great Civil War*, II, 124 seq.

1642, no significant attempt was now made to keep in Parliamentary hands control of the armed forces, though these were much more important in 1660 than in 1642.[10] That the Presbyterians would expect rewards had long been anticipated. Hyde's attitude now towards them was consistent with his view of them eighteen years before. Just as he had failed to perceive any moral fervor behind Puritanism and had attributed the start of the civil war to private ambition, so in 1660 he felt that promises of preferment to leaders like Manchester would suffice to induce them to support the restoration of monarchy. Of Waller, for example, he wrote: "Many think that Sir William Waller hath of late declined that warmth he hath professed towards the King's service, and that he more adheres to the passion and rigour of the Presbyterians than he hath seemed to do, which I hope proceeds rather from his design of converting them, than from being corrupted by them. My Lord Mordaunt will easily discover what place will oblige him." Similarly, Anglican clergymen should try to win over Presbyterian ministers by assuring them "of present good Preferments in the Church."[11] Clearly Hyde hoped that buying up prominent members of the group might prevent the imposition of conditions.

In addition to the harsh terms Presbyterians might impose, there was another possible obstacle to the recall of Charles II—that another "single person" might be preferred. Of the three possible choices, Lambert had thrown away his chances by his conduct during the last three months of 1659. The proposals of some Royalists in October that his daughter Mary should marry the King merely illustrates the proverb that a drowning man will catch at any straw.[12] Lambert missed one opportunity in failing to declare for a free parliament after his break with the Rump. Then he might have anticipated Monck.[13]

According to Royalists' letters Richard Cromwell had some influential supporters. Birch, Fiennes, Mountagu, Pierrepont, St. John, and Thurloe were all named as favoring the restoration of the Protectorate, but direct evidence is lacking, and it is difficult to believe that most of his alleged advocates considered his claims very seriously.[14] Hyde was right in refusing to worry about Richard's pretensions.[15]

[10]In a letter of March 23 a Royalist told Hyde that the severer Presbyterians intended to propose in the new Parliament that the militia for fifteen years be [? controlled by Parliamentary commissioners]—the sentence is incomplete. *Clarendon Calendar*, IV, 616.

[11]*Clarendon State Papers*, II, 657; Barwick, p. 525. Hyde also wrote in his letter of January 13/23, 1660, that "the King doth not look that the Presbyterians shall serve him for nothing, but intends to gratify the several persons who shall serve him eminently with offices and honours."

[12]For the proposals, see Dawson, *Cromwell's Understudy*, ch. xxiii.

[13]Kingsly told Hyde (January 12) that his officers and men despised Lambert most of all because they had offered to stand by him if he declared for a free Parliament. *Clarendon Calendar*, IV, 517.

[14]*Clarendon Calendar*, IV, 543, 572, 581, 584, 586, 592, 595, 602, 610.

[15]Ibid., 588.

Monck, the third possible rival to Charles II, was barred from the list by his convictions as well as by his actions and declarations. He had been perfectly consistent in trying to make the army not the master but the servant of the civil authority. Suggestions had been made to him from time to time that he should assume the Cromwellian mantle but he had rejected them all. He was now about to adhere to the Royalist party. The time when he made up his mind to take the plunge has been variously judged by modern as well as by contemporary writers.[16] The probability is that no time can be definitely fixed, because his was a very gradual conversion. Events and not political theories or arguments converted him. After Oliver's death and Richard's ignominious fall he acquiesced in, rather than welcomed, the recall of the Rump in May. When Lambert sent the Rump packing he supported it not because he cherished any delusions about it but because it represented the civil authority against military dictatorship. He was actuated by two principles, the desire to curb the exorbitancies of the English council of officers and the wish to avoid another civil war. He did not look far ahead. One step at a time was his rule. He gave the Rump a last chance. He may have expected, possibly wished, it to fail but he did not follow Oliver's example and go to Westminster to tell the members to be gone. When its perversity was beyond question he adopted the characteristic compromise of allowing the secluded members to take their seats in order to bring to an end the perpetual Parliament, and to insure that a freely elected House should soon meet.

During his march south he had ample opportunity of studying public opinion which was overwhelmingly hostile to the Rump. He found identical sentiments in London. The remedy the Rump had proposed was to imprison petitioners for a free parliament and to treat London as a center of rebellion. The critical period was from February 9 to 21, 1660. Once Monck had decided to recall the secluded members, he had crossed the Rubicon. Most likely he felt in his heart of hearts that every step he had taken from Coldstream had brought him nearer to the Restoration, but he may have shrunk from recognizing the inevitable consequences of his own actions. Better than his wife, brother, chaplains, and others of his entourage, he perceived that time was essential so that the armed forces could perceive that even from their own selfish point of view the old constitution must be set up again. A too precipitate step, and the army might once again have intervened in politics. He was by nature a cautious man—a waiter on Providence—and yet his step-by-

[16]For some judicious comments see Miss Coate's note, "William Morice and the Restoration of Charles II," in *Eng. Hist. Rev.*, XXXIII (1918), 367-77.

step strategy did keep the restive army under control and did avoid bloodshed.

Clarendon, who did not like Monck, concluded that the general threw in his lot with the Royalists only when he had no other resource. "If he had resolved it sooner, he had been destroyed himself; the whole machine being so infinitely above his strength, that it could be only moved by a divine hand; and it is glory enough to his memory, that he was instrumental in bringing those mighty things to pass, which he had neither wisdom to foresee, nor courage to attempt, nor understanding to contrive."[17] This judgment is harsh, but is correct in so far as the "wisdom to foresee" is concerned, because Monck's whole attitude was one of wait and see. He never tried to force the pace of destiny. A ballad, *The Glory of the West*, likened him to

> Another Fabius, whose wise delayes
> (Like a misty morn, guilt with the Sun's noon'd rayes)
> Have Crown'd him with the Glorious Bayes.

He lagged behind public opinion, but he had an invincible army to conciliate. He used to the greatest advantage the divisions in the army. Meanwhile the civilians were becoming more and more united. To move, stop until the reaction had spent itself, then move again—these were his simple tactics. To prove, even on paper, that any bolder plan than his would have achieved results more quickly and as peacefully would be difficult.

A day or so after the Long Parliament had dissolved itself Monck consented to receive his kinsman, Sir John Grenville, son of the Sir Bevil who had fallen so gallantly at Lansdowne in 1643.[18] Sir John had already waited on Monck in London in the hope of a private conference but had been baffled by the general's rising as soon as the rest of the company had departed and saying, "Goodnight, Cousin; it is late."[19] At last Grenville applied to Morice, who arranged a meeting in his own chamber at St. James's, and who acted as doorkeeper to prevent the intrusion of other visitors. Grenville at once said "that he was infinitely obliged to his Excellency for giving him this opportunity of discharging himself of a trust of great importance both to himself and the whole Kingdom that had been long deposited in his hands; and that, whatsoever became of him, he thought himself very happy to have this good

---

[17]*Rebellion*, XVI, 115.

[18]Baker (*Chronicle*, p. 717) dates the interview the evening after the dissolution of Parliament which he assigns wrongly to March 17.

[19]Maseres, *Select Tracts*, II, 784. Price seems to have learned of the interview from Grenville, to whom he dedicated his *Mystery*, because he claimed to give Grenville's own words on this occasion.

occasion of performing his duty, in obeying the commands of the King, his Master." He then handed over the letter which the King had written on July 21, a royal letter to himself, and the commission he had from the King to treat with the general.[20] The general at first asked his kinsman how he dared speak to him of such a matter, but received the bold reply that the danger he incurred was no greater than he had run before. Monck embraced him, thanked him for the prudence he had shown, read the letters and the commission, and exclaimed: "I hope the King will forgive what is past, both in my words and actions . . . for my heart was ever faithful to him; but I was never in a condition to do him Service till this present time. And you shall assure his Majesty that I am now not only ready to obey his Commands but to sacrifice my Life and Fortune in his Service." He then called Morice to join them.[21]

Two or three days later Monck heard from the Speaker the advice which the latter was sending the King.[22] The heads of Lenthall's advice were eleven in number. Among them were cautions against reliance on the army and acceptance of highly prejudicial conditions which were likely to be patterned on the Newport treaty. The most dangerous of them was the loss of control over the militia without which a king was but half a king. Toleration for all should be the rule because then the Roman Catholics would balance the Presbyterians and sectaries. Royalists in England should refrain from boasting that they would call all others to an account. The advice of the kings of France and Spain should be sought on any proposals from England so that "your Majesty may engage them to see articles performed, which will be of mighty advantage to you . . . I fear you may have need of such friends."[23]

Monck's counsel was briefer and more statesmanlike. At a second interview he told Grenville that, to quiet the fears of the armed forces which he was remodeling, the King should issue a general pardon to all except such as Parliament might exclude from it, promise to accept any acts Parliament might pass to confirm the sales of public lands to soldiers and others, establish liberty of conscience for all his subjects who did

[20] The letter of July 21 is reprinted in *Collection of Letters*, p. 78. The reply there inserted is a forgery. This alleged early communication contradicts the authentic reports of Monck's first Royalist overtures to Charles II. The commission (to Belasyse, Fauconberg, and Grenville) is printed out of place in *Clarendon State Papers*, III, 417-18; it should be dated about July 11, 1659 (see *Clarendon Calendar*, IV, 268). The letter to Grenville I have not identified.

[21] Maseres, II, 755-56. Monck's defense, that he could not have acted sooner, is substantially in agreement with Hyde's verdict, already noted.

[22] Lady Mordaunt in a letter of March 30 (a Friday) told her husband that the Speaker had unburdened himself to Monck "Wednesday-was-sevennight [i.e., the twenty-first]." *Clarendon State Papers*, III, 711. Monck listened but said little and apparently concealed successfully his interview with Grenville, leaving Lenthall under the impression that his counsel was responsible for the meeting which, he thought, was still to take place. Even Mordaunt knew no more on the twenty-fourth than that Monck had promised Morice that he would receive the King's letters from Grenville. Ibid., III, 706.

[23] *Clarendon State Papers*, III, 712-14; Thurloe, VII, 872-73.

not disturb the public peace, and at once withdraw from the Spanish dominions and establish himself at Breda because he [Monck] had certain intelligence that the King would be detained if he lingered on Spanish soil. When Grenville had memorized these counsels he tore up his notes and departed without any written message from the general to his sovereign. Shortly afterwards he left for Brussels in company with Mordaunt.[24] On their arrival they concealed themselves by day and attended the King in Hyde's lodgings at night.

The first of Monck's advices to be considered was removal from Spanish territory. The King had already sought permission to go to Holland. Now his departure was hastened by a report that a guard of horse had been ordered to see that he did not leave Brussels. The King with a few attendants set out in the early morning for Dutch soil, arriving at Breda the night of April 4. On the way he gave Grenville the declaration, to become famous as the Declaration of Breda, and various dispatches for Monck, the Speaker, the Speaker of the House of Lords, Monck and Mountagu, and the Lord Mayor of London.[25] The three subjects which had given Hyde the greatest trouble were the confirmation of all sales, a general toleration, and an indemnity for all past offenses. The first involved the lands of crown and church and delinquents, the second violated many statutes and was inconsistent with the peace of the realm, and the third, if without exceptions, included the regicides, whose pardon the King felt would violate his honor and conscience. The problem was solved by making "a general reference of all things which he could not reserve to himself to the wisdom of the Parliament, upon presumption that they would not exact more from him than he was willing to consent to; since he well knew that, whatever title they assumed or he gave them, they must have another kind of parliament to confirm all that was done by them, and without which they could not be safe and contented nor his majesty obliged."[26] The declaration, together with the other documents dated

[24]Baker, p. 718. It is here stated that Grenville and Mordaunt reached Ostend on March 23. This is an impossible date because they did not leave London until March 26 and because Charles II could not have written as he did to Monck on March 27 (*Clarendon Calendar*, IV, 620) if he had first seen Grenville, who would not require more than a day or two to reach Brussels from Ostend. Also, the narrative in Baker implies only one interview between Monck and Grenville, but I believe there were two at an interval of several days. Apart from the definite statements by Price and Clarendon (*Rebellion*, XVI, 168) that Grenville received his instructions at "the next conference," I think it certain that Monck had conversed with Lenthall before he drew up his own suggestions. When Mordaunt wrote to the King on the twenty-fourth that Monck had consented to receive Grenville, he was correct in one sense—Monck was going to see Grenville but it was for the second, not the first time. Therefore I infer that the second meeting took place late on the twenty-fourth or on the twenty-fifth.

[25]Clarendon, *Rebellion*, XVI, 173-79.

[26]Ibid., pp. 171-72. News of the early parliamentary returns is said to have influenced the decision to adopt the formula used in the declaration. The earliest letter among the Clarendon correspondence which gives any details of elections was dated March 30 from London (*Calendar*, IV, 626), but Grenville and Mordaunt could have reported the first returns.

from Breda, were not published until they had been read in Parliament on May 1, so further discussion of their contents is reserved for later treatment.

The six weeks from the dissolution of the Long Parliament to the meeting of the Convention are remarkable for intense propaganda. In England manifestations of Royalist enthusiasm were to be seen on all sides. The author of a newsbook ventured to begin with some rhymes of which the following is a specimen:

> Religion now will serve no more
> To cloak our false professors;
> There's none so blinde but plainly sees
> Who were the Lands Oppressors.

He ended with "God prosper long our noble King, &c."[27] As a correspondent of Nicholas stated: "The pulpits, the press, the people in city and counties, with much impatience call for their king."[28] On March 18 Pepys heard a sermon of which the substance can be inferred from the text, "Pray for the life of the King and the King's son." The next day he recorded two proclamations, ordering cavaliers and disbanded officers to leave London. The first was generally disregarded with impunity and "all the discourse now-a-day is that the King will come again." The second elicited the arrogant comment from one of its victims, Major Richard Creed, "that he looked upon it as if they had said, that all God's people should depart the town."[29] The Council of State promised £10 to every informer against anyone trying to corrupt the army.[30] Another proclamation was issued for the arrest of Livewell Chapman for publishing seditious books and pamphlets, among which had been Milton's *Readie & Easie Way*. The Council is said to have offered a reward of £20 for the apprehension of the author of *News from Brussels*, allegedly written by one of the King's attendants but generally attributed to Marchamont Nedham, who was dismissed from the editorship of the official newsbook. His successors were Giles Dury and Henry Muddiman, the first a nonentity, the second an able journalist untroubled by political principles.[31]

These measures were insignificant, however, compared with those taken to keep the army loyal. Clarges, alive to the murmurs of discon-

[27]*Mercurius Honestus*, Mar. 14-21. Thomason records only the one issue, which is all I have. Probably there were no more.

[28]*Calendar Domestic*, p. 393.

[29]Creed is said to have been imprisoned, so he may have disobeyed the order. *Clarendon Calendar*, IV, 615.

[30]Steele, *Tudor and Stuart Proclamations*, Nos. 3166, 3170, 3174.

[31]*Thomason Tracts*, II, 291; *Clarendon Calendar*, IV, 629; Masson, *Life of Milton*, V, 670-672.

tent, proposed to Monck to draw up an engagement for all to sign to acquiesce in whatever the next parliament should enact. The general agreed, though thinking such a pledge very hard to exact. Thereupon, his subordinate framed an engagement and consulted with Ashley Cooper and Annesley, and Colonels Howard and Knight, who all approved. Knight undertook to get the signatures of the officers of his own regiment and the general's, together with those of the lifeguard, and Howard the like from his regiment now remodeled. Then the officers of all the regiments in London were summoned to St. James's. There Knight told them of the address some officers had framed to the general and proposed that all should sign it. The address was then read. After mentioning that a wonderful Providence had brought them into a hopeful way of settlement, it alleged there were too many who, seeking their private interests rather than the public good, were trying to return to the old state of confusion. Therefore, the signers declared to their leader that they would as officers obey their superior's orders or any commands that might emanate from the Council or Parliament, and that, according to the late proclamation, they would hold no meetings for drafting declarations concerning matters of state, "thereby avoiding those Mischiefs, which made many lately in Arms, so justly distasteful to the People, by making themselves a divided Interest from the rest of them." The address was soon signed by the officers of the ten regiments in London and the lifeguard, and of the regiments in Yorkshire, and then presented to Monck on April 11. It was then recommended to the other regiments in England and Scotland. Refusal to sign was tantamount to resigning commissions. Vacancies among colonels were filled by giving regiments of horse to Fauconberg, Rossiter, and Mountagu, and one of foot to Sheffield—all four being Royalists.[32] At the same time, in order to insure that those local forces should be led by trustworthy officers, Monck and the Council were busy going over the lists of officers proposed for the militia by the respective commissioners for each county.

Meanwhile the war on paper was being waged most vigorously. One of the few tracts opposing the King's return was Nedham's, a very able caricature in the form of an old Cavalier's letter "which casually became thus publique." It represents him as loathing the Presbyterians not only because they began the Civil War but because they became Royalists not from love of monarchy, but hatred of the fanatics. We must court them now through necessity not choice. "Hug them you cannot hang,

[32]Baker's *Chronicle*, pp. 719-20; *Mercurius Politicus*, p. 1252. Subscriptions from outlying regiments came in for the rest of the month. A Royalist noted that twenty-three of the lifeguard had been cashiered about March 23. *Clarendon Calendar*, IV, 615-16.

at least until you can." As for the attempt to impose conditions on the King, remember Machiavelli—only a fool thinks an oath can tame a prince beyond his pleasure. Even if the King has forgotten his wrongs, there is enough fire in his father's ashes to consume every adversary. To deceive the Presbyterians the King orders us all to be "plaguy-godly," though he can scarcely conceal his laughter when they preach to him. A Roundhead is always a Roundhead; and black and white devils are alike to us. We cannot live in peace so long as one remains alive who was responsible for the execution of Charles I or of his adherents, but we must use all art to make them submit tamely to the halter. Let us press the speedy arming of the City regiments, so that if other means fail we may cut our passage to the throne through traitors' blood.[33]

Nedham's tract was near enough to the true sentiments of a Cavalier to require an immediate answer to what its writer, John Evelyn, described as "fictitious stuff, put into a most malicious dress of Drollery." The reply starts with a remarkable eulogy of Charles II as fictitious as anything Nedham had written—"His person so lovely, amiable and gracefull . . . so meek, gentle, and sweet of Behaviour; so firm, constant, and obliging in his Friendships . . . but above all, so firmly and irremoveably fixed, to the profession of the true Protestant Religion." The tract ends with a most emphatic repudiation of the charge that Loyalists harbored any thoughts of revenge or intended to recoup their losses by confiscating their adversaries' estates.[34] Eulogies of the King and professions of willingness to forget the past are two themes that run through many tracts. One endowed Charles with wisdom, justice, fortitude, courage, clemency, faithfulness, industry, temperance, and steadfastness to his religion.[35] The authorship of this tribute has been assigned, probably doubtfully, to George Morley, later bishop of Winchester, one of whose purposes in coming to England at Hyde's request was to deny that the King was a Roman Catholic. The services of foreign divines were enlisted to testify to the King's constancy to Protestantism, especially when residing in France.[36] As to Nedham's point about imposing terms, Cavaliers waited until the Parliamentary invitation to the King to return, and then repudiated the very idea. As one pamphleteer stated, all cried out for a King, not the shadow of one, a King

[33]This tract or alleged letter is dated March 10 from Brussels.

[34]*The Late News or Message from Bruxels Unmasked.*

[35]*A Character of Charles the Second*, dated by Thomason Apr. 30. Another tract, *Policy no Policy*, has another description of the King's person and character.

[36]See the extracts in Kennet (*Register*, pp. 110-111), the references in Airy's edition of Burnet's *Own Time* (I, 159), and Alexander Robertson, *The Life of Sir Robert Moray* (1922), pp. 102-104. The longest of these testimonials—*A Letter Farther and more fully evidencing the Kings stedfastness in the Protestant religion*, by de l'Angle of the Protestant church at Rouen—was dated by Thomason June 1, so it was too late to serve its immediate purpose.

invested with inviolable authority and power, limited only by the ancient laws. As for those peers who would caress His Majesty's person but betray his authority with a kiss, if they were "present at any of our dayly Clubs," and heard the censures poured on them, they would soon cease their odious machinations.[37]

Apparently the nobility and gentry of Worcestershire were the first to publish a declaration that they had no thought of revenge upon those who had been of a contrary judgment but wished only for peace and the unity of the nation.[38] Their example was widely followed. Perhaps the most impressive of these olive branches emanated from Royalists in and about London. After praising Monck for leading them through the wilderness of confusion without passing the Red Sea of blood, they denied the charge that they were implacable; they intended to wait quietly in expectation that a future parliament would produce a perfect settlement both in church and state, beneath the foundations of which all rancor and animosities should be buried.[39]

There was much direct propaganda in favor of the King and, at least after the invitation to Charles II to return to the throne, some sermons in vindication of the divine right of kings.[40] Yet there were far more tracts which indirectly helped the royal cause by discrediting its opponents, past and present. Ballads, satirical verses, and tracts in the form of queries poured from the press, all holding up to ridicule the Rump, the English army leaders, and the fanatics. Their alleged humble origins, their ambition and hypocrisy, and their greed for confiscated estates, excited many rude rhymes and lively tracts. All restraint was cast aside. The liberty of the press degenerated into such license that no man's reputation was safe.[41] Some of the ablest writers combined personal abuse of an unquotable kind with selected bits of history designed to show the inconsistencies of the Commonwealthsmen. They were reminded that they had taken the oaths of allegiance and supremacy, the Protestation, the Solemn League and Covenant, the Engagement to be true to a government without King or House of Lords, and had subscribed addresses to live and die under Oliver and Richard Cromwell. The names of the regicides, as well as the martyrdom

[37]T. C., *Vox & Votum Populi Anglicani . . . in a letter to . . . the Earle of Manchester* (dated May 7), pp. 4, 8-9.

[38]Mar. 4, *Thomason Tracts*, II, 289.

[39]Apr. 20. Printed both in Baker's *Chronicle*, pp. 722-23, and in Kennet, *Register*, pp. 120-121. About the time Parliament met, many similar declarations were issued. They can be found listed in the *Thomason Tracts*.

[40]An example is a sermon preached on May 24 at East Coker, Somerset, by William Walwyn (to be distinguished from the Leveller of the same name) entitled *God Save the King*.

[41]If used with care, however, the abuse may supply guidance to the original means of livelihood of many officers and public figures of the time.

of Charles I, were kept prominently before the public eye. The opponents of monarchy were declared to have been members of the high courts of justice, sequestrators, excisemen, and trustees for the sale of royal, clerical, and delinquent estates—in short, notorious villains and diabolical hypocrites responsible for all oppressions.[42]

On the other side appeared Milton's last pamphlet before the Restoration. It was entitled *Brief Notes Upon a Late Sermon*, in reply to a discourse Matthew Griffith had delivered in the Mercers' Chapel on March 25, from the text "My son, fear God and the King." The sermon was too outspoken a plea for the restoration of monarchy to be politic at the moment, and the author was summoned before the Council and committed to Newgate.[43] Milton's answer is not one of his happiest efforts but shows how even in April he still dared to argue for a commonwealth against kingship. In its turn it provoked L'Estrange's *No Blinde Guides*, which, after a brief review of Milton's justification of the King's execution, is a page-by-page attempt to show that the passages of Scripture and the references to recent history in *Brief Notes* were misapplied. The contrast between the indifference which had formerly attended most of Milton's political writings and the vehemence with which he was now assailed is most striking. Although some of his critics were content with satirical ridicule and dismissed the *Readie & Easie Way* as "all windy foppery,"[44] others, like G. S. in *The Dignity of Kingship Asserted*, recalled the defense of Charles I's execution and *Eikonoklastes* in order to excite public opinion against their author.[45] In his epistle dedicatory, G. S. praises Milton's language as smooth and tempting, his expressions as political and apt to move the affections, but the subject matter he thought of "desperate consequence." He himself wrote because "dangerous, villanous wits misapplyed, have done more mischief with their Pens, than the Soldier with his weapons, to your Majesties cause, for by such Books and pamphlets the inconsiderate Soldier, that before was but your mercenary Enemy, is now perswaded, that in reviling your sacred Person, casting off Your Authority, and resisting your restauration, he both serves and pleaseth God." The author was right in concluding that

---

[42]A good specimen of this type of pamphlet is *The Qualifications of Persons, declared capable by the Rump Parliament to elect, or be elected, members*. This is, of course, a travesty of the real views of the Rump.

[43]*Calendar Domestic*, p. 572.

[44]*The Censure of the Rota*, reprinted in *Harleian Miscellany* (1810), VII, 122. Although this tract is initialed J. H., it was not written by Harrington. For the suggestion that the tract was written by Samuel Butler, see Paul Bunyan Anderson, in *Studies in Philology*, XLIV (1944), 504-18. Masson, (*Life of Milton*, V, 659-63) analyzes it at greater length than it perhaps deserves. A ballad-writer used the phrase "blinde Guides" (*Rump: or an Exact Collection*, II, 188).

[45]In his introduction to the reproduction he edited for the Facsimile Text Society (No. 54, 1942), William R. Parker plausibly identifies the author as George Starkey, a Harvard graduate, a physician, and an occasional controversial writer.

the army alone stood in the way of a recall of the Stuarts. Milton could hardly make such an admission, and stood forth as the great Republican advocate in 1660, but he probably did his cause no good, and perhaps some harm. It was lost beyond redemption. By presenting the hopeless alternative, he may well have made monarchy seem the more desirable.

Many of the pamphleteers are likely to have hoped to influence the general election even though they did not refer to it specifically. However, certain broadsides, verses, and tracts were issued for the guidance of electors. *The Grand Memorandum* was said to be published "to tell the people who have been their oppressors and fatal betrayers of their liberties, and that they may be the better guided in their future elections." It supplied the names of 176 secluded members, starring the names of about forty to indicate they were absent from Parliament on March 16; it then enumerated the Rumpers with hands pointing to regicides and stars attached to those who did not sit after the readmission of the secluded members. The versifier responsible for England's *Directions for Members Elections* began, "Set a black mark upon whimsical Vane," and then described in the darkest colors many of the chief actors during the Protectorate and later—Disbrowe, Hesilrige, Lambert, Robinson, Scot, and many others. *A Free Parliament Litany*, with the refrain *Libera nos Domine*, lists vow-breakers, king-triers, sellers and buyers of crown and church lands, major generals, army officers, gospel ministers settled by the sword, the rich who made us poor, a Speaker who crept to the House by a back door, regicides, an everlasting mock Parliament, the assessment, blind guides, preaching aldermen, etc., together with many Rumpers by name.

Three items have been found that gave advice to electors, but curiously enough, in each case the appeal is negative—whom not to elect. *The Qualifications of the Succeeding Parliament* urged that no one should be chosen who was an enemy to kingly government, a sectary, a purchaser of the lands of the King, church, and delinquents, or an exciseman. A petition of eight freeholders of manors in Wales alleged that these crown lands had become the property of private owners who used their jurisdictions more rigorously than the petitioners were used to and by threats extorted their voices at elections against their wills. They asked that they should be restored to their old position as tenants of the crown.[46] If this is not an isolated instance the unpopularity of the purchasers of crown lands is easy to understand. *A Necessary and Reasonable Caution* exhorted voters to be against people who preach without a call, who sacrifice the public good to private interests or use parlia-

[46] *Mercurius Publicus*, p. 338.

319

mentary privilege to cheat creditors, or who have been farmers of the revenue or enriched themselves at the price of universal ruin. The broadside ends with the comment that "this may suffice for a caution to all such as are not resolved upon beggars and bondage."[47] The last, longest, and most serious is entitled *Certain Considerations . . . Presented to the Free-holders, and to the Free Men . . . to Regulate their Elections.* It begins with a very partisan account of the many gracious concessions made by Charles I to the Long Parliament, of the evils that followed from the ambitions of men, who, although they had taken the oath of allegiance and supremacy and taken the Covenant, made the greatest atheists their darlings and then murdered their King and set up Cromwell as Protector who trampled under foot all laws from Magna Charta to the Petition of Right. After this introduction the electors are advised not to support purchasers of crown, church, or delinquents' lands; any officeholder or anyone who had profited by the late troubles; commanders of the former or present armies; and tax collectors. The new qualifications for members of parliament should be disregarded and men chosen who were qualified by the old laws of the fifteenth century (they were enumerated). The conclusion is: "Printed for publick good, with hearty desire it may be read before (or at) all Elections."

Naturally, inevitably, William Prynne contributed to this as to all other controversies. His *Seasonable and Healing Instructions Humbly Tendered to the Freeholders* (March 26) is unlike the broadsides and tracts summarized above because it was concerned with the duties of the elected which were: "To procure a speedy honorable, safe, Christian treaty and accord with our long Protestant King and royal posterity, upon moderate, just, righteous terms and propositions on either side, whereby the bleeding Protestant cause and religion (much endangered in all places) may be promoted and secured, the plots of Popish enemies to extirpate them prevented. . . ." This is the sole direct reference noticed in the election literature to the plan of some Presbyterians to make the Restoration conditional.

An account of the general election of 1660 naturally begins with the counties.[48] There the franchise was uniform, the electors most numerous (with certain exceptions), and the proportion of contested elections described much higher than for the boroughs with their diversified qualifications for electors. The best account of a county election is by Sir John Bramston. He describes how in Essex the Earl of Warwick, confident of

<hr />

[47]L'Estrange included this paper in his *Apology* (pp. 99-100) and claimed to have distributed some hundreds of it.

[48]For a more elaborate account of the election see my article in the *Huntington Library Quarterly*, XV (1952), 211-35.

the support of the justices of the peace, committee men, sequestrators, and ministers, "the generalltie of which were in sequestred liveings, or in no orders, not manie in Presbiterian orders," declined an offer to share the representation, declaring he would have both seats or none. Therefore Sir Harbottle Grimston and a Mr. Raymond[49] were nominated in opposition to Bramston and Edward Turner (or Turnor)—the first and last being future Speakers of the House of Commons. Bramston himself was a Cavalier, the son of a judge deprived of his position for loyalty and brother of a captain in the royal army. Turner had no such record because he had sat in Cromwellian parliaments but, as he became attorney general less than three weeks after the King's return, he was no doubt regarded as a Royalist at the election. Bramston headed the poll by 500 voices and Turner came second. They owed their victory to the exertions of the nobility (except Warwick) and the gentry whose lead the freeholders followed, believing them to be "men well affected to peace."[50] This phrase meant that the victors were regarded as men who would promptly invite Charles II to return to the throne rather than risk the disorders which might attend the delays that any negotiations to frame conditions as the price of the Restoration would entail.

The results in two other counties that had been in the old Eastern Association were equally satisfactory to the King's adherents. In Cambridgeshire, Isaac Thornton was willing to withdraw in favor of a person of greater quality and estate if he would pledge himself to support the Restoration of King and church. When Thornton announced that person's refusal to the freeholders, they elected him and Thomas Wendy, who stood on the same platform.[51] In Norfolk Thomas Richardson, Baron Cramond in the Scots peerage, and Sir Horatio Townshend triumphed over Sir William Doyley and Sir John Hobart, though the first of the defeated candidates is said to have polled 2,000 votes.[52] This was a victory of two recognized supporters of the crown over two erstwhile Parliamentarians, and was due to the exertions of the "great" Mr. Coke and other gentlemen.

No less than six candidates sought to represent Middlesex—Sir Gilbert Gerrard and Sir William Waller, who joined forces, Lancelot Leke, Page of Oxinden, and Sir William Roberts and Sir James Harrington,

---

[49]Probably the Oliver Raymond (or a relative) who had been named to various Essex committees during the Puritan Revolution. See index to *Acts and Ordinances*.

[50]*The Autobiography of Sir John Bramston* . . . , ed. Lord Braybrooke (1845), pp. 114-15.

[51]*Clarendon Calendar*, IV, 657. Pepys, Apr. 20, supplies the names of the defeated—Sir Dudley North and Sir Thomas Willis. Who the person of greater quality was I do not know. I should have expected North and Willis to have stood as Royalists.

[52]*Clarendon Calendar*, IV, 640.

who also combined.[53] Waller and Leke were chosen. The first, once a Parliamentary general, was now a staunch Royalist, and the second was a younger son of Francis, Lord Deincourt, created Earl of Scarsdale, a delinquent. Of the defeated candidates, Gerrard had been the Parliamentary treasurer at war at the beginning of the Civil War and sat on various committees, but he was now a Royalist, while Harrington, a Republican, had lately been a member of the notorious committee of safety the army set up after the expulsion of the Rump on October 13, 1659. His record would be fatal to his chances the following spring. In Surrey, Francis, Lord Aungier (created Earl of Longford in the Irish peerage in 1677) and Daniel Harvey defeated Sir Richard Onslow and his son (who were, however, elected at Guildford). Onslow relied overmuch on local influence and ruined his chances by insisting on his son's standing with him. The Royalists strongly opposed him and shouted: "Noe Rumpers, no Presbiterians that will put bad conditions on the King."[54] Lord Aungier had sat in Richard Cromwell's one Parliament but may have been a crypto-Royalist then. Too little is known about Harvey to identify him with any group, but he probably stood as a Royalist. Sir Richard Onslow had been an original member of the Long Parliament, and had sat, with his son, in Oliver Cromwell's two Parliaments, and had been called to the "House of Lords" in 1657 which told heavily against him at the election. As he had been one of the Surrey commissioners for ejecting alleged scandalous ministers, the whole weight of Anglicanism was probably against him.[55]

In Berkshire there are said to have been three candidates, of whom a correspondent of Hyde's writes that he knew all the writer could tell of the first, Sir Robert Pye, that the second candidate, Richard Powell, was honest (i.e., loyalist), and that the third, Sorbye, was neither "fish nor good flesh," presumably a non-party man.[56] Pye had attracted attention early in 1660 as an enemy to the army's intervention in politics and as an advocate for the readmission of the members of Parliament excluded by Pride's Purge. Sent to the Tower by the Rump, he defiantly sued for a writ of habeas corpus. These actions no doubt commended him to the electors. As for Buckinghamshire, Bulstrode Whitelocke noted not only the names of, but even the votes given to, the four candidates—Sir William Bowyer, 1,499, Colonel Terringham, 1,379, Richard Hampden (second son of the famous John Hampden), 1,315, and Mr. Wynwood

[53]Ibid., p. 644.

[54]Hist. MSS Comm. *Fourteenth Report*, App. IX, 482; *Laing MSS*, I, 310-311.

[55]*Clarendon Calendar*, IV, 642; *Complete Peerage*, eds. Cokayne, Gibbs, et al, under Longford; and *DNB* s.v. "Onslow, Sir Richard."

[56]*Clarendon Calendar*, IV, 664.

(Richard Winwood), 1,242. He added the comment that the last pair had many more voices than the first pair if right had been done.[57] Both Hampden and Winwood had been Cromwellians. The victors seem not to have played a noteworthy role in national politics previously.[58]

In Worcestershire John Talbot and John Bromley, described to Hyde in disguised language by a lady as "arrant Cavaliers by generation and education," triumphed over two Presbyterian local worthies, Foley and Colonel Richard Graves, in spite of the interference of the soldiery and the opposition of Richard Baxter and other eminent divines.[59] In Herefordshire a correspondent of Colonel Edward Harley regretted a rival candidate. "Popery is both the ultimate end of their giddy proceedings, and the primary engine that sets all their wheels agoing." The opposition candidate, a Mr. Price, was disqualified and incompetent in respect of "years, estates, etc.," but contracted to "a very forward, argumentative Romanist, and that is all in all."[60] The return is torn and supplies only Christian names. The "Edward" was Harley, and the "William" was "William Hinson, alias Powell, Esq., made his election for *Dover*. New writ ordered to be issued *June* 4."[61] Hinson was no doubt the William Hinston, alias Powell, appointed a Herefordshire commissioner for the assessment in January, 1660, and for the militia two months later.[62] Cornwall was the only county for which there is a double return. After one of the few divisions on disputed election results, the House decided that Sir John Carew had the most votes, that Hugh Boscawen had 862 against Robartes' 843, and that Elliot had the least, the number not being stated.[63] Probably all the candidates were moderate Presbyterians, desirous of the King's speedy return. At Exeter the freeholders "met in such numbers as never were known before on such an occasion, and did with one voice in a full election, *nemine contradicente*, choose" Monck.[64] Cheshire elected Sir George Booth and Denbighshire Sir Thomas Middleton, two leaders of the rising against the Rump the previous August.

The impression left by these contests is that the freeholders eagerly

[57]*Memorials*, fol. 699.

[58]Whitelocke probably erred in making Bowyer a knight and in naming Terringham because, according to the *Official Returns*, William Terringham was returned only at a by-election, August 22, 1660. There is no official return for Buckinghamshire for the general election. Probably the contemporary list is correct in giving the victors' names as William Bowyer (or Bower) and Thomas Tyrrell.

[59]*Clarendon Calendar*, IV, 642, 644; Hist. MSS Comm. *Laing MSS*, I, 310-311. The Foley may be Thomas, elected for Bewdley.

[60]Hist. MSS Comm. *Portland MSS*, III, 220. Perhaps the unsuccessful candidate was Thomas Price who represented the county from 1661 to 1679.

[61]The old *Parliamentary History*, XXII, 215.

[62]*Acts and Ordinances*, II, 1369, 1432.

[63]*Journals*, VIII, 47, 87, 95. For some interesting particulars see Mary Coate, *Cornwall in the Great Civil War . . .* (Oxford, 1933), p. 314.

[64]*Mercurius Publicus*, Apr. 12-19, p. 245.

supported Cavaliers or their sons whenever there were such candidates, or, when there were none, gave their voices to Presbyterian Royalists. No extreme sectarian or Republican was returned for an English county. A search in the *Calendar of the Committee for Compounding* fully confirms the view that Cavaliers or their sons were popular with the freeholders. The most notable example is the election for Derbyshire of Henry Cavendish, Viscount Mansfield (second son and successor of the Marquis—later Duke—of Newcastle who commanded the King's forces in the north until after the battle of Marston Moor), and John Ferrers (the son of Anne, Countess of Chesterfield by a former marriage—the earl being a delinquent).

Another group of county members which was well represented in the Convention was composed of recent opponents of the English army leaders, even if themselves officers, past or present. Charles Howard sat for Cumberland, Monck for Devonshire, Norton for Hampshire, Rossiter for Lincolnshire, Ashley Cooper for Wiltshire, and Fairfax for Yorkshire. All of them had made their peace with the exiled monarch before the elections began. Men who had declared first for the readmission of the secluded members and then for a free parliament or were known to be Cavaliers, though not technically delinquents, account for the rest of the county members. Taking the seventy-eight who sat for English shires, at least a quarter were Cavaliers or their sons, and probably ninety per cent or more would vote, if voting were necessary, for the unconditional restoration of Charles II. These results can scarcely have surprised contemporaries because they were in complete accord with a trend noticeable at least from the elections to Cromwell's second Parliament.

All contemporary writers agree that competition for seats in the boroughs was very keen, but few give details. For the City of London, Alderman Robinson informed Charles II that thirty or forty were nominated but that he himself, Major General Browne, the recorder, Wilde, and William Vincent were chosen without any dispute which was unprecedented. Presumably the others canvassed but withdrew at the hustings, perhaps after a show of hands or shouting as each name was read out because none of the reports mentions any polling. A letter to the King informed him that all four were men of honest principles.[65] He might have added that Browne and Robinson had been deep in the plotting prior to Booth's rising. At Hull six candidates offered themselves for election, the largest number known to have received votes in any constituency. All six were Yorkshiremen, three of whom had played minor

[65]*Clarendon Calendar*, IV, 630, 634.

roles on the national stage. Francis Thorpe had served in the Parliamentary army, sat in the Long Parliament as a recruiter [one chosen at a by-election], became a judge, justified the King's execution though he declined to attend the court that condemned him, tried the Cavaliers captured after Penruddock's rising in 1655, quarrelled with the Protector, and had been elected for the West Riding in 1656. This record placed him at the bottom of the poll. The next lowest was Matthew Alured, who had commanded a regiment of foot raised in his native county, but lost his colonelcy for joining in an Anabaptist movement against Oliver Cromwell in 1654. The Rump gave him a regiment of foot and he supported it against Lambert and other leaders of the army in England, being a leader of the forces that returned to their obedience to Parliament at the end of December, 1659. He was employed by Monck to induce Overton peacefully to surrender his governorship of Hull early the next year. Apparently these last actions were insufficient to overcome the prejudice against an Anabaptist. William Lister and Edward Barnard were local worthies only, like John Ramsden, a former mayor and member who headed the poll by a substantial majority. Andrew Marvell's services as a Latin secretary and his verses on Cromwell's death did not prevent his election.[66] A royal supporter, summing up the Yorkshire results, lamented Luke Robinson's success at Scarborough which he ascribed to Vice-Admiral Lawson's influence but estimated that "we shall not have above three scabbed sheep in our flock."[67] The writer was too optimistic, but if the regicide Francis Lascelles won at Allerton, John Lambert[68] and Thomas Harrison lost at Ripon and Thirsk. Among the victors were two officers whose assistance had been of the greatest value to Monck in his contest with the English army leaders, Hugh Bethell and John Clobery. Two other notable winners were Sir George Savile, son of a Cavalier and destined to attain to the marquisate of Halifax, and Sir John Hotham, whose father and grandfather had been executed for treason to the Parliamentary cause.

Those who had attended any of the sessions of the high court set up to try Charles I as well as the actual regicides fared ill at the election and worse in the House of Commons when it assembled. Only one regicide was allowed to retain his seat—Richard Ingoldsby who received the thanks of the House for his capture of Lambert and so putting an end to his revolt. Lascelles, Robert Wallop (Whitchurch), Hutchinson (Not-

[66]The figures (*The Complete Works of Andrew Marvell*, ed. A. B. Grosart [1875], II, 15) are: Ramsden, 227; Marvell, 141; Barnard, 113; Lister, 80; Alured, 55; Thorpe, 35.

[67]Hist. MSS Comm. *Fifth Report*, 199.

[68]His major, Breman, was said to have been elected at Stockbridge while in prison as a suspect, but the rumor was false. *Leyborne-Popham MSS*, p. 178. He may well have been a candidate.

tingham), and Ludlow (Hindon) all lost their seats, the first three being expelled and the fourth declared not duly elected.[69] Hutchinson received the suffrages of Nottingham because the citizens looked upon him as their deliverer from a threatened sack of their town by Hacker's regiment. His colleague, Anthony Stanhope, gained popular sympathy as a victim of plunder by the soldiery. Their opponent, a Dr. Plumptre, an old enemy of those he styled "puritanical prick-eared rascals," is said to have spread the basest scandals about Hutchinson, but no indication of their nature is given.[70]

Ludlow claimed to have been elected with George Grubham Howe at Hindon, which he described as part of his manor of Knoyle, because he had nineteen voices out of twenty-six. The agents of Sir Thomas Thynne, however, expecting that the House would welcome the chance to decide a disputed election against Ludlow, signed another indenture for Howe and Thynne, "making up in number what they wanted in quality, taking the subscriptions of the rabble, who not only paid nothing either to the state, church, or poor, but also received the publick alms of the parish: and to gain these they were obliged to descend to the most unworthy artifices, affirming that I was already fled, and that they would certainly be destroyed by the King if they elected me." The committee on elections submitted an interim report in Ludlow's favor which the House at first accepted but later concluded that the freemen in general were allowed to vote and not the payers of scot and lot (rates) only, so Thynne was declared the member.[71] Thomas Scot was returned by one indenture as the second member for Chipping Wycombe (now High Wycombe), and Richard Browne, son of the major general of that name, by another. As early as May 5 the House voted that Browne had the majority of qualified voices. The brief record in the *Journals*, however, contains no mention of the unscrupulous campaigning against Scot. His opponents produced a woman with a bastard whom she laid to his account, and alleged that he had been summoned before the Council of State for inciting Colonel Okey to mutiny.[72] At Leicester two hundred gentlemen announced that, if Hesilrige were elected, they would spend no more money in the town and hold no sessions or meetings there.

[69]Luke Robinson, not a regicide, was also expelled for unspecified reasons. *Journals*, June 9, 11.

[70]*Life of Hutchinson*, pp. 127, 320-321. In the *Records of the Borough of Nottingham* (V, 305) is an entry of forty shillings to defray the expenses of twelve persons going to London to testify at a court martial against soldiers suspected of killing two inhabitants.

[71]Ludlow, II, 256-57, 262, 477-78; *Journals*, May 3 and 18.

[72]*Clarendon Calendar*, IV, 625-26, 628, 643. The father is sometimes said to have been Scot's opponent but as he was certainly elected for the City of London and was never called upon to choose for which constituency he would sit, I think *Mercurius Politicus* (p. 1222) is correct in describing the candidate as the major general's son.

Whether due to this threat or to his general unpopularity, Hesilrige, if he stood, was defeated and did not find a seat elsewhere.[73]

Massey sat for Gloucester, but nearly lost his life there. After listening to a sermon on the text, "When the righteous are in authority, the people rejoice: but when the wicked rule, the people mourn" (Prov. 29:2), he was on his way with the preacher to dine with the mayor when the inferior officers of the garrison raised a shout. "Fall on, kill the rogues," and surrounded them with drawn swords. The citizens, at the rumor that Massey and the minister had been killed, rushed to arms and three hundred were soon on the scene. Counter-demonstrations lasted for two hours before order was restored, the mayor making himself responsible for Massey's appearance if necessary. This hostility between citizenry and soldiery is likely to have been a feature of many local elections when the candidates were known Royalists.[74]

After this excitement the statement that there seem to have been no contests for the Cinque Ports may be tame. Yet two interesting points emerge about them. Samuel Pepys, acting on behalf of Edward Mountagu, one of the generals at sea, waited on Widdrington, a commissioner for the great seal, to request the disposal of the writs, which was granted. Mountagu, having qualified himself by securing the grant of the freedom of Dover, was duly elected there, but failed to get his kinsman of the same name accepted at Hastings because the freemen had already promised their votes.[75] Much more significant is the fortunate survival of letters from the town authorities to Mountagu. This is the sole example of what a body of electors expected of its member and is most revealing. The first letter is from Thomas Browne, the mayor, Andrew Day, Thomas White, and John Price, who state that several gentlemen of the country have appeared in person and others have signified their desires to represent Dover at Westminster, and that if Mountagu will honor the town by acting as one of its barons, its electors "will so far understand their own and [the] Commonwealth's interest as very freely and cheerfully to make choice of your lordship before any others." They add that some persons have pre-engaged themselves to some of the gentlemen above mentioned, so Captains Thomas Tiddeman and Valentine Tatnell should be sent to canvass them. Much more revealing is a letter from Thomas White, written after Mountagu had agreed to stand, and now quoted in part: "Besides the sad condition of our peer which is

[73]*Eng. Hist. Rev.* XXXIII (1918), 376. After the election was over a Richard Dudley promised ten loads of coals to be disposed of by the mayor for the use of the poor. Perhaps hints were dropped before the polling that if the result was satisfactory such a gift would be made. *Records of the Borough of Leicester*, ed. Helen Stocks, et al (1923), IV, 462.

[74]Rugge, "Mercurius Politicus Redivivus," p. 116.

[75]Pepys, *Diary*, March 21, 25; April 3, 14, 18.

unrecoverable without the assistance and help of the great council in parliament in order to a supply for maintenance thereof, we poor inhabitants are near 3000 £ out for the reparation of the navy, in refitting and furnishing necessaries to boatswains and carpenters, not having received any stores from London this eighteen months, and the money due to us unpaid of part of the quarter from the 25 December 1658 to the 25 March 1659, besides all the time since, so that we have here neither stores nor money but are greatly indebted for such things that we have taken up upon trust, here being 52 families who are creditors to the state on this account. Right honourable, my humble desire in the behalf of myself and creditors is to intreat your honourable lordship to [? write to] the commissioners of the admiralty to order us our arrears."[76] Not a single word about national politics but only about local needs! How far Dover is typical there is no means of telling, but it does not seem fanciful to suggest that one potent cause of the Restoration was the general indebtedness of the governments that preceded it. Material grievances may have played a larger part in shaping events than political or religious preferences in not a few elections.

A few other elections for boroughs merit attention. One of the first decisions by the Commons of disputed elections was for Bury St. Edmunds. The resolution was most laconic—that Thomas Chaplyn and Thomas Clarke ought not to sit and that Sir Henry Crofts and Sir John Duncombe ought to sit. The first pair had been members of Richard Cromwell's Parliament, now no recommendation. Crofts was inactive during the interregnum, but Duncombe had attended Prince Charles at Oxford as his gentleman server, been knighted in 1646, and compounded for his delinquency in 1650. The House, therefore, at the earliest moment, winked at a gross breach of the act passed by the expiring Long Parliament to regulate the general election.[77] Not infrequently the dispute turned on whether the prescriptive or charter rights should prevail. At Chichester, for the second seat, the question was whether the franchise was restricted to the free citizens or open to the commonalty at large. The decision was for the larger body because for twenty-one parliaments that had been the custom. The mayor was committed to the sergeant at arms because he had ignored the precedents brought to his attention at the time. Without impugning the fairness of the proceedings, it may be mentioned that the candidate thus rejected was an obscure regicide, William Cawley.[78]

[76]Bodleian Library, Carte MS. 73, fols. 357, 382.
[77]*Journals*, May 5, 14. The result was one of the first printed. See *Mercurius Politicus*, p. 1205, under Mar. 26.
[78]*Journals*, May 21, 24. Whether the successful candidate, John Farmington, was the sequestered Papist listed under Kent in 1648 is probably doubtful.

The Contests for the university seats are revealing. Monck declined to stand for Oxford himself but wrote a letter recommending William Lenthall, the Speaker of the Long Parliament, as a patriot and a friend to learning and the university. At one meeting of convocation the recommendation was read together with a letter from Lenthall himself who claimed to have conferred benefits upon the university during the late times and promised, if elected, to be as active on his constituents' behalf as in settling the nation. The vice-chancellor, John Conant, a Presbyterian, tried to help Lenthall by summoning convocation again. Another letter from Monck was read. He began in an apologetic tone. Understanding there was severe opposition to Lenthall, he assured the masters of arts that he would never have intervened if he had not thought them willing to grant the boon he sought because of the favor they had intended him [i.e. to choose him as the one of their representatives]. "Gentlemen," he wrote, "it is really the desire of my Heart, to be an instrument in the hand of God to doe good in my best Services, both to your Selves, and the whole Nation, and had I known any Person more able and ready to assist in that Great Work, I had certainly with the same freedome proposed him: But you must give me leave to say, it was not Favour but Choyce, and that in order to the best Ends, that fixt and determined my Thoughts upon that Worthy Person [Lenthall]; and therefore, not withstanding his Modesty, and selfe-deniall herein to mee, I take the freedome still to insist upon my first desires; Your Condescention whereunto will oblige him to continue his Regards to You and the Whole Church." According to the great annalist, Anthony Wood, the Presbyterians and fanatics caused this letter to be printed and distributed about the university. A copy is in his collection of papers at Bodley's Library—one of the very few pieces of election literature known to have been distributed then.

In spite of Monck's letters, the filial efforts of John Lenthall, much canvassing, and gifts of beef and ale at the Mitre, the electors chose Thomas Clayton and John Mills—the one, the Regius Professor of Medicine, had been all things to all men during the interregnum, the other, a canon of Christ Church, had been deprived, restored, and was about to be ejected again.[79] Wood supplies a hint about Lenthall's defeat —that men remembered him as the rogue who had run away with the mace to join the army in 1647. To have adhered to the army against the Presbyterian majority in Parliament would not commend Lenthall to an electorate probably largely Presbyterian. Another disadvantage was

[79]Wood, *Life and Times*, I, 311-12; Bodleian Library, Wood MSS, 515 (25); *Register of the Visitors of the University of Oxford*, ed. Montagu Burrows (1881), pp. 489, 539.

that he had left the university without taking a degree—a point on which Oxonians are touchy. Unfortunately, it is impossible to discover what interpretation the masters of arts placed upon the last sentence in Monck's letter. If they felt that "the Whole Church" meant the Anglican Church, they may well have taken alarm because many of them would be likely to be ejected in the event of a restoration of that church to her former exclusive position.

At Cambridge the candidates were Monck, Thomas Crouch, an ejected fellow of King's and a fellow-commoner of Trinity Hall, and Oliver St. John, appointed chancellor in 1651 by the obnoxious committee for the reformation of the university. For the first, 341 votes were cast, for the second, 211, and for the third, 157. The vice-chancellor reported the result to Monck: "As it hath pleased God to make your Excellencie eminently instrumental for the raising up of these gasping and dying nations, into the faire hopes and prospect of peace and settlement, so hath He engraven your name in characters of gratitude upon the hearts of all to whom the welfare of this Church and State is deare and pretious." Monck replied that nothing could be more welcome than this testimony of the affections of "your famous University," because he had always been ambitious to serve those eminent foundations which were the glory of the nation. But he warned that if his native county should require his service, he was bound by nature and promise not to refuse it. Devonshire did choose Monck as one of its knights of the shire, and at the ensuing by-election William Mountagu was returned.[80]

The *Journals* supply less information than usual about disputed elections and often print nothing more than the recommendations of the committee on privileges and elections and their normal acceptance, or occasional rejection, by the House. Decisions were reached for about sixty irregular elections but the total may have been larger. Inasmuch as the *Journals* do not always record decisions in cases of which cognizance was taken, some may have been omitted altogether. Henry Coventry, recommended by Hyde for a Cornish seat which he failed to gain, reported to his sponsor that there were seventy or eighty double returns. Another Royalist thought that many of the double returns were made in order to prevent good men from sitting immediately.[81] The Commons resolved on April 26, 1660 (as on May 11, 1661), that, upon all double returns of members, none were to sit until the returns were

80James Bass Mullinger, *The University of Cambridge*, III (1911), 552-53. The author makes two curious errors. He dates the vice-chancellor's letter about August 8 and Monck's reply August 10, but Monck must have written before his election as M.P. for Devonshire, of which the exact date is unknown but was before April 25. The second error is to state that Mountagu represented the university when Parliament met on April 25. His election was on June 22.

81*Clarendon Calendar*, IV, 670, 685.

determined, except such members as were named in the several inden-
tures. Nevertheless, the House did reach promptly many interim decisions—that so-and-so should sit until the issue was determined—and
thus foiled the device if it was used. The House also tried to insure a
full representation by setting a date by which a member elected for two
constituencies should declare his choice and thus allow another writ to
be issued. Twenty-one members were returned twice. This plurality
may represent national reputation or local popularity. Monck was
chosen by Devonshire and the University of Cambridge, Edward Mountagu by Dover and Weymouth, Sir Thomas Widdrington by York and
Berwick, and Lord Falkland at Oxford and Arundel. More often the two
constituencies were not far distant from each other. Sir William Morice
was elected for Plymouth and Newport (Cornwall), Colonel Norton for
Hampshire and Portsmouth, Colonel Bethell for Hedon and Beverley,
and so on. Prynne's election for Bath and Ludgershall may be used as
an illustration of either kind.[82]

The unpopularity of members of the Long Parliament who had sat
after their recall by the army in May, 1659, is proved by the election
of sixteen only—omitting from this total Edmund Ludlow and John
Lenthall who were permitted to sit until the double returns from Hindon
and Abingdon were decided but then declared not elected.[83] Of the sixteen three were expelled—Hutchinson and Wallop for having attended
the earlier sittings of the court set up to try Charles I, and Robinson for
unspecified offenses, among which may well have been his spying on
Monck during the later stages of the march from Coldstream to London.[84] Of the remaining thirteen, none had been in any way conspicuous
for opposition to Monck's measures during the first months of 1660, and
four at least had actively assisted the general. The restored Rump had
appointed a Council of State of twenty-one Parliamentary and ten non-
Parliamentary members. Morley alone of the first group was both
elected to and retained his seat in the convention, though three of the
second group were sent to Westminster—Fairfax, Sir Horatio Townshend, and Sir Anthony Ashley Cooper, the only one of the three to
attend the sessions of the Council. None of the committee of safety set
up by the army after Lambert had excluded the Rumpers in October
was duly elected for the convention. The Council of State chosen by the

[82]The constituency named first is the one for which the member elected to sit.

[83]According to the list in Masson's *Life of Milton* (V, 453-54), there were 122 Rumpers who took
their seats during the five months which elapsed before the army closed the House of Commons on
October 13, 1659.

[84]Robinson is reported to have recanted and promised to be a loyal subject. Hist. MSS Comm. *Fifth
Report*, pp. 146b, 149b.

Rump after its return to Westminster at the end of December was better represented, because out of thirty-one members, ten were chosen, though Robinson and Wallop were soon expelled. The tally for the Council nominated on February 21 and 23 after the readmission of the secluded members is very different. Twenty-six were returned, and of these no less than ten represented counties and five were returned for two constituencies (Monck being in both categories). Among the five councillors who were not elected, Oliver St. John may have owed his failure to find a seat to the reputation he had acquired as an opponent of the King's unconditional restoration or as an advocate of recalling Richard Cromwell to be Protector. John Weaver was defeated at Stamford, perhaps because his Republicanism was repugnant to the nascent Royalism. Whether the remaining three—Knightly, Thompson, and Trevor—were candidates is unknown. Clearly Republicans found little favor in the sight of the electors, though those who had opposed the coup d'état of Lambert and other leaders of the army in England fared better than those who accepted it.

These figures, like most of the election literature, are rather negative. They show what classes of politicians, and indirectly what platforms, the voters rejected. With few exceptions, all wished to make a clean sweep of the political and constitutional changes effective since the second Civil War. The annihilation of the English army leaders responsible for the ejection of Parliament in October and of the civilians who supported them showed the general hatred of military rule. The heavy taxes to support the armed forces, and the soldiers' living at free quarters in spite of the taxes, accentuated antimilitarism. The crushing defeat of regicides and Republicans demonstrated their unpopularity. The animosity toward sectaries may be due to a combination of causes—they were the main supporters of the Republic and they may have been blamed for the interference with the daily lives of Englishmen which Puritan morality prompted. Their advocacy of toleration and the attempt some made to abolish tithes would anger both Anglicans and Presbyterians. The attacks on the newly rich, together with the reiteration in ballads of the alleged humble origins of the army leaders and their supporters, suggest that they had made an ostentatious display of the wealth and estates they had acquired.

Also rather negative but nevertheless important was the general feeling of disappointment and disillusionment. Economic, legal, and social reforms seemed as far off as ever. The war with Spain was unpopular with the loss of many ships to the Dunkirkers. Complaints of this decay of trade were loud during the winter of 1659-1660 when the bitter cold must have aggravated distress.[85] Hard times usually are fatal to those in power when they occur and there is no reason to believe that the election of 1660 was an exception to the rule. The dearness of food and the decay of trade were in part due to the bad weather which prevailed at the end of the interregnum. Thus in September, 1658, an Essex vicar noted that strong winds had laid flat an abundant harvest and that heavy rains had completed the ruin of much of it. On January 15, 1660, he recorded that the season from November 11 till then had been "very vehement cold," and by May 6 the spring was "very excellent."[86] Even the elements seem to have fought against the Republicans.

On the positive side generalizations are more difficult.[87] Probably at least ninety per cent of the members of the Convention hoped Charles II would be recalled.[88] How many of this huge majority were Anglican Cavaliers and how many Presbyterian Royalists is a difficult question, but it is probable that the Cavaliers were the more numerous if to this side should be added those who were more Royalist than Presbyterian.[89] The issue of the House of Lords does not seem to have been raised, possibly because its restoration may have been regarded as certain after the Parliament's declaration in its favor before the late dissolution. Little was said about the church. Whether the several advices not to vote for those who had bought church lands may be regarded as a sign that men desired the re-establishment of Anglicanism is by no means certain.[90] No one apparently urged that the bishops should resume their former positions. Perhaps the desire not to risk offending the Presbyterians, or Monck, or the army may explain this reticence. The Republicans are said to have tried to frighten Presbyterians by arguing that the King's return would necessarily bring back the bishops. Appeals to Parliament

[85]For many quotations and references, see Scott, *Joint-Stock Companies*, I, 259-62.

[86]*The Diary of the Rev. Ralph Josselin*, ed. Ernest Hockliffe (1908), pp. 126, 132, 134.

[87]Louise F. Brown, in an article entitled "The Religious Factors in the Convention Parliament" (*Eng. Hist. Rev.*, XXII [1907], 51-63), supplies a good sample of the opinions expressed by contemporaries and by later writers as to the election results. Her conclusion is that the Presbyterians did not have a clear majority.

[88]That the King's return was "the unanimous wish of the people" is the Venetian resident's verdict, *Calendar Venetian, 1659-1661*, p. 138.

[89]Bordeaux mentions a proposal to exclude from the House 100 or 120 members disqualified by the act passed by the expiring Long Parliament (Guizot, II, 412). Even if these figures be accepted as the total for the Cavaliers and their sons, there were other relations as well as Cavalier sympathizers to be reckoned in.

[90]The Venetian resident interpreted "the fixed aim of the communes" not to elect any possessors of land of the crown, church, or delinquents to fear that private interests might prevail over public. *Calendar Venetian*, op. cit. Some time in April, Sharp wrote to Douglas at Edinburgh that moderate episcopacy was the fairest accommodation. By the end of May he found "very few or none" who desired Presbyterianism to be established in England. Wodrow, *Sufferings of the Church of Scotland*, I, 20b, 30a. The Episcopalian Scot James Fraser noted that he saw in London bishops appearing in the streets "crouded with affectionat salutations, and accosted for benedictions; such a veneration ther people have for that holy order, now so long ecclipsed. I saw 8 Bishopes in London at the sitting of the Parliament" (*Chronicles of the Frasers* [Edinburgh, 1905], p. 426).

to restore the ejected clergy to their benefices were too late to influence voters.[91] Certainly no guidance was furnished from the exiled court. Charles urged that as many Royalists should be elected as possible but gave no hint what program they should adopt. Perhaps he realized that precedents, especially that of 1614, proved that royal attempts to influence elections were unsuccessful. More likely he did not yet know what ecclesiastical policy to adopt. Prudence rather than affection for the Presbyterian party was responsible for the failure to announce the restoration of the church as one of the issues at the election. The Cavaliers, in spite of the support Presbyterians had given to the royal cause since 1648, in private still denounced them as the originators of the rebellion.[92]

Two considerations suggest that the Cavaliers might have won a decisive victory if they had been bolder. The first is the success of the more outspoken candidates. The second is the ecstatic welcome of the King at the end of May. Perhaps they had been disappointed so often in the past that they failed to recognize that now they had the game in their hands. However, if they failed to achieve all the success that might have been theirs, the lack of any central organization or recognized leader in England may account for their caution. At least they achieved enough to restore the monarchy. The rest could wait.

The escape of Lambert from the Tower threatened to undo all that had been recently accomplished. Upon him the hopes of the Republicans had been focused as their only possible leader. They had been raising money to pay soldiers willing to take the field against Monck, and to go bail for Lambert. Ludlow, a principal conspirator, proposed that seven of the Council of State named by the restored Rump and three of the army commissioners appointed by it should assume command and order the regiments of Moss and Fagge (then led by Lieutenant Colonel Farley) to march to the Tower where Morley was expected to welcome them. Slingsby Bethel was the emissary to Hesilrige but found him convinced that the good old cause was ruined.[93] Scot found it impossible to get together a sufficient number of the former Council of State and left London to go electioneering. After these disappointments Ludlow himself began to think of his own safety and withdrew into the country. Apparently some conspirators remained in town to assist Lambert. He escaped during the evening of April 10 by climbing down a rope

[91]*The Army's Declaration Being a True Alarum*, p. 7. This is not an official publication, but claims to be written by a member of the army; Robert Mossom, *An Apology in the behalf of the Sequestred Clergy* (1660).

[92]Bosher, *The Making of the Restoration Settlement*, p. 47.

[93]There is no reason to doubt Hesilrige's assertion that he was not privy to Lambert's rising. See his letter to Monck of April 30, cited in Ludlow, II, 252, n.1.

and into a barge ready to receive him. To give him a start before discovery of his flight a maid is said to have occupied his bed, put on his nightcap, and replied to the warder who came to lock the door of Lambert's room—a service which is reported to have earned her £100.[94] As soon as news of the escape reached the Council, a proclamation was issued offering £100 for Lambert's recapture.[95] He is supposed to have remained hidden in London for two days, probably exploring the possibility of a rising in the capital[96] but abandoning this in favor of an appeal to the regiments in the midlands and the north. Among the precautions taken were arresting sectaries, changing the garrison of the Tower, and announcing that all arrears of pay would be satisfied for all soldiers that remained with their colors.[97] Though Moss is not known to have helped Lambert, his regiment was disbanded on April 20 after receiving full arrears of pay, the need for economy being the excuse.[98] At York Hugh Bethell promptly secured a Lieutenant Merry, whom he described as the chief agitator, but two others slipped through his fingers.[99] Hull again gave trouble. A mutinous petition was presented to the officers but suppressed: its promoters were sentenced to thirty-one lashes apiece.[100] Elsewhere, officers who had been cashiered tried to seduce their former troops or companies but with little success. Small groups deserted to join Lambert but no complete regiments and very few complete units. Monck's plan of scattering the component parts of most regiments made any concerted action difficult. Altogether, four troops only are known to have reached Lambert's rendezvous at Edgehill, and these apparently not at full strength, but no companies of foot.[101] This may be explained by two reasons—the horse throughout the civil war had been more politically minded than the foot, and cavalry could more quickly make their way across country than infantry. Lambert also had with him a number of field officers who were probably each attended by a few adherents.

[94]These romantic details are in *Mercurius Aulicus*, transcribed by Dawson (p. 390) and incorporated by Rugge, who is quoted in a note to Pepys' *Diary* for April 14. Other accounts state that two or more of the Tower garrison connived at the escape. *Clarendon Calendar*, IV, 653, 656-57; *Calendar Venetian*, p. 139. As his escape was not known until the eleventh, it is often dated the eleventh.

[95]See Kennet, *Register*, pp. 114-15.

[96]Some particulars about Lambert's evading arrest in London are in Hist. MSS Comm. *Fifth Report*, p. 146b. I cannot accept as genuine the two letters numbered 65 and 70, dated April 4 and 8, in the *Calendar Domestic*, pp. 407, 409-11. They are so at variance with the facts of the situation that their author's purpose is obscure.

[97]*Mercurius Publicus*, p. 261.

[98]Bordeaux to Mazarin, Apr. 16/26 (Guizot, II, 410).

[99]*Leyborne-Popham MSS*, pp. 175-82; *Mercurius Publicus*, p. 261.

[100]*Mercurius Publicus*, p. 256.

[101]The troops of Colonel Alured and Major Nelthorpe (though neither officer took part) and of Captains Clair and Hesilrige (son of Sir Arthur). A few particulars of local risings or attempts at rising may be gleaned from *Letters to the Council of State from the Commissioners of the Militia*. The letters are from Gloucester, Nottingham, and Coventry.

As soon as Monck received intelligence of Lambert's rendezvous, he sent for Richard Ingoldsby, one of the most capable and popular officers in the army, and ordered him to join Colonel Streeter at Northampton with his regiment by Saturday, April 21. Ingoldsby promised to do his best, hastened to collect his horse, quartered in Norfolk and Suffolk, at Cambridge, and reached Northampton Saturday evening.[102] On Easter Sunday they found Lambert's little army in a ploughed field near Daventry. On the way Captain Hesilrige was surprised but released on a promise to bring over his troop, which he did. Ingoldsby had with him his own regiment, a troop commanded by Captain Linley, and two companies led by Streeter.

Ingoldsby did not permit his men to fraternize with Lambert's, but himself rode to the front and argued with the scouts to such good purpose that twenty-five troopers and a quartermaster crossed over—probably Hesilrige's men. As the distance between the two forces narrowed, a wordy battle ensued. Their object, said Lambert's men, was to restore Richard to his Protectorship. The answer was that they meant only to set up one they had learned to pull down. Their duty was to submit to the orders they received from their superiors. Then a welcome reinforcement came for the loyal force, Captain Barker's troop, which formed part of Ingoldsby's regiment but apparently had not previously caught up with the main body. After a short pause Alured's troop deserted Lambert. Streeter's two companies advanced and fired a few shots, but the opposing horse pointed their pistols to the ground to show they had no thought of fighting. Lambert and the officers about him begged that he should be allowed to escape but Ingoldsby refused to be a traitor to those who had sent him thither. Lambert turned his horse, a swift barb, in flight but, hampered in a ploughed field, was soon overtaken by Ingoldsby, pistol in hand, whereupon he ignominiously surrendered.[103] Other captives were Cobbet, Creed, Young, and three captains. Axtell, Okey, and his son-in-law, Clare, escaped.[104]

When the victors in the skirmish reached Northampton they were greeted with loud applause. Lambert reminded his captor of an incident in 1650 when Cromwell and he were marching northward to invade Scotland. When the crowd cheered them Lambert remarked to Cromwell that he was glad to see they had the nation on their side. His com-

[102]Baker's *Chronicle*, p. 720.

[103]The official account in *Mercurius Politicus*, p. 269, is reprinted in Firth and Davies, *Regimental History*, I, 160-161, where the other authorities are cited.

[104]There were two captains Clare present. Probably Henry was captured and Timothy escaped. Both had been in Okey's dragoons and may have been relations, but this is unsupported by any evidence known to me.

panion warned him not to "trust to that; for these very persons would shout as much if you and I were going to be hanged." Lambert said to Ingoldsby that it looked as if Cromwell had been prophetic.[105] He may have felt more convinced of this when he reached London, where he was forced to stand under the gallows at Tyburn before being recommitted to the Tower.[106] That some of the bravest leaders of the Cromwellian army surrendered without striking a blow in self-defense is proof of their demoralization. They really had no cause to support. When Ludlow wanted to know whether Lambert stood for a Commonwealth, he was answered that "it was not now a time to declare what we would be for but what we would be against." This negative attitude was as fatal as the last-minute adoption of Richard. That Lambert had never stood for any cause but his own advancement was now clear. The Republicans would never lift a finger to restore Richard, and many of his erstwhile supporters were Royalists. As Ludlow remarked of the Commonwealth party, "Thus our enemies were those of our own house." It is true that they did not owe their defeat to their original enemies, but the Cavaliers were the real beneficiaries of Lambert's failure. Monck had proposed, if the fortune of battle went against Ingoldsby, to proclaim the King and call the Royalists to arms in the three kingdoms.[107] As it happened, they triumphed without taking up arms.

[105]Burnet, *Own Time*, I, 85.

[106]*Clarendon Calendar*, IV, 674.

[107]Maseres, *Select Tracts*, II, 793-94; *Clarendon Calendar*, IV, 682. *Mercurius Publicus*, under April 21, announced that if Monck himself took the field he would bring with him a large train of gentry.

CHAPTER XVII

The Restoration

THE CONVENTION duly assembled on Wednesday, April 25, 1660. Apprehensions that there might be disputes in both Houses about membership were soon set at rest. The Lords did not follow the precedent set by the secluded members when they were allowed to return to their seats by ordering certain resolutions excluding them to be erased from the *Journals*. They simply ignored all that had taken place since they had ceased to sit after the vote of the Commons on February 6, 1649, that "the House of Peers in Parliament is useless and dangerous, and ought to be abolished." Their *Journals* recorded that they met "in the Twelfth year of the Reign of our Most Serene Lord *Charles* the Second, by the Grace of God, King of *England, Scotland, France,* and *Ireland*, Defender of the Faith." There were present five earls: Manchester, appointed Speaker *pro tempore*, Northumberland, Lincoln, Suffolk, and Denbigh; Viscount Saye and Sele; and four barons, Wharton, Hunsdon, Grey de Wark, and Maynard. The first business was the appointment of the following Monday as a day of fasting to seek a blessing upon the Parliament, in which the House of Commons was invited to concur. Monck was then nominated captain general of the forces, and Henry Scobell was ordered to turn over all records of the House of Lords to Richard Browne, clerk of the Parliaments. A message was approved to summon six more peers to attend, but it proved a dead letter because three more earls, all "young Lords" none of whom had sat before, attended that afternoon and another the next day, none of them being on the list. On the twenty-seventh there were present nineteen earls, three viscounts, and fourteen barons, including eight peers who had never sat in the House since their ancestors' deaths. As the eight included Derby, Strafford, and Capel, the lords did not visit the sins of their fathers upon them, if indeed a majority regarded the older Derby, Strafford, and Capel as sinners.[1] Soon all peers, Royalists and even Roman Catholics, were free to take their seats. The total was about 145.

[1] An order of May 4 that no peers created since 1642 should sit was vacated on May 31. On that day Charles II signified his desire that the peers created by his father at Oxford should be allowed to take their seats, and the House at once acquiesced because "Matters of Honour do belong to His Majesty." A bill was introduced on May 19 into the Commons to void all titles of honors and grants of manors, lands, etc., since an unnamed day in May, 1642, and was read a second time on May 22. It never became law. For all questions about admissions, see C. H. Firth, *House of Lords during the Civil War* (1910), pp. 282-91.

In the Commons some wished to debate whether the House of Lords should be acknowledged, but the argument prevailed that the re-establishment of the hereditary chamber was a step toward the restoration of the monarchy.[2] No questions seem to have been asked about the qualifications of a hundred or more Cavaliers and their sons who had been elected in spite of the act passed by the expiring Long Parliament.[3] To allow Cavaliers to sit in the Commons and all peers in the Lords (except new creations) made certain the restoration of monarchy without any new legal restrictions on the prerogative. The rising tide of Royalism could not be stemmed much longer. The almost universal demand was for a return to the old constitution without innovations. Had Charles II landed he might well have entered Whitehall without opposition, but he realized the advantage of waiting for an invitation from the Convention. That was soon forthcoming. Those Presbyterians who expected that Monck would aid them in imposing conditions on Charles II were woefully disappointed.[4] Whether Monck had made up his mind what tactics to adopt before the Parliament met may be doubted, because he participated in the prompt election of the Presbyterian Sir Harbottle Grimston as Speaker immediately after the Parliament assembled without waiting for a full house.[5] He did nothing further for the Presbyterians. The appointment of the committee of privileges and elections, naming May 10 as a day of thanksgiving to Monck and others instrumental in delivering the nation from thralldom and misery, and a vote of thanks to Ingoldsby for capturing Lambert occupied the second day. On Friday a motion was made to recall the King but deferred until the following Tuesday when the representatives from the West, thought to be "royally affected," would have arrived.[6]

On Saturday the twenty-eighth, Grenville appeared before the Council. There he delivered to Monck the letter addressed to him but to be communicated to the Council and to the officers of the army. After Grenville had been called in he explained that he had received the letter from

[2] Parliamentary Diary of Sir Edward Dering, Thursday, Apr. 26.

[3] Bordeaux told Mazarin (Guizot, II, 412) there were a hundred or six score members not qualified, and he was probably correct. He added (II, 417) that Monck, after promising the Presbyterians not to allow any other Lords to sit, actually had done no more than exclude the "young Lords" for two days, and that he had agreed that all members should sit in the Commons "without regard to qualifications."

[4] Mountagu told Pepys on April 29 that he expected the King would be brought in without conditions though the Presbyterians had wished to fetter him. The ambiguity of pronouns renders the passage obscure as to whether Monck or Mountagu had prompted the Presbyterians to try to exclude from Parliament the lords and M.P.'s "that came not within the qualifications."

[5] Mordaunt (Clarendon State Papers, III, 734) names Holles, Lewis, and Monck, but Sir John Bramston (Autobiography, pp. 116-17) omits the General but mentions the old Parliamentarians, Holles, Pierrepont, Annesley, and Swinton. The Journals show that Pierrepont proposed Grimston and, together with Monck and Holles, led him to the chair.

[6] Henry Coventry to Ormonde, April 27 (Carte, Ormonde Papers, II, 328).

the King's own hands at Breda. The decision was taken not to open it but to leave it with Grenville to present to Parliament, Monck guaranteeing his appearance at the next sitting.[7]

On Tuesday, the House of Lords was informed that Grenville was in the lobby with a letter from the King. Manchester received from him a letter addressed to the Speaker of the House of Peers and the Lords there assembled and a Declaration, both signed at Breda on April 4. They were read twice. The letter was a model of tact. The King hailed as a happy augury for his own restoration the acknowledgment[8] that the peers should enjoy the authority and jurisdiction which had always been theirs by their birth and the fundamental laws. He claimed their counsel in composing the distractions of the kingdom. Knowing from their own experience how violation succeeded violation when the rules of justice were once transgressed, they would be zealous for the rights of the Crown, and establish King, Lords, and Commons upon the foundation which could alone support them.

The Declaration was Hyde's masterpiece. Insofar as the Restoration was in any way conditional, the conditions were therein stated. Carefully designed to conciliate all likely opponents and to place the King in the "just and peaceful possession" of the throne, and the people in the enjoyment of "what by law is theirs," it promised a free and general pardon to all who within forty days claimed it and asserted their loyalty, except to those who should be exempted by Parliament. No crime whatsoever should ever be brought in question against any to endanger their lives, liberties, and estates, so that "all notes of discord, separation, and difference of parties" should be utterly abolished, and all subjects were invited to "a perfect union among themselves, under our protection, for the re-settlement of our just rights and theirs, in a free Parliament." To assuage animosities in religion, "we do declare a liberty to tender consciences," and none was to be called in question for differences which did not cause disturbances of the peace. Any act to this end which, after mature deliberation, Parliament should offer would receive the royal assent. The King further asserted his willingness that Parliament should determine the ownership of estates which by grants and purchases had passed into the possession of officers, soldiers, and others, and should satisfy all arrears due to the officers and soldiers under Monck's command, who should be received into the royal service upon as good conditions as they now enjoyed.

[7]Maseres, *Select Tracts*, II, 797; *Clarendon State Papers*, III, 736. The letter is printed, among other places, in Clarendon, *Rebellion*, XVI, 181.

[8]In the resolution passed by the Long Parliament just prior to its dissolution.

Every line of the Declaration suggests careful preparation. The promise to accept bills passed by Parliament to settle the vexed questions of a general pardon, toleration, forfeited estates, and army pay was very wise. The odium of a settlement which could not but be disappointing to many was thus to be borne by Parliament. To bring that body prominently to share in the Restoration was most politic, because it had never wholly lost the popularity it had enjoyed in 1640. Nothing is more remarkable during the interregnum than the lasting attachment to the principle of representative government, though that devotion had been severely strained by the Rump when it mistook a belief in parliamentary institutions for acceptance of its own permanency. No doubt Hyde, when framing the Declaration, fully expected that a future parliament would not pardon regicides, grant full toleration, permit the present possessors of royal and church lands to keep them, or maintain the army, though he was to be surprised at the violence of the reaction at the election in 1661. He also showed his statesmanship by mentioning only the subjects which especially concerned the opponents of monarchy, past and present. His object was to restore the King. That he never mentioned the Anglican church, or all the restrictions on the prerogative imposed since 1640 was certainly not due to indifference but to the decision to postpone these troublesome questions until the King enjoyed his own again.

In the Commons the King's letter and the Declaration were both read. In the letter addressed to the Speaker the King asserted his belief that parliaments were vital to the constitution, and claimed that their preservation depended on the preservation of the royal authority. His trust in them was proved by the Declaration he enclosed as well as by his refusal of other assistance, "which we have assurance of."[9] He had given the world ample testimony of his zeal for Protestantism, and he would consent to any proposals which would manifest his affection for it. In due time he hoped to propose a method of propagation which would prove that he had always made it his care and study.[10] He left to Parliament to provide security for transgressors and for those whose rights have been violated, and by a just computation of what men have done and suffered, to take care, as near as possible, that all men be satisfied. If there was a crying sin which involved the nation in infamy, Parliament would be as eager as the King to vindicate the nation from it. After this hint of the necessity of punishing the regicides, the King expressed his desire to

[9]Whether he meant foreign assistance or offers from England, Scotland, or Ireland to proclaim him king without waiting for Parliamentary action is uncertain.

[10]What inspired this cryptic remark can be only a matter for conjecture—possibly a plan of comprehension.

be sworn to obey the fundamental laws. After the pious hope that he had made a "right Christian use" of his sufferings, he concluded by invoking the divine blessings on Parliament.

Monck, in a set speech, enlarged on "the King's goodnesse & our happinesse in him," and was seconded by Finch "with his usual eloquence." Many followed with dutiful reflections on the royal letter[11] The Commons then named a committee to answer the royal letter, which was to be printed, voted £50,000 to the King, and resolved that the King's letter to Monck should be communicated to the army. They then adjourned in order that a committee of their members might attend a conference. There Manchester spoke briefly, reminding his auditors of the maxim, "'where the word of a King is, there is Power'; and where the word of our King is, as it is now received, there is Truth; and Power and Truth are the best Supports of Government." Reference to "some new State Builders" evoked consideration of "our ancient government, the best in the world." He then read the votes the Lords had passed: "That, according to the ancient and fundamental Laws of this Kingdom, the Government is, and ought to be, by King, Lords, and Commons; that the Lords . . . conceiving, that the separating the Head from the Members hath been the chiefest occasion of all our Disorders and Confusions; they desire that some ways may be considered how to make up these Breaches, and to obtain the King's Return again to his People"; and that a joint committee should be set up to accomplish these ends.[12] The Commons, meeting again that afternoon after the conference, at once passed the first vote, but ignored the other two.

That evening Monck summoned to a meeting all the officers in or near London and communicated to them the letter he had received from Charles II and the Declaration. The King again claimed that to effect his restoration he preferred to rely upon his subjects' affections than to invade any of his kingdoms with foreign aid. He appealed to Monck to avert a ruinous war and to make the nation indebted to him for the peace and happiness it would enjoy. He acknowledged that the army had complied with the obligations for which they were first raised, the preservation of Protestantism, the King's honor and dignity, the privileges of parliament, and the subjects' liberty and property. His Declaration would show how greatly he desired to contribute to these good ends. Power and authority assumed by passion and appetite had given the people no peace or happiness and had not received their obedience.

[11]Parliamentary Diary of Sir Edward Dering, Tuesday, May 1.

[12]*Commons Journals*, May 1, VIII, 8, Morice proposed the above-mentioned resolutions. *Clarendon State Papers*, III, 737, Grenville to the King, May 2.

Therefore, the reasonable conclusion was "that God hath not been well pleased with the attempts that have been made," but had sanctified the very means which ill men had designed for private ambition to wholesome and public ends.

Leonard Lytcott, who had replaced Cobbet when the latter adhered to Lambert's faction, praised the royal clemency as expressed in the Declaration. He borrowed the sentence from the letter to explain why they had first taken up arms, but alleged that some implacable spirits had improved their successes to make the breach between King and Parliament irreparable. Now they were complying with the obligations for which they were originally raised, and were acknowledged by the King to be the instruments to reconcile him with his people. These specious arguments seemed to have prevailed, and Colonel Knight obtained Monck's permission to refer to a committee the drafting of an address in compliance with the King's letter and Declaration. The address was presented the next morning. His excellency was assured of their obedience and adherence to their former promise to accept whatever the Parliament should enact. The King's letter and Declaration had given "a great measure of quiet" to their minds. The concessions from Breda were enumerated—general indemnity, liberty to tender consciences, satisfaction of arrears, confirmation of sales of estates to those now in possession of them—and confidence expressed in their fulfillment because left to the determination of Parliament. The signatories professed their loyalty to the King and their compliance with the principles for which they were first raised.[13] Monck acquainted the Commons with the address and readily obtained leave for Clarges, a member, to carry a letter and the address to the King. This was the last time the army participated in the politics of the time. Its approval insured a bloodless restoration.

The turn of the navy came next. From Breda Charles had addressed a letter to Monck and Mountagu. He wrote of the comfort he felt on learning that the ships of the navy, "the walls of the kingdom," were now commanded by the generals at sea and that officers and seamen were rather inclined to return to their duty than to "raise their fortunes by rapine and violence." He enclosed the Declaration and desired that it should be read throughout the fleet. He promised to provide for the payment of all arrears and of rewards according to merit.[14] Mountagu had by this time grown confident that the fleet shared the loyal sentiments daily reported from the shore. His secretary noted that at the news that Parliament had voted for a government by King, Lords, and Commons,

[13]Baker's *Chronicle*, pp. 727-28; *Clarendon State Papers*, III, 737; Clarendon MSS 72, ff. 131-32.
[14]Clarendon, *Rebellion*, XVI, 199-200.

the commanders rejoiced "which a week ago they would not do." The seamen who had money or credit were busy drinking loyal toasts. On May 3, Mountagu, having previously dictated to Pepys the resolution he wanted passed, summoned a council of war. When the commanders had assembled, Pepys read to them the letter and the Declaration, and then pretended to draft Mountagu's resolution. "Not one man seemed to say no to it, though I am confident many in their heart were against it." All then proceeded to the quarter-deck where Pepys again read the two documents and then asked the seamen what they thought. They replied with shouts of "'God bless King Charles!' with the greatest joy imaginable." He visited each ship in turn and found none that evinced the least dislike of the proceedings. The fleet was now ready to obey the King's command as Parliament ordered it to do.[15]

The last of the royal letters from Breda was addressed to the Lord Mayor, aldermen, and common council of the City of London. They had just ordered to be printed a vindication of themselves from any responsibility for the acts of the unrepresentative common council of 1648 which tended "to the murder of the late king and total extinguishment of kingly government." Thenceforth, it was asserted, supporters of a personal treaty with Charles I were excluded from all share in the City's government, and their places taken by a "mechanicke juncto." Now they hoped for a return to a hereditary monarchy. Thus they were in a frame of mind to listen with approval to the King's letter. It paid a just tribute to the Londoners' efforts to restore the form of government under which England had for hundreds of years "enjoyed as great felicity as any nation in Europe" and in opposing the constitutional changes by which, to gratify a few men's ambitions, the most arbitrary and tyrannical power had been introduced. It referred to the Declaration and the King's intention to restore the fundamental laws. Because of his extraordinary kindness for his native city, the King promised not only the renewal of the charter and traditional privileges, but new favors to advance the trade, wealth, and honor of London. The common council thanked the King for his condescension towards the City and said they were willing to submit to his Majesty, in proof of which the arms of the commonwealth had already been replaced by those of the King. Permission was then sought and obtained from Parliament to send a formal reply. The next day the common council agreed to cooperate in raising a loan of £100,000 at the request of Parliament, and itself voted £10,000 to the King, £2,000 to the Dukes of York and Gloucester, and £300 to buy

[15]*Commons Journals*, May 9. Mountagu's letter to the King of May 4, which confirms what Pepys says about the rejoicing in the fleet, is printed by Lister, *Life of Clarendon*, III, 104-106.

rings for Mordaunt and Grenville, the bearers of the royal letter.[16]

These events contributed to make this the happiest May Day for many a year. In London there were more bonfires than ever, and ringing of bells, and men drinking the King's health upon their knees which, thought Pepys, "is a little too much." One sign of the times was the setting up of maypoles, which the Puritans so abominated. At Oxford, according to Wood, a maypole was erected to vex the Presbyterians and Independents. When the vice-chancellor appeared with his beadles and servants to cut it down, the mob interfered and prevented its destruction.[17]

Having reached the great decision to recall the King, Parliament speedily dealt with the necessary preliminaries. All proceedings involving the use of the great seal[18] were to be in the King's name from May 5, and all ministers in the three kingdoms were ordered to pray for "Our Sovereign Lord Charles the Second, by the Grace of God, King of England, Scotland, France, and Ireland, Defender of the Faith, &c." Both Houses chose representatives to carry answers to his Majesty's letters. On May 8 the form of a proclamation was adopted. According to it the King's right and title to the crown were completed by his father's death. Nevertheless, because proclamations have always given good subjects an opportunity of testifying their duty and respect and because this had been denied by violence for many years, the Lords and Commons, together with the Lord Mayor, aldermen, and commons of the City of London and other freemen, proclaimed that immediately upon the decease of the late King Charles the imperial crown did, "by inherent Birthright, and lawful and undoubted Succession," descend to King Charles the Second. "God save the King." The members of the two Houses assembled at the palace gate where the King was proclaimed by William Ryley, created Clarenceux king of arms by Richard Cromwell. They proceeded in coaches to Whitehall and thence to the City where, on the approach of the procession the gate at Temple Bar was closed, to be opened again after the king of arms had knocked and demanded

---

[16]Sharpe, *London and the Kingdom*, II, 378-79. According to Dering's Parliamentary Diary (Wednesday, May 2), Finch, Annesley, and Ashley Cooper were sent to the City to borrow the £100,000, half for the King and half for the soldiers' pay. A correspondent had told Nicholas on March 9 (*Nicholas Papers*, IV, 196) that only money from the City would restrain the fickleness of Monck's army. Here is a fine example of the importance of London. If its purses were open, the army could be paid and disciplined but, if closed, the soldiers might again become politicians.

[17]*Life and Times*, I, 314. The same writer notes that on May 31 a dozen maypoles were set up, but as the Puritans made no opposition, one or two sufficed in the future—a striking example of the folly of trying to change social habits by prohibitions. Perhaps the fullest account of the proclamation of Charles II is in the *Diary of Henry Townshend*, ed. J. W. Willis Bund, for the Worcestershire Historical Society, 1915, I, 38-39. It was fitting that Worcester, one of the last cities to hold out for Charles I, should be pre-eminent in welcoming the proclamation of his son. The three issues of *Mercurius Publicus*, for May 3/10, 10/17, and 17/24, are full of notices of celebrations.

[18]The seal to be used was the one remaining in the hands of the Earl of Manchester and the commissioners. This was probably the old great seal of which Manchester was in charge from 1646 to 1648.

entrance. Then the proclamation was read in three different places. Everywhere the procession was greeted with acclamations, and "the numberless numbers of bonfires, the ringing of bells, and shooting off of guns, and the joyful expressions of the people did declare beyond the art of any pen" their satisfaction.[19] Throughout the country the same enthusiasm was manifested at the restoration of the monarchy. Oxford showed the old and unfeigned loyalty which the city had always borne to Charles I, and bread, wine, and beer were freely dispensed. At Cambridge the celebrations lasted two days.[20]

About this time took place a debate upon a motion by Matthew Hale that a committee should be appointed to ascertain which of the propositions of the treaty of Newport Charles I had accepted were suitable to be presented to Charles II. Monck opposed the motion. He urged that although the peacefulness of the nation exceeded all men's expectations, he knew incendiaries were still at work trying to start a flame. He could not answer for the nation or army if any delay occurred in sending for the King, and moved that commissioners should be sent immediately to bring him over. This "was echoed with such a shout over the house, that the motion was no more insisted on."[21]

The instructions to the representatives of both Houses, who were to begin their journey to the King at Breda on May 11, referred to the earnest desire that he should speedily return to his Parliament and to the exercise of his kingly office.[22] In preparation for his arrival, Whitehall was to be evacuated, and furnishings provided. Every effort was made to recover the royal furniture, and the Council, hearing that Elizabeth Cromwell was detaining some of his Majesty's goods at a warehouse, ordered an inspection. Seven horses of Cromwell's and his coach were to be reserved for the King's use. Laud's library, in Hugh Peters' hands, and books from the royal library in Selden's possession, were to be secured.[23]

One of the first tasks of the Convention was to provide funds for current expenses and for the disbandment of the forces. An assessment of £70,000 a month for three months was an obvious resource. A curious

[19]*Mercurius Publicus*, p. 302. Dugdale proclaimed the King at Coleshill on May 10. *Life, Diary, and Correspondence of Sir William Dugdale*, ed. William Hamper (1827), p. 105.

[20]Ibid., pp. 310, 324.

[21]Burnet, *Own Time*, I, 160-161, or fo. 61. The instruction to the committees of both Houses were agreed to on May 10. An interesting tract against "capitulating" with the King was entitled *Vox & Votum Populi Anglicani*, by T. C.

[22]*Commons Journals*, May 10.

[23]*Mercurius Politicus*, p. 320; *Commons Journals*, May 26 and 28; 16 and 19. The report that ten cart loads of rich goods were found in her possession was probably a gross exaggeration. Hist. MSS Comm. *Fifth Report*, pp. 206-207. For various particulars of "the late King's goods" see Hist. MSS Comm. *Seventh Report* (1879), pp. 88-93.

resolution was that the titles of honor which commissioners for executing the act had received from Oliver, Richard, and Henry Cromwell were to be omitted, and the names of various obnoxious individuals—Slingsby Bethel and Thurloe among them—were deleted. This ordinance was to go into force on June 24 when the six months' assessment voted the previous December would end.[24] The two Houses joined in an order (May 17) for the prompt payment of the older assessment ("though not originally imposed by such an authority as was legal") because otherwise there would be no money to pay his Majesty's armies and they would be necessitated to live at free quarters.[25] The Commons, adopting a report of a grand committee, resolved that a further sum of £400,000 should be raised to disband and pay off such of the land and sea forces "as are now thought not necessary any longer to be continued." The decision reached was to raise this sum by a poll tax.[26]

Parliament was busy with various bills. It may not be without significance that a bill to abolish tenures *in capite*, by knights' service, and by socage *in capite*, and to provide £100,000 as compensation to the crown, and the court of wards was the first to be ordered and that its preparation was entrusted to the committee to consider the King's letter and Declaration.[27] These vexatious burdens had been removed from tenants in chief by ordinances passed during the interregnum and there was now every intention not to allow them to be reimposed.[28] It is noteworthy that the feudal dues had been paid by a relatively few but that the excise on beer which provided the compensation would be paid by many. The second bill was to prevent any disputes about the assembling and sitting of the Convention. It declared that the Lords and Commons then in session were the two Houses of Parliament, in spite of the fact that they had not been summoned by royal writs. It passed its three readings in the Commons on May 4 and 5. Two days later the Lords returned it to the Commons with the amendment that the Parliament could be dissolved by the King just as if he had summoned it. The Commons concurred and the bill was the first to receive the royal assent.[29]

The bill for a general pardon, indemnity, and oblivion was introduced

[24]The bill was introduced May 1 and passed the Commons on May 18. The resolution about titles was taken on May 17.

[25]According to the sums of money charged by the Council of State from February 25 to May 15, much of the army received no pay during this period (*Journals*, VIII, 28-31).

[26]May 18, 19. Unfortunately, the only estimate of arrears was for the ships not employed in the summer guard which showed £130,000 due. As the monthly cost of these ships was £11,000, pay was nearly a year in arrears. *Journals*, May 16.

[27]*Commons Journals*, May 3. See *Select Statutes, Cases, and Documents to Illustrate English Constitutional History*, ed. Charles Grant Robertson (1935), pp. 13-18.

[28]Ordinances of Feb. 24, 1646, and Nov. 27, 1656.

[29]*Commons Journals*, May 7; *Lords Journals*, June 1.

and read a second time. The debate was prefaced by the recital of the vote of December 12, 1650, when the Commons had resolved that the persons entrusted with the trial of the late king had discharged their duty with great courage and fidelity, and ordered that the account of the proceedings "be recorded, to remain among the records of Parliament, for the transmitting the memory thereof to posterity." Then Prynne produced a journal of the proceedings which was read. After that divers members present in the House explained how far they had been concerned.[30] Among these apologists was Richard Ingoldsby, who with many tears professed his repentance for the murder and had the effrontery to say that Cromwell had forced him to sign the death warrant, though an examination of that document shows that his is one of the clearest signatures attached to it. Colonel Hutchinson was satisfied with the defense that if he had erred at that time, inexperience and defect of judgment and not malice had prompted him. As to the King's execution he felt about it as befitted "an Englishman, a Christian, and a gentleman." One speaker pointed out that Hutchinson seemed more sorry for the consequences than the actions, but another urged that when a man's words admitted of more than one interpretation, gentlemen should adopt the most favorable.[31] John Lenthall went so far as to assert that "he who first drew his sword against the King committed as high an offence as he that cut off the King's head." Such a reflection upon the Parliamentary cause affronted many and he was severely reprimanded by the Speaker for so poisonous a remark. When the debate was resumed two days later, Prynne arraigned William Lenthall as the worst criminal, but Finch's defense averted a vote of censure.[32] A resolution was passed to secure all who sat in judgment on the King, together with the executioners, Joyce, who had seized the King at Holmby House, and a few others. The decision was also taken to execute seven regicides as yet unnamed. To attaint as from January 1, 1649, Bradshaw, Cromwell, Ireton, and Pride caused no trouble: they were all dead.[33] An order to seize the estates, both real and personal, of regicides, living and dead, seems to have excited no opposition.[34] A most rigorous hunt began, and the ports were ordered to

[30]*Commons Journals*, May 9, 12; Parliamentary Diary of Sir Edward Dering, Saturday, May 12. See Preface to J. G. Muddiman, *Trial of King Charles the First* (Edinburgh and London, [1928]) for an identification of the journal mentioned above with "Bradshawe's Journal," printed in App. A.

[31]Hutchinson, *Life*, pp. 323-24; Clarendon, *Rebellion*, XVI, 225.

[32]Parliamentary Diary of Sir Edward Dering, Monday, May 14.

[33]*Journals*, May 12, 14, 15. Broderick was very anxious to impeach Thurloe or include him in the seven, Clarendon MSS 72.

[34]The Lords objected to the Commons' proceedings because they intrenched upon the privileges of the Upper House to which judicature in Parliament solely belonged. However, they issued out their own order to the same effect. *Lords Journals*, May 19; *Commons Journals*, May 21.

be stopped lest any regicides should escape abroad.[35] The authorities at Stafford, who had seized Thomas Harrison, and the Earl of Winchelsea, who arrested Sir Henry Mildmay at Dover, received the thanks of the House.[36] Probably more surrendered voluntarily within the forty days allowed by the Declaration than were arrested. Among those secured for high treason who were not concerned in the King's trial was John Thurloe, but charges against him were never presented and he was set free six weeks later.[37]

Perhaps in accordance with Monck's suggestion that, instead of imposing conditions before the King's return, they should be presented after it, an interesting bill was introduced in the Commons on May 23 and read a first time. Its purpose was to maintain the just rights and privileges of Parliament and to confirm the fundamental laws, which were later described as *"Magna Charta, Statutum de Talagio non concedendo, the Petition of Right, and other Acts."* It was sent to a committee on May 29. Its failure to pass into law or to survive as a bill is regrettable, because a statement of what the Convention judged the constitution to be in 1660 could hardly fail to be significant.[38]

The last hours before the King's arrival in London were devoted to two proclamations, both concerned with the present occupations of estates of which previous occupants felt they had been unjustly deprived. Both in Ireland and in England the forcible entry upon the possessions, temporal and ecclesiastical, of those now settled in them "by any lawful or pretended authority" was forbidden till Parliament should take order therein.[39] Having disposed temporarily of two of the thorniest questions of the day, members of both Houses made their solemn way to Whitehall to await their lawful sovereign. On May 3 the Lords had approved an answer to his Majesty's gracious letter and named the Earls of Oxford, Warwick, and Middlesex, Viscount Hereford, and Lords Berkeley and Brooke to carry it to the King.[40] Two days later no less than 408 members attended in the Commons to elect twelve of their number to attend the King with the answer of the House. At the top of the list appeared

---

[35]According to the lists compiled by Masson (VI, 28), there were sixty-seven present when sentence was pronounced on January 27, 1649, and fifty-nine signers of the death warrant. Of the sixty-seven, twenty-three were dead.

[36]May 19. William Cawley, also at Dover, managed to escape.

[37]May 15.

[38]It was brought very appropriately by William Prynne to the Lords on June 3, and by them referred to a committee the next day, but then dropped.

[39]*Lords Journals*, May 29.

[40]The letter is reprinted in the old *Parliamentary History*, XXII, 259-60. It pointed out that the same power that usurped the scepter had deprived the peers of their rights and privileges, and claimed that they owned "a more particular Dependence and subserviency to the throne of Majesty."

Booth, Falkland, and Holles, one of the Five Members Charles I had tried to arrest eighteen years before. In the middle were Ashley Cooper and Townshend. The last three were Fairfax, Cholmley, and Mandeville, son and heir of the only peer Charles I joined to the Five Members in an accusation of high treason.[41] The only noteworthy feature of the letter from the Commons was the repudiation of Parliament's responsibility for the execution of Charles I, "the Act of some few ambitious and bloody Persons."[42] The instructions to the members of both Houses directed them to start on May 11, acquaint the King with the great rejoicings at his proclamation, with their desires that he make a speedy return to his Parliament and to the exercise of his kingly office, and with the order to Mountagu to observe the royal command.

Preparations were now taken in hand for the ejection from Whitehall of all persons who did not "necessarily attend upon the Council," and the equipment of the royal palace with beds, linen, carpets, and other furniture.[43] Carpenters and painters were busy on board the fleet, tearing down or painting out the arms of the Commonwealth, and soon tailors were cutting out cloth into the fashion of a crown with letters C. R. and inserting it into the flag. The report that Charles II found hateful the addition of the Irish harp to the crosses of St. George and St. Andrew was responsible for an order from the Council that it must be removed from the Union Jack.[44]

Apparently Parliament and the Council of State intended that the fleet should remain in the Downs until Charles II ordered it to fetch him home. But Monck, still obsessed with the notion that delay was dangerous, sent a verbal message by Grenville to Mountagu to weigh anchor at once.[45] The next day Mountagu set sail for Scheveningen, the port of The Hague, arriving off the Dutch coast on May 14. Stormy weather made communications with the shore difficult, but it did not prevent Pepys from landing and gazing with curious eyes at the foreign scene.

Charles arrived at The Hague soon after his fleet. Lately despised and rejected, he received at Breda pressing invitations to spend his last days on the Continent in the Spanish Netherlands, in France, and in the United Provinces. He accepted invitations from the States General and the States of Holland to come to The Hague as their guest, probably because he thought it expedient to be in a Protestant country and he wished

[41]The Lord Mandeville of 1642 was the Earl of Manchester, Speaker of the House of Lords in 1660.

[42]The old *Parliamentary History*, XXII, 263-67 .

[43]An interesting list is in *Commons Journals*, VIII, 21.

[44]Pepys' *Diary*, May 11, 13.

[45]Sandwich, *Journal*, p. 75. A list of the ships at Scheveningen is in *Memorials of Sir William Penn*, II, 220-221.

to be near his sister, the widow of William II, the Prince of Orange. There he received the representatives of both Houses of Parliament, a deputation of the citizens of London, and a group of Presbyterian ministers, and impressed all by his graciousness, finding the right phrase for all occasions. One discordant note only was heard. The ministers urged the King not to use the Book of Common Prayer regularly in the royal chapel and were told that in granting them liberty he did not intend to sacrifice his own.[46] On the twenty-third the King came on board, dined, and altered the names of some ships which recalled unpleasant memories of the Civil War. In the afternoon the fleet set sail and Charles's interest in maritime affairs was at once manifested. He regaled those near him with an account of his wanderings after the battle of Worcester which moved Pepys almost to tears. On the morning of the twenty-fifth, the fleet being near the shore, the King and his two brothers, the Dukes of York and Gloucester, breakfasted like the seamen on pease and pork and boiled beef. Then they went on shore.

At Dover a huge multitude had assembled to greet the King. On landing he knelt down and gave God thanks. He then approached Monck, who was on his knees, lifted him up, embraced and kissed him, and called him father. When the mayor presented him with a very rich Bible, he said he valued it above all things.[47] He did not stop at Dover but, taking a coach, hastened towards Canterbury. On Barham Down he found seven troops of horse led by Buckingham, Oxford, and other Cavalier noblemen, several regiments of foot of Kentishmen, and great crowds of countrymen. He stopped at Canterbury from Saturday night to Monday morning, attending service at the cathedral and finding it "very much dilapidated and out of repair," an eloquent protest against the usage of the Church of England during two decades. There he invested with the Order of the Garter George Monck, Edward Mountagu, the Marquis of Hertford and the Earl of Southampton, the last two having been nominated at Jersey ten years before.[48] Monck was especially honored as the Dukes of York and Gloucester put on the Garter and the George. His confidant Morice was appointed secretary of state and knighted. The King held his first meeting of the Privy Council on English soil at Canterbury. Apart from the two royal dukes, three only of the members who had attended him abroad were present —Ormonde, Culpepper, and Sir Edward Nicholas, secretary of state.

[46]Clarendon, *Rebellion*, XVI, 243-44.

[47]*The Flemings in Oxford*, ed. J. R. Magrath (Oxford), I (1904), 129; Pepys, May 25. Sir Owen Morshead, the librarian at Windsor, kindly informs me that neither this Bible nor the one given the King in London is now in the royal possession.

[48]The first two on May 26, the last two next day.

Four new members were now sworn in—Monck, Southampton, Morice, and Ashley Cooper.[49]

Hyde describes two mortifications the King suffered at Canterbury. The first was inflicted by old Cavaliers who, anxious not to lose the first opportunity, insisted on recounting "the insupportable losses undergone by themselves or their fathers." Each demanded the grant or promise of this or that office as his reward, and pressed his suit so confidently and at such length that the King "was extremely nauseated" and contracted an extreme prejudice against some of the highest quality.[50] The second was caused by Monck who produced a long list of persons he recommended as "most grateful to the people, and in respect of their pasts and interests were best able to serve him." The King did not wish to discuss the merits of any individual, so pocketed the list and assured the General he would always be ready to receive his advice and to gratify him in any way he could. When the list was examined it was found to recommend seventy people as Privy Councillors, of whom two only, Southampton and Hertford, had ever served the King. All the rest were ex-Parliamentarians, including the leaders of the Presbyterians, inserted, Hyde thought, "to satisfy the foolish and unruly inclinations" of Mrs. Monck. Charles, not wishing to affront the General, "in whose absolute power he now was," handed the list to Hyde in order that Morice should be consulted. Morice talked to Monck and discovered that he, like the King, had been beset by suitors, so had promised them his good offices and inserted their names without any expectation that the King would grant their desires.[51] Both incidents were revealing. They demonstrated an insoluble problem—how to distribute a limited number of favors so as to satisfy a much greater number of applicants. Whether the recipients of the royal bounty should be old Cavaliers or recent converts to Royalism or a selection from both groups had soon to be decided. The King went on the twenty-eighth to Rochester, paid a visit to Chatham to inspect the "Royal Sovereign," and returned to spend the night at the house of Colonel Gibbon who presented him with a loyal address from his regiment, first raised in 1656.

On May 29, his birthday, the King proceeded to Blackheath, where the army was drawn up. Colonel Knight gave him a declaration describing the army's joy at the presence of his Majesty among them and promising a ready obedience to his command.[52] Whether these were sentiments

[49]Edward Raymond Turner, *The Privy Council of England* (Baltimore, 1927), I, 375.

[50]Clarendon, *Life*, I, 274-75. Council Note 22. Two of the suitors may have been the Marquis of Worcester and Lord J. Somerset. See Lister, *Life of Clarendon*, III, 108-109, 499-500.

[51]Clarendon, *Life*, I, 277-78.

[52]Baker's *Chronicle*, pp. 733-34.

truly representative of what the officers and men felt is dubious. Their very countenances are said to have revealed that they "were drawn thither to a service they were not delighted in."[53] Thence the royal party made its way through Deptford to St. George's Fields where the Lord Mayor, aldermen, common councillors, and others waited for him in a large tent. The King knighted Aleyne, the only dignity granted this day.[54] After refreshments, the procession was formed for the progress through the City to Whitehall. He was again given a Bible, this time by the ministers of London, headed by Edward Reynolds, and in acknowledgment said that the greatest part of the day's solemnity he must ascribe to God's providence, and that he would make that book the rule both of his life and government.[55] The enthusiasm was inexpressible and caused him to remark that it was "his own fault that he had been abroad so long, for he saw nobody that did not protest he had ever wished for his return."[56]

At Whitehall he listened to addresses from the Speakers of both Houses of Parliament. Manchester, after tendering the peers' loyal joy at his Majesty's safe return, asserted that during recent times strangers had "ruled over us, even with a rod of iron" but now "our native King . . . holds forth a golden scepter. . . . Be you the powerful defender of the true Protestant faith; the just asserter and maintainer of the laws and liberties of your subjects." The King apologized for the brevity of his reply because he was disordered by the warmth of his reception. He intended to promote the happiness of his subjects by the advice of Parliament, and concluded by repeating the last two clauses of Manchester's address. Grimston said that the King had conquered the hearts and affections of his people—an incomparable conquest for which God alone had the glory. The King was content to reply: "I shall be as ready to grant as you shall be to ask." He then retired.[57] His subjects celebrated the occasion with toasts, bonfires three or four stories high, sometimes with an effigy of Cromwell on top, and bell-ringing. The King and his people were enjoying their own again.

A passage in the diary of John Evelyn expresses admirably the feelings of a Cavalier who was also a Christian gentleman: "I stood in the

[53]Clarendon, *Life*, I, 284. The writer (p. 279) grossly exaggerated when he spoke of above 50,000 men. All the armies and garrisons in the three kingdoms could not make up such a total. The tract *England's Joy* (in *Harleian Miscellany* VII, 111-14), mentions five regiments of horse—less than 3,000 men.

[54]Clarendon (*Life*, I, 279), asserted that in addition to the Lord Mayor, all the aldermen, etc., were knighted. See William A. Shaw, *The Knights of England*, 1906, II, 225-26.

[55]This version of the King's remarks I have taken from Magrath, *Flemings in Oxford*, I, 132.

[56]Clarendon, *Rebellion*, XVI, 246.

[57]Whether to the arms of Barbara Palmer is uncertain. The well-established tradition to that effect is possibly premature for May 29.

Strand, & beheld it, & blessed God: And all this without one drop of bloud, & by that very army, which rebell'd against him: but it was the Lords doing, . . . for such a Restauration was never seene in the mention of any history, antient or modern, since the returne of the *Babylonian Captivity* nor so joyfule a day, & so bright, ever seene in this nation: this hapning when to expect it or effect it, was past all humane policy." Clarendon, ten years later, wrote of the "wonderful manner" and "miraculous expedition" with which God put an end to the rebellion.[58]

But perhaps the feelings of the members of the Church of England were best expressed by a woman. She described the agonizing uncertainties felt in 1659—how men looked at each other with anxious eyes not knowing whom to trust or how to save themselves from "the raige, rapine, and destruction from the soldiery." Groaning under tyranny they prayed daily that their sovereign and the church might be restored. At the very time that they most feared destruction an instrument of deliverance appeared, General Monck, who was induced by the petitions he received from all quarters to call a free parliament. When it recalled the King, the hearts and tongues of all faithful, loyal people were full of gratitude to Him who had delivered their souls and bodies from thralldom and restored true doctrine and His viceregent on earth.[59] Just or unjust this may be accepted as the Cavalier view of the Restoration.

---

[58]Evelyn's *Diary*, May 29; *Rebellion*, XVI, 247.

[59]*The Autobiography of Mrs. Alice Thornton* (Edinburgh, 1875), pp. 98-100, 127-28. The feelings of two other women are briefly quoted in *Memoirs of the Verney Family*, III, 479-80. Roger North described admirably his brother's gradual conversion to the view that religion had been a hypocritical cloak for power and tyranny. *Lives of the Norths*, ed. Augustus Jessopp (1890), II, § 25.

EPILOGUE

ONE OF THE FEW safe generalizations about the Restoration is that it happened because the vast majority of Englishmen wanted it to happen. The Parliamentarians, like the Cavaliers, had constituted only a minority of the nation at the start of the Civil War. In between the two parties was a large body of neutrals, not interested enough to take up arms, but in sympathy with Parliament rather than with the King. This preference was derived more from dislike of the personal government of the King and of the Laudian church, which many regarded as a halfway house on the road to Rome, than from affection for Puritanism. Attempts by acts and ordinances to make sins legal crimes, and to treat innocent amusements as sins, usually converted the indifferent into enemies. They were not sufficiently roused to fight, and they had few opportunities of showing their resentment by votes. No general election took place from 1640 until 1654 —a longer period than the eleven years of unparliamentary government of Charles I—and at the elections of 1654, 1656, 1659, and 1660 the candidates for whom many may have wished to vote—the Royalists—were disqualified.

In spite of this handicap, Cromwell's opponents elected enough members to cause him to dissolve his first Parliament in the shortest possible time and to exclude arbitrarily a hundred members from his second. When they were allowed to take their seats, he had once again summarily to dismiss them. Richard Cromwell's Parliament may seem more co-operative, because on most questions he could command a majority, but it supported him mainly because it feared the alternatives—the Rump or the army. The Convention, the most freely elected parliament since 1640, restored the monarchy. Another proof that the Commonwealth and Protectorate were never popular is indirect but conclusive. The supporters of a republic, whatever form it took, were so conscious that a free election would yield a hostile majority that many of them advocated unalterable written constitutions. Others pinned their faith to perpetuating the existing fragment of the Long Parliament which came to be called the Rump in derision. Even if the almost universal demand for a full parliament grew too strong to be resisted, the Rumpers hoped to satisfy it by filling vacancies, themselves retaining their seats. Their last, dying effort was further to restrict the franchise by prohibiting the election of sons of Royalists, whereas previously to disqualify the fathers had seemed sufficient.

How far the former neutrals who applauded the Restoration were actuated by love of the Stuarts is a very difficult question. Some at least of the cheers that welcomed Charles II on his return may have been prompted by no higher motive than the desire to shout with the largest mob. Not until the very eve of the Restoration was enthusiasm for the royal cause very noticeable. Probably people rejoiced most of all because the Puritan Revolution was ended. It may have been, like a recent episode in American history, "an experiment, noble in motive and far-reaching in purpose," but, like Prohibition, it failed to retain the support of many of its early champions. It created greater evils than it cured. The greatest was the constant interference of the army in politics. The army became violently unpopular, not because the populace suffered from an unruly soldiery, though the iron discipline of Cromwell's day was breaking down after his death, but because it insisted that Britain should be governed as it willed. Second only to the army in unpopularity was the remnant of the Long Parliament with its absurd claim to represent the people. Because the work of reformation was often declared to be a main plank in the platforms of army leaders and "saints," both incurred the bitter resentment of many who might otherwise have remained mere spectators of the constantly changing political scene.

Perhaps as serious as the alienation of the erstwhile neutrals were the divisions that developed among the Puritans. The first large split occurred after the first Civil War when Independents parted company with Presbyterians, defeated them in the second Civil War, excluded one hundred and forty members of Parliament, executed the King, and abolished the House of Lords. The second breach was between the military and civilian supporters of a republic in 1653 when Cromwell turned out the remainder of the Long Parliament. The breach was never repaired, though temporarily plastered over in the spring of 1659 when the Rump was invited to return to Westminster. Its second ejection caused a schism in the rapidly diminishing group of civilian adherents of a commonweath and fatally divided the army.

Cromwell's army had never been a homogeneous body. To use modern terminology, the right had been composed of ex-Royalists and Presbyterians, the center of Congregationalists and the more restrained sectarians, and the left of Baptists (including Fifth Monarchy men), Levellers, and the more extreme groups both in politics and religion. Although the Levellers practically disappeared from the army as an organized group after the Bedford mutiny their doctrine of political equality was not forgotten by the inferior officers and the rank and file, and helped to create what contemporaries called "a divided interest" between the aspiring grandees and their subordinates. Other leftist elements were weakened during the Protectorate as Oliver was gradually transforming the republic into a monarchy. Had he lived longer he probably would have accepted the crown and made a clean sweep of the politicians in the army opposed to his rule. But at his death the conversion of the armed forces into a professional army was far from completed. The grandees were still powerful enough to compel Richard to dissolve his Parliament but found they had won a barren victory because their subordinates obliged them to recall the Rump. In October came the cleavage between the English and the Scottish armies, when Monck upheld the Rump after Lambert had sent it packing once again.

Many reasons can be assigned for Monck's prevailing over Lambert. The most important is that he had a very high percentage of Englishmen on his side. If Lambert's men had been recruited like the Janissaries in Turkey, from foreign elements, the feelings of the people among whom they lived might have mattered little, but, being Englishmen, they were affected by public opinion and became more and more uneasy at their unpopularity.[1] They never had an opportunity of showing how gladly they welcomed fraternizing with civilians such as Monck's soldiers enjoyed in London during and after "the roasting of the Rump," but the meager response when Lambert escaped from the Tower and called his old comrades to arms is significant. Cromwell had said of his Ironsides that they knew what they were fighting for and loved what they knew. Lambert's men had no such knowledge. Beyond the selfish desire to retain their commissions and to lord it over the land, their leaders had no distinctive program.

The army in the past had often cheerfully endured hardships when fighting for a cause it held sacred. When it was deprived of this stimulus the vacuum was filled by material grievances. That the soldiers were irregularly paid, and would remain irregularly paid until a parliament sat again, were themes most skillfully used in all the propaganda against the English army leaders. Because a soldier's rations consisted only of a pound of bread and a half or quarter of a pound of cheese—and these were no longer always available—the need of subsistence money was imperative. To grant him his due the soldier trusted first Monck, and then the Convention and Charles II, rather than the council of the army and any sham parliament it might summon. Their empty pockets were to some officers and many privates the decisive factor. Once the movement started to pay no taxes until a free and full parliament was elected,

[1] L'Estrange (*Apology*, p. 51) seems to have been among the first to recognize this point. "The Army is necessitous, and without pay, they must or Steal, or Perish. *Let us consider, they are our Countreymen, and many* of them (the *necessity apart*) *our Friends*."

the Republicans were powerless. Here was the opportunity for the former neutrals to act decisively at little risk. They had only to close their purses and the republic would collapse like a house of cards.

Another economic question which occupied much space in the pamphlets of the day concerned forfeited lands. A large vested interest had been created in England and, especially, in Ireland, which would oppose a restoration tooth and nail if the restitution of all confiscated property was in prospect. Hence Monck wanted a complete guarantee for all purchasers of such property, and Charles was willing that a partial assurance should be given them. Cavaliers were urged by the King's councillors not to start suits to recover their estates but to wait and see what Parliament would advise.[2] To return lands to their former owners, however, was not likely to be unpopular in England. Because so many pamphleteers denounced the purchasers of forfeited estates, the inference seems safe that to represent the new landlords as harsher than the old was good propaganda. In the army, the grandees and their satellites but not the lower officers had been the great beneficiaries of the confiscations. Hence the majors and captains that Monck promoted during the six months prior to the King's return had little to lose if royal and ecclesiastical lands were restored.[3] But they did have a stake in the Restoration because they would receive their pay, whereas if the grandees triumphed they would be displaced and forfeit all arrears. Few sailors had acquired fortunes during the interregnum, but all had arrears of pay.

The third group with much to lose in the event of a restoration was composed of the civilians who held offices and the ministers who held benefices from both of which supporters of the monarchy had been evicted —some in each category had succeeded to positions left vacant through the death of their holders. The number of officials was small in those days and not all had reason to fear that their services would not be required whatever the form of government. The ministers were more numerous, probably between three and four thousand. The majority of them, the Presbyterians, welcomed a restoration which would end the rule of "the Saints." Both the Presbyterian ministers who foresaw what was likely to be their fate after the King's restoration and those who wrote after they had been ejected in 1662 agreed in rejoicing that all danger from rule by the sectaries was past.[4] Others may have believed

[2]*Nicholas Papers*, IV, 207-208.

[3]Barwick was right in his assurance to Hyde that "it is no small happiness, that most of his [Monck's] officers are *post-nati* to the spoyles both of the church and crown; for there the shoe pincheth most." Mar. 19, 1660. Thurloe, VII, 861.

[4]*Oliver Haywood's Life of John Angier*, ed. Ernest Axon (Manchester, 1937), p. 69; Newcome's *Autobiography*, pp. 118-19; Martindale's *Life*, p. 143.

that the promise from Breda of liberty for tender consciences would shield them. Both groups may well have felt uneasy, however, when they reflected on the way they had treated Anglicans, the oaths they had imposed on them, and the prohibition of the Book of Common Prayer. The few may have perceived at last that, in order that they might enjoy liberty of worship, they had prohibited both the religion and the politics of the many. The Quakers had a foretaste of what might be in store for them during the last months prior to the King's arrival.

The propertied classes, with the exception of the possessors of for-feited estates, welcomed the King. Many were permeated with a class consciousness and eagerly welcomed the day when those they regarded as their social inferiors would cease to dominate over them. Practically every city or town of importance had shown its hatred of the English section of the army and of the Rump. Pre-eminent among the opponents of the Rump was the City of London. As Macaulay remarked: "In truth, it is no exaggeration to say, that, but for the hostility of the City, Charles the First would never have been vanquished, and that, without the help of the City, Charles the Second could scarcely have been restored." But in 1660, as in 1642, London did not stand alone: it was in the van of a movement supported by the country at large. It focused all the discon-tent throughout the land, but it did not create the discontent. That already existed.

One element in the prevalent anti-republicanism was the mob. It was never, or hardly ever, on the side of the army or the Rump. "We hear all the common people crying for the coming of King Charles," reported the Venetian ambassador.[5] With a few very notable exceptions, Puri-tanism seems not to have attracted the lowest classes. Rigid Sabbatarian-ism denied laborers their amusements on the one day when they had the leisure to enjoy them. Nothing had been accomplished to ease their burdens and they had no reason to be grateful to the Puritans. They came to prefer the publican to the Pharisee.

The editor of the works of the communist Gerrard Winstanley has stated that probably, "even when the Revolution was at its height, there were ten Puritans who were interested in reforming the church for one who cared what happened to the government of England."[6] Judging from the pamphlet literature of the years immediately preceding the Restora-

---

[5] July 8-18, 1659. In his sermon before the Lord Mayor on May 10, 1660, entitled *Right Rejoycing*, Baxter bitterly complained (p. 50) that many ministers in cities and counties "have their persons as-saulted, their windows battered, their ministrations openly reviled, and that go in danger of their lives, from the brutish rabble," exasperated by the magistrates' punishing them or the ministers' reproof. Else-where in the same sermon he refers to the abusive terms applied to Presbyterian ministers: "Pres-biters, Drivines, Jack-Presbyters, Blackcoats, Pulpeteers, &c."

[6] Ithaca, New York, 1941, ed. George H. Sabine. Introduction, p. 3.

tion, this dictum would not apply then. Two of the most vocal groups, the Baptists and the Quakers, opposed any kind of state church. Independents and Presbyterians supported different kinds of national churches. Both groups favored the retention of tithes and submitted to the examination of ministers by "triers," but the one regarded each congregation as an independent unit while the other wanted a rigid structure starting with the parish and ending with the general assembly. Apart from the Quakers, who were generally not in a position to influence politics, the various sectarians were very eager that the constitution should be molded to their wishes. They demanded toleration but their various proposals for a written constitution usually did not include any reforms of the church. Two explanations can be offered for the few suggestions for ecclesiastical change other than the abolition of tithes. One is that the majority of constitution-mongers was satisfied with the status quo or that men had ceased to care for the work of reformation. The leading ministers at least had every reason to be content—they largely controlled the commissions that approved nominations to benefices or ejected the alleged scandalous holders of them, and they received larger stipends than ever before. The ordinary minister had little opportunity of directing events which were probably by no means all to his liking. The second explanation is that the many had become tired of religious issues. The constitutionalist with the Bible under one arm and Magna Charta under the other was becoming more popular than the preacher.[7] A most significant incident had happened during the election of 1656. When Edmund Chillenden was told that one of the candidates for Middlesex was not a godly man, he answered: "Pish, let religion alone; give me my small liberty."[8] The speaker, as a lieutenant, had been a vehement friend of the Levellers in 1647 and had been promoted to a captaincy in Whalley's regiment of horse. When he became a Fifth Monarchy enthusiast he had lost his commission. Yet this former lay preacher was by 1656 convinced that godliness, as the Saints interpreted it, could be purchased at too high a price. By 1659 the minister and the soldier—the blackcoat and the redcoat—had become accursed. They stood between the citizen and his "small liberty."

The failure to distinguish between social evils and harmless amusements was fatal to the Puritan cause. George Fox, with all his tolerance, was guilty of this error. He describes "one of the wickedest men in the country, one who was a common drunkard, a noted whore-master, and

[7]Aubrey (*Brief Lives*, II, 6) describes David Jenkins as resolved, if he was going to be hanged, to be thus equipped.

[8]Thurloe, V, 287.

a rhyme-maker."[9] Had the Puritan confined his repressive zeal to sinners like the first two, he would have carried with him the great majority of Englishmen, but when he tried to prohibit all sorts of innocent recreations he became hated. The rhymester was not the only one with cause to complain that

> The bigots of the iron time
> Had call'd his harmless art a crime.

The enforcement of the various acts and ordinances designed to make men and women moral was rigid enough to irritate but not to reform people. Fox, in an eloquent passage, tells how he was moved to denounce wakes or feasts, May-games, sports, plays, and shows, "which trained up people to vanity and looseness." In fairs and markets he reproved "deceitful merchandise, and cheating and cozening."[10] No doubt his countrymen would have been as grateful for efforts to prevent them from being swindled as they were resentful of the attempts to restrict their enjoyments. Evidence abounds that the legislator who wished to improve the hard lot of many Englishmen had ample opportunity.

> You people which be wise,
>   Will Freedom highly prize;
>   For experience you have
> What 'tis to be a slave:
>   This have you been all your life long,
>   But chiefly since the Wars begun.[11]

The last line does not suggest that the poor had benefited from the Puritan Revolution.

Whether Englishmen were especially religious during the years from 1640 to 1660 is doubtful. They assuredly professed more loudly and more often than in any other age that they were obeying the divine will. At no other time were the Scriptures so often on the tongues of politicians. How far familiarity with Holy Writ bred contempt for it cannot be categorically asserted. The number of hypocrites may have been no greater than at other times. In one respect at least triumphant Puritanism sinned grievously. The oaths an office holder swore and broke during the twenty years were many. The first three—the oath of allegiance, the Protestation, and the Covenant—all bound him to defend the King's person. After the Negative Oath, which pledged Cavaliers not to assist the King, came the various Engagements—to be faithful to a republic, to two Pro-

[9]*Journal*, pp. 26-27.
[10]Ibid., p. 37.
[11]"The Diggers Christmas-Caroll," in *The Works of Gerrard Winstanley*, p. 667.

tectors, and to a republic again. The Covenant was resuscitated during the last months of the interregnum, only to be declared no longer obligatory by the Act of Uniformity of 1662. Well might Samuel Butler conclude

> Oaths are but words, and words but wind;
> Too feeble implements to bind.[12]

Puritanism is seen at its worst just before the Restoration. To some extent it furnishes an example of the corruption of power. To use an analogy based on *Pilgrims Progress*, Christian was gradually being transformed into Worldly Wise man.[13] Many Puritans had relaxed their missionary ardor and those who retained it ceased to attract disciples. The success that attended the preaching of George Fox proves that the more orthodox preachers had lost their grip, because many of his adherents were drawn from the ranks of the sectaries. The Puritans in power were less admirable than under persecution. Once they were in the saddle they seemed to forget the steps by which they had ascended. In one of his speeches Cromwell said: "Religion was not the thing at first contested for, but God brought it to that issue at last; and gave it unto us by way of redundancy; and at last it proved that which was most dear to us." No doubt such a culmination was inevitable because the motive power of Puritanism was supplied by the sermons, by far the most influential of the organs of public opinion. Once a minority became convinced that it had a divine mission to reform England, it lost sight of all else. In its headlong course it dropped followers at every turn. The smaller it grew the more strident its claims to represent the people and to comprise "the Saints." Similarly the officers forgot why the army was raised and how to fill the ranks of the New Model half of the men were pressed. They overestimated the privates' zeal and grew certain that their victories demonstrated that Providence approved their cause. A clash became inevitable when a civilian and a martial group each felt called upon to rule the three nations.

Oliver Cromwell's greatness is never so apparent as when the period immediately following his death is studied. Whether viewed as a commander in chief or as a ruler he appears a colossus beside his successors. Probably the history of England to 1649 would not have been essen-

---

[12]*Hudibras*, pt. II, pp. 107-108. For the oaths see Prynne, *Concordia Discors, or the Dissonant Harmony of Sacred Publique Oaths, Protestations, Leagues, Covenants, Ingagements lately taken by many Time-Serving Saints, Officers*. 1659 repr. 1683. Whether the Quaker was at all influenced in his refusal to take oaths by the prevalent habit of taking and breaking them is a question that merits consideration.

[13]Fox reports that Oliver Cromwell said that he could not win the Quakers "with honour[?s], high places, or gifts, but all other people he could." *Journal*, p. 200. Cromwell should have excepted others. See *The Autobiography of Richard Baxter*, ed. J. M. Lloyd Thomas (n.d.), p. 128.

tially different had he never been born. The material resources at the disposal of Parliament should have sufficed to win the first Civil War. Given the temper of the army the clash between Independents and Presbyterians in 1647-1648 and the King's execution would have occurred without Cromwell. Perhaps Ireland and Scotland would have been conquered under another leader. But then without him, events might well have followed the pattern of 1659-1660, and Charles II might have returned six or seven years earlier. As time was to prove, Cromwell alone could control the army with its many cliques.

Burnet remarks that the King's execution "was the true occasion of the great turn of the nation in the year 1660."[14] The postponement of the "great turn" until 1660 was due to Cromwell. That the Puritan Revolution lasted for the eleven additional years was of the greatest importance. What above all Puritanism owed to Cromwell was time to spread its roots deeply and widely so that the Clarendon Code could not eradicate them. Individual follies and sectarian eccentricities mattered only temporarily.

Puritanism survived, not in the seats of power, but in the hearts of men. The best of Puritanism is to be found not in the Milton of *The Tenure of Kings* or *The Readie & Easie Way* but in the Milton of *Paradise Lost*. Its permanent legacy cannot be discovered in the dull tones of those who

reason'd high
Of providence, foreknowledge, will and fate,
Fix'd fate, free will, foreknowledge absolute,
And found no end, in wand'ring mazes lost.

It should rather be sought in the record of the humble pilgrim who at the end of his journey was content to be going "to see *that* head that was Crowned with Thorns, and *that* Face that was spit upon for me."

---

[14] *Own Time*, § 50.

Charles X, King of Sweden: sent envoy to Richard, 13; saw Baltic as Swedish lake, 191-92; found treaty of Roskilde insufficient, 192-93; attacked Denmark, 195; aided by England, 196; Parliament debated relations with, 197-99; Republicans suspected, 199; attempted mediation with, 203-206; death of, 207

Chepstow, 129, 132

Cheshire: Booth's rising in, 129 seq.; elected Booth, 323

Chester: occupied by Booth, 135; surrendered, 140

Chesterfield, Earl of. See Stanhope

Chichester, 131-32, 328

Chillenden, Edmund, advocate of liberty, 360

Chirk Castle, 138, 140, 246

Chiverton, Richard, lord mayor of London, 4-6, 115

Cholmley, Sir Henry, 286, 350

Christian IV, King of Denmark: accepted treaty of Roskilde, 192

Church during the Interregnum. See State church

Church of England: position in 1658, 22-23; proscribed, 95; confiscated lands, 269; not an issue at election, 333; not mentioned in Declaration of Breda, 341

Chute, Chaloner: elected Speaker, 50; on disorderly debates, 54

Cinque Ports, the: parliamentary representation, 46, 327

Clarendon, Earl of. See Hyde, Edward

Clarges, Anne: marriage to Monck, 216. See Monck, Anne

Clarges, Thomas: sent to Monck, 19; brought back Monck's letter, 21; blamed lower officers for unrest, 37; his tract, 168; mission to England, 179; commissary general, 273; urged Monck to remonstrate with Rump, 280-81; for secluded members, 288; reassured officers, 299; proposed address from army, 314-15; 172-73, 177

Claypole, John, 42

Clayton, Thomas, M.P., 329

Clerk (Clark), John, colonel, 74, 158

Clinton, Theophilus, 4th Earl of Lincoln, 338

Clobery, John, colonel, 162, 171-72, 177, 180, 265, 281-82, 288, 308, 325

Clotworthy, Sir John, 253-54

Coal, sea: tax on, 70

Cobbet, Ralph, colonel, 148, 151, 156, 163, 336

Cock fighting, 104

Cockermouth, 47

Colchester, 301

Coldstream: Monck's headquarters, 176, 264; Foot Guards called after, 176-77

Committee of safety: in May 1659, 96, 106-108; in October to December 1659, 157 seq., 184-87

Commons, the House of: election of, 46-48, 320-32; bill to recognize Richard debated in, 52 seq.; vote to recognize Richard, 56; discussed Moyer's petition, 57-58; debated constitution, 59 seq.; discussed finance, 70-72; Butler attacked in, 72-73; relations with Lords, 73; antimilitarism of, 78, 80; last proceedings in, 84; reassembled, 90, 339; Royalists not challenged, 339; King's letter and Declaration read in, 341-42; voted for proclaiming Charles II, 345; bill to abolish feudal tenures, 347; bill for a general pardon, 347-48; measures against regicides, 348-49; bill to secure fundamental laws, 349; named members to attend the King, 349-50. See Parliament, the Long

Commonwealth, a: always tyrannical, 56; established, 97; oath to maintain, 102. See also Republicans

Compton, James, 12th Earl of Northampton, 307

Compton, Sir William, Royalist, 125

Conant, John, vice-chancellor, 329

Conference between two Souldiers, A, 170-71

Confession of Faith, the, 297

Congregationalists, the: associated with Presbyterians, 25-26, 238; Declaration of Faith, 26; preparation for the Lord's Supper, 26-27; in Ireland, 237-38

Connaught: transplantation, 234, 254; population, 235; secured by Coote, 248

Conservators of liberty, twenty-one, 184, 186

Constantinople, 212

Convention, Irish, the, 250n, 252-54

Convention of royal burghs, 230

Convention Parliament, the: election literature, 319-20; elections, 320-32; proceedings in, ch. xvii; declared to be a true parliament, 347. See separate headings as House of Lords

Cook, John, Irish judge, 252-53

Cooper, Sir Anthony Ashley: against a nominated second chamber, 60; in Council of State, 101, 180, 260, 295; did not rise, 129; tried to seize Tower, 182-83; on Monck's tactics, 284-85; met secluded members, 288-89; 189, 227, 263, 268, 282, 315, 324, 350, 352

Cooper, Thomas, colonel, 37, 237, 247-48

Cooper, William, Puritan minister, 20

Coote, Sir Charles, president of Connaught: in Parliament, 68; not a Republican, 249; Royalist, 250, 252-53; his brothers, 251; in touch with Monck, 251, 267; 180, 241, 245, 247-48

Copenhagen: besieged by Swedes, 195; treaty of, 207

Copplestone, Sir John, sheriff, 66

Corbet, Miles, baron of Irish exchequer, 243, 247

Cork, 235, 238, 254

Cornwall: parliamentary representation, 46, 323; 128

Council of officers, the. See Army

Council, the Privy: proclaimed Richard Protector, 3-6; Register, 4n; membership, 4n, 29-30; oath, 6; control of, 9, 29; lacked initiative, 15; treatment of Quakers by, 27-28; divisions in, 29-31, 39; officers wished to remodel, 39; decided to summon Parliament, 45; quarrels in, 46; discussed foreign policy, 195; first meeting of Charles II's, 351-52; 48-49

Council of State, the: created, 29, 96; members of, in May 1659, 101-102; act constituting, 102; its committees, 103; compared with cabinet, 103; hampered by lack of money, 103-104, 115; arrested Royalists, 127; measures against rising, 131-33, 139; debate in about Parliament, 152-53; ceased to sit, 154; revived, 180n; in authority, 189; recalled Henry Cromwell, 243-44; newly constituted, 260, 331; question of abjuring Charles II, 263, 285; measures against London, 278; chosen in March 1660, 294-95, 332; considered conditional Restoration, 295; issued reward for Lambert, 335; Grenville before, 339-40; searched for royal property, 346

Court-martial: demands that soldiers be cashiered only by, 40, 57

Coventry, 132

Cowley, Abraham: on Cromwell's funeral, 42

Cox, Samuel, Irish Presbyterian, 252

Crawford, Earl of. See Lindsay

Creed, Richard, major, 74, 146-47, 151, 314, 336

Crew, John, 288, 295, 305

Crofts, Sir Henry, M.P., 328

Croke, Unton, sheriff of Oxfordshire, 7, 293

Cromwell, Elizabeth, 346

Cromwell, Henry, lord lieutenant, Ireland: on address from army in Ireland, 11; his coming to England opposed, 31-32, 242; on army's influence, 32; criticisms of army officers, 35-36; against oath for Irish Catholics, 236; moderation towards Presbyterians, 237; lost his Irish regiment, 240; character, 241-42; complained of Council, 242-43; recalled to England, 243-44; letter of resignation, 244-45; 8, 17, 86

Cromwell, Mary: marriage to Fauconberg, 31

Cromwell, Oliver: death, 3; names successor, 4; body to be embalmed, 4-5; news of death abroad, 11-12; compared with his son Richard, 17; on his enemies, 17-18; approved accommodation in religion, 25-26; lying in state at Somerset House, 40-41; funeral procession, 41-42; comments on his funeral, 43-45; became Protector, 53; cashiered Packer, 55; debts of Protectorate of, 70-71; comments on Fleetwood, 170, 188; foreign policy, 190-91, 213-14; anecdote about, 336-37; to be attainted, 348; burned in effigy, 353; relations with Parliament, 355; greatness, 362-63; 63

Cromwell, Richard: nominated as Protector, 3-5; proclaimed, 5-6; took oath as Protector, 6; addressed by army, 8-10; other addresses to, 242; acknowledged abroad, 12-13; character, 14-17; his enemies, 17-18; Monck's advice to, 20-21; supported state church, 23; to consult Fleetwood about army, 34-35; tried to conciliate the army, 35-36, 65; speeches to the officers, 36-37, 39-40; sided with Mountagu, 46; opened Parliament, 48, 51; Republicans wished to limit authority of, 52-56; vote to recognize passed, 56; denounced Ingoldsby's cornet, 64; alienated the godly, 64; called "the young gentleman," 74-75; received army petition, 78; sent petition to Parliament, 79; declared army council dissolved, 80-81; orders Fleetwood's arrest, 82-83; lost all authority, 86; debts, 98;

did not co-operate with Royalists, 99; resigned, 100; foreign policy under, ch. xi; compared to Henry, 242; proclaimed in Ireland, 242; left Henry without instructions, 243; recall considered, 295, 309; Lambert wished to restore, 336-37; 59

Crouch, Thomas, M.P., 330

Culpepper, C., 229

Culpepper (Colepeper), John, First Lord, 210, 351

Cumberland, 47

Cunningham, William, 9th Earl of Glencairn, 218, 226

Customs: bill to abolish, 68; yield of, 70

Cuttance, Roger, naval captain, 303

Dakins, George, naval captain, 303

Daniel, William, colonel, 111, 223

Darnall, Ralph, 50

Davenport, ———, captain lieutenant, 223

Daventry: Lambert captured near, 336-37

Dean, Richard, captain: clerk of the Council, 102

Dean, Forest of, 118

Debt: imprisonment for, 93

Debt, the national: amount of, in April 1659, 70-71

Declaration of the Faith [of] Congregational Churches, 26

Declaration of the General Council of the Officers, A, 108, 114

Declaration of the Lords, The: issued by Booth, 135-36

Denbigh, Earl of. See Feilding

Denbighshire, 323

Dendy, Edward, sergeant at arms, 181

Denham, John: lame, 104

Denmark: at war with Sweden, 33, 191, 195; aided by Dutch, 195; attempted mediation to end Swedish war, 203-207; gained at treaty of Copenhagen, 207

Derby, Earl of. See Stanley

Derby: assizes at, 27; petition, 147 seq., 246-47

De Vere, Aubrey, 20th Earl of Oxford, 125, 349

Devonshire: Monck's letter to gentlemen of, 269-70; elected Monck, 323; 66, 128

De Witt, John, Grand Pensionary of Holland: recognized Richard, 12; negotiations about Danish-Swedish war, 196-97

Dickson, David, Scottish minister, 227

Directions for Members, 319

Directory, the, 228, 297, 308

Disbrowe, John: Richard's councillor, 4n, 30, 39; accepted Richard's nomination, 4; feud with Mountagu, 30, 46; opposed Henry Cromwell's visit to England, 31-32; urged raising taxes by force, 32; a leader of discontented officers, 34-35, 37-38, 58-59, 74, 79-81; threatened Richard, 84; in Council of State, 101; slighted Parliament, 106; commanded in West, 132, 139; to command the horse, 147; presented Derby petition, 149; cashiered, 151; at the Council, 153; in committee of safety, 157; speech, 159; his regiment, 185, 261; submission, 301; 182-83, 187-88, 260, 298, 319

Disbrowe, Samuel, 217, 224

Dixmude, 190

Dorset, Earl of. See Sackville

Douglas, Sir Joseph, 267

Douglas, Robert, Scottish minister, 227-28, 233

Douglas, family of, 218

Dover: elected Mountagu, 327-28; Charles II landed at, 351

Downing, Sir George, English resident in Holland, 12, 39, 194, 196, 200-202, 209

Doyley, Sir William, 321

Dublin: Richard proclaimed in, 7; population, 235; castle seized, 248, 251

Duckenfield, William, lieutenant colonel, 146

Duckett, Charles, captain, 107

Duncannon, 248

Duncombe, Sir John, 328

Dunkirk: Richard proclaimed at, 7; mutiny at, 38; garrison at, 98-99, 111-12; cession to England, 191, 194, 200

Durham, 141

Durham College: address from, 10

Dury, Giles, journalist, 314

Dutch East India Company, the: seized English ships, 194

East India Company, the: lent Council money, 104

Eastland Company, the, 210

Edgehill: Lambert's rendezvous at, 335

Edinburgh: Richard proclaimed at, 7; meeting of nobles and magistrates, 226, 230; ministers in, 227

Edmundson, William, founder of Irish Quakerism, 238

Glynn, Robert, captain, 110
Goffe, William: on Richard's nomination, 3-5; in army council, 8; his regiment of horse, 14; speech by, 36; 34, 74, 80, 175
Good old cause, the. See Republicans
Goodrich, William, major, 74
Goodson, William, vice-admiral, 195-96
Goodwin, Robert, 250
Goodwin, Thomas: independent divine, 3, 6; on Richard's nomination, 4; presented address, 10; sermon at opening of Parliament, 49, 50; 26
Gordon, family of, 218
Gorges, John, lieutenant colonel, 61
Gough, William, lieutenant colonel, 65, 109, 162
Grand Memorandum, The, 319
Gravelines, 190
Greenhill, William, Congregational minister, 26
Grenville, Sir John, Royalist, 131, 133-34, 307; carried Monck's message to King, 311-13; brought royal letters, 339-40
Grey, Henry, 1st Earl of Stamford, 138
Griffith, John: sermon of, 79
Grimston, Sir Harbottle: Speaker, 339; 321
Grove, Thomas, M.P., 73
Gumble, Thomas: Monck's chaplain and biographer, 162, 173-74, 175; reported to Monck, 268
Guthrie, James, 231

Habeas corpus, writ of: denied, 53
Hacker, Francis, colonel: received commission from Speaker, 106; 179, 326
Hague, The: treaties signed at, 203, 205; Charles II at, 350-51
Hale, Matthew, 346
Hamburg, 210
Hamilton, family of, 218
Hampden, John, 20
Hampden, Richard, 322-23
Harley, Edward, 288, 323
Haro, Don Luis Mendez de, Spanish minister, 208-209
Harrington, James: his Oceana, 54, 291; disciples of, 62; model constitution, 91; advocated a militia, 94; his Aphorisms, 95; on ideal foreign policy, 213-14; the Rota, 291; 293, 298
Harrington, Sir James, 157, 321-22
Harrison, Thomas, major general, 18, 157, 325, 349

Hart, Theophilus, major, 31
Harvey, Daniel, M.P., 322
Hastings, Henry, Lord Loughborough, Royalist, 125
Hatnell, Henry, captain: sold slaves, 66
Hatton, Sir Thomas, 72
Hay, John, 2nd Earl of Tweeddale, 224
Henrietta Maria, Queen of England, 12
Henry, Duke of Gloucester, 351
Herbert, Philip, 5th Earl of Pembroke, 157
Hertford, Marquis of. See Seymour
Hesilrige, Robert, captain, 336-37
Hesilrige, Sir Arthur: praised Richard Cromwell, 16; on sermons before the Commons, 50; declares Speaker the greatest man in England, 51; long speech on bill of Recognition, 53; against a nominated second chamber, 60, 62; defended Long Parliament, 65; on violations of freedom, 67; on losses at sea, 71; in Council of State, 101; against army's domination, 109, 145; on Act of Indemnity, 113-14; wanted a "pure republic," 114; character, 145; quarreled with Vane, 146, 154; angered by Derby petition, 148; army commissioner, 151, 260-61, 282; at the Council, 153; at Portsmouth, 180; conferences with London authorities, 257, 272; importance early in 1660, 260; regiment, 273; told he must fall, 282; met secluded members, 287-88; submitted, 301; not elected M.P., 326; did not join Lambert, 334; 48, 57, 58, 63, 68, 75, 79, 80, 88, 103, 106, 108, 141, 178-81, 199, 247, 263, 284, 319
Hewson, John, colonel: in army council, 8; sided with Commonwealthsmen, 38; helped defeat Booth, 139; fired on London apprentices, 182; 158, 240
Highlands of Scotland, the, 217-19
Hinston, William, M.P., 323
Hobart, Sir John, 20, 272, 321
Hobson, John, 213
Holdenby (Holmby), manor of, 72-73, 348
Holland, Cornelius, 158
Holland: rejoicing at Cromwell's death, 12; recognized Richard, 12; Englishmen jealous of, 198-99; helped Spaniards, 194, 198, 201-203; complained of detention of ships, 201; fleet in the Sound, 203-207
Holles, Denzil, 300, 350
Hollings, Marjory: on Willis, 142-43
Holmes, Abraham, lieutenant colonel, 110, 162

claimed in, 345-46; King's reception in, 353; share in Restoration, 359; lord mayor of, see Thomas Aleyne, Richard Chiverton, John Ireton

London, Tower of: attempt to seize, 182-83; secured for Parlament, 189; Lambert escaped from, 334-35; Morley lieutenant of, 334

Lords, House of: Monck recommended calling old lords to, 20; swordsmen in, 48; Richard's speech in, 49; Packer refused to acknowledge, 55; debates on, 59-62; officers in, 60, 62; Commons to transact with, 62, 67-68, 73-74; debated fast, 73-74; the "young Lords", 296; resolution in favor of, 305; met in April 1660, 338; King's letter read in, 340; voted Charles II was king, 342, 345; lords to attend the King, 349; 14, 82

Loughborough, Lord. See Hastings

Louis XIV, King of France: marriage, 191, 208

Ludlow, Edmund: on Cromwell's funeral, 42; on election of 1659, 46; elected M.P., 46; sat without taking the oath, 51; on Richard's indifference about religion, 64; on Lords' debate, 73-74; met army leaders, 75, 88-89; in Council of State, 101-102; on Act of Indemnity, 113-14; army commissioner, 151; conciliatory efforts, 158-59; on conservators of liberty, 186; Irish regiments, 240, 245; commander in chief in Ireland, 245-47; sent Irish brigade against Booth, 246; repudiated in Ireland, 249; impeached, 250, 282; received Monck's assurances, 284; on his election, 326, 334; on Lambert's rising, 337; 60, 106, 108, 109, 131, 152, 157-58, 261

Lytcott, Leonard, colonel, 177, 265, 271, 273, 281, 343

Mabbott, Thomas, 118

Macaulay, Thomas Babington, Lord: on Long Parliament, 305-306; on influence of London, 359

Magna Charta, 53, 62, 178, 349, 360

Maitland, John, 2nd Earl of Lauderdale, 228, 233, 293

Major, Dorothy, Richard Cromwell's wife, 14, 17

Man, William, 266

Manchester, Earl of. See Mountagu

Manchester: ministers at agreed about the Lord's Supper, 26

Manley, Robert, 72

Manley, Sir Roger, 193-94

Manton, Thomas, Presbyterian minister, 20, 50, 221, 227, 297

Maria Theresa, Infanta, 191, 208

Markham, Henry, colonel, 156, 240, 250, 266

Marston Moor: Fairfax held rendezvous on, 265

Marten, Henry: M.P., 90; councillor, 260; 298, 304

Martindale, Adam, minister, 137

Marvell, Andrew: poem on Cromwell's death, 16, 43; at Cromwell's funeral, 41, 43-44; lodged at Whitehall, 104; on Cromwell's foreign policy, 214; M.P., 325

Mary, Princess of Orange, sister of Charles II, 351

Mason, John, lieutenant colonel, 74, 107

Massey, Sir Edward: Royalist, 127-28, 131, 133-34; elected for Gloucester, 327

Masson, David: on number of M.P.'s, 97

Maynard, John: elected for three places, 47; on purge of Parliament, 56; 198

Maynard, Thomas, consul, 211

Mazarin, Giulio [Jules], cardinal: visited Henrietta Maria, 12; acknowledged Richard, 12-13; foreign policy of, 190-91, 200; made truce with Spain, 200; negotiated treaty of the Pyrenees, 208

Meadowe, Philip, English envoy: modified treaty of Roskilde, 192; unable to persuade Charles X, 194

Meath, 237

Merchant Adventurers, the, 210

Mercurius Britanicus, newspaper, 170

Mercurius Politicus, official newspaper, 3, 10, 170

Message sent from the King, A, 229-30

Middlesex: election in, 321-22

Middleton, Sir Hugh, 133

Middleton, Sir Thomas: ready to rise, 129; proclaimed the King, 138; released, 293; M.P., 323

Mildmay, Sir Henry, 349

Militia, the: reorganized, 115, 298; paid by decimation tax, 123; during Booth's rising, 132; insisted on being paid, 144-45; of London, 82, 115, 182, 294; Act, 298, 300

Mill, John, colonel: lost his regiment, 86

Miller, John, adjutant general, 162, 289

Miller, John, lieutenant colonel, 183, 189

Mills, John, M.P., 329

Milton, John: at Cromwell's funeral, 41, 43-44; against a state church, 119-20; against tithes, 121; denounced army, 155; *Samson Agonistes*, 188; *Readie & Easie Way*, 291-92, 318, 363; *Brief Notes*, 318; exponent of Puritanism, 363; 29, 117, 146

Mitchell, William, colonel, 147

Model of a Democraticall Government, A, 90-91

Monck, Anne: for admission of secluded members, 288

Monck, George, commander in Scotland: army full of extremists, 18; against military tyranny, 20; advice to Richard Cromwell, 20-21; on Ashfield, 65; might have helped Richard, 98-99; accepted Commonwealth, 99-100; wished his officers unchanged, 110-11; on obedience to civil authority, 110-11, 215; to command the foot, 147; refused to sign Derby petition, 148; army commissioner, 151; upheld the Rump, 162; remodeled his army, 162-64; defended his stand, 164; three tasks, 167; propaganda, 168-71; consulted his council, 169; rejected treaty with English army, 174; answered minister, 175; correspondence with Owen, 175-76; at Coldstream, 176-80; Fairfax promised assistance, 177-80; welcomed Morgan, 178; character and career, 215-16; disliked Quakers as soldiers, 223; on Scottish representatives, 224; measures in Scotland, 225-26; favored moderate Presbyterianism, 226; marched into England, 227, 265 seq.; correspondence with Irish army, 247-48; promotions approved, 260-61; member of Council, 260, 284; crossed the Tweed, 265; assured Speaker of army's loyalty, 266; met Fairfax, 267; correspondence with Londoners, 266; letter to gentlemen of Devon, 269-70; an opportunist, 270, 311; plan to scatter regiments, 273; entered London, 276; speech to Parliament, 276-77; coerced London, 278-80; persuaded to remonstrate with the Rump, 280-81; stiff letter to Rump, 281-82; slighted by Parliament, 282-83; for a Commonwealth, 284; deception, 284; on Parliament's filling vacancies, 287; meetings with secluded members, 287-89; readmitted them, 289-90; Milton's

letter to, 292; rewarded by Parliament, 293; general at sea, 294; expected army to obey Parliament, 299; puzzled Royalists, 307-308; decided to support the Restoration, 310-11; sent loyal message to Charles II, 311-12; advice to Charles II, 312-13; M.P., 323-24, 330-31; letter on Lenthall's behalf, 329-30; sent Ingoldsby against Lambert, 336-37; part in Speaker's election, 339; loyal speech, 342; told Commons of army address, 343; against conditional Restoration, 346; sent fleet for the King, 350; received the King at Dover, 351; K.G., 351; recommendations to the King, 352; why he prevailed over Lambert, 357; 8, 86

Monckton, Sir Philip, 265

Monthly assessment, the, 70, 71-72, 144

Moore, Sir Henry: arrest ordered, 127

Mordaunt, John: roused Knightley, 61; in touch with Richard, 99; Royalist leader, 123, 125 seq.; critical of Booth, 140; puzzled by Monck, 307; thought Restoration certain, 308; accompanied Grenville to Charles II, 313; 141, 258

Morgan, Anthony, 73, 85

Morgan, Ethelbert, captain, 162

Morgan, Sir Thomas, major general: joined Monck, 178; commanded in Flanders, 190; to command in Scotland, 267, 287; 177, 265

Morice, Sir William: against a nominated second chamber, 60; M.P., 331; secretary of state, 351-52; 300, 311

Morland, Samuel: exposed Willis, 130

Morley, George, bishop, 296-97, 316

Morley, Herbert: loyal to Parliament, 151-52; dismissed, 156; army commissioner, 260-61, 282; regiment, 273, 280; councillor, 295; lieutenant of the Tower, 334; 180, 287-88

Moss, Richard, lieutenant colonel: loyal to Parliament, 151-52; his regiment purged, 261; expected to join Lambert, 334-35; 74

Mountagu, Edward: Richard's councillor, 4n, 29-30, 39; drew up navy's address, 10-11; a strong Cromwellian, 30, 38; quarrel with Disbrowe, 30, 46; a colonel of horse, 31; in the Sound, 87, 128, 203-207; might have helped Richard, 99; complained that Dutch were unneutral, 194; general at sea, 294; reorganized navy, 302-304; given a regiment, 315; M.P., 327-28, 331; dictated naval ad-

Prideaux, William, envoy to Russia, 210
Pride's Purge. See Pride
Prince, ——, goldsmith, 134
Privy Council. See Council
Proclamation: of Richard, 5-6; of Charles II, 345-46
Propaganda: for the Rump, 87-88; for the English army, 165-66; for Charles II, 166-67, 314-18; for Monck, 167-71; against English army, 182; election literature, 319-20, 329
Prostitutes, 107
Protesters, in Scotland, 220-22
Prussia, 192
Prynne, William: secluded member, 96; for tithes, 121; pamphlet for secluded members, 259; entered Parliament, 289-90; not a councillor, 295; argued for old constitution, 304; advice to electors, 320; M.P., 331; and trial of Charles I, 348
Pulpits, the: influence of, 24-25
Puritanism: work of reformation, 8, 104, 262-63; unpopular, 96, 332, 355, 359; divisions among supporters, 356-57; at its worst when triumphant, 362-63
Pye, Sir Robert, 293, 322
Pyrenees, treaty of the, 208

Quakers, the: sufferings, 27, 119, 359; Declaration by, 28; released, 118; against tithes, 119; rumors they were in arms, 137; in Scotland, 222-23; in Ireland, 238-39; 157, 360
Qualifications of the Succeeding Parliament, The, 319

Raleigh, Carew, 288
Raleigh, Sir Walter: Cromwell recommends his History, 14; his History cited in Parliament, 56
Ramsden, John, M.P., 325
Raymond, [?Oliver], 321
Reade, Thomas, colonel, 162, 177, 265
Recognition, bill of: beginning of, 3; introduced and debated, 52 seq.; a blunder, 84-85
"Recruiters": to Long Parliament, 97
Redhill, 134
Redman, Daniel: led Irish brigade, 240, 269; dismissed, 245
Reformation, the work of. See Puritanism
Regicides, the: expelled from Convention, 325-26; to be punished, 340; to be secured, 348-49

Religion: parties in 1658, 22-28; commissioners to approve ministers, 23-24; admission to communion, 26-27; during Puritan Revolution, 361-62. See separate headings as Quakers or Toleration
Republicans, the: opposed to Protectorate, 18, 22, 35; many junior officers were, 19, 22, 87; officers intrigued with, 38, 74, 76, 82; electioneering by, 45; parliamentary tactics, 54; against fixed revenue, 72; good old cause, the, 77, 87, 90, 95; adroit tactics in Parliament, 84; supported the Rump, 109; differences among, 114, 145, 186; and foreign policy, 204-206; inconsistencies of, 317; unpopular in 1660, 332; wished written constitution, 355
Resolutioners, the Scottish, 221-22, 231
Revenue, the: bill to abolish excise, 68; state of in 1659; 70-72; expenditures, 70, 104; sources, 70; debts, 70-71; farmers of, unpopular, 71; taxation a grievance, 95; cost of army and navy, 115-16; of Ireland, 240-41; financial measures, December 1659, 260; refusal to pay taxes, 272, 286; taxes in January 1660, 294; additional taxes, 346-47
Reynolds, Edward, Presbyterian minister, 20, 50, 297, 353
Reynolds, Robert, 180, 288
Rhine, League of the, 190-91
Rich, Charles, 4th Earl of Warwick, 320-21, 349
Rich, Nathaniel, colonel: cashiered, 18; his regiment, 107, 301-302
Richardson, Thomas, Lord Cramond, 272, 321
Rivers, Marcellus, Royalist, 66
Robinson, George, captain, 172
Robinson, John, alderman, 139, 257, 281, 324
Robinson, Luke, 271, 282, 293, 319, 325, 331
Robson, Yaxley, colonel, 163
Rogers, John, Fifth Monarchy preacher, 18, 104
Rogers, Wroth, lieutenant colonel, 111
Rolle, Robert, 270
Roman Catholics, the: little persecution of, 22-23, 119; taxed, 70; not to be tolerated, 95; in Ireland, 236-37
Roskilde, treaty of, 192-93, 203
Rossiter, Edward, colonel, 129, 179, 295, 315, 324
Rota, the debating club, 291